D1247090

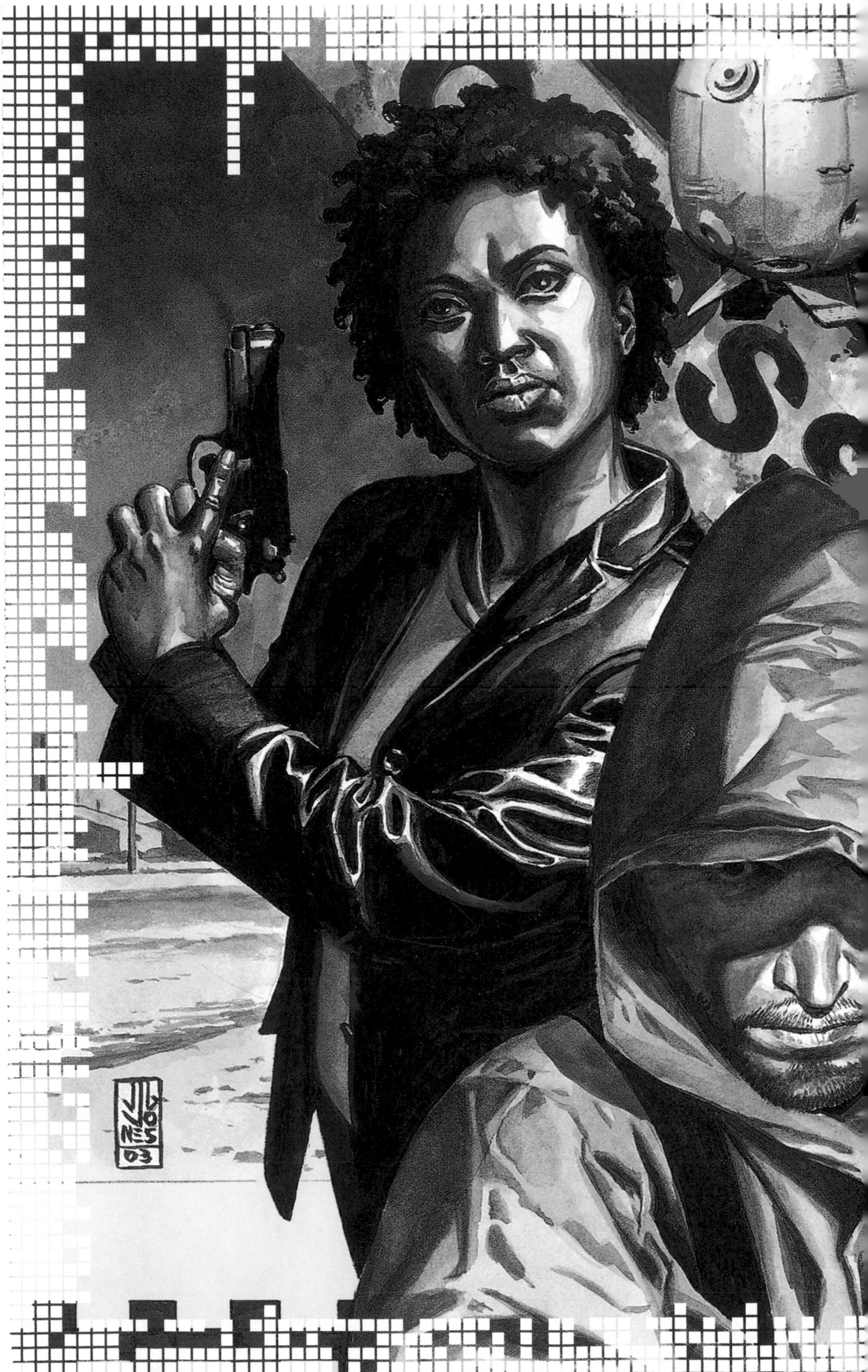

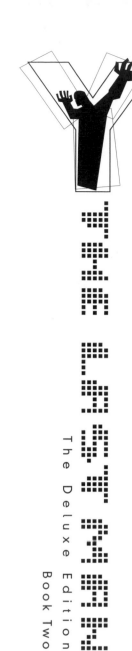

Y: THE LAST MAN

The Deluxe Edition

Book Two

Brian K. Vaughan Writer

Pia Guerra, Goran Parlov, Paul Chadwick Pencillers

José Marzán, Jr. Inker

Pamela Rambo, Zylonol Colorists

Clem Robins Letterer

J.G. Jones, Aron Wiesenfeld,
Massimo Carnevale Original Series Covers

Y: THE LAST MAN created by Brian K. Vaughan and Pia Guerra

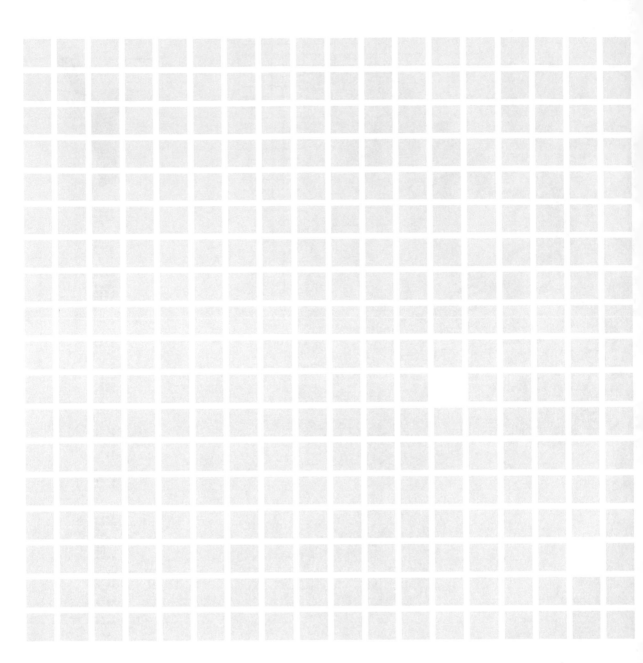

Steve Bunche, Will Dennis Editors – original series
Zachary Rau, Casey Seijas Assistant Editors – original series
Scott Nybakken Editor – collected edition
Robbin Brosterman Design Director – Books
Louis Prandi Publication Design

Karen Berger Senior VP – Executive Editor, Vertigo
Bob Harras VP – Editor-in-Chief

Diane Nelson President
Dan DiDio and Jim Lee Co-Publishers
Geoff Johns Chief Creative Officer
John Rood Executive VP – Sales, Marketing and Business Development
Amy Genkins Senior VP – Business and Legal Affairs
Nairi Gardiner Senior VP – Finance
Jeff Boison VP – Publishing Operations
Mark Chiarello VP – Art Direction and Design
John Cunningham VP – Marketing
Terri Cunningham VP – Talent Relations and Services
Alison Gill Senior VP – Manufacturing and Operations
Hank Kanalz Senior VP – Digital
Jay Kogan VP – Business and Legal Affairs, Publishing
Jack Mahan VP – Business Affairs, Talent
Nick Napolitano VP – Manufacturing Administration
Sue Pohja VP – Book Sales
Courtney Simmons Senior VP – Publicity
Bob Wayne Senior VP – Sales

Cover illustration by
Massimo Carnevale.

Logo design by
Terry Marks.

Y: THE LAST MAN —
THE DELUXE EDITION
BOOK TWO

Published by DC Comics.
Cover and compilation
Copyright © 2009
DC Comics. All Rights
Reserved. Script Copyright
© 2003 Brian K. Vaughan
and Pia Guerra.
All Rights Reserved.

DC Comics,
1700 Broadway,
New York, NY 10019
A Warner Bros.
Entertainment Company.
Printed in the USA.
Fourth Printing.
ISBN: 978-1-4012-2235-2

SUSTAINABLE
FORESTRY
INITIATIVE

Certified Sourcing
www.sfiprogram.org
SFI-01042
APPLIES TO TEXT STOCK ONLY

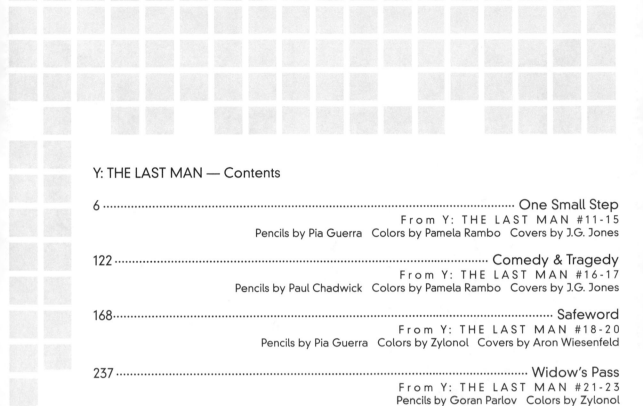

Y: THE LAST MAN — Contents

6 .... One Small Step

From Y: THE LAST MAN #11-15
Pencils by Pia Guerra   Colors by Pamela Rambo   Covers by J.G. Jones

122 .... Comedy & Tragedy

From Y: THE LAST MAN #16-17
Pencils by Paul Chadwick   Colors by Pamela Rambo   Covers by J.G. Jones

168 .... Safeword

From Y: THE LAST MAN #18-20
Pencils by Pia Guerra   Colors by Zylonol   Covers by Aron Wiesenfeld

237 .... Widow's Pass

From Y: THE LAST MAN #21-23
Pencils by Goran Parlov   Colors by Zylonol
Covers by Aron Wiesenfeld (#21-22) and Massimo Carnevale (#23)

306 .... Y: THE LAST MAN #18 Script by Brian K. Vaughan

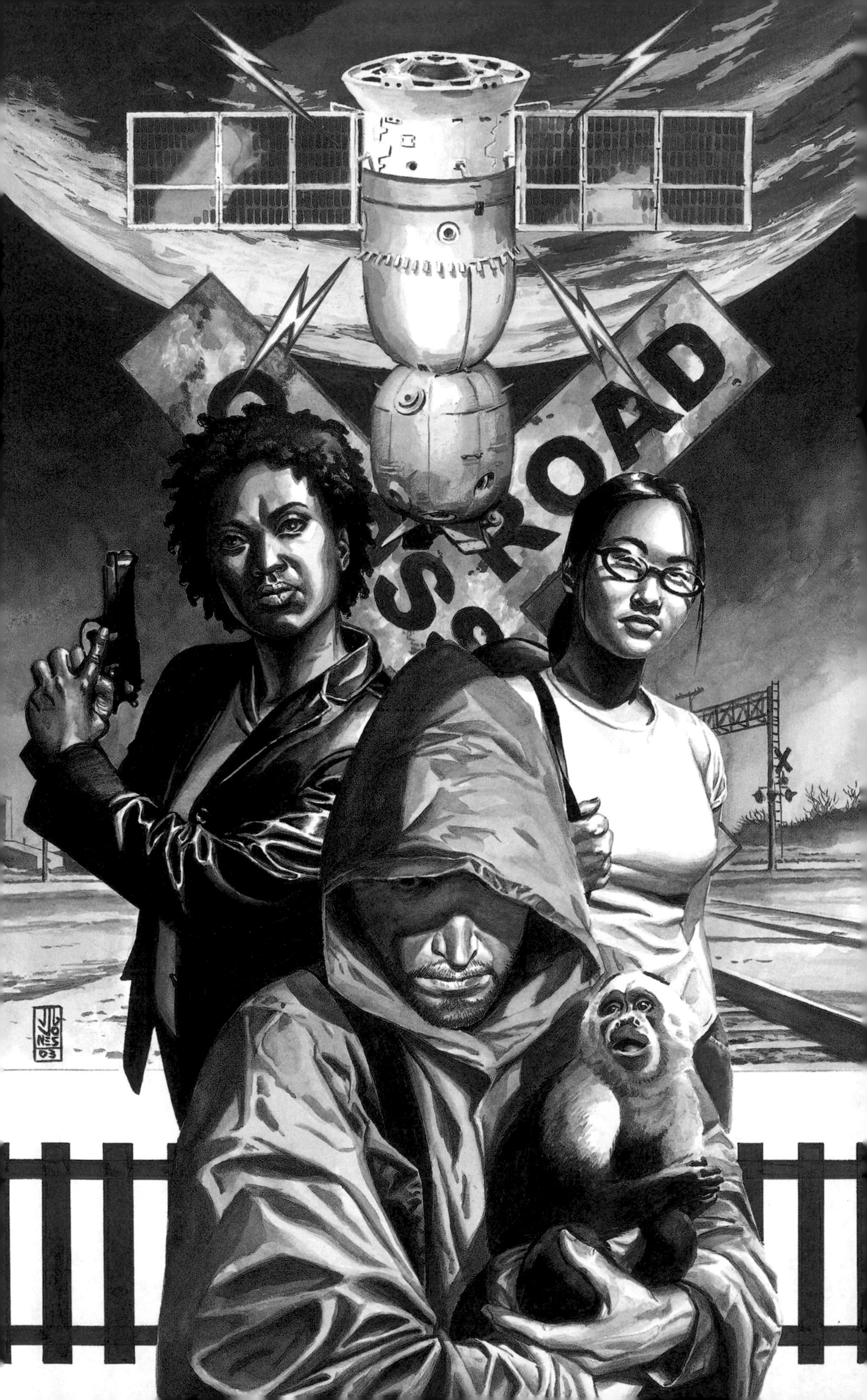
ROAD

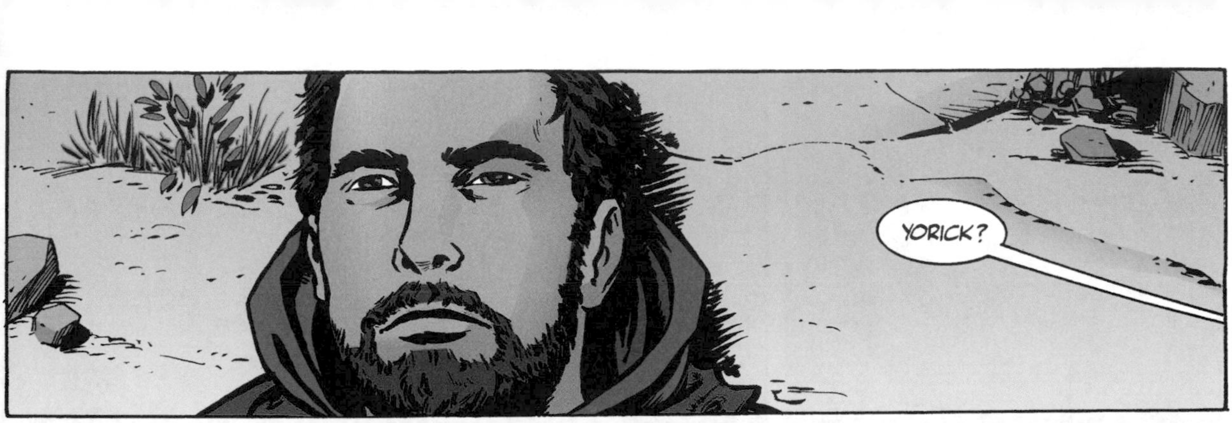
YORICK?

Marquand, Missouri
Now

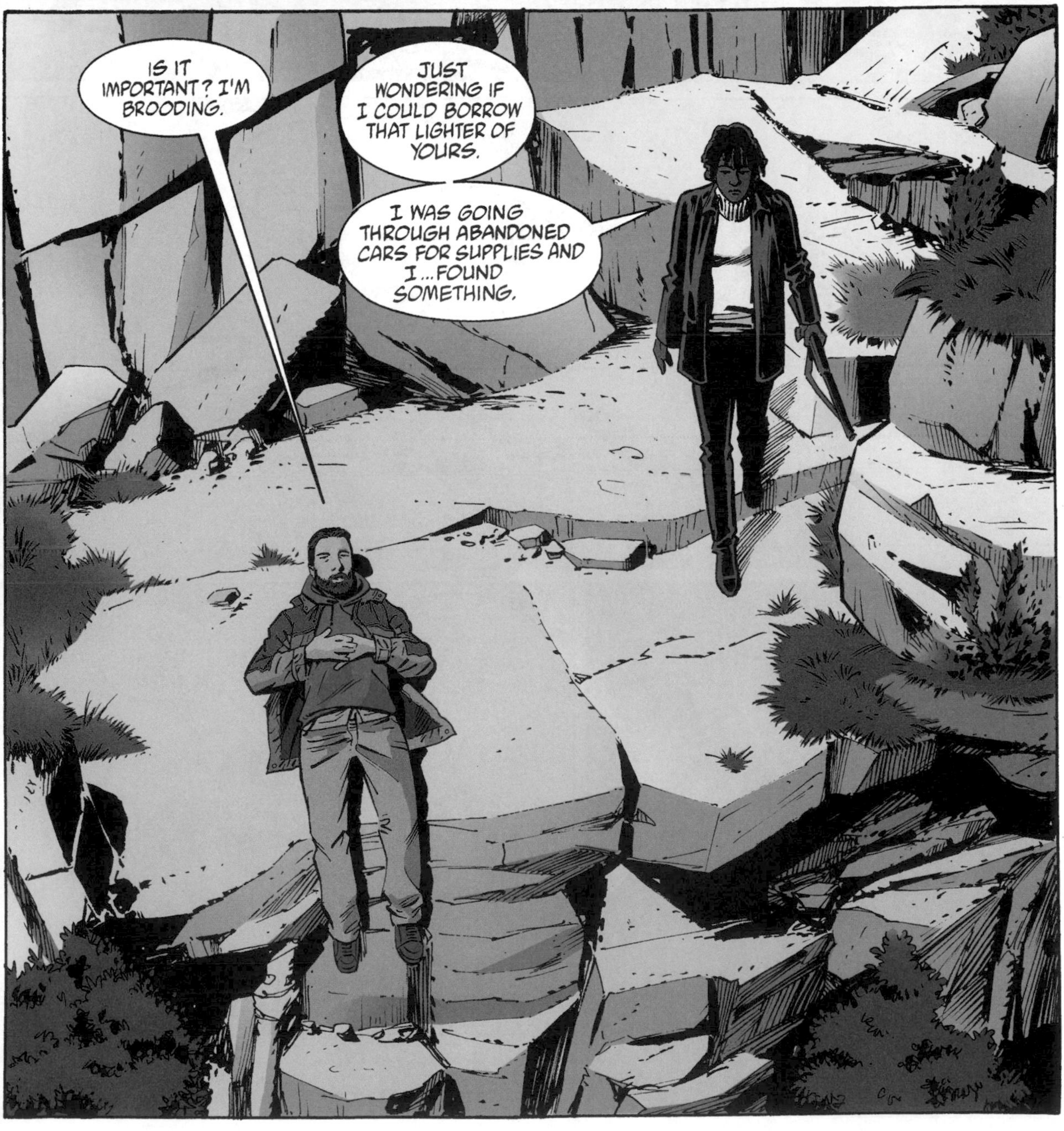
IS IT IMPORTANT? I'M BROODING.
JUST WONDERING IF I COULD BORROW THAT LIGHTER OF YOURS.
I WAS GOING THROUGH ABANDONED CARS FOR SUPPLIES AND I...FOUND SOMETHING.

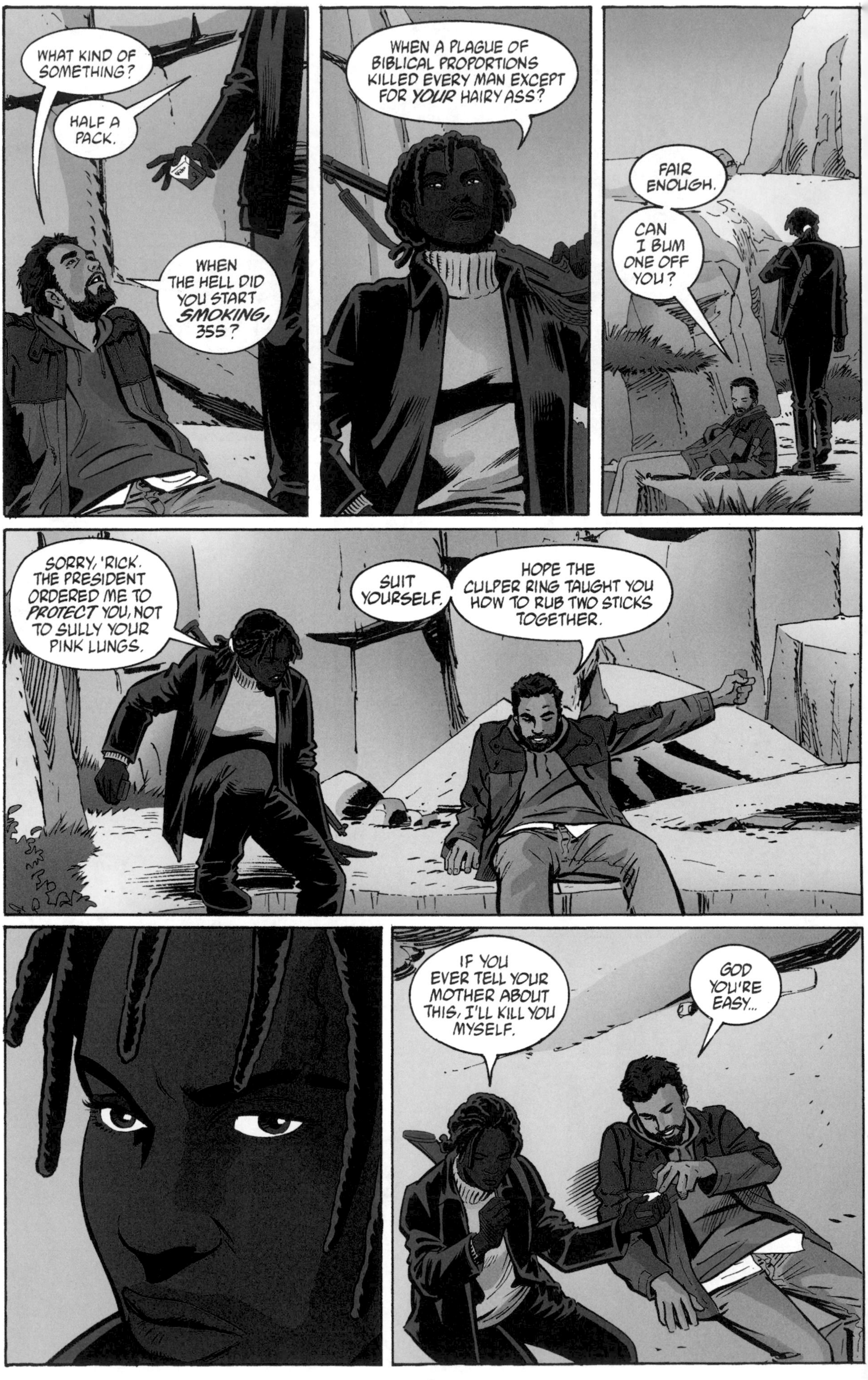
WHAT KIND OF SOMETHING?
HALF A PACK.
WHEN THE HELL DID YOU START SMOKING, 355?
WHEN A PLAGUE OF BIBLICAL PROPORTIONS KILLED EVERY MAN EXCEPT FOR YOUR HAIRY ASS?
FAIR ENOUGH.
CAN I BUM ONE OFF YOU?
SORRY, 'RICK. THE PRESIDENT ORDERED ME TO PROTECT YOU, NOT TO SULLY YOUR PINK LUNGS.
SUIT YOURSELF.
HOPE THE CULPER RING TAUGHT YOU HOW TO RUB TWO STICKS TOGETHER.
IF YOU EVER TELL YOUR MOTHER ABOUT THIS, I'LL KILL YOU MYSELF.
GOD YOU'RE EASY...

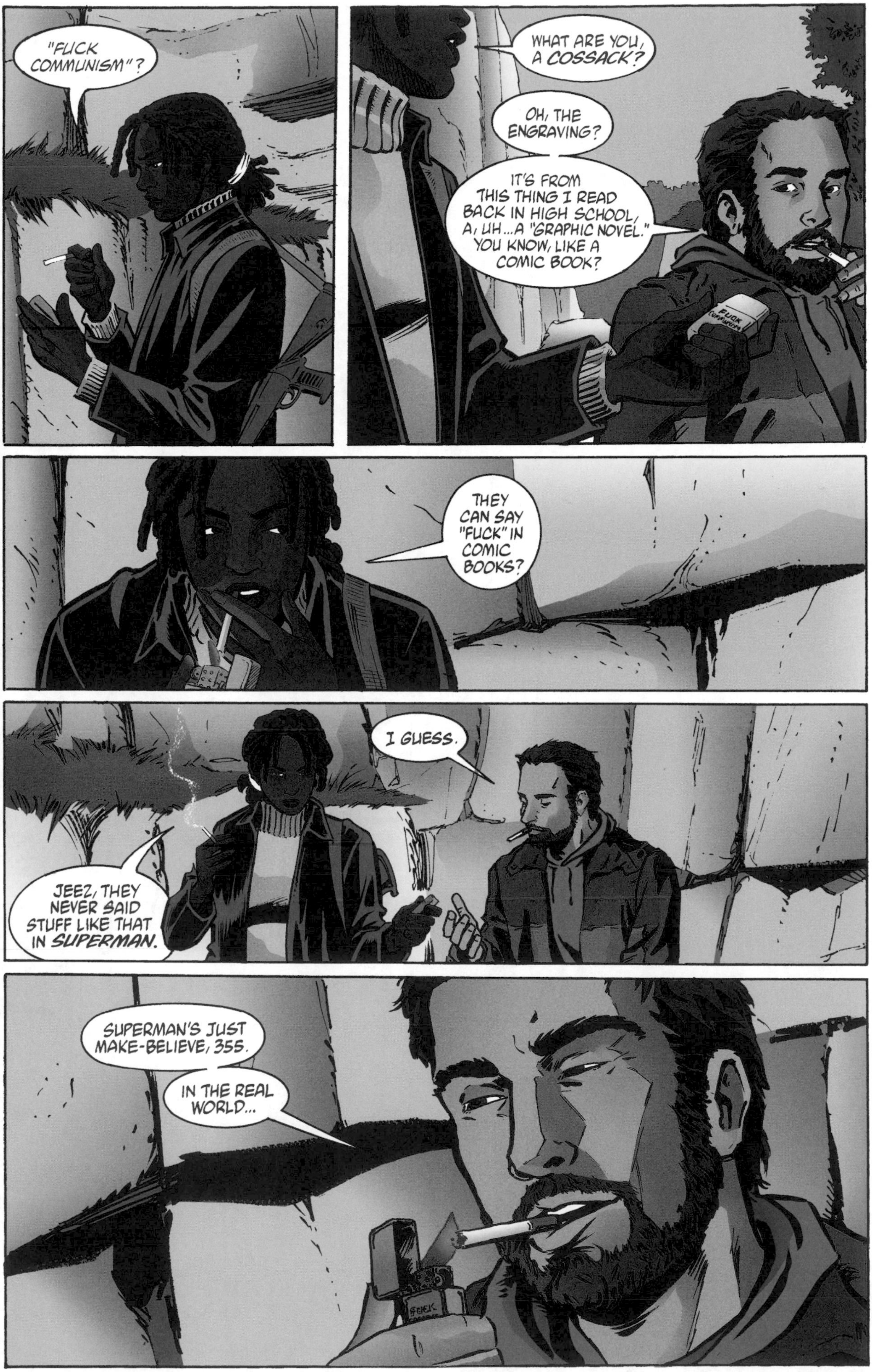
"FUCK COMMUNISM"?
WHAT ARE YOU, A COSSACK?
OH, THE ENGRAVING?
IT'S FROM THIS THING I READ BACK IN HIGH SCHOOL, A, UH...A "GRAPHIC NOVEL." YOU KNOW, LIKE A COMIC BOOK?
THEY CAN SAY "FUCK" IN COMIC BOOKS?
I GUESS.
JEEZ, THEY NEVER SAID STUFF LIKE THAT IN SUPERMAN.
SUPERMAN'S JUST MAKE-BELIEVE, 355.
IN THE REAL WORLD...

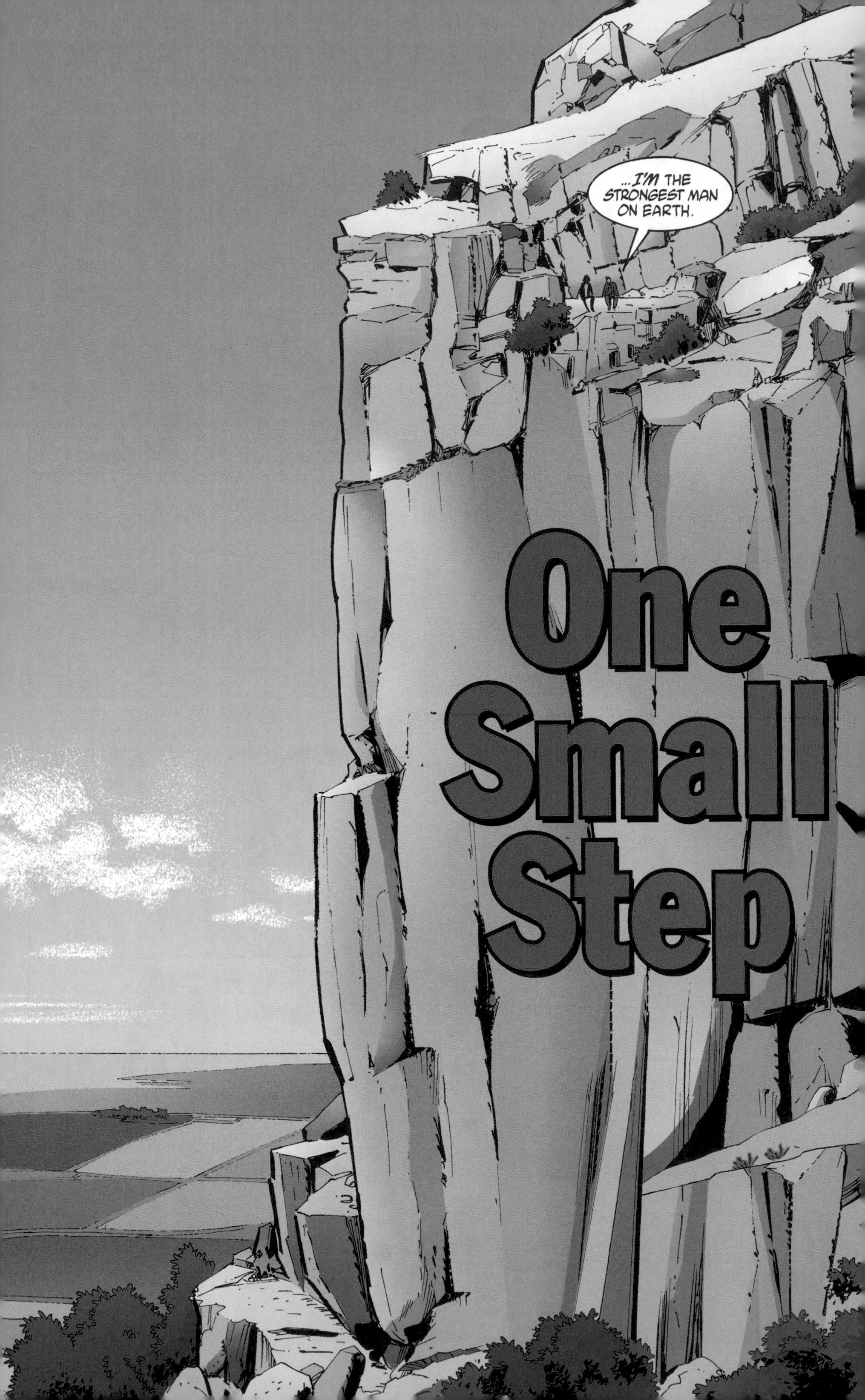
...I'M THE STRONGEST MAN ON EARTH.
One Small Step

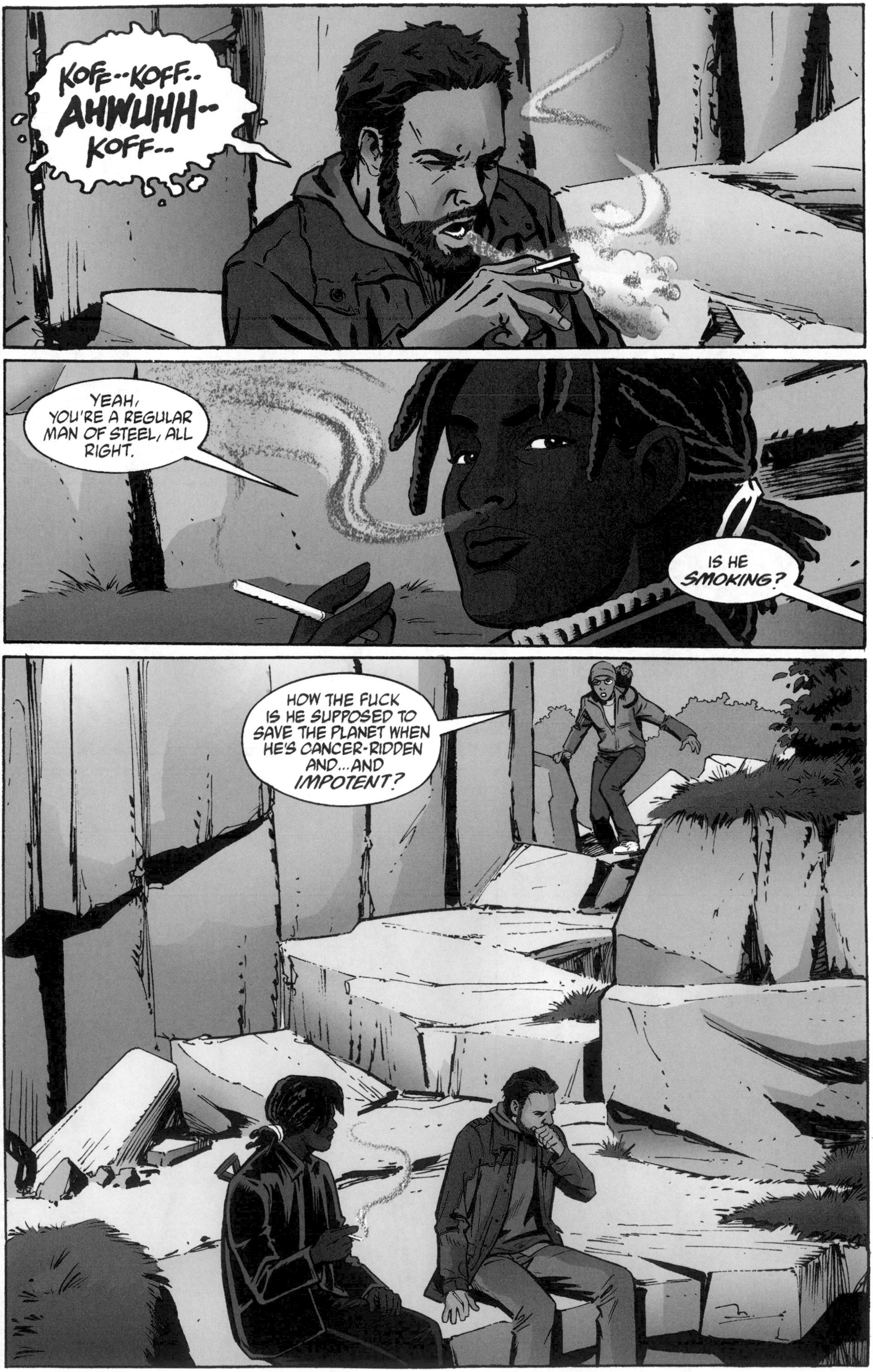
KOFF--KOFF--
AHWUHH--
KOFF--
YEAH, YOU'RE A REGULAR MAN OF STEEL, ALL RIGHT.
IS HE SMOKING?
HOW THE FUCK IS HE SUPPOSED TO SAVE THE PLANET WHEN HE'S CANCER-RIDDEN AND...AND IMPOTENT?

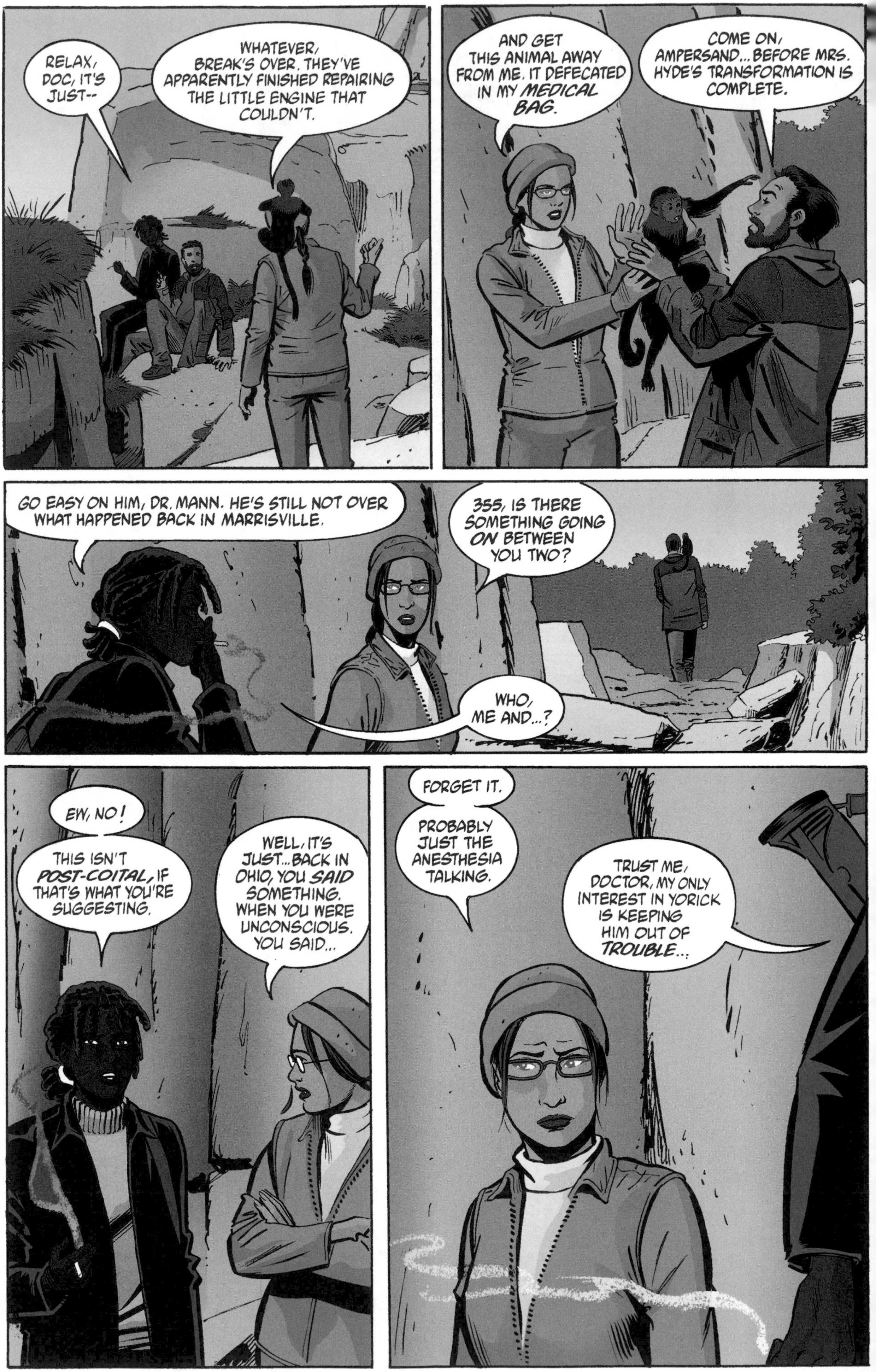
RELAX, DOC, IT'S JUST--
WHATEVER, BREAK'S OVER. THEY'VE APPARENTLY FINISHED REPAIRING THE LITTLE ENGINE THAT COULDN'T.
AND GET THIS ANIMAL AWAY FROM ME. IT DEFECATED IN MY MEDICAL BAG.
COME ON, AMPERSAND... BEFORE MRS. HYDE'S TRANSFORMATION IS COMPLETE.
GO EASY ON HIM, DR. MANN. HE'S STILL NOT OVER WHAT HAPPENED BACK IN MARRISVILLE.
355, IS THERE SOMETHING GOING ON BETWEEN YOU TWO?
WHO, ME AND...?
EW, NO!
THIS ISN'T POST-COITAL, IF THAT'S WHAT YOU'RE SUGGESTING.
WELL, IT'S JUST... BACK IN OHIO, YOU SAID SOMETHING. WHEN YOU WERE UNCONSCIOUS. YOU SAID...
FORGET IT.
PROBABLY JUST THE ANESTHESIA TALKING.
TRUST ME, DOCTOR, MY ONLY INTEREST IN YORICK IS KEEPING HIM OUT OF TROUBLE...

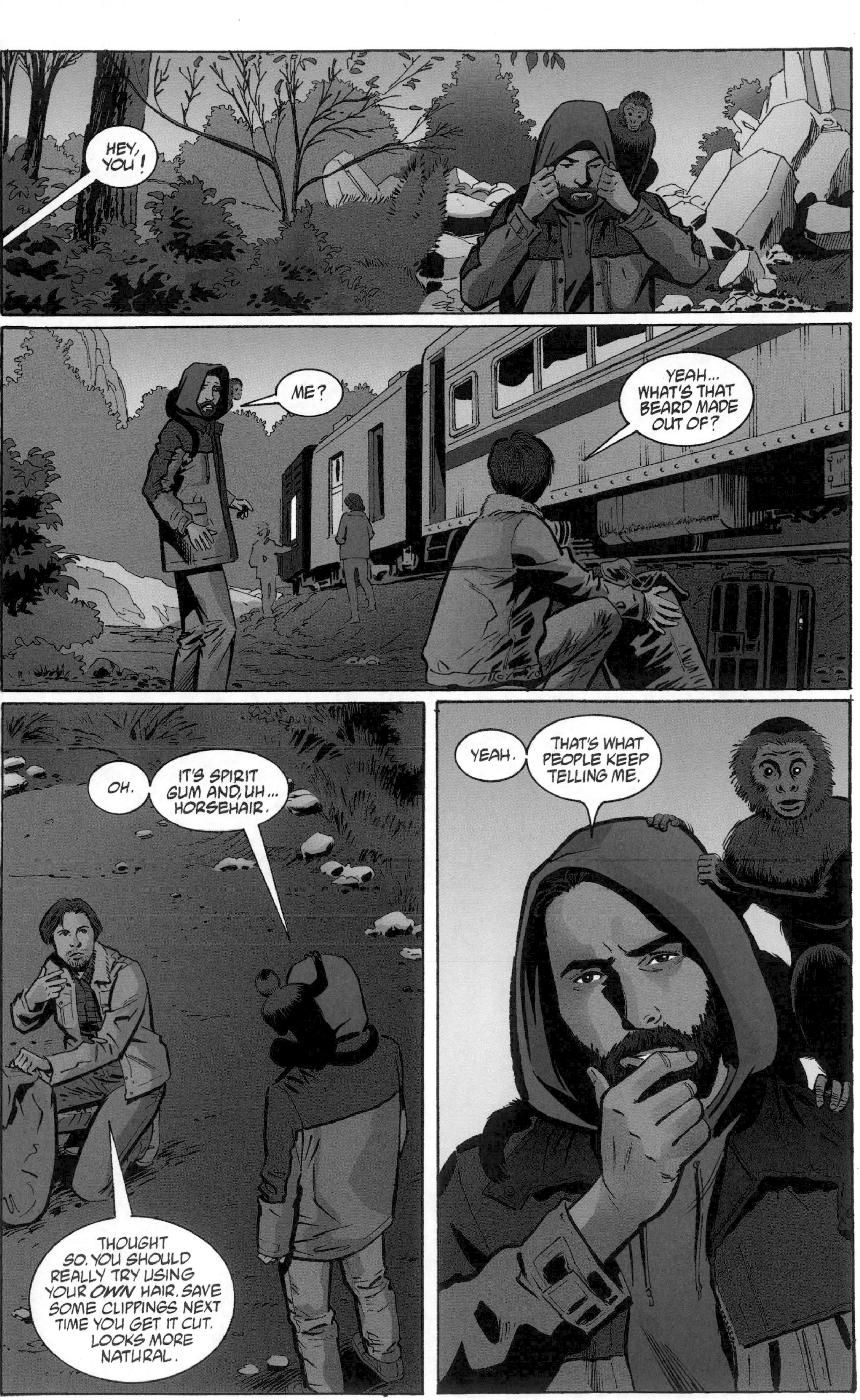
HEY, YOU!
ME?
YEAH... WHAT'S THAT BEARD MADE OUT OF?
OH.
IT'S SPIRIT GUM AND, UH... HORSEHAIR.
THOUGHT SO. YOU SHOULD REALLY TRY USING YOUR OWN HAIR. SAVE SOME CLIPPINGS NEXT TIME YOU GET IT CUT. LOOKS MORE NATURAL.
YEAH.
THAT'S WHAT PEOPLE KEEP TELLING ME.

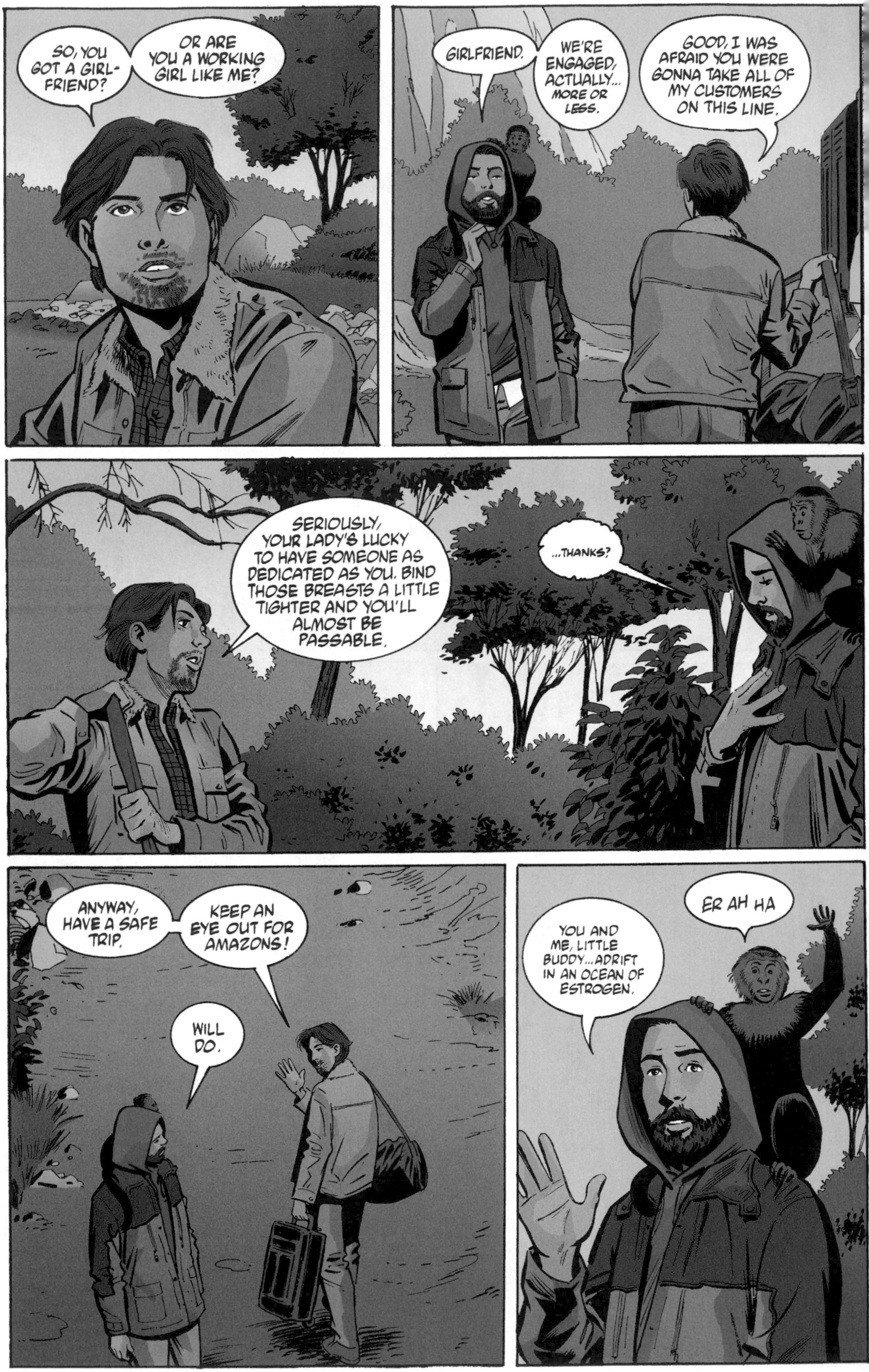
SO, YOU GOT A GIRL-FRIEND?
OR ARE YOU A WORKING GIRL LIKE ME?
GIRLFRIEND.
WE'RE ENGAGED, ACTUALLY... MORE OR LESS.
GOOD, I WAS AFRAID YOU WERE GONNA TAKE ALL OF MY CUSTOMERS ON THIS LINE.
SERIOUSLY, YOUR LADY'S LUCKY TO HAVE SOMEONE AS DEDICATED AS YOU. BIND THOSE BREASTS A LITTLE TIGHTER AND YOU'LL ALMOST BE PASSABLE.
...THANKS?
ANYWAY, HAVE A SAFE TRIP.
KEEP AN EYE OUT FOR AMAZONS!
WILL DO.
YOU AND ME, LITTLE BUDDY...ADRIFT IN AN OCEAN OF ESTROGEN.
ER AH HA

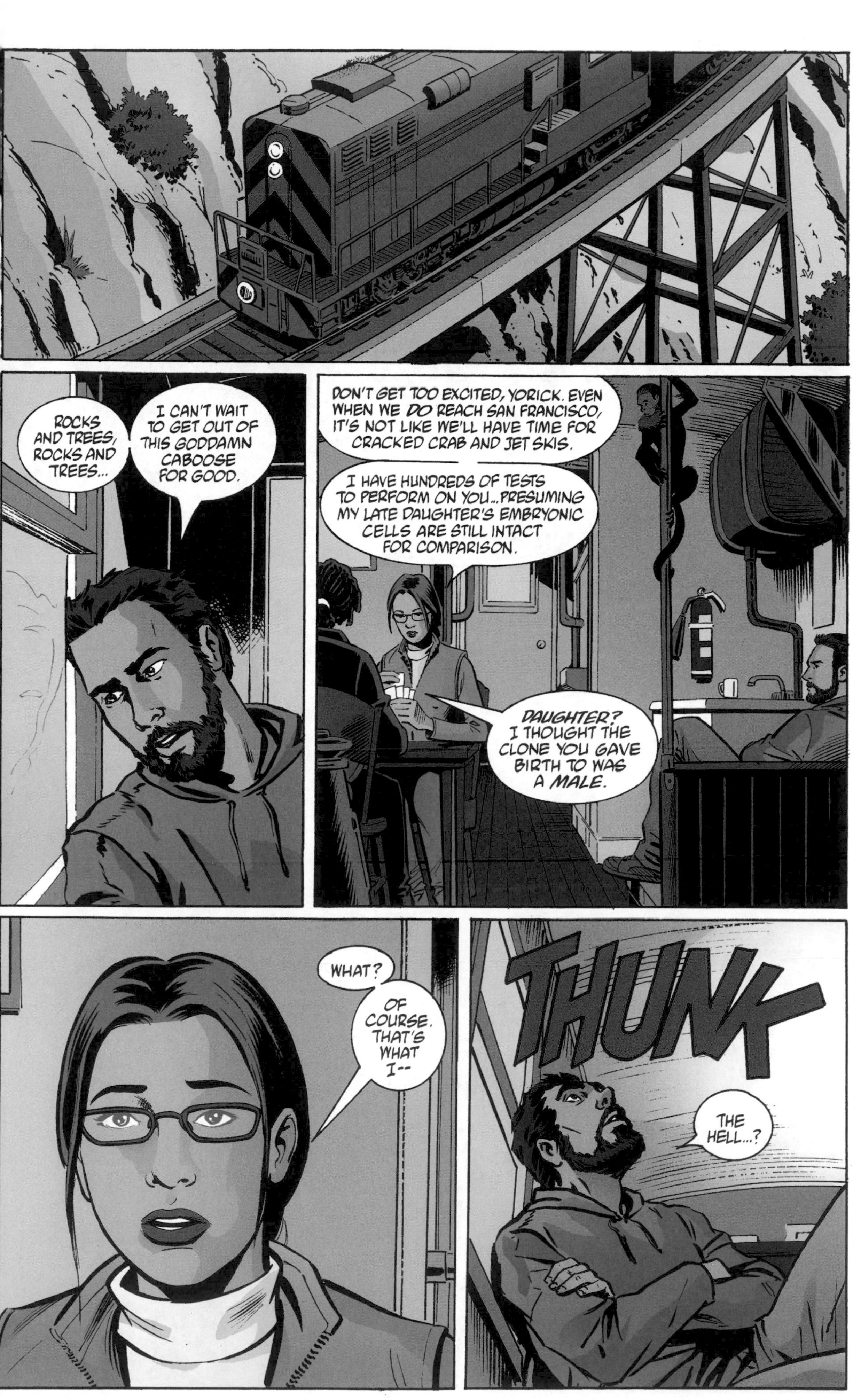
ROCKS AND TREES, ROCKS AND TREES...
I CAN'T WAIT TO GET OUT OF THIS GODDAMN CABOOSE FOR GOOD.
DON'T GET TOO EXCITED, YORICK. EVEN WHEN WE DO REACH SAN FRANCISCO, IT'S NOT LIKE WE'LL HAVE TIME FOR CRACKED CRAB AND JET SKIS.
I HAVE HUNDREDS OF TESTS TO PERFORM ON YOU...PRESUMING MY LATE DAUGHTER'S EMBRYONIC CELLS ARE STILL INTACT FOR COMPARISON.
DAUGHTER? I THOUGHT THE CLONE YOU GAVE BIRTH TO WAS A MALE.
WHAT?
OF COURSE. THAT'S WHAT I--
THUNK
THE HELL...?

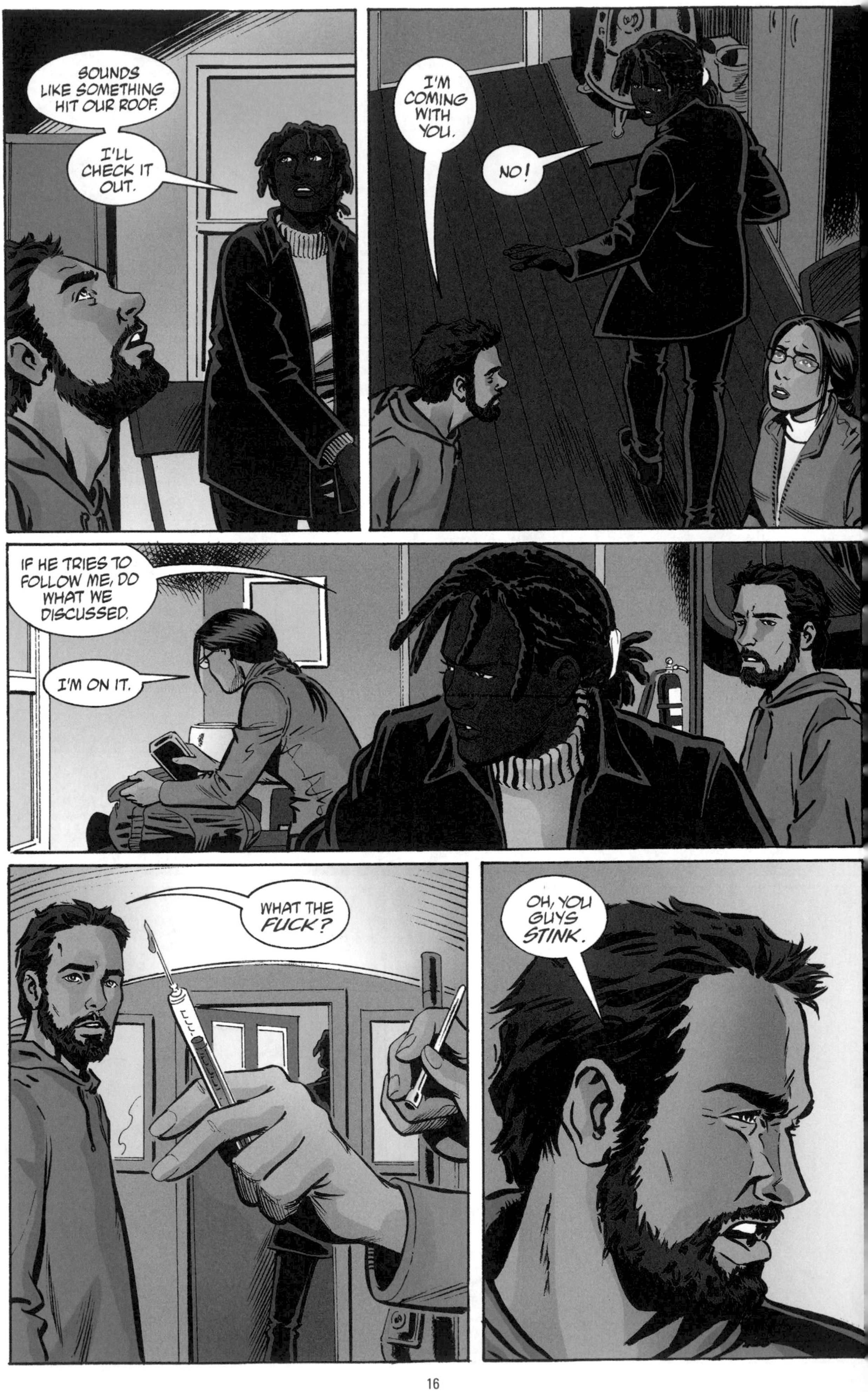
SOUNDS LIKE SOMETHING HIT OUR ROOF.
I'LL CHECK IT OUT.
I'M COMING WITH YOU.
NO!
IF HE TRIES TO FOLLOW ME, DO WHAT WE DISCUSSED.
I'M ON IT.
WHAT THE *FUCK*?
OH, YOU GUYS *STINK*.

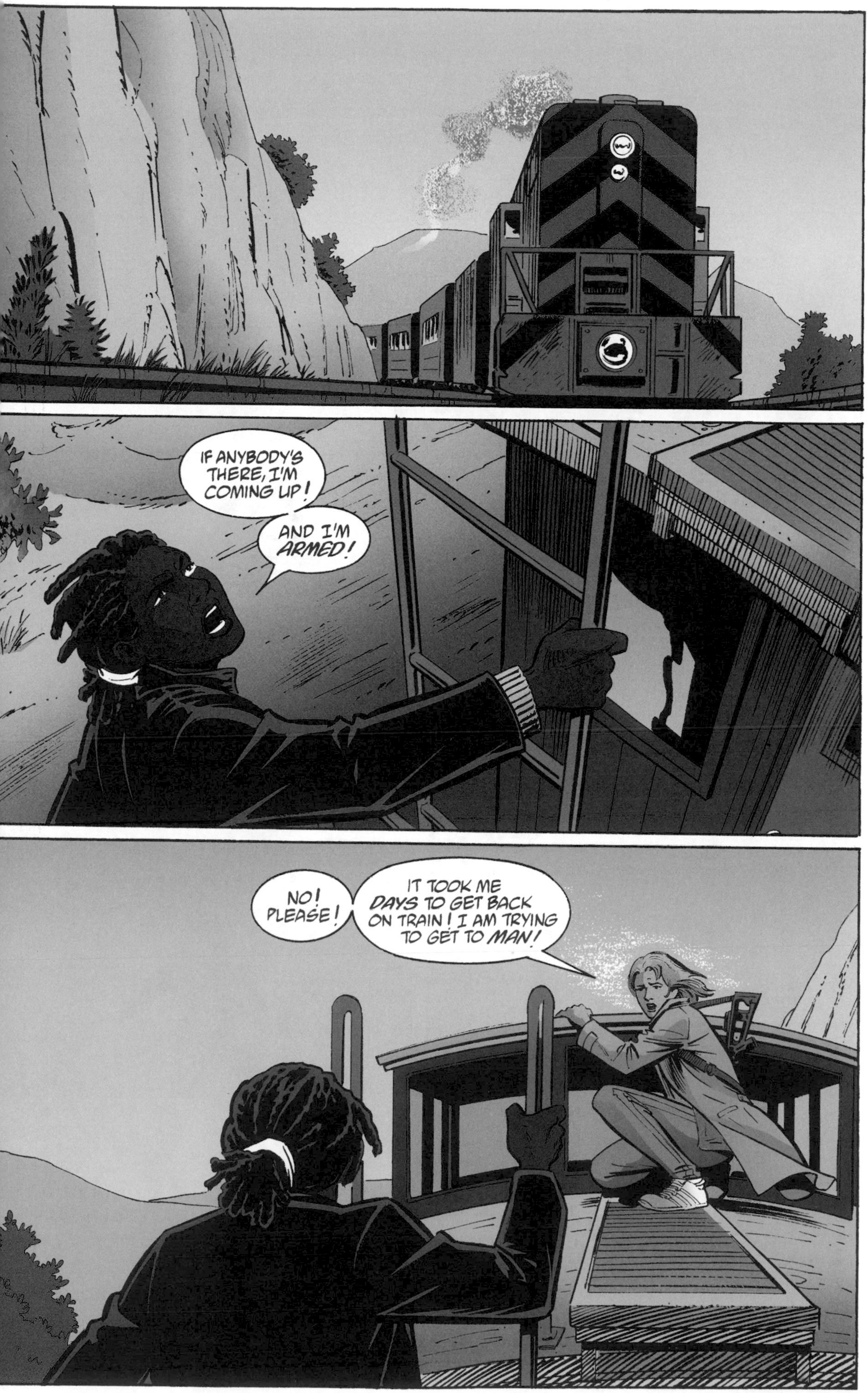
IF ANYBODY'S THERE, I'M COMING UP!
AND I'M ARMED!
NO! PLEASE!
IT TOOK ME DAYS TO GET BACK ON TRAIN! I AM TRYING TO GET TO MAN!

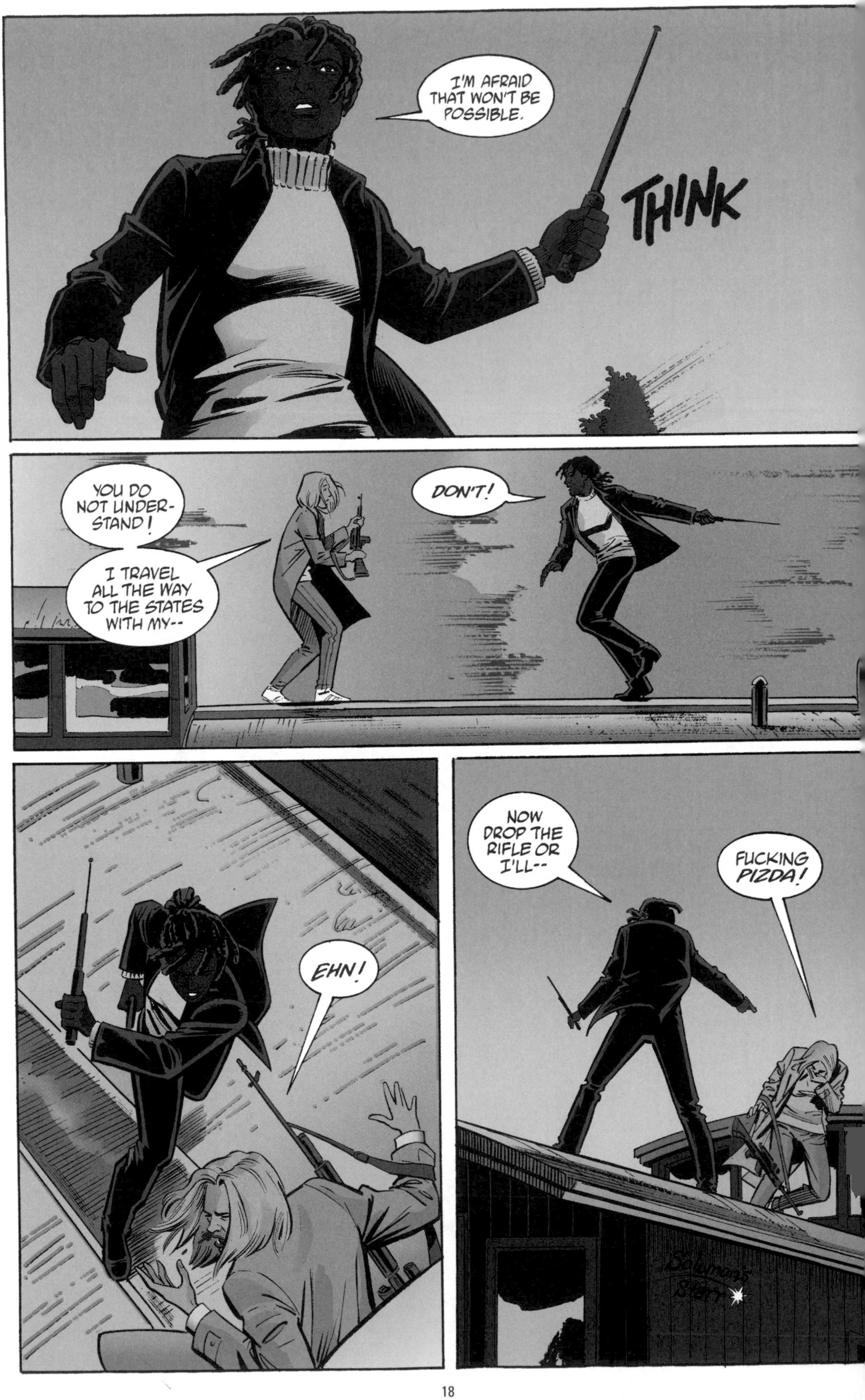
I'M AFRAID THAT WON'T BE POSSIBLE.
THINK
YOU DO NOT UNDER-STAND!
I TRAVEL ALL THE WAY TO THE STATES WITH MY--
DON'T!
EHN!
NOW DROP THE RIFLE OR I'LL--
FUCKING PIZDA!

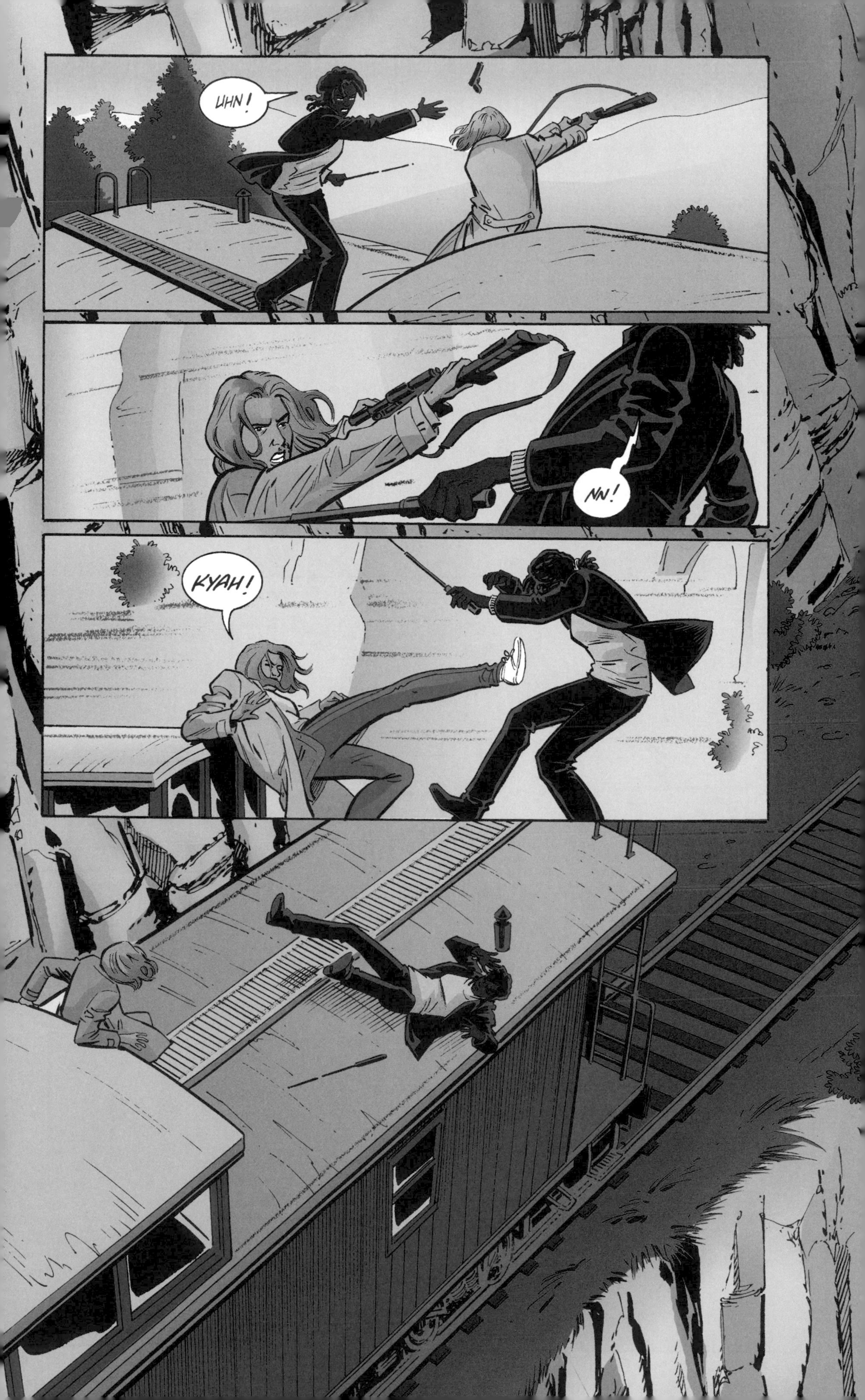
UHN!
NN!
KYAH!

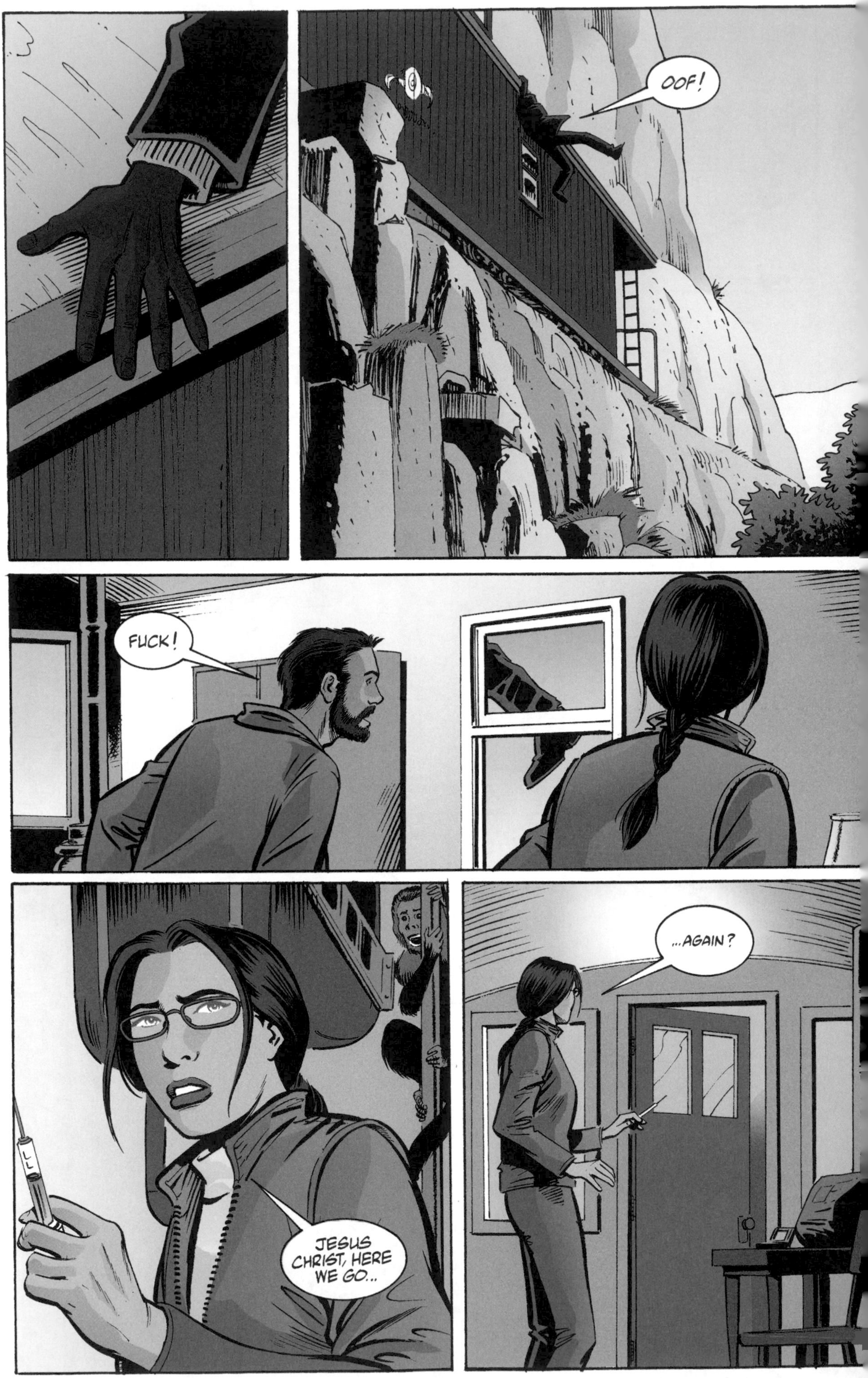
OOF!
FUCK!
JESUS CHRIST, HERE WE GO...
...AGAIN?

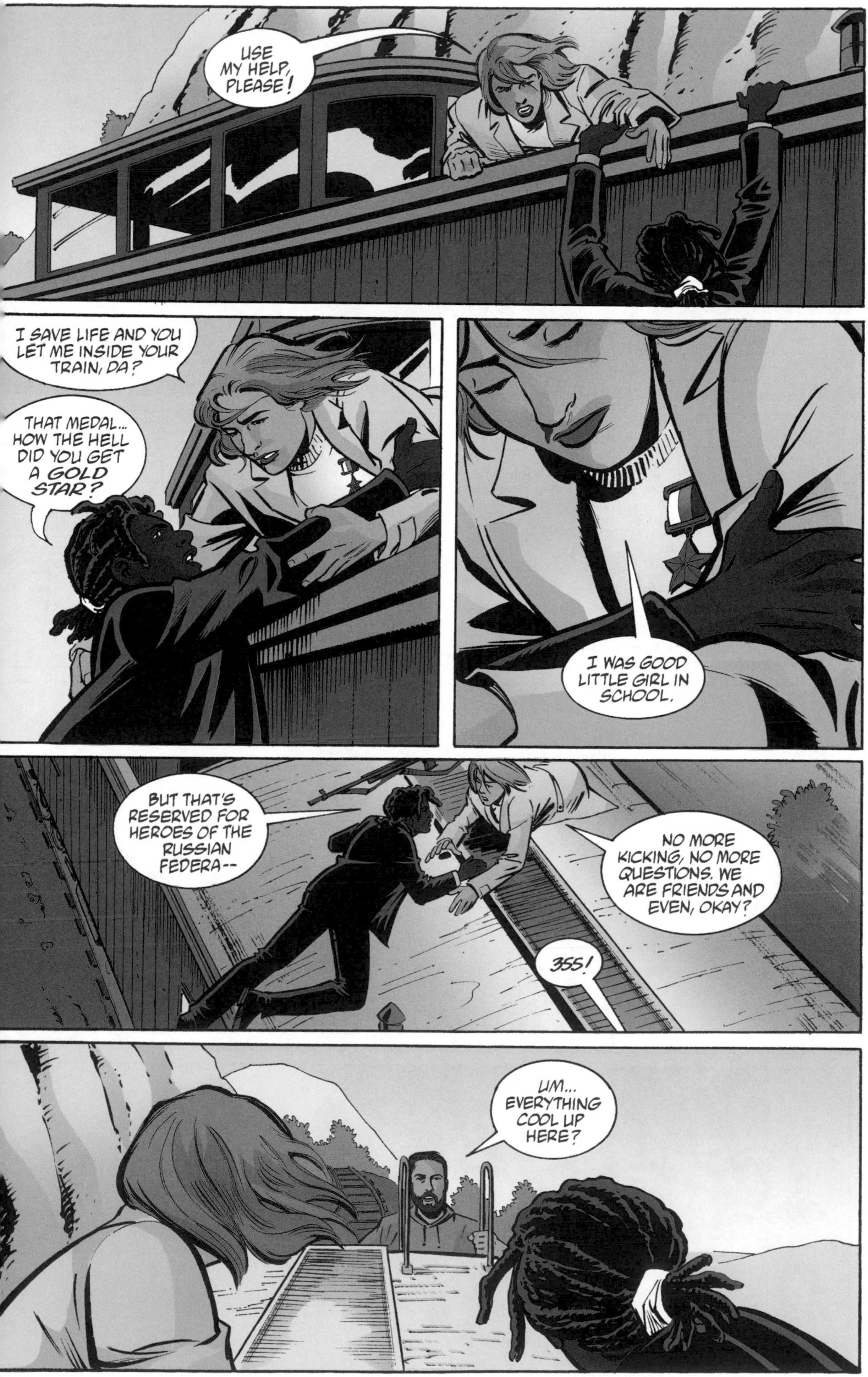
USE MY HELP, PLEASE!
I SAVE LIFE AND YOU LET ME INSIDE YOUR TRAIN, DA?
THAT MEDAL... HOW THE HELL DID YOU GET A GOLD STAR?
I WAS GOOD LITTLE GIRL IN SCHOOL.
BUT THAT'S RESERVED FOR HEROES OF THE RUSSIAN FEDERA--
NO MORE KICKING, NO MORE QUESTIONS. WE ARE FRIENDS AND EVEN, OKAY?
355!
UM... EVERYTHING COOL UP HERE?

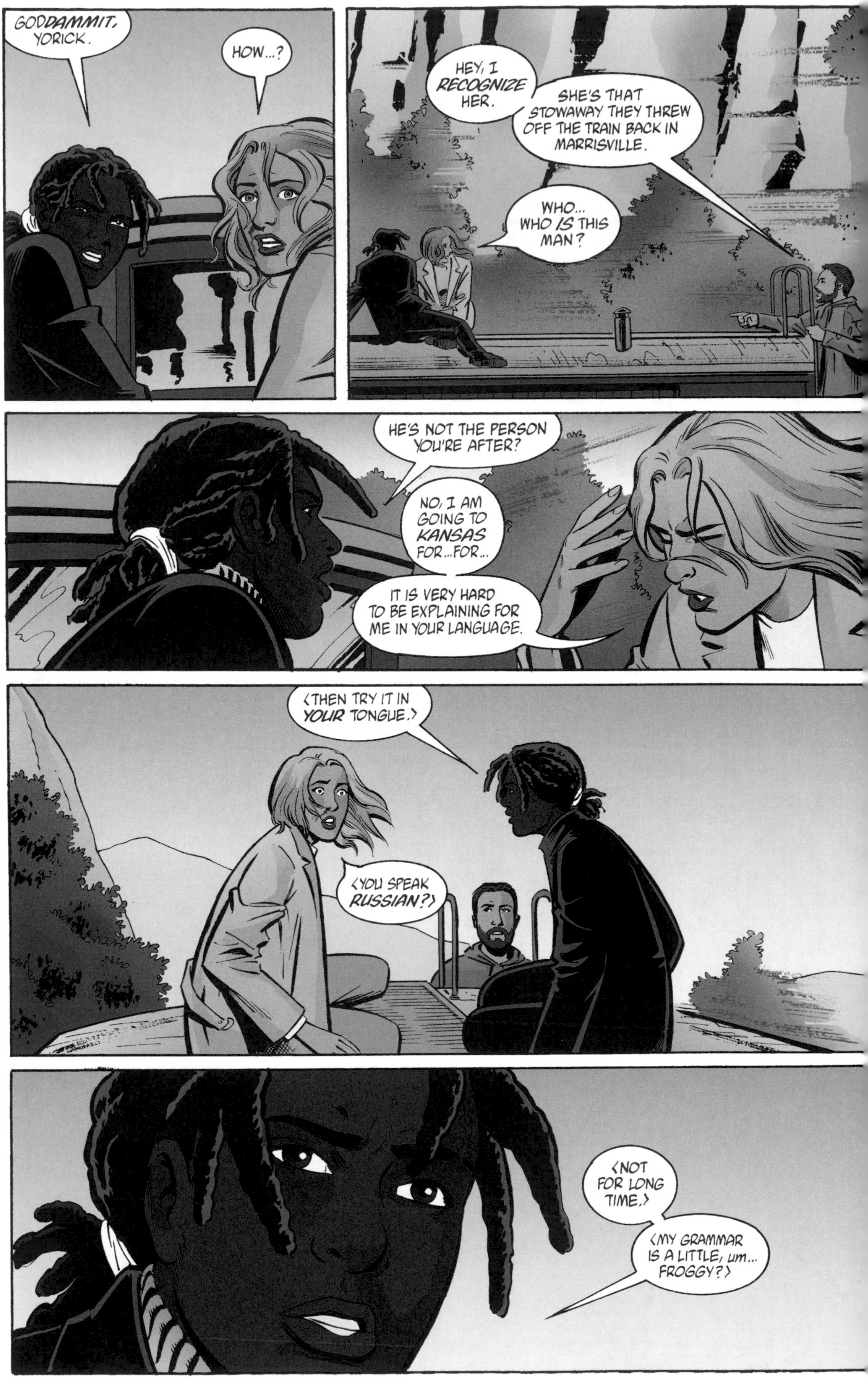
GODDAMMIT, YORICK.
HOW...?
HEY, I RECOGNIZE HER.
SHE'S THAT STOWAWAY THEY THREW OFF THE TRAIN BACK IN MARRISVILLE.
WHO... WHO IS THIS MAN?
HE'S NOT THE PERSON YOU'RE AFTER?
NO, I AM GOING TO KANSAS FOR...FOR...
IT IS VERY HARD TO BE EXPLAINING FOR ME IN YOUR LANGUAGE.
‹THEN TRY IT IN YOUR TONGUE.›
‹YOU SPEAK RUSSIAN?›
‹NOT FOR LONG TIME.›
‹MY GRAMMAR IS A LITTLE, um... FROGGY?›

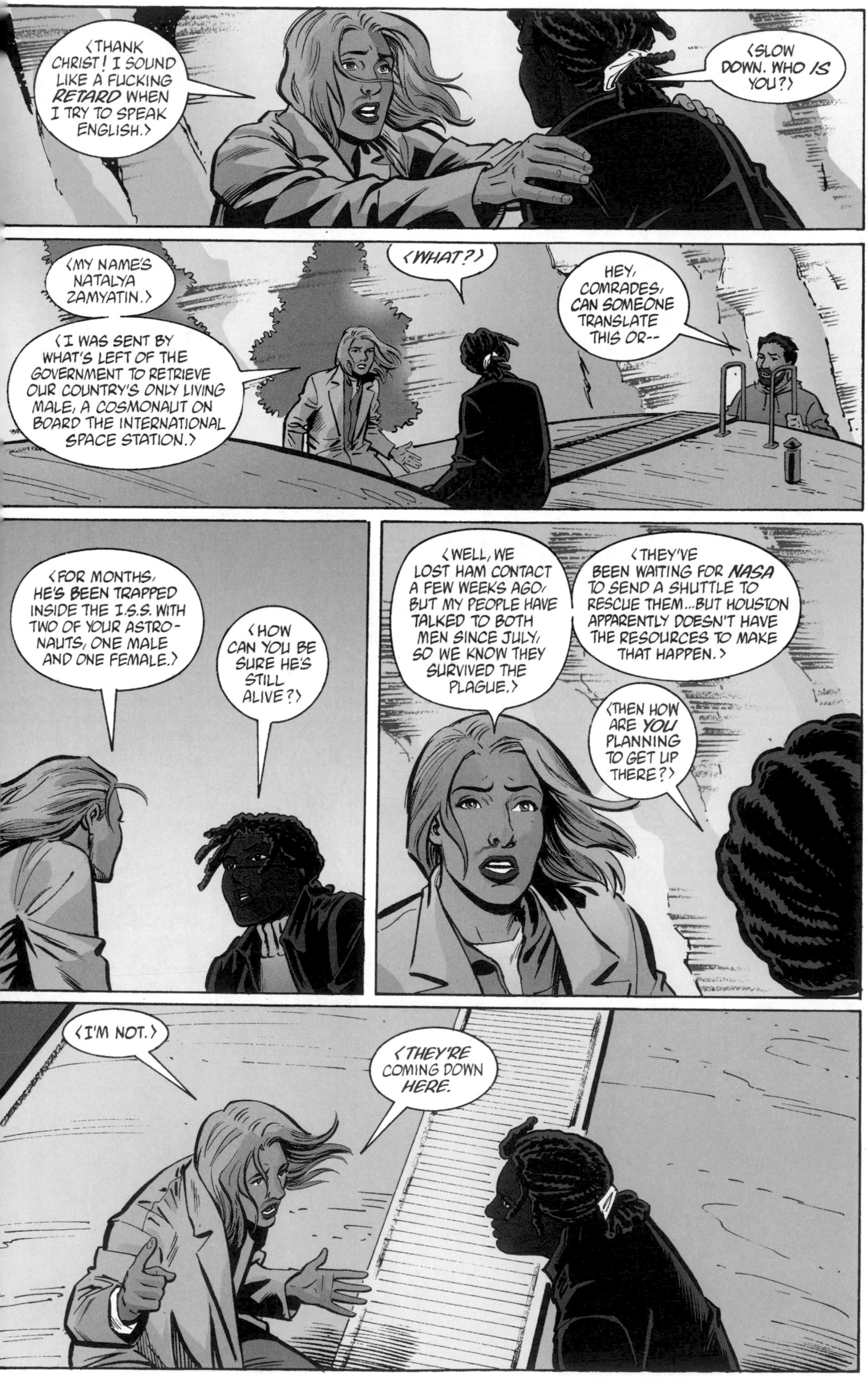
‹THANK CHRIST! I SOUND LIKE A FUCKING RETARD WHEN I TRY TO SPEAK ENGLISH.›
‹SLOW DOWN. WHO IS YOU?›
‹MY NAME'S NATALYA ZAMYATIN.›
‹I WAS SENT BY WHAT'S LEFT OF THE GOVERNMENT TO RETRIEVE OUR COUNTRY'S ONLY LIVING MALE, A COSMONAUT ON BOARD THE INTERNATIONAL SPACE STATION.›
‹WHAT?›
HEY, COMRADES, CAN SOMEONE TRANSLATE THIS OR--
‹FOR MONTHS, HE'S BEEN TRAPPED INSIDE THE I.S.S. WITH TWO OF YOUR ASTRO-NAUTS, ONE MALE AND ONE FEMALE.›
‹HOW CAN YOU BE SURE HE'S STILL ALIVE?›
‹WELL, WE LOST HAM CONTACT A FEW WEEKS AGO, BUT MY PEOPLE HAVE TALKED TO BOTH MEN SINCE JULY, SO WE KNOW THEY SURVIVED THE PLAGUE.›
‹THEY'VE BEEN WAITING FOR NASA TO SEND A SHUTTLE TO RESCUE THEM...BUT HOUSTON APPARENTLY DOESN'T HAVE THE RESOURCES TO MAKE THAT HAPPEN.›
‹THEN HOW ARE YOU PLANNING TO GET UP THERE?›
‹I'M NOT.›
‹THEY'RE COMING DOWN HERE.

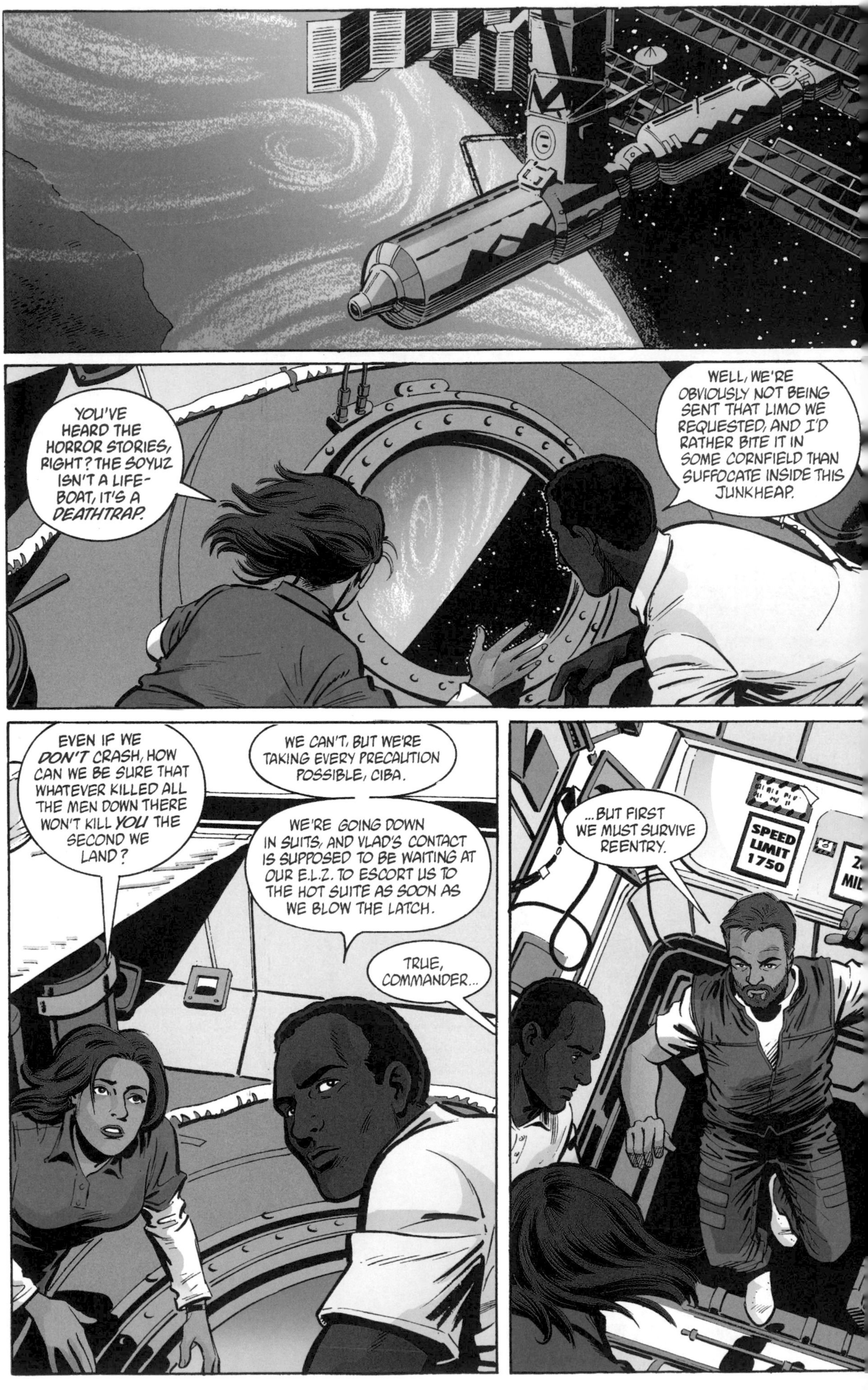
YOU'VE HEARD THE HORROR STORIES, RIGHT? THE SOYUZ ISN'T A LIFE-BOAT, IT'S A DEATHTRAP.
WELL, WE'RE OBVIOUSLY NOT BEING SENT THAT LIMO WE REQUESTED, AND I'D RATHER BITE IT IN SOME CORNFIELD THAN SUFFOCATE INSIDE THIS JUNKHEAP.
EVEN IF WE DON'T CRASH, HOW CAN WE BE SURE THAT WHATEVER KILLED ALL THE MEN DOWN THERE WON'T KILL YOU THE SECOND WE LAND?
WE CAN'T, BUT WE'RE TAKING EVERY PRECAUTION POSSIBLE, CIBA.
WE'RE GOING DOWN IN SUITS, AND VLAD'S CONTACT IS SUPPOSED TO BE WAITING AT OUR E.L.Z. TO ESCORT US TO THE HOT SUITE AS SOON AS WE BLOW THE LATCH.
TRUE, COMMANDER...
...BUT FIRST WE MUST SURVIVE REENTRY.
SPEED LIMIT 1750

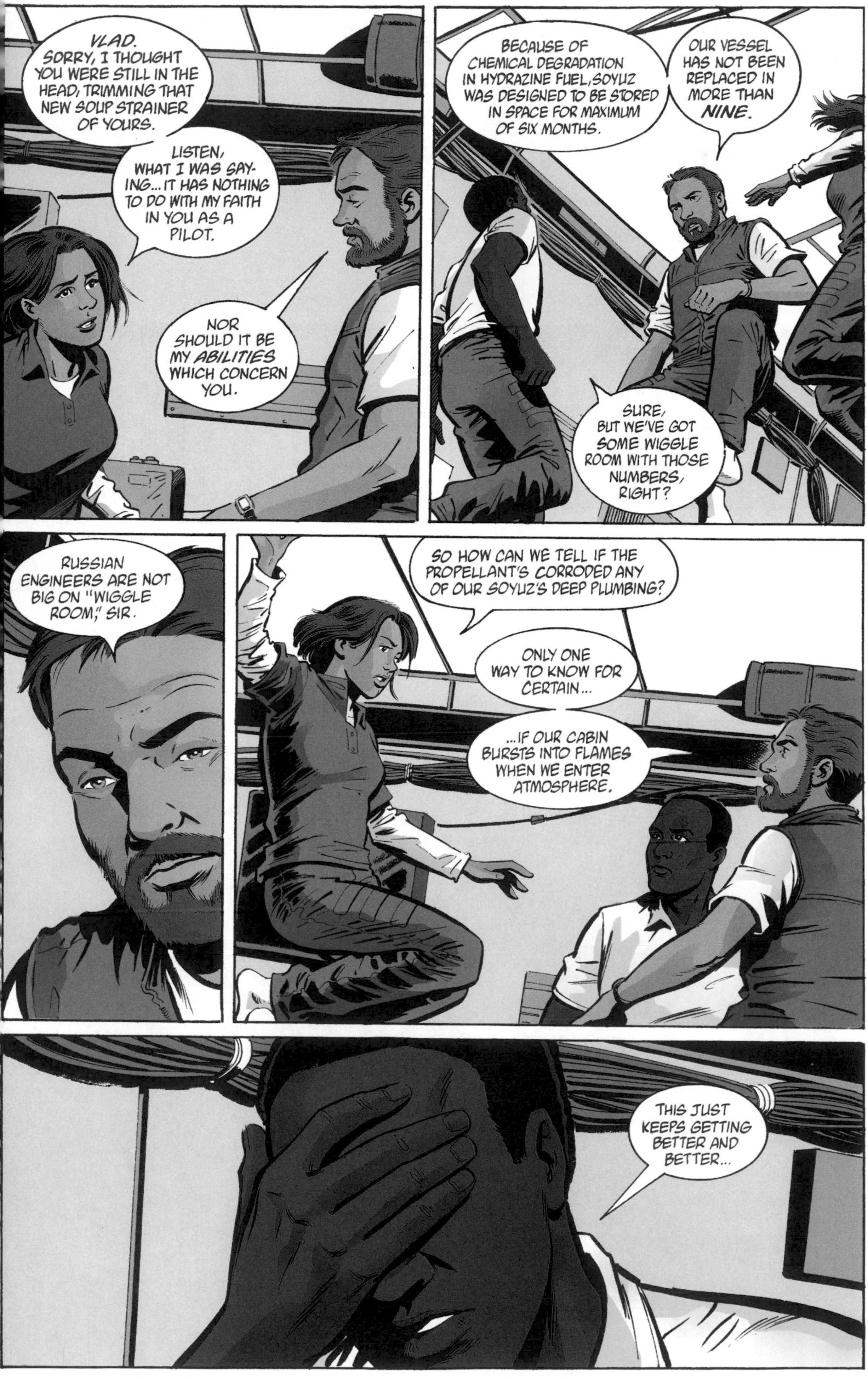
VLAD. SORRY, I THOUGHT YOU WERE STILL IN THE HEAD, TRIMMING THAT NEW SOUP STRAINER OF YOURS.
LISTEN, WHAT I WAS SAY-ING... IT HAS NOTHING TO DO WITH MY FAITH IN YOU AS A PILOT.
NOR SHOULD IT BE MY *ABILITIES* WHICH CONCERN YOU.
BECAUSE OF CHEMICAL DEGRADATION IN HYDRAZINE FUEL, SOYUZ WAS DESIGNED TO BE STORED IN SPACE FOR MAXIMUM OF SIX MONTHS.
OUR VESSEL HAS NOT BEEN REPLACED IN MORE THAN **NINE**.
SURE, BUT WE'VE GOT SOME WIGGLE ROOM WITH THOSE NUMBERS, RIGHT?
RUSSIAN ENGINEERS ARE NOT BIG ON "WIGGLE ROOM," SIR.
SO HOW CAN WE TELL IF THE PROPELLANT'S CORRODED ANY OF OUR SOYUZ'S DEEP PLUMBING?
ONLY ONE WAY TO KNOW FOR CERTAIN...
...IF OUR CABIN BURSTS INTO FLAMES WHEN WE ENTER ATMOSPHERE.
THIS JUST KEEPS GETTING BETTER AND BETTER...

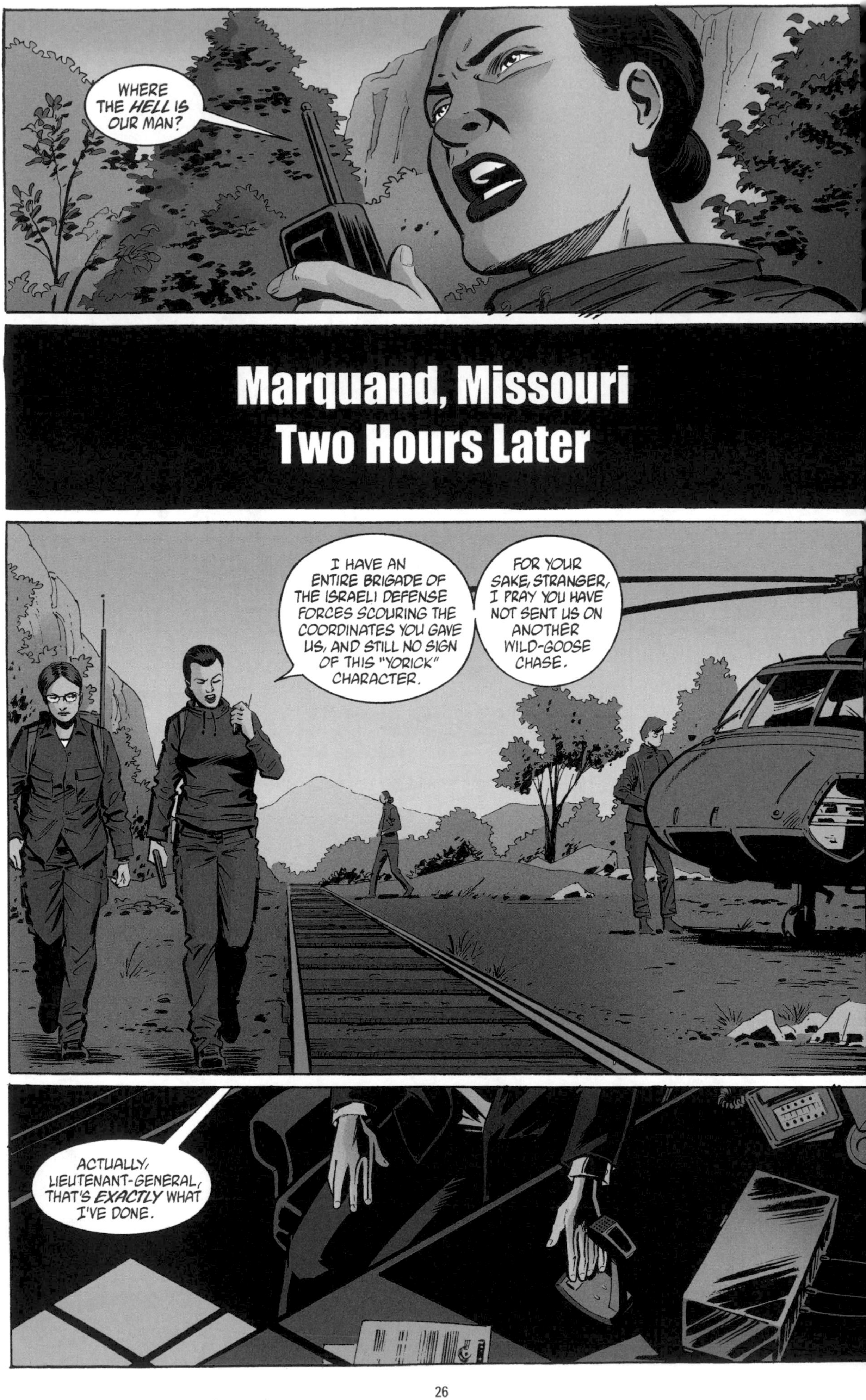
WHERE THE HELL IS OUR MAN?
Marquand, Missouri
Two Hours Later
I HAVE AN ENTIRE BRIGADE OF THE ISRAELI DEFENSE FORCES SCOURING THE COORDINATES YOU GAVE US, AND STILL NO SIGN OF THIS "YORICK" CHARACTER.
FOR YOUR SAKE, STRANGER, I PRAY YOU HAVE NOT SENT US ON ANOTHER WILD-GOOSE CHASE.
ACTUALLY, LIEUTENANT-GENERAL, THAT'S EXACTLY WHAT I'VE DONE.

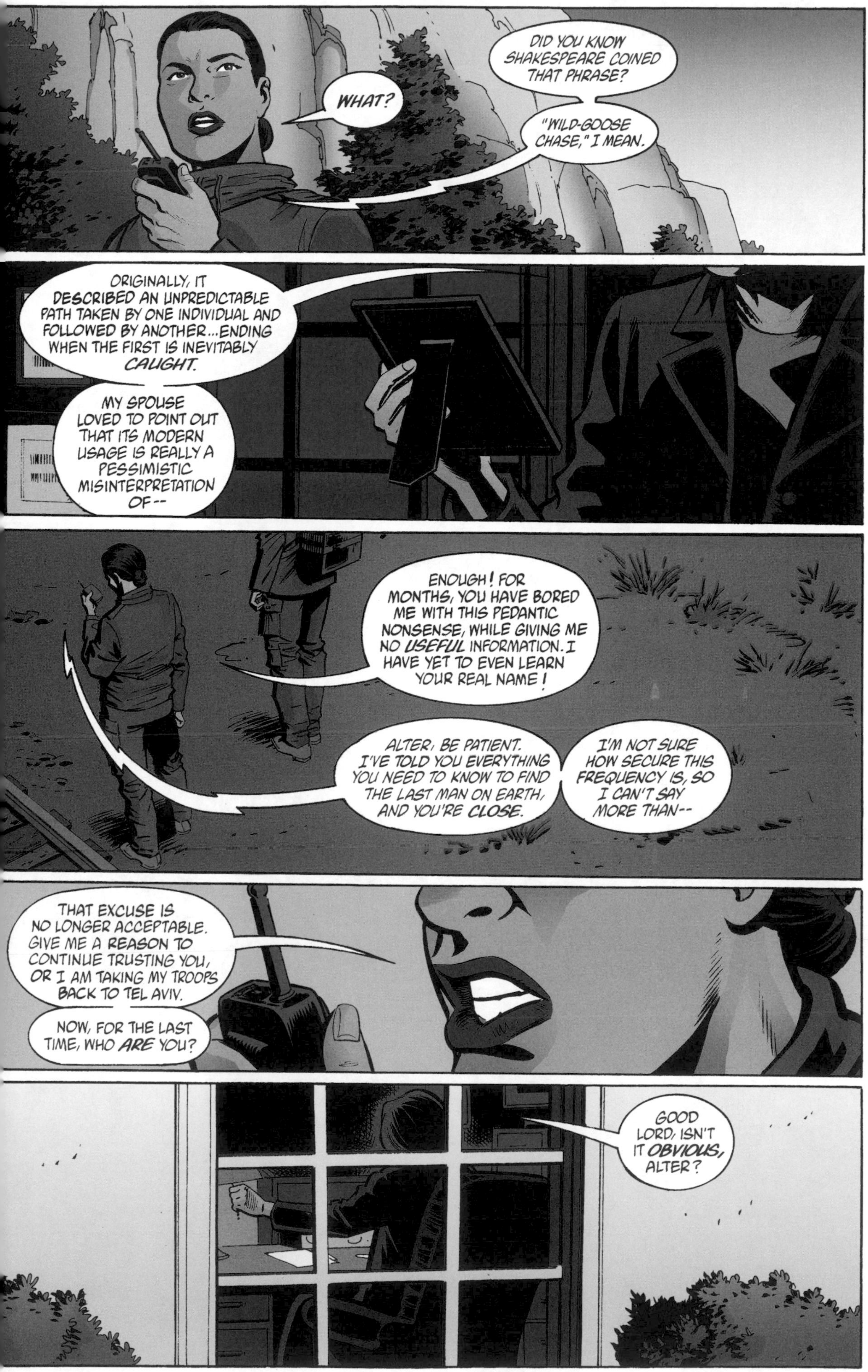
WHAT?
DID YOU KNOW SHAKESPEARE COINED THAT PHRASE?
"WILD-GOOSE CHASE," I MEAN.
ORIGINALLY, IT DESCRIBED AN UNPREDICTABLE PATH TAKEN BY ONE INDIVIDUAL AND FOLLOWED BY ANOTHER...ENDING WHEN THE FIRST IS INEVITABLY CAUGHT.
MY SPOUSE LOVED TO POINT OUT THAT ITS MODERN USAGE IS REALLY A PESSIMISTIC MISINTERPRETATION OF--
ENOUGH! FOR MONTHS, YOU HAVE BORED ME WITH THIS PEDANTIC NONSENSE, WHILE GIVING ME NO USEFUL INFORMATION. I HAVE YET TO EVEN LEARN YOUR REAL NAME!
ALTER, BE PATIENT. I'VE TOLD YOU EVERYTHING YOU NEED TO KNOW TO FIND THE LAST MAN ON EARTH, AND YOU'RE CLOSE.
I'M NOT SURE HOW SECURE THIS FREQUENCY IS, SO I CAN'T SAY MORE THAN--
THAT EXCUSE IS NO LONGER ACCEPTABLE. GIVE ME A REASON TO CONTINUE TRUSTING YOU, OR I AM TAKING MY TROOPS BACK TO TEL AVIV.
NOW, FOR THE LAST TIME, WHO ARE YOU?
GOOD LORD, ISN'T IT OBVIOUS, ALTER?

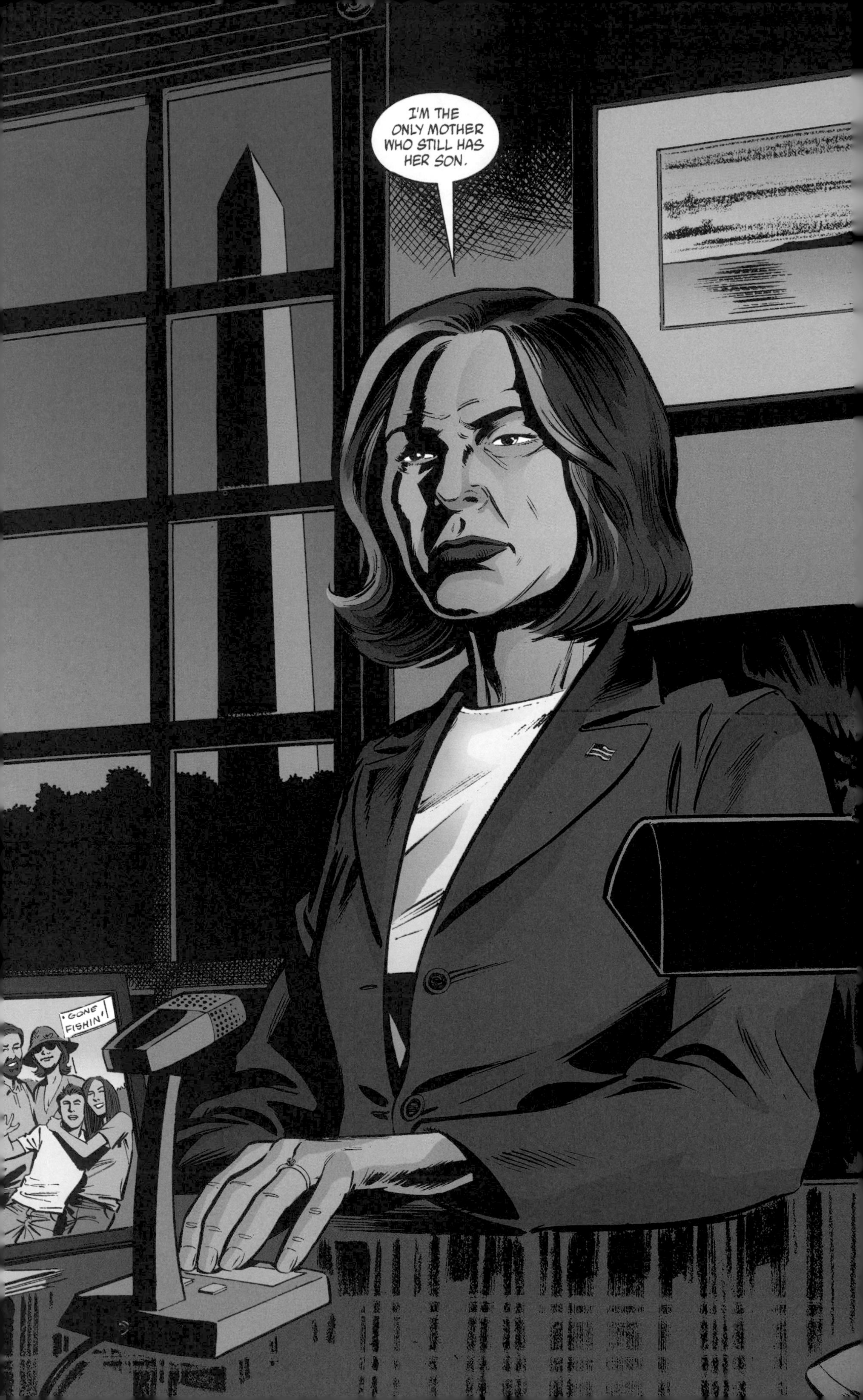
I'M THE ONLY MOTHER WHO STILL HAS HER SON.
'GONE FISHIN'!

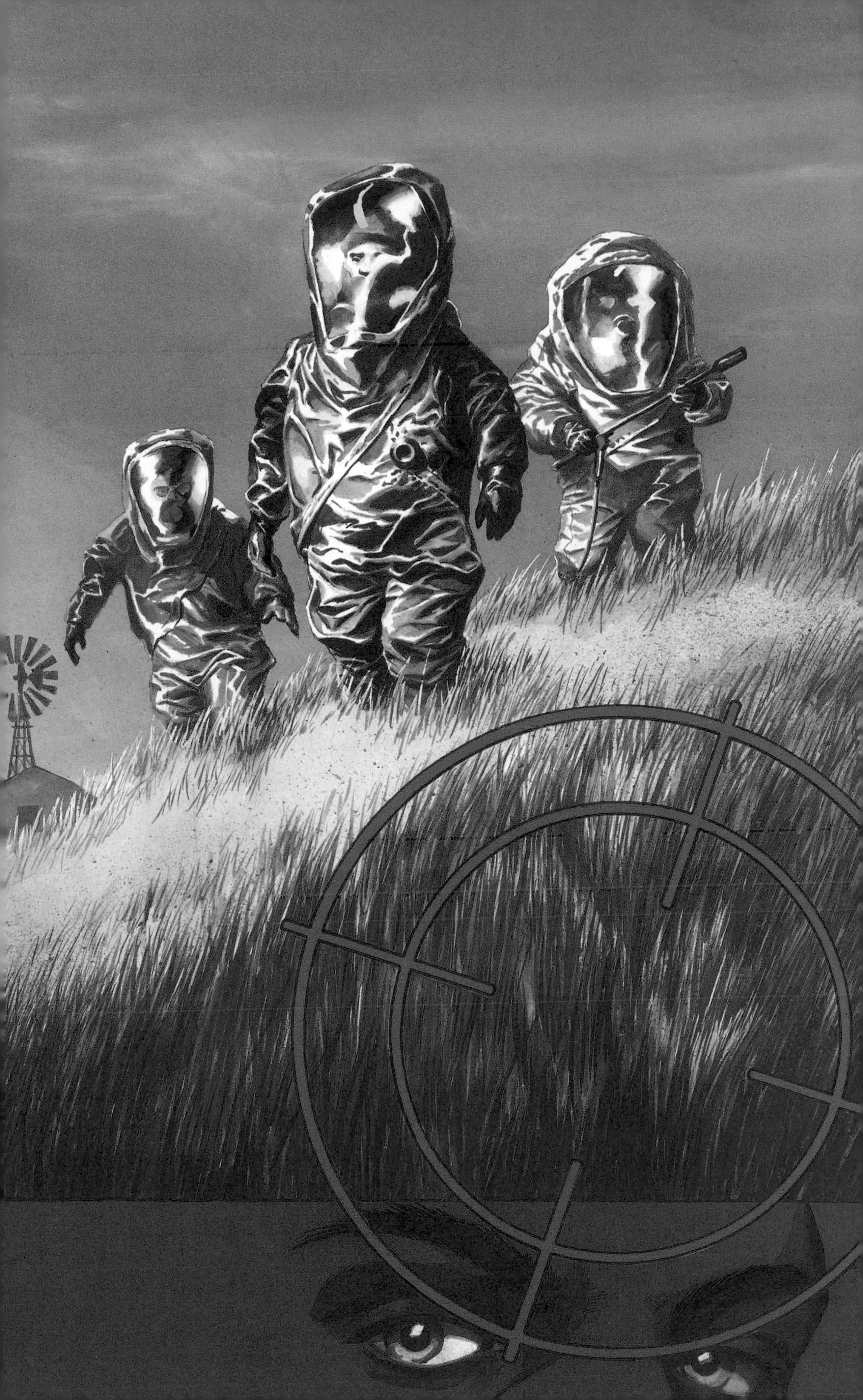

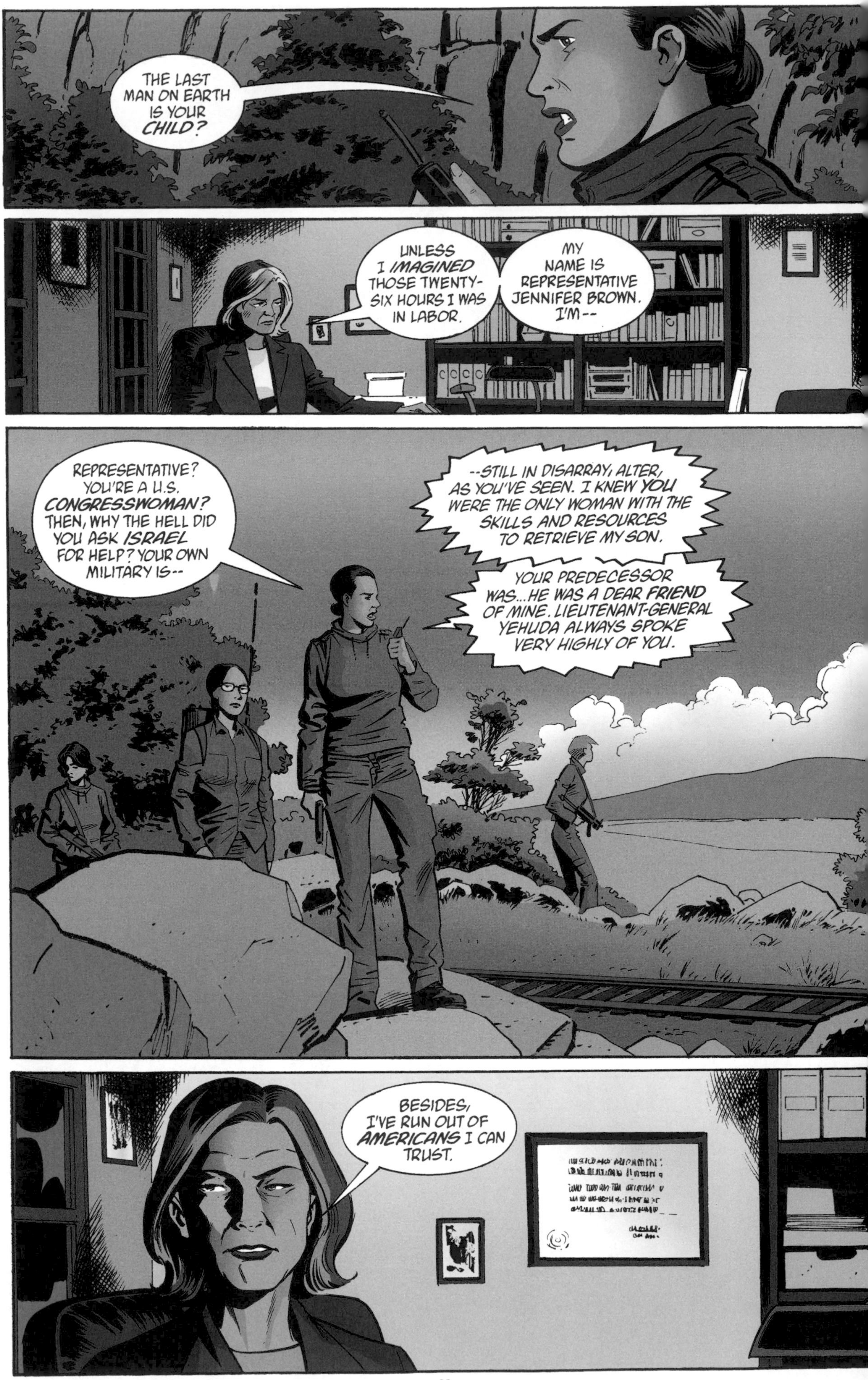
THE LAST MAN ON EARTH IS YOUR CHILD?
UNLESS I IMAGINED THOSE TWENTY-SIX HOURS I WAS IN LABOR.
MY NAME IS REPRESENTATIVE JENNIFER BROWN. I'M--
REPRESENTATIVE? YOU'RE A U.S. CONGRESSWOMAN? THEN, WHY THE HELL DID YOU ASK ISRAEL FOR HELP? YOUR OWN MILITARY IS--
--STILL IN DISARRAY, ALTER, AS YOU'VE SEEN. I KNEW YOU WERE THE ONLY WOMAN WITH THE SKILLS AND RESOURCES TO RETRIEVE MY SON.
YOUR PREDECESSOR WAS...HE WAS A DEAR FRIEND OF MINE. LIEUTENANT-GENERAL YEHUDA ALWAYS SPOKE VERY HIGHLY OF YOU.
BESIDES, I'VE RUN OUT OF AMERICANS I CAN TRUST.

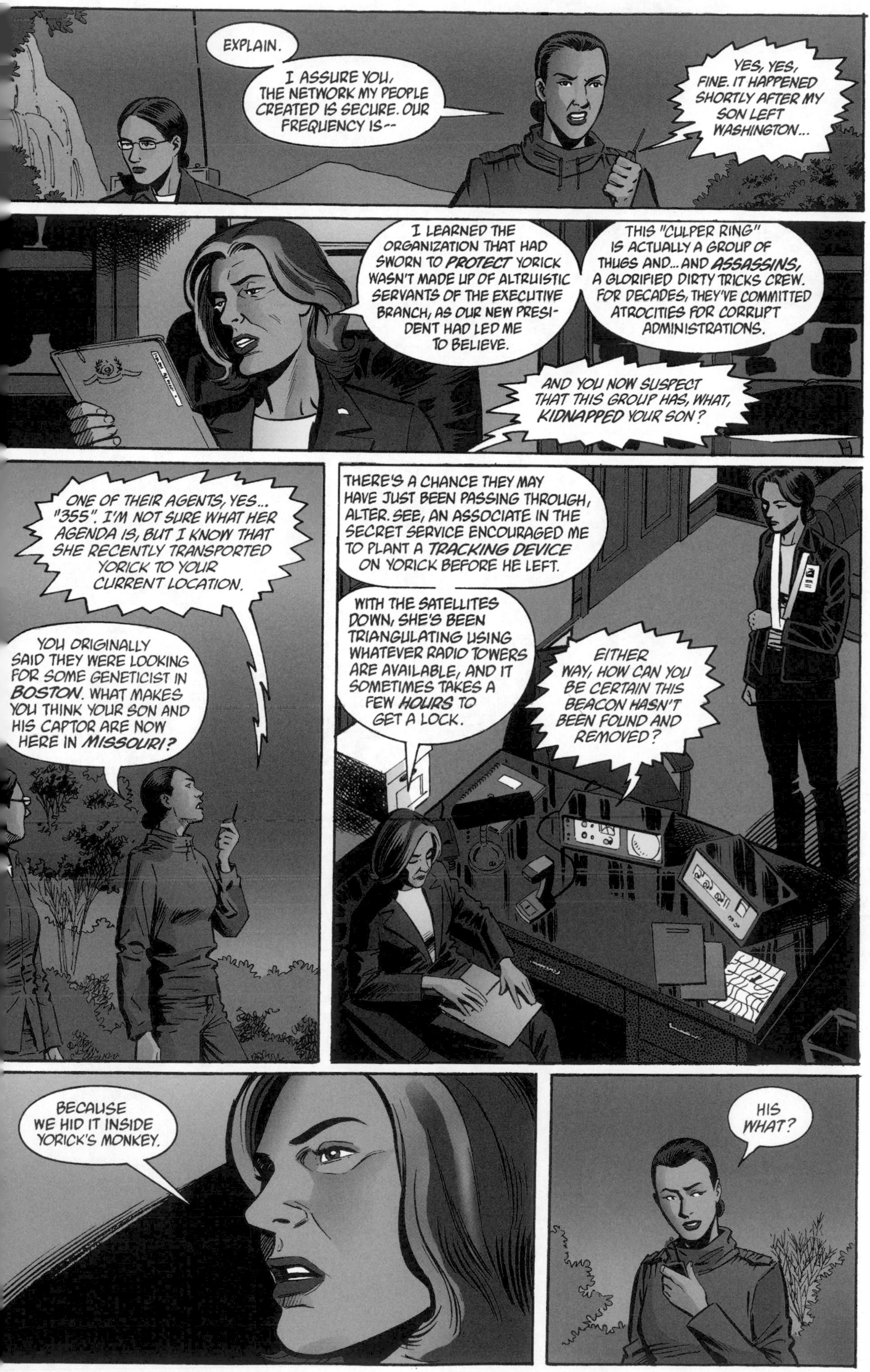
EXPLAIN.
I ASSURE YOU, THE NETWORK MY PEOPLE CREATED IS SECURE. OUR FREQUENCY IS--
YES, YES, FINE. IT HAPPENED SHORTLY AFTER MY SON LEFT WASHINGTON...
I LEARNED THE ORGANIZATION THAT HAD SWORN TO PROTECT YORICK WASN'T MADE UP OF ALTRUISTIC SERVANTS OF THE EXECUTIVE BRANCH, AS OUR NEW PRESIDENT HAD LED ME TO BELIEVE.
THIS "CULPER RING" IS ACTUALLY A GROUP OF THUGS AND... AND ASSASSINS, A GLORIFIED DIRTY TRICKS CREW. FOR DECADES, THEY'VE COMMITTED ATROCITIES FOR CORRUPT ADMINISTRATIONS.
AND YOU NOW SUSPECT THAT THIS GROUP HAS, WHAT, KIDNAPPED YOUR SON?
ONE OF THEIR AGENTS, YES... "355". I'M NOT SURE WHAT HER AGENDA IS, BUT I KNOW THAT SHE RECENTLY TRANSPORTED YORICK TO YOUR CURRENT LOCATION.
YOU ORIGINALLY SAID THEY WERE LOOKING FOR SOME GENETICIST IN BOSTON. WHAT MAKES YOU THINK YOUR SON AND HIS CAPTOR ARE NOW HERE IN MISSOURI?
THERE'S A CHANCE THEY MAY HAVE JUST BEEN PASSING THROUGH, ALTER. SEE, AN ASSOCIATE IN THE SECRET SERVICE ENCOURAGED ME TO PLANT A TRACKING DEVICE ON YORICK BEFORE HE LEFT.
WITH THE SATELLITES DOWN, SHE'S BEEN TRIANGULATING USING WHATEVER RADIO TOWERS ARE AVAILABLE, AND IT SOMETIMES TAKES A FEW HOURS TO GET A LOCK.
EITHER WAY, HOW CAN YOU BE CERTAIN THIS BEACON HASN'T BEEN FOUND AND REMOVED?
BECAUSE WE HID IT INSIDE YORICK'S MONKEY.
HIS WHAT?

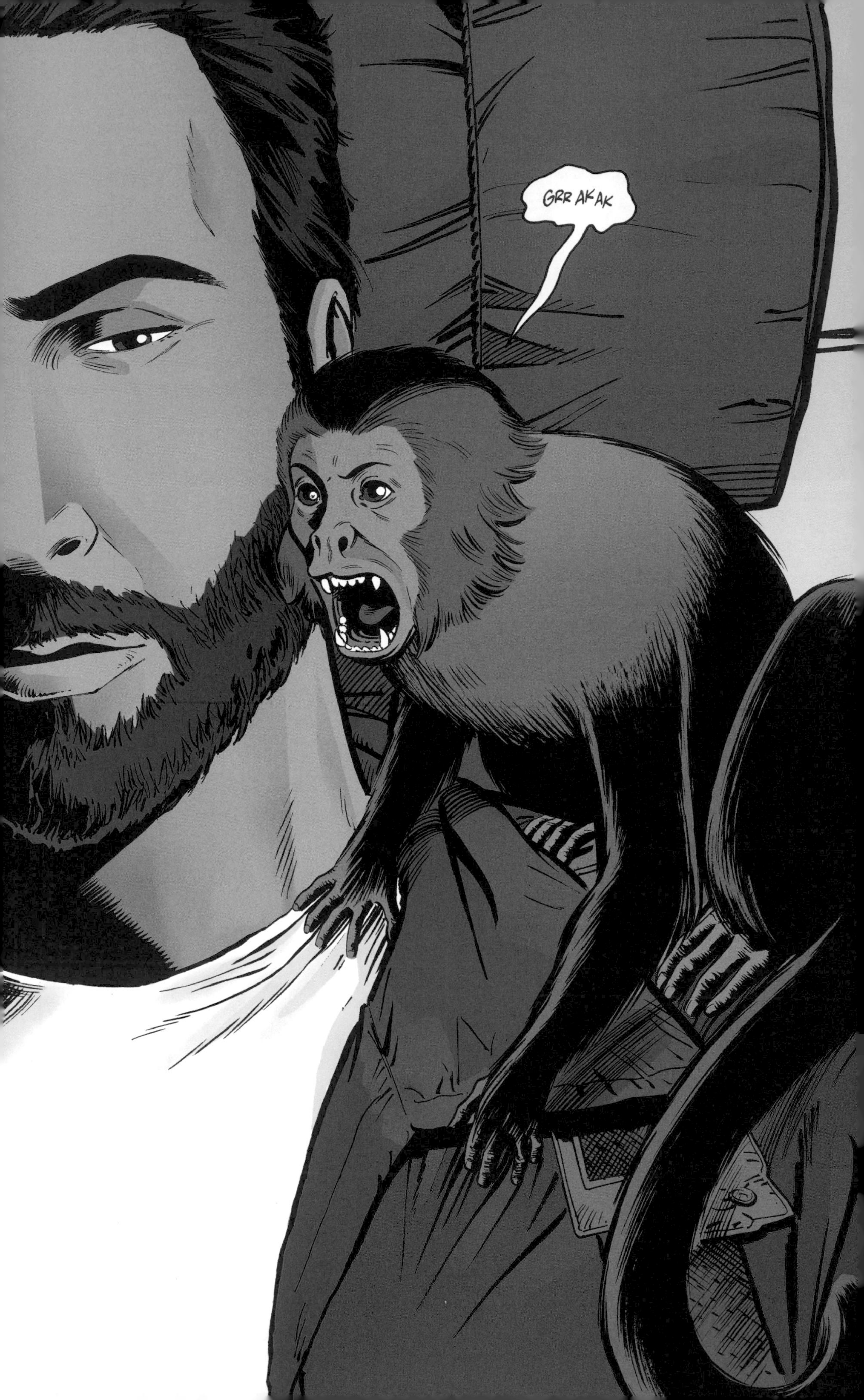
GRR AKAK

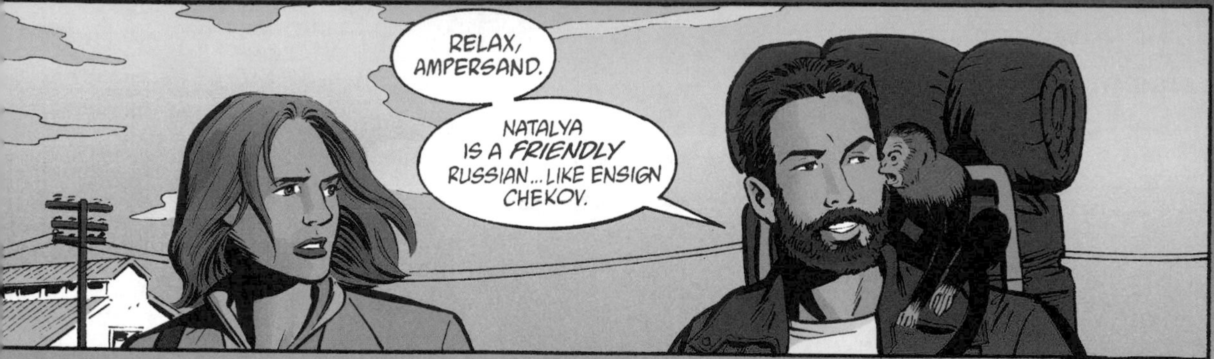
RELAX, AMPERSAND.
NATALYA IS A FRIENDLY RUSSIAN... LIKE ENSIGN CHEKOV.

Oldenbrook, Kansas
Ten Hours Later

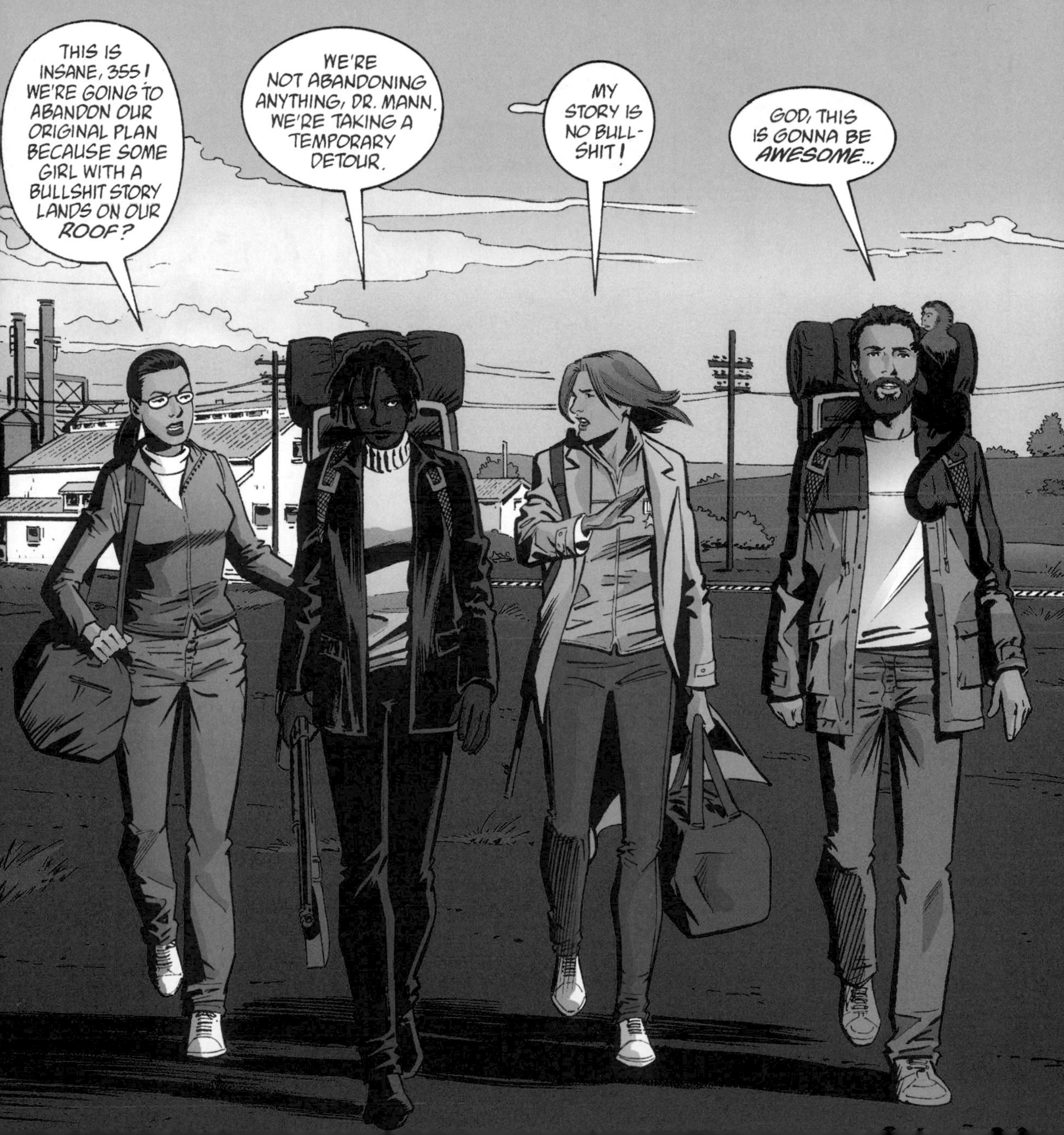
THIS IS INSANE, 355! WE'RE GOING TO ABANDON OUR ORIGINAL PLAN BECAUSE SOME GIRL WITH A BULLSHIT STORY LANDS ON OUR ROOF?
WE'RE NOT ABANDONING ANYTHING, DR. MANN. WE'RE TAKING A TEMPORARY DETOUR.
MY STORY IS NO BULL-SHIT!
GOD, THIS IS GONNA BE AWESOME...

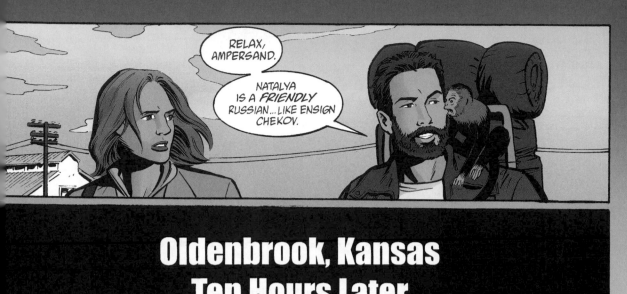

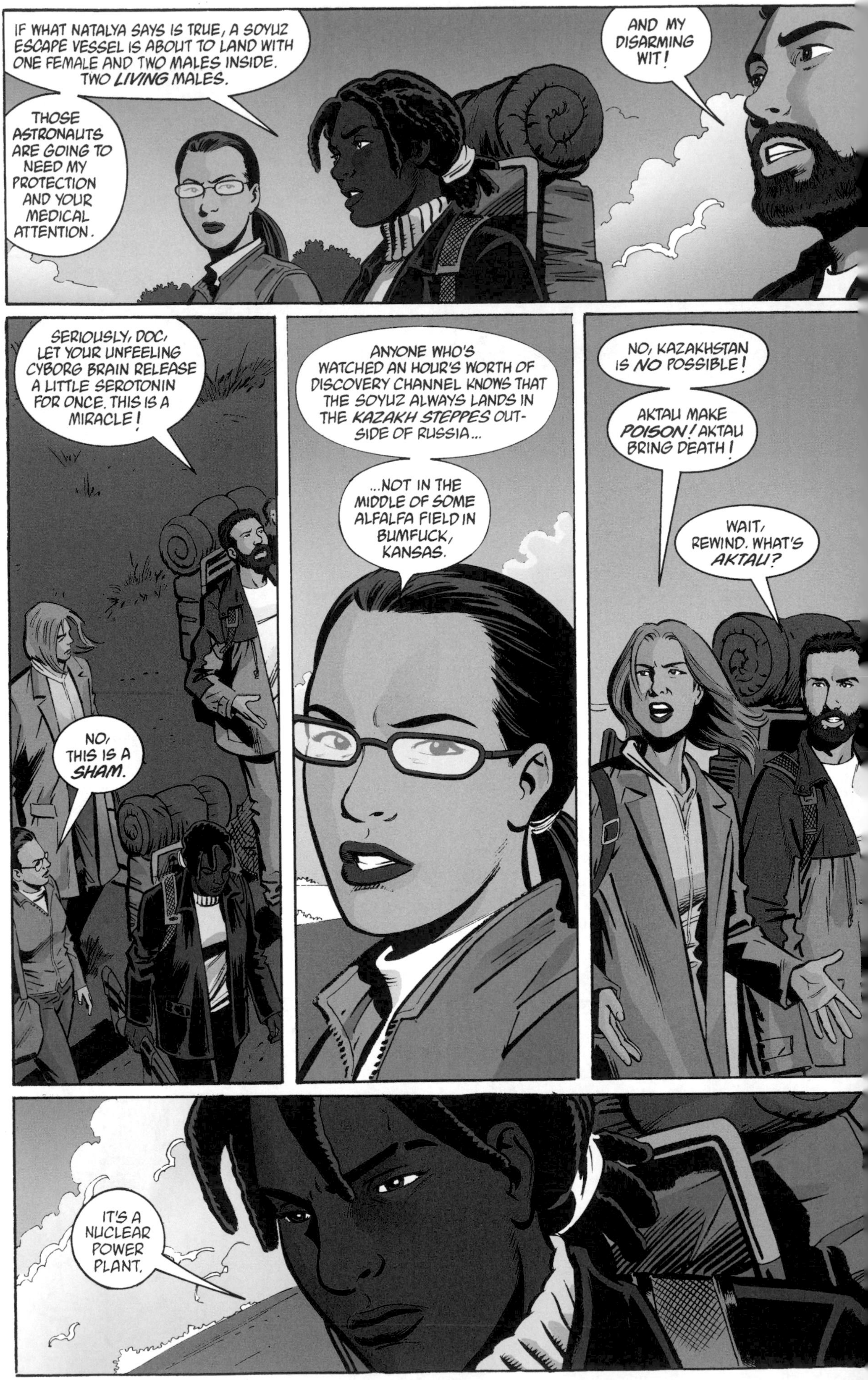
IF WHAT NATALYA SAYS IS TRUE, A SOYUZ ESCAPE VESSEL IS ABOUT TO LAND WITH ONE FEMALE AND TWO MALES INSIDE. TWO *LIVING* MALES.
THOSE ASTRONAUTS ARE GOING TO NEED MY PROTECTION AND YOUR MEDICAL ATTENTION.
AND MY DISARMING WIT!
SERIOUSLY, DOC, LET YOUR UNFEELING CYBORG BRAIN RELEASE A LITTLE SEROTONIN FOR ONCE. THIS IS A MIRACLE!
NO, THIS IS A *SHAM*.
ANYONE WHO'S WATCHED AN HOUR'S WORTH OF DISCOVERY CHANNEL KNOWS THAT THE SOYUZ ALWAYS LANDS IN THE *KAZAKH STEPPES* OUT-SIDE OF RUSSIA...
...NOT IN THE MIDDLE OF SOME ALFALFA FIELD IN BUMFUCK, KANSAS.
NO, KAZAKHSTAN IS *NO* POSSIBLE!
AKTAU MAKE *POISON!* AKTAU BRING DEATH!
WAIT, REWIND. WHAT'S *AKTAU?*
IT'S A NUCLEAR POWER PLANT.

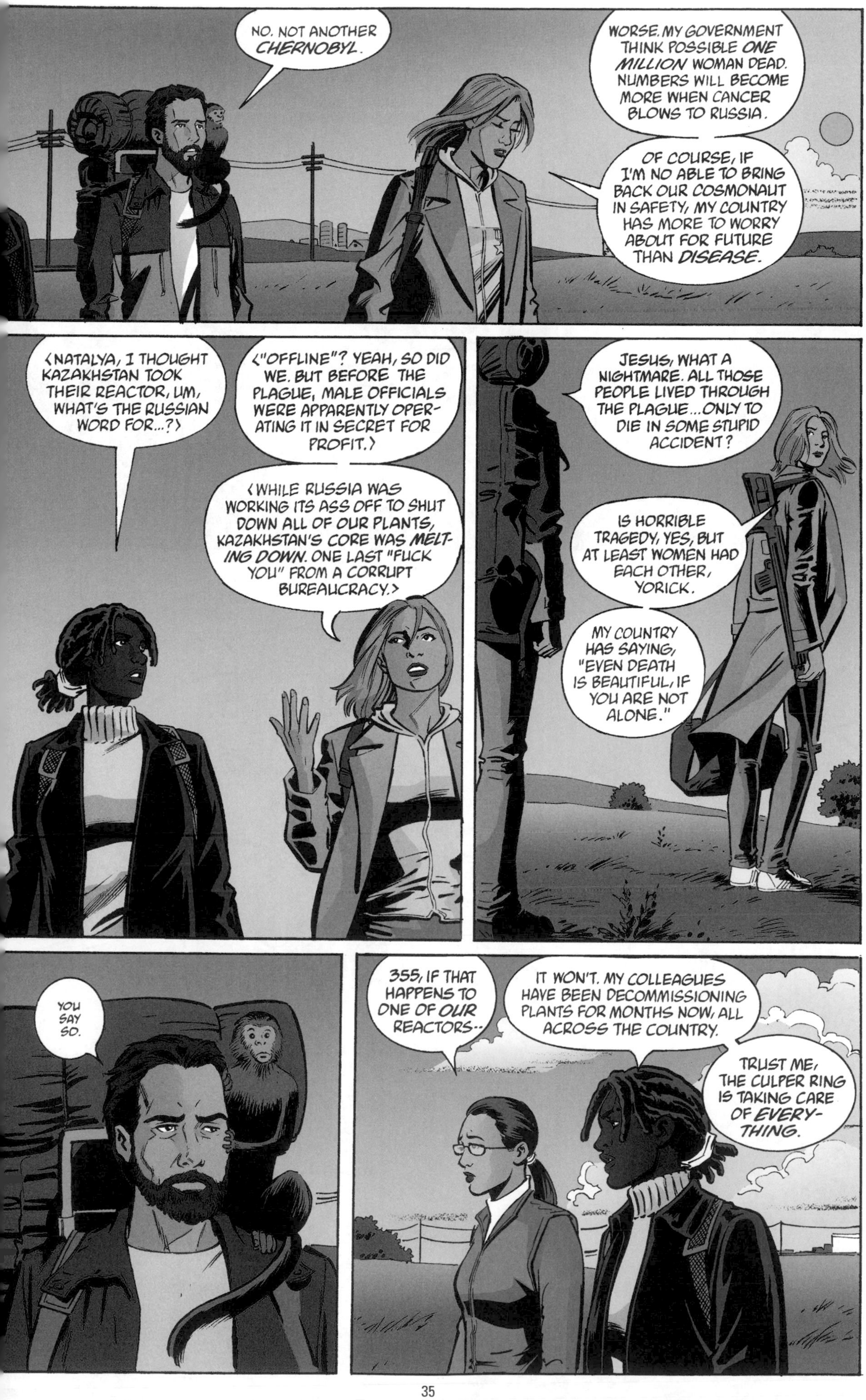
NO. NOT ANOTHER CHERNOBYL.
WORSE. MY GOVERNMENT THINK POSSIBLE ONE MILLION WOMAN DEAD. NUMBERS WILL BECOME MORE WHEN CANCER BLOWS TO RUSSIA.
OF COURSE, IF I'M NO ABLE TO BRING BACK OUR COSMONAUT IN SAFETY, MY COUNTRY HAS MORE TO WORRY ABOUT FOR FUTURE THAN DISEASE.
‹NATALYA, I THOUGHT KAZAKHSTAN TOOK THEIR REACTOR, UM, WHAT'S THE RUSSIAN WORD FOR...?›
‹"OFFLINE"? YEAH, SO DID WE. BUT BEFORE THE PLAGUE, MALE OFFICIALS WERE APPARENTLY OPERATING IT IN SECRET FOR PROFIT.›
‹WHILE RUSSIA WAS WORKING ITS ASS OFF TO SHUT DOWN ALL OF OUR PLANTS, KAZAKHSTAN'S CORE WAS MELTING DOWN. ONE LAST "FUCK YOU" FROM A CORRUPT BUREAUCRACY.›
JESUS, WHAT A NIGHTMARE. ALL THOSE PEOPLE LIVED THROUGH THE PLAGUE...ONLY TO DIE IN SOME STUPID ACCIDENT?
IS HORRIBLE TRAGEDY, YES, BUT AT LEAST WOMEN HAD EACH OTHER, YORICK.
MY COUNTRY HAS SAYING, "EVEN DEATH IS BEAUTIFUL, IF YOU ARE NOT ALONE."
YOU SAY SO.
355, IF THAT HAPPENS TO ONE OF OUR REACTORS--
IT WON'T. MY COLLEAGUES HAVE BEEN DECOMMISSIONING PLANTS FOR MONTHS NOW, ALL ACROSS THE COUNTRY.
TRUST ME, THE CULPER RING IS TAKING CARE OF EVERYTHING.

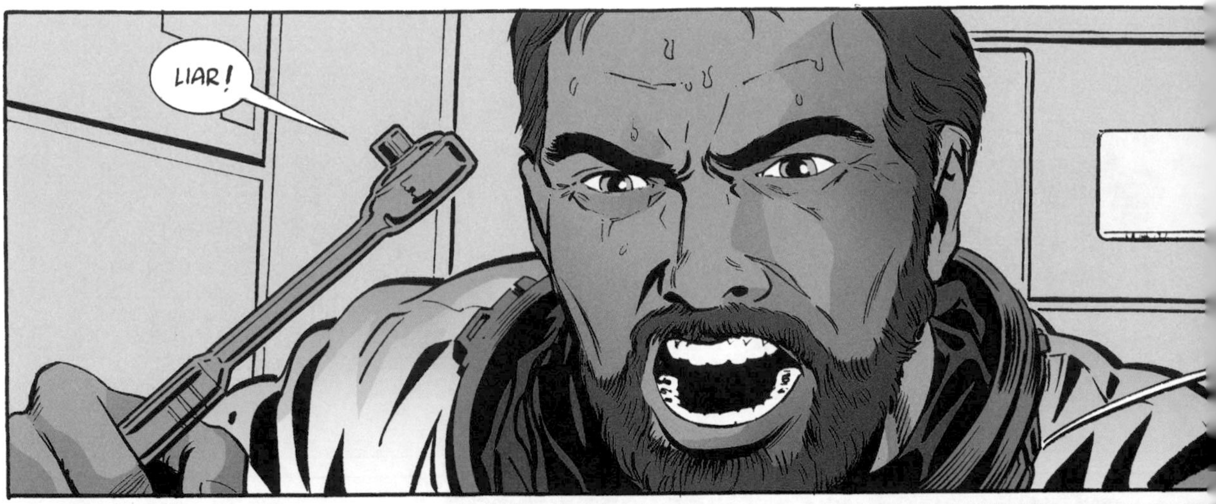
LIAR!

International Space Station
Now

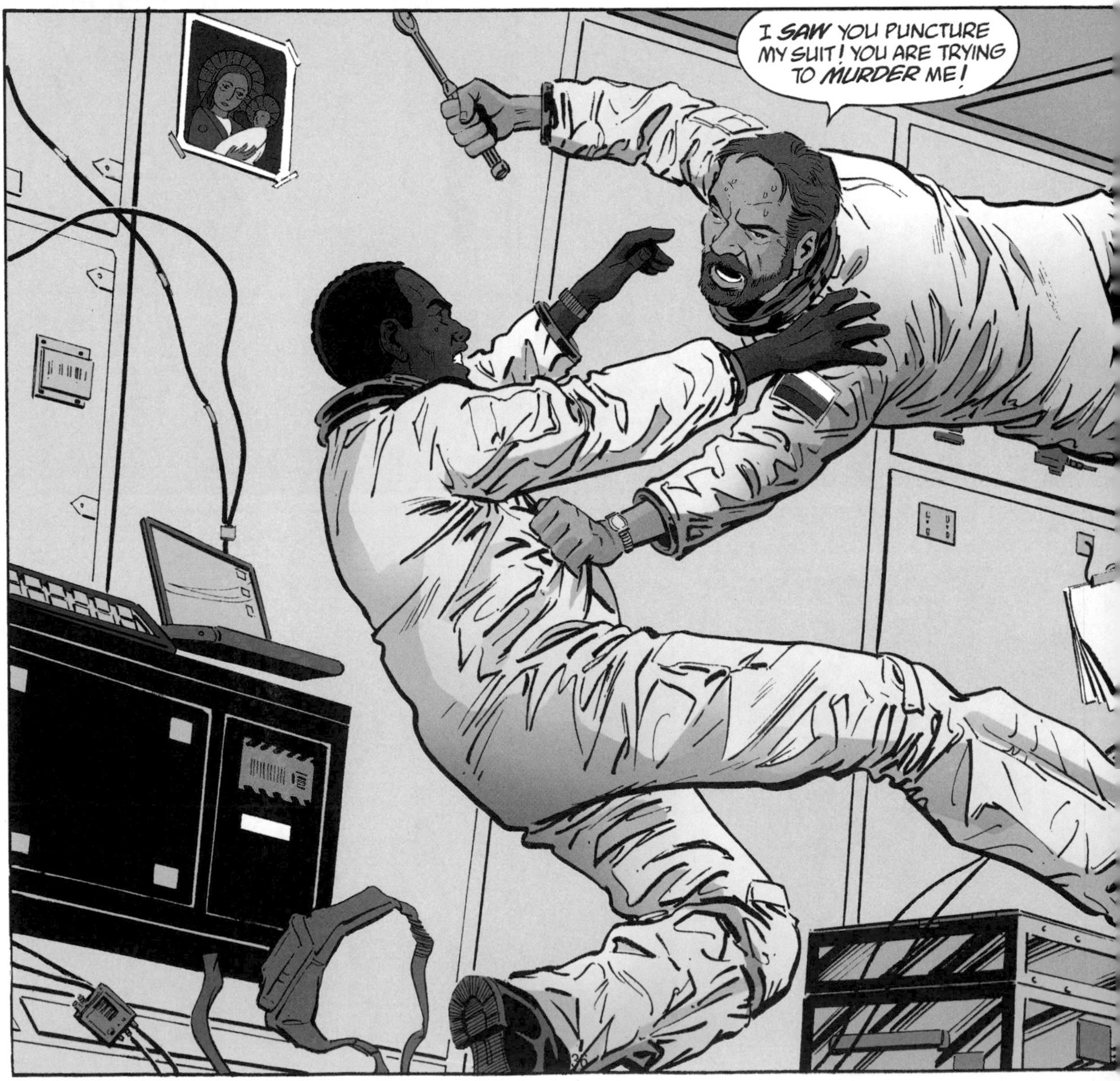
I SAW YOU PUNCTURE MY SUIT! YOU ARE TRYING TO MURDER ME!

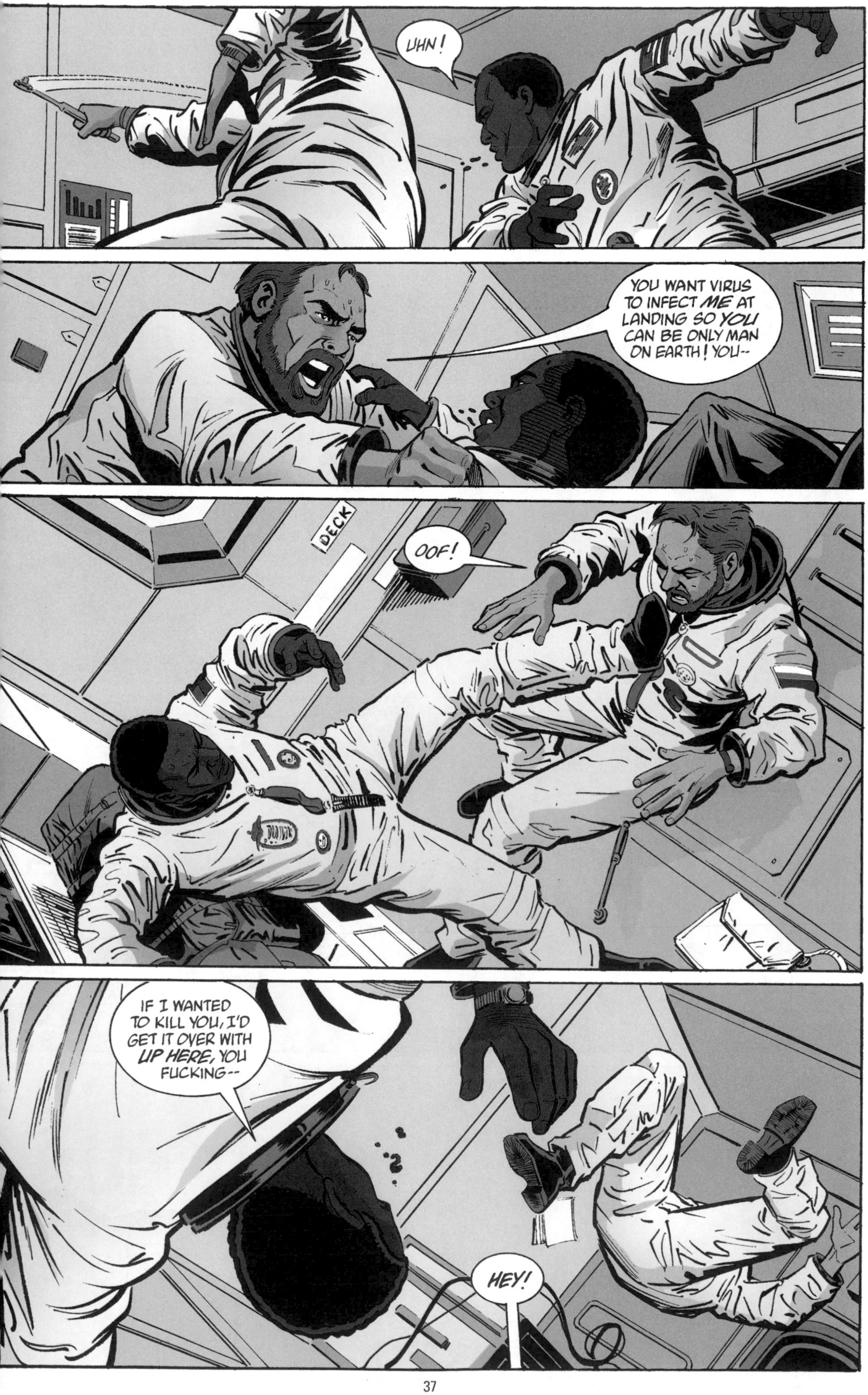
UHN!
YOU WANT VIRUS TO INFECT ME AT LANDING SO YOU CAN BE ONLY MAN ON EARTH! YOU--
DECK
OOF!
IF I WANTED TO KILL YOU, I'D GET IT OVER WITH UP HERE, YOU FUCKING--
HEY!

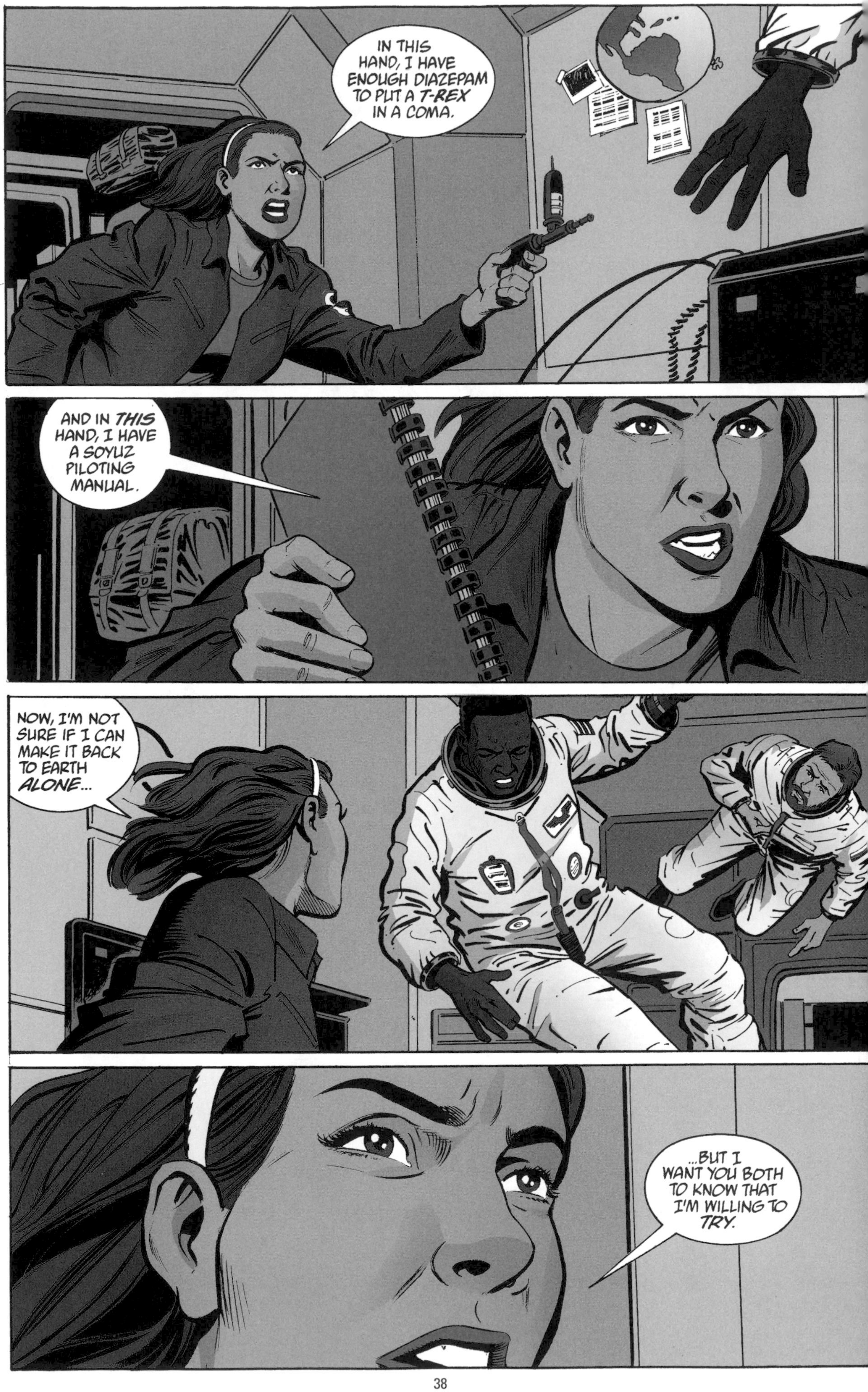
IN THIS HAND, I HAVE ENOUGH DIAZEPAM TO PUT A T-REX IN A COMA.
AND IN THIS HAND, I HAVE A SOYUZ PILOTING MANUAL.
NOW, I'M NOT SURE IF I CAN MAKE IT BACK TO EARTH ALONE...
...BUT I WANT YOU BOTH TO KNOW THAT I'M WILLING TO TRY.

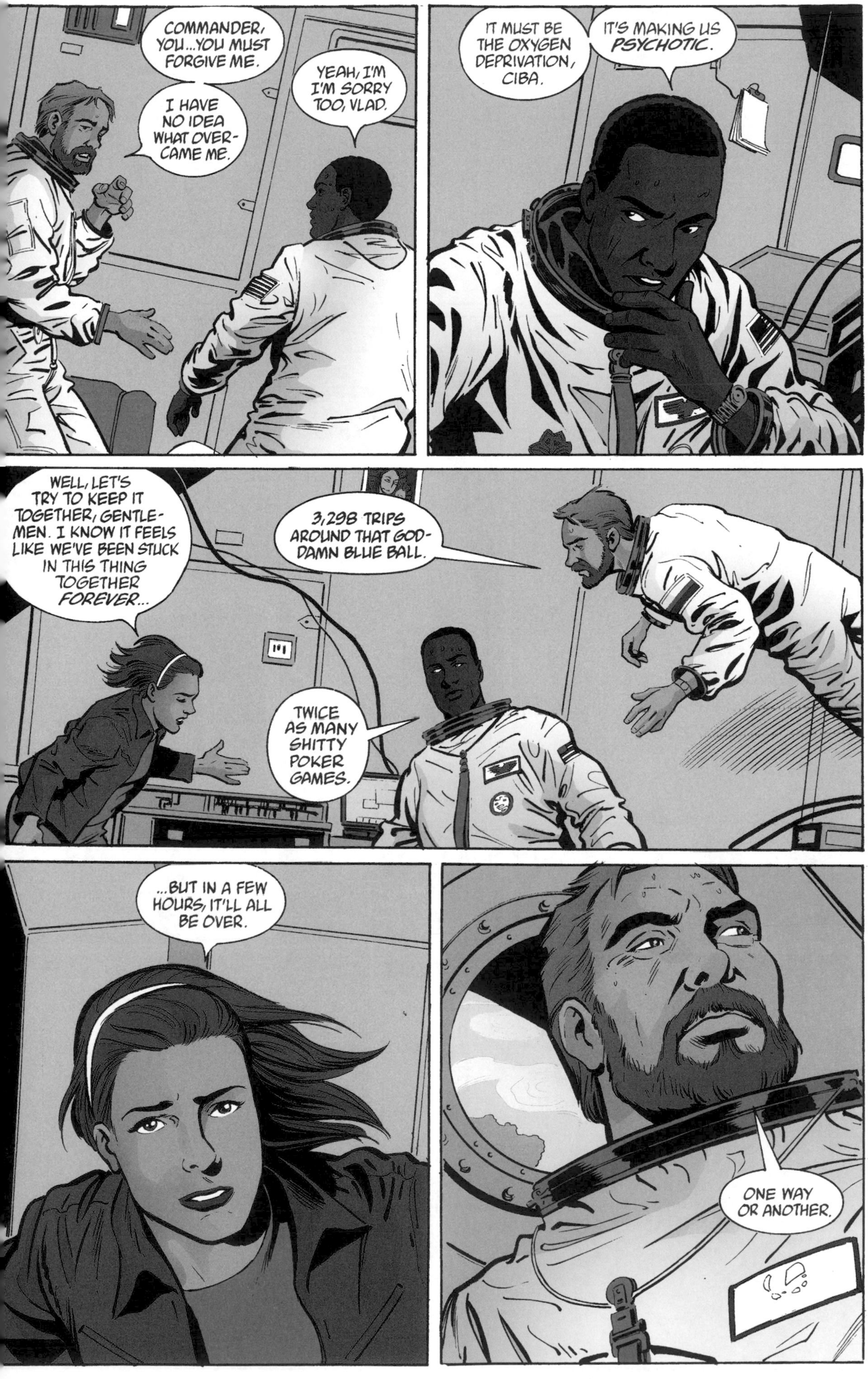
COMMANDER, YOU...YOU MUST FORGIVE ME.
I HAVE NO IDEA WHAT OVER-CAME ME.
YEAH, I'M I'M SORRY TOO, VLAD.
IT MUST BE THE OXYGEN DEPRIVATION, CIBA.
IT'S MAKING US PSYCHOTIC.
WELL, LET'S TRY TO KEEP IT TOGETHER, GENTLE-MEN. I KNOW IT FEELS LIKE WE'VE BEEN STUCK IN THIS THING TOGETHER FOREVER...
3,298 TRIPS AROUND THAT GOD-DAMN BLUE BALL.
TWICE AS MANY SHITTY POKER GAMES.
...BUT IN A FEW HOURS, IT'LL ALL BE OVER.
ONE WAY OR ANOTHER.

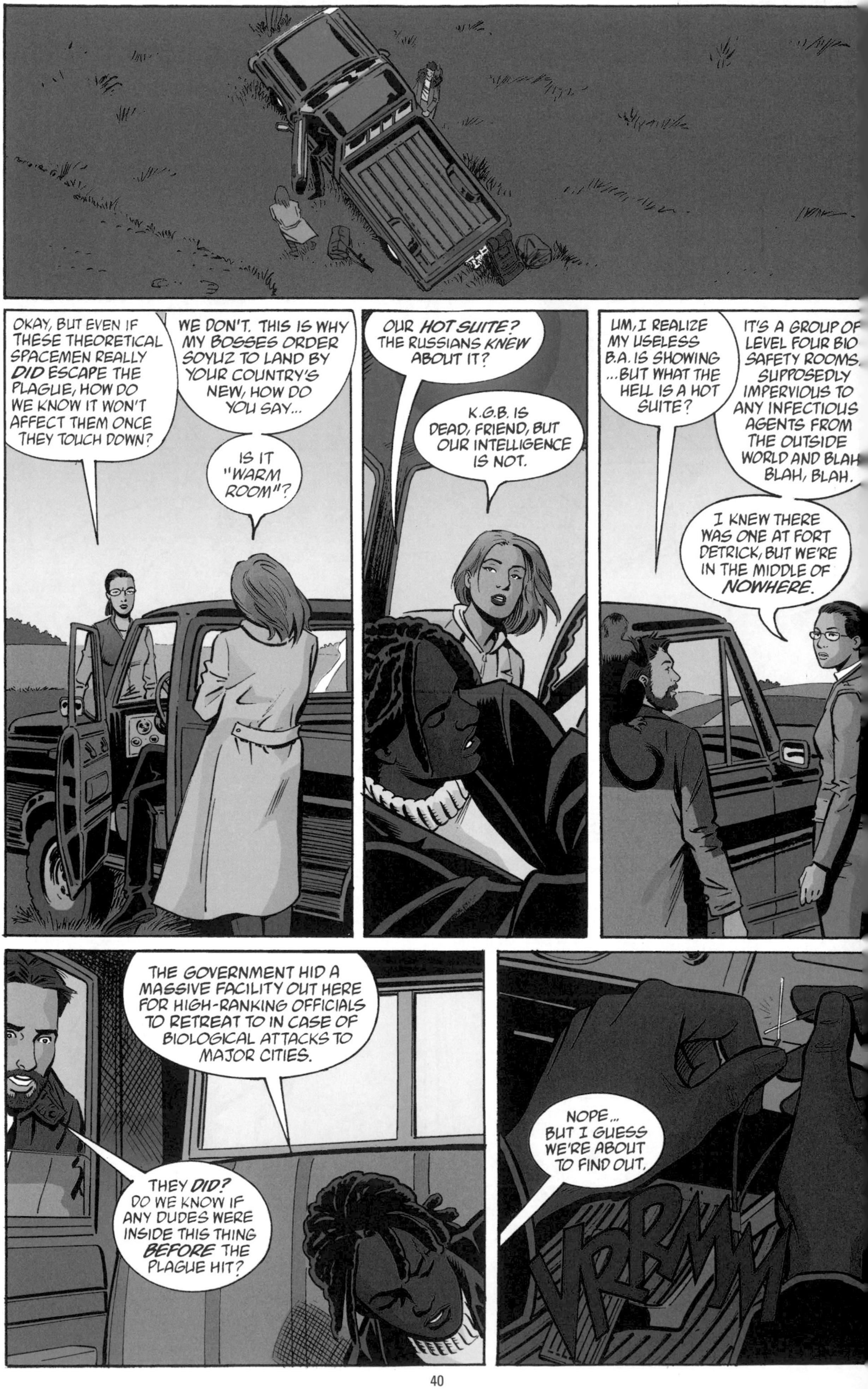
OKAY, BUT EVEN IF THESE THEORETICAL SPACEMEN REALLY DID ESCAPE THE PLAGUE, HOW DO WE KNOW IT WON'T AFFECT THEM ONCE THEY TOUCH DOWN?
WE DON'T. THIS IS WHY MY BOSSES ORDER SOYUZ TO LAND BY YOUR COUNTRY'S NEW, HOW DO YOU SAY...
IS IT "WARM ROOM"?
OUR HOT SUITE? THE RUSSIANS KNEW ABOUT IT?
K.G.B. IS DEAD, FRIEND, BUT OUR INTELLIGENCE IS NOT.
UM, I REALIZE MY USELESS B.A. IS SHOWING ...BUT WHAT THE HELL IS A HOT SUITE?
IT'S A GROUP OF LEVEL FOUR BIO SAFETY ROOMS, SUPPOSEDLY IMPERVIOUS TO ANY INFECTIOUS AGENTS FROM THE OUTSIDE WORLD AND BLAH BLAH, BLAH.
I KNEW THERE WAS ONE AT FORT DETRICK, BUT WE'RE IN THE MIDDLE OF NOWHERE.
THE GOVERNMENT HID A MASSIVE FACILITY OUT HERE FOR HIGH-RANKING OFFICIALS TO RETREAT TO IN CASE OF BIOLOGICAL ATTACKS TO MAJOR CITIES.
THEY DID? DO WE KNOW IF ANY DUDES WERE INSIDE THIS THING BEFORE THE PLAGUE HIT?
NOPE... BUT I GUESS WE'RE ABOUT TO FIND OUT.
VRRM

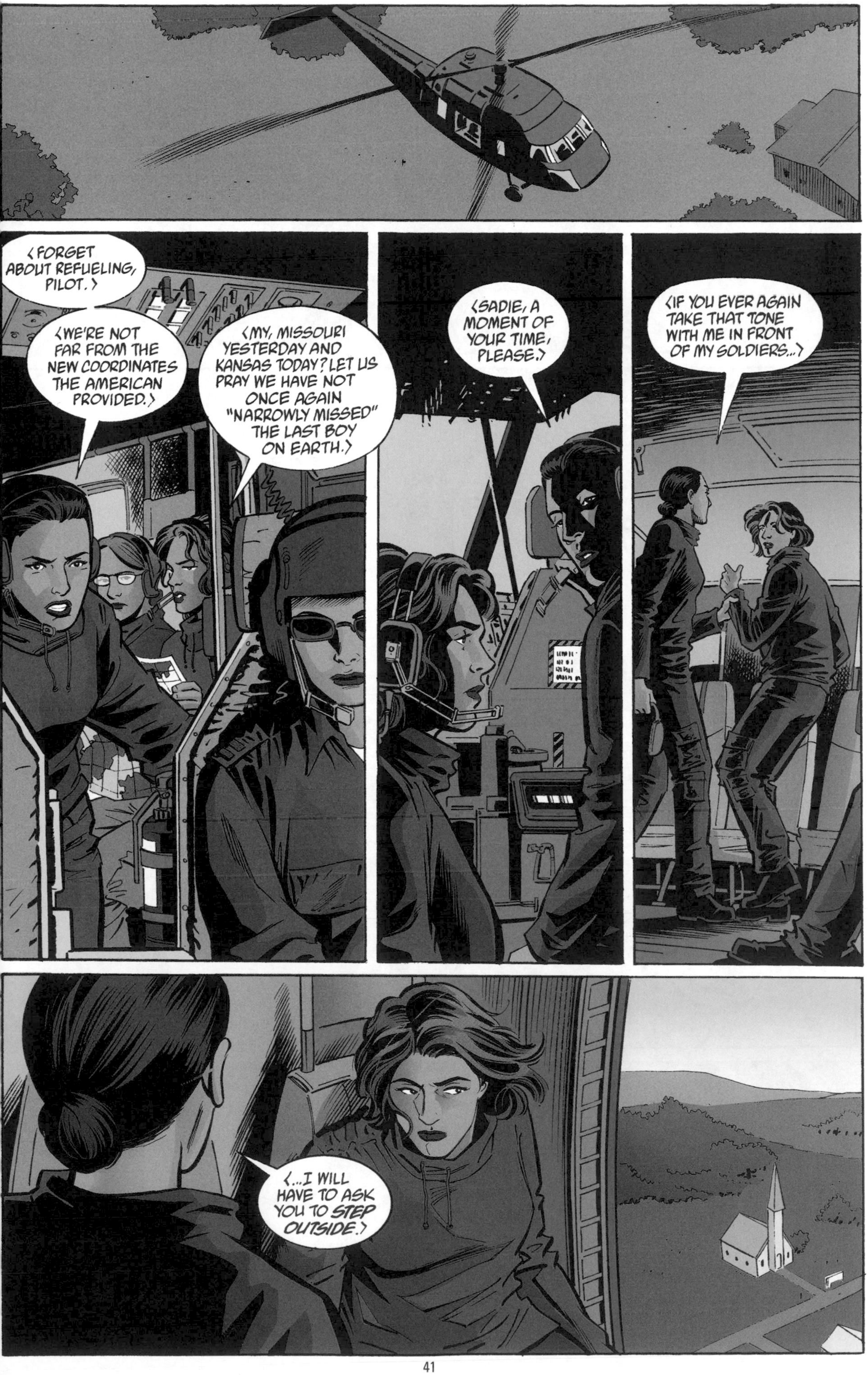
‹FORGET ABOUT REFUELING, PILOT.›
‹WE'RE NOT FAR FROM THE NEW COORDINATES THE AMERICAN PROVIDED.›
‹MY, MISSOURI YESTERDAY AND KANSAS TODAY? LET US PRAY WE HAVE NOT ONCE AGAIN "NARROWLY MISSED" THE LAST BOY ON EARTH.›
‹SADIE, A MOMENT OF YOUR TIME, PLEASE.›
‹IF YOU EVER AGAIN TAKE THAT TONE WITH ME IN FRONT OF MY SOLDIERS...›
‹...I WILL HAVE TO ASK YOU TO *STEP OUTSIDE*.›

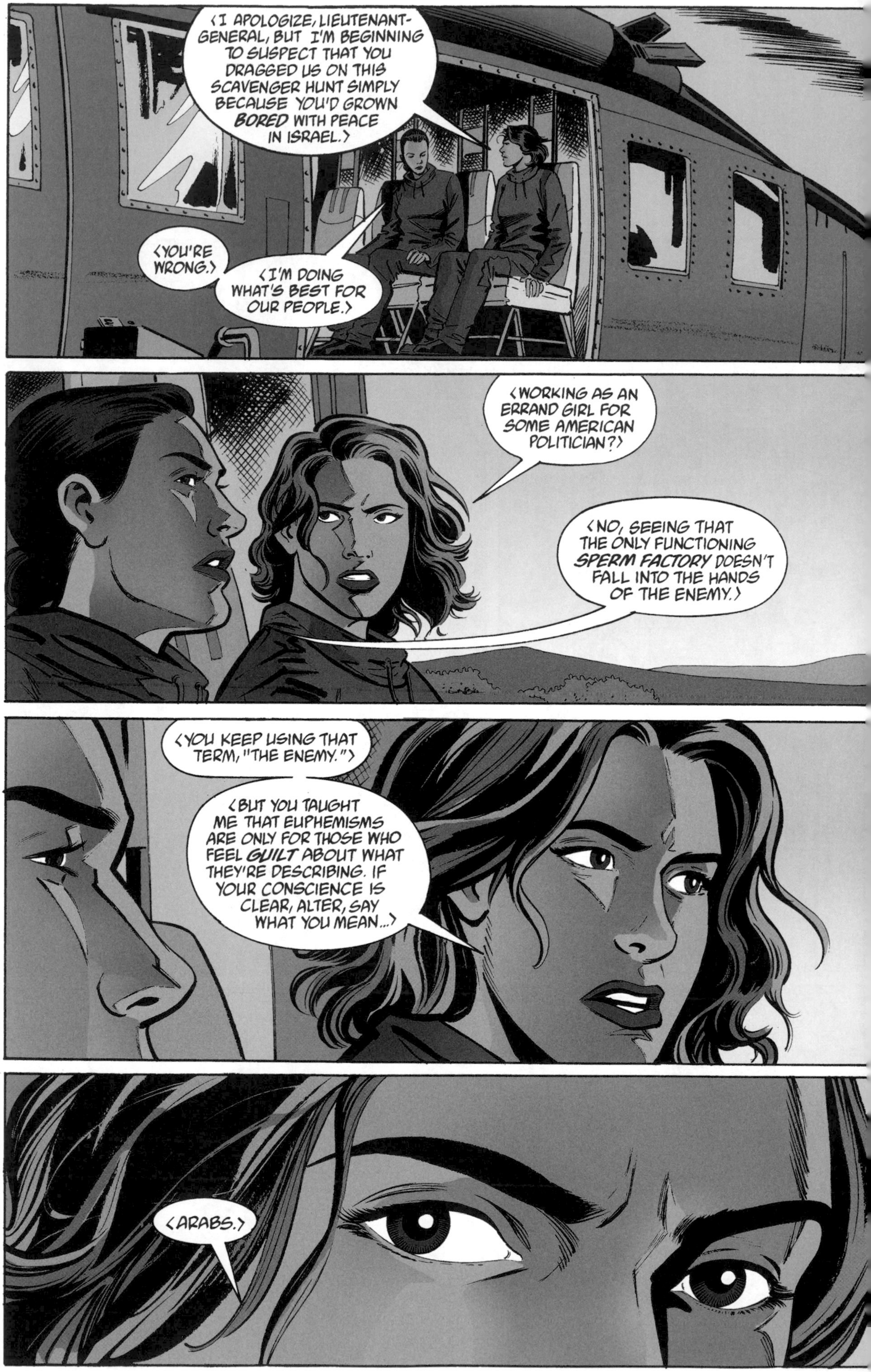

<I APOLOGIZE, LIEUTENANT-GENERAL, BUT I'M BEGINNING TO SUSPECT THAT YOU DRAGGED US ON THIS SCAVENGER HUNT SIMPLY BECAUSE YOU'D GROWN BORED WITH PEACE IN ISRAEL.>
<YOU'RE WRONG.>
<I'M DOING WHAT'S BEST FOR OUR PEOPLE.>
<WORKING AS AN ERRAND GIRL FOR SOME AMERICAN POLITICIAN?>
<NO, SEEING THAT THE ONLY FUNCTIONING SPERM FACTORY DOESN'T FALL INTO THE HANDS OF THE ENEMY.>
<YOU KEEP USING THAT TERM, "THE ENEMY.">
<BUT YOU TAUGHT ME THAT EUPHEMISMS ARE ONLY FOR THOSE WHO FEEL GUILT ABOUT WHAT THEY'RE DESCRIBING. IF YOUR CONSCIENCE IS CLEAR, ALTER, SAY WHAT YOU MEAN...>
<ARABS.>

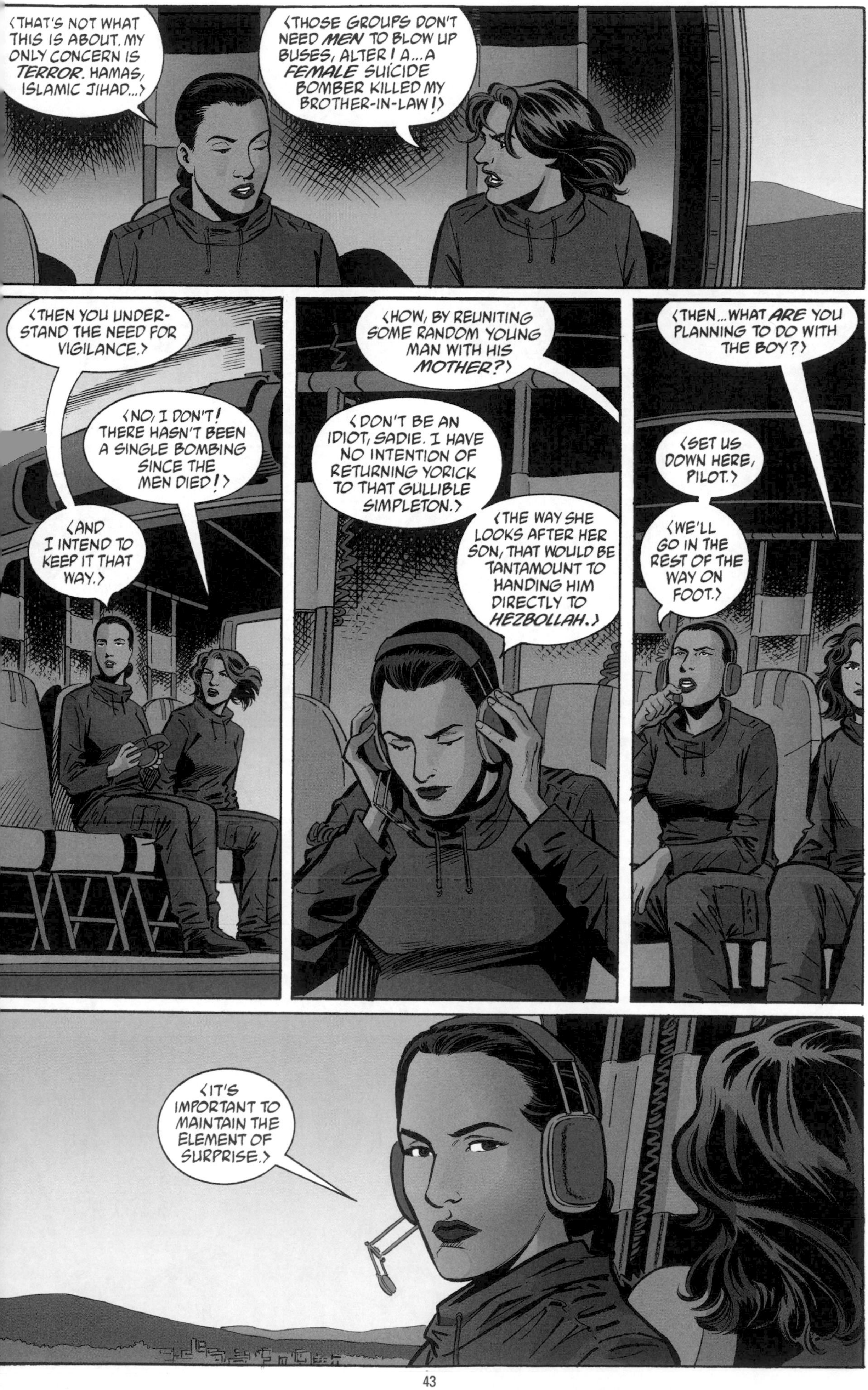
<THAT'S NOT WHAT THIS IS ABOUT. MY ONLY CONCERN IS TERROR. HAMAS, ISLAMIC JIHAD...>
<THOSE GROUPS DON'T NEED MEN TO BLOW UP BUSES, ALTER! A...A FEMALE SUICIDE BOMBER KILLED MY BROTHER-IN-LAW!>
<THEN YOU UNDER-STAND THE NEED FOR VIGILANCE.>
<NO, I DON'T! THERE HASN'T BEEN A SINGLE BOMBING SINCE THE MEN DIED!>
<AND I INTEND TO KEEP IT THAT WAY.>
<HOW, BY REUNITING SOME RANDOM YOUNG MAN WITH HIS MOTHER?>
<DON'T BE AN IDIOT, SADIE. I HAVE NO INTENTION OF RETURNING YORICK TO THAT GULLIBLE SIMPLETON.>
<THE WAY SHE LOOKS AFTER HER SON, THAT WOULD BE TANTAMOUNT TO HANDING HIM DIRECTLY TO HEZBOLLAH.>
<THEN...WHAT ARE YOU PLANNING TO DO WITH THE BOY?>
<SET US DOWN HERE, PILOT.>
<WE'LL GO IN THE REST OF THE WAY ON FOOT.>
<IT'S IMPORTANT TO MAINTAIN THE ELEMENT OF SURPRISE.>

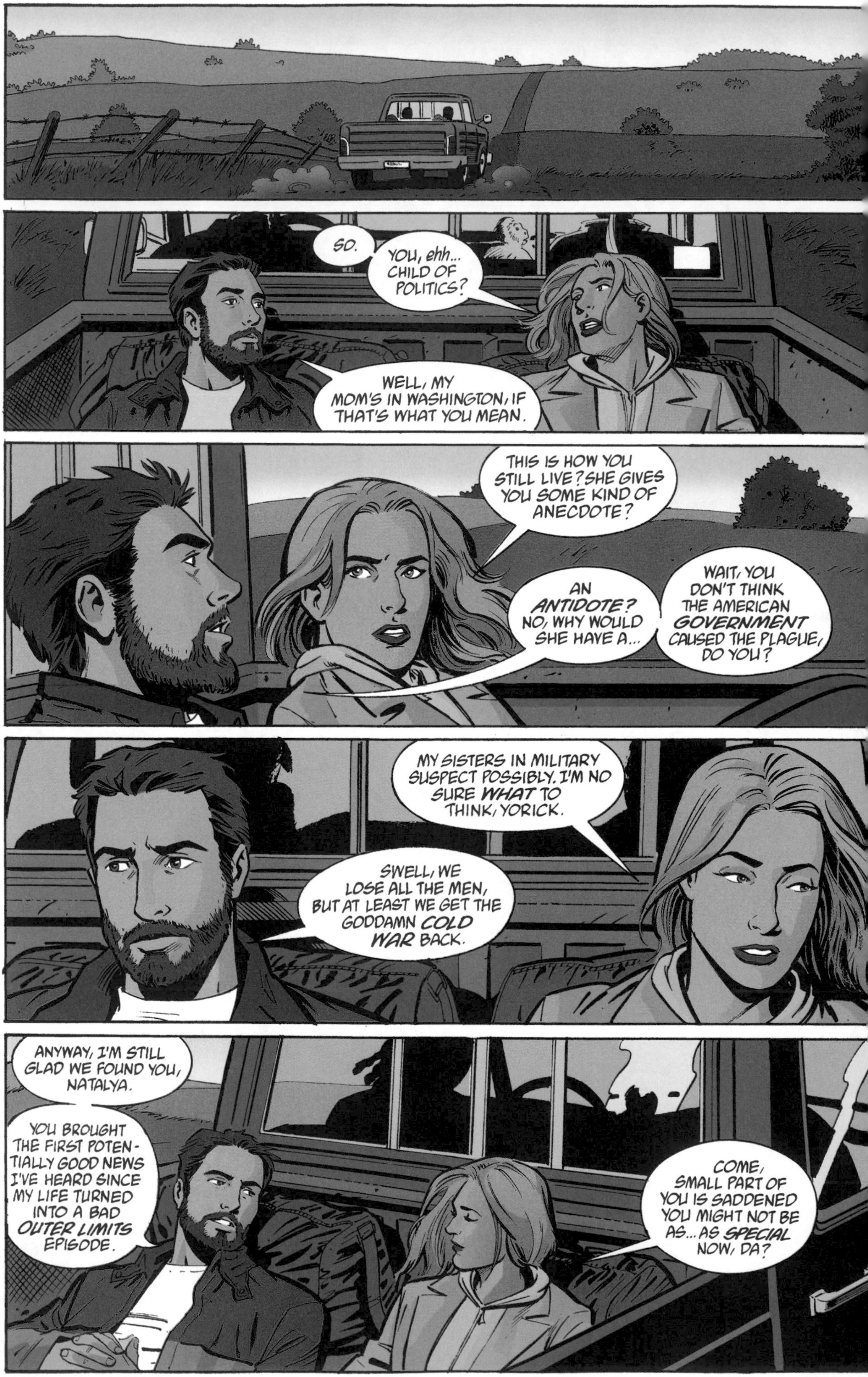
SO.
YOU, ehh... CHILD OF POLITICS?
WELL, MY MOM'S IN WASHINGTON, IF THAT'S WHAT YOU MEAN.
THIS IS HOW YOU STILL LIVE? SHE GIVES YOU SOME KIND OF ANECDOTE?
AN ANTIDOTE? NO, WHY WOULD SHE HAVE A...
WAIT, YOU DON'T THINK THE AMERICAN GOVERNMENT CAUSED THE PLAGUE, DO YOU?
MY SISTERS IN MILITARY SUSPECT POSSIBLY. I'M NO SURE WHAT TO THINK, YORICK.
SWELL, WE LOSE ALL THE MEN, BUT AT LEAST WE GET THE GODDAMN COLD WAR BACK.
ANYWAY, I'M STILL GLAD WE FOUND YOU, NATALYA.
YOU BROUGHT THE FIRST POTEN-TIALLY GOOD NEWS I'VE HEARD SINCE MY LIFE TURNED INTO A BAD OUTER LIMITS EPISODE.
COME, SMALL PART OF YOU IS SADDENED YOU MIGHT NOT BE AS... AS SPECIAL NOW, DA?

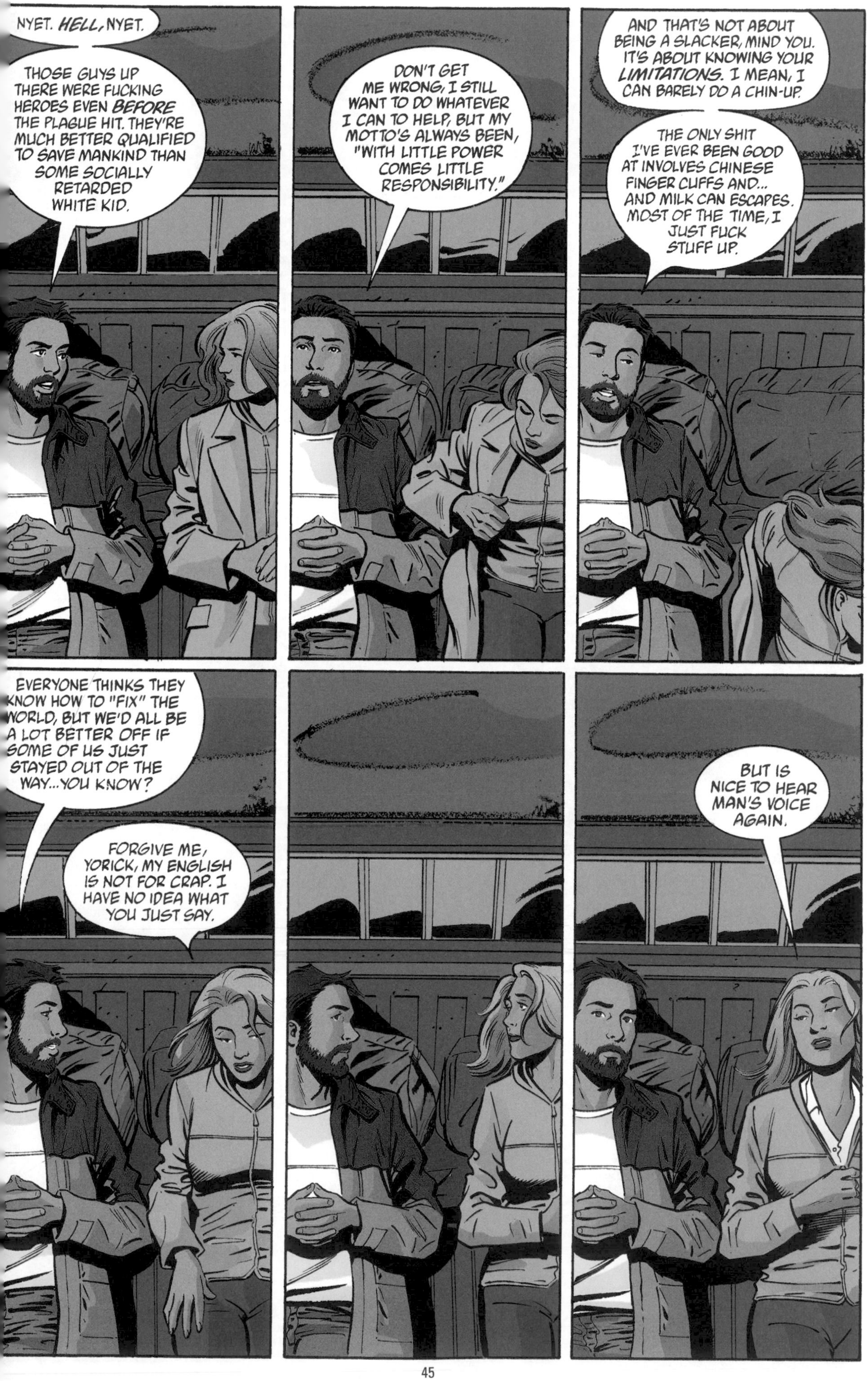
NYET. HELL, NYET.
THOSE GUYS UP THERE WERE FUCKING HEROES EVEN BEFORE THE PLAGUE HIT. THEY'RE MUCH BETTER QUALIFIED TO SAVE MANKIND THAN SOME SOCIALLY RETARDED WHITE KID.
DON'T GET ME WRONG, I STILL WANT TO DO WHATEVER I CAN TO HELP, BUT MY MOTTO'S ALWAYS BEEN, "WITH LITTLE POWER COMES LITTLE RESPONSIBILITY."
AND THAT'S NOT ABOUT BEING A SLACKER, MIND YOU. IT'S ABOUT KNOWING YOUR LIMITATIONS. I MEAN, I CAN BARELY DO A CHIN-UP.
THE ONLY SHIT I'VE EVER BEEN GOOD AT INVOLVES CHINESE FINGER CUFFS AND... AND MILK CAN ESCAPES. MOST OF THE TIME, I JUST FUCK STUFF UP.
EVERYONE THINKS THEY KNOW HOW TO "FIX" THE WORLD, BUT WE'D ALL BE A LOT BETTER OFF IF SOME OF US JUST STAYED OUT OF THE WAY...YOU KNOW?
FORGIVE ME, YORICK, MY ENGLISH IS NOT FOR CRAP. I HAVE NO IDEA WHAT YOU JUST SAY.
BUT IS NICE TO HEAR MAN'S VOICE AGAIN.

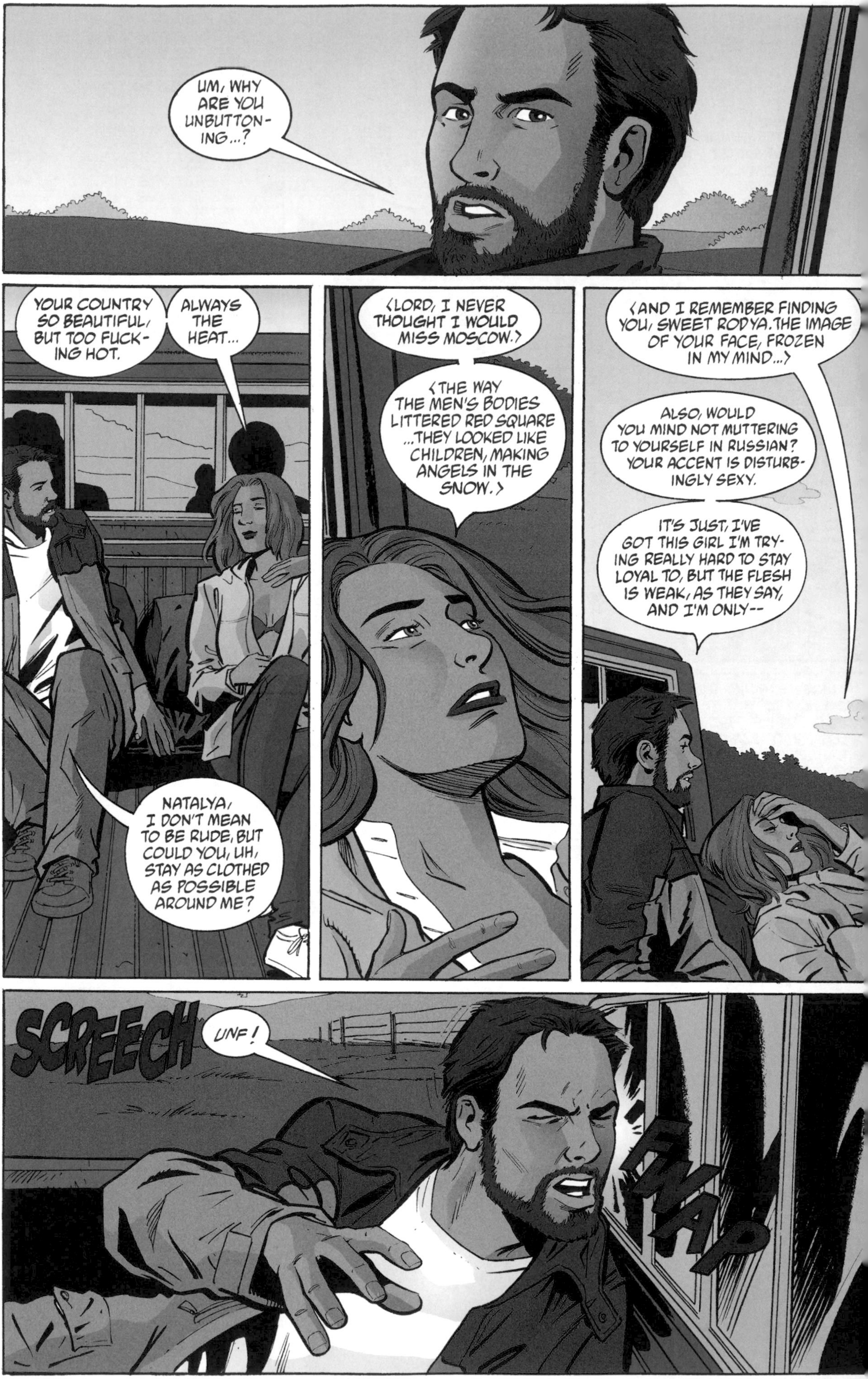
UM, WHY ARE YOU UNBUTTONING...?
YOUR COUNTRY SO BEAUTIFUL, BUT TOO FUCKING HOT.
ALWAYS THE HEAT...
NATALYA, I DON'T MEAN TO BE RUDE, BUT COULD YOU, UH, STAY AS CLOTHED AS POSSIBLE AROUND ME?
<LORD, I NEVER THOUGHT I WOULD MISS MOSCOW.>
<THE WAY THE MEN'S BODIES LITTERED RED SQUARE ...THEY LOOKED LIKE CHILDREN, MAKING ANGELS IN THE SNOW.>
<AND I REMEMBER FINDING YOU, SWEET RODYA. THE IMAGE OF YOUR FACE, FROZEN IN MY MIND...>
ALSO, WOULD YOU MIND NOT MUTTERING TO YOURSELF IN RUSSIAN? YOUR ACCENT IS DISTURBINGLY SEXY.
IT'S JUST, I'VE GOT THIS GIRL I'M TRYING REALLY HARD TO STAY LOYAL TO, BUT THE FLESH IS WEAK, AS THEY SAY, AND I'M ONLY--
SCREECH
UNF!
FWAP

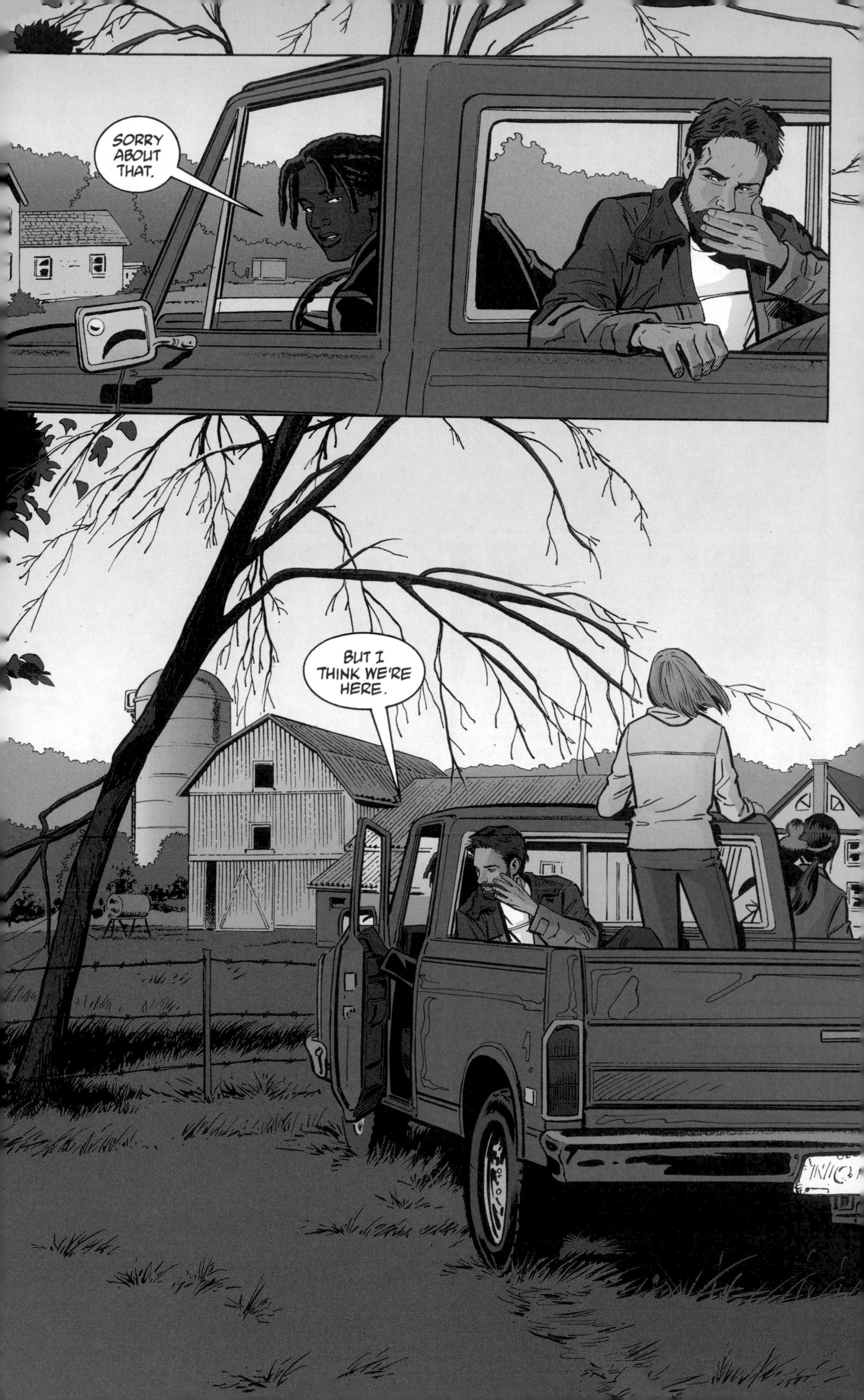
SORRY ABOUT THAT.
BUT I THINK WE'RE HERE.

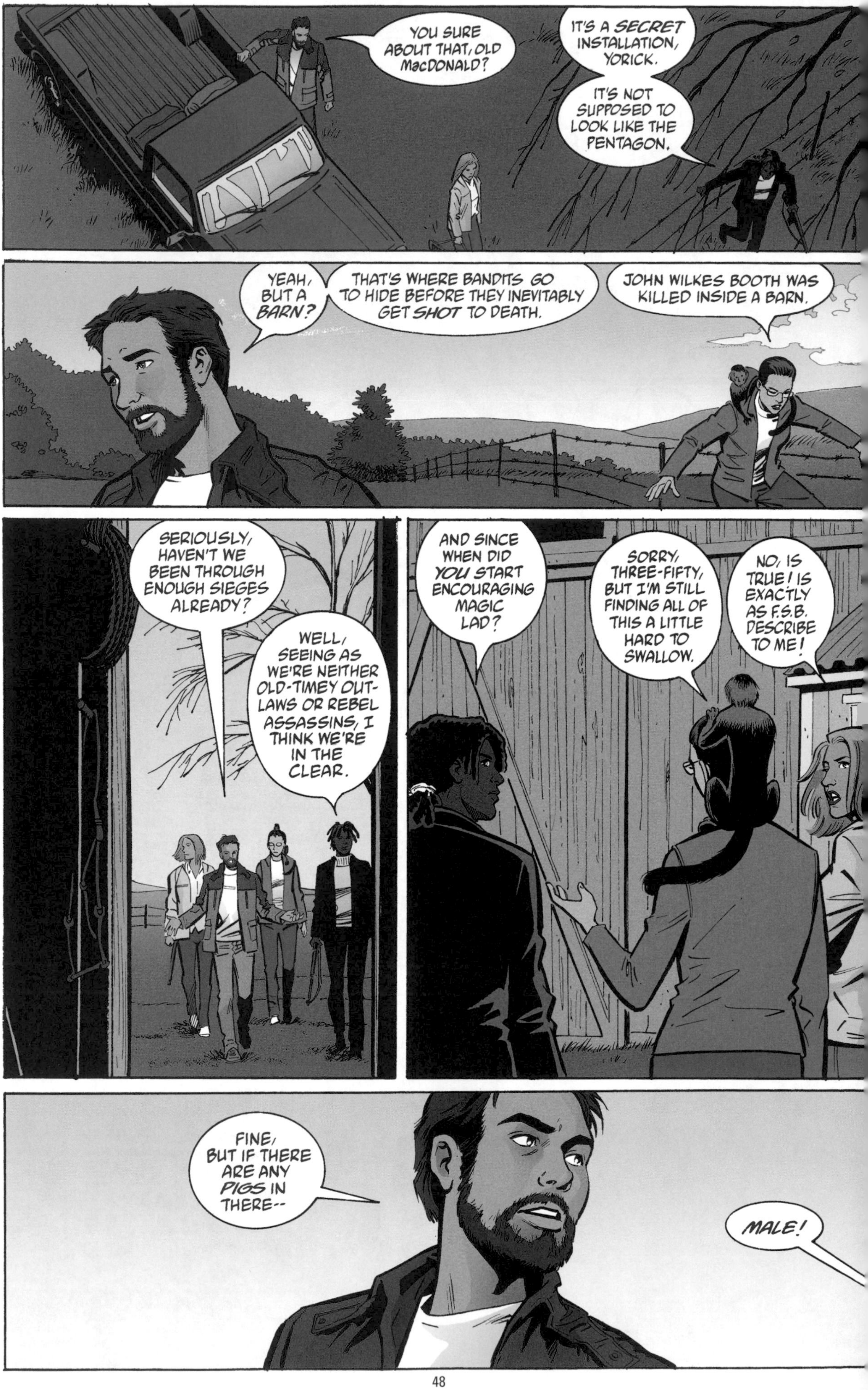
YOU SURE ABOUT THAT, OLD MacDONALD?
IT'S A SECRET INSTALLATION, YORICK.
IT'S NOT SUPPOSED TO LOOK LIKE THE PENTAGON.
YEAH, BUT A BARN?
THAT'S WHERE BANDITS GO TO HIDE BEFORE THEY INEVITABLY GET SHOT TO DEATH.
JOHN WILKES BOOTH WAS KILLED INSIDE A BARN.
SERIOUSLY, HAVEN'T WE BEEN THROUGH ENOUGH SIEGES ALREADY?
WELL, SEEING AS WE'RE NEITHER OLD-TIMEY OUT-LAWS OR REBEL ASSASSINS, I THINK WE'RE IN THE CLEAR.
AND SINCE WHEN DID YOU START ENCOURAGING MAGIC LAD?
SORRY, THREE-FIFTY, BUT I'M STILL FINDING ALL OF THIS A LITTLE HARD TO SWALLOW.
NO, IS TRUE! IS EXACTLY AS F.S.B. DESCRIBE TO ME!
FINE, BUT IF THERE ARE ANY PIGS IN THERE--
MALE!

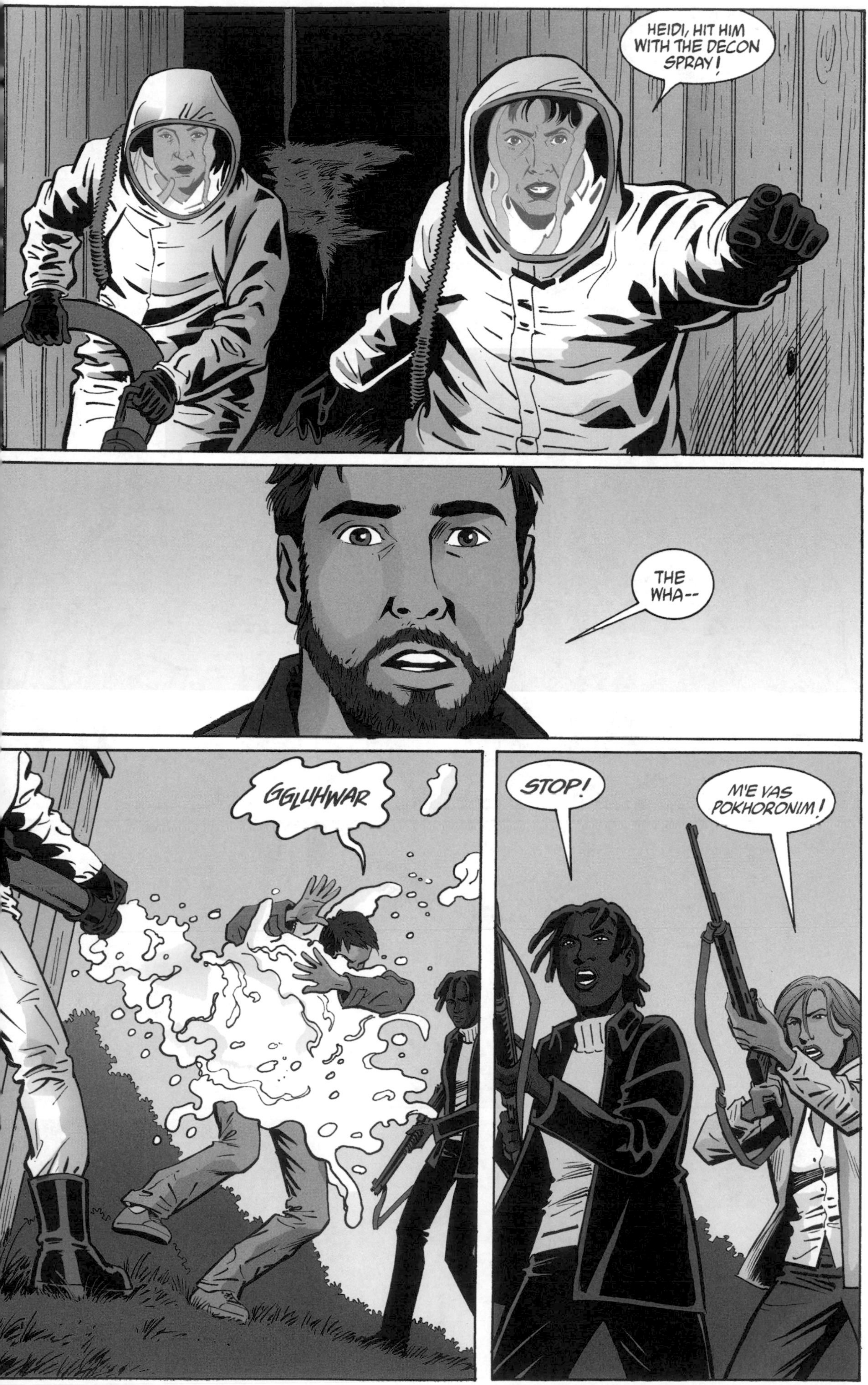
HEIDI, HIT HIM WITH THE DECON SPRAY!
THE WHA--
GGLUHWAR
STOP!
M'E VAS POKHORONIM!

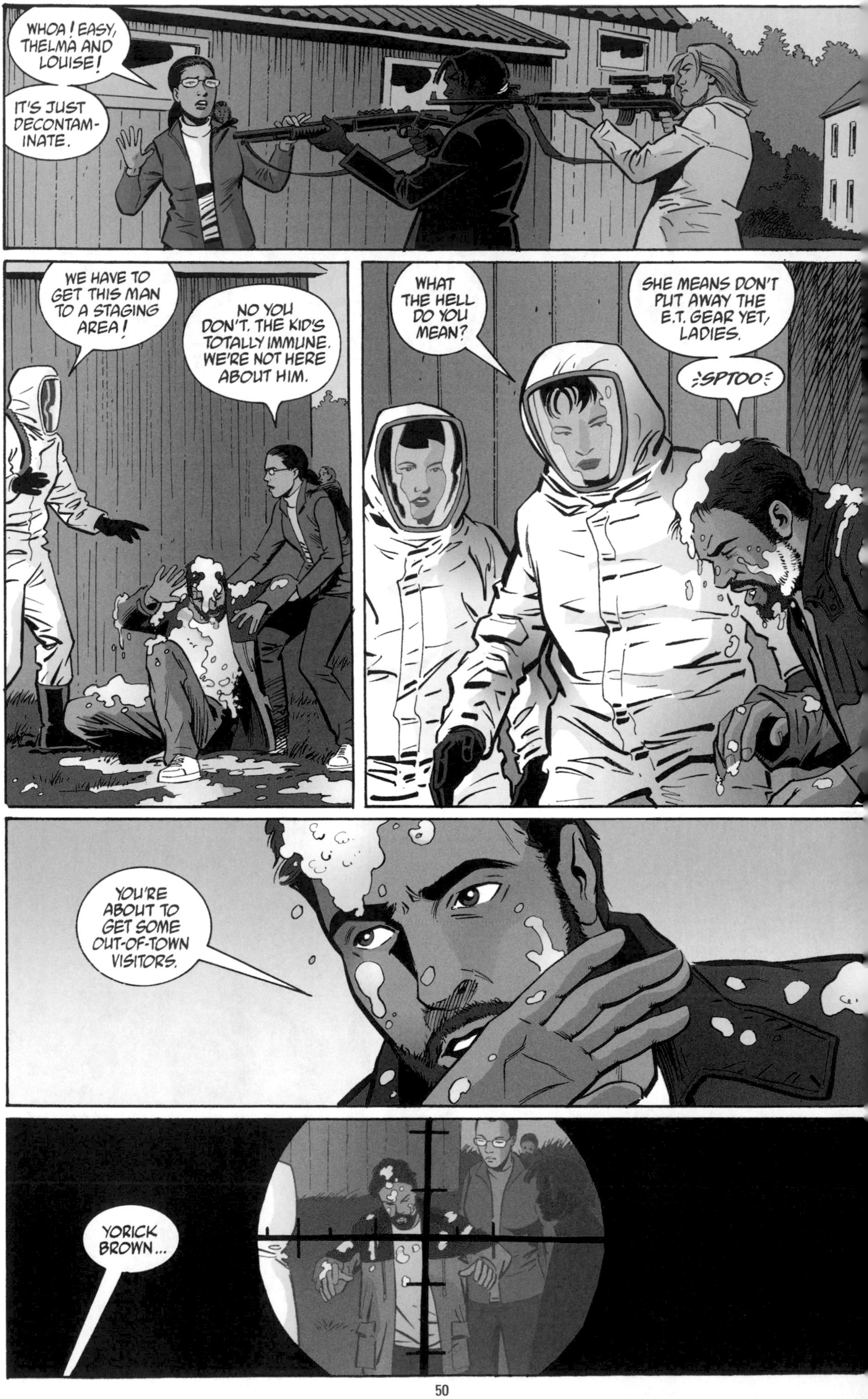
WHOA! EASY, THELMA AND LOUISE!
IT'S JUST DECONTAMINATE.
WE HAVE TO GET THIS MAN TO A STAGING AREA!
NO YOU DON'T. THE KID'S TOTALLY IMMUNE. WE'RE NOT HERE ABOUT HIM.
WHAT THE HELL DO YOU MEAN?
SHE MEANS DON'T PUT AWAY THE E.T. GEAR YET, LADIES.
SPTOO
YOU'RE ABOUT TO GET SOME OUT-OF-TOWN VISITORS.
YORICK BROWN...

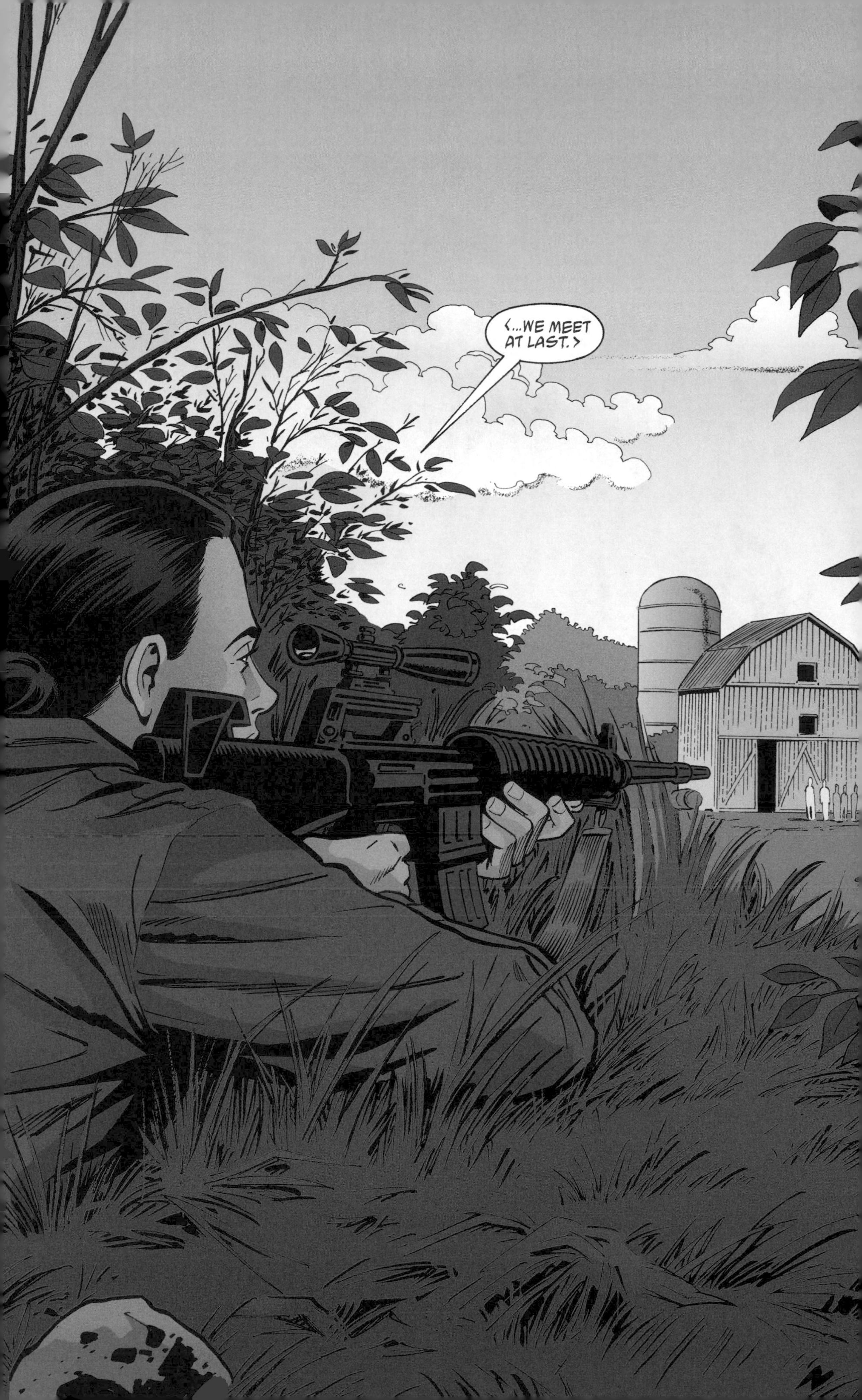
<...WE MEET AT LAST.>

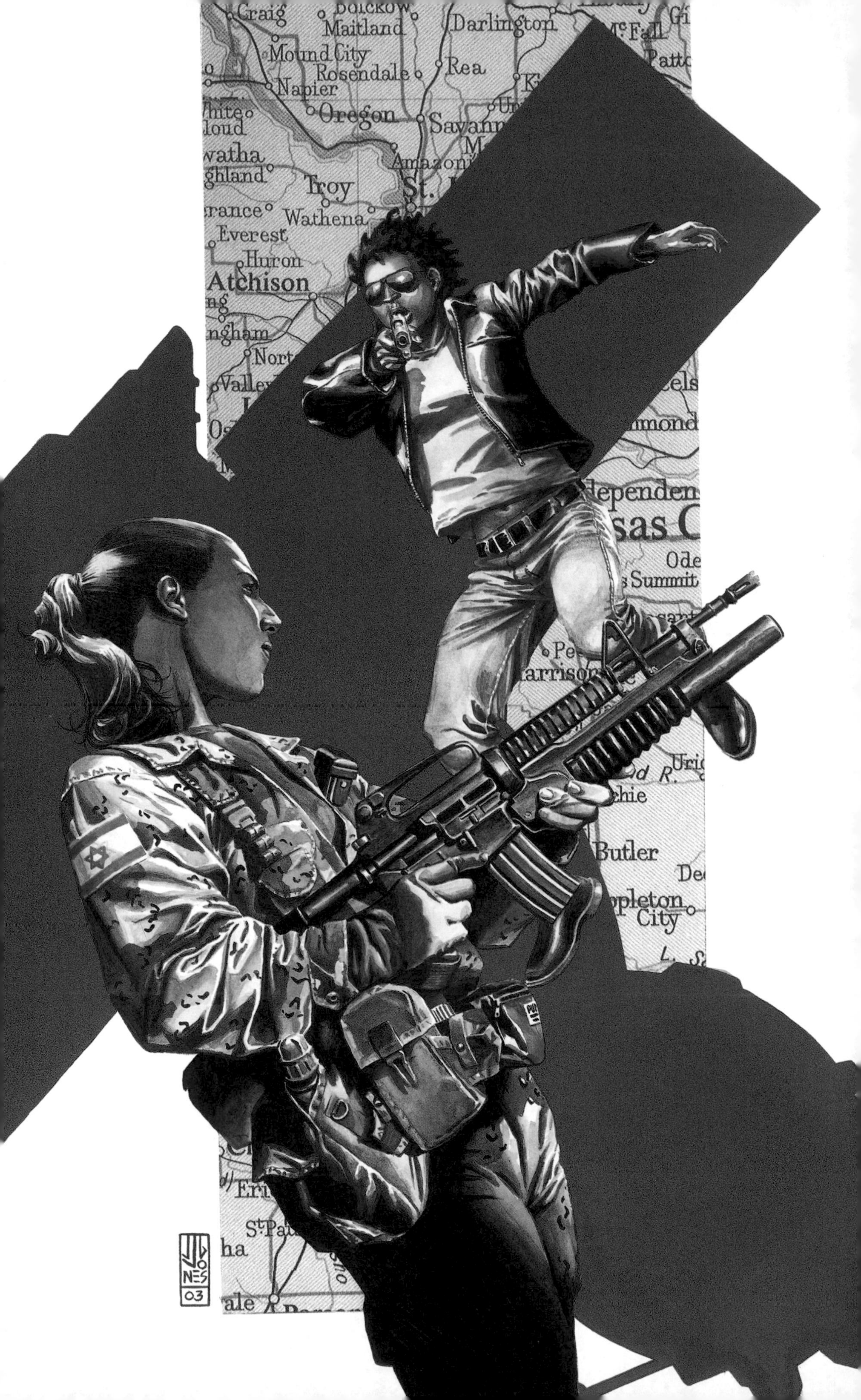
Craig
Maitland
Darlington
Mound City
Rosendale
Rea
Napier
Oregon
Troy
Wathena
Everest
Huron
Atchison
Butler
City

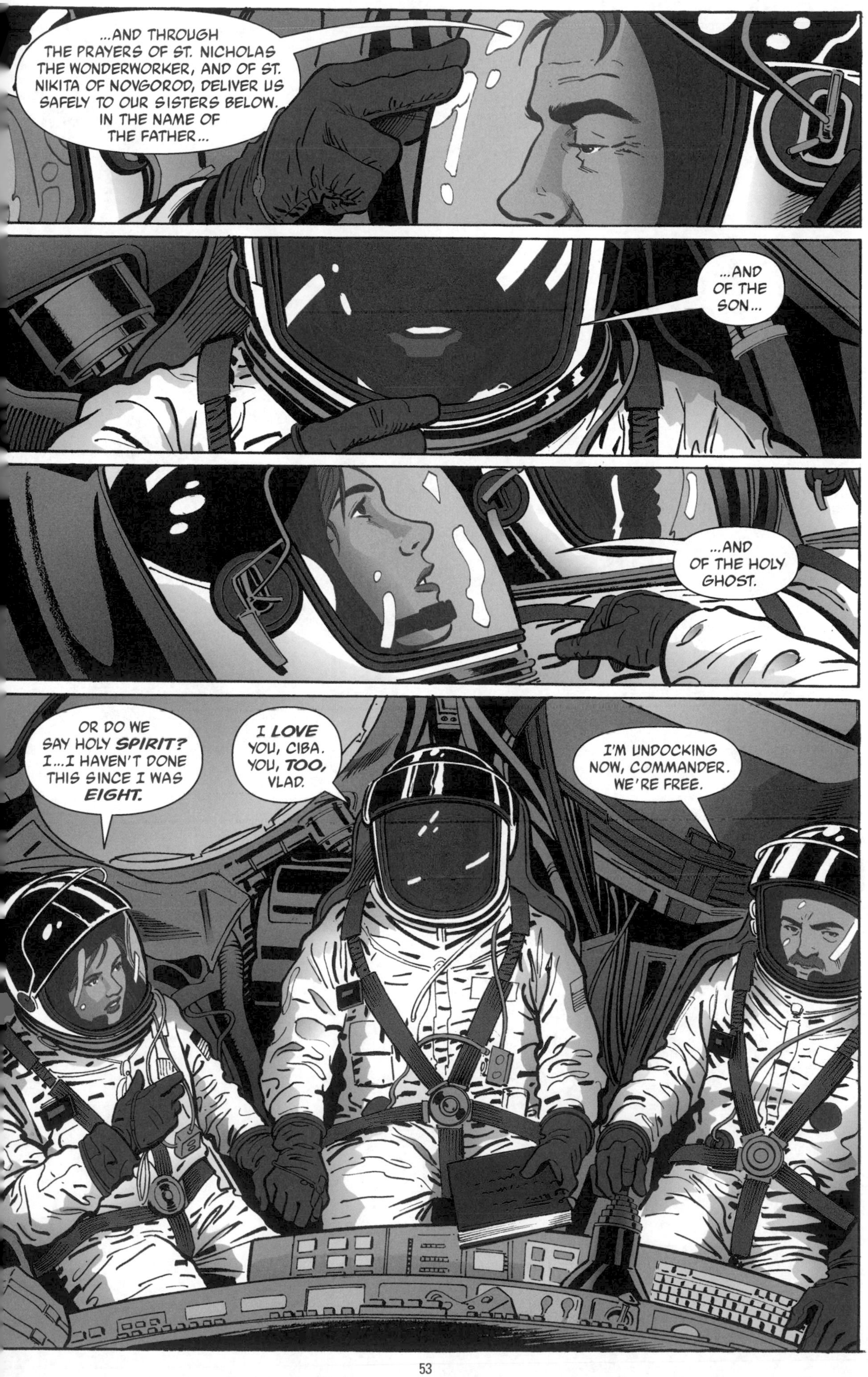
...AND THROUGH THE PRAYERS OF ST. NICHOLAS THE WONDERWORKER, AND OF ST. NIKITA OF NOVGOROD, DELIVER US SAFELY TO OUR SISTERS BELOW. IN THE NAME OF THE FATHER...
...AND OF THE SON...
...AND OF THE HOLY GHOST.
OR DO WE SAY HOLY *SPIRIT?* I...I HAVEN'T DONE THIS SINCE I WAS *EIGHT.*
I *LOVE* YOU, CIBA. YOU, *TOO,* VLAD.
I'M UNDOCKING NOW, COMMANDER. WE'RE FREE.

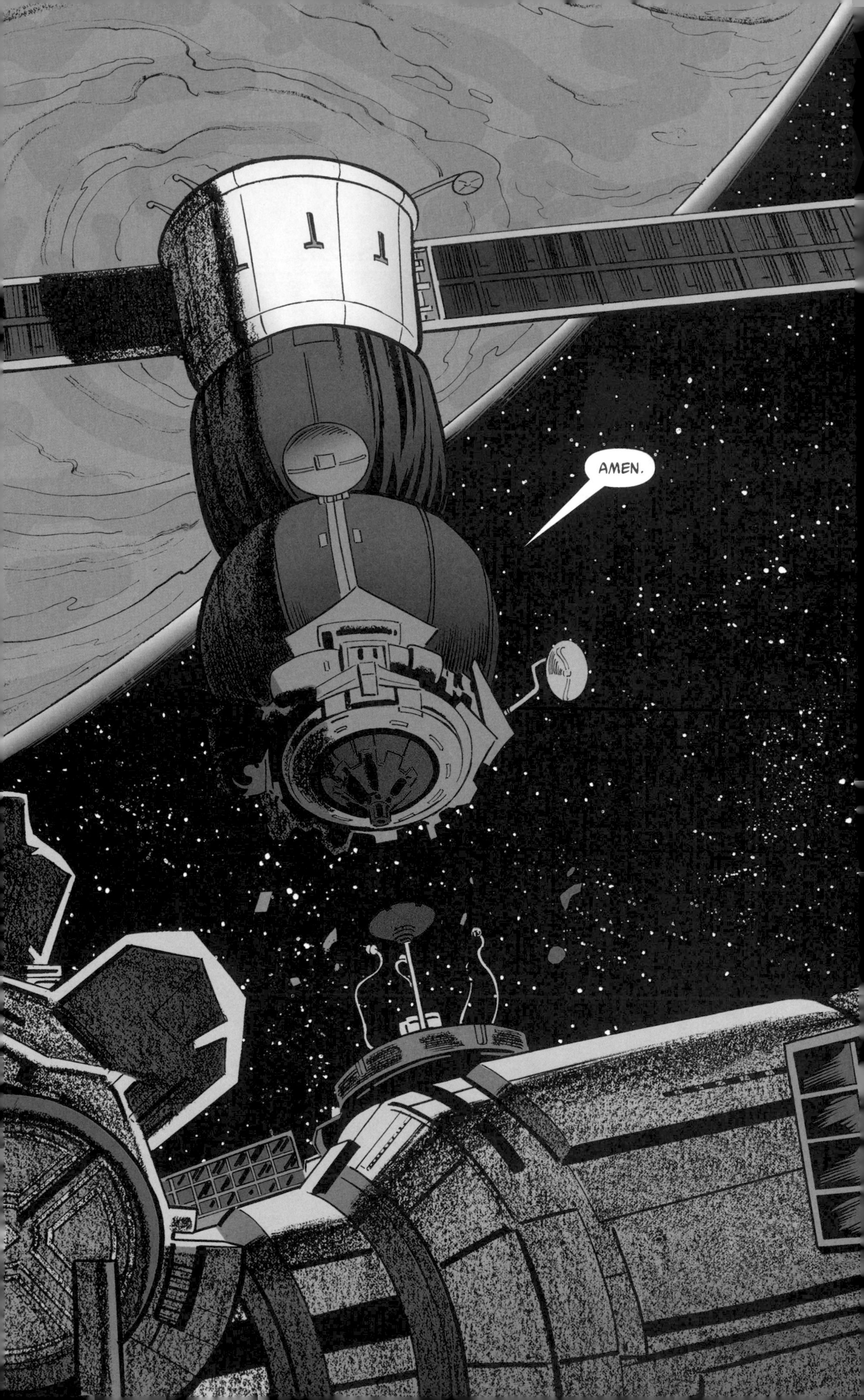
AMEN.

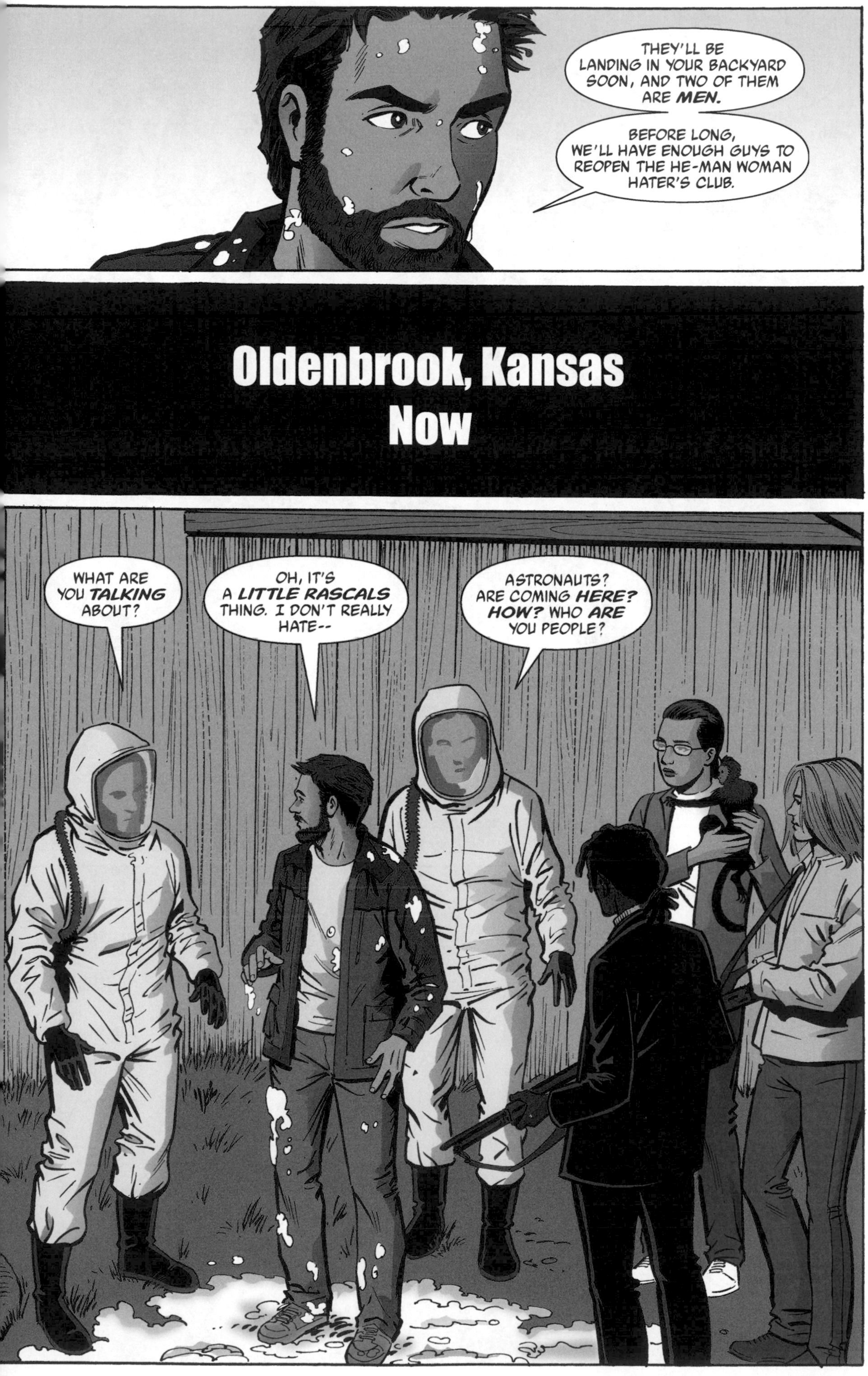
THEY'LL BE LANDING IN YOUR BACKYARD SOON, AND TWO OF THEM ARE **MEN.**
BEFORE LONG, WE'LL HAVE ENOUGH GUYS TO REOPEN THE HE-MAN WOMAN HATER'S CLUB.
Oldenbrook, Kansas
Now
WHAT ARE YOU **TALKING** ABOUT?
OH, IT'S A ***LITTLE RASCALS*** THING. I DON'T REALLY HATE--
ASTRONAUTS? ARE COMING **HERE? HOW?** WHO **ARE** YOU PEOPLE?

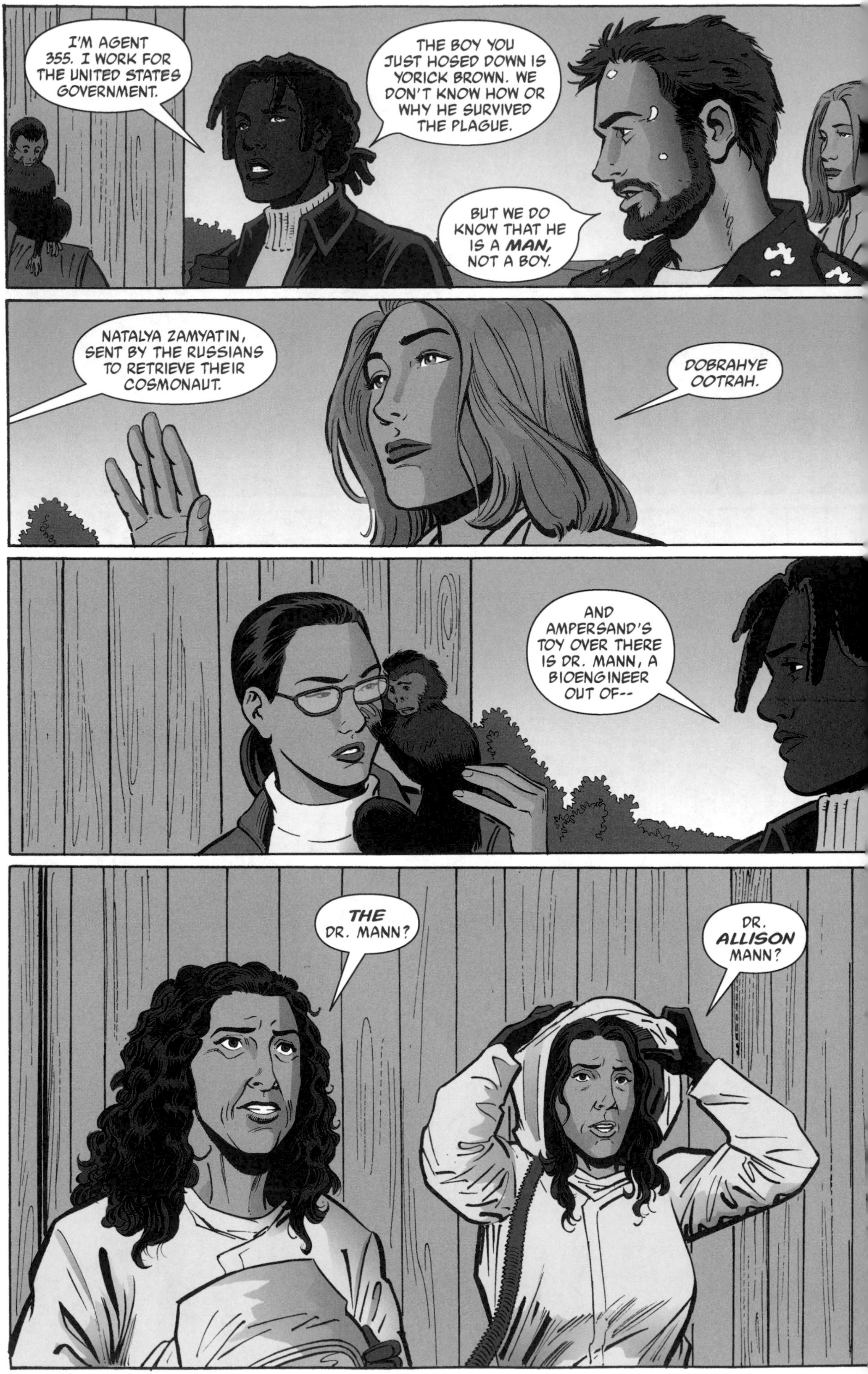
I'M AGENT 355. I WORK FOR THE UNITED STATES GOVERNMENT.
THE BOY YOU JUST HOSED DOWN IS YORICK BROWN. WE DON'T KNOW HOW OR WHY HE SURVIVED THE PLAGUE.
BUT WE DO KNOW THAT HE IS A **MAN,** NOT A BOY.
NATALYA ZAMYATIN, SENT BY THE RUSSIANS TO RETRIEVE THEIR COSMONAUT.
DOBRAHYE OOTRAH.
AND AMPERSAND'S TOY OVER THERE IS DR. MANN, A BIOENGINEER OUT OF--
THE DR. MANN?
DR. **ALLISON** MANN?

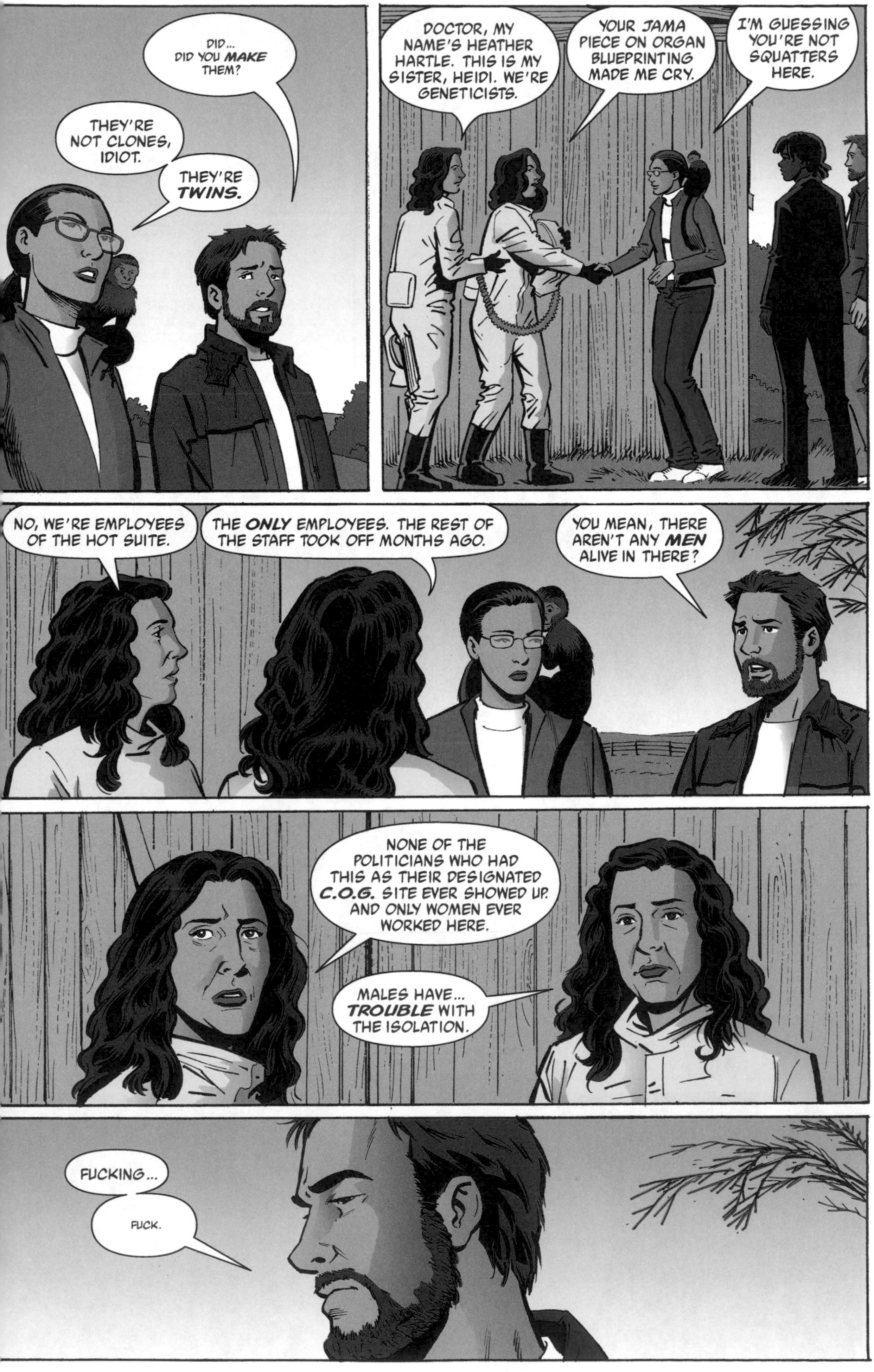
DID... DID YOU MAKE THEM?
THEY'RE NOT CLONES, IDIOT.
THEY'RE TWINS.
DOCTOR, MY NAME'S HEATHER HARTLE. THIS IS MY SISTER, HEIDI. WE'RE GENETICISTS.
YOUR JAMA PIECE ON ORGAN BLUEPRINTING MADE ME CRY.
I'M GUESSING YOU'RE NOT SQUATTERS HERE.
NO, WE'RE EMPLOYEES OF THE HOT SUITE.
THE ONLY EMPLOYEES. THE REST OF THE STAFF TOOK OFF MONTHS AGO.
YOU MEAN, THERE AREN'T ANY MEN ALIVE IN THERE?
NONE OF THE POLITICIANS WHO HAD THIS AS THEIR DESIGNATED C.O.G. SITE EVER SHOWED UP. AND ONLY WOMEN EVER WORKED HERE.
MALES HAVE... TROUBLE WITH THE ISOLATION.
FUCKING...
FUCK.

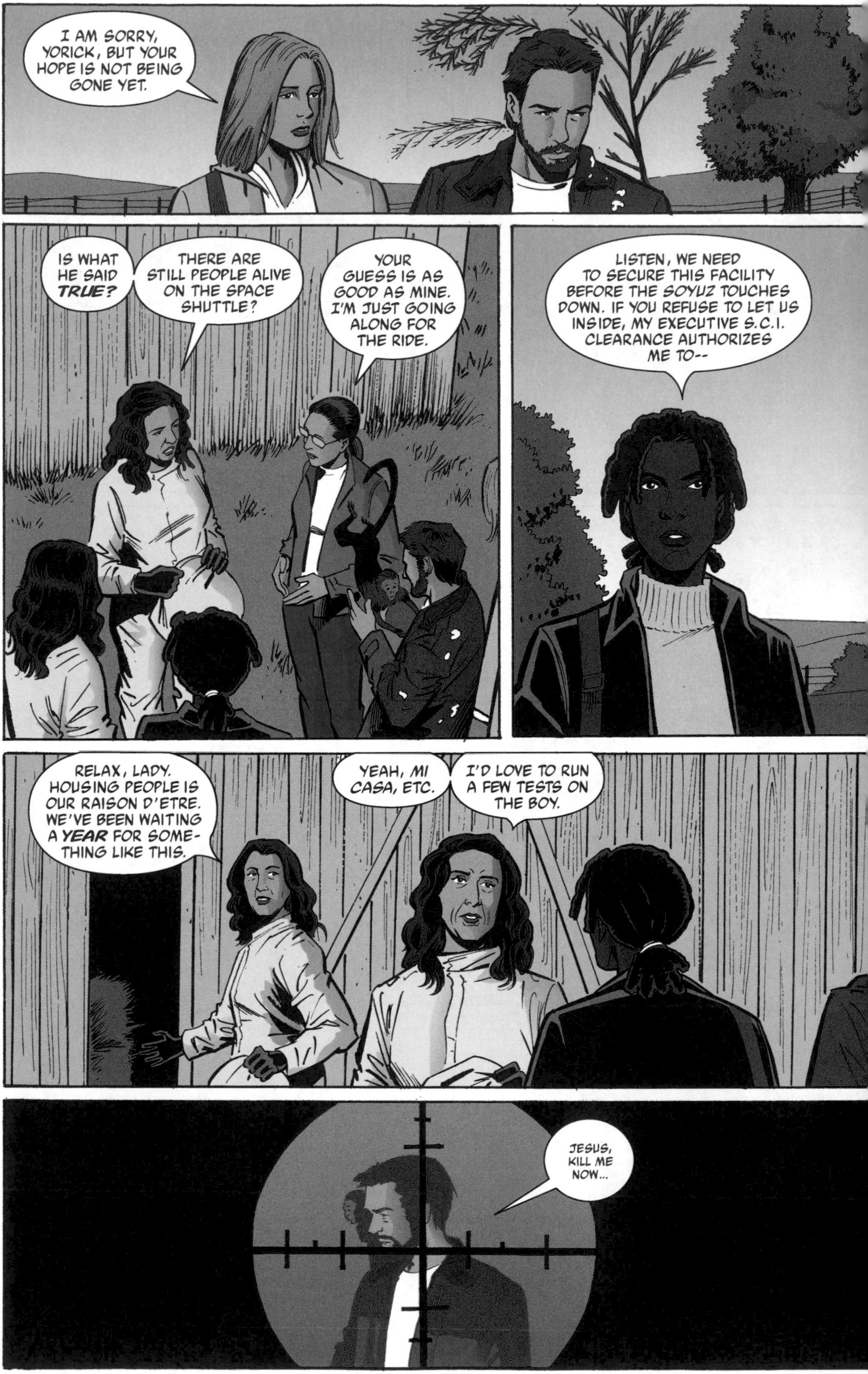
I AM SORRY, YORICK, BUT YOUR HOPE IS NOT BEING GONE YET.
IS WHAT HE SAID ***TRUE?***
THERE ARE STILL PEOPLE ALIVE ON THE SPACE SHUTTLE?
YOUR GUESS IS AS GOOD AS MINE. I'M JUST GOING ALONG FOR THE RIDE.
LISTEN, WE NEED TO SECURE THIS FACILITY BEFORE THE *SOYUZ* TOUCHES DOWN. IF YOU REFUSE TO LET US INSIDE, MY EXECUTIVE S.C.I. CLEARANCE AUTHORIZES ME TO--
RELAX, LADY. HOUSING PEOPLE IS OUR RAISON D'ETRE. WE'VE BEEN WAITING A ***YEAR*** FOR SOME-THING LIKE THIS.
YEAH, *MI* CASA, ETC.
I'D LOVE TO RUN A FEW TESTS ON THE BOY.
JESUS, KILL ME NOW...

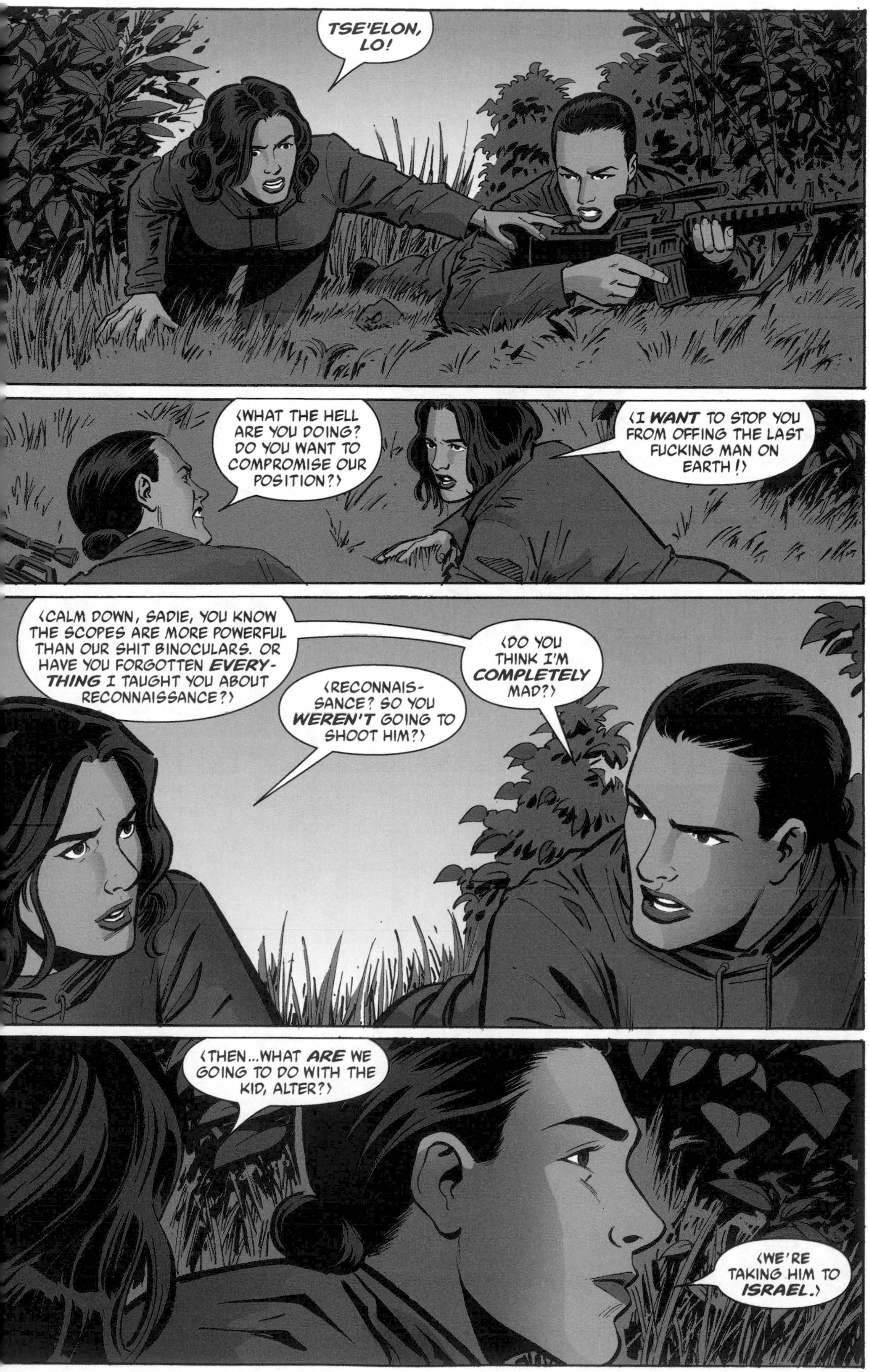
TSE'ELON, LO!
‹WHAT THE HELL ARE YOU DOING? DO YOU WANT TO COMPROMISE OUR POSITION?›
‹I **WANT** TO STOP YOU FROM OFFING THE LAST FUCKING MAN ON EARTH!›
‹CALM DOWN, SADIE, YOU KNOW THE SCOPES ARE MORE POWERFUL THAN OUR SHIT BINOCULARS. OR HAVE YOU FORGOTTEN **EVERYTHING** I TAUGHT YOU ABOUT RECONNAISSANCE?›
‹RECONNAISSANCE? SO YOU **WEREN'T** GOING TO SHOOT HIM?›
‹DO YOU THINK I'M **COMPLETELY** MAD?›
‹THEN...WHAT **ARE** WE GOING TO DO WITH THE KID, ALTER?›
‹WE'RE TAKING HIM TO **ISRAEL**.›

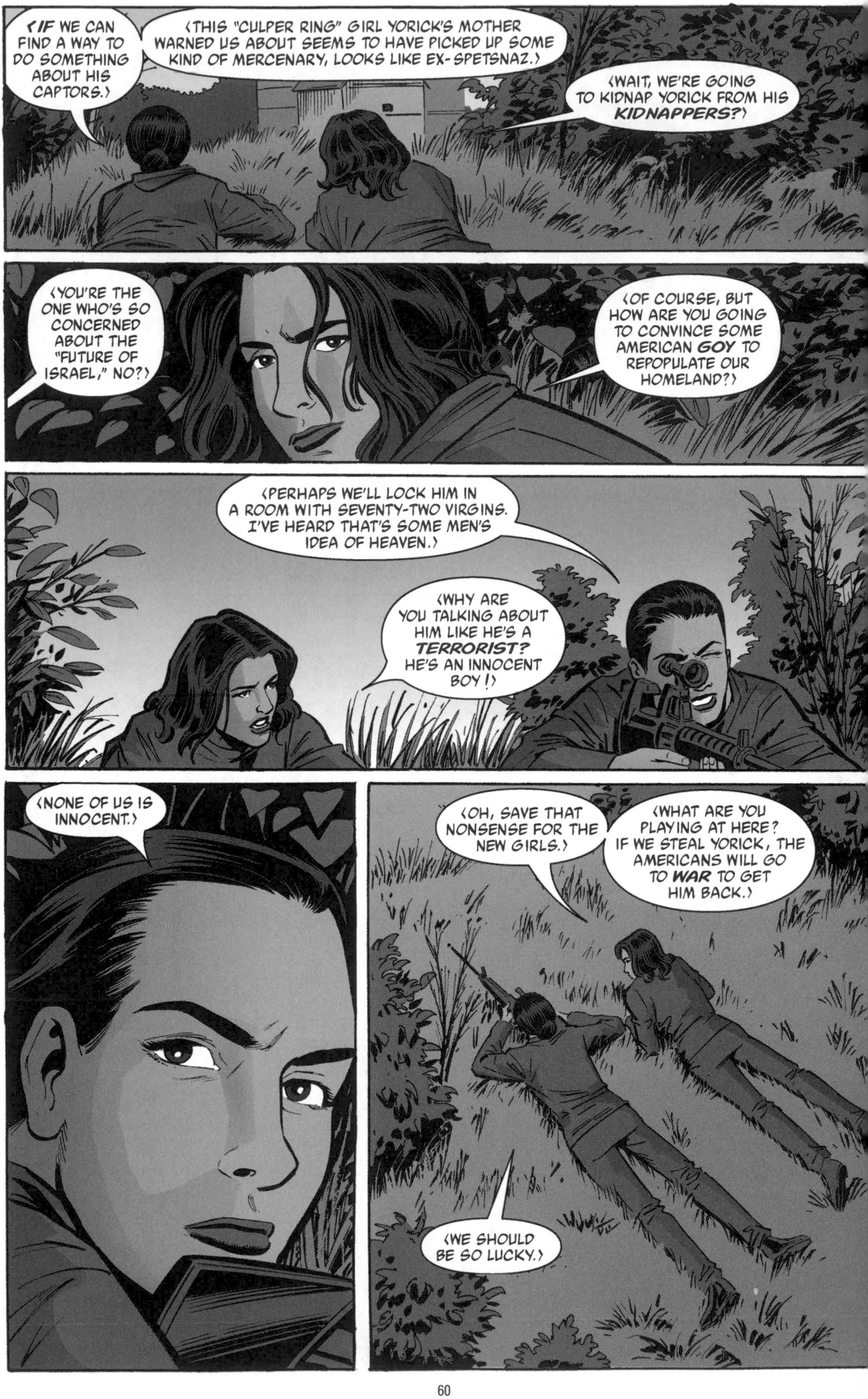
‹IF WE CAN FIND A WAY TO DO SOMETHING ABOUT HIS CAPTORS.›
‹THIS "CULPER RING" GIRL YORICK'S MOTHER WARNED US ABOUT SEEMS TO HAVE PICKED UP SOME KIND OF MERCENARY, LOOKS LIKE EX-SPETSNAZ.›
‹WAIT, WE'RE GOING TO KIDNAP YORICK FROM HIS KIDNAPPERS?›
‹YOU'RE THE ONE WHO'S SO CONCERNED ABOUT THE "FUTURE OF ISRAEL," NO?›
‹OF COURSE, BUT HOW ARE YOU GOING TO CONVINCE SOME AMERICAN GOY TO REPOPULATE OUR HOMELAND?›
‹PERHAPS WE'LL LOCK HIM IN A ROOM WITH SEVENTY-TWO VIRGINS. I'VE HEARD THAT'S SOME MEN'S IDEA OF HEAVEN.›
‹WHY ARE YOU TALKING ABOUT HIM LIKE HE'S A TERRORIST? HE'S AN INNOCENT BOY!›
‹NONE OF US IS INNOCENT.›
‹OH, SAVE THAT NONSENSE FOR THE NEW GIRLS.›
‹WHAT ARE YOU PLAYING AT HERE? IF WE STEAL YORICK, THE AMERICANS WILL GO TO WAR TO GET HIM BACK.›
‹WE SHOULD BE SO LUCKY.›

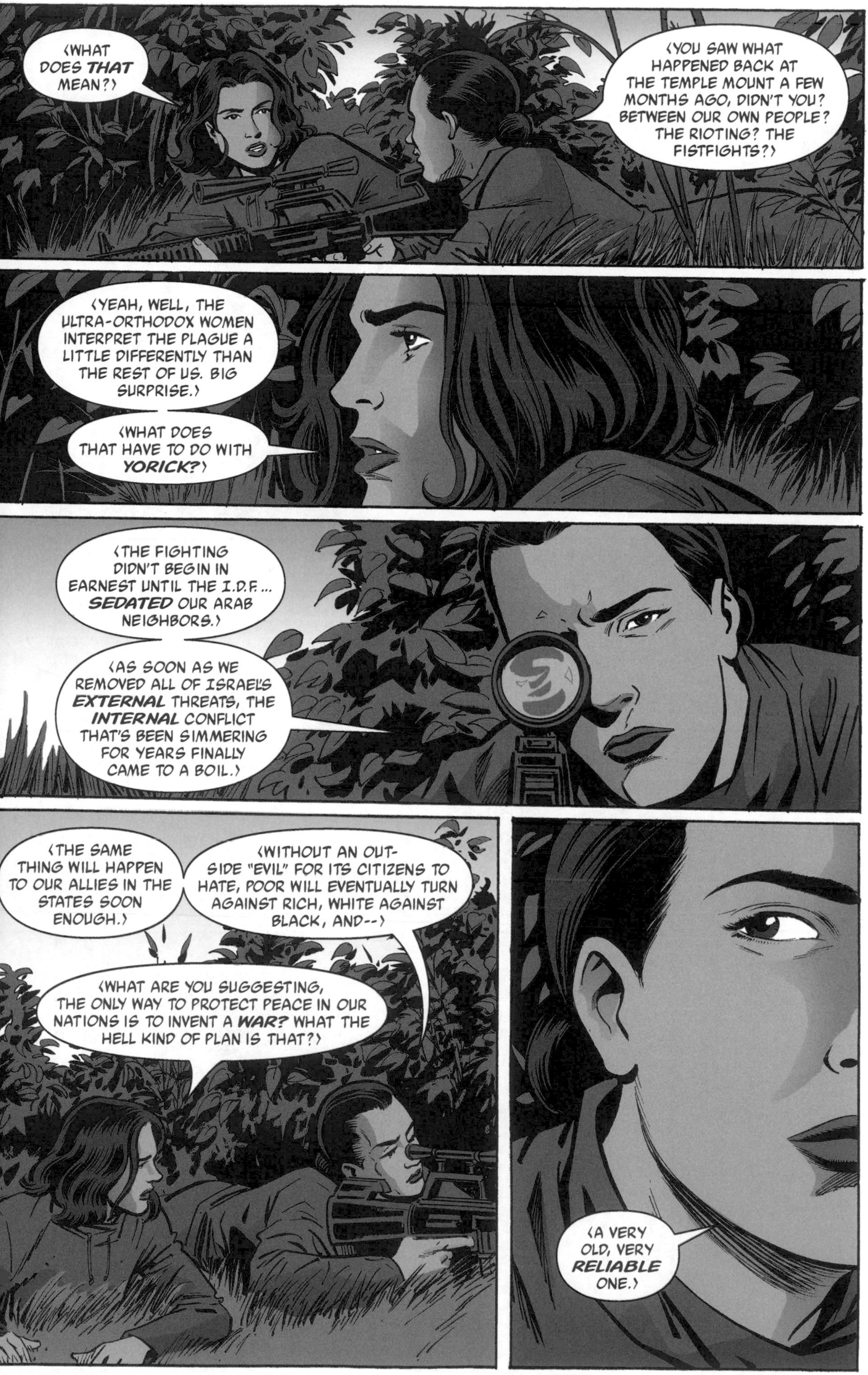
‹WHAT DOES THAT MEAN?›
‹YOU SAW WHAT HAPPENED BACK AT THE TEMPLE MOUNT A FEW MONTHS AGO, DIDN'T YOU? BETWEEN OUR OWN PEOPLE? THE RIOTING? THE FISTFIGHTS?›
‹YEAH, WELL, THE ULTRA-ORTHODOX WOMEN INTERPRET THE PLAGUE A LITTLE DIFFERENTLY THAN THE REST OF US. BIG SURPRISE.›
‹WHAT DOES THAT HAVE TO DO WITH YORICK?›
‹THE FIGHTING DIDN'T BEGIN IN EARNEST UNTIL THE I.D.F. ... SEDATED OUR ARAB NEIGHBORS.›
‹AS SOON AS WE REMOVED ALL OF ISRAEL'S EXTERNAL THREATS, THE INTERNAL CONFLICT THAT'S BEEN SIMMERING FOR YEARS FINALLY CAME TO A BOIL.›
‹THE SAME THING WILL HAPPEN TO OUR ALLIES IN THE STATES SOON ENOUGH.›
‹WITHOUT AN OUT-SIDE "EVIL" FOR ITS CITIZENS TO HATE, POOR WILL EVENTUALLY TURN AGAINST RICH, WHITE AGAINST BLACK, AND--›
‹WHAT ARE YOU SUGGESTING, THE ONLY WAY TO PROTECT PEACE IN OUR NATIONS IS TO INVENT A WAR? WHAT THE HELL KIND OF PLAN IS THAT?›
‹A VERY OLD, VERY RELIABLE ONE.›

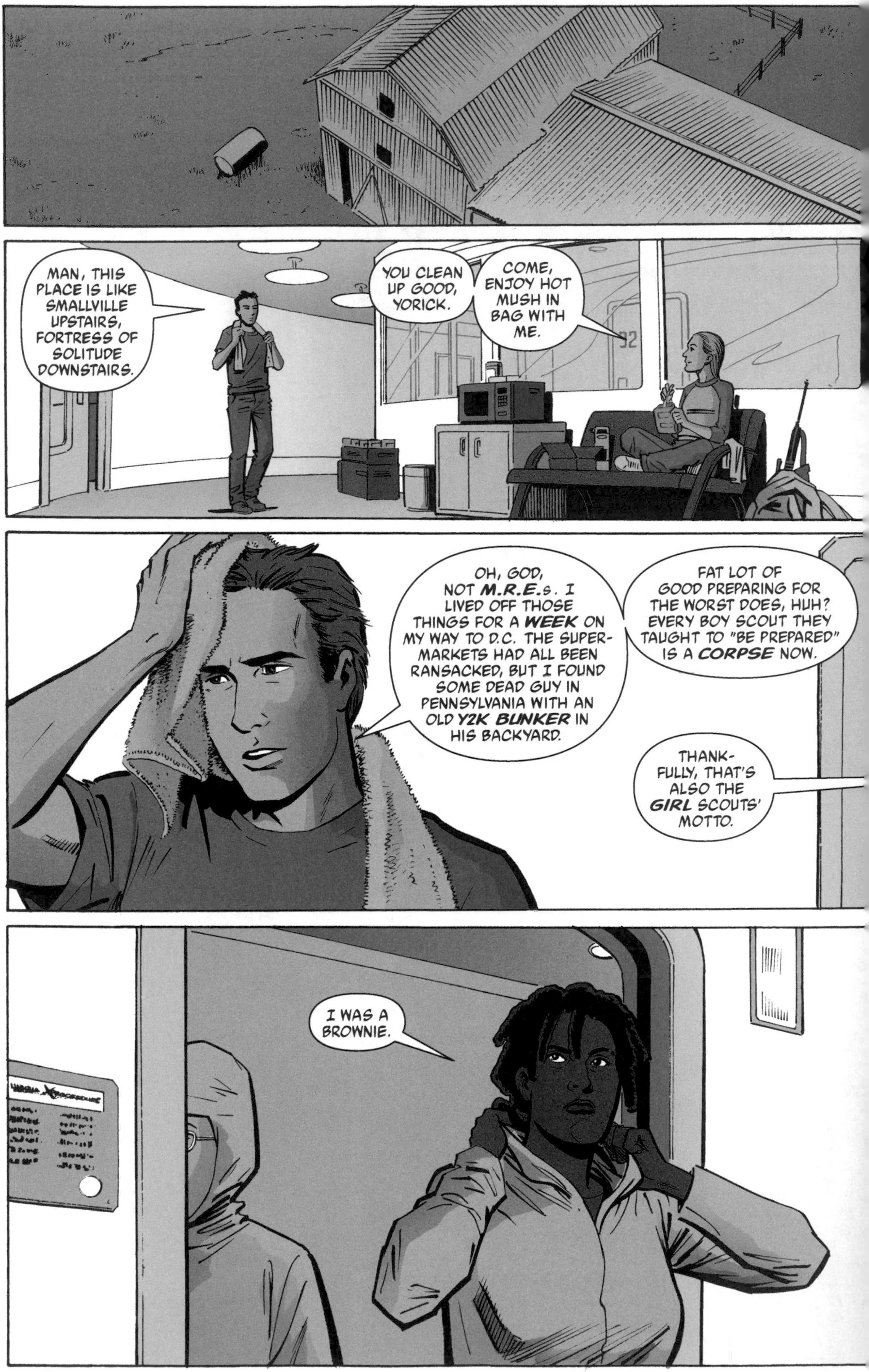
MAN, THIS PLACE IS LIKE SMALLVILLE UPSTAIRS, FORTRESS OF SOLITUDE DOWNSTAIRS.
YOU CLEAN UP GOOD, YORICK.
COME, ENJOY HOT MUSH IN BAG WITH ME.
OH, GOD, NOT M.R.E.s. I LIVED OFF THOSE THINGS FOR A WEEK ON MY WAY TO D.C. THE SUPER-MARKETS HAD ALL BEEN RANSACKED, BUT I FOUND SOME DEAD GUY IN PENNSYLVANIA WITH AN OLD Y2K BUNKER IN HIS BACKYARD.
FAT LOT OF GOOD PREPARING FOR THE WORST DOES, HUH? EVERY BOY SCOUT THEY TAUGHT TO "BE PREPARED" IS A CORPSE NOW.
THANK-FULLY, THAT'S ALSO THE GIRL SCOUTS' MOTTO.
I WAS A BROWNIE.

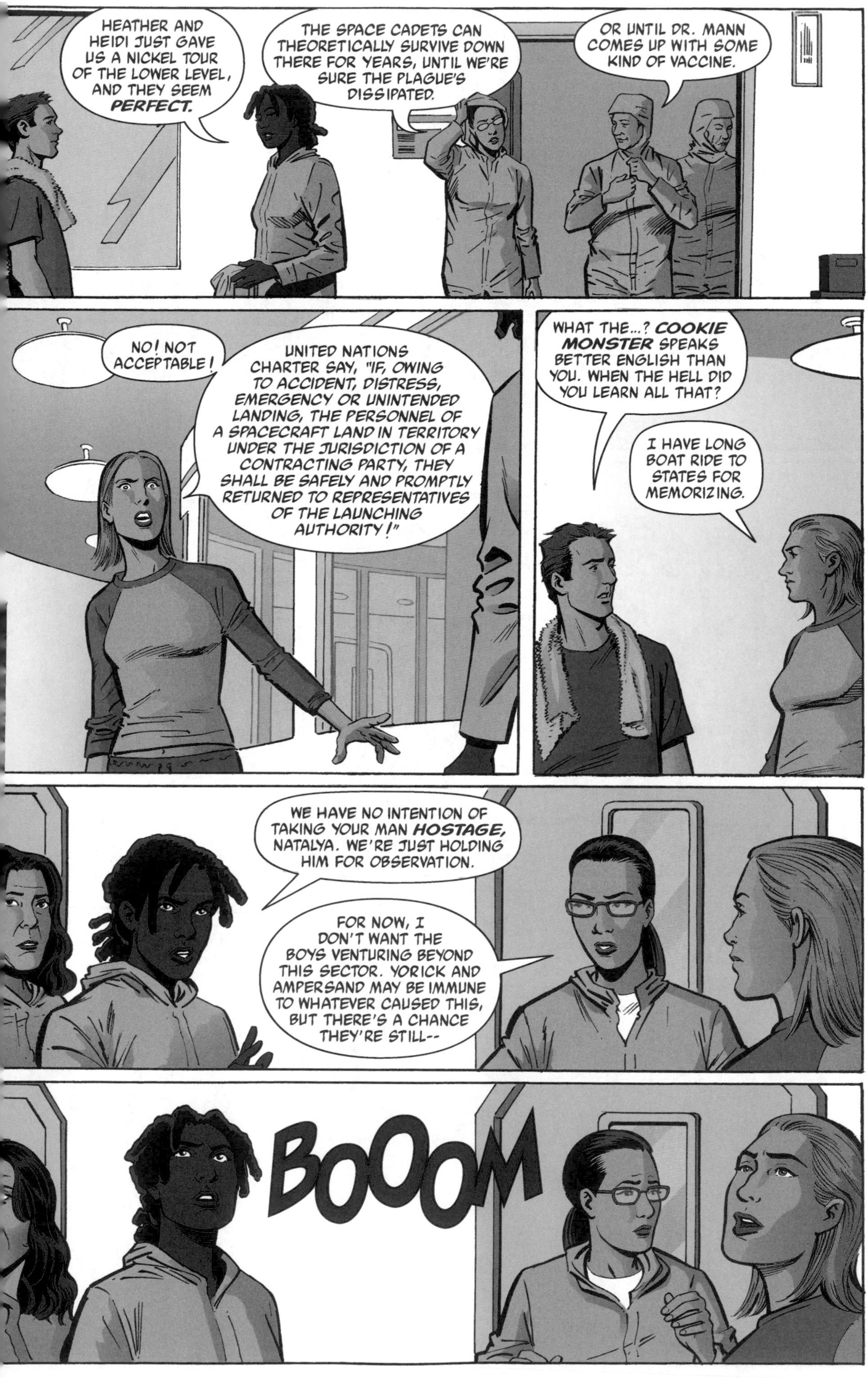
HEATHER AND HEIDI JUST GAVE US A NICKEL TOUR OF THE LOWER LEVEL, AND THEY SEEM PERFECT.
THE SPACE CADETS CAN THEORETICALLY SURVIVE DOWN THERE FOR YEARS, UNTIL WE'RE SURE THE PLAGUE'S DISSIPATED.
OR UNTIL DR. MANN COMES UP WITH SOME KIND OF VACCINE.
NO! NOT ACCEPTABLE!
UNITED NATIONS CHARTER SAY, "IF, OWING TO ACCIDENT, DISTRESS, EMERGENCY OR UNINTENDED LANDING, THE PERSONNEL OF A SPACECRAFT LAND IN TERRITORY UNDER THE JURISDICTION OF A CONTRACTING PARTY, THEY SHALL BE SAFELY AND PROMPTLY RETURNED TO REPRESENTATIVES OF THE LAUNCHING AUTHORITY!"
WHAT THE...? COOKIE MONSTER SPEAKS BETTER ENGLISH THAN YOU. WHEN THE HELL DID YOU LEARN ALL THAT?
I HAVE LONG BOAT RIDE TO STATES FOR MEMORIZING.
WE HAVE NO INTENTION OF TAKING YOUR MAN HOSTAGE, NATALYA. WE'RE JUST HOLDING HIM FOR OBSERVATION.
FOR NOW, I DON'T WANT THE BOYS VENTURING BEYOND THIS SECTOR. YORICK AND AMPERSAND MAY BE IMMUNE TO WHATEVER CAUSED THIS, BUT THERE'S A CHANCE THEY'RE STILL--
BOOOM

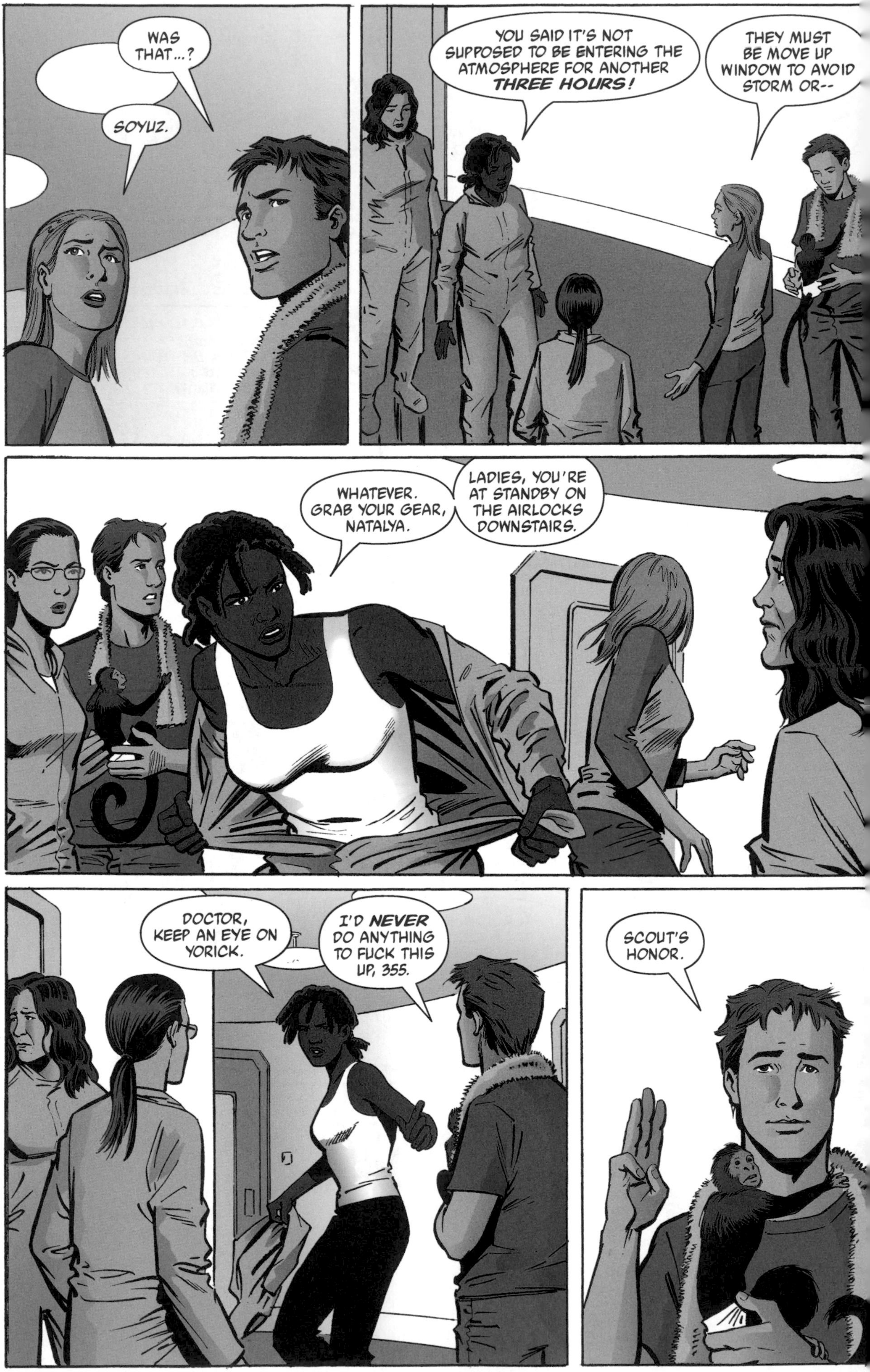
WAS THAT...?
SOYUZ.
YOU SAID IT'S NOT SUPPOSED TO BE ENTERING THE ATMOSPHERE FOR ANOTHER THREE HOURS!
THEY MUST BE MOVE UP WINDOW TO AVOID STORM OR--
WHATEVER. GRAB YOUR GEAR, NATALYA.
LADIES, YOU'RE AT STANDBY ON THE AIRLOCKS DOWNSTAIRS.
DOCTOR, KEEP AN EYE ON YORICK.
I'D NEVER DO ANYTHING TO FUCK THIS UP, 355.
SCOUT'S HONOR.

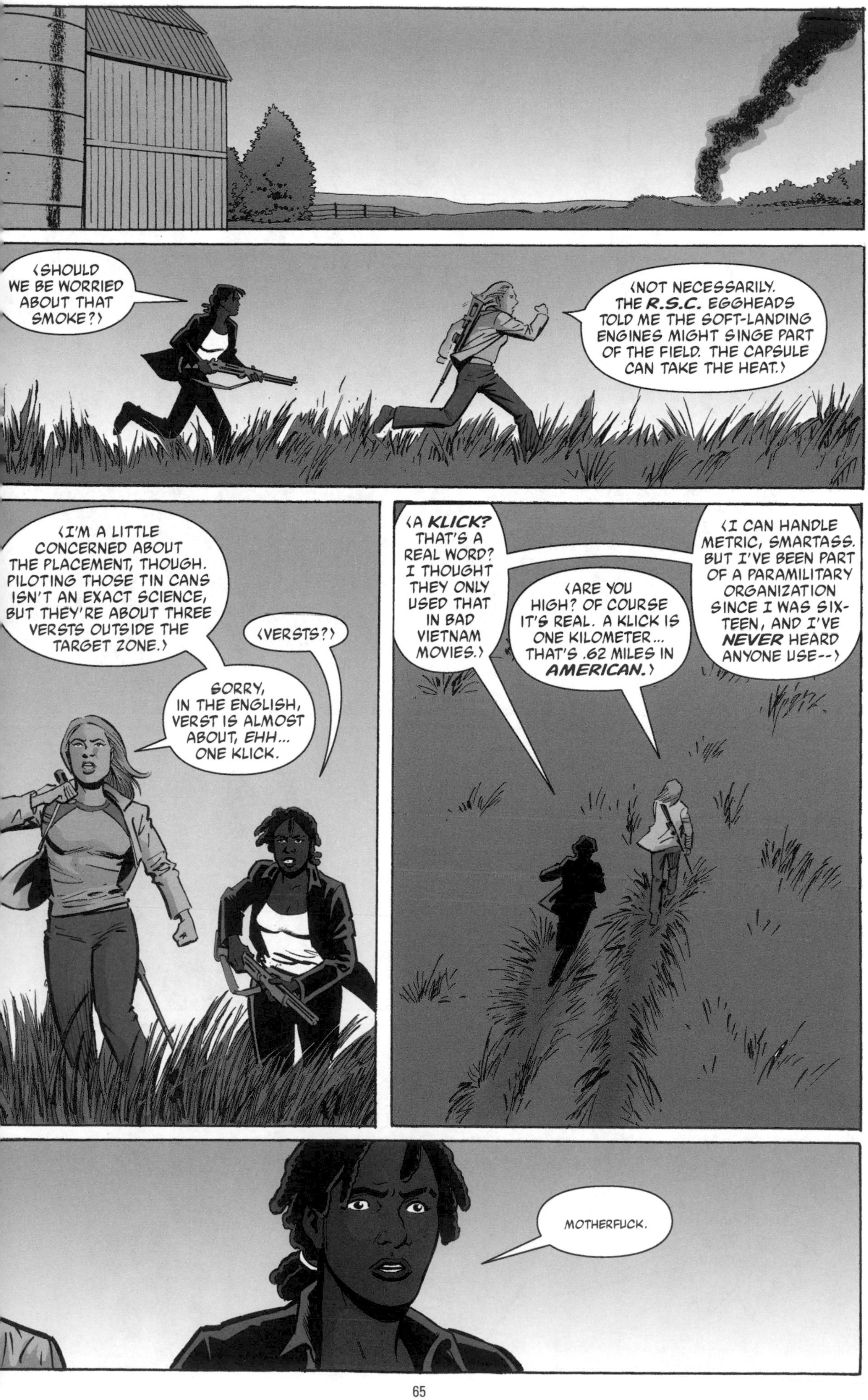
‹SHOULD WE BE WORRIED ABOUT THAT SMOKE?›
‹NOT NECESSARILY. THE R.S.C. EGGHEADS TOLD ME THE SOFT-LANDING ENGINES MIGHT SINGE PART OF THE FIELD. THE CAPSULE CAN TAKE THE HEAT.›
‹I'M A LITTLE CONCERNED ABOUT THE PLACEMENT, THOUGH. PILOTING THOSE TIN CANS ISN'T AN EXACT SCIENCE, BUT THEY'RE ABOUT THREE VERSTS OUTSIDE THE TARGET ZONE.›
‹VERSTS?›
SORRY, IN THE ENGLISH, VERST IS ALMOST ABOUT, EHH... ONE KLICK.
‹A KLICK? THAT'S A REAL WORD? I THOUGHT THEY ONLY USED THAT IN BAD VIETNAM MOVIES.›
‹ARE YOU HIGH? OF COURSE IT'S REAL. A KLICK IS ONE KILOMETER... THAT'S .62 MILES IN AMERICAN.›
‹I CAN HANDLE METRIC, SMARTASS. BUT I'VE BEEN PART OF A PARAMILITARY ORGANIZATION SINCE I WAS SIXTEEN, AND I'VE NEVER HEARD ANYONE USE--›
MOTHERFUCK.

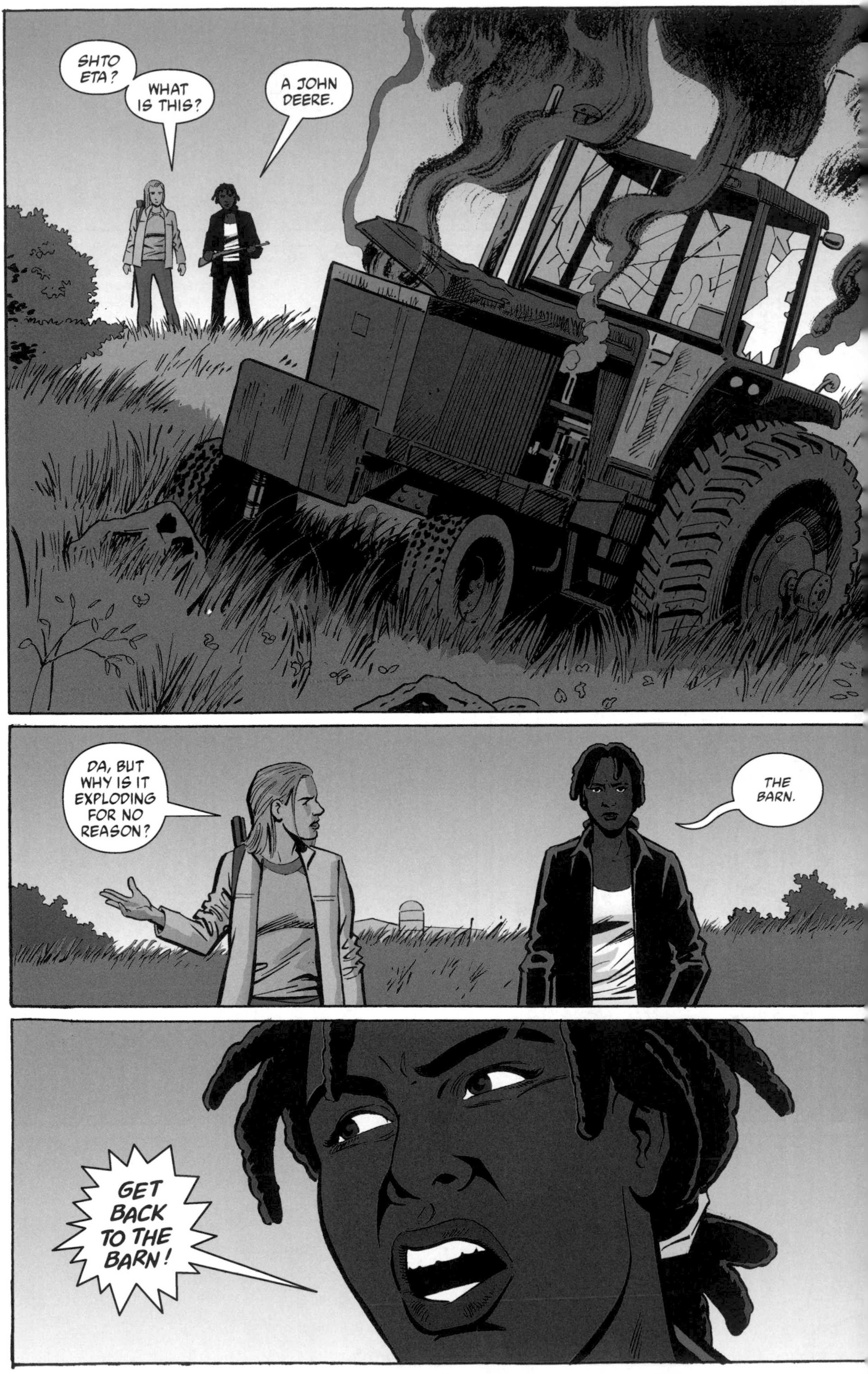

SHTO ETA?
WHAT IS THIS?
A JOHN DEERE.
DA, BUT WHY IS IT EXPLODING FOR NO REASON?
THE BARN.
GET BACK TO THE BARN!

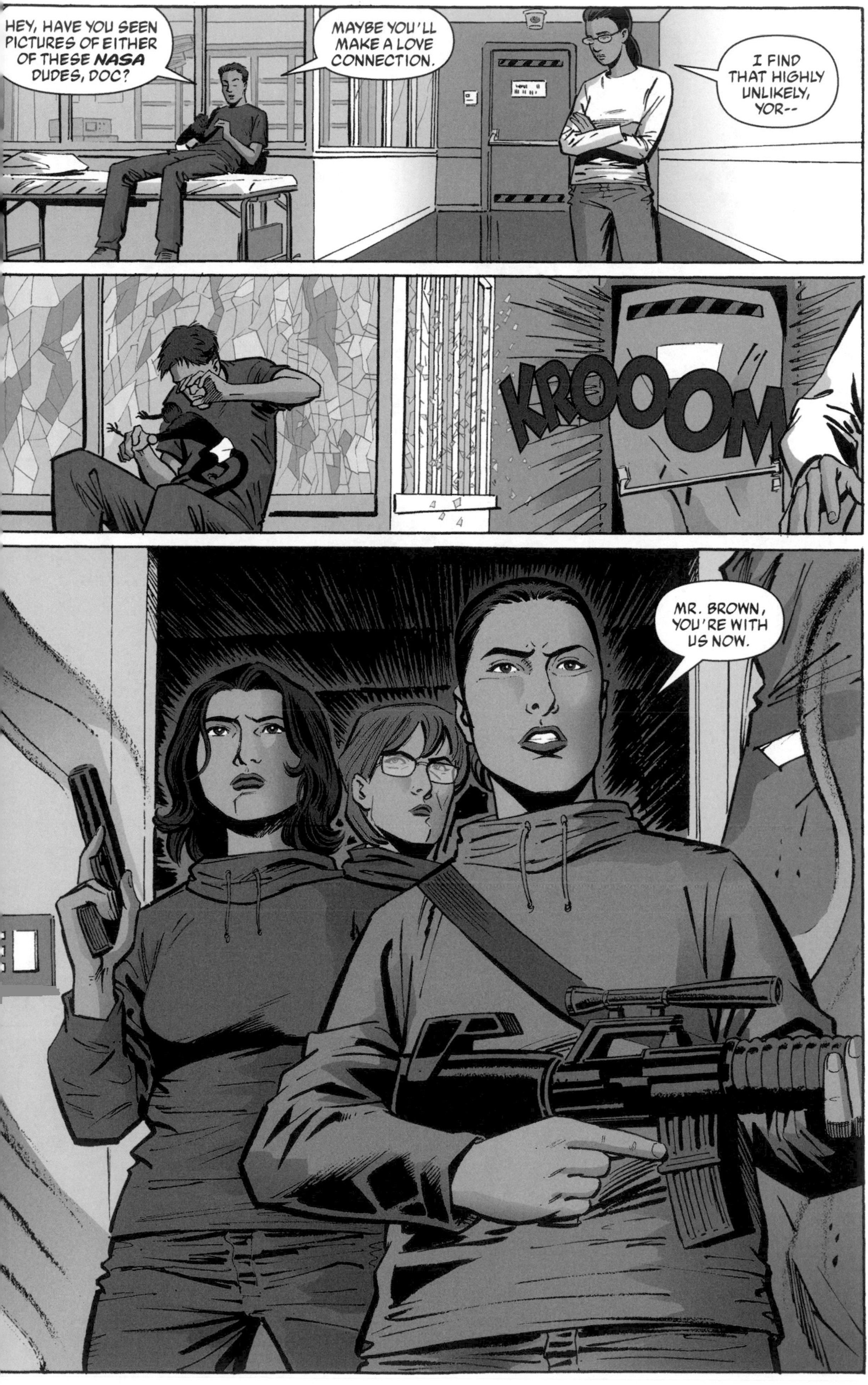
HEY, HAVE YOU SEEN PICTURES OF EITHER OF THESE NASA DUDES, DOC?
MAYBE YOU'LL MAKE A LOVE CONNECTION.
I FIND THAT HIGHLY UNLIKELY, YOR--
KROOOM
MR. BROWN, YOU'RE WITH US NOW.

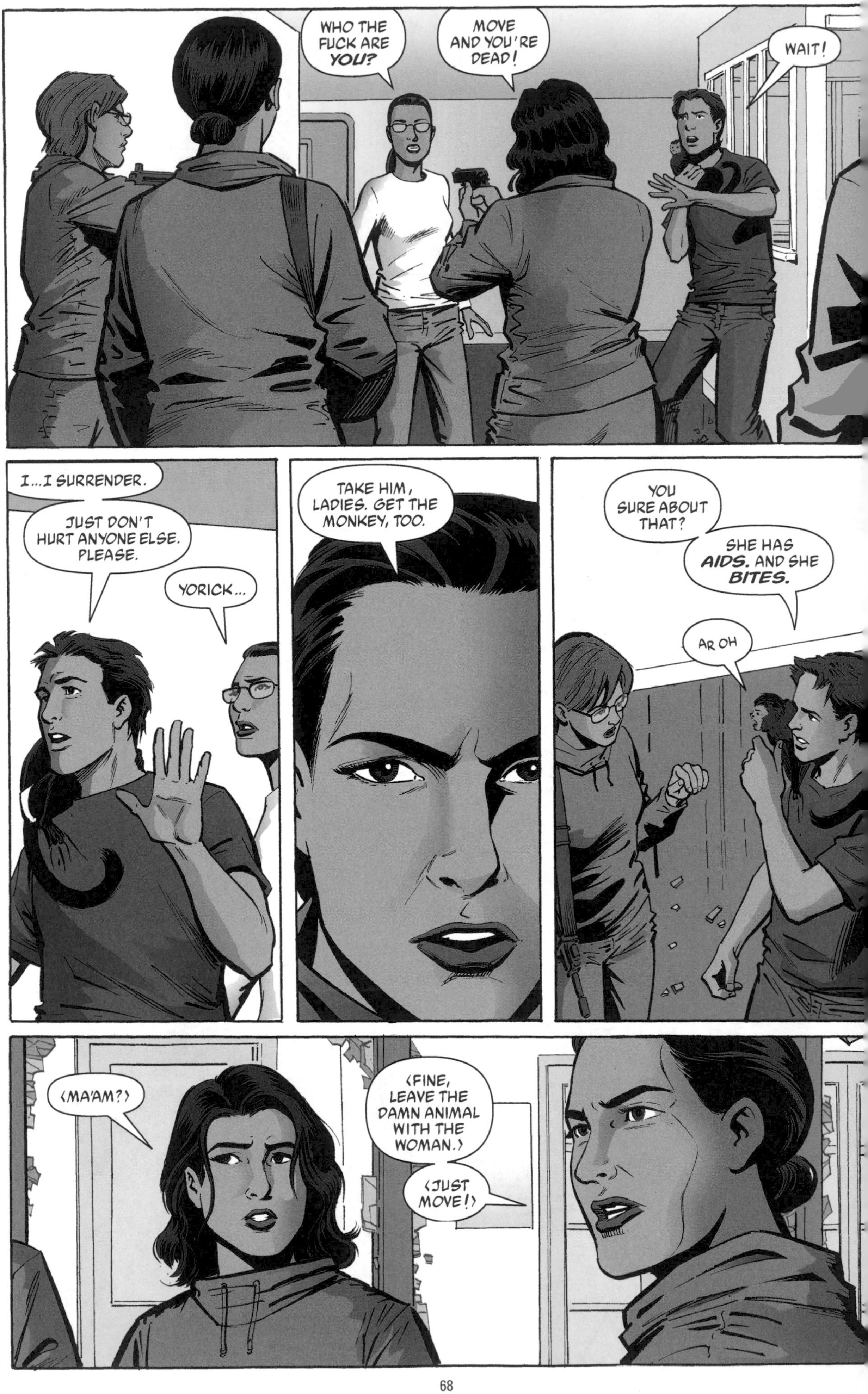
WHO THE FUCK ARE YOU?
MOVE AND YOU'RE DEAD!
WAIT!
I...I SURRENDER.
JUST DON'T HURT ANYONE ELSE. PLEASE.
YORICK...
TAKE HIM, LADIES. GET THE MONKEY, TOO.
YOU SURE ABOUT THAT?
SHE HAS AIDS. AND SHE BITES.
AR OH
‹MA'AM?›
‹FINE, LEAVE THE DAMN ANIMAL WITH THE WOMAN.›
‹JUST MOVE!›

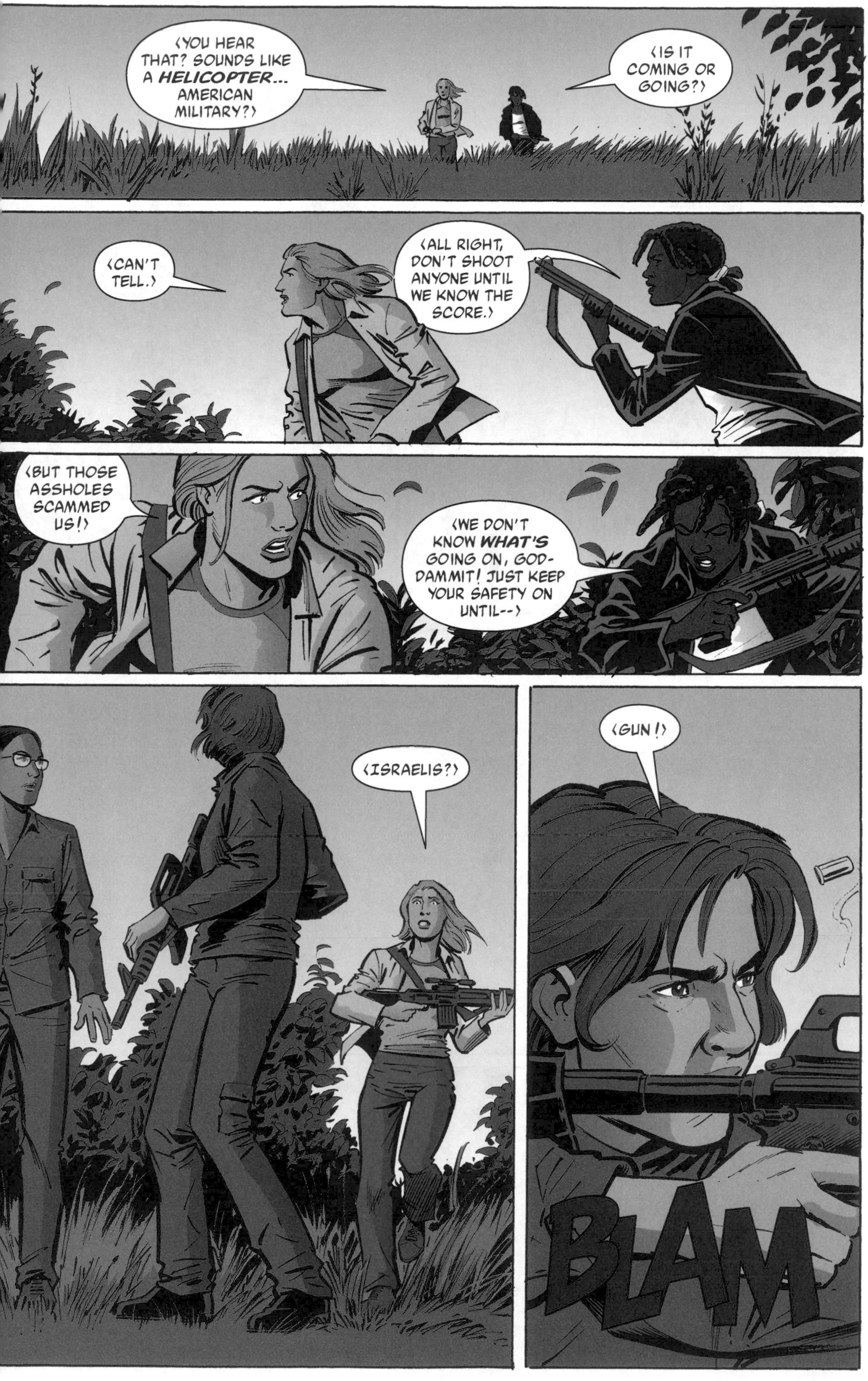
‹YOU HEAR THAT? SOUNDS LIKE A **HELICOPTER...** AMERICAN MILITARY?›
‹IS IT COMING OR GOING?›
‹CAN'T TELL.›
‹ALL RIGHT, DON'T SHOOT ANYONE UNTIL WE KNOW THE SCORE.›
‹BUT THOSE ASSHOLES SCAMMED US!›
‹WE DON'T KNOW ***WHAT'S*** GOING ON, GOD-DAMMIT! JUST KEEP YOUR SAFETY ON UNTIL--›
‹ISRAELIS?›
‹GUN!›
BLAM

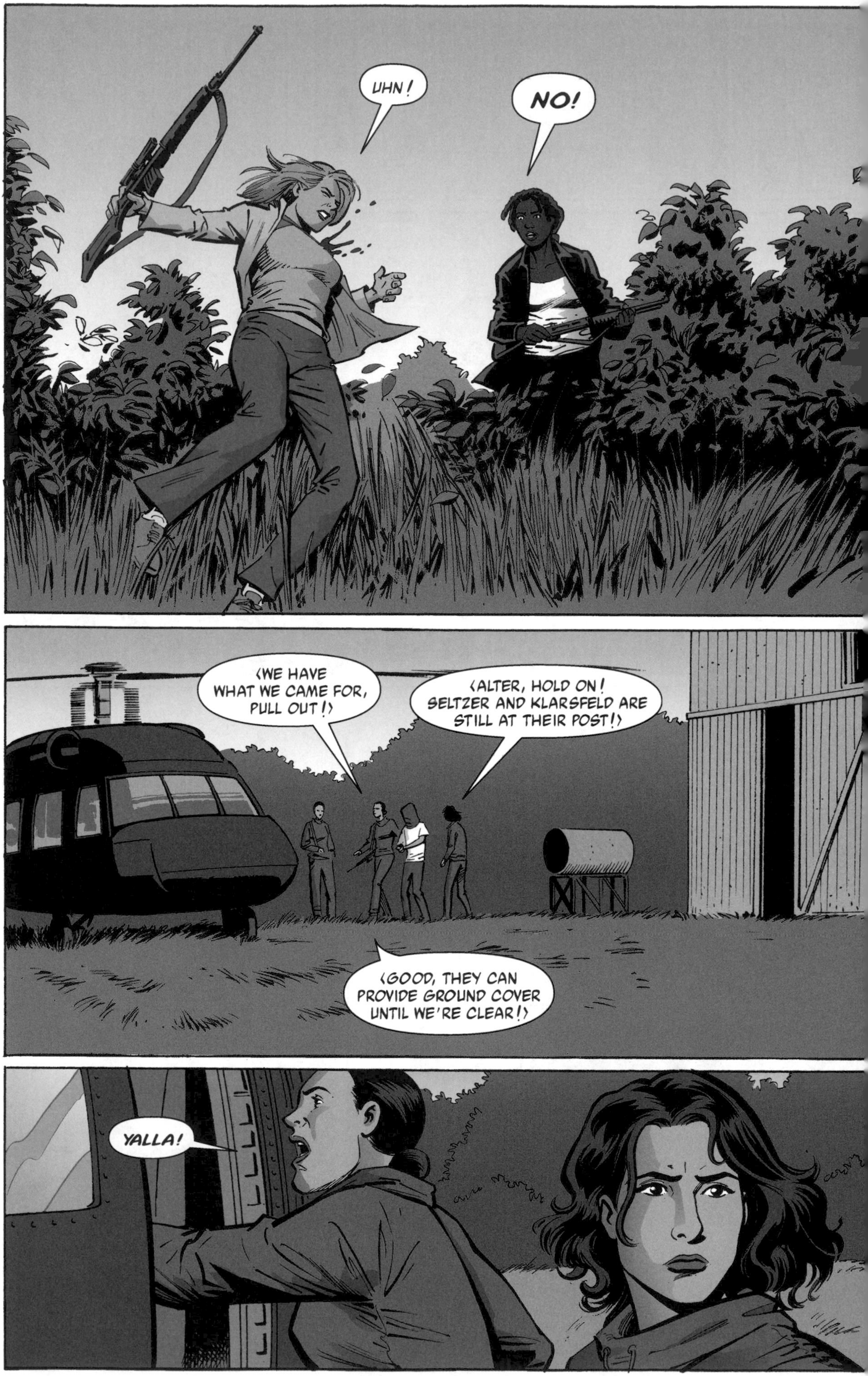
UHN!
NO!
‹WE HAVE WHAT WE CAME FOR, PULL OUT!›
‹ALTER, HOLD ON! SELTZER AND KLARSFELD ARE STILL AT THEIR POST!›
‹GOOD, THEY CAN PROVIDE GROUND COVER UNTIL WE'RE CLEAR!›
YALLA!

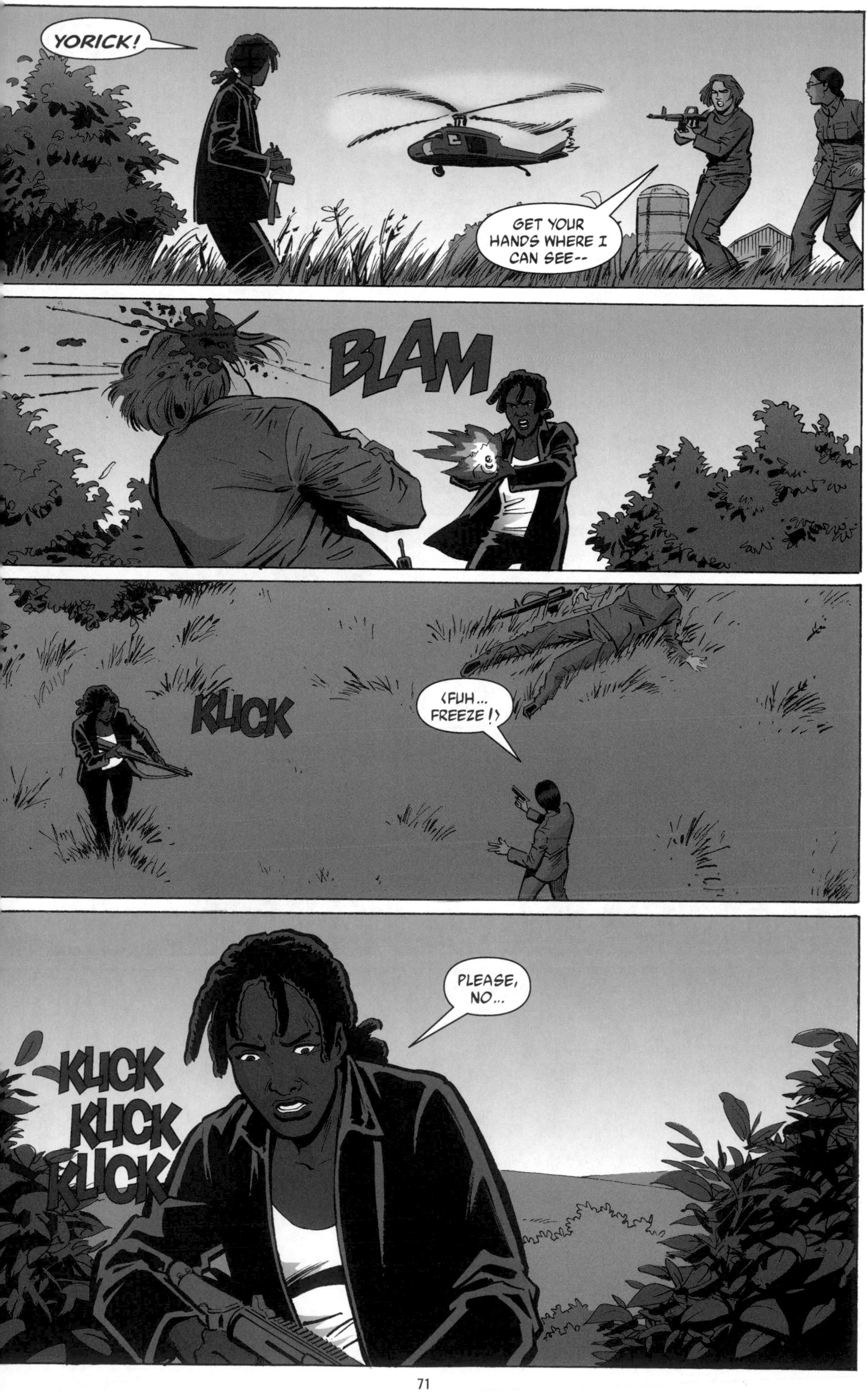
YORICK!
GET YOUR HANDS WHERE I CAN SEE--
BLAM
KLICK
‹FUH... FREEZE!›
PLEASE, NO...
KLICK
KLICK
KLICK

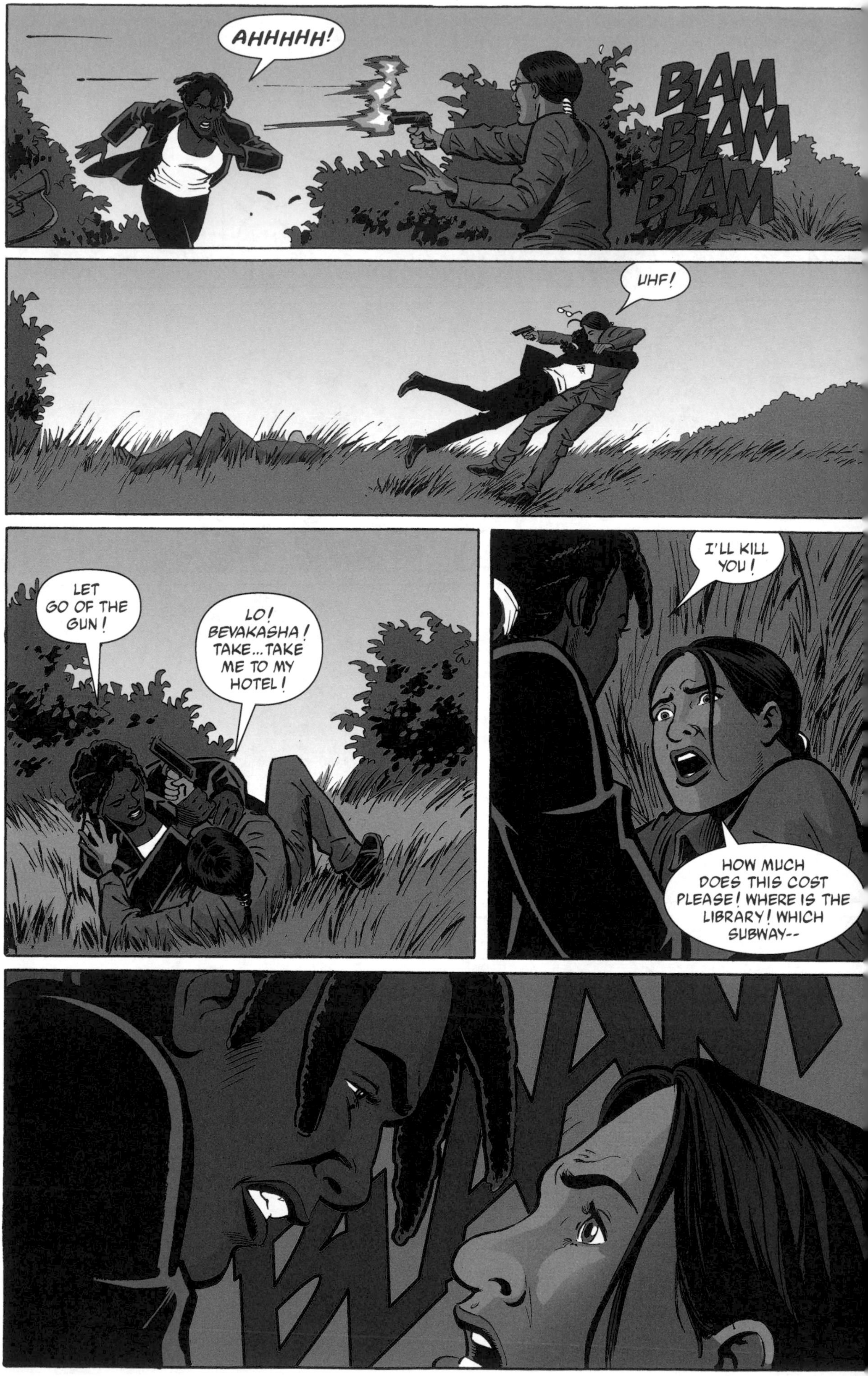
AHHHHH!
BLAM BLAM BLAM
UHF!
LET GO OF THE GUN!
LO! BEVAKASHA! TAKE...TAKE ME TO MY HOTEL!
I'LL KILL YOU!
HOW MUCH DOES THIS COST PLEASE! WHERE IS THE LIBRARY! WHICH SUBWAY--

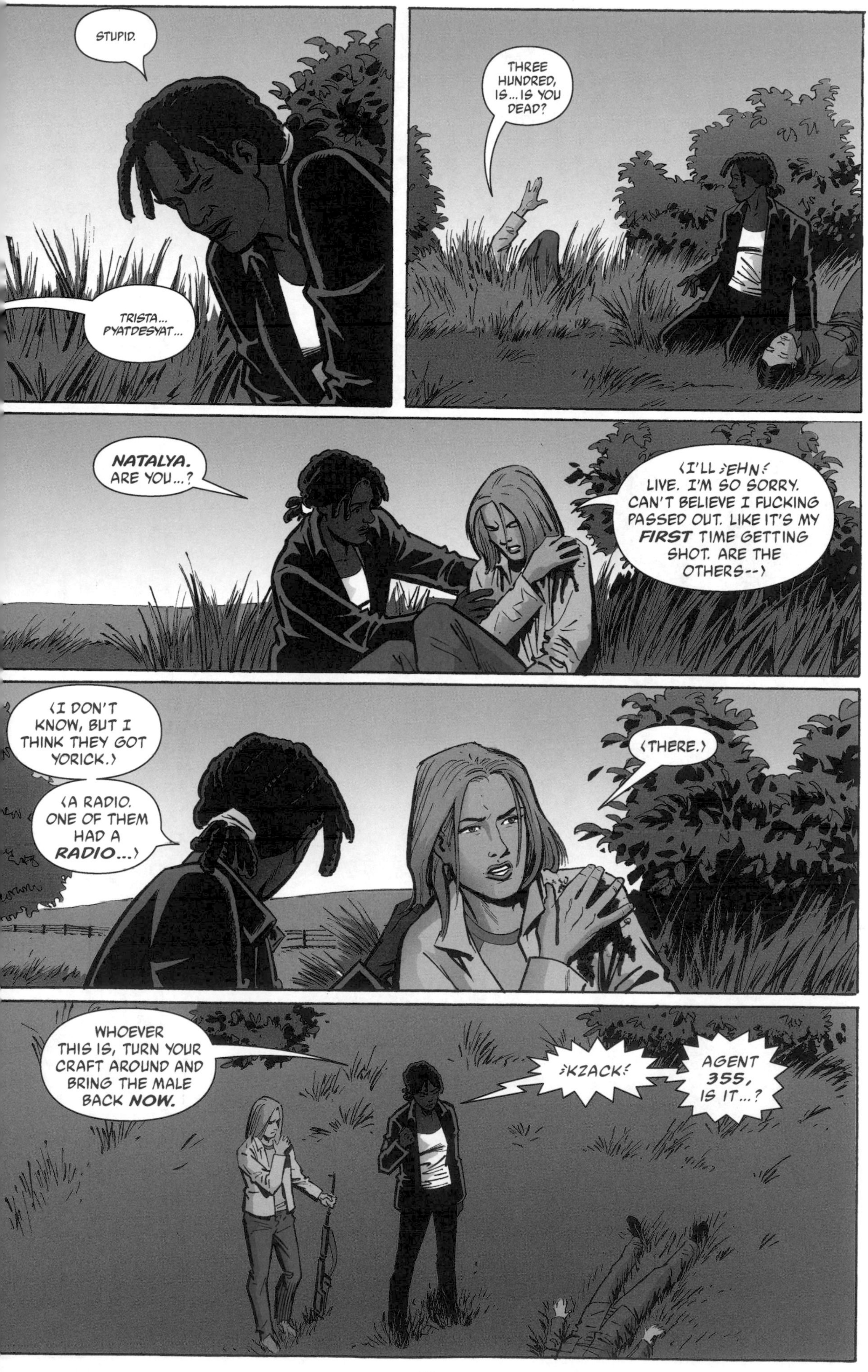
STUPID.
TRISTA... PYATDESYAT...
THREE HUNDRED, IS... IS YOU DEAD?
NATALYA. ARE YOU...?
‹I'LL ›EHN‹ LIVE. I'M SO SORRY. CAN'T BELIEVE I FUCKING PASSED OUT. LIKE IT'S MY FIRST TIME GETTING SHOT. ARE THE OTHERS--›
‹I DON'T KNOW, BUT I THINK THEY GOT YORICK.›
‹A RADIO. ONE OF THEM HAD A RADIO...›
‹THERE.›
WHOEVER THIS IS, TURN YOUR CRAFT AROUND AND BRING THE MALE BACK NOW.
›KZACK‹
AGENT 355, IS IT...?

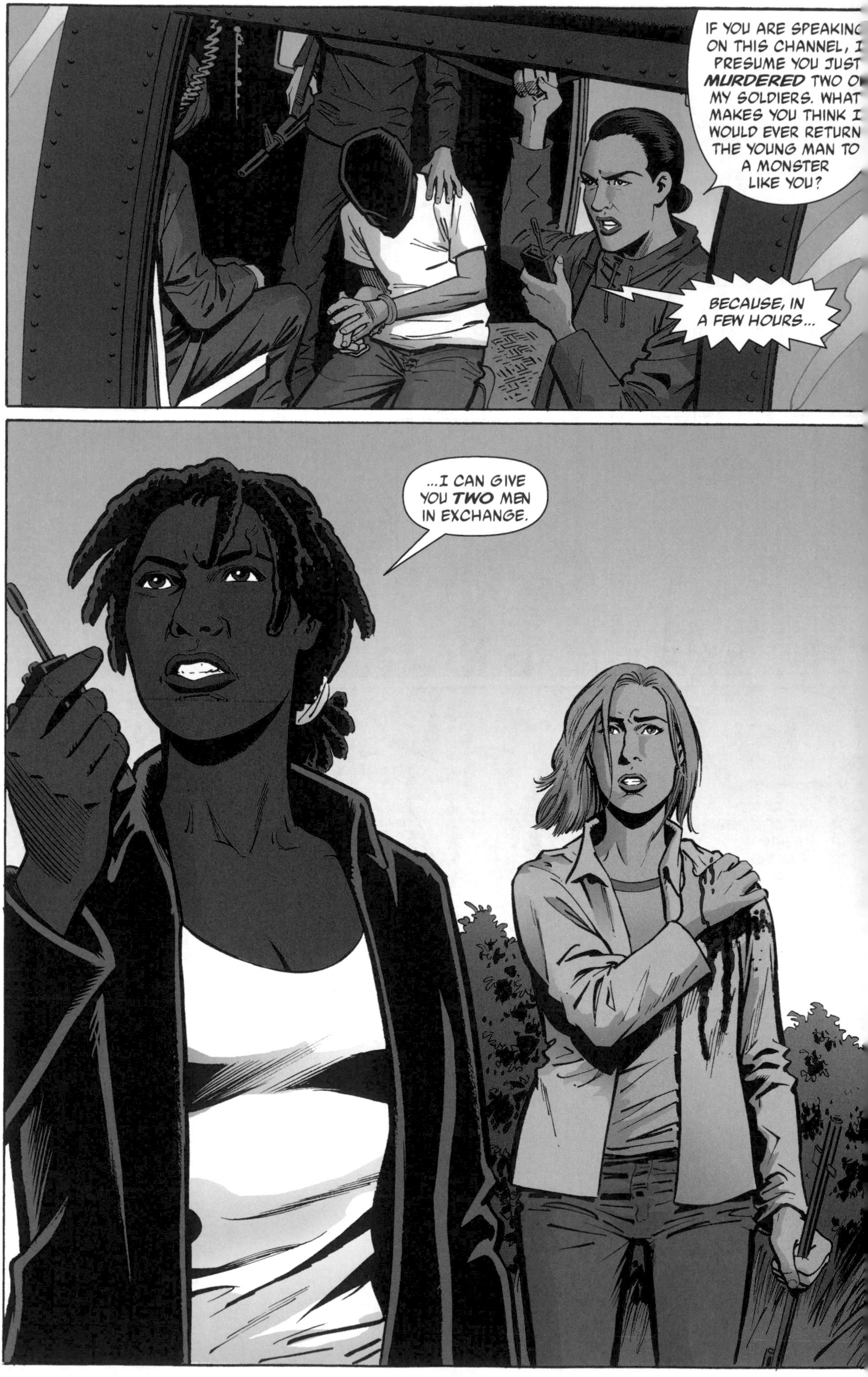
IF YOU ARE SPEAKING ON THIS CHANNEL, I PRESUME YOU JUST MURDERED TWO OF MY SOLDIERS. WHAT MAKES YOU THINK I WOULD EVER RETURN THE YOUNG MAN TO A MONSTER LIKE YOU?
BECAUSE, IN A FEW HOURS...
...I CAN GIVE YOU TWO MEN IN EXCHANGE.

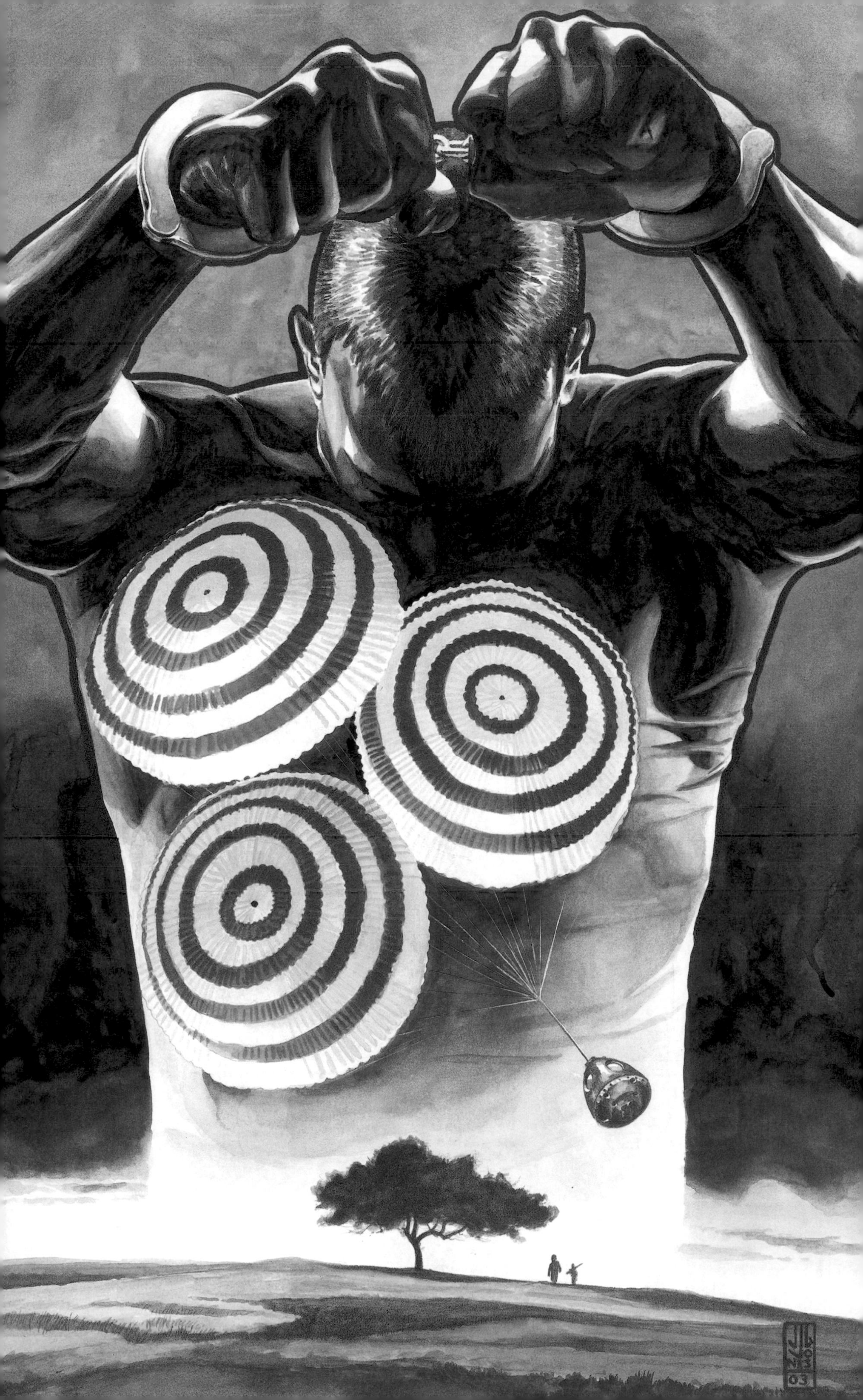

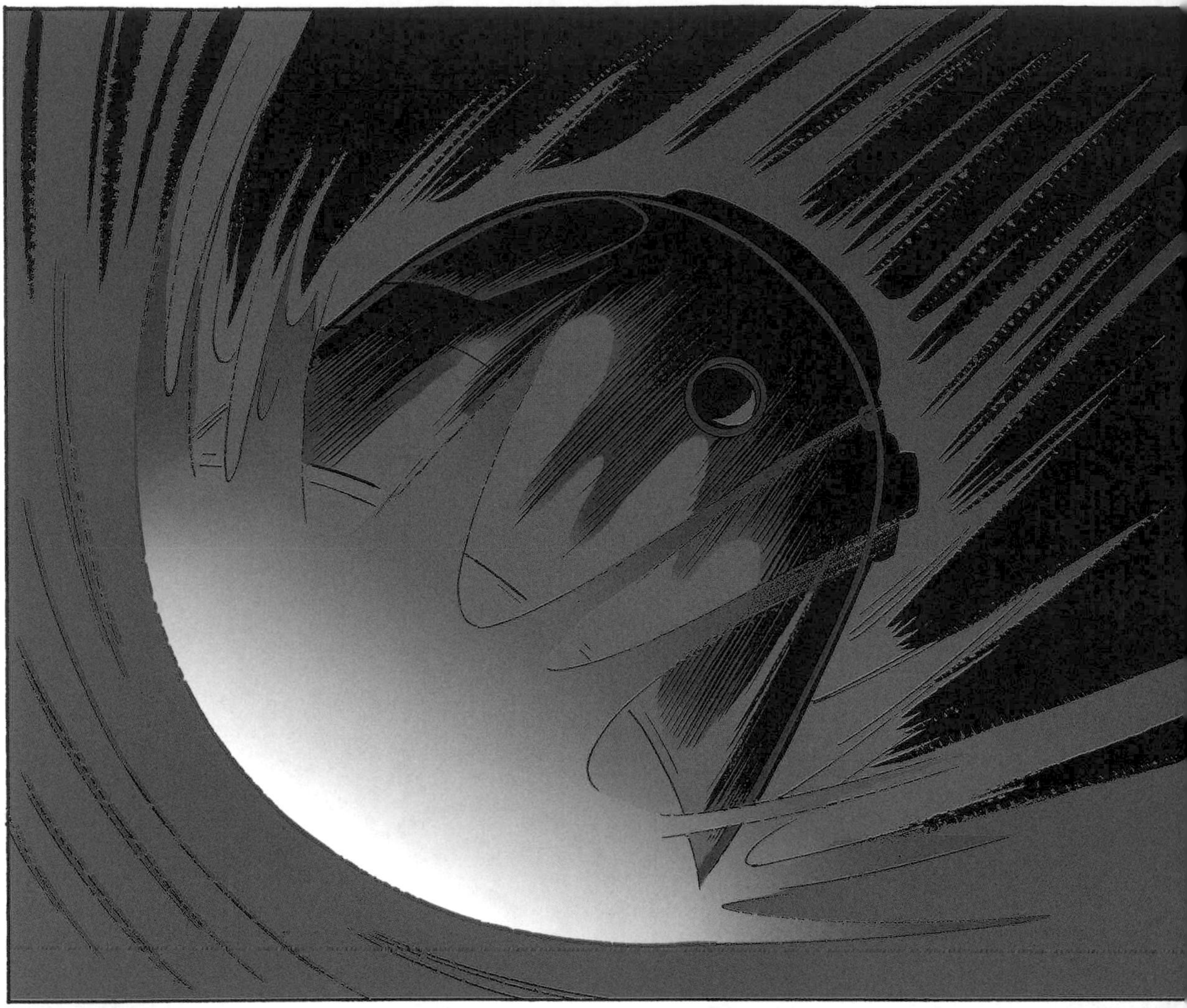

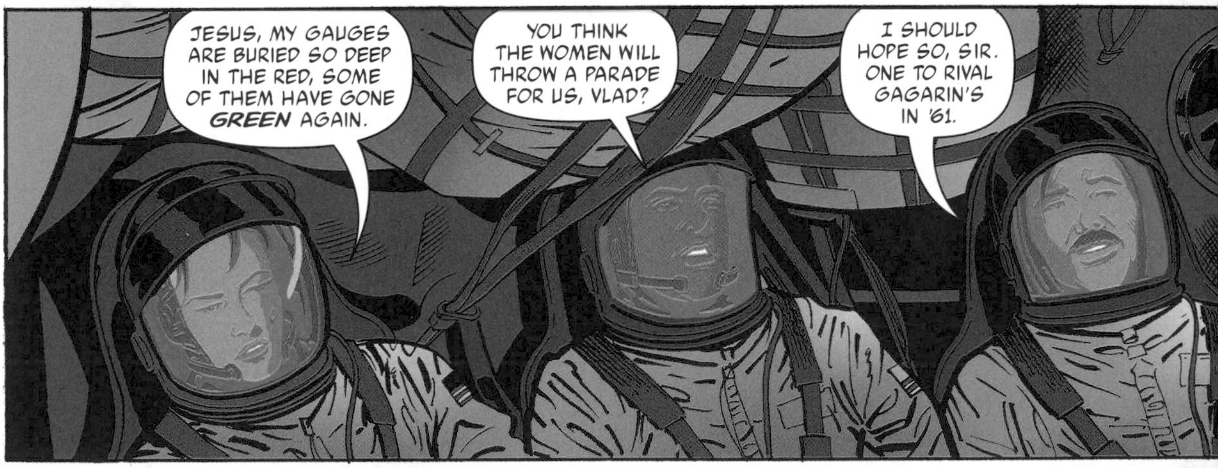
JESUS, MY GAUGES ARE BURIED SO DEEP IN THE RED, SOME OF THEM HAVE GONE **GREEN** AGAIN.
YOU THINK THE WOMEN WILL THROW A PARADE FOR US, VLAD?
I SHOULD HOPE SO, SIR. ONE TO RIVAL GAGARIN'S IN '61.

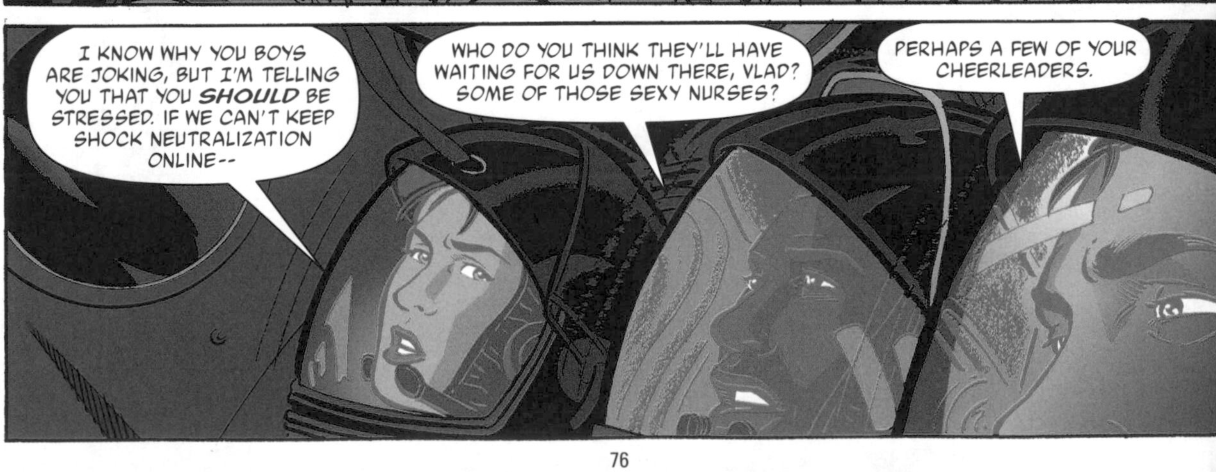
I KNOW WHY YOU BOYS ARE JOKING, BUT I'M TELLING YOU THAT YOU **SHOULD** BE STRESSED. IF WE CAN'T KEEP SHOCK NEUTRALIZATION ONLINE--
WHO DO YOU THINK THEY'LL HAVE WAITING FOR US DOWN THERE, VLAD? SOME OF THOSE SEXY NURSES?
PERHAPS A FEW OF YOUR CHEERLEADERS.

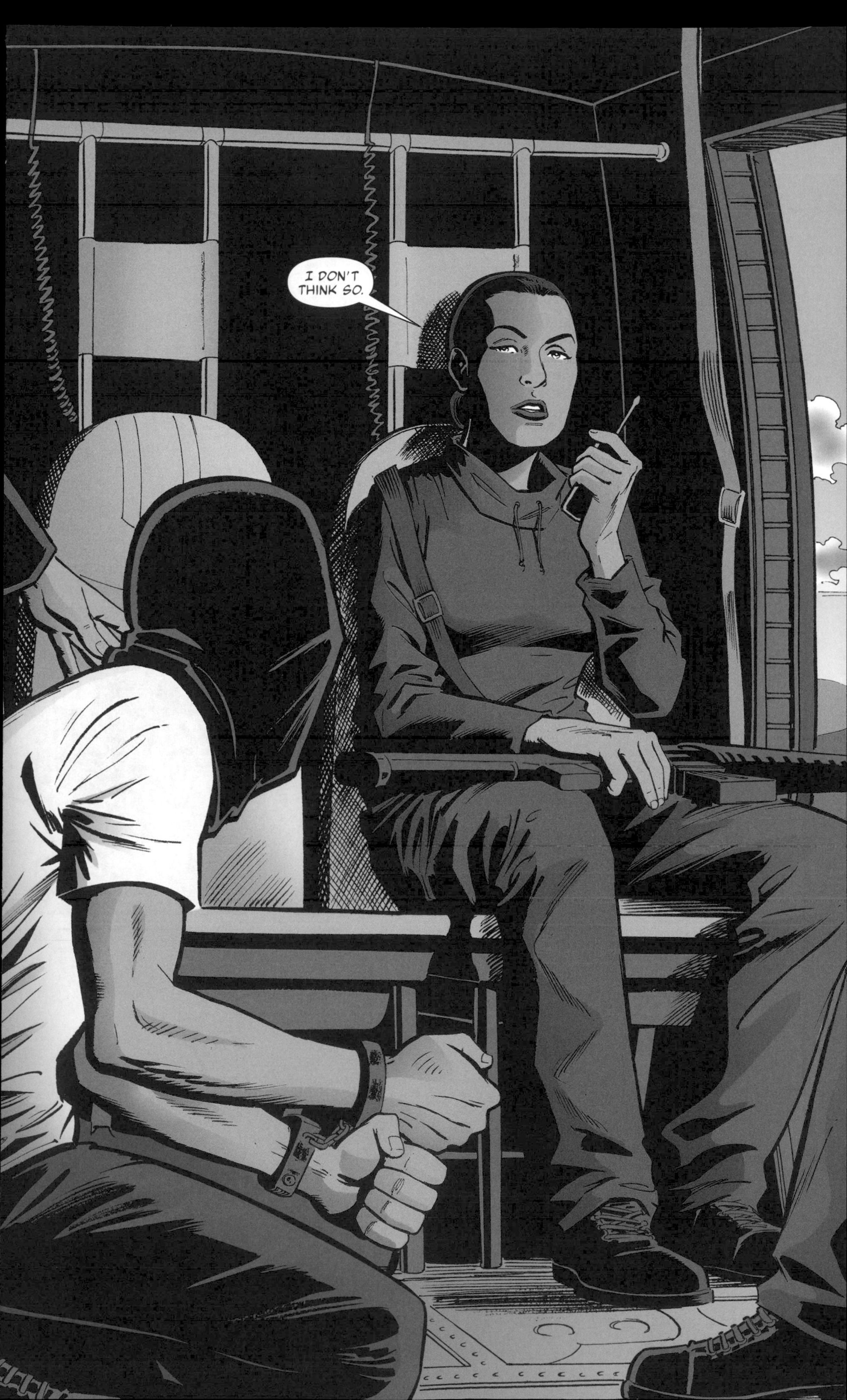
I DON'T THINK SO.

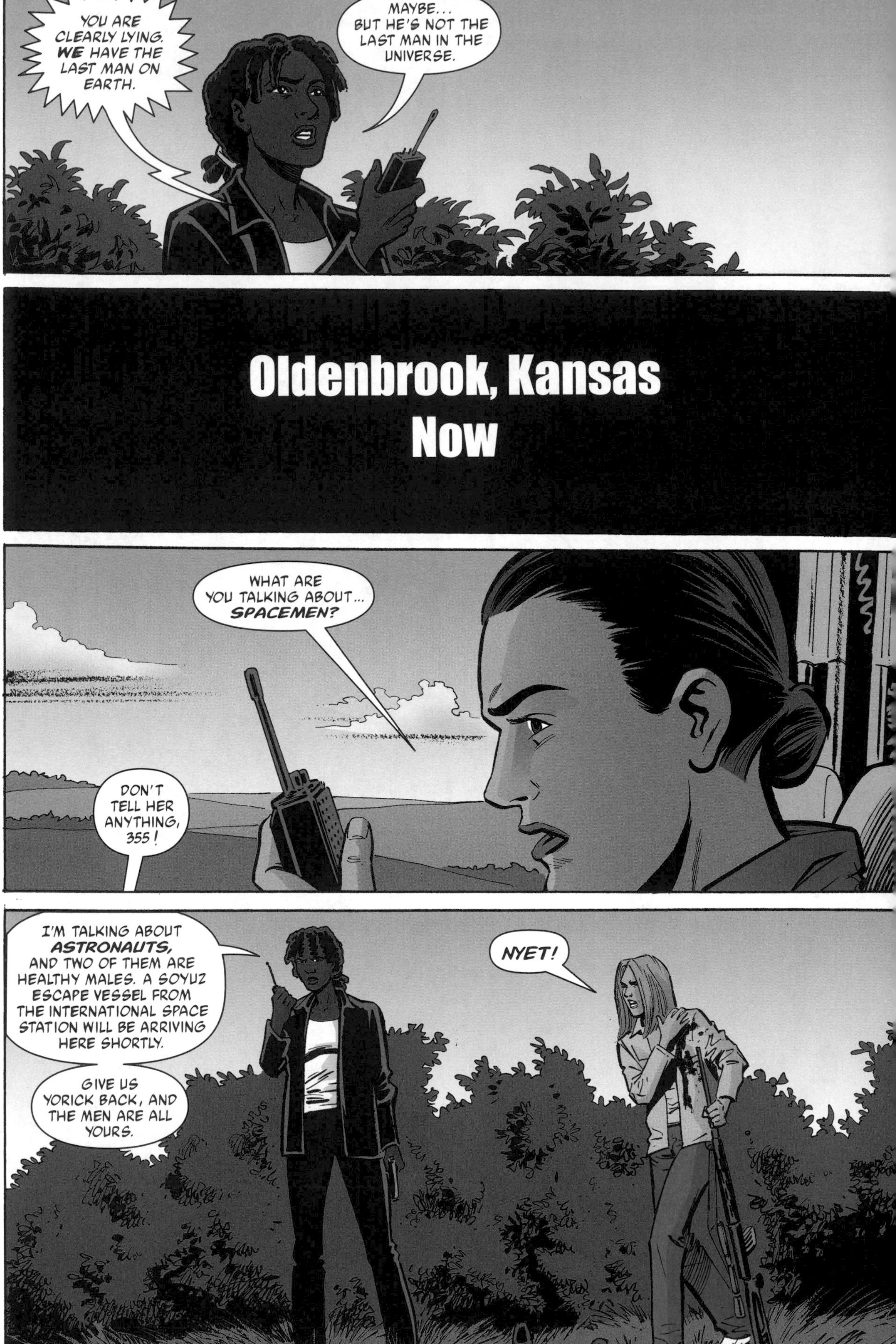
YOU ARE CLEARLY LYING. WE HAVE THE LAST MAN ON EARTH.
MAYBE... BUT HE'S NOT THE LAST MAN IN THE UNIVERSE.
Oldenbrook, Kansas
Now
WHAT ARE YOU TALKING ABOUT... SPACEMEN?
DON'T TELL HER ANYTHING, 355!
I'M TALKING ABOUT ASTRONAUTS, AND TWO OF THEM ARE HEALTHY MALES. A SOYUZ ESCAPE VESSEL FROM THE INTERNATIONAL SPACE STATION WILL BE ARRIVING HERE SHORTLY.
GIVE US YORICK BACK, AND THE MEN ARE ALL YOURS.
NYET!

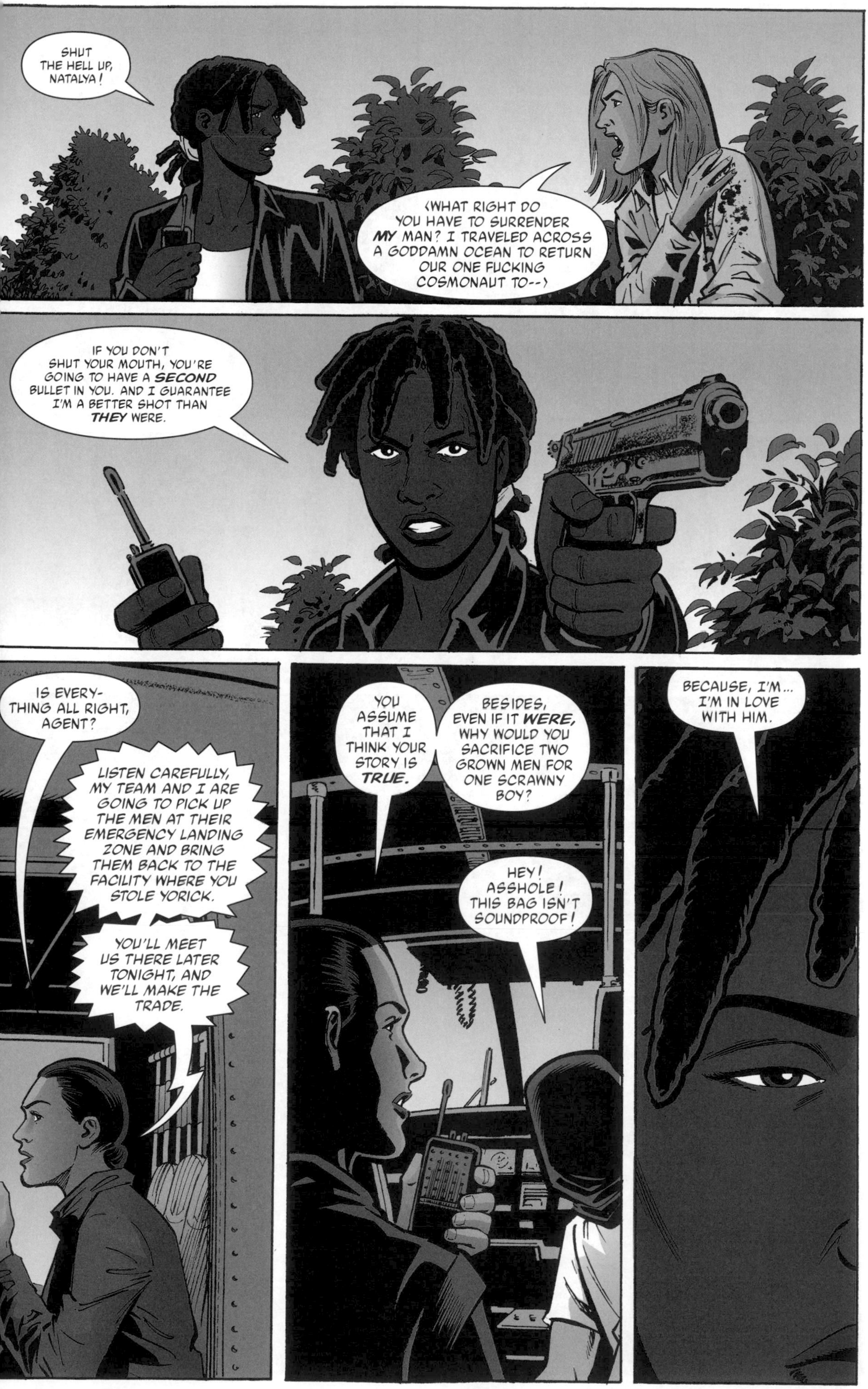
SHUT THE HELL UP, NATALYA!
‹WHAT RIGHT DO YOU HAVE TO SURRENDER MY MAN? I TRAVELED ACROSS A GODDAMN OCEAN TO RETURN OUR ONE FUCKING COSMONAUT TO--›
IF YOU DON'T SHUT YOUR MOUTH, YOU'RE GOING TO HAVE A SECOND BULLET IN YOU. AND I GUARANTEE I'M A BETTER SHOT THAN THEY WERE.
IS EVERYTHING ALL RIGHT, AGENT?
LISTEN CAREFULLY, MY TEAM AND I ARE GOING TO PICK UP THE MEN AT THEIR EMERGENCY LANDING ZONE AND BRING THEM BACK TO THE FACILITY WHERE YOU STOLE YORICK.
YOU'LL MEET US THERE LATER TONIGHT, AND WE'LL MAKE THE TRADE.
YOU ASSUME THAT I THINK YOUR STORY IS TRUE.
BESIDES, EVEN IF IT WERE, WHY WOULD YOU SACRIFICE TWO GROWN MEN FOR ONE SCRAWNY BOY?
HEY! ASSHOLE! THIS BAG ISN'T SOUNDPROOF!
BECAUSE, I'M... I'M IN LOVE WITH HIM.

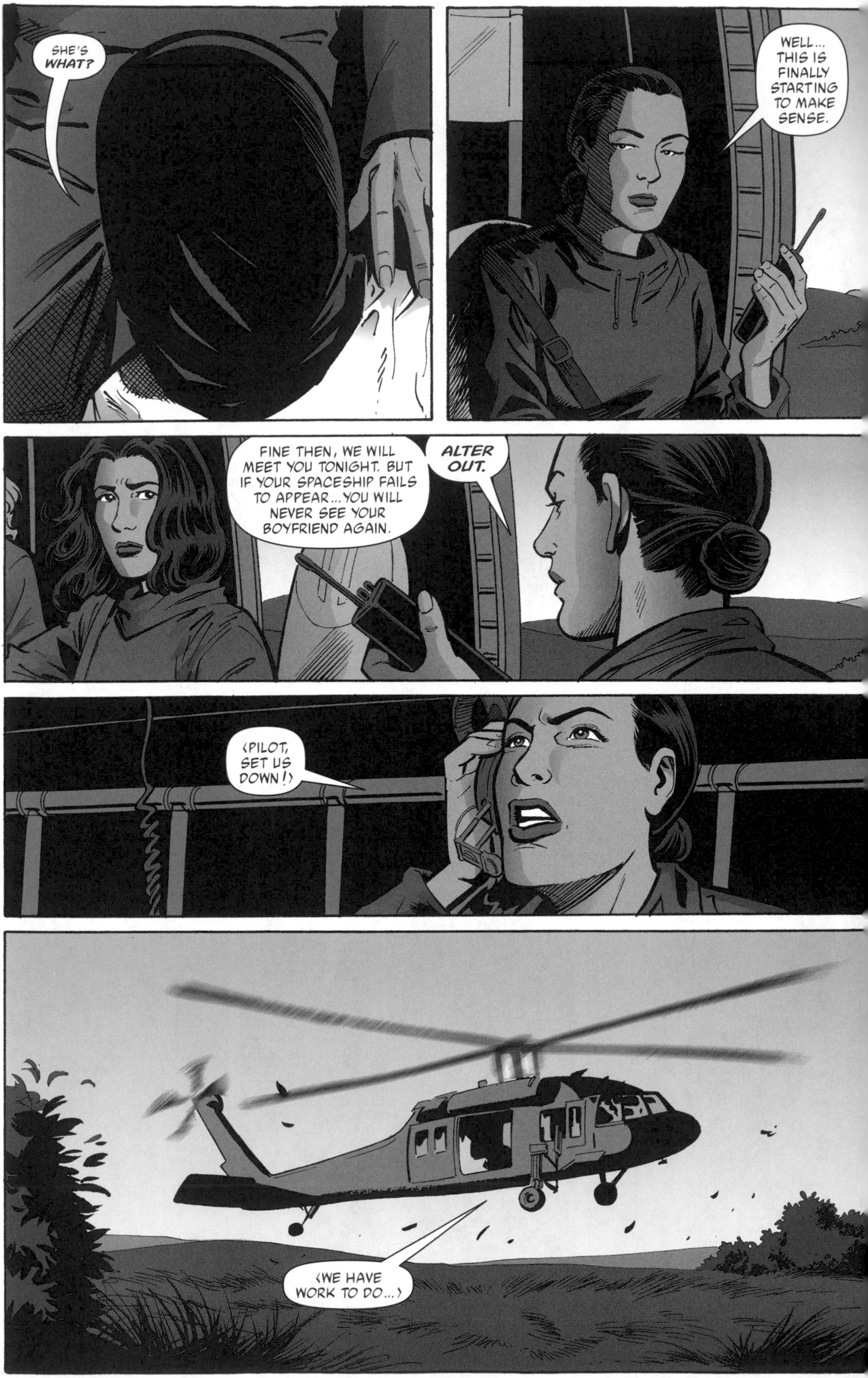
SHE'S *WHAT?*
WELL... THIS IS FINALLY STARTING TO MAKE SENSE.
FINE THEN, WE WILL MEET YOU TONIGHT. BUT IF YOUR SPACESHIP FAILS TO APPEAR... YOU WILL NEVER SEE YOUR BOYFRIEND AGAIN.
ALTER OUT.
‹PILOT, SET US DOWN!›
‹WE HAVE WORK TO DO...›

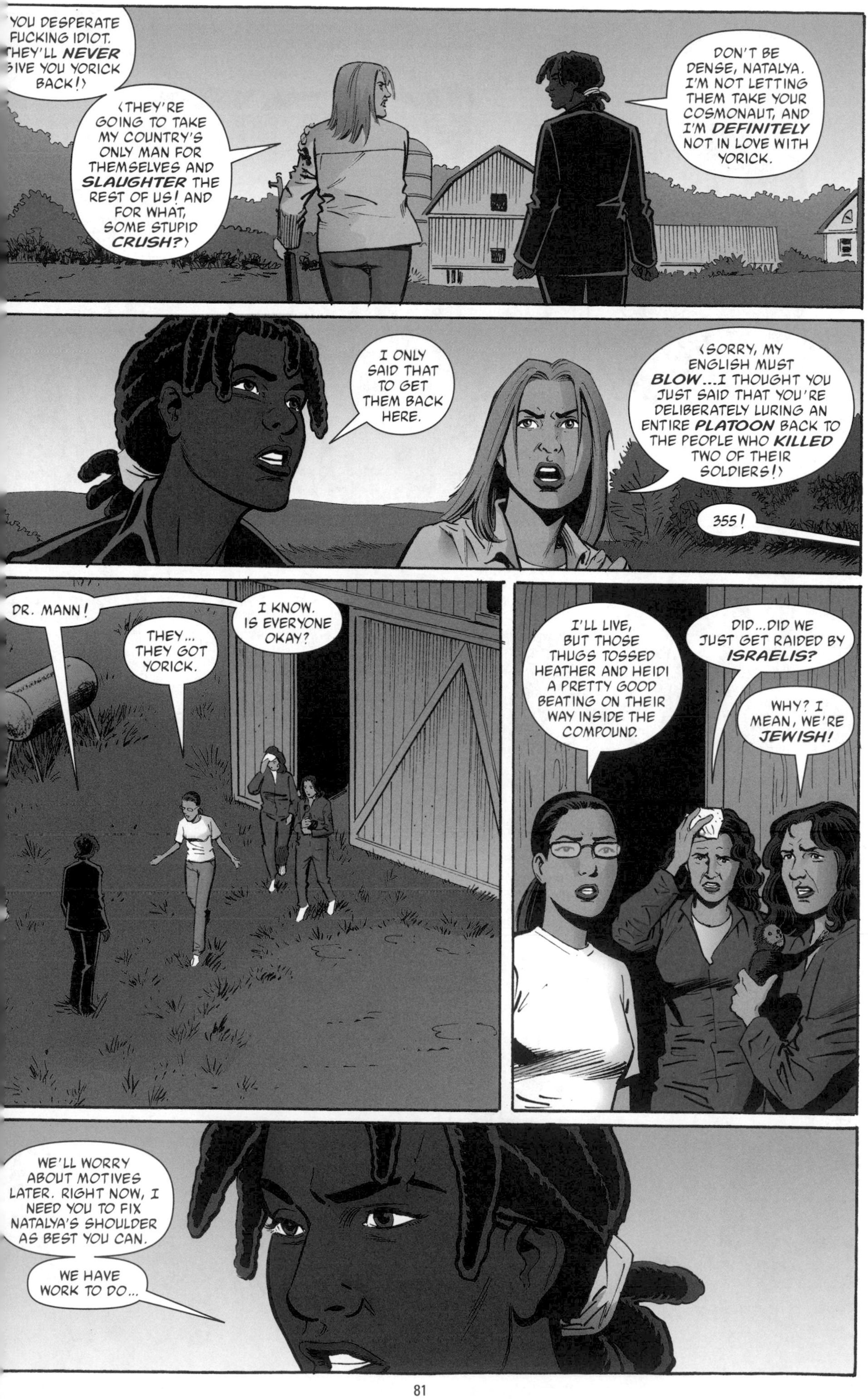
YOU DESPERATE FUCKING IDIOT. THEY'LL NEVER GIVE YOU YORICK BACK!›
‹THEY'RE GOING TO TAKE MY COUNTRY'S ONLY MAN FOR THEMSELVES AND SLAUGHTER THE REST OF US! AND FOR WHAT, SOME STUPID CRUSH?›
DON'T BE DENSE, NATALYA. I'M NOT LETTING THEM TAKE YOUR COSMONAUT, AND I'M DEFINITELY NOT IN LOVE WITH YORICK.
I ONLY SAID THAT TO GET THEM BACK HERE.
‹SORRY, MY ENGLISH MUST BLOW...I THOUGHT YOU JUST SAID THAT YOU'RE DELIBERATELY LURING AN ENTIRE PLATOON BACK TO THE PEOPLE WHO KILLED TWO OF THEIR SOLDIERS!›
355!
DR. MANN!
I KNOW. IS EVERYONE OKAY?
THEY... THEY GOT YORICK.
I'LL LIVE, BUT THOSE THUGS TOSSED HEATHER AND HEIDI A PRETTY GOOD BEATING ON THEIR WAY INSIDE THE COMPOUND.
DID...DID WE JUST GET RAIDED BY ISRAELIS?
WHY? I MEAN, WE'RE JEWISH!
WE'LL WORRY ABOUT MOTIVES LATER. RIGHT NOW, I NEED YOU TO FIX NATALYA'S SHOULDER AS BEST YOU CAN.
WE HAVE WORK TO DO...

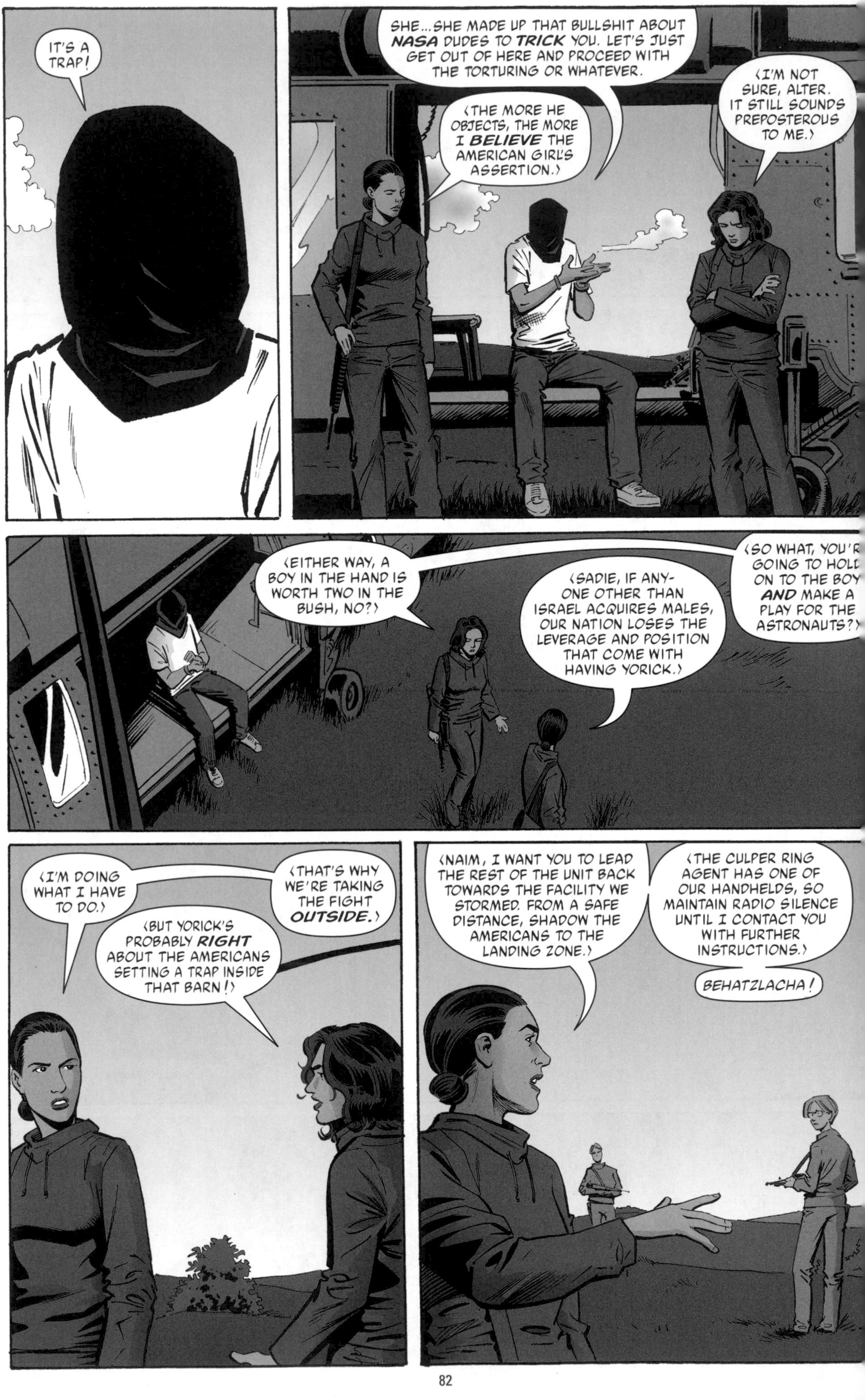
IT'S A TRAP!
SHE... SHE MADE UP THAT BULLSHIT ABOUT NASA DUDES TO TRICK YOU. LET'S JUST GET OUT OF HERE AND PROCEED WITH THE TORTURING OR WHATEVER.
‹THE MORE HE OBJECTS, THE MORE I BELIEVE THE AMERICAN GIRL'S ASSERTION.›
‹I'M NOT SURE, ALTER. IT STILL SOUNDS PREPOSTEROUS TO ME.›
‹EITHER WAY, A BOY IN THE HAND IS WORTH TWO IN THE BUSH, NO?›
‹SADIE, IF ANY-ONE OTHER THAN ISRAEL ACQUIRES MALES, OUR NATION LOSES THE LEVERAGE AND POSITION THAT COME WITH HAVING YORICK.›
‹SO WHAT, YOU'R GOING TO HOLD ON TO THE BOY AND MAKE A PLAY FOR THE ASTRONAUTS?›
‹I'M DOING WHAT I HAVE TO DO.›
‹THAT'S WHY WE'RE TAKING THE FIGHT OUTSIDE.›
‹BUT YORICK'S PROBABLY RIGHT ABOUT THE AMERICANS SETTING A TRAP INSIDE THAT BARN!›
‹NAIM, I WANT YOU TO LEAD THE REST OF THE UNIT BACK TOWARDS THE FACILITY WE STORMED. FROM A SAFE DISTANCE, SHADOW THE AMERICANS TO THE LANDING ZONE.›
‹THE CULPER RING AGENT HAS ONE OF OUR HANDHELDS, SO MAINTAIN RADIO SILENCE UNTIL I CONTACT YOU WITH FURTHER INSTRUCTIONS.›
BEHATZLACHA!

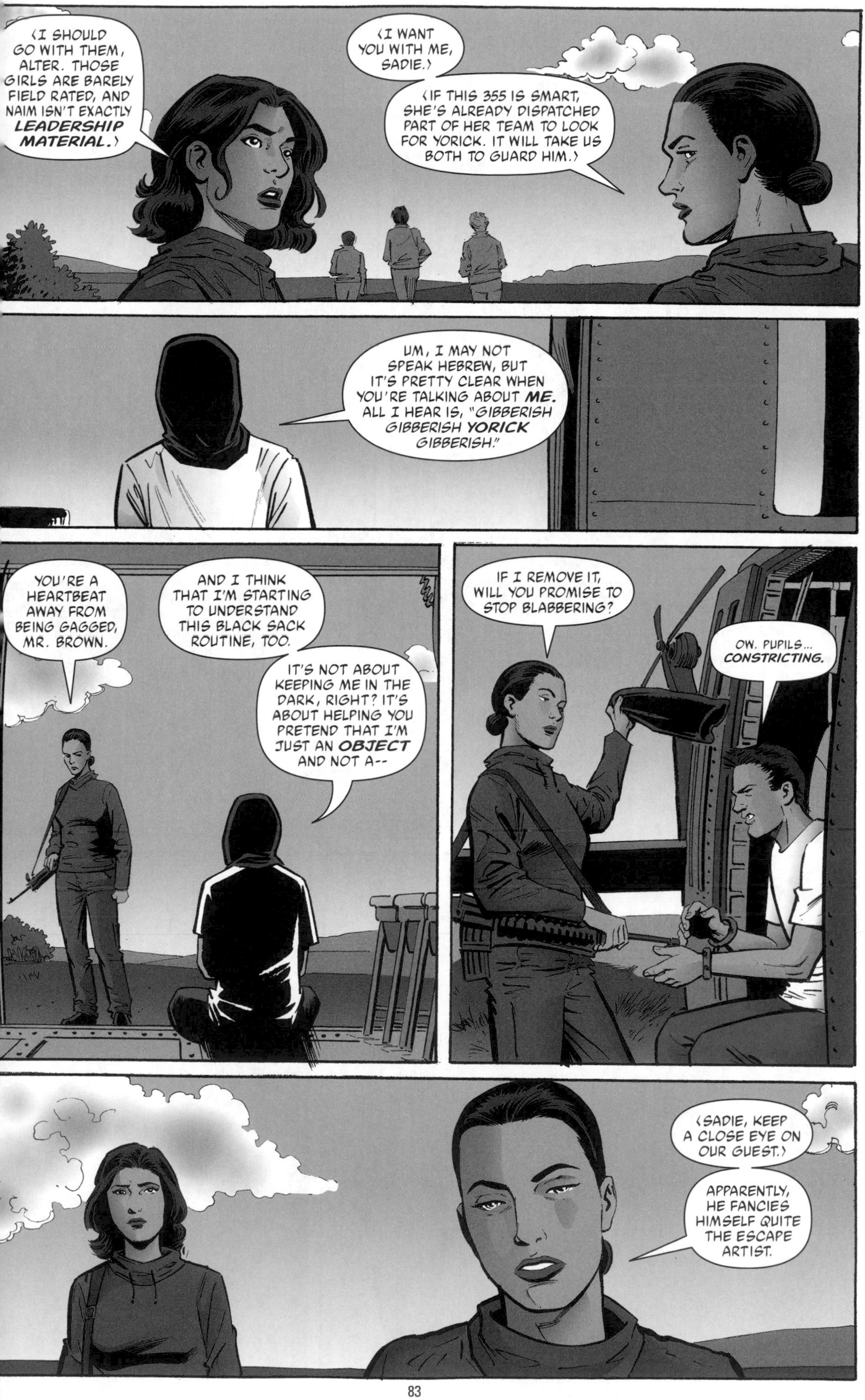
‹I SHOULD GO WITH THEM, ALTER. THOSE GIRLS ARE BARELY FIELD RATED, AND NAIM ISN'T EXACTLY LEADERSHIP MATERIAL.›
‹I WANT YOU WITH ME, SADIE.›
‹IF THIS 355 IS SMART, SHE'S ALREADY DISPATCHED PART OF HER TEAM TO LOOK FOR YORICK. IT WILL TAKE US BOTH TO GUARD HIM.›
UM, I MAY NOT SPEAK HEBREW, BUT IT'S PRETTY CLEAR WHEN YOU'RE TALKING ABOUT ME. ALL I HEAR IS, "GIBBERISH GIBBERISH YORICK GIBBERISH."
YOU'RE A HEARTBEAT AWAY FROM BEING GAGGED, MR. BROWN.
AND I THINK THAT I'M STARTING TO UNDERSTAND THIS BLACK SACK ROUTINE, TOO.
IT'S NOT ABOUT KEEPING ME IN THE DARK, RIGHT? IT'S ABOUT HELPING YOU PRETEND THAT I'M JUST AN OBJECT AND NOT A--
IF I REMOVE IT, WILL YOU PROMISE TO STOP BLABBERING?
OW. PUPILS... CONSTRICTING.
‹SADIE, KEEP A CLOSE EYE ON OUR GUEST.›
APPARENTLY, HE FANCIES HIMSELF QUITE THE ESCAPE ARTIST.

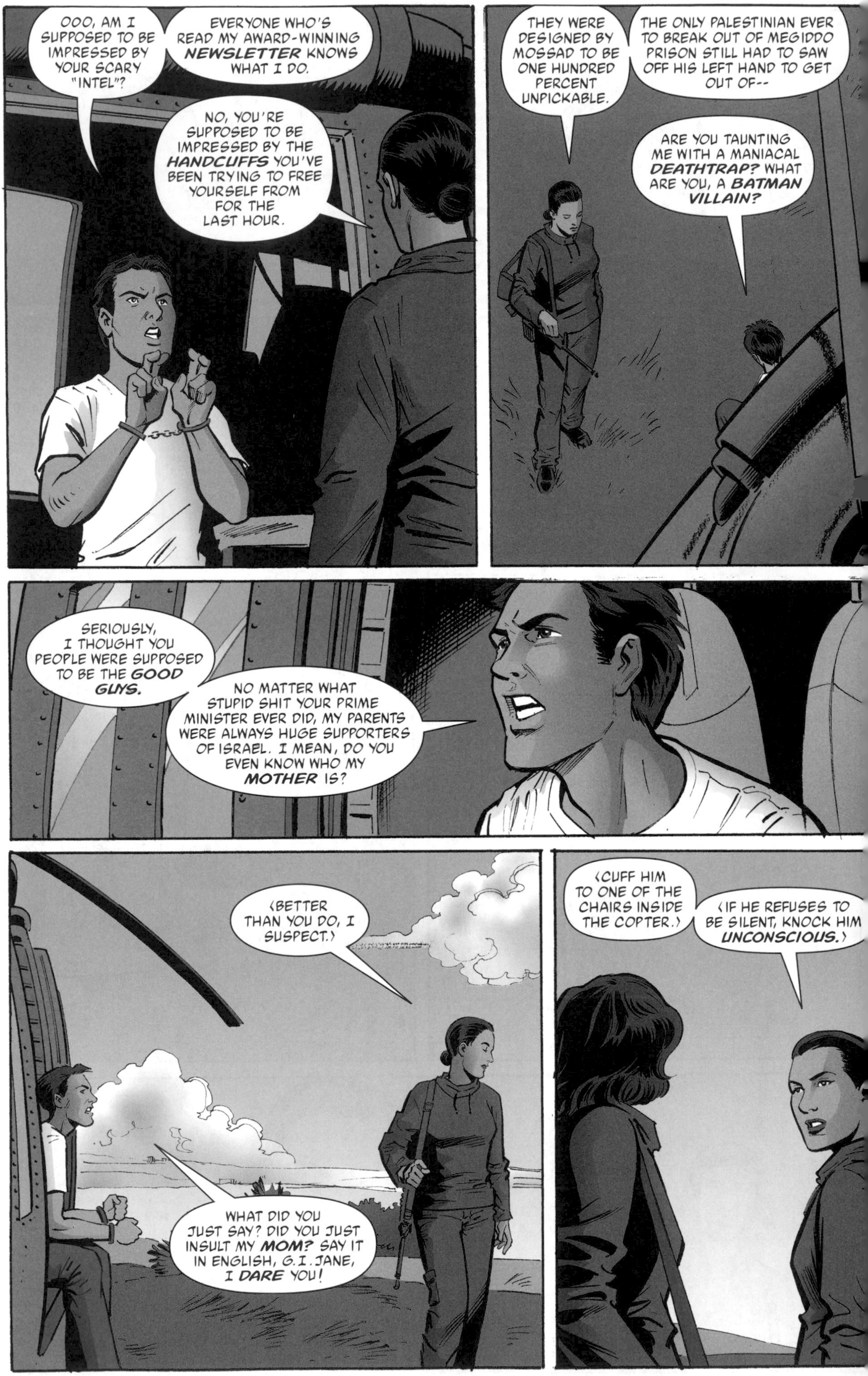
OOO, AM I SUPPOSED TO BE IMPRESSED BY YOUR SCARY "INTEL"?
EVERYONE WHO'S READ MY AWARD-WINNING NEWSLETTER KNOWS WHAT I DO.
NO, YOU'RE SUPPOSED TO BE IMPRESSED BY THE HANDCUFFS YOU'VE BEEN TRYING TO FREE YOURSELF FROM FOR THE LAST HOUR.
THEY WERE DESIGNED BY MOSSAD TO BE ONE HUNDRED PERCENT UNPICKABLE.
THE ONLY PALESTINIAN EVER TO BREAK OUT OF MEGIDDO PRISON STILL HAD TO SAW OFF HIS LEFT HAND TO GET OUT OF--
ARE YOU TAUNTING ME WITH A MANIACAL DEATHTRAP? WHAT ARE YOU, A BATMAN VILLAIN?
SERIOUSLY, I THOUGHT YOU PEOPLE WERE SUPPOSED TO BE THE GOOD GUYS.
NO MATTER WHAT STUPID SHIT YOUR PRIME MINISTER EVER DID, MY PARENTS WERE ALWAYS HUGE SUPPORTERS OF ISRAEL. I MEAN, DO YOU EVEN KNOW WHO MY MOTHER IS?
‹BETTER THAN YOU DO, I SUSPECT.›
WHAT DID YOU JUST SAY? DID YOU JUST INSULT MY MOM? SAY IT IN ENGLISH, G.I. JANE, I DARE YOU!
‹CUFF HIM TO ONE OF THE CHAIRS INSIDE THE COPTER.›
‹IF HE REFUSES TO BE SILENT, KNOCK HIM UNCONSCIOUS.›

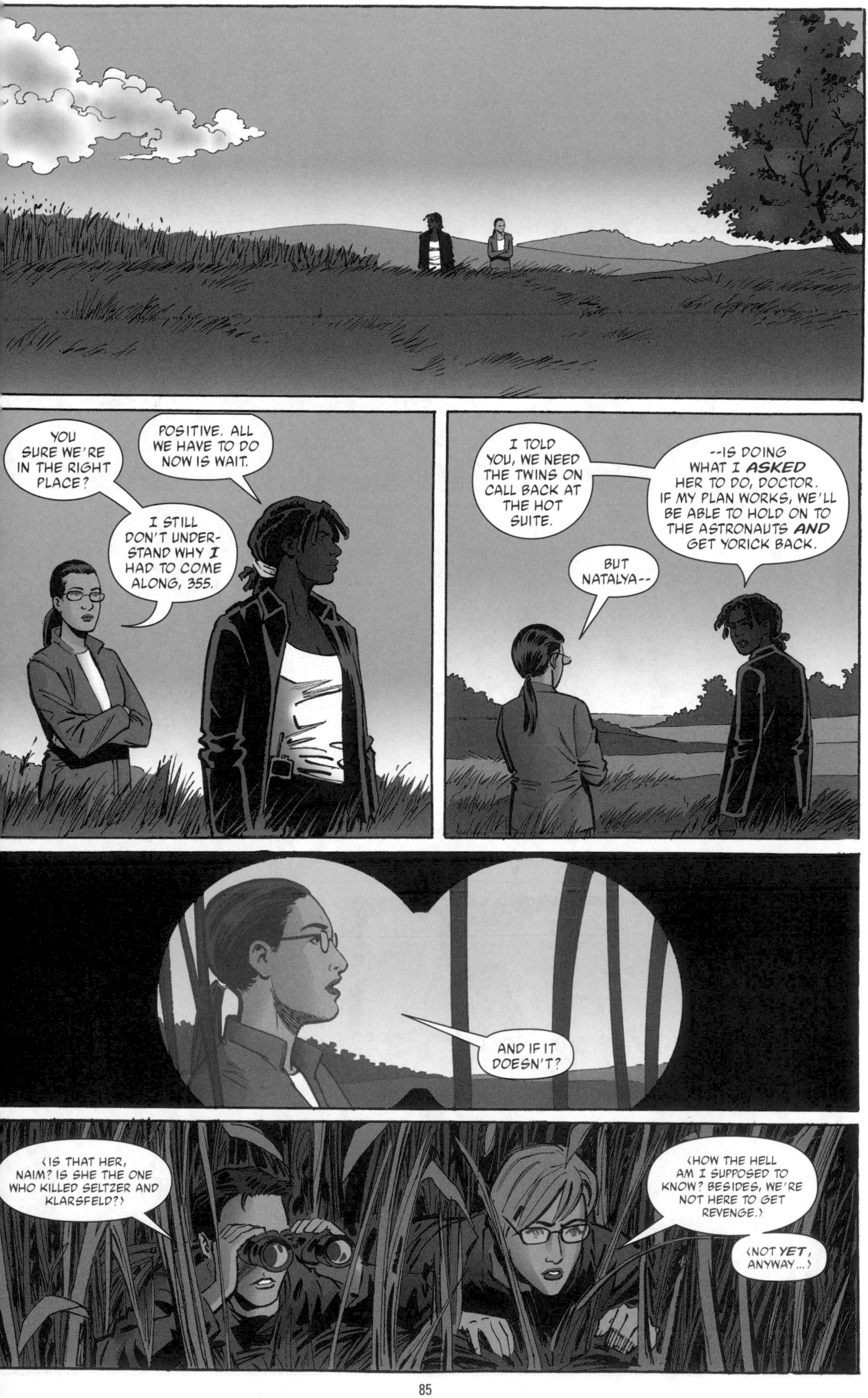
YOU SURE WE'RE IN THE RIGHT PLACE?
POSITIVE. ALL WE HAVE TO DO NOW IS WAIT.
I STILL DON'T UNDER-STAND WHY I HAD TO COME ALONG, 355.
I TOLD YOU, WE NEED THE TWINS ON CALL BACK AT THE HOT SUITE.
--IS DOING WHAT I ASKED HER TO DO, DOCTOR. IF MY PLAN WORKS, WE'LL BE ABLE TO HOLD ON TO THE ASTRONAUTS AND GET YORICK BACK.
BUT NATALYA--
AND IF IT DOESN'T?
‹IS THAT HER, NAIM? IS SHE THE ONE WHO KILLED SELTZER AND KLARSFELD?›
‹HOW THE HELL AM I SUPPOSED TO KNOW? BESIDES, WE'RE NOT HERE TO GET REVENGE.›
‹NOT YET, ANYWAY...›

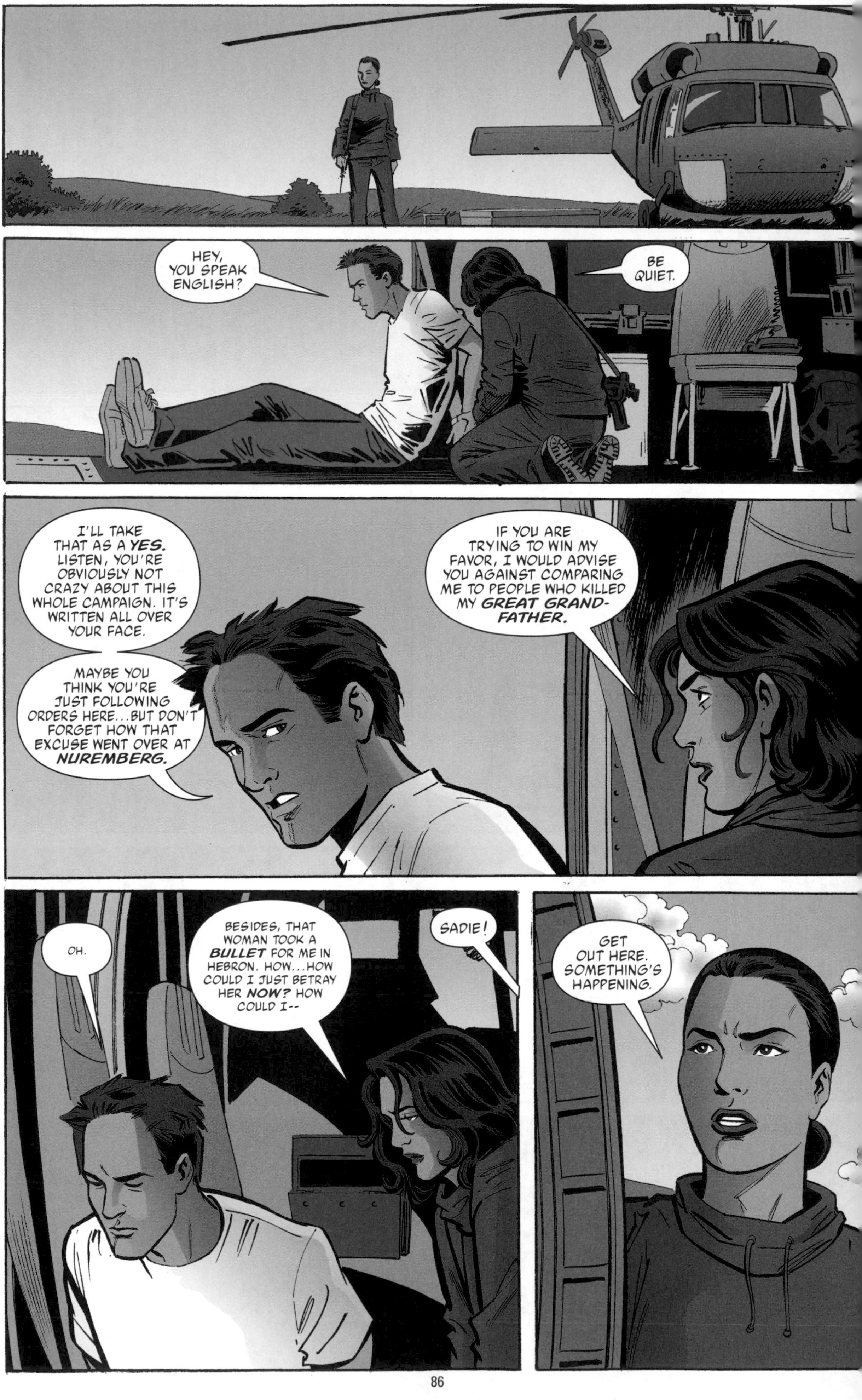

HEY, YOU SPEAK ENGLISH?
BE QUIET.
I'LL TAKE THAT AS A **YES.** LISTEN, YOU'RE OBVIOUSLY NOT CRAZY ABOUT THIS WHOLE CAMPAIGN. IT'S WRITTEN ALL OVER YOUR FACE.
MAYBE YOU THINK YOU'RE JUST FOLLOWING ORDERS HERE...BUT DON'T FORGET HOW THAT EXCUSE WENT OVER AT **NUREMBERG.**
IF YOU ARE TRYING TO WIN MY FAVOR, I WOULD ADVISE YOU AGAINST COMPARING ME TO PEOPLE WHO KILLED MY **GREAT GRAND-FATHER.**
OH.
BESIDES, THAT WOMAN TOOK A **BULLET** FOR ME IN HEBRON. HOW...HOW COULD I JUST BETRAY HER **NOW?** HOW COULD I--
SADIE!
GET OUT HERE. SOMETHING'S HAPPENING.

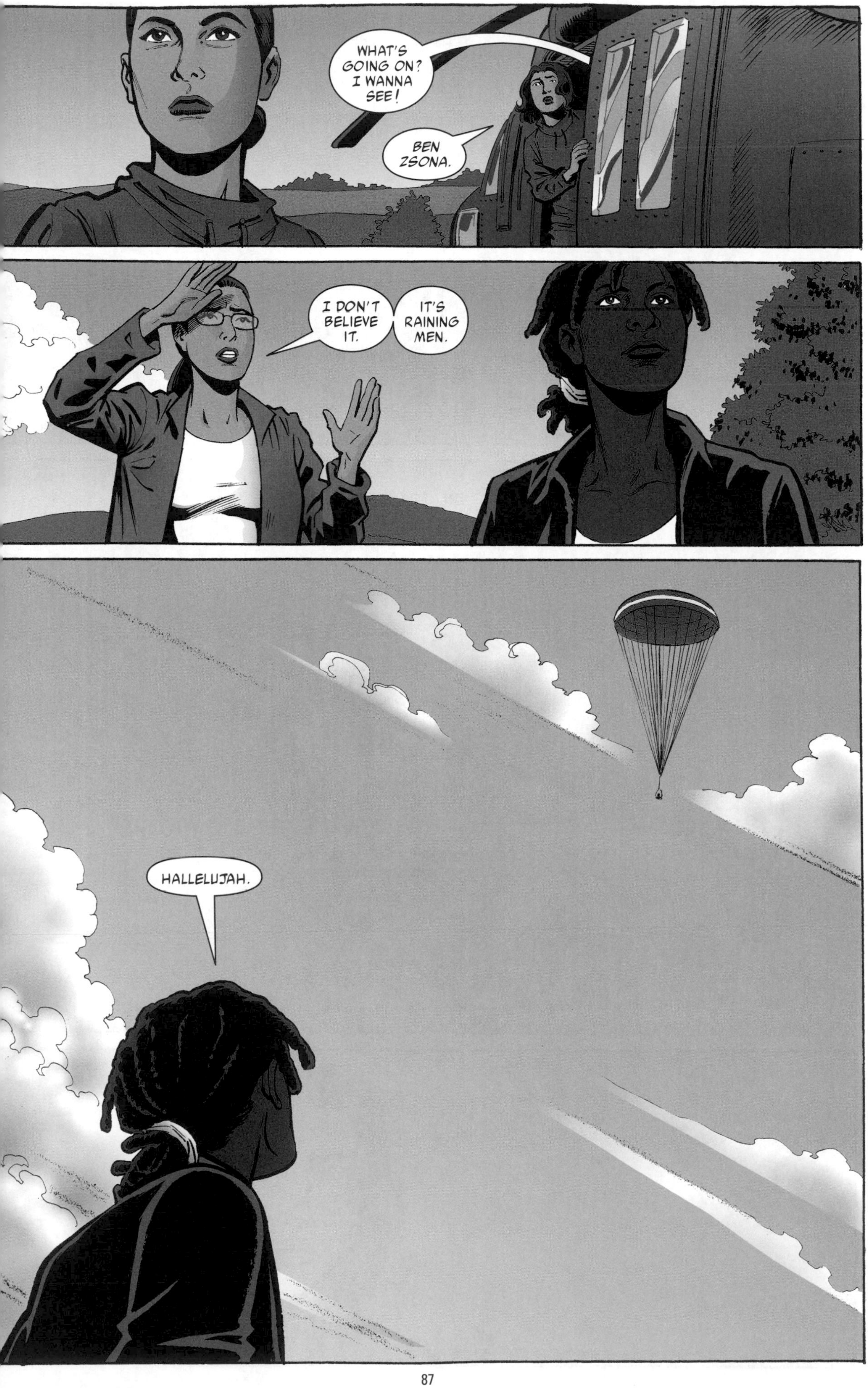
WHAT'S GOING ON? I WANNA SEE!
BEN ZSONA.
I DON'T BELIEVE IT.
IT'S RAINING MEN.
HALLELUJAH.

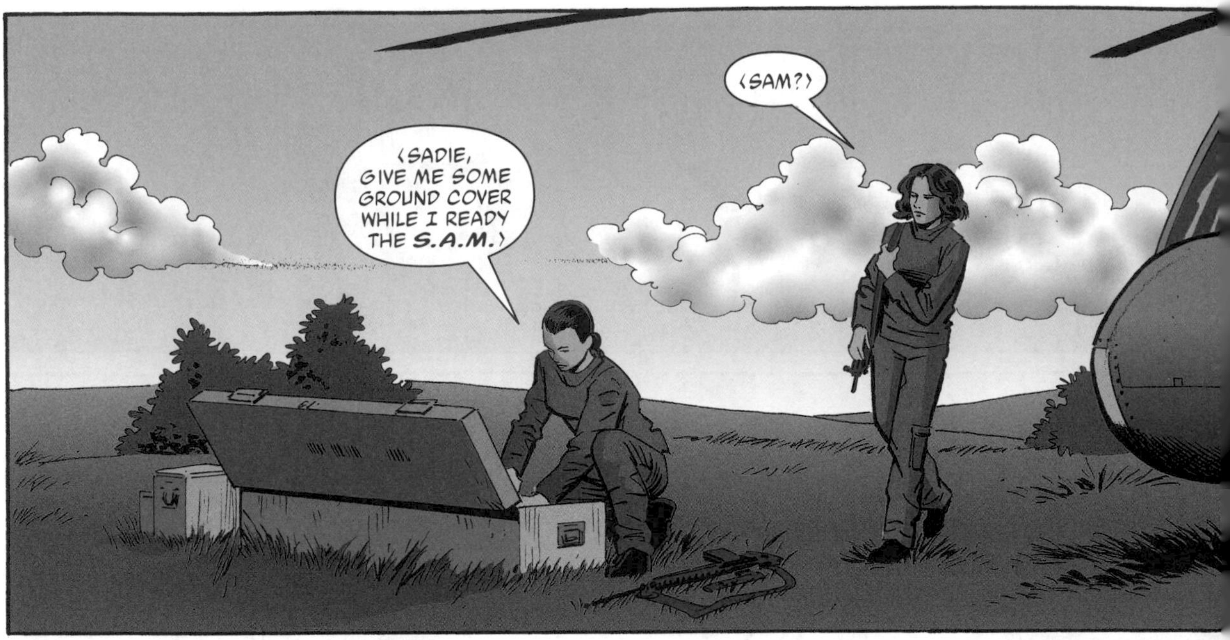
‹SADIE, GIVE ME SOME GROUND COVER WHILE I READY THE S.A.M.›
‹SAM?›

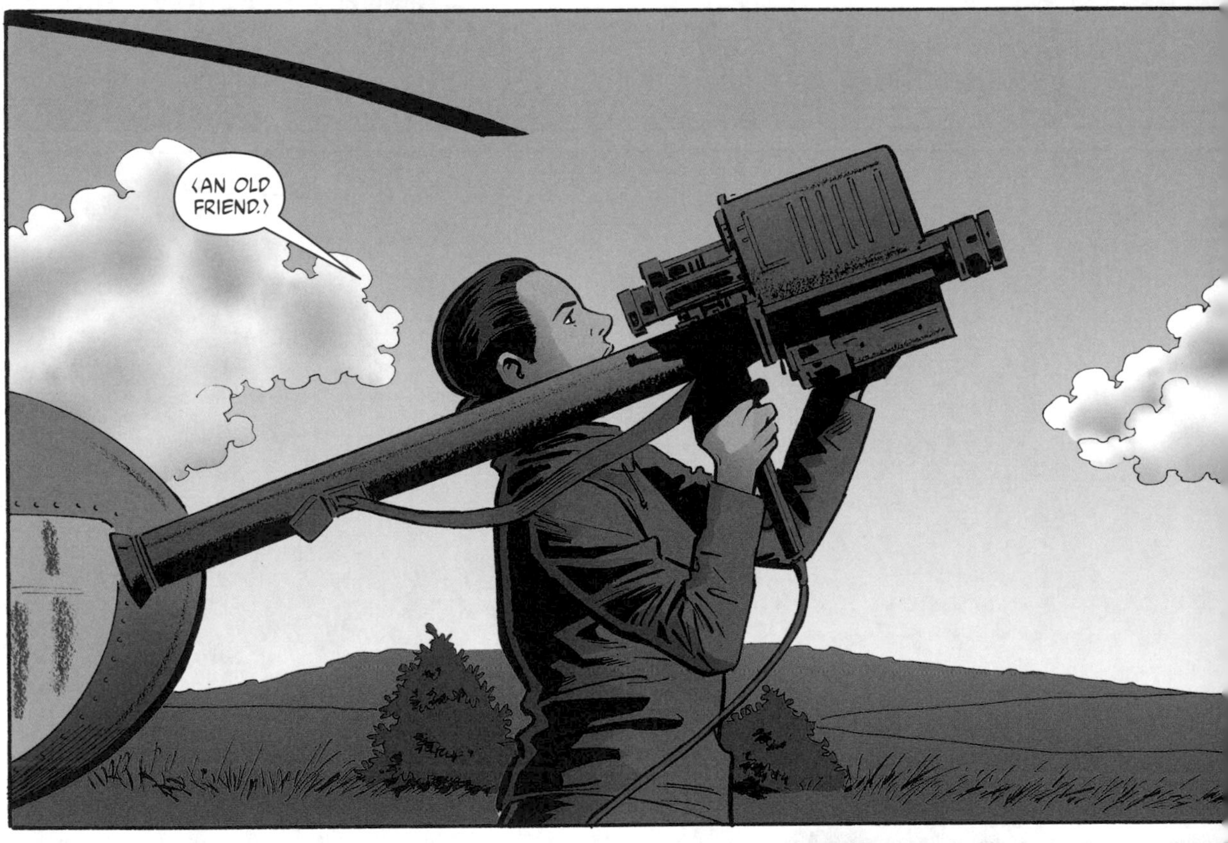
‹AN OLD FRIEND.›

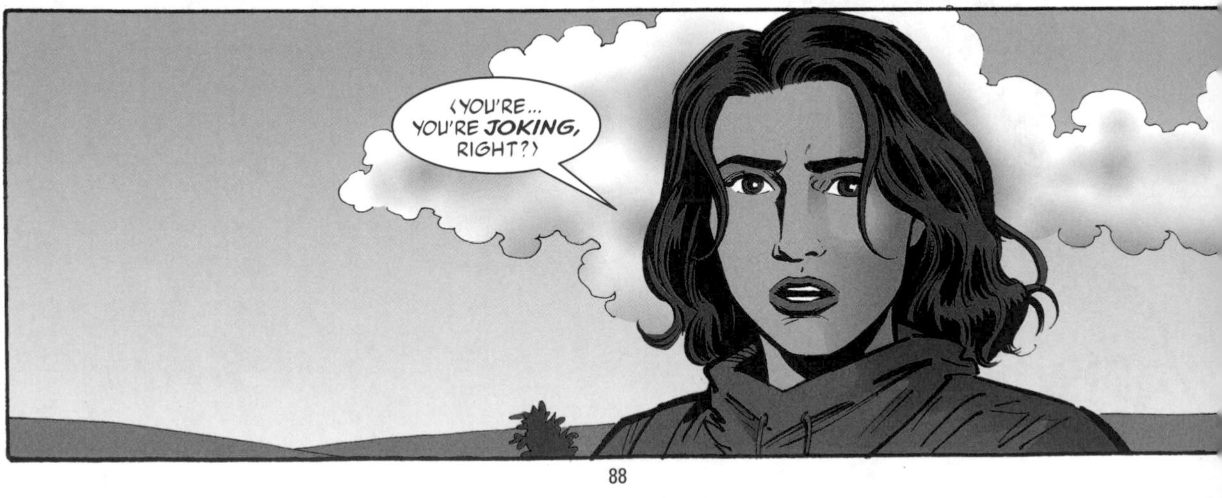
‹YOU'RE... YOU'RE JOKING, RIGHT?›

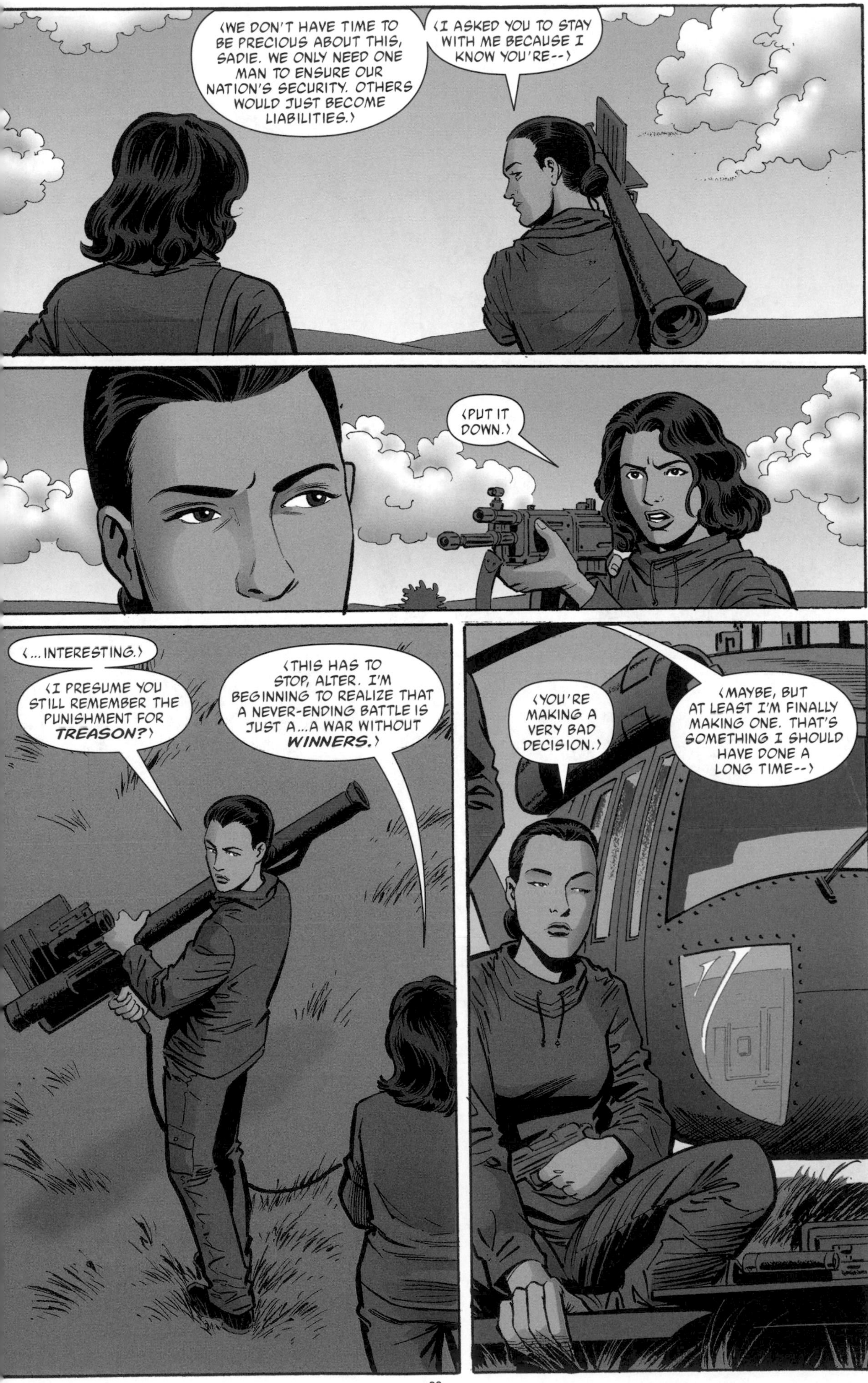

‹WE DON'T HAVE TIME TO BE PRECIOUS ABOUT THIS, SADIE. WE ONLY NEED ONE MAN TO ENSURE OUR NATION'S SECURITY. OTHERS WOULD JUST BECOME LIABILITIES.›
‹I ASKED YOU TO STAY WITH ME BECAUSE I KNOW YOU'RE--›
‹PUT IT DOWN.›
‹...INTERESTING.›
‹I PRESUME YOU STILL REMEMBER THE PUNISHMENT FOR TREASON?›
‹THIS HAS TO STOP, ALTER. I'M BEGINNING TO REALIZE THAT A NEVER-ENDING BATTLE IS JUST A...A WAR WITHOUT WINNERS.›
‹YOU'RE MAKING A VERY BAD DECISION.›
‹MAYBE, BUT AT LEAST I'M FINALLY MAKING ONE. THAT'S SOMETHING I SHOULD HAVE DONE A LONG TIME--›

⟨I AM SORRY, LITTLE ONE.⟩

⟨YOU ARE A GOOD GIRL...⟩

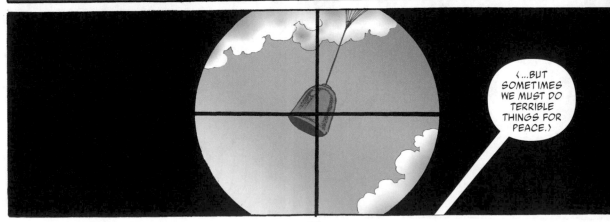

⟨...BUT SOMETIMES WE MUST DO TERRIBLE THINGS FOR PEACE.⟩

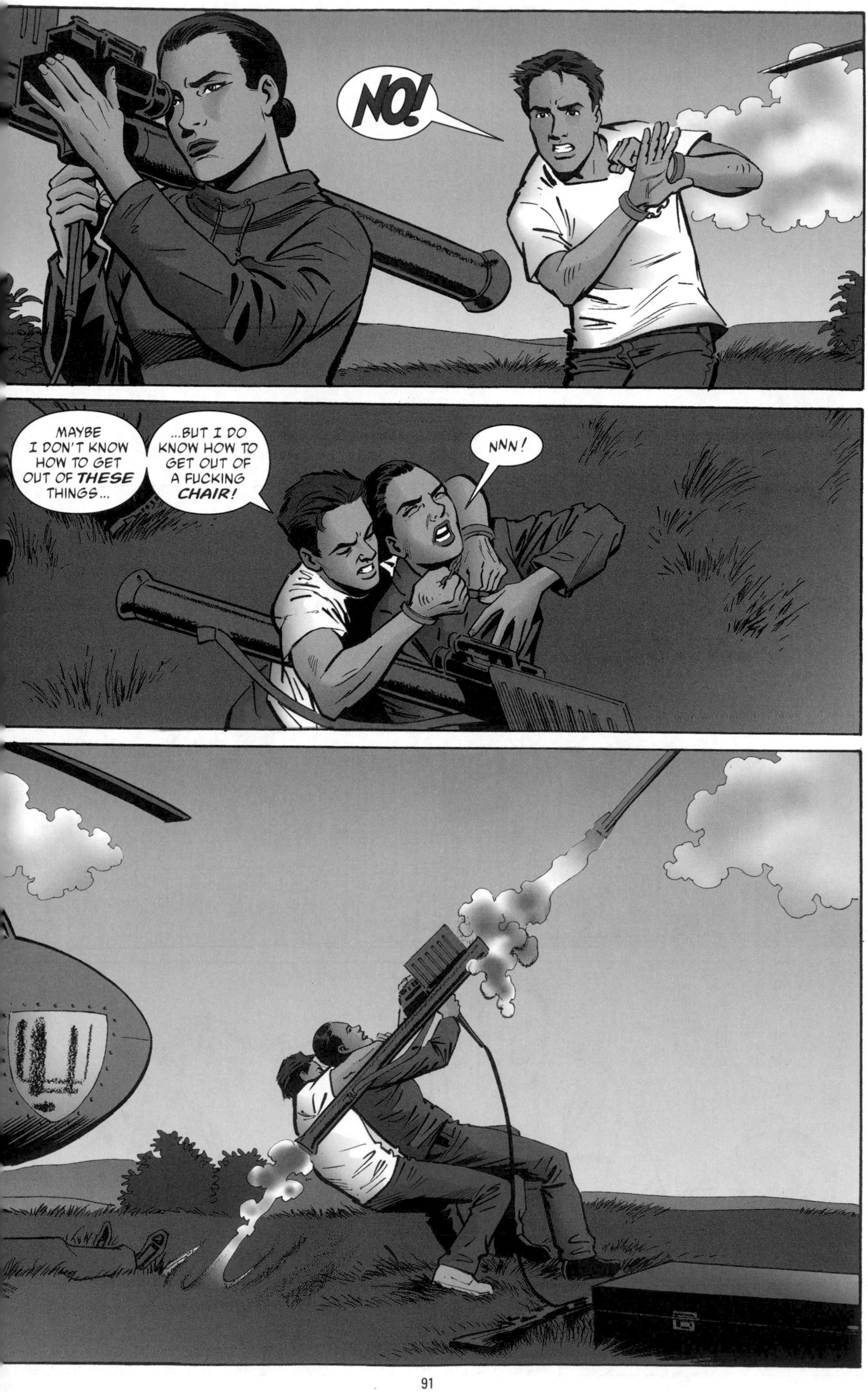
NO!
MAYBE I DON'T KNOW HOW TO GET OUT OF THESE THINGS...
...BUT I DO KNOW HOW TO GET OUT OF A FUCKING CHAIR!
NNN!

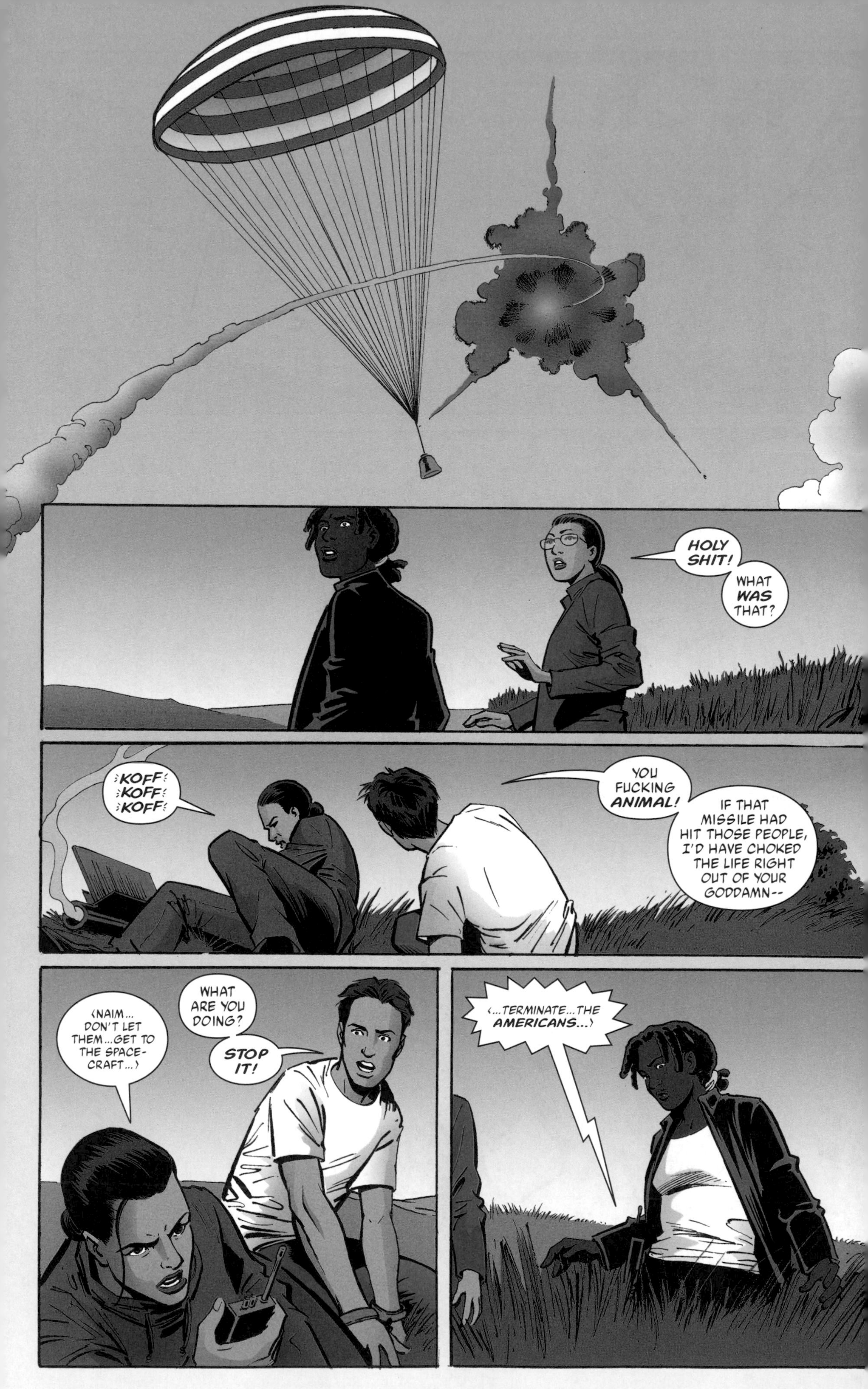
HOLY SHIT!
WHAT WAS THAT?
KOFF KOFF KOFF
YOU FUCKING ANIMAL!
IF THAT MISSILE HAD HIT THOSE PEOPLE, I'D HAVE CHOKED THE LIFE RIGHT OUT OF YOUR GODDAMN--
‹NAIM... DON'T LET THEM...GET TO THE SPACE-CRAFT...›
WHAT ARE YOU DOING?
STOP IT!
‹...TERMINATE...THE AMERICANS...›

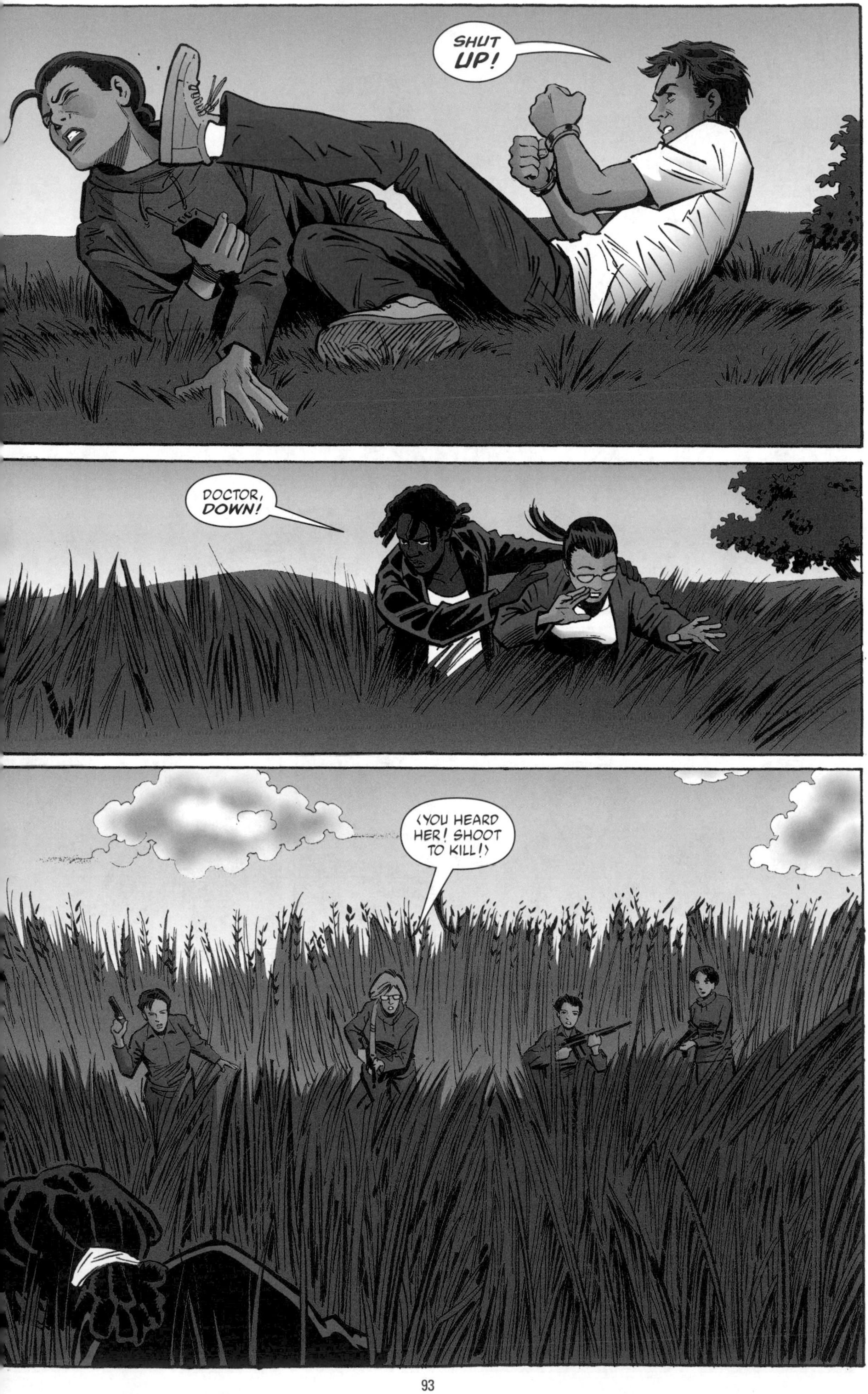
SHUT UP!
DOCTOR, DOWN!
‹YOU HEARD HER! SHOOT TO KILL!›

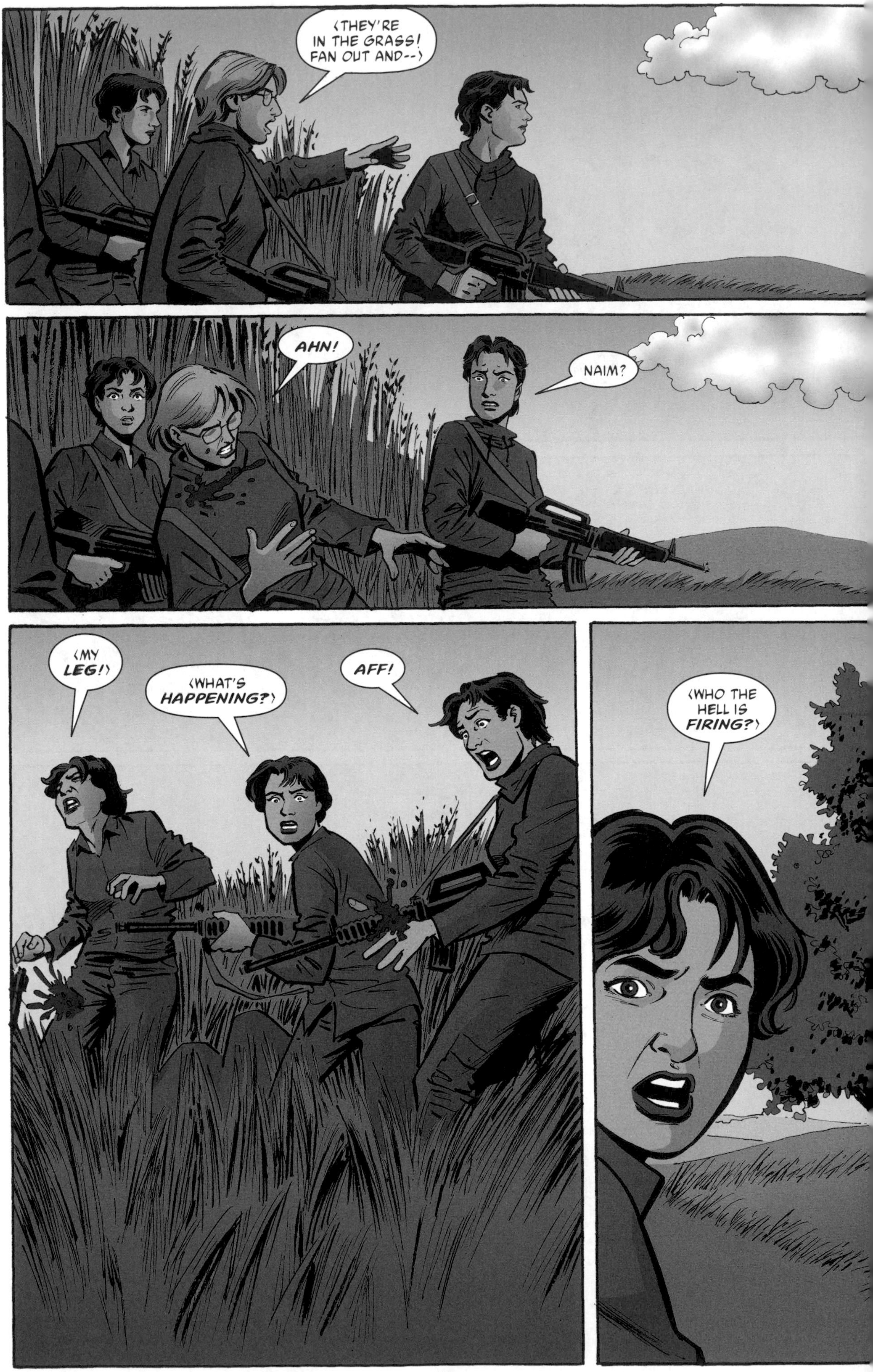

‹THEY'RE IN THE GRASS! FAN OUT AND--›
AHN!
NAIM?
‹MY LEG!›
‹WHAT'S HAPPENING?›
AFF!
‹WHO THE HELL IS FIRING?›

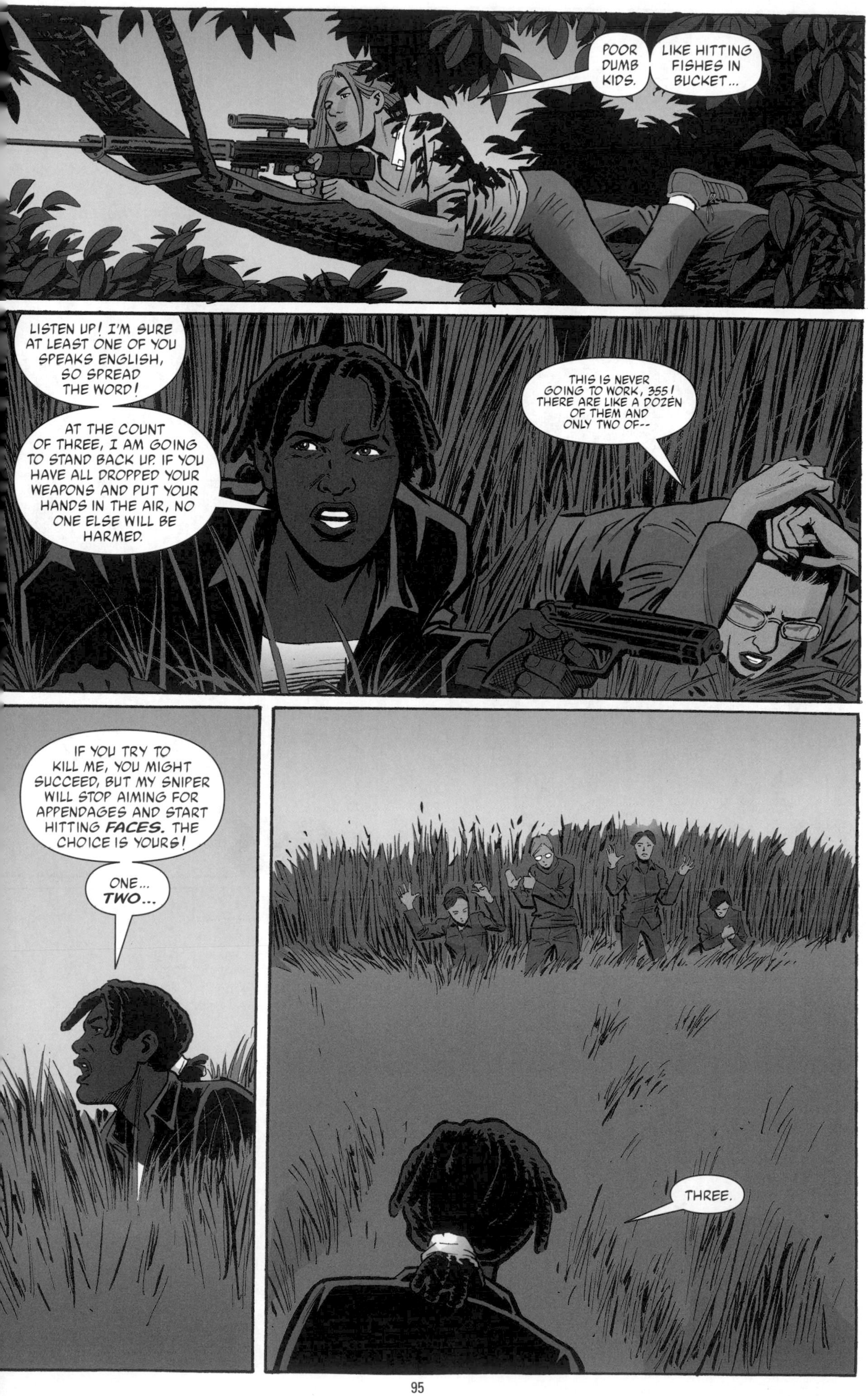
POOR DUMB KIDS.
LIKE HITTING FISHES IN BUCKET...
LISTEN UP! I'M SURE AT LEAST ONE OF YOU SPEAKS ENGLISH, SO SPREAD THE WORD!
AT THE COUNT OF THREE, I AM GOING TO STAND BACK UP. IF YOU HAVE ALL DROPPED YOUR WEAPONS AND PUT YOUR HANDS IN THE AIR, NO ONE ELSE WILL BE HARMED.
THIS IS NEVER GOING TO WORK, 355! THERE ARE LIKE A DOZEN OF THEM AND ONLY TWO OF--
IF YOU TRY TO KILL ME, YOU MIGHT SUCCEED, BUT MY SNIPER WILL STOP AIMING FOR APPENDAGES AND START HITTING FACES. THE CHOICE IS YOURS!
ONE... TWO...
THREE.

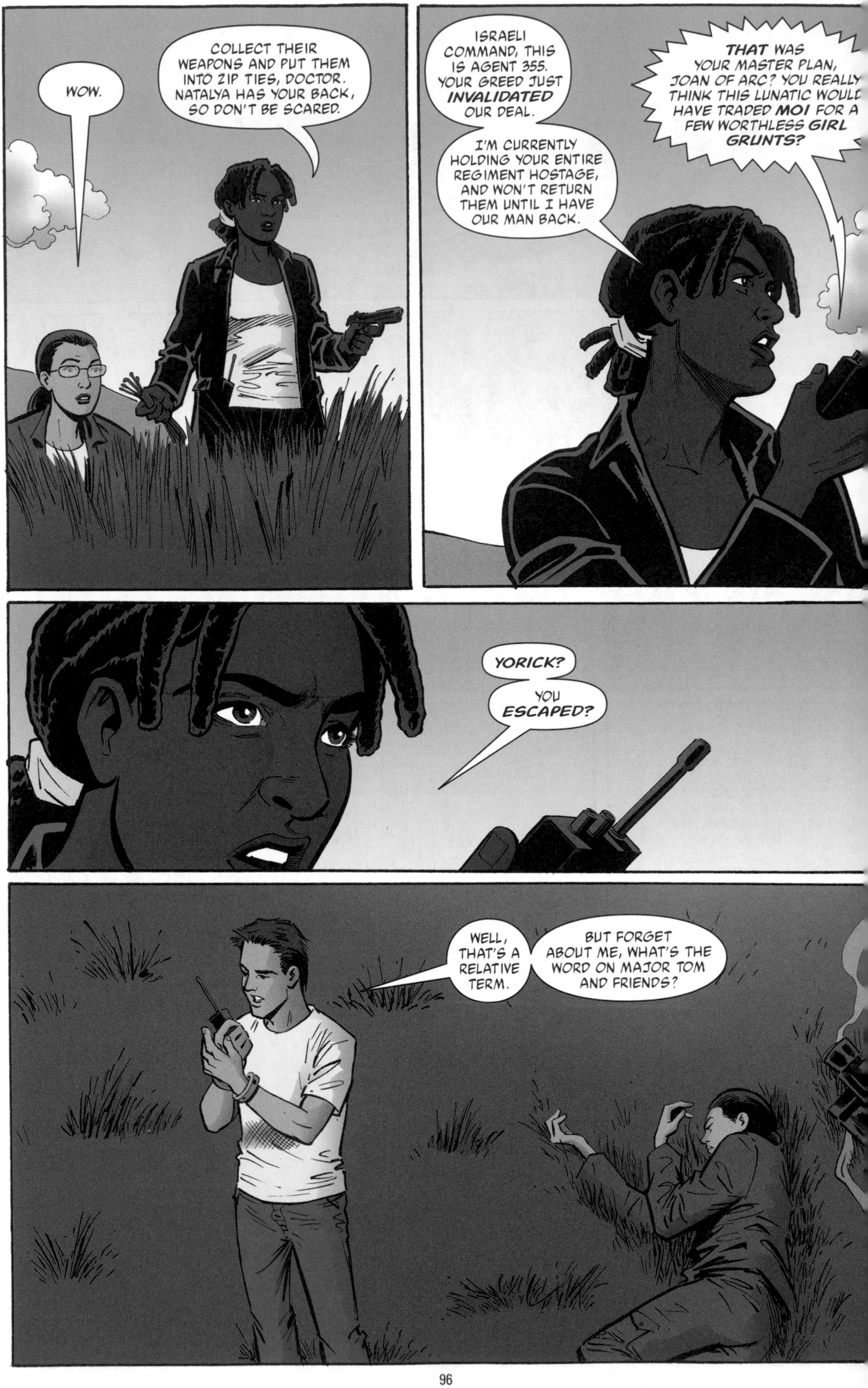
WOW.
COLLECT THEIR WEAPONS AND PUT THEM INTO ZIP TIES, DOCTOR. NATALYA HAS YOUR BACK, SO DON'T BE SCARED.
ISRAELI COMMAND, THIS IS AGENT 355. YOUR GREED JUST INVALIDATED OUR DEAL.
I'M CURRENTLY HOLDING YOUR ENTIRE REGIMENT HOSTAGE, AND WON'T RETURN THEM UNTIL I HAVE OUR MAN BACK.
THAT WAS YOUR MASTER PLAN, JOAN OF ARC? YOU REALLY THINK THIS LUNATIC WOULD HAVE TRADED MOI FOR A FEW WORTHLESS GIRL GRUNTS?
YORICK?
YOU ESCAPED?
WELL, THAT'S A RELATIVE TERM.
BUT FORGET ABOUT ME, WHAT'S THE WORD ON MAJOR TOM AND FRIENDS?

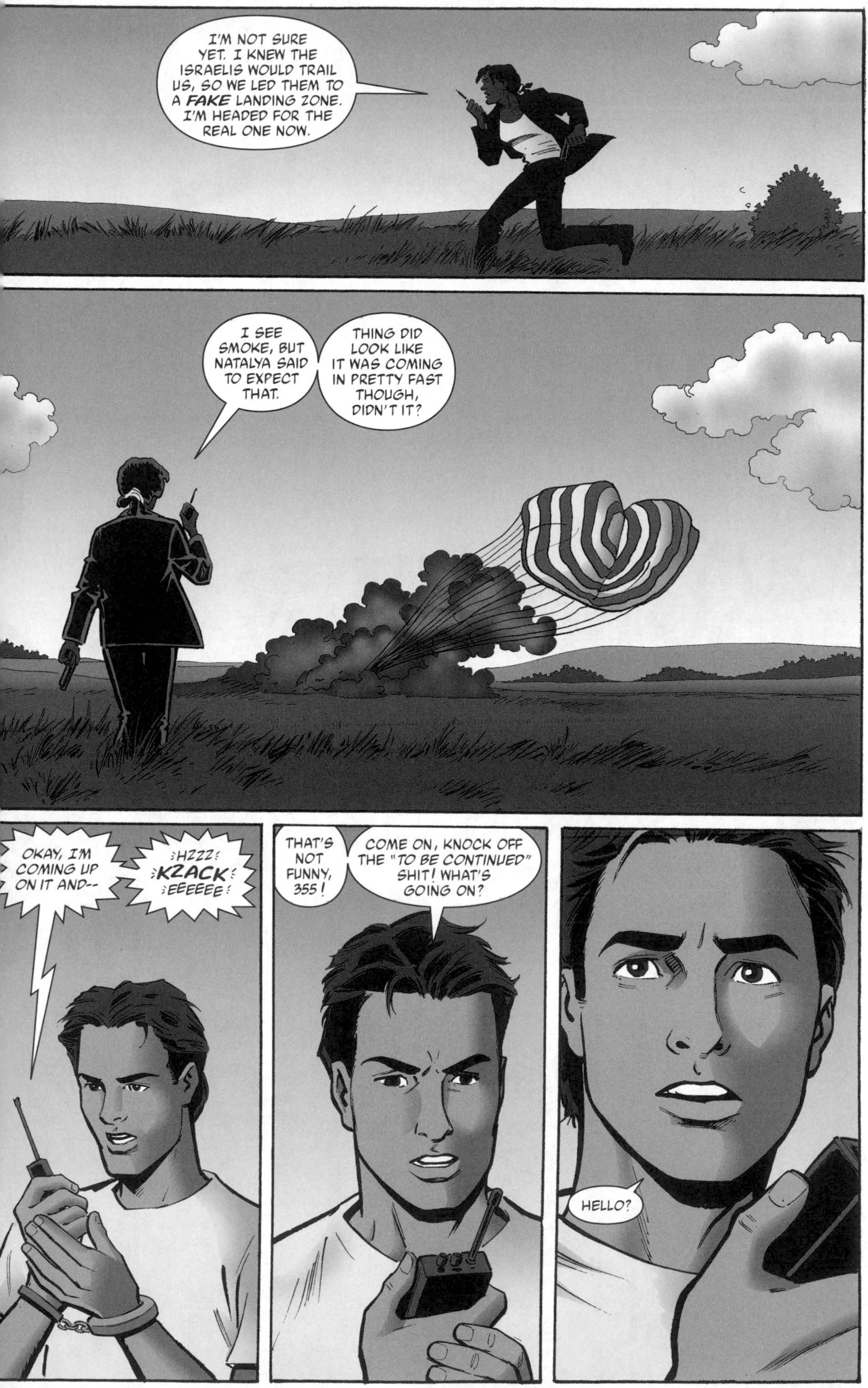
I'M NOT SURE YET. I KNEW THE ISRAELIS WOULD TRAIL US, SO WE LED THEM TO A **FAKE** LANDING ZONE. I'M HEADED FOR THE REAL ONE NOW.
I SEE SMOKE, BUT NATALYA SAID TO EXPECT THAT.
THING DID LOOK LIKE IT WAS COMING IN PRETTY FAST THOUGH, DIDN'T IT?
OKAY, I'M COMING UP ON IT AND--
HZZZ KZACK EEEEEE
THAT'S NOT FUNNY, 355!
COME ON, KNOCK OFF THE "TO BE CONTINUED" SHIT! WHAT'S GOING ON?
HELLO?

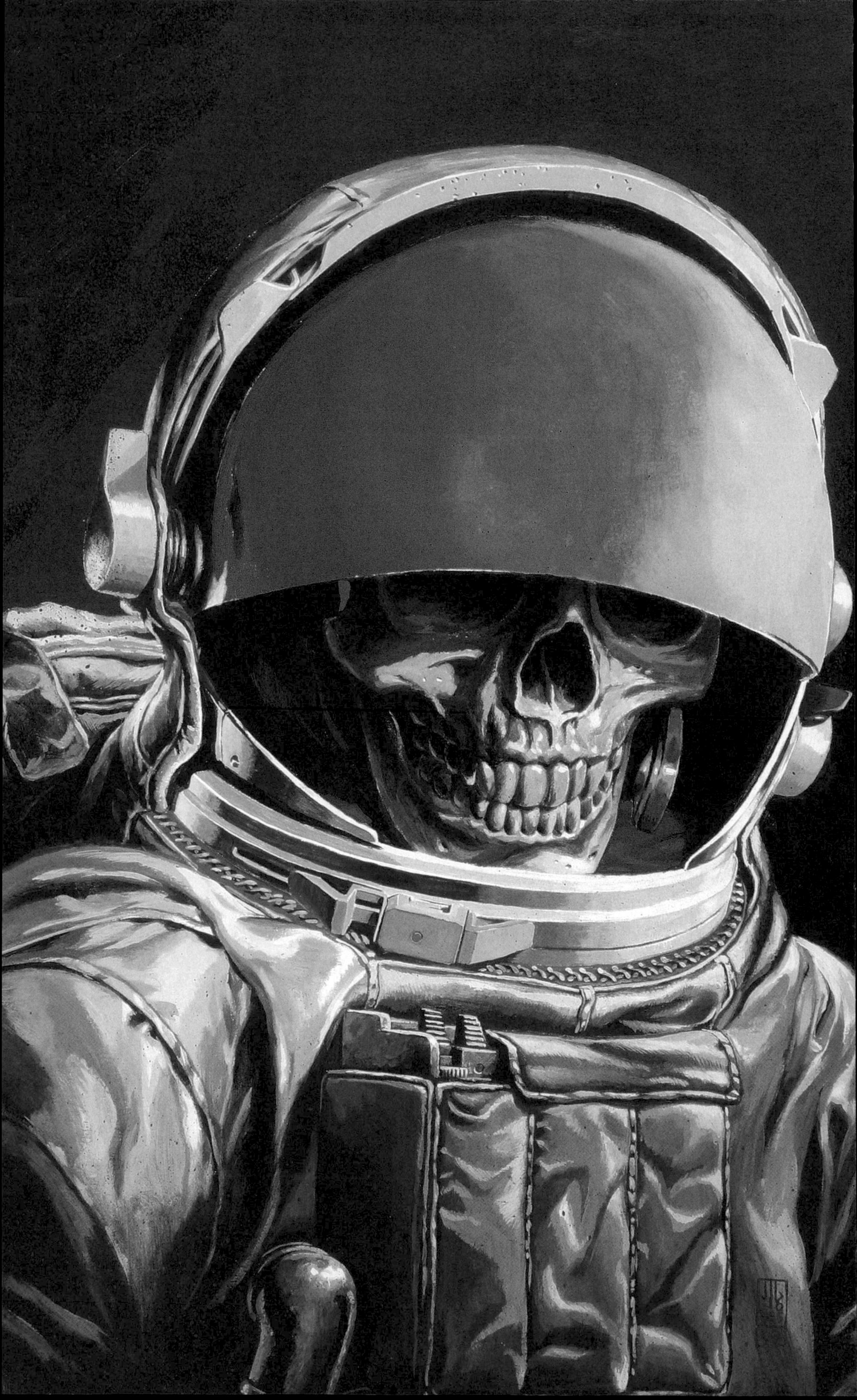

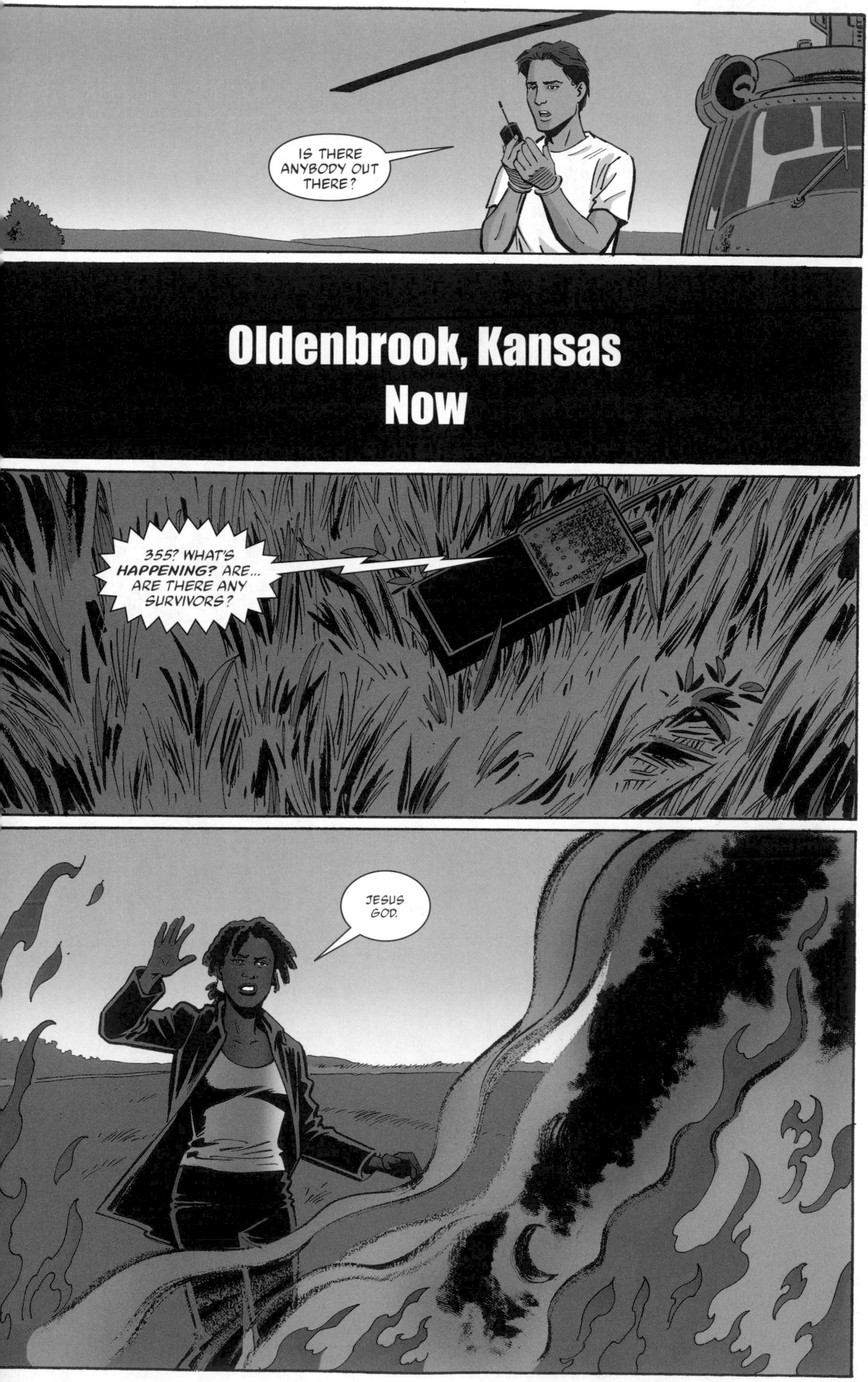
IS THERE ANYBODY OUT THERE?
Oldenbrook, Kansas
Now
355? WHAT'S HAPPENING? ARE... ARE THERE ANY SURVIVORS?
JESUS GOD.

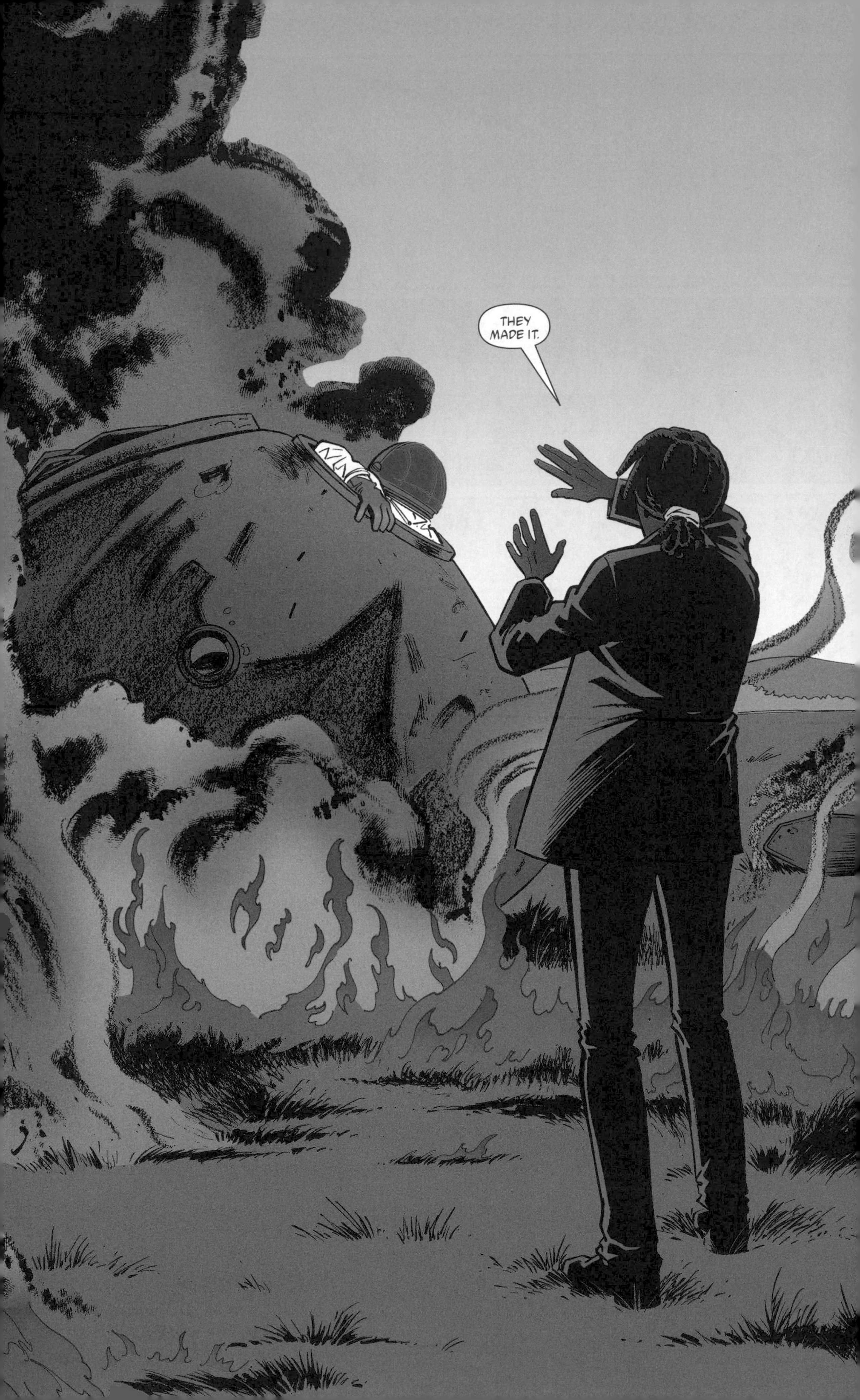
THEY MADE IT.

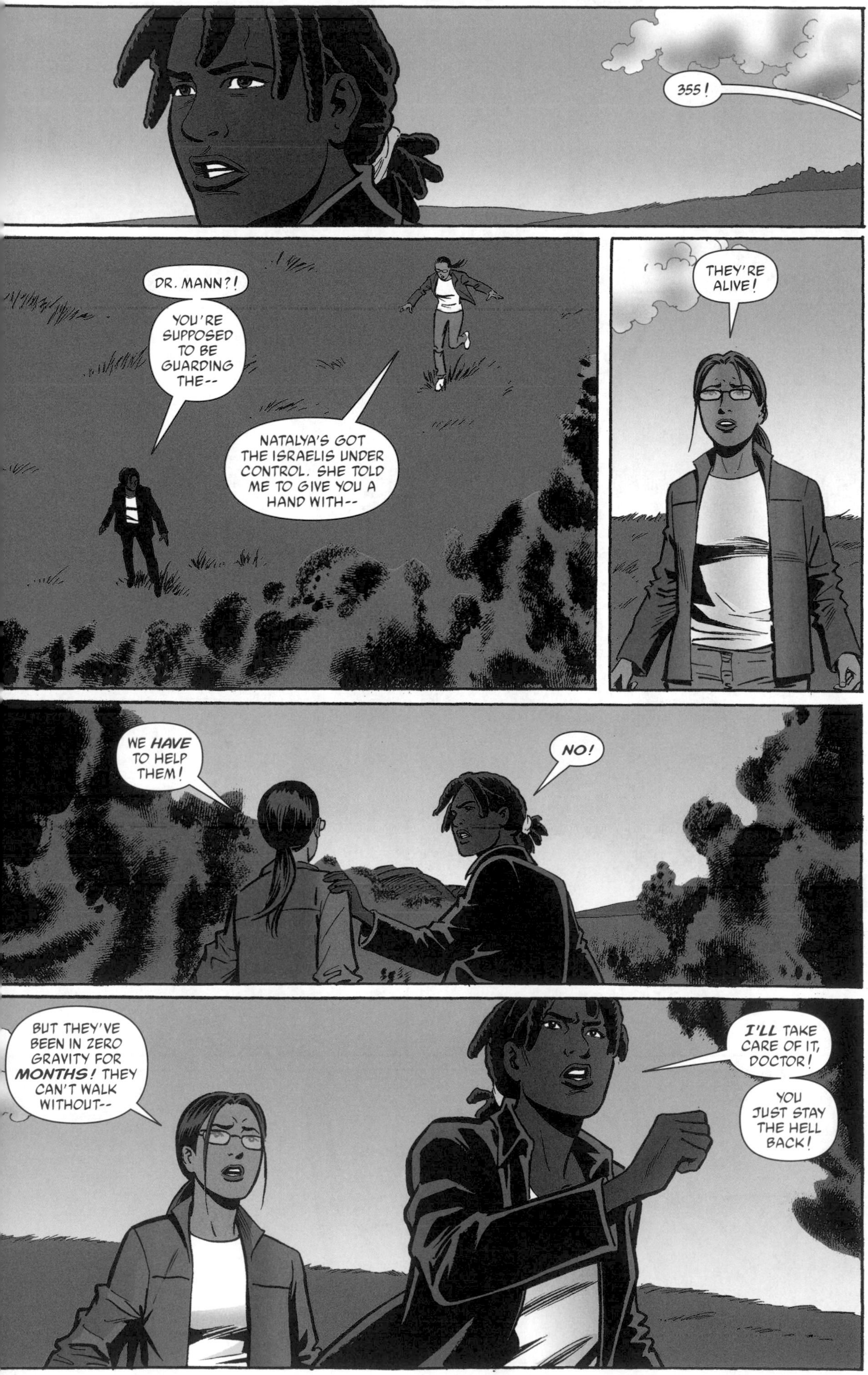
355!
DR. MANN?!
YOU'RE SUPPOSED TO BE GUARDING THE--
NATALYA'S GOT THE ISRAELIS UNDER CONTROL. SHE TOLD ME TO GIVE YOU A HAND WITH--
THEY'RE ALIVE!
WE HAVE TO HELP THEM!
NO!
BUT THEY'VE BEEN IN ZERO GRAVITY FOR MONTHS! THEY CAN'T WALK WITHOUT--
I'LL TAKE CARE OF IT, DOCTOR!
YOU JUST STAY THE HELL BACK!

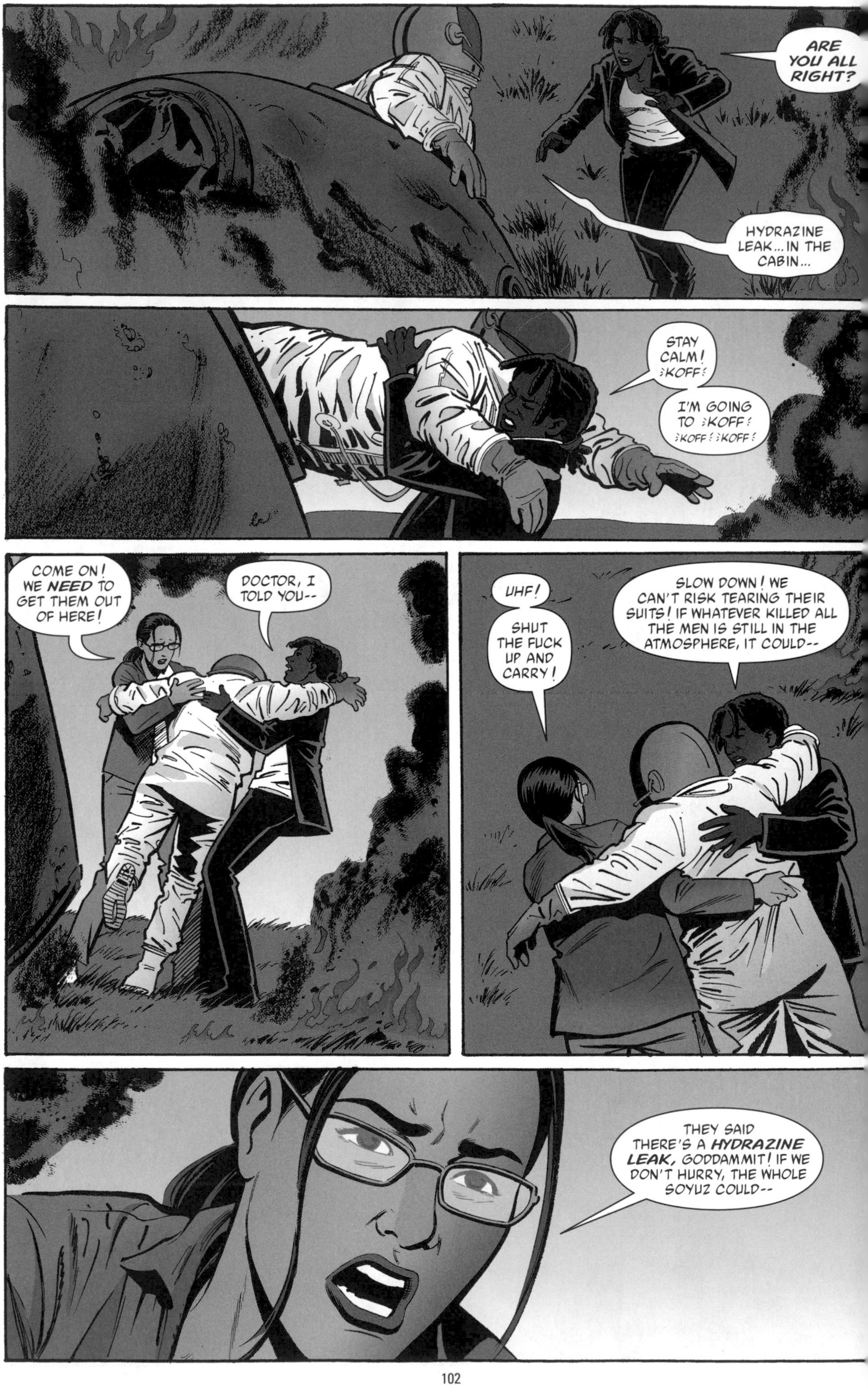
ARE YOU ALL RIGHT?
HYDRAZINE LEAK... IN THE CABIN...
STAY CALM! KOFF
I'M GOING TO KOFF KOFF KOFF
COME ON! WE NEED TO GET THEM OUT OF HERE!
DOCTOR, I TOLD YOU--
UHF!
SHUT THE FUCK UP AND CARRY!
SLOW DOWN! WE CAN'T RISK TEARING THEIR SUITS! IF WHATEVER KILLED ALL THE MEN IS STILL IN THE ATMOSPHERE, IT COULD--
THEY SAID THERE'S A HYDRAZINE LEAK, GODDAMMIT! IF WE DON'T HURRY, THE WHOLE SOYUZ COULD--

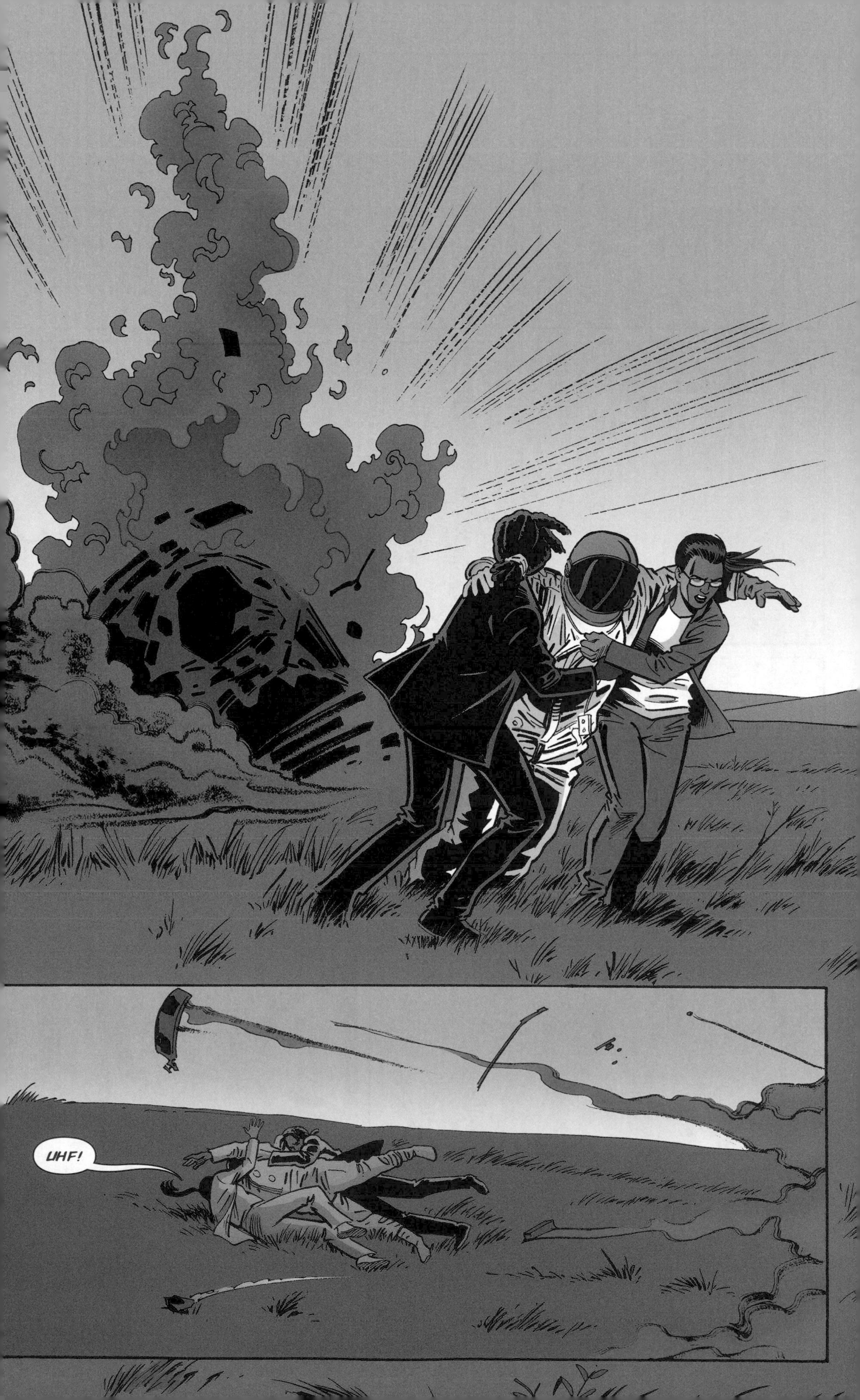
UHF!

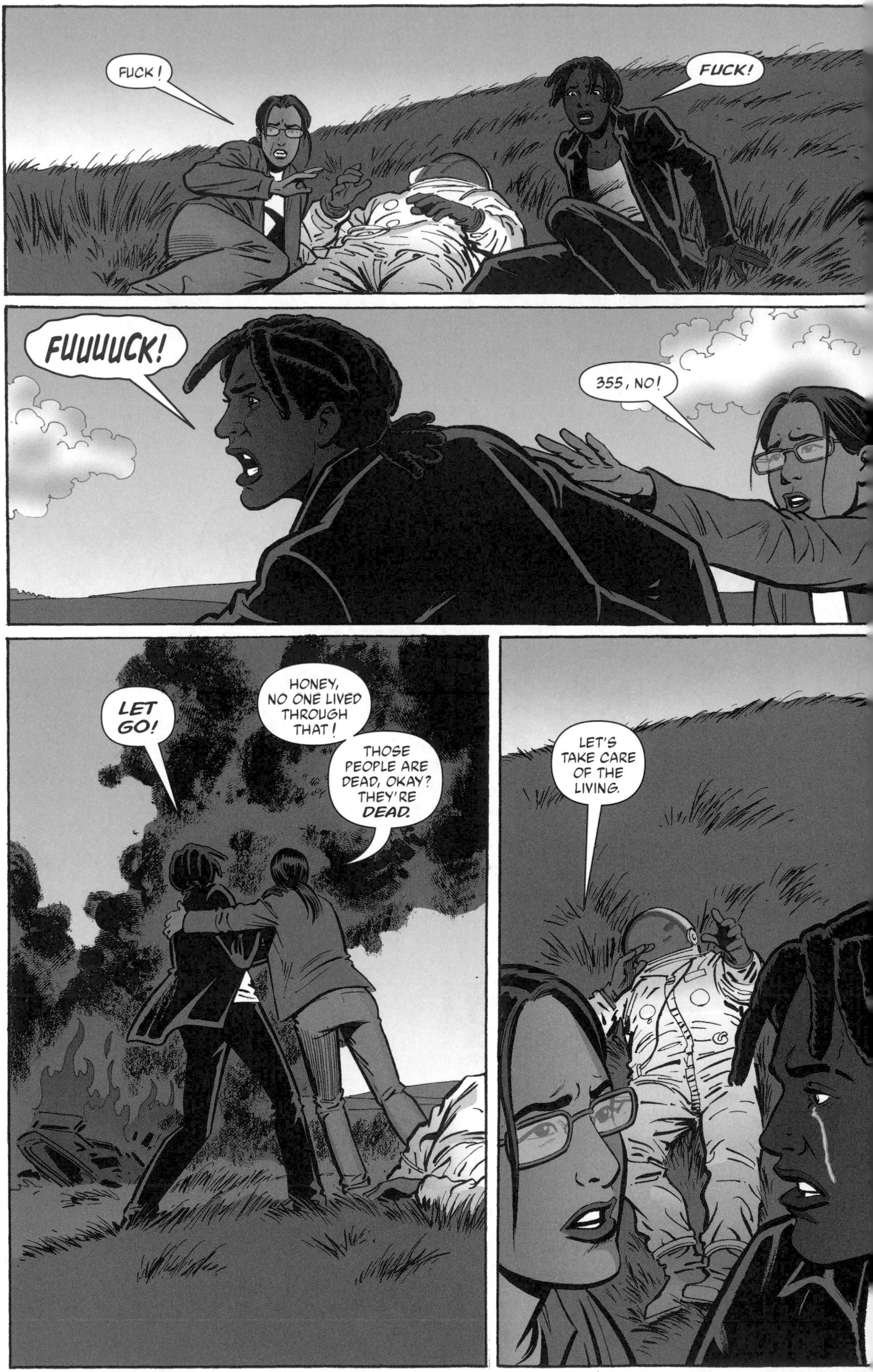
FUCK!
FUCK!
FUUUUCK!
355, NO!
LET GO!
HONEY, NO ONE LIVED THROUGH THAT!
THOSE PEOPLE ARE DEAD, OKAY? THEY'RE DEAD.
LET'S TAKE CARE OF THE LIVING.

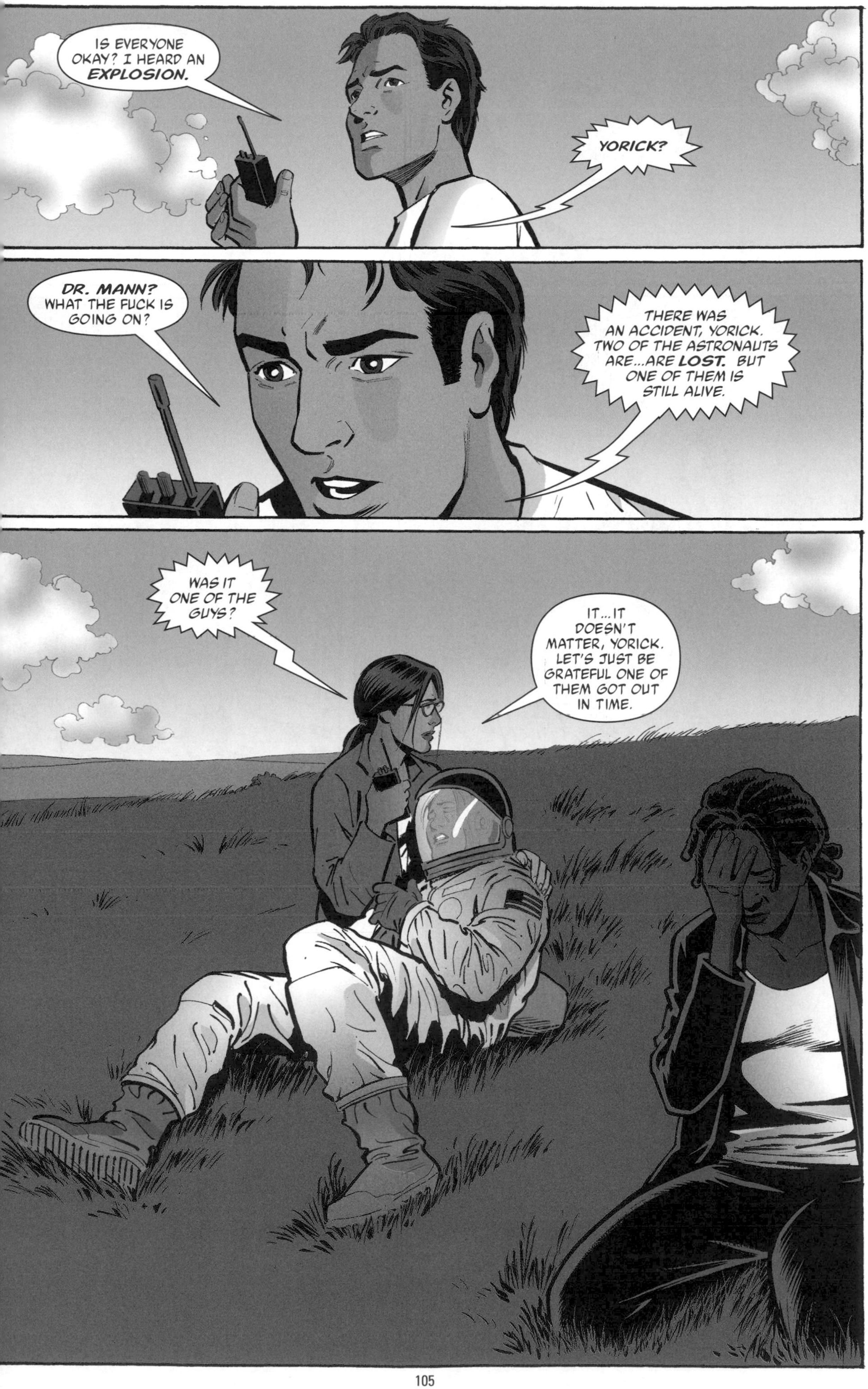
IS EVERYONE OKAY? I HEARD AN EXPLOSION.
YORICK?
DR. MANN? WHAT THE FUCK IS GOING ON?
THERE WAS AN ACCIDENT, YORICK. TWO OF THE ASTRONAUTS ARE...ARE LOST. BUT ONE OF THEM IS STILL ALIVE.
WAS IT ONE OF THE GUYS?
IT...IT DOESN'T MATTER, YORICK. LET'S JUST BE GRATEFUL ONE OF THEM GOT OUT IN TIME.

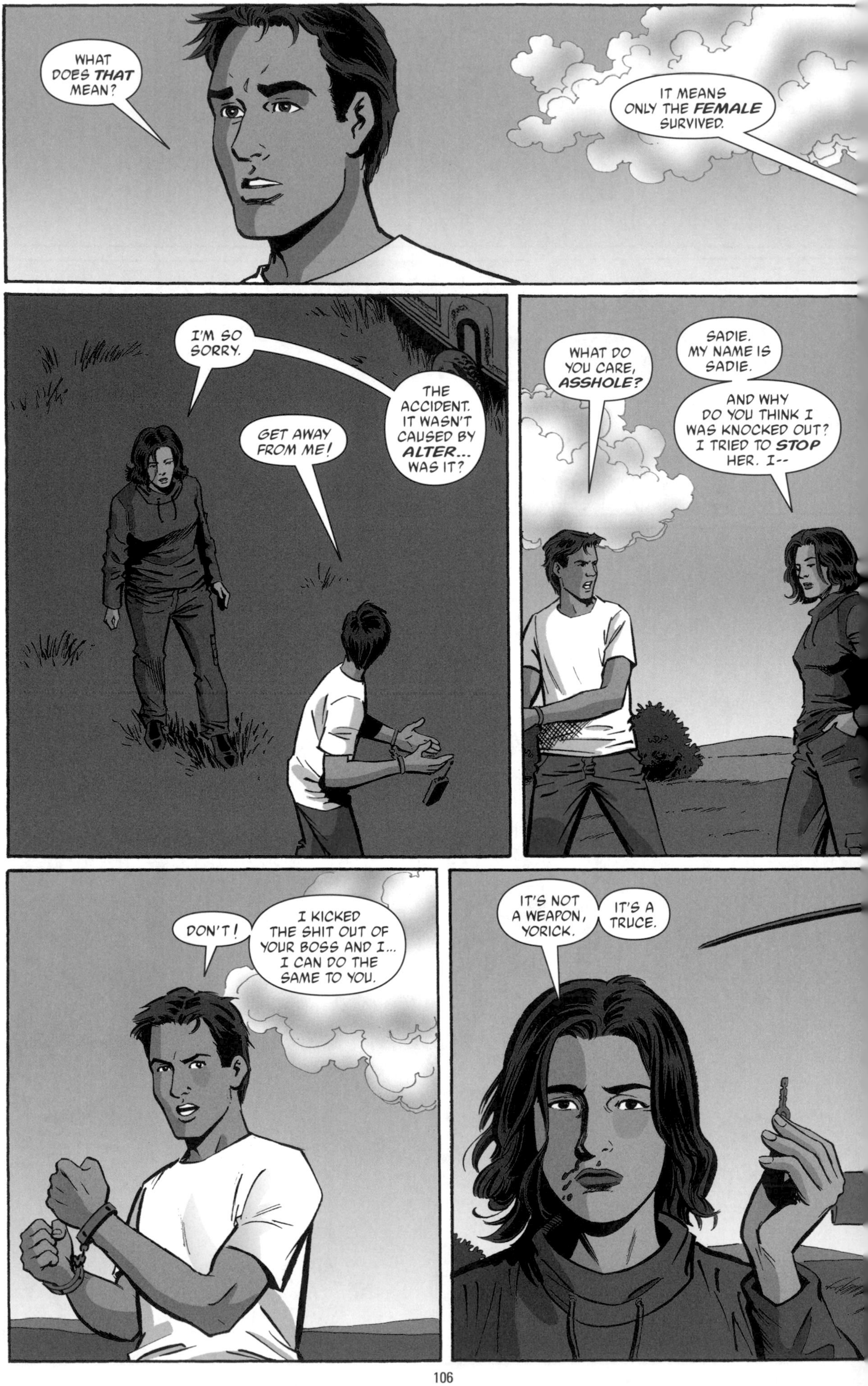
WHAT DOES THAT MEAN?
IT MEANS ONLY THE FEMALE SURVIVED.
I'M SO SORRY.
THE ACCIDENT. IT WASN'T CAUSED BY ALTER... WAS IT?
GET AWAY FROM ME!
WHAT DO YOU CARE, ASSHOLE?
SADIE. MY NAME IS SADIE.
AND WHY DO YOU THINK I WAS KNOCKED OUT? I TRIED TO STOP HER. I--
DON'T!
I KICKED THE SHIT OUT OF YOUR BOSS AND I... I CAN DO THE SAME TO YOU.
IT'S NOT A WEAPON, YORICK.
IT'S A TRUCE.

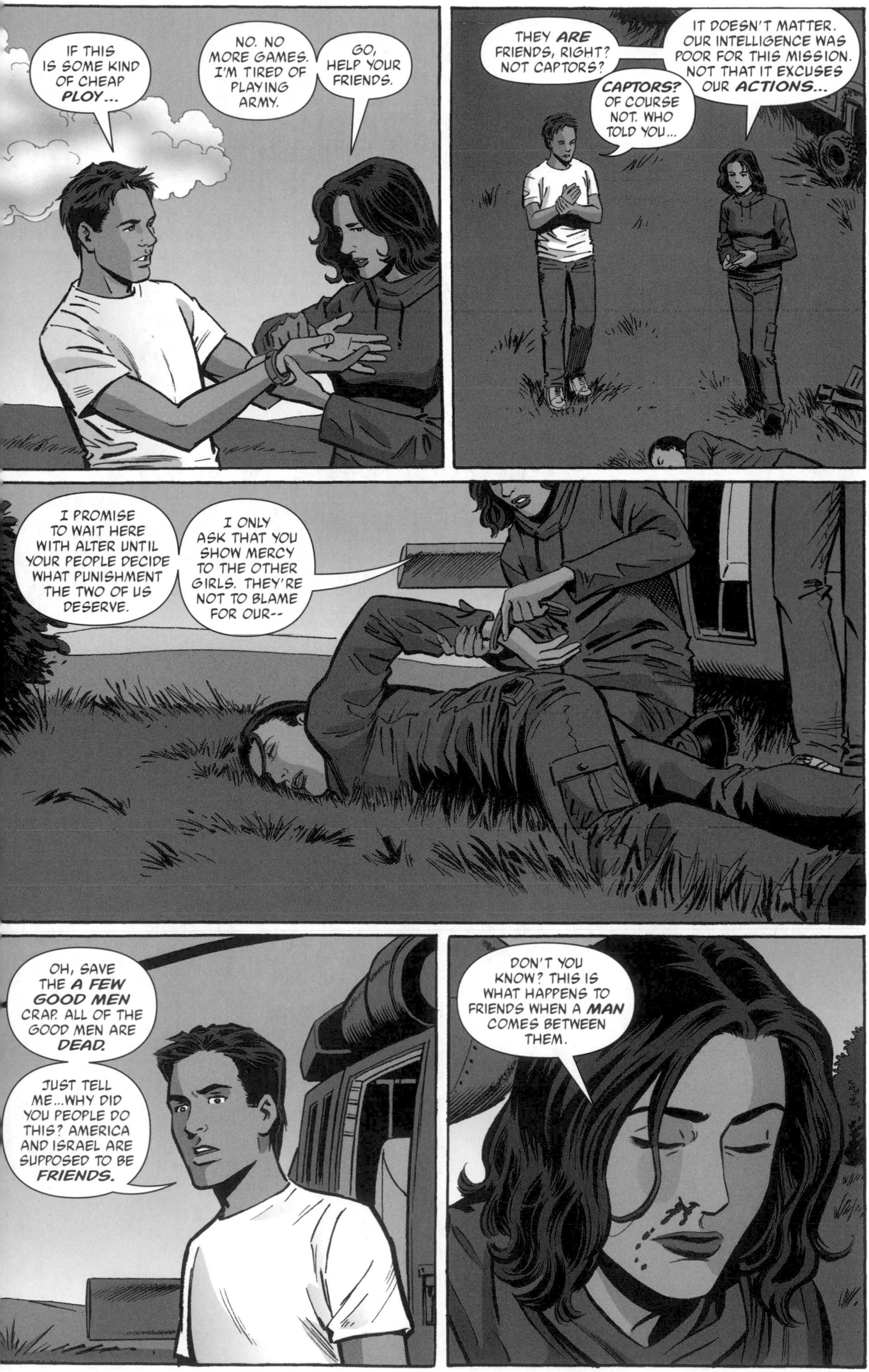
IF THIS IS SOME KIND OF CHEAP *PLOY*...
NO. NO MORE GAMES. I'M TIRED OF PLAYING ARMY.
GO, HELP YOUR FRIENDS.
THEY *ARE* FRIENDS, RIGHT? NOT CAPTORS?
CAPTORS? OF COURSE NOT. WHO TOLD YOU...
IT DOESN'T MATTER. OUR INTELLIGENCE WAS POOR FOR THIS MISSION. NOT THAT IT EXCUSES OUR *ACTIONS*...
I PROMISE TO WAIT HERE WITH ALTER UNTIL YOUR PEOPLE DECIDE WHAT PUNISHMENT THE TWO OF US DESERVE.
I ONLY ASK THAT YOU SHOW MERCY TO THE OTHER GIRLS. THEY'RE NOT TO BLAME FOR OUR--
OH, SAVE THE *A FEW GOOD MEN* CRAP. ALL OF THE GOOD MEN ARE *DEAD.*
JUST TELL ME...WHY DID YOU PEOPLE DO THIS? AMERICA AND ISRAEL ARE SUPPOSED TO BE *FRIENDS.*
DON'T YOU KNOW? THIS IS WHAT HAPPENS TO FRIENDS WHEN A *MAN* COMES BETWEEN THEM.

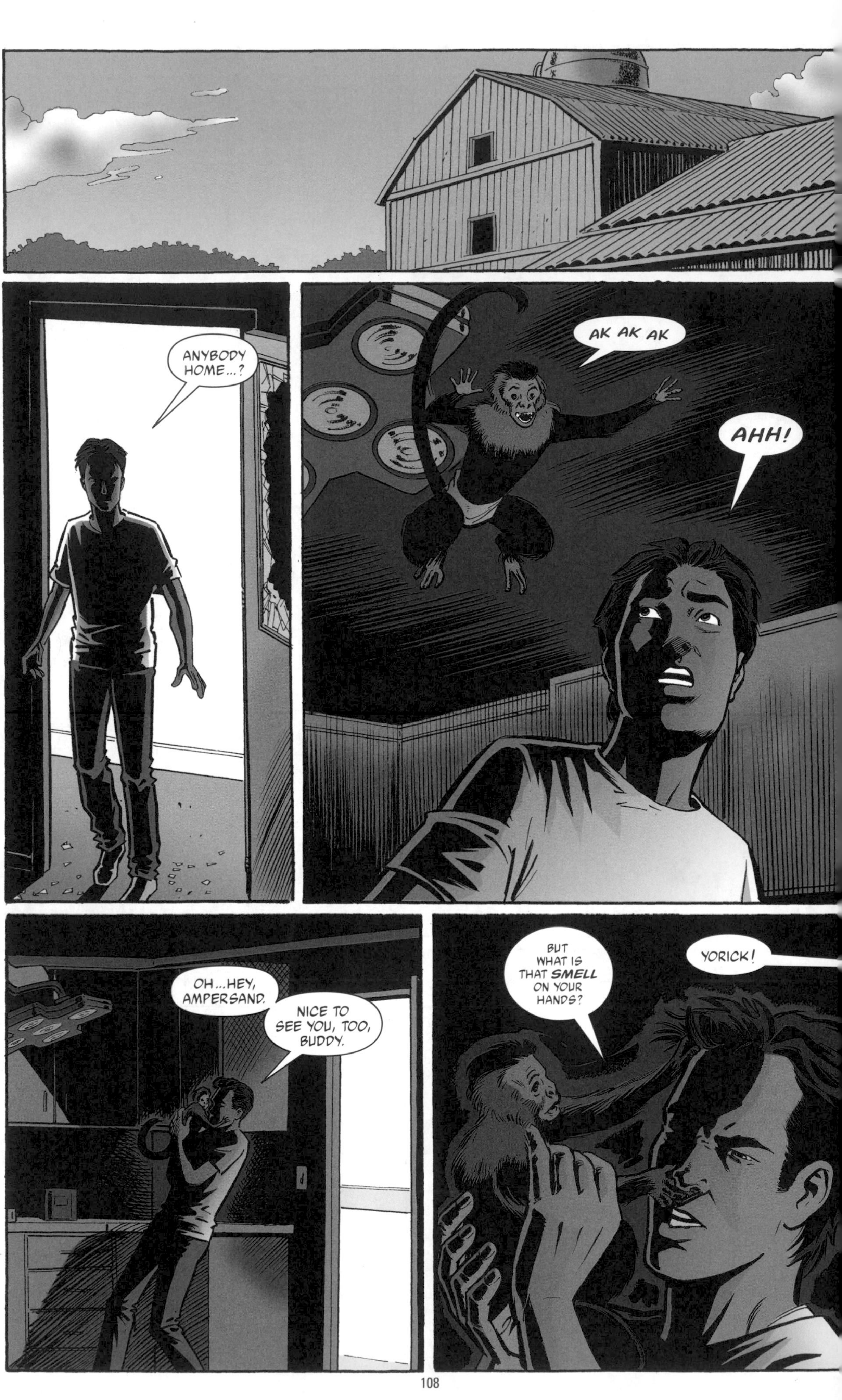
ANYBODY HOME...?
AK AK AK
AHH!
OH...HEY, AMPERSAND.
NICE TO SEE YOU, TOO, BUDDY.
YORICK!
BUT WHAT IS THAT SMELL ON YOUR HANDS?

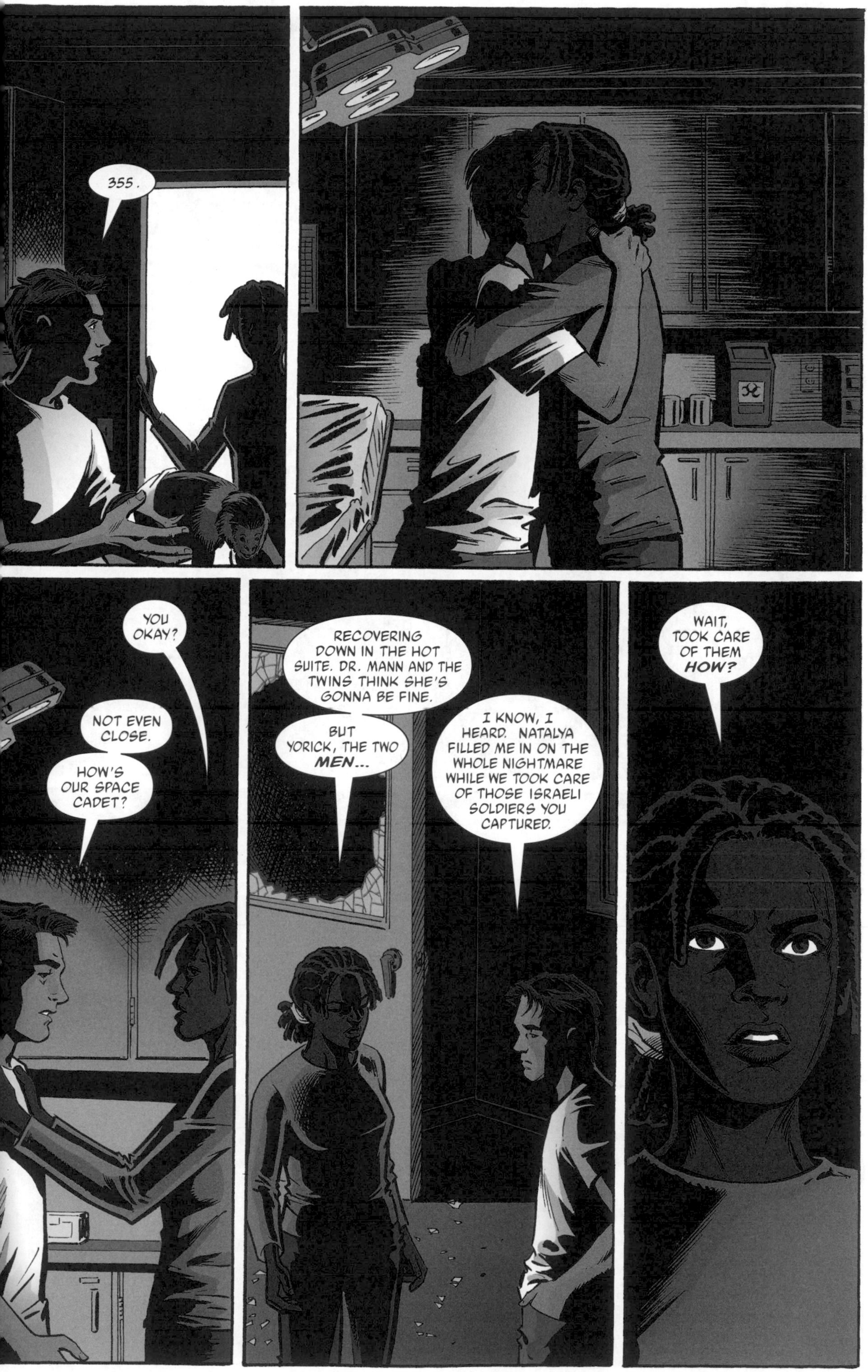
355.
YOU OKAY?
NOT EVEN CLOSE.
HOW'S OUR SPACE CADET?
RECOVERING DOWN IN THE HOT SUITE. DR. MANN AND THE TWINS THINK SHE'S GONNA BE FINE.
BUT YORICK, THE TWO MEN...
I KNOW, I HEARD. NATALYA FILLED ME IN ON THE WHOLE NIGHTMARE WHILE WE TOOK CARE OF THOSE ISRAELI SOLDIERS YOU CAPTURED.
WAIT, TOOK CARE OF THEM HOW?

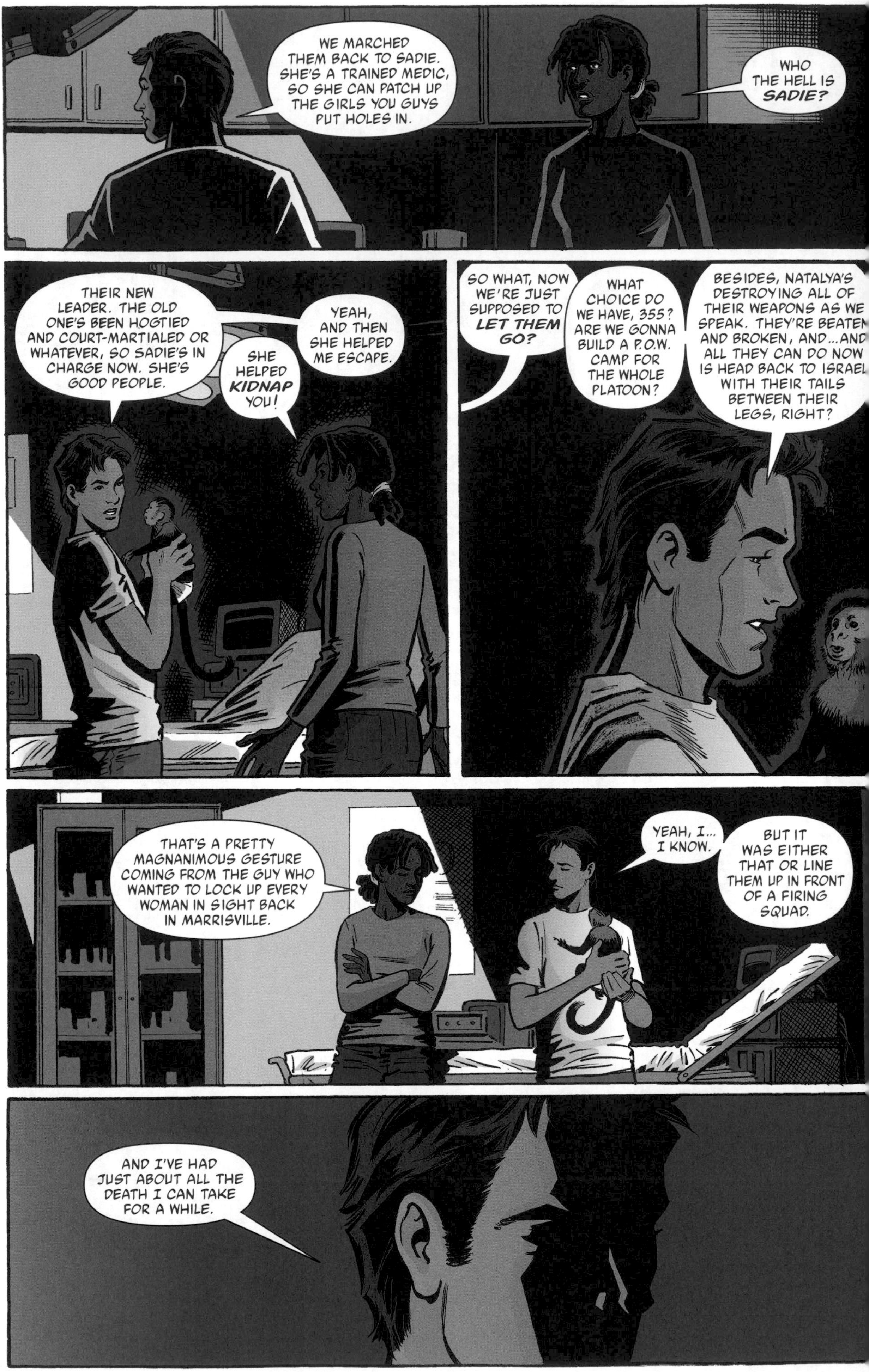

WE MARCHED THEM BACK TO SADIE. SHE'S A TRAINED MEDIC, SO SHE CAN PATCH UP THE GIRLS YOU GUYS PUT HOLES IN.
WHO THE HELL IS SADIE?
THEIR NEW LEADER. THE OLD ONE'S BEEN HOGTIED AND COURT-MARTIALED OR WHATEVER, SO SADIE'S IN CHARGE NOW. SHE'S GOOD PEOPLE.
SHE HELPED KIDNAP YOU!
YEAH, AND THEN SHE HELPED ME ESCAPE.
SO WHAT, NOW WE'RE JUST SUPPOSED TO LET THEM GO?
WHAT CHOICE DO WE HAVE, 355? ARE WE GONNA BUILD A P.O.W. CAMP FOR THE WHOLE PLATOON?
BESIDES, NATALYA'S DESTROYING ALL OF THEIR WEAPONS AS WE SPEAK. THEY'RE BEATEN AND BROKEN, AND...AND ALL THEY CAN DO NOW IS HEAD BACK TO ISRAEL WITH THEIR TAILS BETWEEN THEIR LEGS, RIGHT?
THAT'S A PRETTY MAGNANIMOUS GESTURE COMING FROM THE GUY WHO WANTED TO LOCK UP EVERY WOMAN IN SIGHT BACK IN MARRISVILLE.
YEAH, I... I KNOW.
BUT IT WAS EITHER THAT OR LINE THEM UP IN FRONT OF A FIRING SQUAD.
AND I'VE HAD JUST ABOUT ALL THE DEATH I CAN TAKE FOR A WHILE.

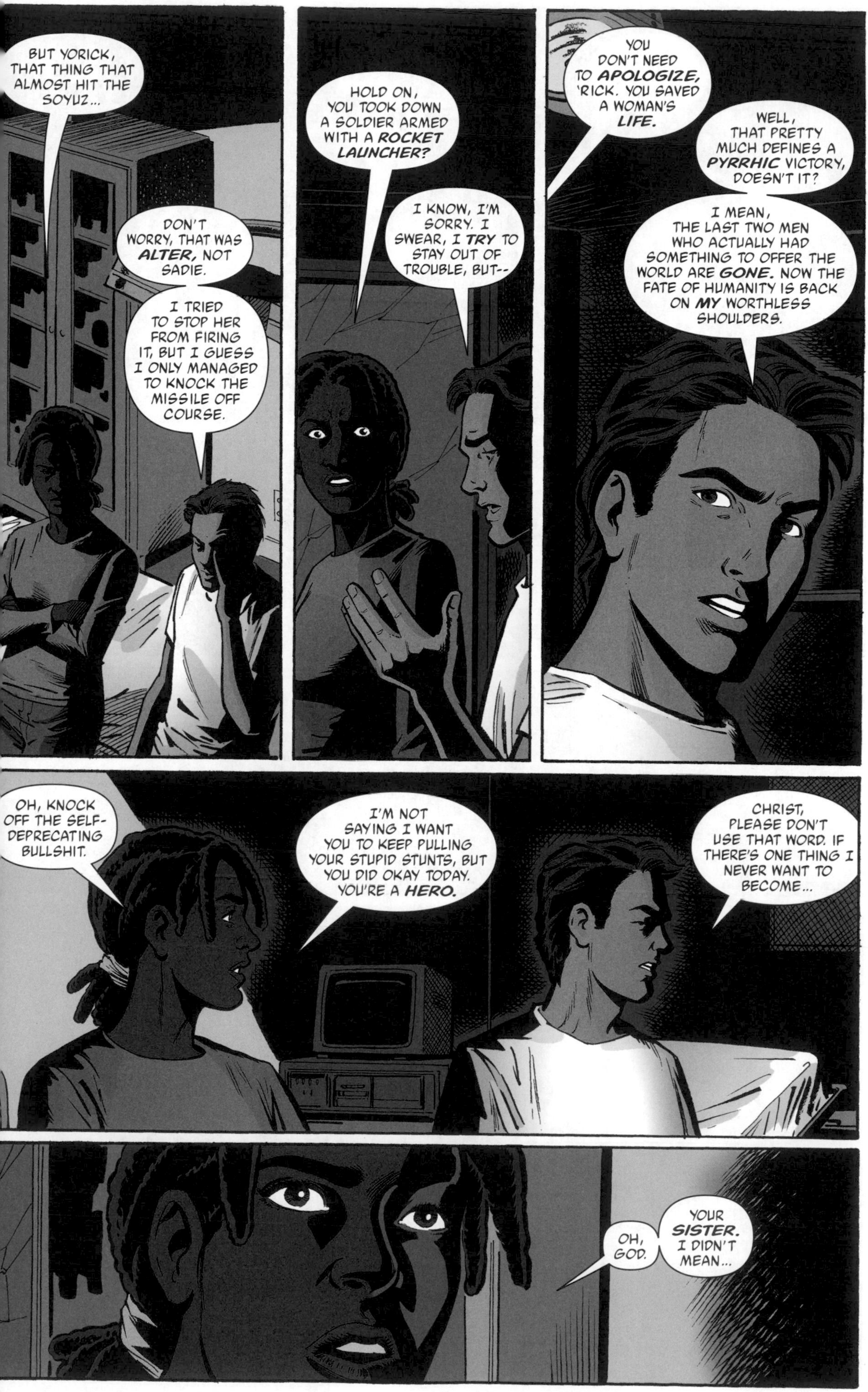
BUT YORICK, THAT THING THAT ALMOST HIT THE SOYUZ...
DON'T WORRY, THAT WAS **ALTER,** NOT SADIE.
I TRIED TO STOP HER FROM FIRING IT, BUT I GUESS I ONLY MANAGED TO KNOCK THE MISSILE OFF COURSE.
HOLD ON, YOU TOOK DOWN A SOLDIER ARMED WITH A **ROCKET LAUNCHER?**
I KNOW, I'M SORRY. I SWEAR, I **TRY** TO STAY OUT OF TROUBLE, BUT--
YOU DON'T NEED TO **APOLOGIZE,** 'RICK. YOU SAVED A WOMAN'S **LIFE.**
WELL, THAT PRETTY MUCH DEFINES A **PYRRHIC** VICTORY, DOESN'T IT?
I MEAN, THE LAST TWO MEN WHO ACTUALLY HAD SOMETHING TO OFFER THE WORLD ARE **GONE.** NOW THE FATE OF HUMANITY IS BACK ON **MY** WORTHLESS SHOULDERS.
OH, KNOCK OFF THE SELF-DEPRECATING BULLSHIT.
I'M NOT SAYING I WANT YOU TO KEEP PULLING YOUR STUPID STUNTS, BUT YOU DID OKAY TODAY. YOU'RE A **HERO.**
CHRIST, PLEASE DON'T USE THAT WORD. IF THERE'S ONE THING I NEVER WANT TO BECOME...
OH, GOD.
YOUR **SISTER.** I DIDN'T MEAN...

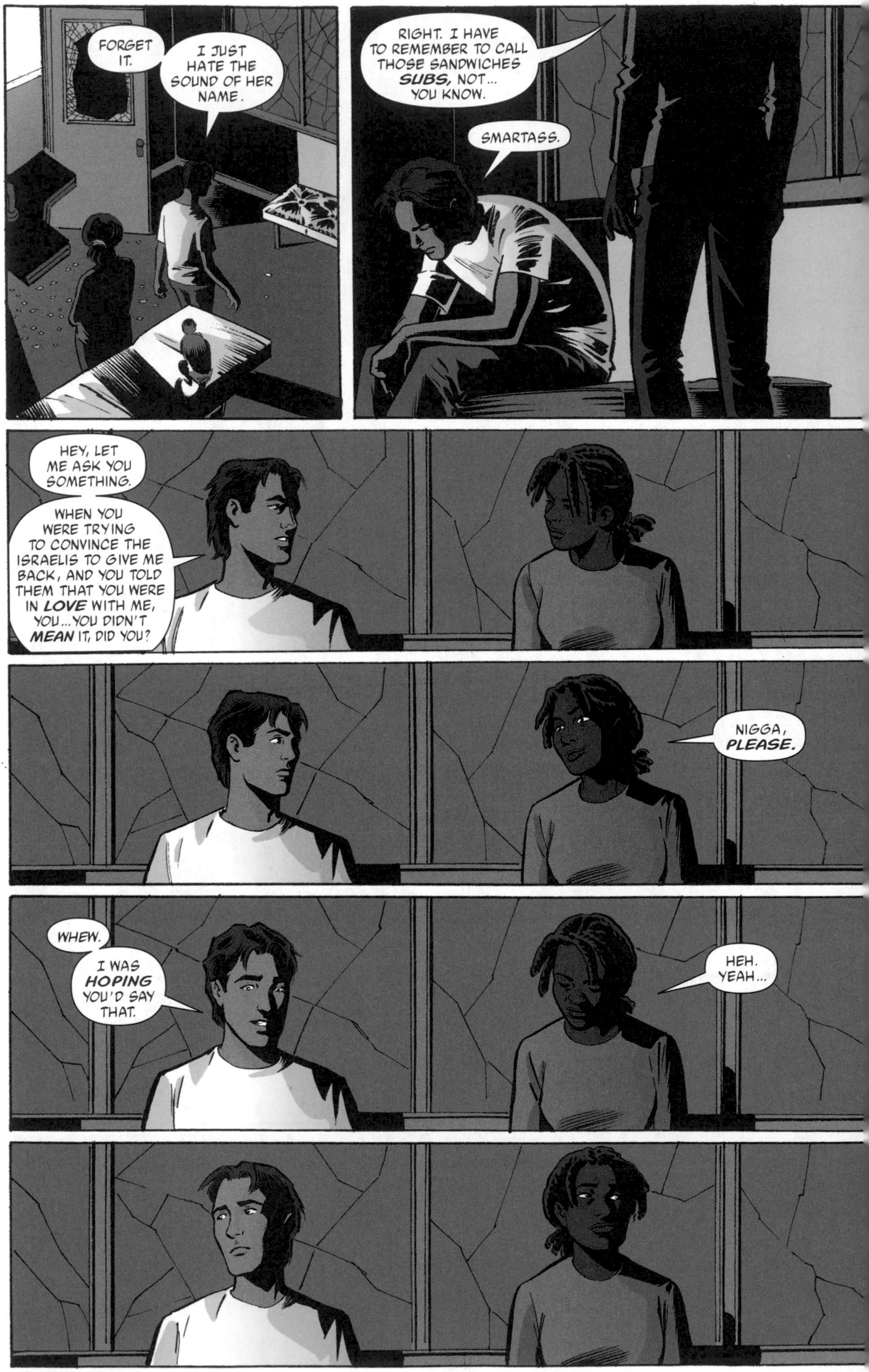
FORGET IT.
I JUST HATE THE SOUND OF HER NAME.
RIGHT. I HAVE TO REMEMBER TO CALL THOSE SANDWICHES SUBS, NOT... YOU KNOW.
SMARTASS.
HEY, LET ME ASK YOU SOMETHING.
WHEN YOU WERE TRYING TO CONVINCE THE ISRAELIS TO GIVE ME BACK, AND YOU TOLD THEM THAT YOU WERE IN LOVE WITH ME, YOU...YOU DIDN'T MEAN IT, DID YOU?
NIGGA, PLEASE.
WHEW.
I WAS HOPING YOU'D SAY THAT.
HEH. YEAH...

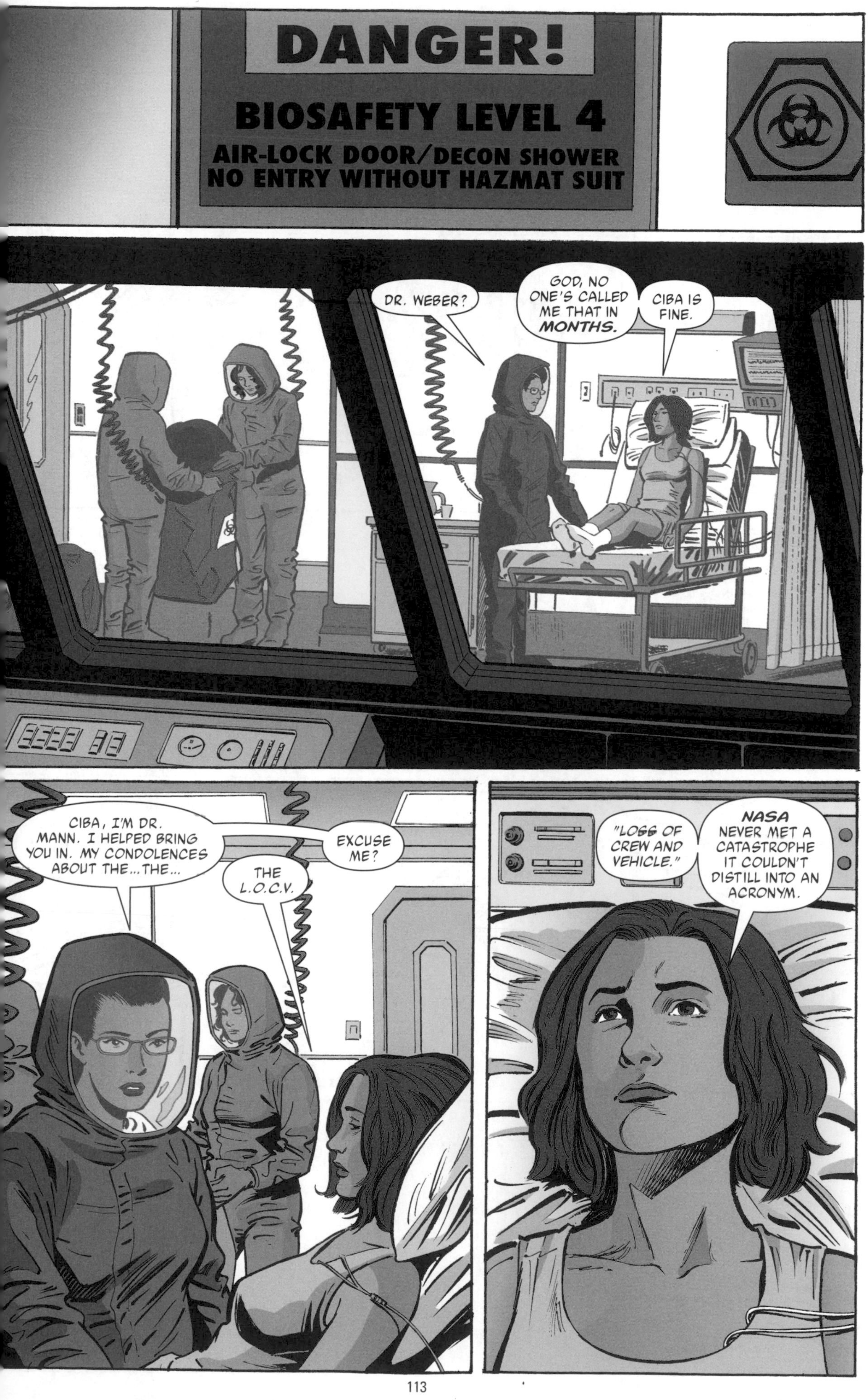
DANGER!
BIOSAFETY LEVEL 4
AIR-LOCK DOOR/DECON SHOWER
NO ENTRY WITHOUT HAZMAT SUIT
DR. WEBER?
GOD, NO ONE'S CALLED ME THAT IN MONTHS.
CIBA IS FINE.
CIBA, I'M DR. MANN. I HELPED BRING YOU IN. MY CONDOLENCES ABOUT THE...THE...
EXCUSE ME?
THE L.O.C.V.
"LOSS OF CREW AND VEHICLE."
NASA NEVER MET A CATASTROPHE IT COULDN'T DISTILL INTO AN ACRONYM.

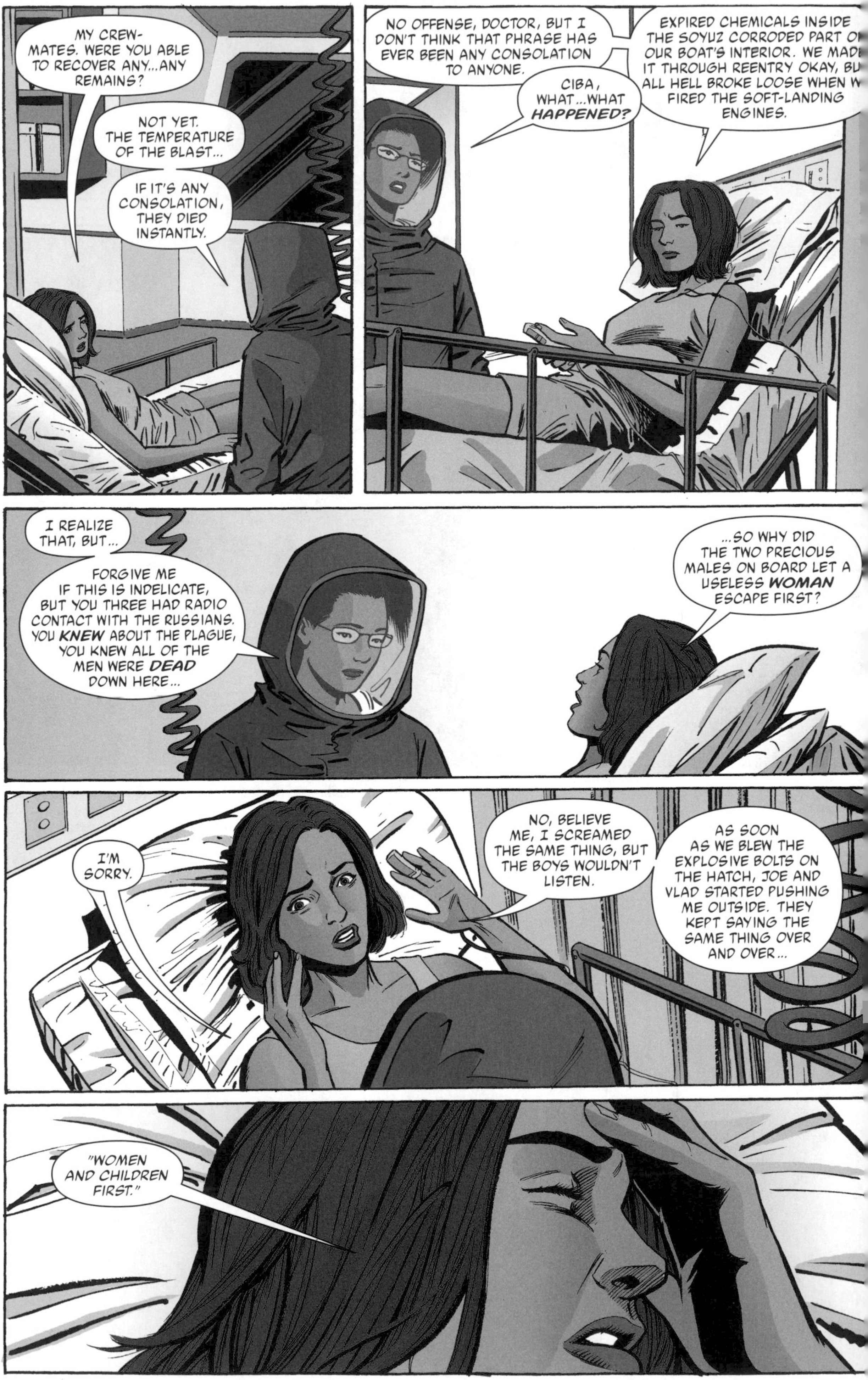
MY CREW-MATES. WERE YOU ABLE TO RECOVER ANY...ANY REMAINS?
NOT YET. THE TEMPERATURE OF THE BLAST...
IF IT'S ANY CONSOLATION, THEY DIED INSTANTLY.
NO OFFENSE, DOCTOR, BUT I DON'T THINK THAT PHRASE HAS EVER BEEN ANY CONSOLATION TO ANYONE.
CIBA, WHAT...WHAT *HAPPENED?*
EXPIRED CHEMICALS INSIDE THE SOYUZ CORRODED PART O OUR BOAT'S INTERIOR. WE MAD IT THROUGH REENTRY OKAY, BU ALL HELL BROKE LOOSE WHEN W FIRED THE SOFT-LANDING ENGINES.
I REALIZE THAT, BUT...
FORGIVE ME IF THIS IS INDELICATE, BUT YOU THREE HAD RADIO CONTACT WITH THE RUSSIANS. YOU *KNEW* ABOUT THE PLAGUE, YOU KNEW ALL OF THE MEN WERE *DEAD* DOWN HERE...
...SO WHY DID THE TWO PRECIOUS MALES ON BOARD LET A USELESS *WOMAN* ESCAPE FIRST?
I'M SORRY.
NO, BELIEVE ME, I SCREAMED THE SAME THING, BUT THE BOYS WOULDN'T LISTEN.
AS SOON AS WE BLEW THE EXPLOSIVE BOLTS ON THE HATCH, JOE AND VLAD STARTED PUSHING ME OUTSIDE. THEY KEPT SAYING THE SAME THING OVER AND OVER...
"WOMEN AND CHILDREN FIRST."

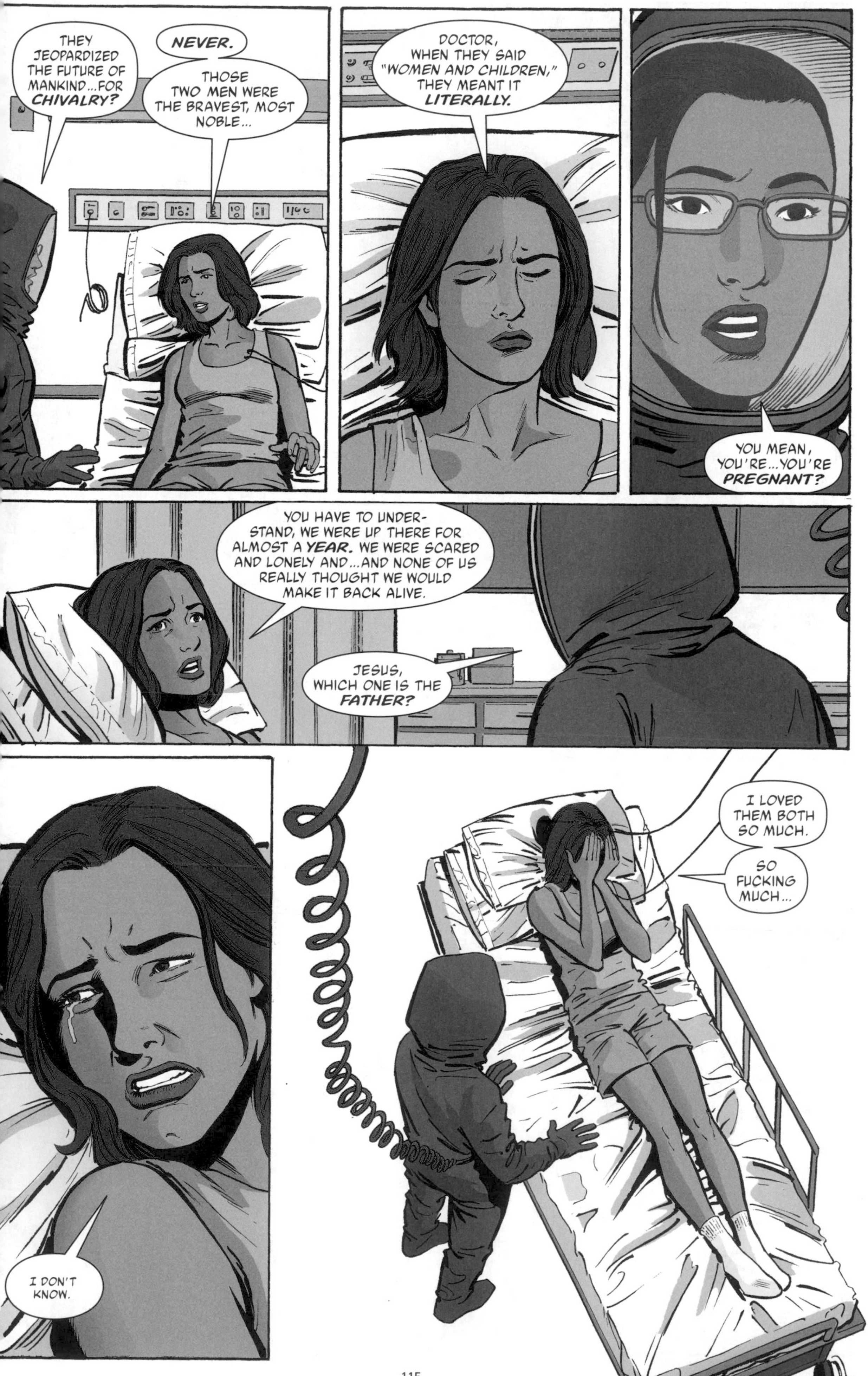
THEY JEOPARDIZED THE FUTURE OF MANKIND...FOR CHIVALRY?
NEVER.
THOSE TWO MEN WERE THE BRAVEST, MOST NOBLE...
DOCTOR, WHEN THEY SAID "WOMEN AND CHILDREN," THEY MEANT IT LITERALLY.
YOU MEAN, YOU'RE...YOU'RE PREGNANT?
YOU HAVE TO UNDER-STAND, WE WERE UP THERE FOR ALMOST A YEAR. WE WERE SCARED AND LONELY AND...AND NONE OF US REALLY THOUGHT WE WOULD MAKE IT BACK ALIVE.
JESUS, WHICH ONE IS THE FATHER?
I DON'T KNOW.
I LOVED THEM BOTH SO MUCH.
SO FUCKING MUCH...

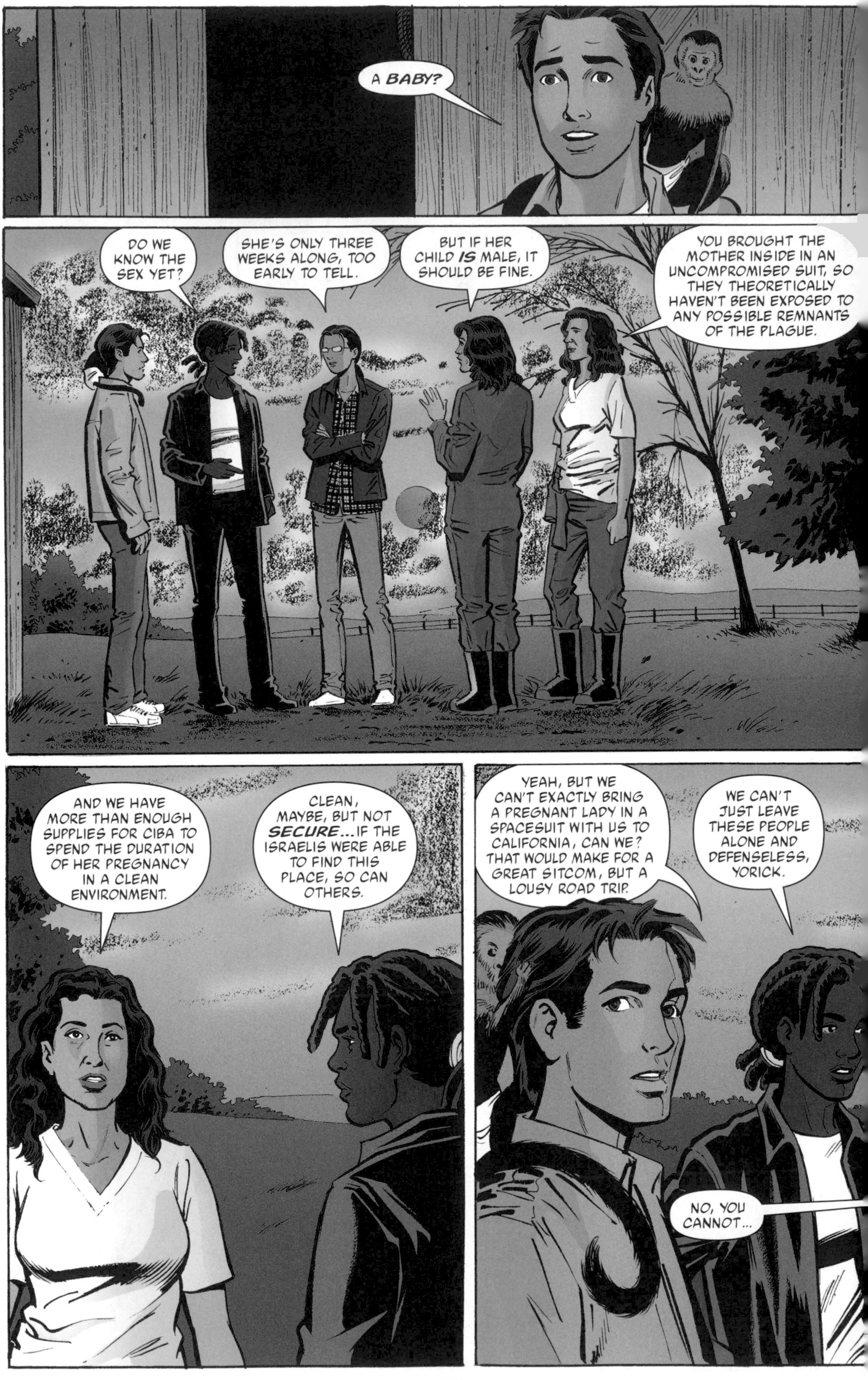
A BABY?
DO WE KNOW THE SEX YET?
SHE'S ONLY THREE WEEKS ALONG, TOO EARLY TO TELL.
BUT IF HER CHILD IS MALE, IT SHOULD BE FINE.
YOU BROUGHT THE MOTHER INSIDE IN AN UNCOMPROMISED SUIT, SO THEY THEORETICALLY HAVEN'T BEEN EXPOSED TO ANY POSSIBLE REMNANTS OF THE PLAGUE.
AND WE HAVE MORE THAN ENOUGH SUPPLIES FOR CIBA TO SPEND THE DURATION OF HER PREGNANCY IN A CLEAN ENVIRONMENT.
CLEAN, MAYBE, BUT NOT SECURE... IF THE ISRAELIS WERE ABLE TO FIND THIS PLACE, SO CAN OTHERS.
YEAH, BUT WE CAN'T EXACTLY BRING A PREGNANT LADY IN A SPACESUIT WITH US TO CALIFORNIA, CAN WE? THAT WOULD MAKE FOR A GREAT SITCOM, BUT A LOUSY ROAD TRIP.
WE CAN'T JUST LEAVE THESE PEOPLE ALONE AND DEFENSELESS, YORICK.
NO, YOU CANNOT...

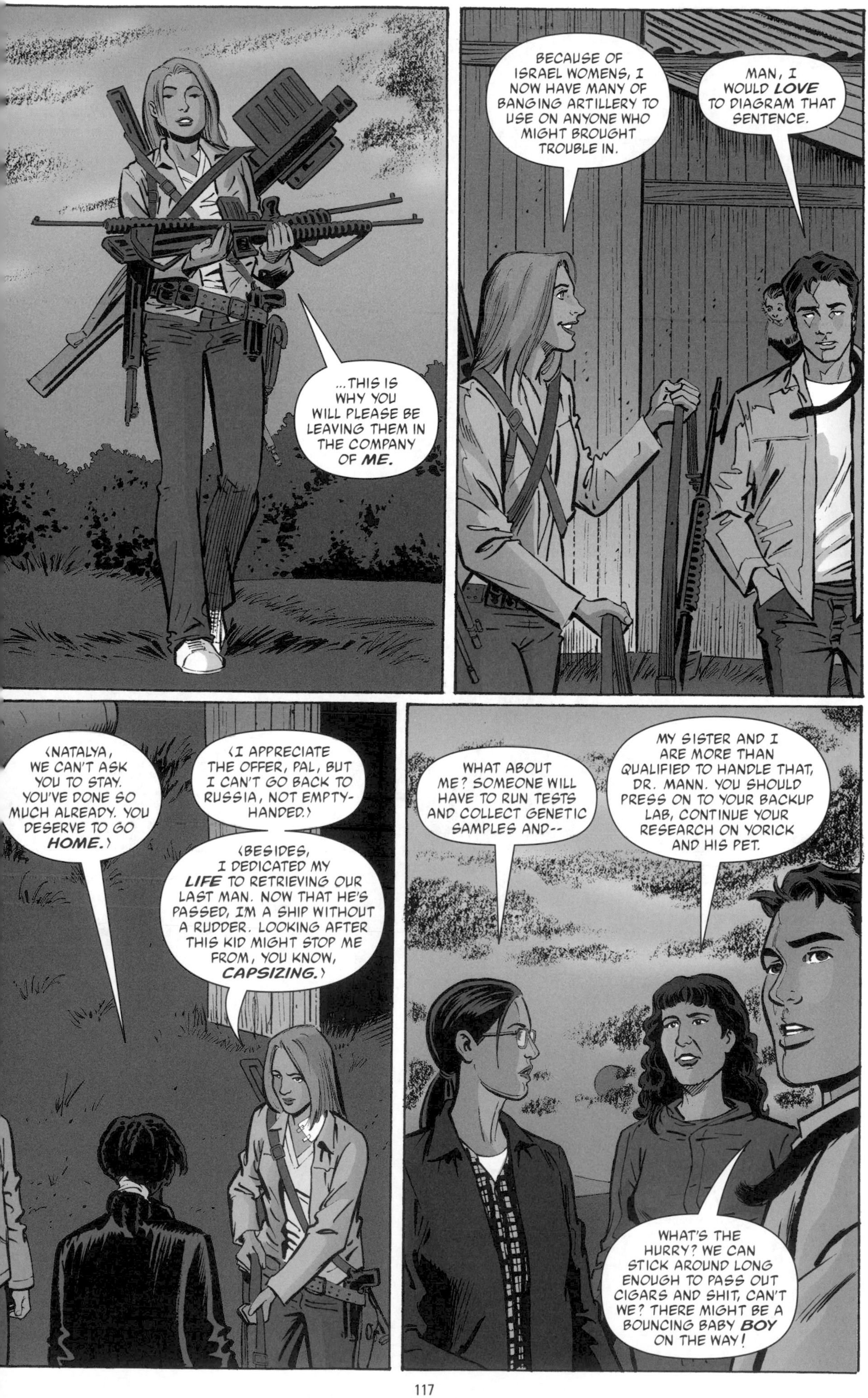
...THIS IS WHY YOU WILL PLEASE BE LEAVING THEM IN THE COMPANY OF ME.
BECAUSE OF ISRAEL WOMENS, I NOW HAVE MANY OF BANGING ARTILLERY TO USE ON ANYONE WHO MIGHT BROUGHT TROUBLE IN.
MAN, I WOULD LOVE TO DIAGRAM THAT SENTENCE.
‹NATALYA, WE CAN'T ASK YOU TO STAY. YOU'VE DONE SO MUCH ALREADY. YOU DESERVE TO GO HOME.›
‹I APPRECIATE THE OFFER, PAL, BUT I CAN'T GO BACK TO RUSSIA, NOT EMPTY-HANDED.›
‹BESIDES, I DEDICATED MY LIFE TO RETRIEVING OUR LAST MAN. NOW THAT HE'S PASSED, I'M A SHIP WITHOUT A RUDDER. LOOKING AFTER THIS KID MIGHT STOP ME FROM, YOU KNOW, CAPSIZING.›
WHAT ABOUT ME? SOMEONE WILL HAVE TO RUN TESTS AND COLLECT GENETIC SAMPLES AND--
MY SISTER AND I ARE MORE THAN QUALIFIED TO HANDLE THAT, DR. MANN. YOU SHOULD PRESS ON TO YOUR BACKUP LAB, CONTINUE YOUR RESEARCH ON YORICK AND HIS PET.
WHAT'S THE HURRY? WE CAN STICK AROUND LONG ENOUGH TO PASS OUT CIGARS AND SHIT, CAN'T WE? THERE MIGHT BE A BOUNCING BABY BOY ON THE WAY!

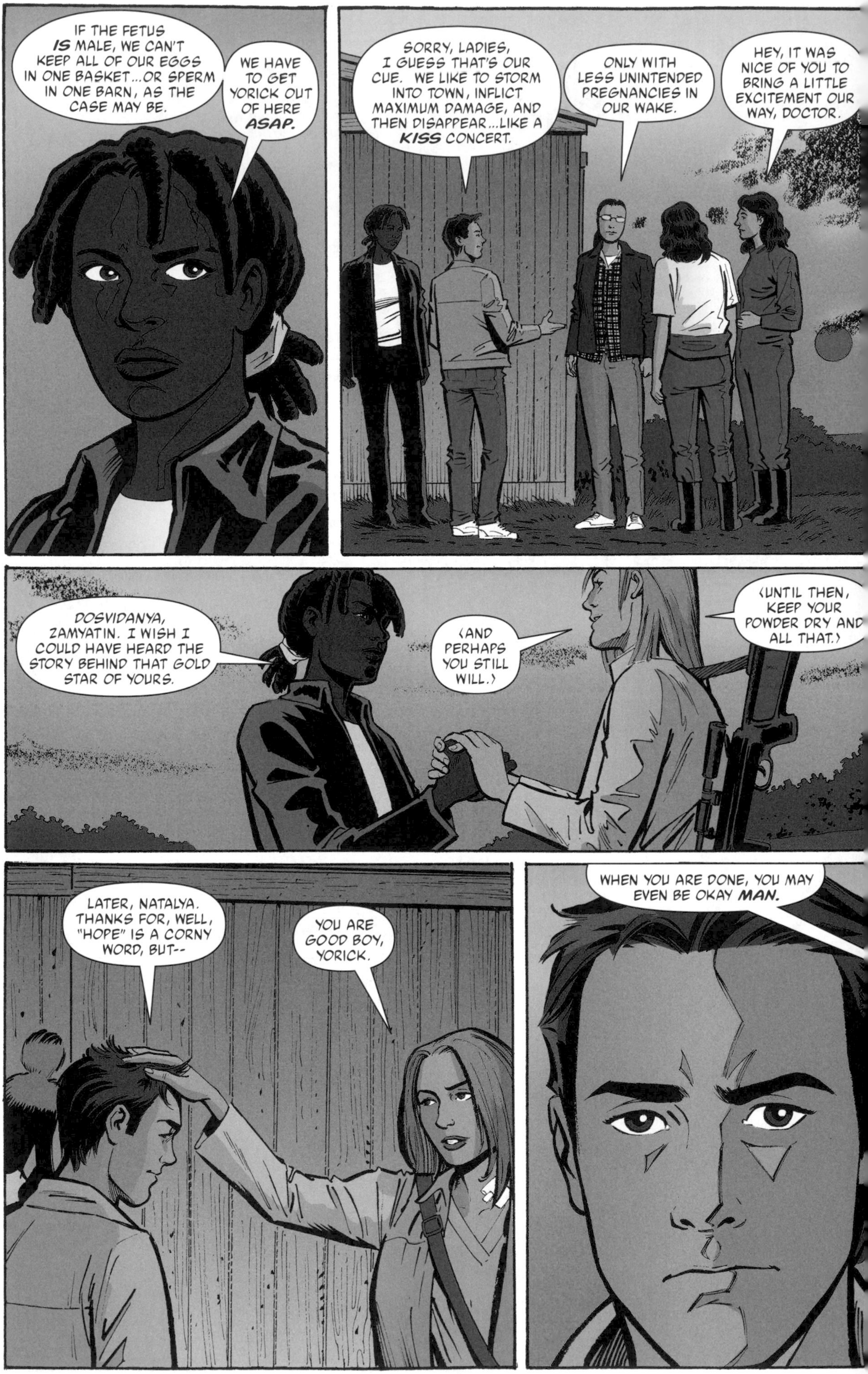
IF THE FETUS IS MALE, WE CAN'T KEEP ALL OF OUR EGGS IN ONE BASKET...OR SPERM IN ONE BARN, AS THE CASE MAY BE.
WE HAVE TO GET YORICK OUT OF HERE ASAP.
SORRY, LADIES, I GUESS THAT'S OUR CUE. WE LIKE TO STORM INTO TOWN, INFLICT MAXIMUM DAMAGE, AND THEN DISAPPEAR...LIKE A KISS CONCERT.
ONLY WITH LESS UNINTENDED PREGNANCIES IN OUR WAKE.
HEY, IT WAS NICE OF YOU TO BRING A LITTLE EXCITEMENT OUR WAY, DOCTOR.
DOSVIDANYA, ZAMYATIN. I WISH I COULD HAVE HEARD THE STORY BEHIND THAT GOLD STAR OF YOURS.
<AND PERHAPS YOU STILL WILL.>
<UNTIL THEN, KEEP YOUR POWDER DRY AND ALL THAT.>
LATER, NATALYA. THANKS FOR, WELL, "HOPE" IS A CORNY WORD, BUT--
YOU ARE GOOD BOY, YORICK.
WHEN YOU ARE DONE, YOU MAY EVEN BE OKAY MAN.

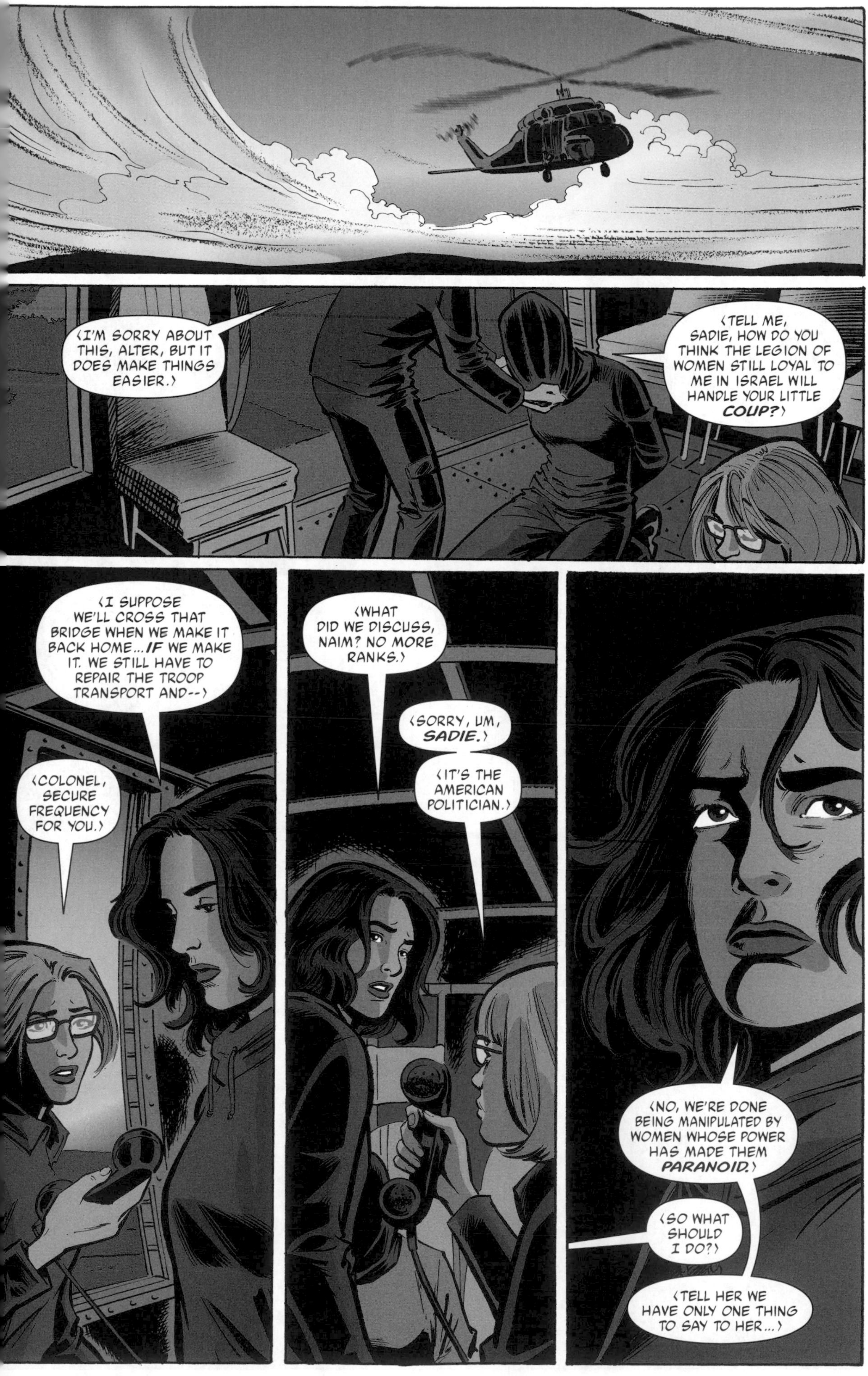

‹I'M SORRY ABOUT THIS, ALTER, BUT IT DOES MAKE THINGS EASIER.›
‹TELL ME, SADIE, HOW DO YOU THINK THE LEGION OF WOMEN STILL LOYAL TO ME IN ISRAEL WILL HANDLE YOUR LITTLE COUP?›
‹I SUPPOSE WE'LL CROSS THAT BRIDGE WHEN WE MAKE IT BACK HOME... IF WE MAKE IT. WE STILL HAVE TO REPAIR THE TROOP TRANSPORT AND--›
‹COLONEL, SECURE FREQUENCY FOR YOU.›
‹WHAT DID WE DISCUSS, NAIM? NO MORE RANKS.›
‹SORRY, UM, SADIE.›
‹IT'S THE AMERICAN POLITICIAN.›
‹NO, WE'RE DONE BEING MANIPULATED BY WOMEN WHOSE POWER HAS MADE THEM PARANOID.›
‹SO WHAT SHOULD I DO?›
‹TELL HER WE HAVE ONLY ONE THING TO SAY TO HER...›

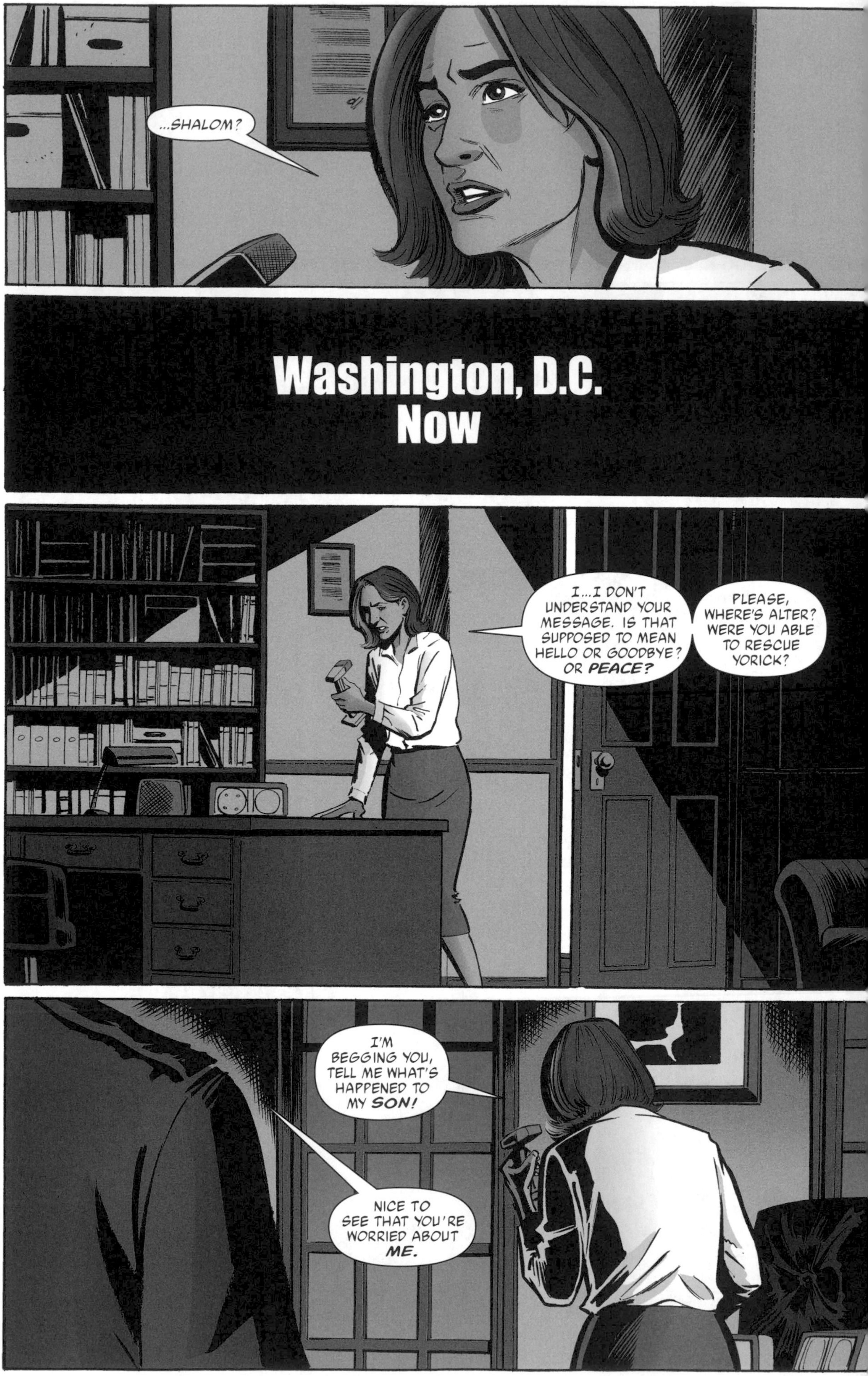
...SHALOM?
Washington, D.C.
Now
I...I DON'T UNDERSTAND YOUR MESSAGE. IS THAT SUPPOSED TO MEAN HELLO OR GOODBYE? OR PEACE?
PLEASE, WHERE'S ALTER? WERE YOU ABLE TO RESCUE YORICK?
I'M BEGGING YOU, TELL ME WHAT'S HAPPENED TO MY SON!
NICE TO SEE THAT YOU'RE WORRIED ABOUT ME.

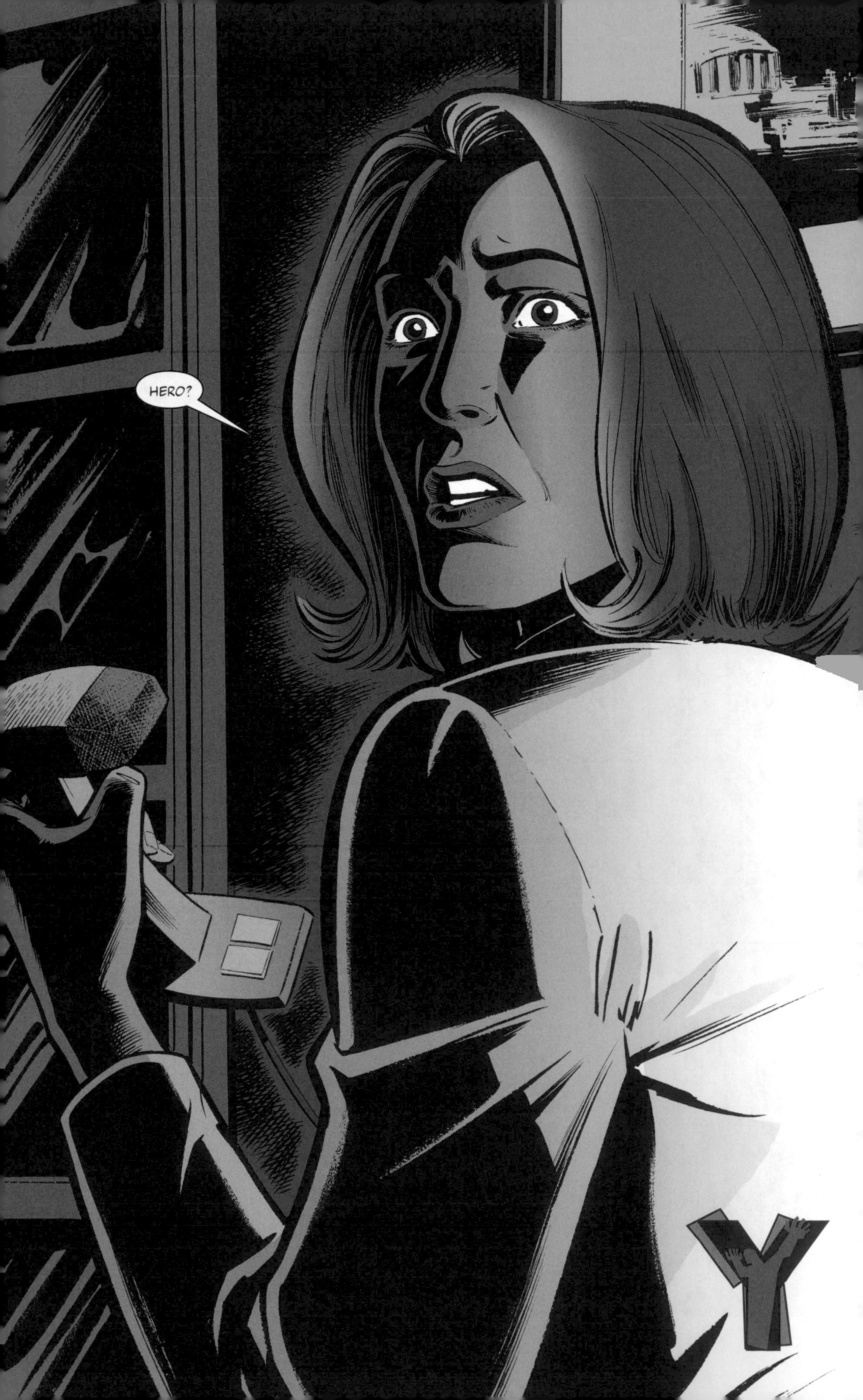
HERO?

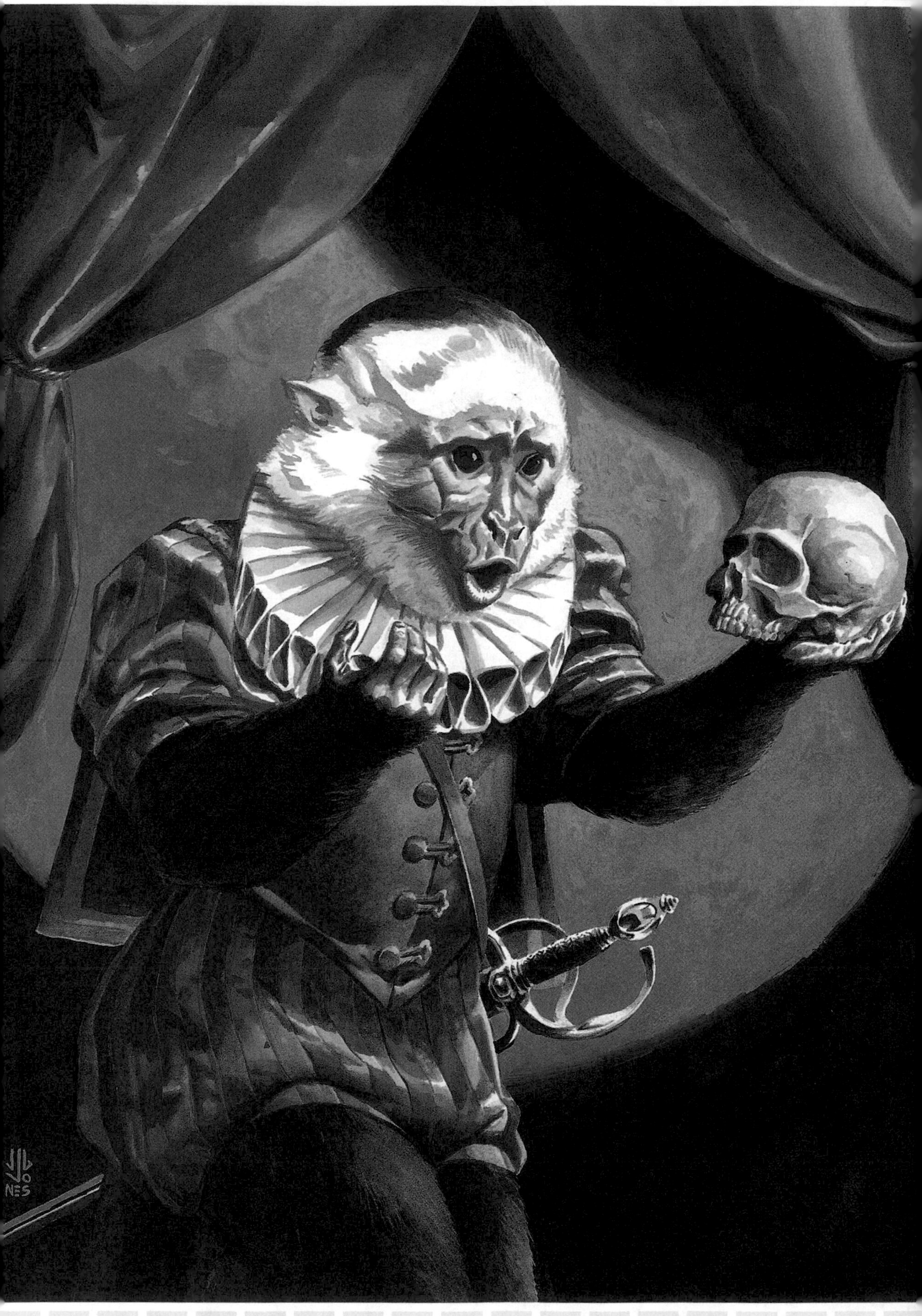

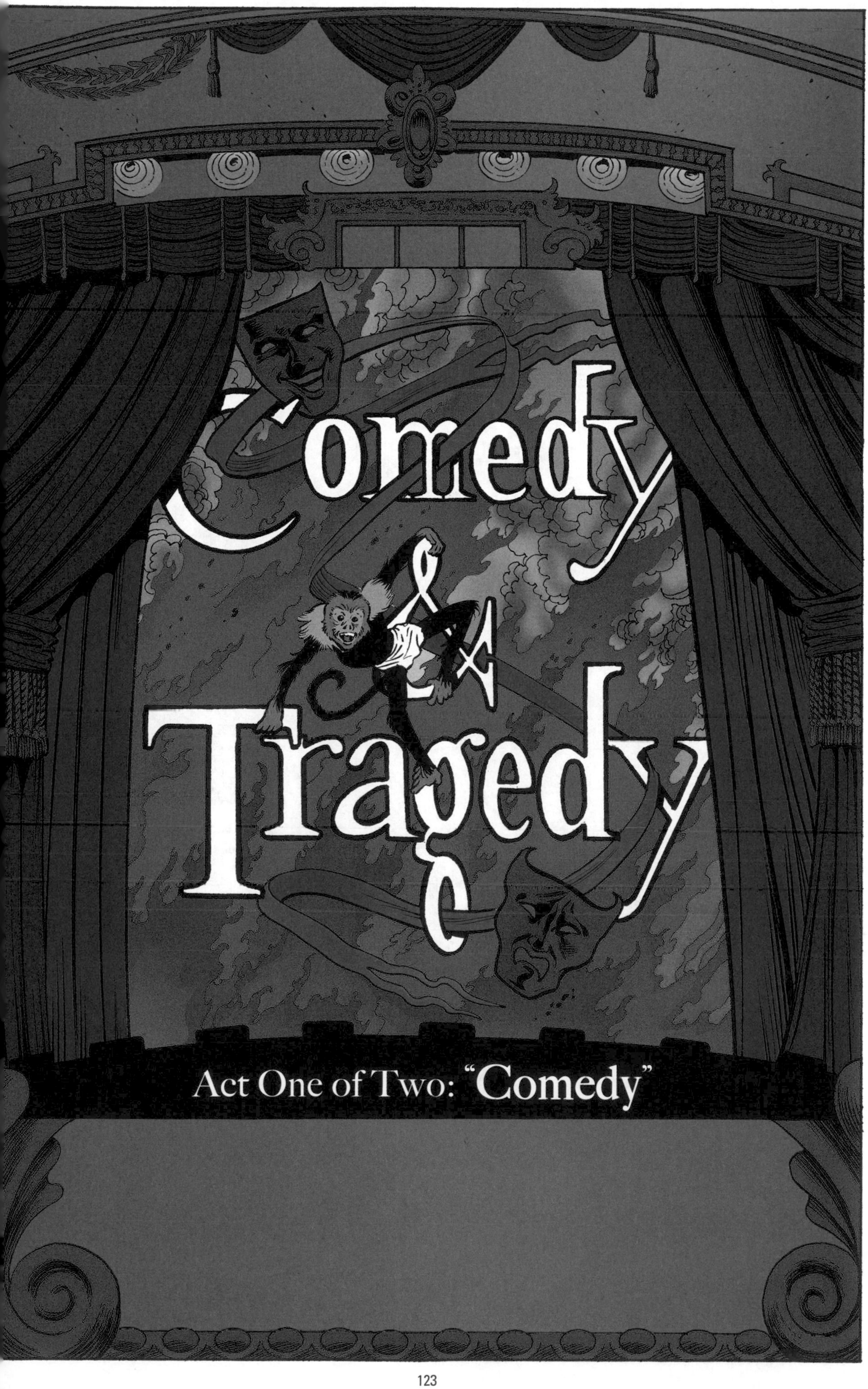
Comedy
&
Tragedy
Act One of Two: "Comedy"

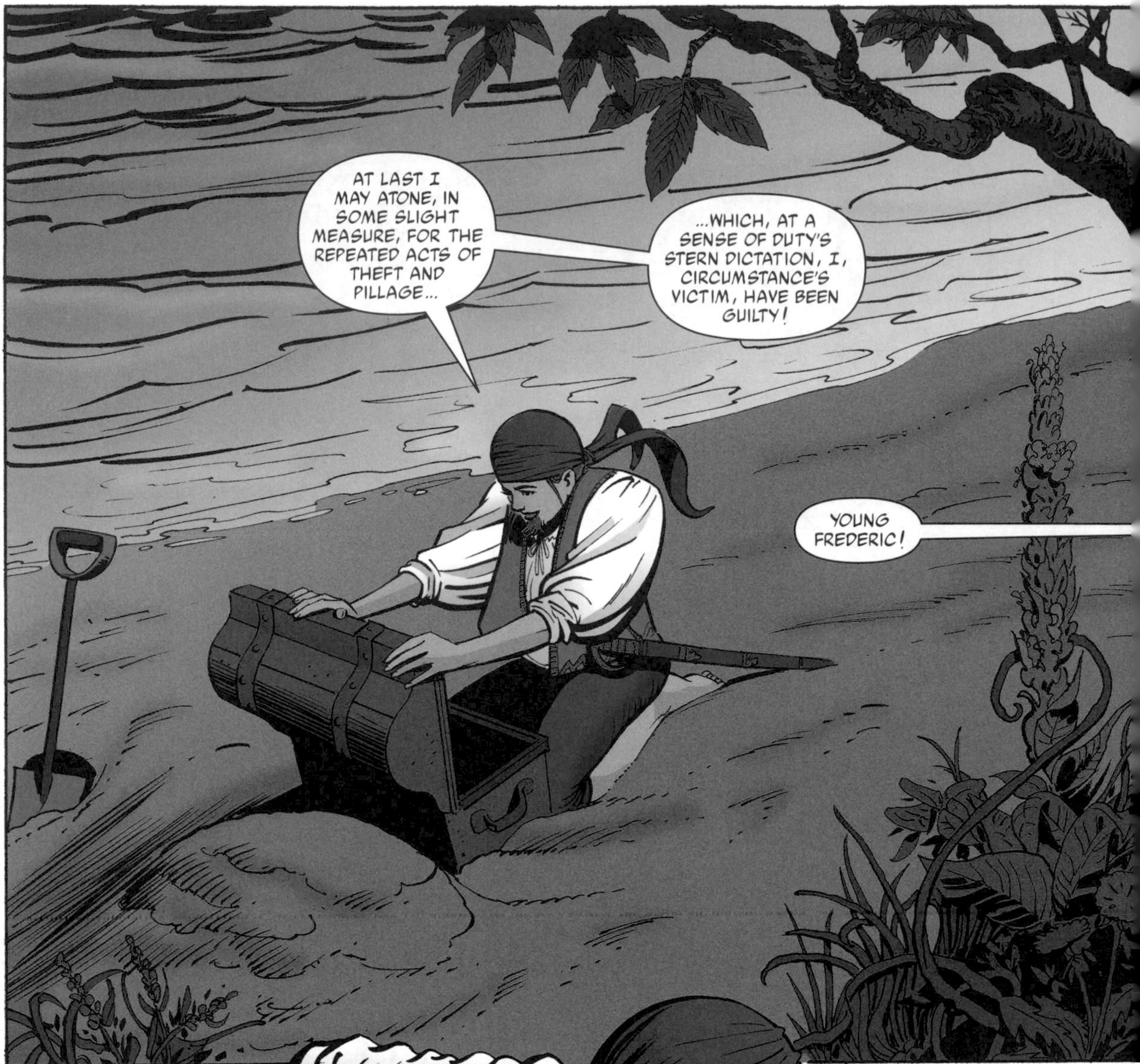
AT LAST I MAY ATONE, IN SOME SLIGHT MEASURE, FOR THE REPEATED ACTS OF THEFT AND PILLAGE...
...WHICH, AT A SENSE OF DUTY'S STERN DICTATION, I, CIRCUMSTANCE'S VICTIM, HAVE BEEN GUILTY!
YOUNG FREDERIC!

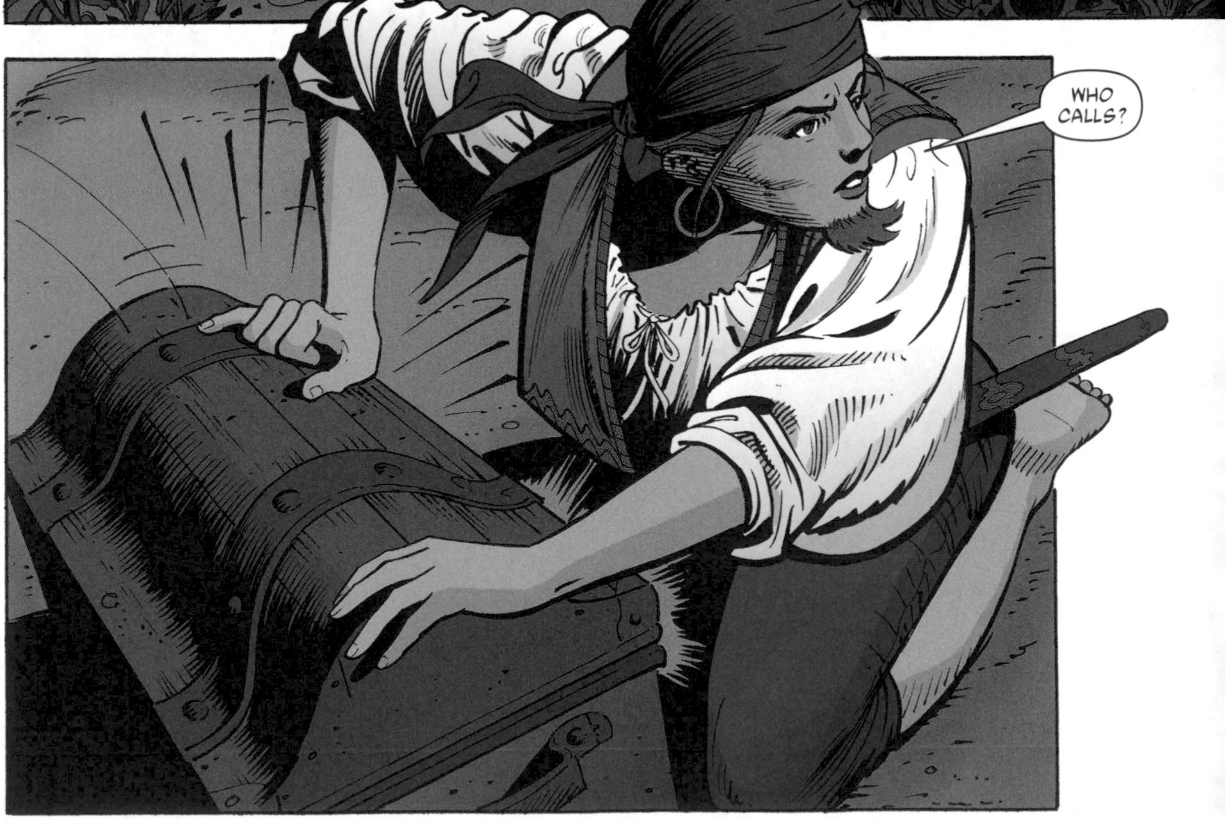
WHO CALLS?

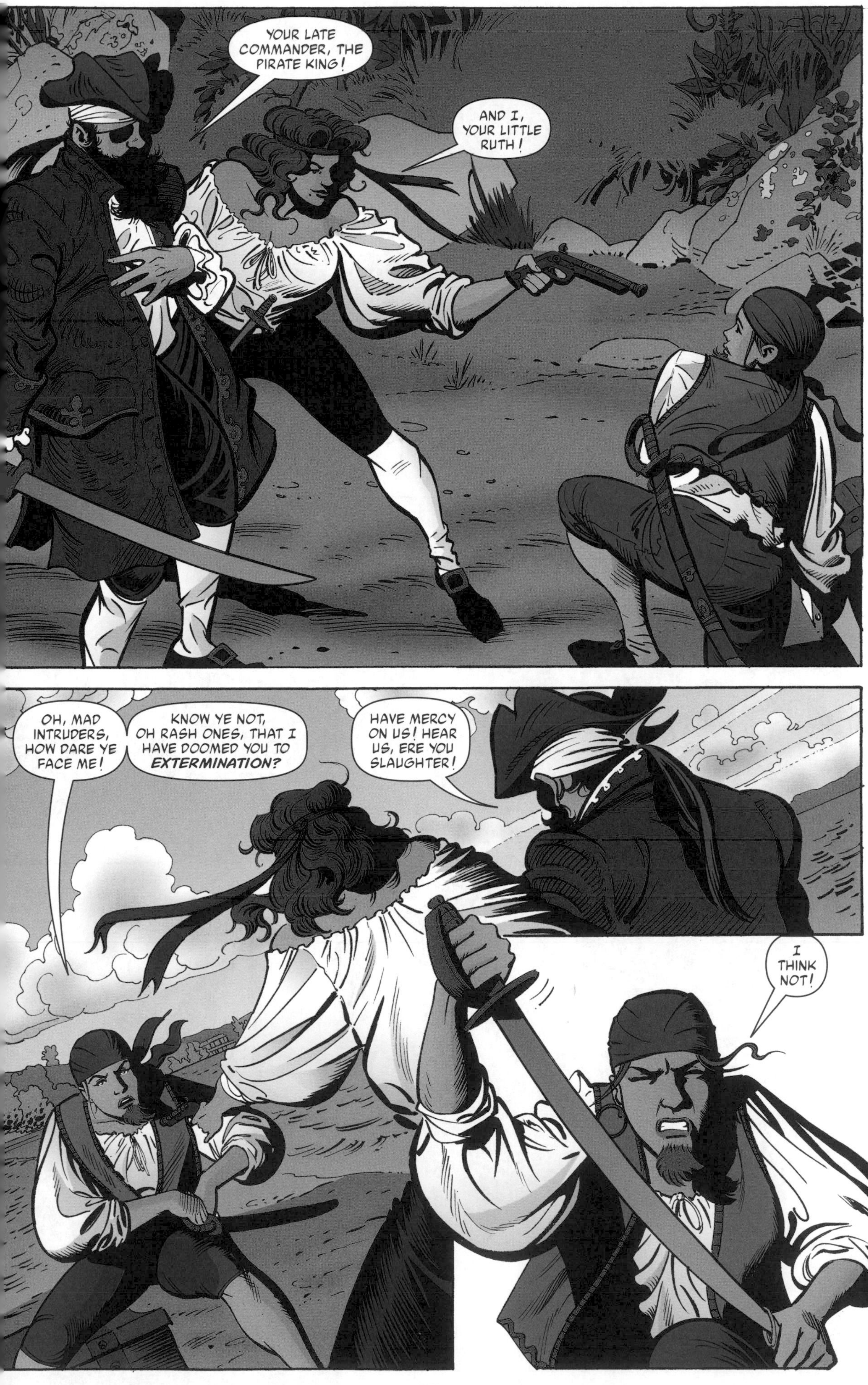
YOUR LATE COMMANDER, THE PIRATE KING!
AND I, YOUR LITTLE RUTH!
OH, MAD INTRUDERS, HOW DARE YE FACE ME!
KNOW YE NOT, OH RASH ONES, THAT I HAVE DOOMED YOU TO **EXTERMINATION?**
HAVE MERCY ON US! HEAR US, ERE YOU SLAUGHTER!
I THINK NOT!

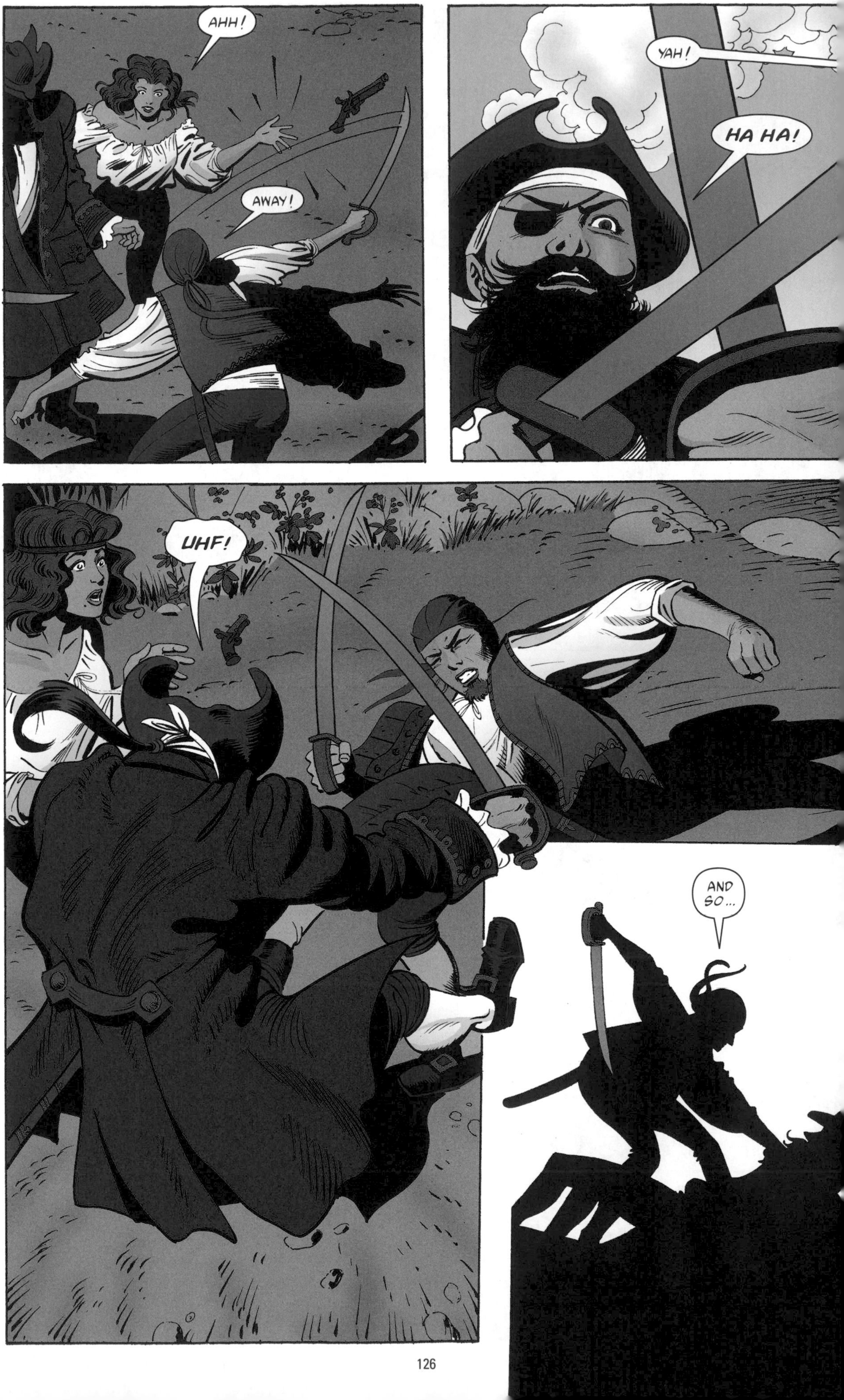
AHH!
AWAY!
YAH!
HA HA!
UHF!
AND SO...

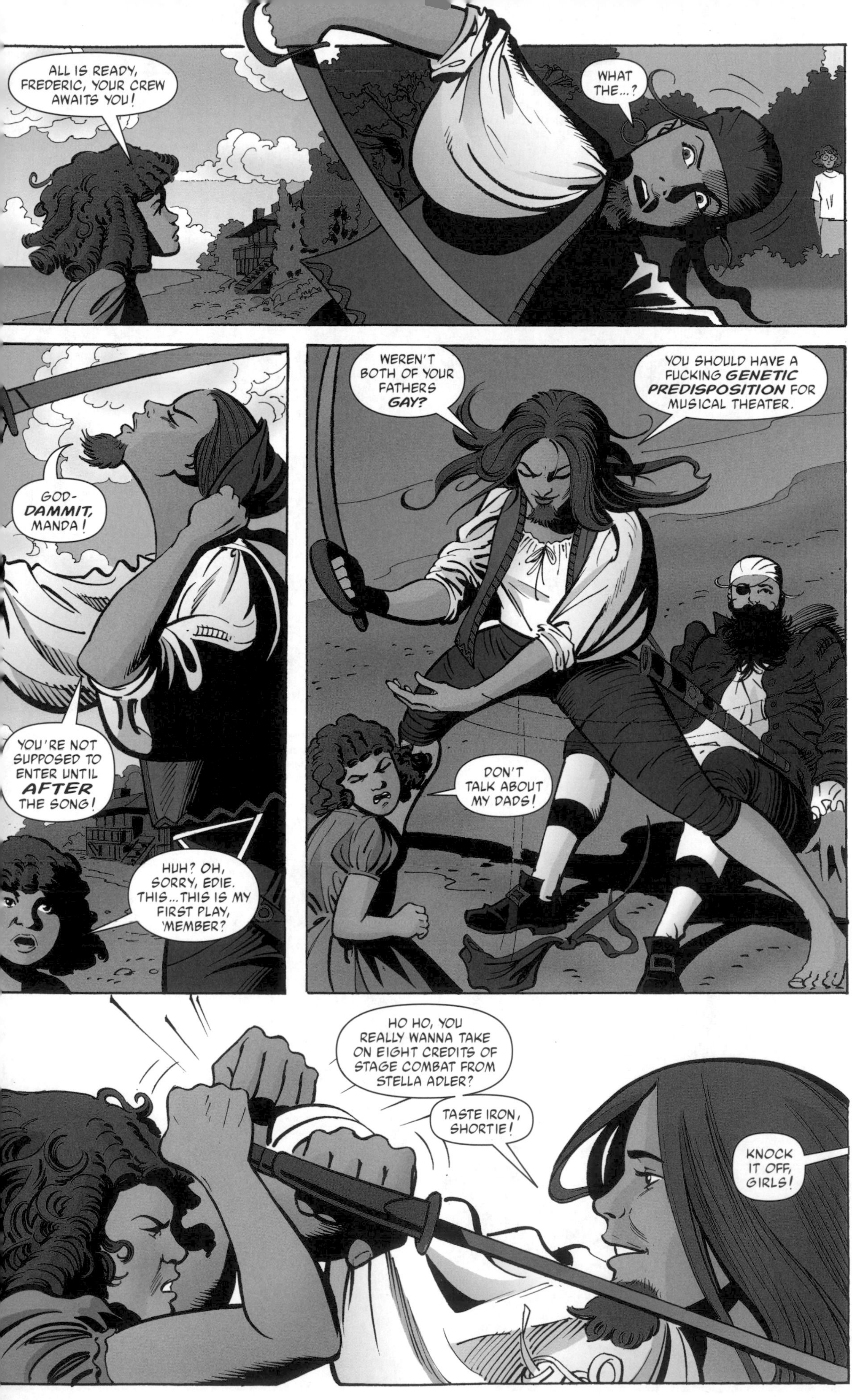
ALL IS READY, FREDERIC, YOUR CREW AWAITS YOU!
WHAT THE...?
GOD-DAMMIT, MANDA!
YOU'RE NOT SUPPOSED TO ENTER UNTIL AFTER THE SONG!
HUH? OH, SORRY, EDIE. THIS...THIS IS MY FIRST PLAY, 'MEMBER?
WEREN'T BOTH OF YOUR FATHERS GAY?
YOU SHOULD HAVE A FUCKING GENETIC PREDISPOSITION FOR MUSICAL THEATER.
DON'T TALK ABOUT MY DADS!
HO HO, YOU REALLY WANNA TAKE ON EIGHT CREDITS OF STAGE COMBAT FROM STELLA ADLER?
TASTE IRON, SHORTIE!
KNOCK IT OFF, GIRLS!

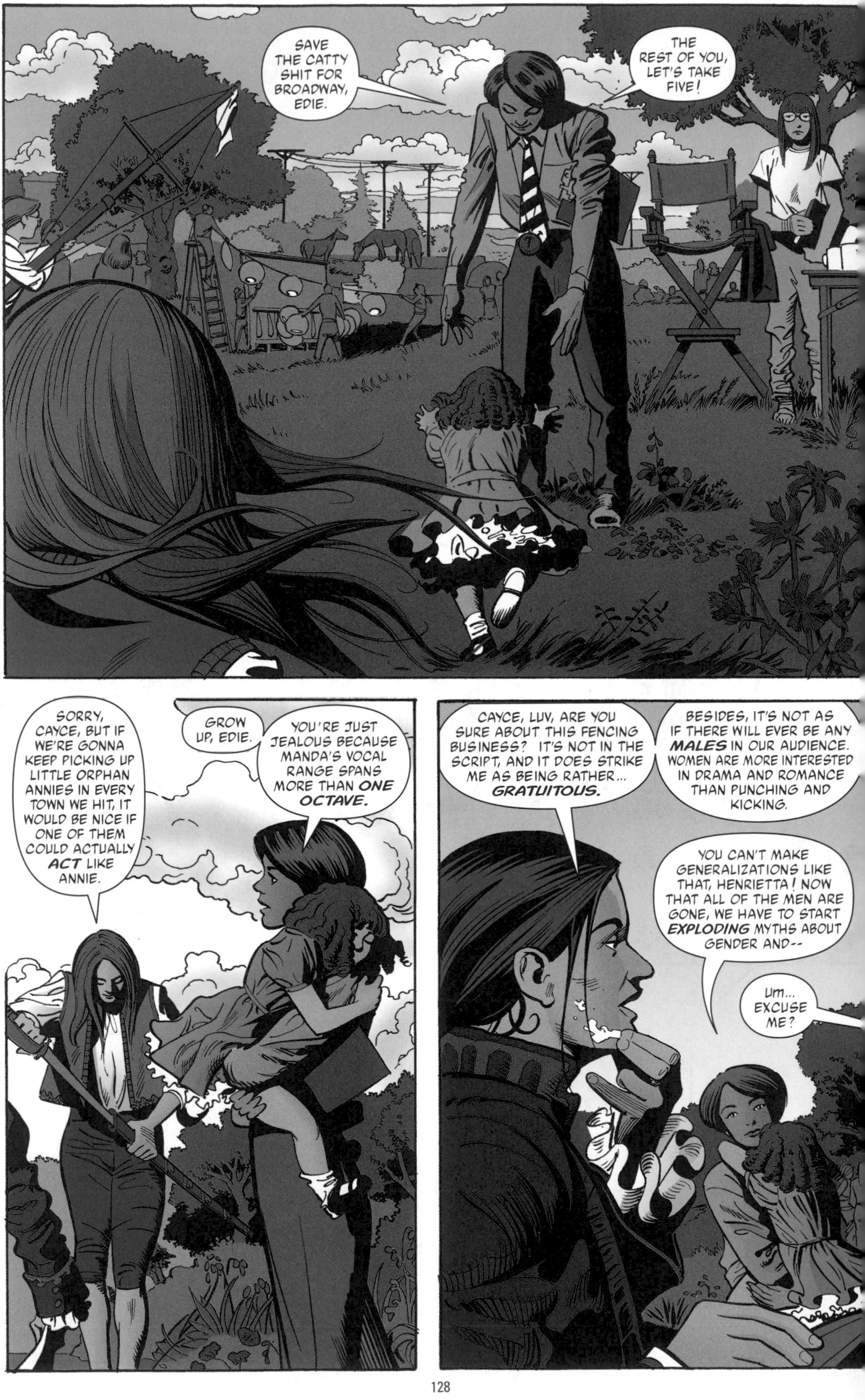
SAVE THE CATTY SHIT FOR BROADWAY, EDIE.
THE REST OF YOU, LET'S TAKE FIVE!
SORRY, CAYCE, BUT IF WE'RE GONNA KEEP PICKING UP LITTLE ORPHAN ANNIES IN EVERY TOWN WE HIT, IT WOULD BE NICE IF ONE OF THEM COULD ACTUALLY ACT LIKE ANNIE.
GROW UP, EDIE.
YOU'RE JUST JEALOUS BECAUSE MANDA'S VOCAL RANGE SPANS MORE THAN ONE OCTAVE.
CAYCE, LUV, ARE YOU SURE ABOUT THIS FENCING BUSINESS? IT'S NOT IN THE SCRIPT, AND IT DOES STRIKE ME AS BEING RATHER... GRATUITOUS.
BESIDES, IT'S NOT AS IF THERE WILL EVER BE ANY MALES IN OUR AUDIENCE. WOMEN ARE MORE INTERESTED IN DRAMA AND ROMANCE THAN PUNCHING AND KICKING.
YOU CAN'T MAKE GENERALIZATIONS LIKE THAT, HENRIETTA! NOW THAT ALL OF THE MEN ARE GONE, WE HAVE TO START EXPLODING MYTHS ABOUT GENDER AND--
UM... EXCUSE ME?

ARE YOU PEOPLE THE PLAY ACTORS?

I...I WAS GIVEN A *FLYER.*

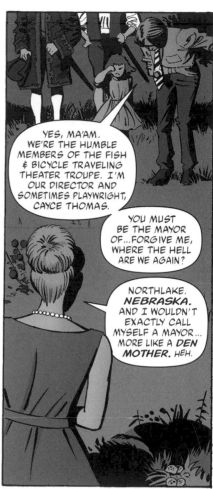

YES, MA'AM. WE'RE THE HUMBLE MEMBERS OF THE FISH & BICYCLE TRAVELING THEATER TROUPE. I'M OUR DIRECTOR AND SOMETIMES PLAYWRIGHT, CAYCE THOMAS.

YOU MUST BE THE MAYOR OF...FORGIVE ME, WHERE THE HELL ARE WE AGAIN?

NORTHLAKE. *NEBRASKA.* AND I WOULDN'T EXACTLY CALL MYSELF A MAYOR... MORE LIKE A *DEN MOTHER.* HEH.

SO, YOU FOLKS PUT ON SHOWS AND WHATNOT?

WE TRY OUR BEST. MY COMPANIONS AND I REPRESENT A CONFEDERATION OF CREATORS AND PERFORMERS WHO BANDED TOGETHER AFTER THE PLAGUE STRUCK.

WITH THE LACK OF DEPENDABLE ELECTRICITY THROUGHOUT THE COUNTRY, WE REALIZE THAT MOVIES, TELEVISION AND EVEN RADIO ARE LARGELY UNAVAILABLE, SO WE BRING OUR LO-TECH BRAND OF ART FROM TOWN TO TOWN AND--

DO YOU TAKE REQUESTS?

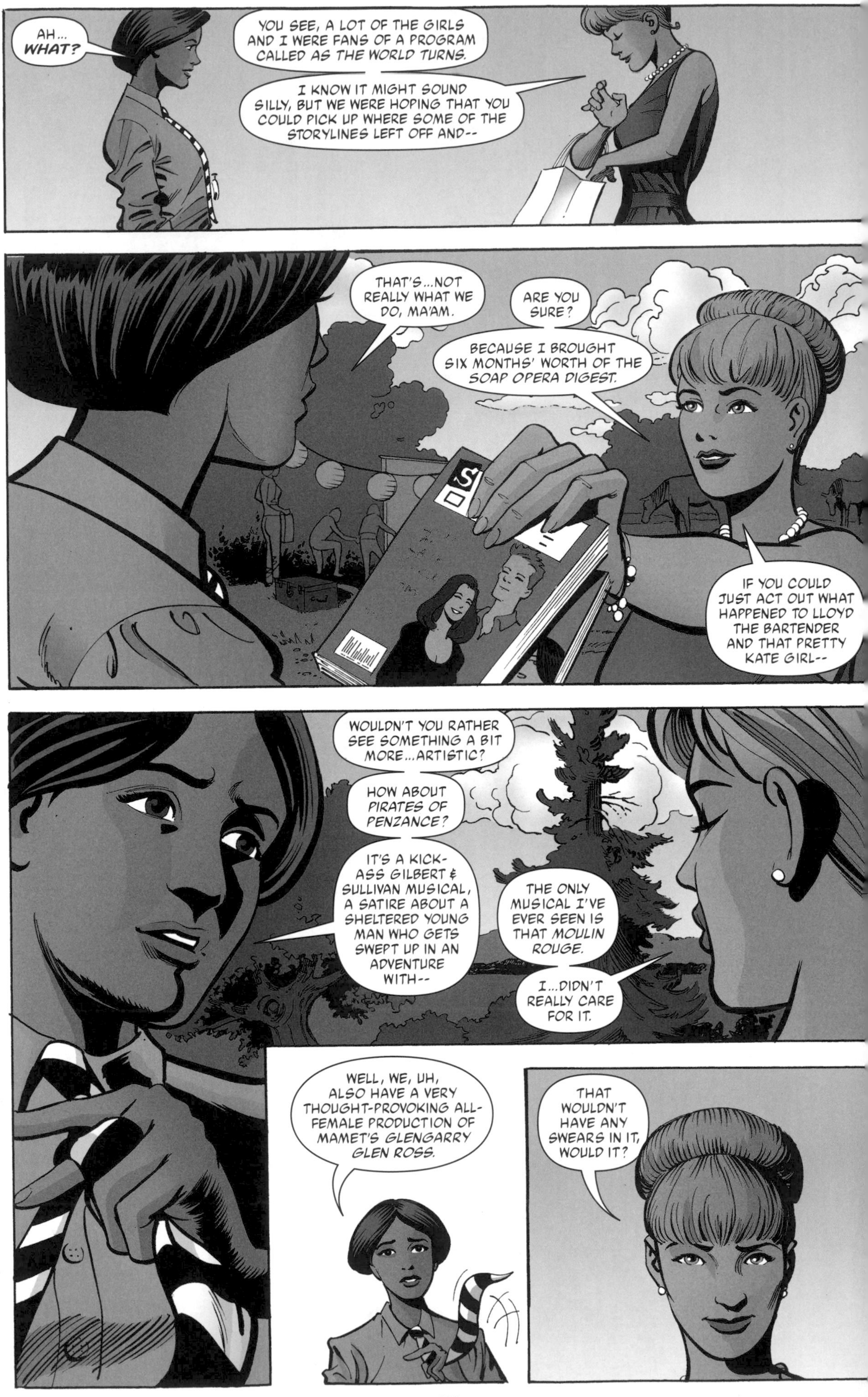
AH... WHAT?
YOU SEE, A LOT OF THE GIRLS AND I WERE FANS OF A PROGRAM CALLED AS THE WORLD TURNS.
I KNOW IT MIGHT SOUND SILLY, BUT WE WERE HOPING THAT YOU COULD PICK UP WHERE SOME OF THE STORYLINES LEFT OFF AND--
THAT'S...NOT REALLY WHAT WE DO, MA'AM.
ARE YOU SURE?
BECAUSE I BROUGHT SIX MONTHS' WORTH OF THE SOAP OPERA DIGEST.
IF YOU COULD JUST ACT OUT WHAT HAPPENED TO LLOYD THE BARTENDER AND THAT PRETTY KATE GIRL--
WOULDN'T YOU RATHER SEE SOMETHING A BIT MORE...ARTISTIC?
HOW ABOUT PIRATES OF PENZANCE?
IT'S A KICK-ASS GILBERT & SULLIVAN MUSICAL, A SATIRE ABOUT A SHELTERED YOUNG MAN WHO GETS SWEPT UP IN AN ADVENTURE WITH--
THE ONLY MUSICAL I'VE EVER SEEN IS THAT MOULIN ROUGE.
I...DIDN'T REALLY CARE FOR IT.
WELL, WE, UH, ALSO HAVE A VERY THOUGHT-PROVOKING ALL-FEMALE PRODUCTION OF MAMET'S GLENGARRY GLEN ROSS.
THAT WOULDN'T HAVE ANY SWEARS IN IT, WOULD IT?

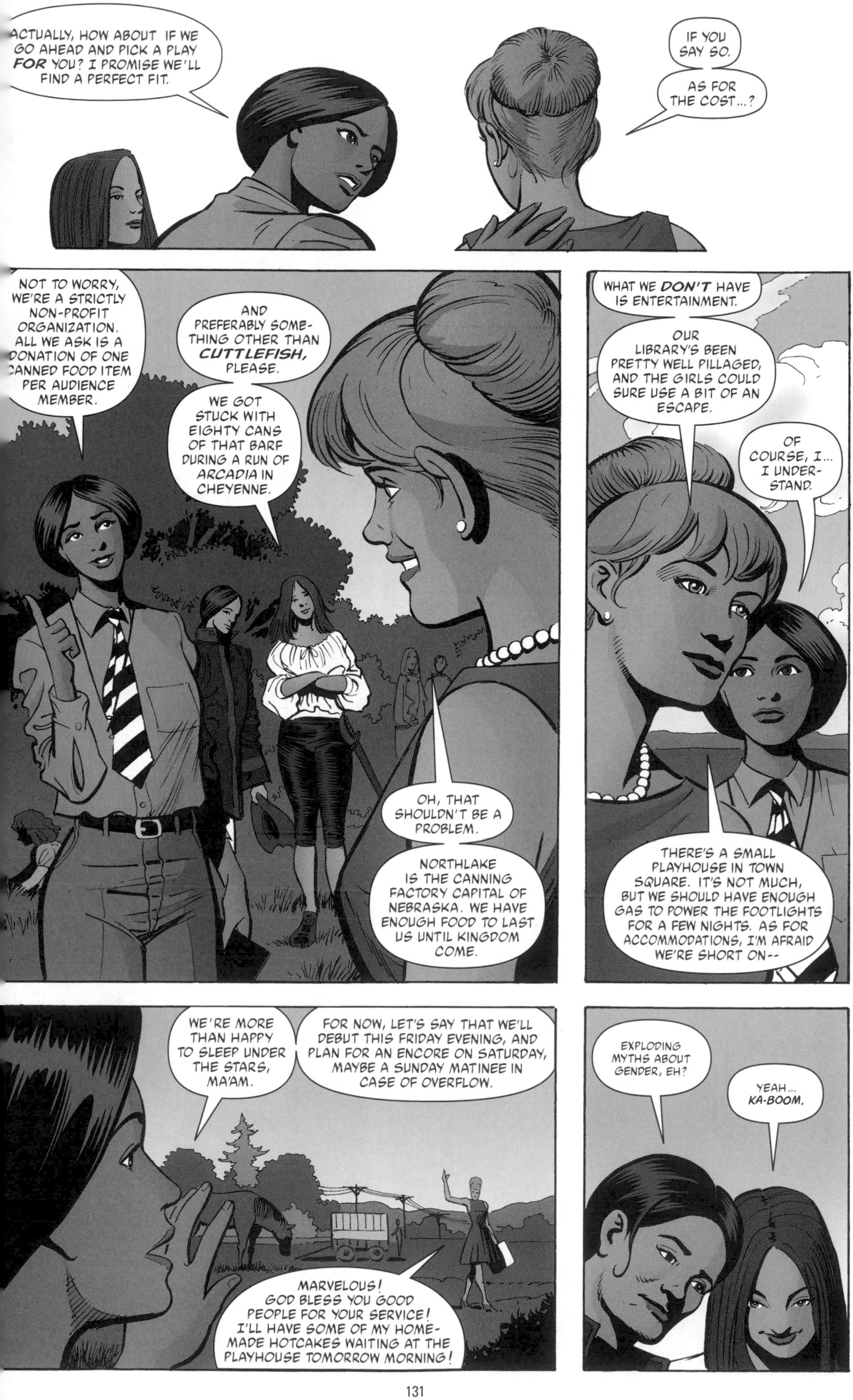
ACTUALLY, HOW ABOUT IF WE GO AHEAD AND PICK A PLAY **FOR** YOU? I PROMISE WE'LL FIND A PERFECT FIT.
IF YOU SAY SO.
AS FOR THE COST...?
NOT TO WORRY, WE'RE A STRICTLY NON-PROFIT ORGANIZATION. ALL WE ASK IS A DONATION OF ONE CANNED FOOD ITEM PER AUDIENCE MEMBER.
AND PREFERABLY SOMETHING OTHER THAN **CUTTLEFISH,** PLEASE.
WE GOT STUCK WITH EIGHTY CANS OF THAT BARF DURING A RUN OF ARCADIA IN CHEYENNE.
OH, THAT SHOULDN'T BE A PROBLEM.
NORTHLAKE IS THE CANNING FACTORY CAPITAL OF NEBRASKA. WE HAVE ENOUGH FOOD TO LAST US UNTIL KINGDOM COME.
WHAT WE **DON'T** HAVE IS ENTERTAINMENT.
OUR LIBRARY'S BEEN PRETTY WELL PILLAGED, AND THE GIRLS COULD SURE USE A BIT OF AN ESCAPE.
OF COURSE, I... I UNDERSTAND.
THERE'S A SMALL PLAYHOUSE IN TOWN SQUARE. IT'S NOT MUCH, BUT WE SHOULD HAVE ENOUGH GAS TO POWER THE FOOTLIGHTS FOR A FEW NIGHTS. AS FOR ACCOMMODATIONS, I'M AFRAID WE'RE SHORT ON--
WE'RE MORE THAN HAPPY TO SLEEP UNDER THE STARS, MA'AM.
FOR NOW, LET'S SAY THAT WE'LL DEBUT THIS FRIDAY EVENING, AND PLAN FOR AN ENCORE ON SATURDAY, MAYBE A SUNDAY MATINEE IN CASE OF OVERFLOW.
MARVELOUS! GOD BLESS YOU GOOD PEOPLE FOR YOUR SERVICE! I'LL HAVE SOME OF MY HOME-MADE HOTCAKES WAITING AT THE PLAYHOUSE TOMORROW MORNING!
EXPLODING MYTHS ABOUT GENDER, EH?
YEAH... **KA-BOOM.**

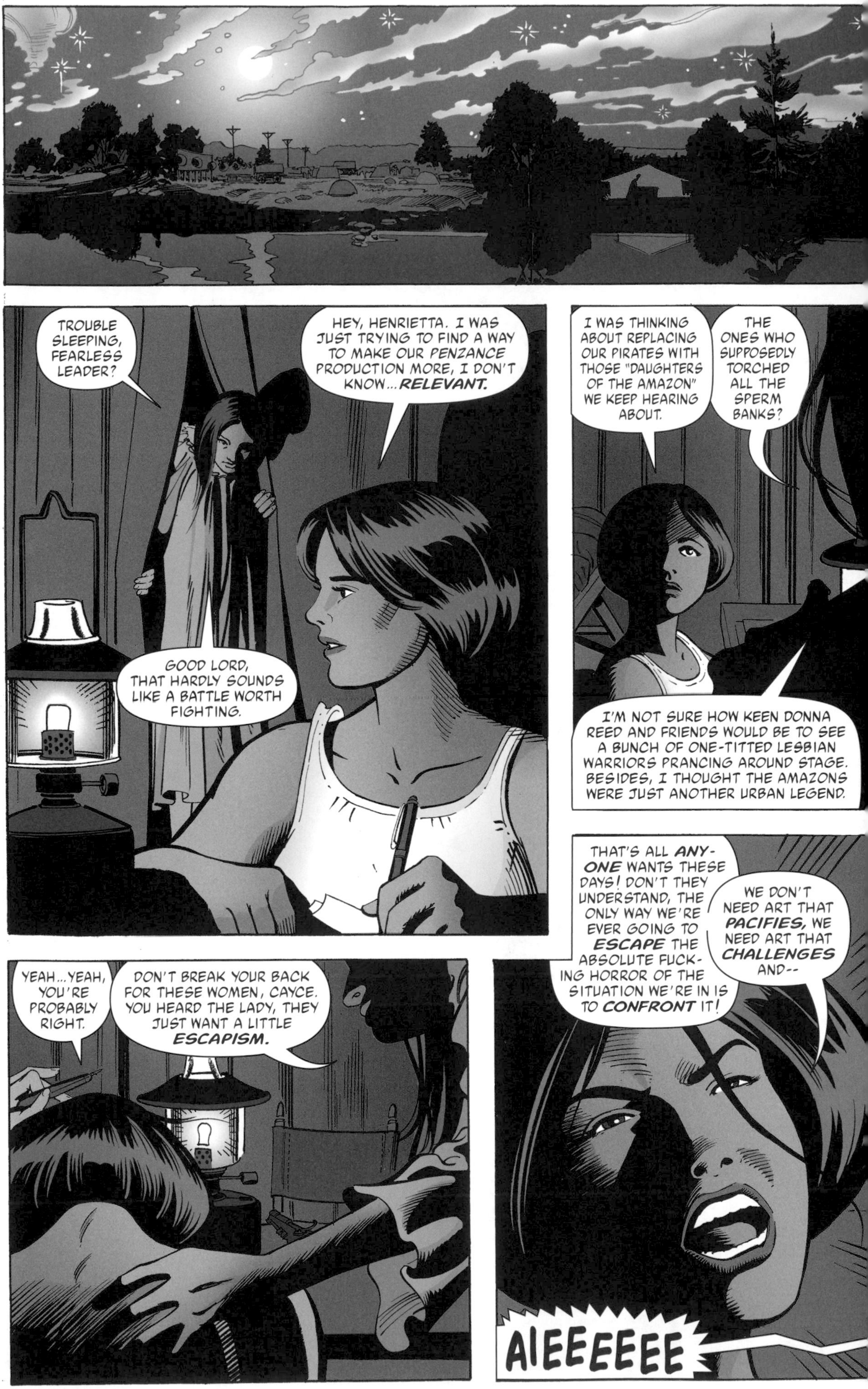
TROUBLE SLEEPING, FEARLESS LEADER?
HEY, HENRIETTA. I WAS JUST TRYING TO FIND A WAY TO MAKE OUR PENZANCE PRODUCTION MORE, I DON'T KNOW... RELEVANT.
GOOD LORD, THAT HARDLY SOUNDS LIKE A BATTLE WORTH FIGHTING.
I WAS THINKING ABOUT REPLACING OUR PIRATES WITH THOSE "DAUGHTERS OF THE AMAZON" WE KEEP HEARING ABOUT.
THE ONES WHO SUPPOSEDLY TORCHED ALL THE SPERM BANKS?
I'M NOT SURE HOW KEEN DONNA REED AND FRIENDS WOULD BE TO SEE A BUNCH OF ONE-TITTED LESBIAN WARRIORS PRANCING AROUND STAGE. BESIDES, I THOUGHT THE AMAZONS WERE JUST ANOTHER URBAN LEGEND.
YEAH... YEAH, YOU'RE PROBABLY RIGHT.
DON'T BREAK YOUR BACK FOR THESE WOMEN, CAYCE. YOU HEARD THE LADY, THEY JUST WANT A LITTLE ESCAPISM.
THAT'S ALL ANY-ONE WANTS THESE DAYS! DON'T THEY UNDERSTAND, THE ONLY WAY WE'RE EVER GOING TO ESCAPE THE ABSOLUTE FUCK-ING HORROR OF THE SITUATION WE'RE IN IS TO CONFRONT IT!
WE DON'T NEED ART THAT PACIFIES, WE NEED ART THAT CHALLENGES AND--
AIEEEEEE

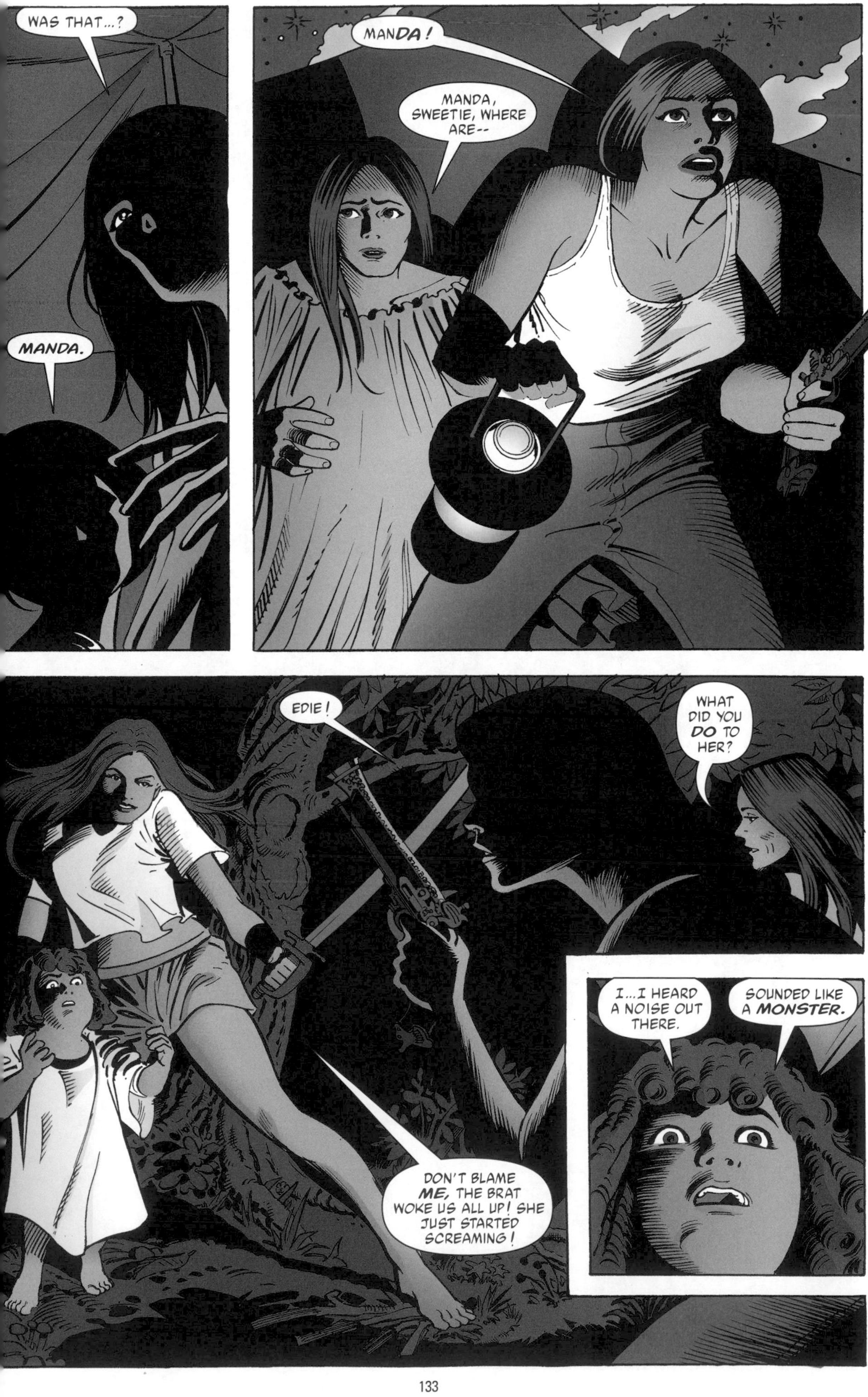
WAS THAT...?
MANDA.
MANDA!
MANDA, SWEETIE, WHERE ARE--
EDIE!
WHAT DID YOU DO TO HER?
DON'T BLAME ME, THE BRAT WOKE US ALL UP! SHE JUST STARTED SCREAMING!
I...I HEARD A NOISE OUT THERE.
SOUNDED LIKE A MONSTER.

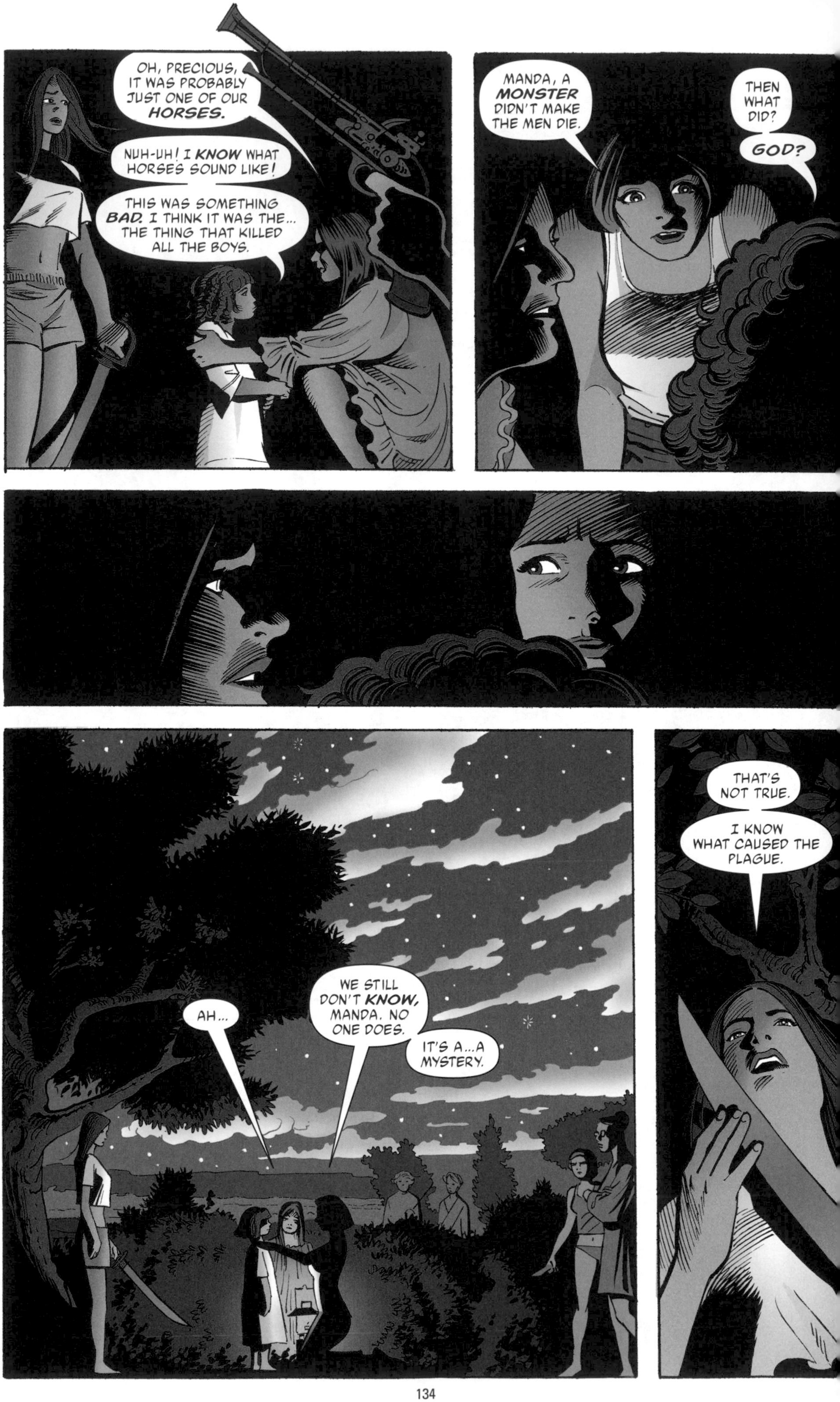

OH, PRECIOUS, IT WAS PROBABLY JUST ONE OF OUR HORSES.
NUH-UH! I KNOW WHAT HORSES SOUND LIKE!
THIS WAS SOMETHING BAD. I THINK IT WAS THE... THE THING THAT KILLED ALL THE BOYS.
MANDA, A MONSTER DIDN'T MAKE THE MEN DIE.
THEN WHAT DID?
GOD?
AH...
WE STILL DON'T KNOW, MANDA. NO ONE DOES.
IT'S A...A MYSTERY.
THAT'S NOT TRUE.
I KNOW WHAT CAUSED THE PLAGUE.

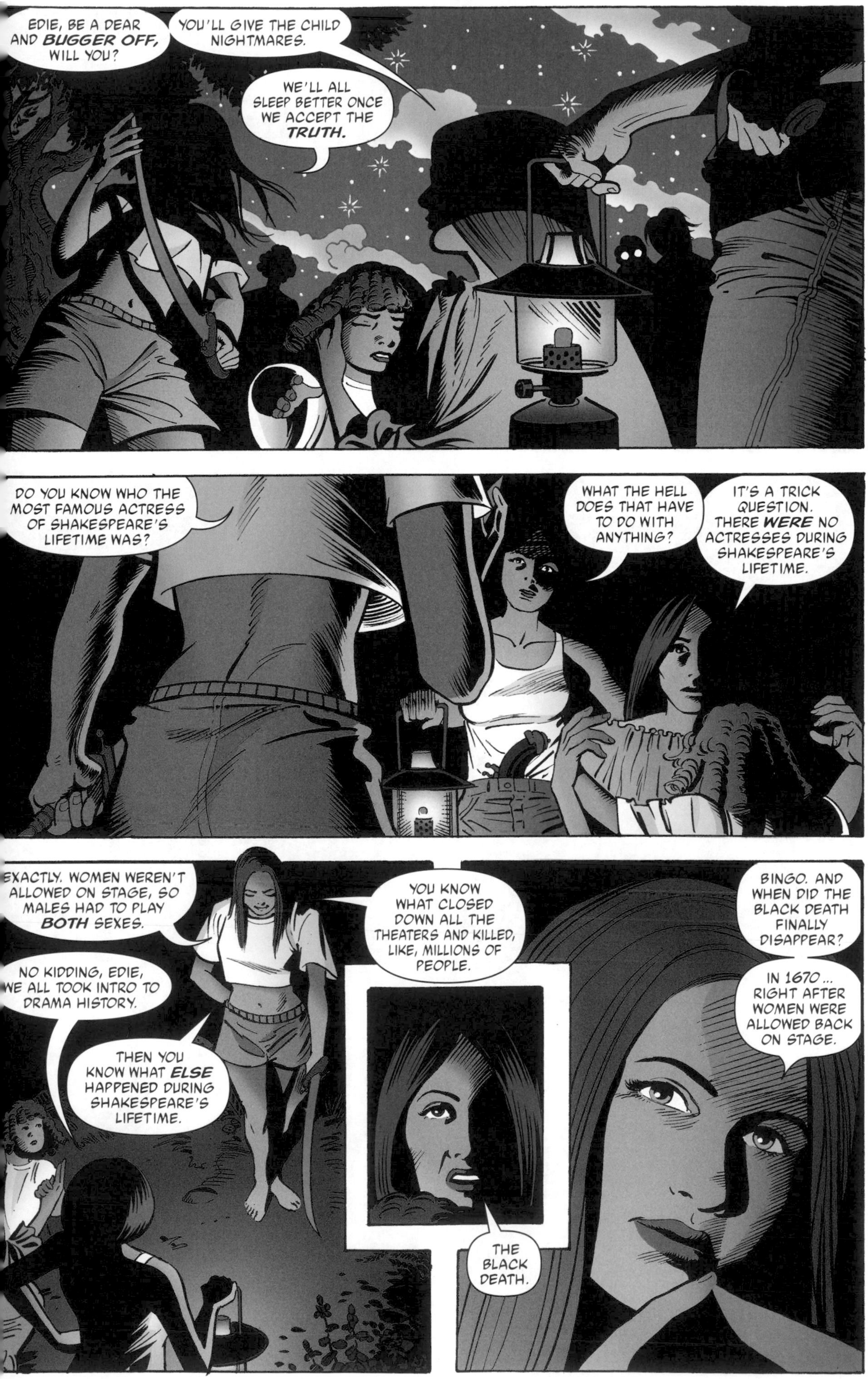
EDIE, BE A DEAR AND BUGGER OFF, WILL YOU?
YOU'LL GIVE THE CHILD NIGHTMARES.
WE'LL ALL SLEEP BETTER ONCE WE ACCEPT THE TRUTH.
DO YOU KNOW WHO THE MOST FAMOUS ACTRESS OF SHAKESPEARE'S LIFETIME WAS?
WHAT THE HELL DOES THAT HAVE TO DO WITH ANYTHING?
IT'S A TRICK QUESTION. THERE WERE NO ACTRESSES DURING SHAKESPEARE'S LIFETIME.
EXACTLY. WOMEN WEREN'T ALLOWED ON STAGE, SO MALES HAD TO PLAY BOTH SEXES.
NO KIDDING, EDIE, WE ALL TOOK INTRO TO DRAMA HISTORY.
THEN YOU KNOW WHAT ELSE HAPPENED DURING SHAKESPEARE'S LIFETIME.
YOU KNOW WHAT CLOSED DOWN ALL THE THEATERS AND KILLED, LIKE, MILLIONS OF PEOPLE.
THE BLACK DEATH.
BINGO. AND WHEN DID THE BLACK DEATH FINALLY DISAPPEAR?
IN 1670... RIGHT AFTER WOMEN WERE ALLOWED BACK ON STAGE.

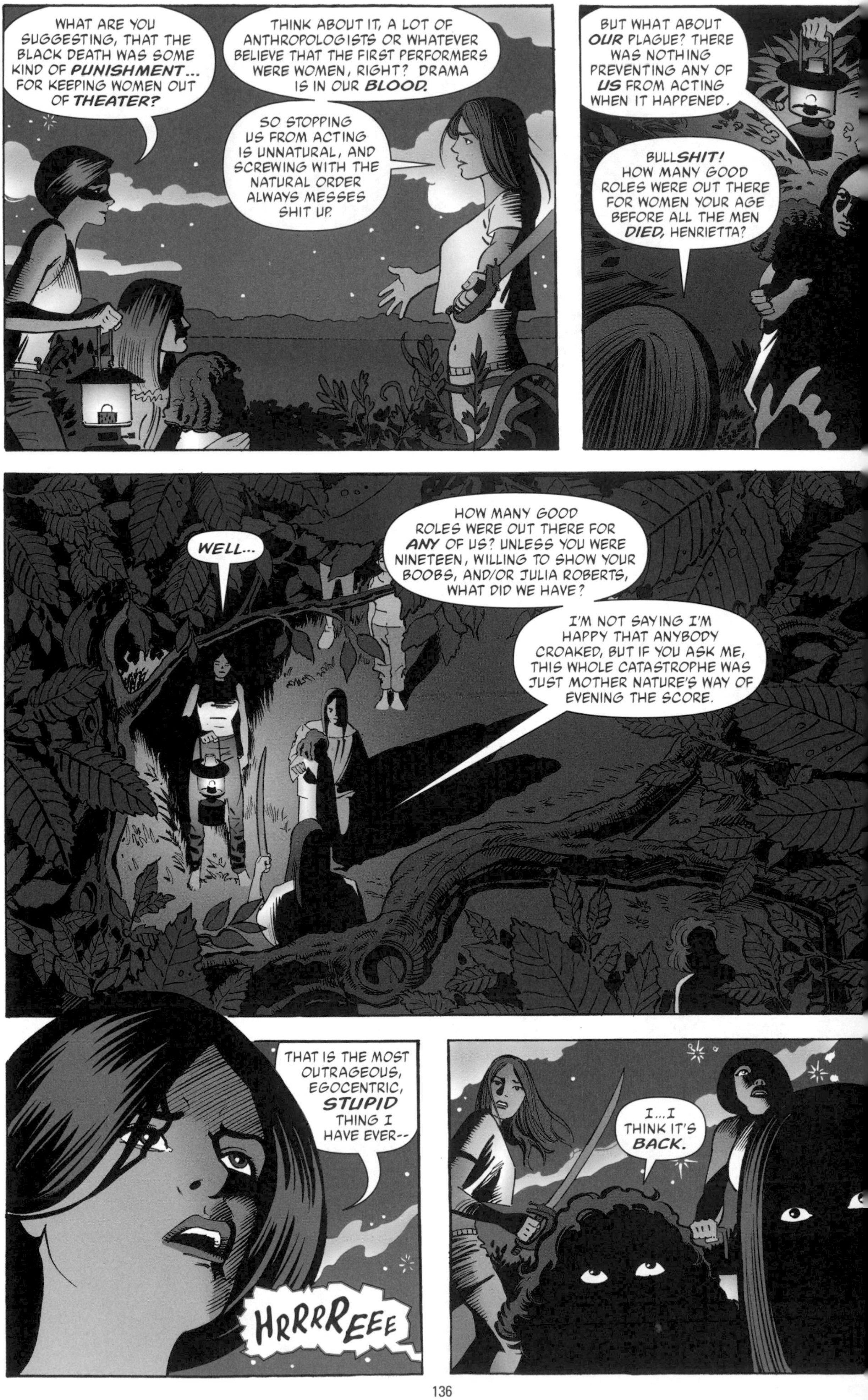
WHAT ARE YOU SUGGESTING, THAT THE BLACK DEATH WAS SOME KIND OF **PUNISHMENT...** FOR KEEPING WOMEN OUT OF **THEATER?**
THINK ABOUT IT, A LOT OF ANTHROPOLOGISTS OR WHATEVER BELIEVE THAT THE FIRST PERFORMERS WERE WOMEN, RIGHT? DRAMA IS IN OUR **BLOOD.**
SO STOPPING US FROM ACTING IS UNNATURAL, AND SCREWING WITH THE NATURAL ORDER ALWAYS MESSES SHIT UP.
BUT WHAT ABOUT **OUR** PLAGUE? THERE WAS NOTHING PREVENTING ANY OF **US** FROM ACTING WHEN IT HAPPENED.
BULL**SHIT!** HOW MANY GOOD ROLES WERE OUT THERE FOR WOMEN YOUR AGE BEFORE ALL THE MEN **DIED,** HENRIETTA?
WELL...
HOW MANY GOOD ROLES WERE OUT THERE FOR **ANY** OF US? UNLESS YOU WERE NINETEEN, WILLING TO SHOW YOUR BOOBS, AND/OR JULIA ROBERTS, WHAT DID WE HAVE?
I'M NOT SAYING I'M HAPPY THAT ANYBODY CROAKED, BUT IF YOU ASK ME, THIS WHOLE CATASTROPHE WAS JUST MOTHER NATURE'S WAY OF EVENING THE SCORE.
THAT IS THE MOST OUTRAGEOUS, EGOCENTRIC, **STUPID** THING I HAVE EVER--
HRRRREEE
I...I THINK IT'S **BACK.**

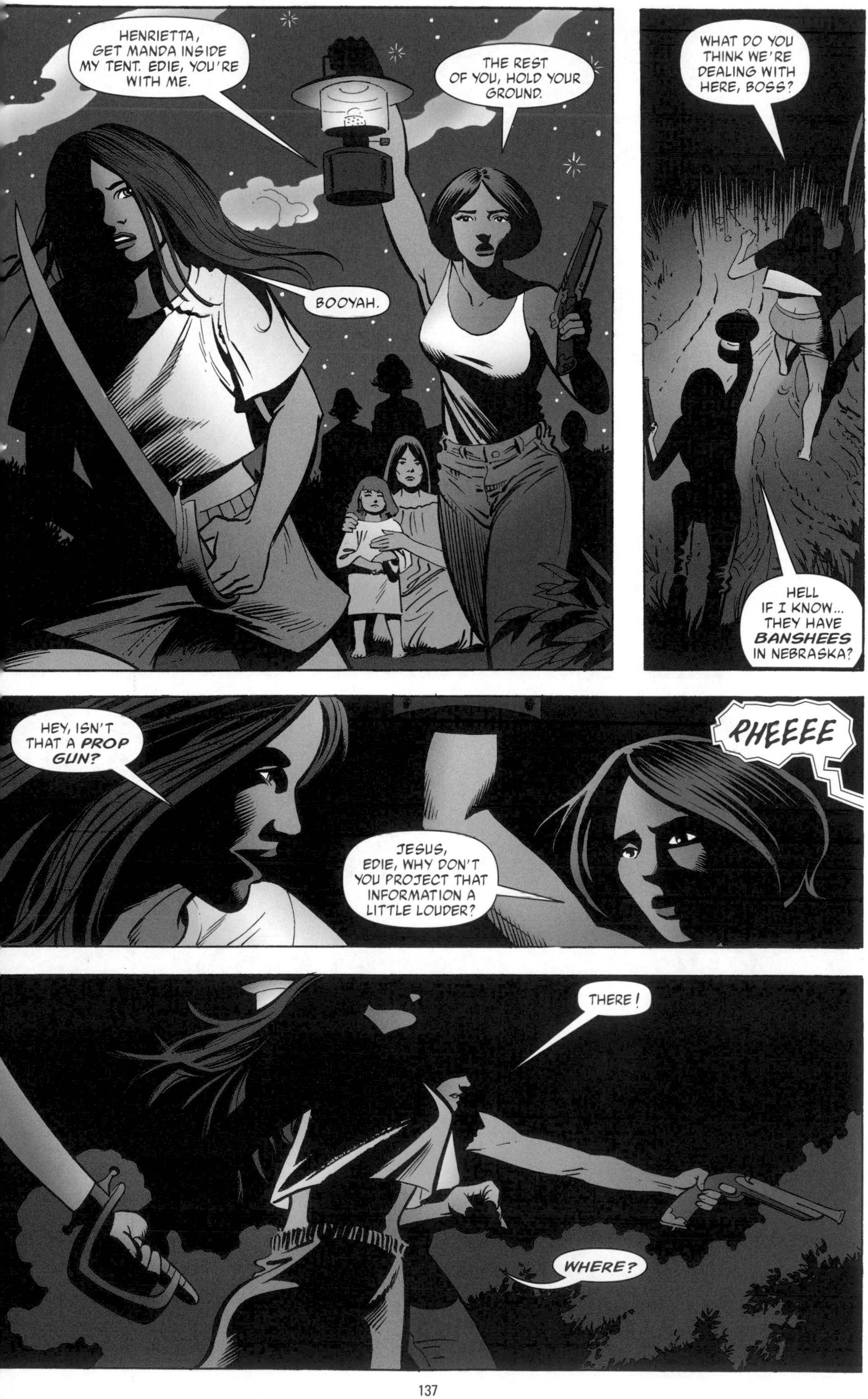
HENRIETTA, GET MANDA INSIDE MY TENT. EDIE, YOU'RE WITH ME.
THE REST OF YOU, HOLD YOUR GROUND.
BOOYAH.
WHAT DO YOU THINK WE'RE DEALING WITH HERE, BOSS?
HELL IF I KNOW... THEY HAVE BANSHEES IN NEBRASKA?
HEY, ISN'T THAT A PROP GUN?
RHEEEE
JESUS, EDIE, WHY DON'T YOU PROJECT THAT INFORMATION A LITTLE LOUDER?
THERE!
WHERE?

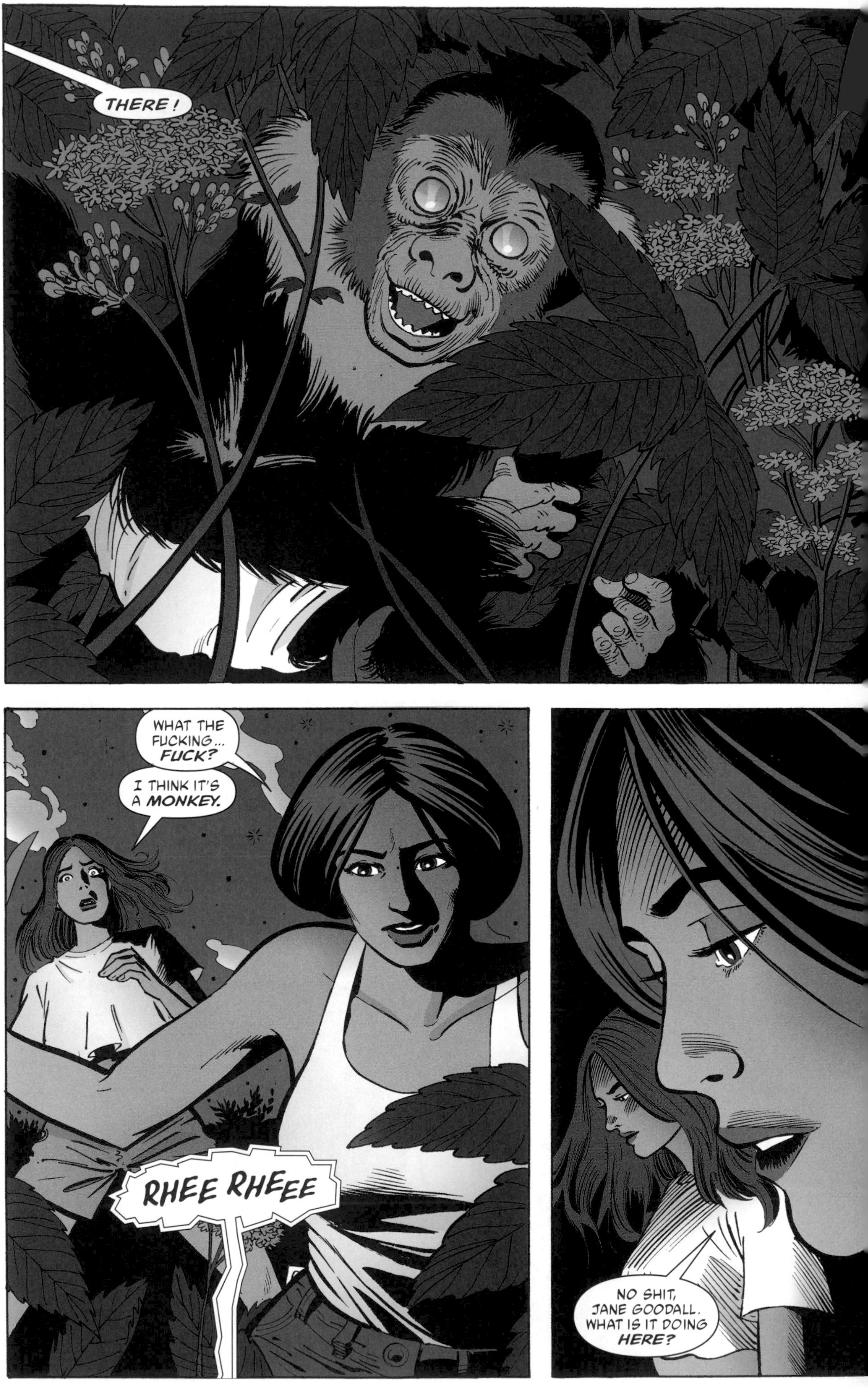
THERE!
WHAT THE FUCKING... FUCK?
I THINK IT'S A MONKEY.
RHEE RHEEEE
NO SHIT, JANE GOODALL. WHAT IS IT DOING HERE?

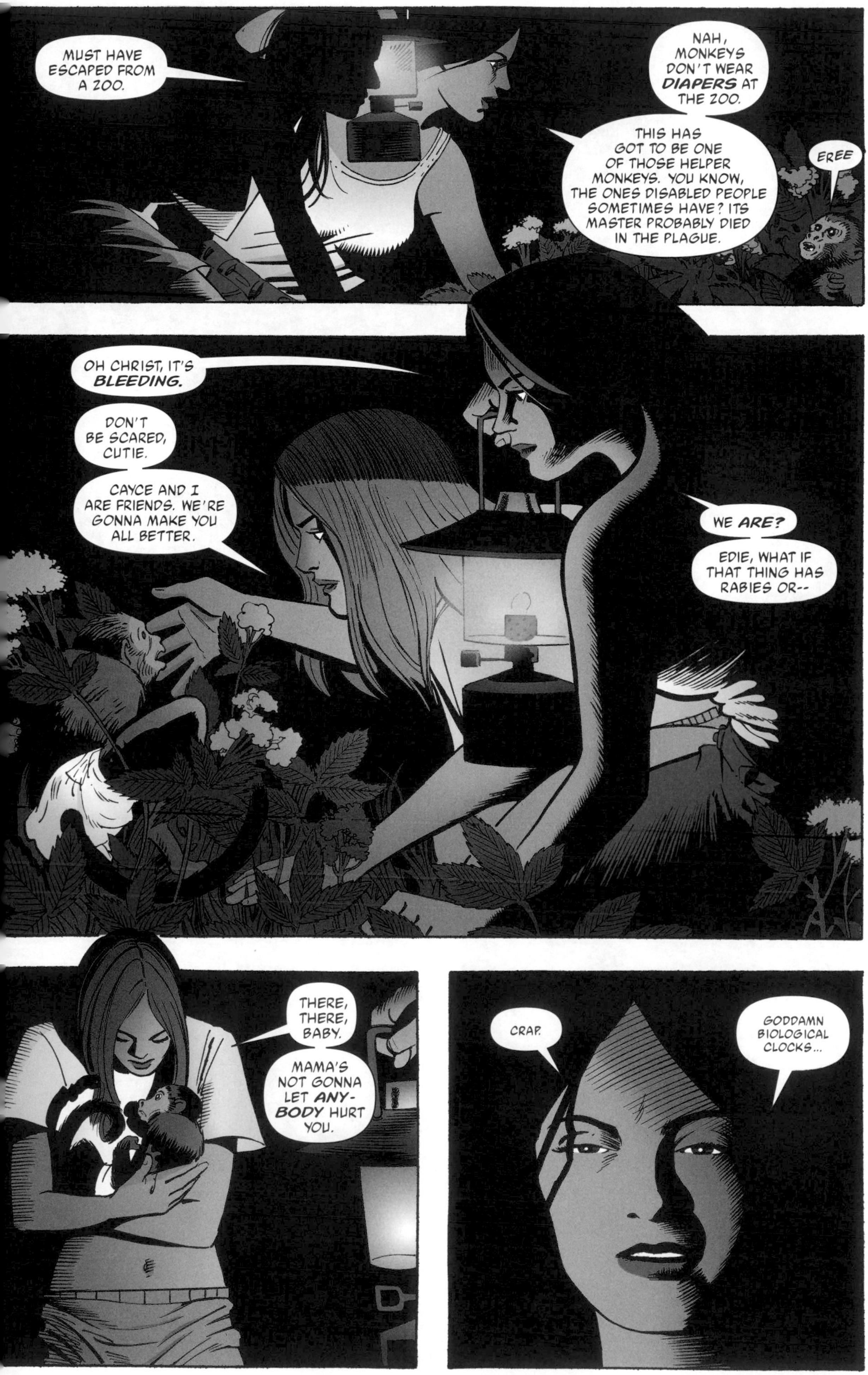
MUST HAVE ESCAPED FROM A ZOO.
NAH, MONKEYS DON'T WEAR DIAPERS AT THE ZOO.
THIS HAS GOT TO BE ONE OF THOSE HELPER MONKEYS. YOU KNOW, THE ONES DISABLED PEOPLE SOMETIMES HAVE? ITS MASTER PROBABLY DIED IN THE PLAGUE.
EREE
OH CHRIST, IT'S BLEEDING.
DON'T BE SCARED, CUTIE.
CAYCE AND I ARE FRIENDS. WE'RE GONNA MAKE YOU ALL BETTER.
WE ARE?
EDIE, WHAT IF THAT THING HAS RABIES OR--
THERE, THERE, BABY.
MAMA'S NOT GONNA LET ANYBODY HURT YOU.
CRAP.
GODDAMN BIOLOGICAL CLOCKS...

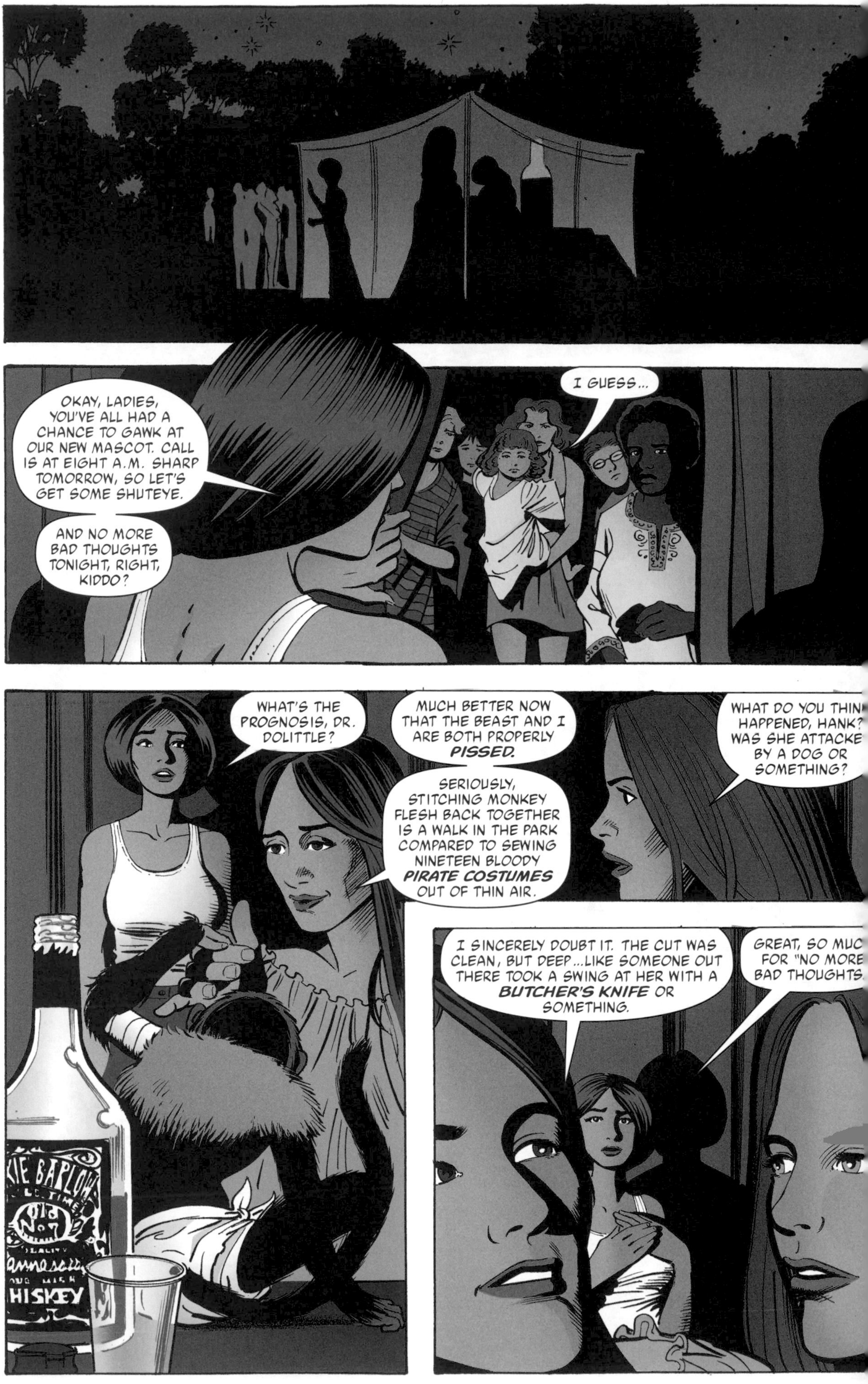
OKAY, LADIES, YOU'VE ALL HAD A CHANCE TO GAWK AT OUR NEW MASCOT. CALL IS AT EIGHT A.M. SHARP TOMORROW, SO LET'S GET SOME SHUTEYE.
AND NO MORE BAD THOUGHTS TONIGHT, RIGHT, KIDDO?
I GUESS...
WHAT'S THE PROGNOSIS, DR. DOLITTLE?
MUCH BETTER NOW THAT THE BEAST AND I ARE BOTH PROPERLY **PISSED.**
SERIOUSLY, STITCHING MONKEY FLESH BACK TOGETHER IS A WALK IN THE PARK COMPARED TO SEWING NINETEEN BLOODY **PIRATE COSTUMES** OUT OF THIN AIR.
WHAT DO YOU THIN HAPPENED, HANK? WAS SHE ATTACKE BY A DOG OR SOMETHING?
I SINCERELY DOUBT IT. THE CUT WAS CLEAN, BUT DEEP...LIKE SOMEONE OUT THERE TOOK A SWING AT HER WITH A **BUTCHER'S KNIFE** OR SOMETHING.
GREAT, SO MUC FOR "NO MORE BAD THOUGHTS.

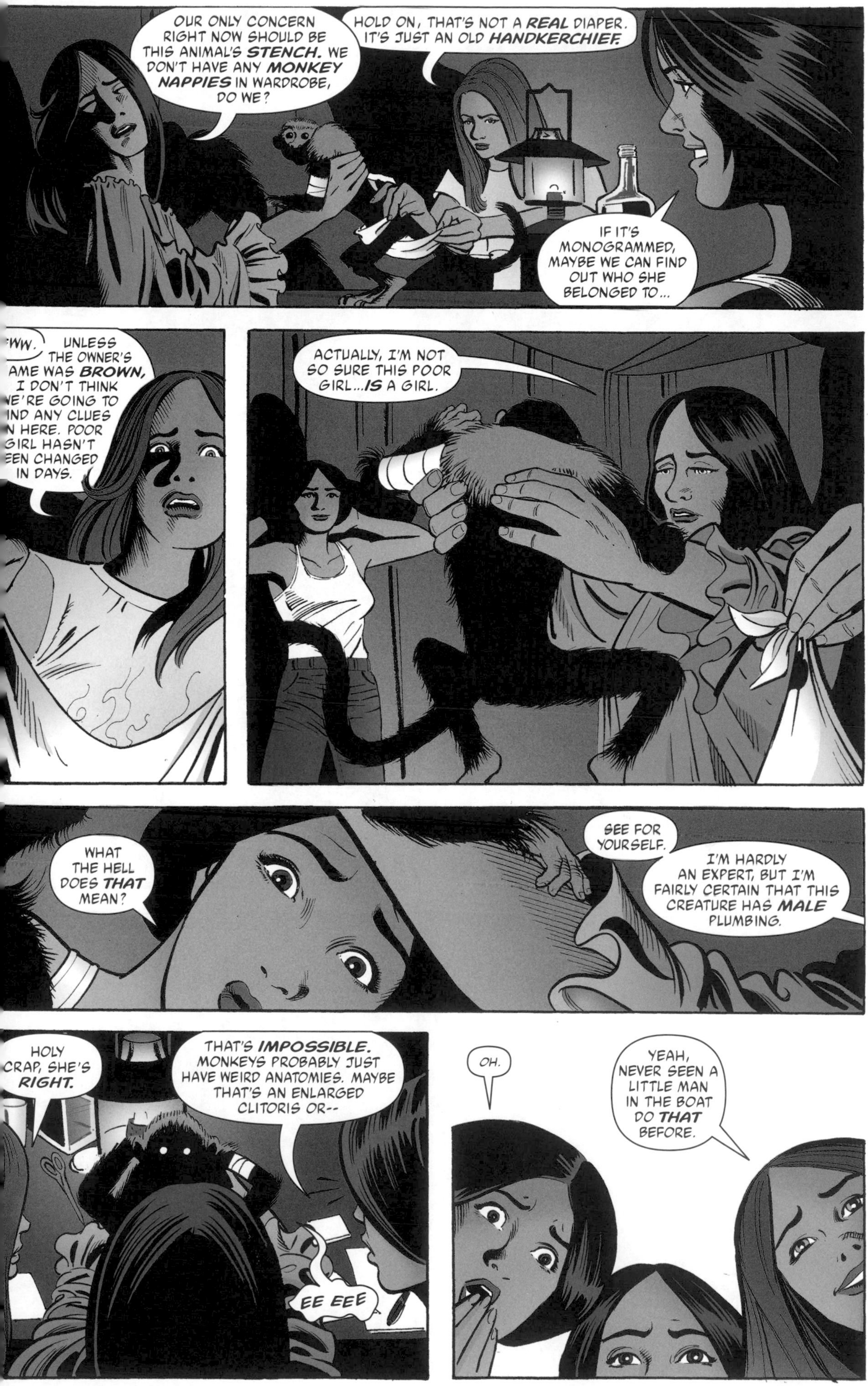
OUR ONLY CONCERN RIGHT NOW SHOULD BE THIS ANIMAL'S STENCH. WE DON'T HAVE ANY MONKEY NAPPIES IN WARDROBE, DO WE?
HOLD ON, THAT'S NOT A REAL DIAPER. IT'S JUST AN OLD HANDKERCHIEF.
IF IT'S MONOGRAMMED, MAYBE WE CAN FIND OUT WHO SHE BELONGED TO...
UNLESS THE OWNER'S AME WAS BROWN, I DON'T THINK E'RE GOING TO IND ANY CLUES N HERE. POOR GIRL HASN'T EEN CHANGED IN DAYS.
ACTUALLY, I'M NOT SO SURE THIS POOR GIRL...IS A GIRL.
WHAT THE HELL DOES THAT MEAN?
SEE FOR YOURSELF.
I'M HARDLY AN EXPERT, BUT I'M FAIRLY CERTAIN THAT THIS CREATURE HAS MALE PLUMBING.
HOLY CRAP, SHE'S RIGHT.
THAT'S IMPOSSIBLE. MONKEYS PROBABLY JUST HAVE WEIRD ANATOMIES. MAYBE THAT'S AN ENLARGED CLITORIS OR--
EE EEE
OH.
YEAH, NEVER SEEN A LITTLE MAN IN THE BOAT DO THAT BEFORE.

BUT I THOUGHT THE PLAGUE KILLED *EVERY* MAMMAL WITH A Y CHROMOSOME. I MEAN, I LOST BOTH MY MALE CATS. AND ALL OF MY BOYFRIEND'S *STALLIONS* DIED.

HALF OF THE MICE IN MY APARTMENT FINALLY PASSED ON, AND I'D BEEN TRYING TO KILL THEM FOR *YEARS.*

SO THE PLAGUE AFFECTED EVERYTHING BUT *MONKEYS?* HOW THE FUCK DOES THAT MAKE ANY SENSE? ISN'T THEIR *DNA,* LIKE, ALMOST IDENTICAL TO OURS?

LORD, WHAT IF IT *DID* AFFECT MONKEYS...JUST NOT *THIS* ONE?

WHAT IF THIS IS THE *LAST MALE ON EARTH?*

YOU'RE STARTING TO SOUND LIKE *EDIE,* HENRIETTA.

BUBBLES HERE IS PROBABLY JUST SOME KIND OF FREAK ANOMALY...LIKE THE HANDFUL OF PEOPLE WHO ARE SUPPOSEDLY IMMUNE TO *HIV* INFECTION, YOU KNOW?

THAT STILL MAKES THIS AN *ENORMOUS* DISCOVERY. WE HAVE TO TELL--

NO! THIS STAYS BETWEEN THE THREE OF US.

IF WORD SPREADS, WOMEN MIGHT START HOLDING OUT HOPE THAT A *HUMAN* MALE IS ALIVE SOME-WHERE, TOO.

WHAT'S SO BAD ABOUT GIVING PEOPLE A LITTLE HOPE?

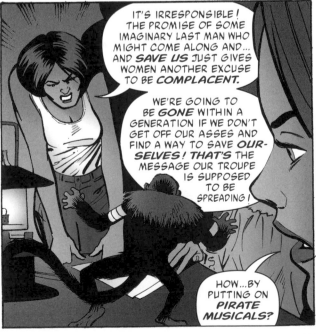

IT'S IRRESPONSIBLE! THE PROMISE OF SOME IMAGINARY LAST MAN WHO MIGHT COME ALONG AND... AND *SAVE US* JUST GIVES WOMEN ANOTHER EXCUSE TO BE *COMPLACENT.*

WE'RE GOING TO BE *GONE* WITHIN A GENERATION IF WE DON'T GET OFF OUR ASSES AND FIND A WAY TO SAVE *OUR-SELVES! THAT'S* THE MESSAGE OUR TROUPE IS SUPPOSED TO BE SPREADING!

HOW...BY PUTTING ON *PIRATE MUSICALS?*

I'M SORRY, CAYCE, BUT--

NO.

YOU'RE... YOU'RE ABSOLUTELY RIGHT.

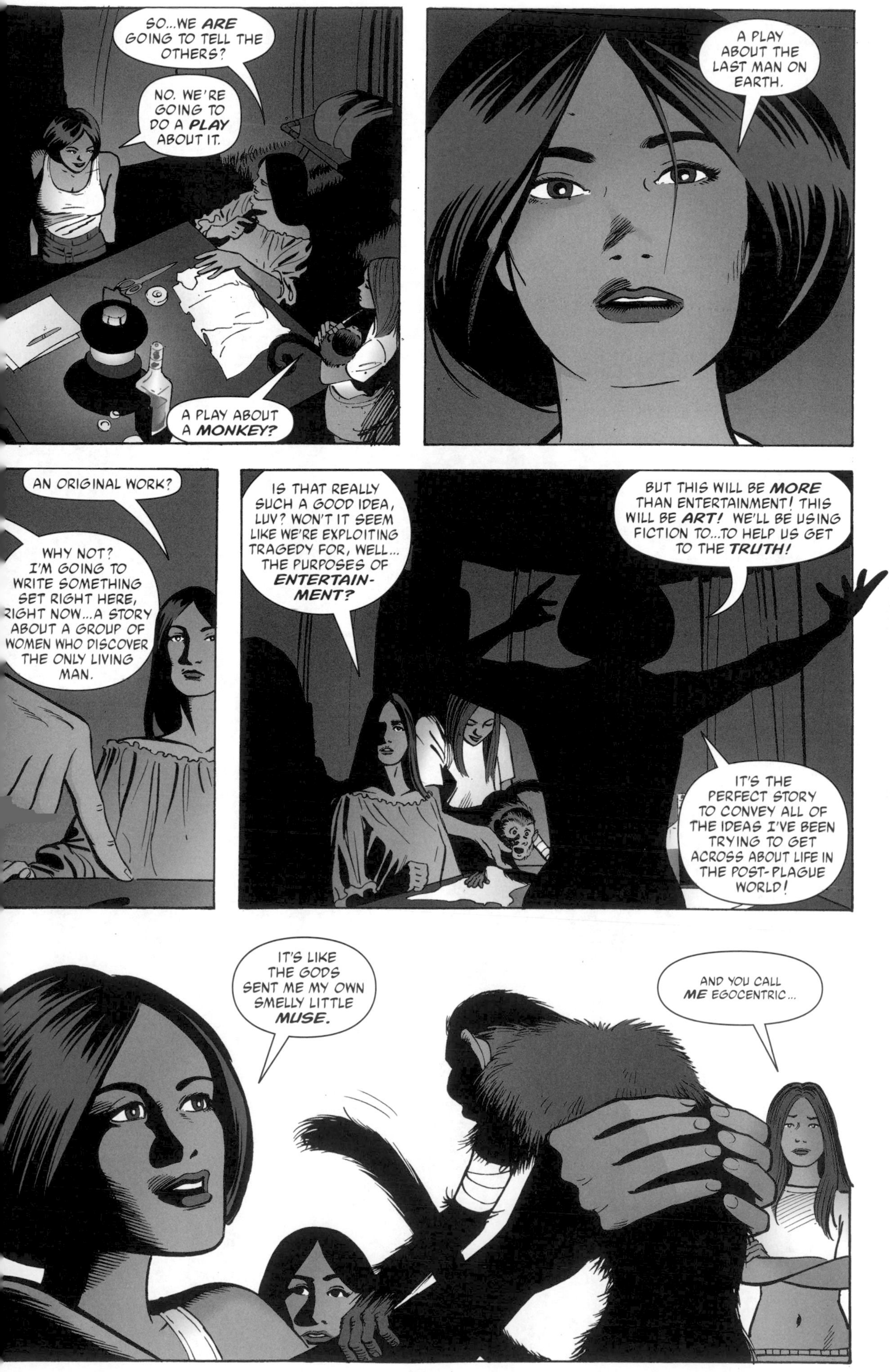
SO...WE ARE GOING TO TELL THE OTHERS?
NO. WE'RE GOING TO DO A PLAY ABOUT IT.
A PLAY ABOUT A MONKEY?
A PLAY ABOUT THE LAST MAN ON EARTH.
AN ORIGINAL WORK?
WHY NOT? I'M GOING TO WRITE SOMETHING SET RIGHT HERE, RIGHT NOW...A STORY ABOUT A GROUP OF WOMEN WHO DISCOVER THE ONLY LIVING MAN.
IS THAT REALLY SUCH A GOOD IDEA, LUV? WON'T IT SEEM LIKE WE'RE EXPLOITING TRAGEDY FOR, WELL... THE PURPOSES OF ENTERTAIN-MENT?
BUT THIS WILL BE MORE THAN ENTERTAINMENT! THIS WILL BE ART! WE'LL BE USING FICTION TO...TO HELP US GET TO THE TRUTH!
IT'S THE PERFECT STORY TO CONVEY ALL OF THE IDEAS I'VE BEEN TRYING TO GET ACROSS ABOUT LIFE IN THE POST-PLAGUE WORLD!
IT'S LIKE THE GODS SENT ME MY OWN SMELLY LITTLE MUSE.
AND YOU CALL ME EGOCENTRIC...

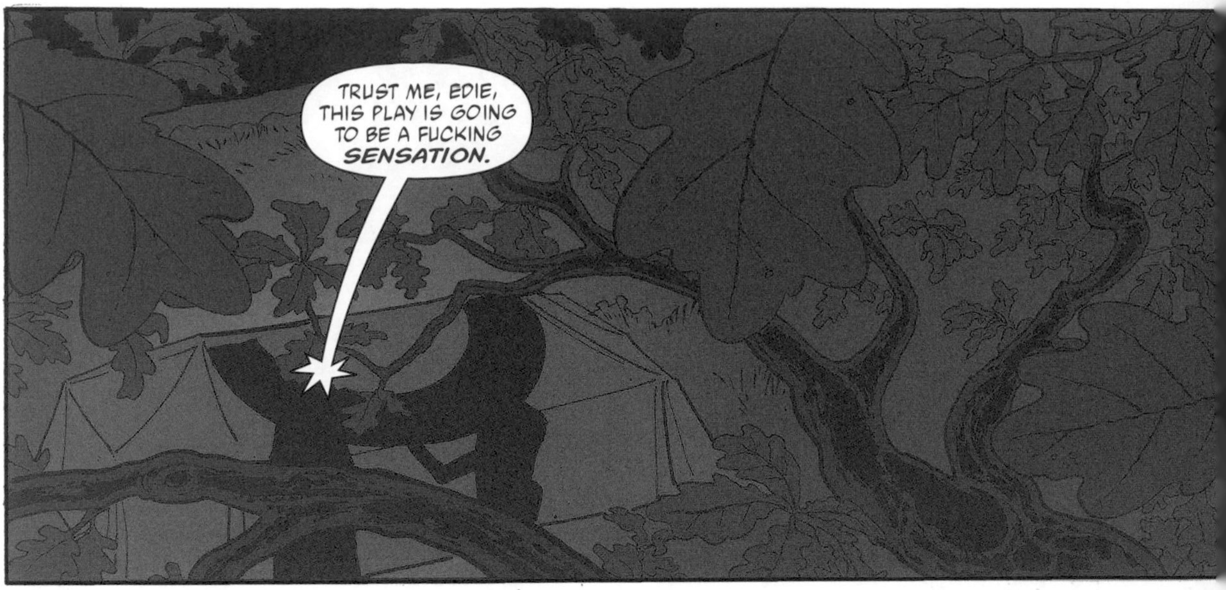
TRUST ME, EDIE, THIS PLAY IS GOING TO BE A FUCKING SENSATION.

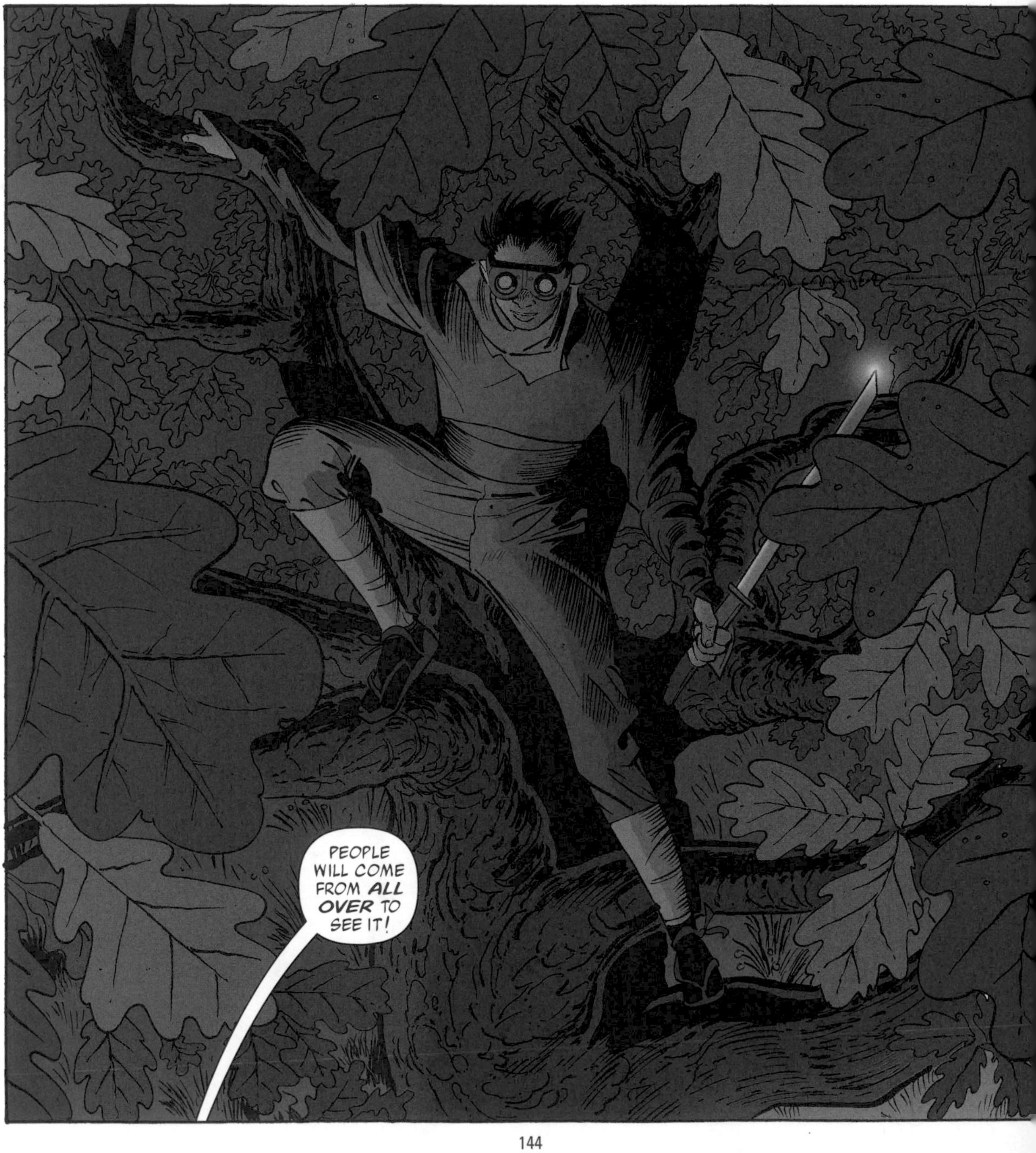
PEOPLE WILL COME FROM ALL OVER TO SEE IT!

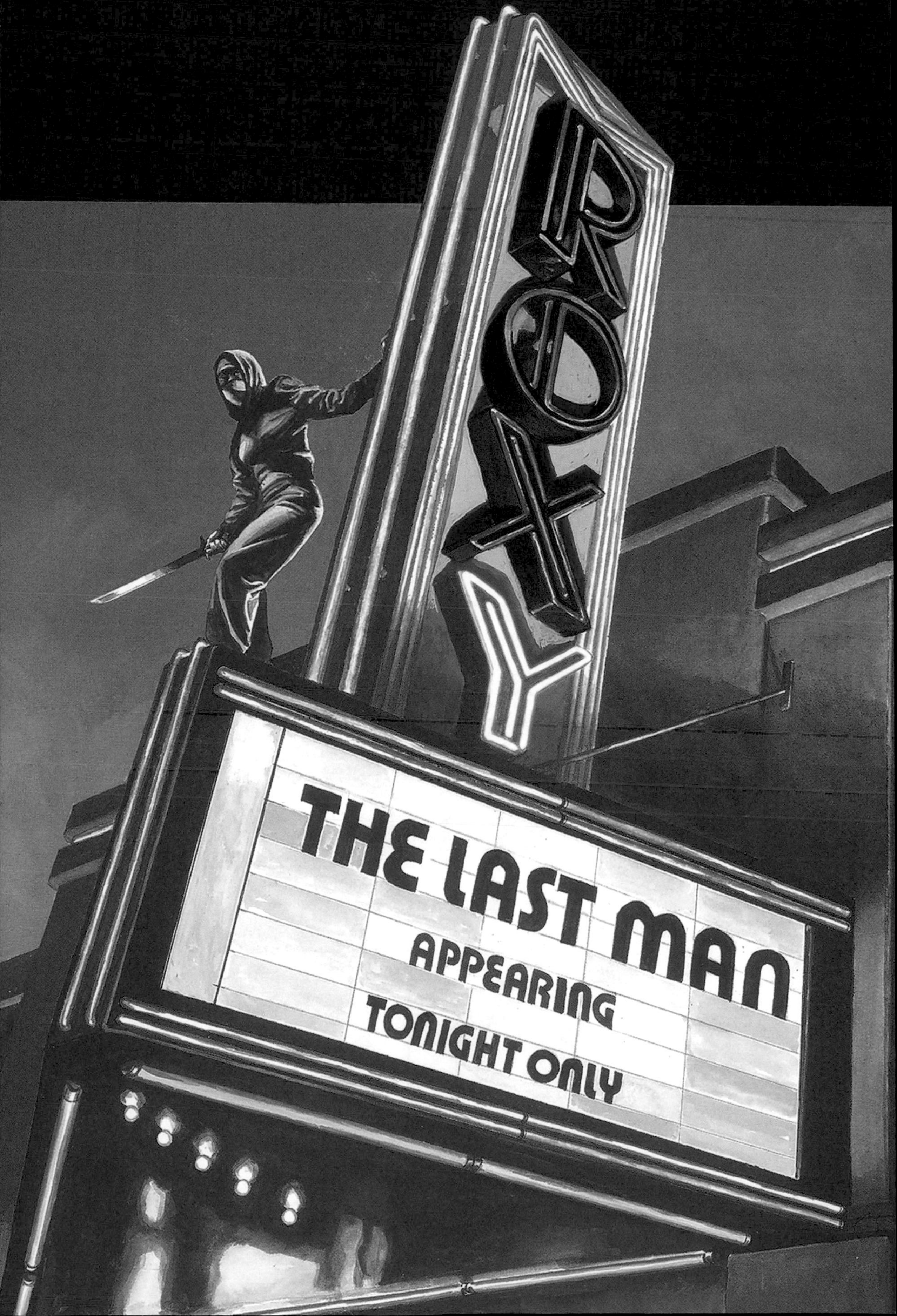
ROXY
THE LAST MAN
APPEARING
TONIGHT ONLY

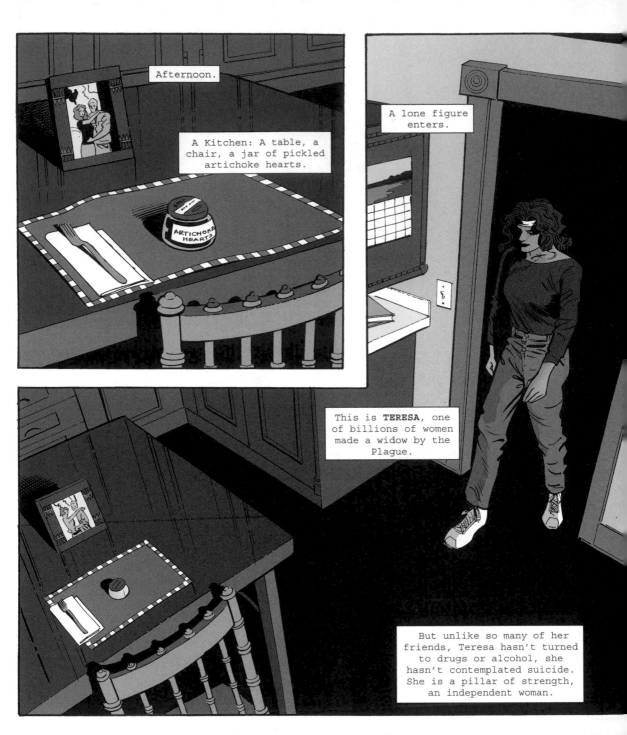

Afternoon.

A Kitchen: A table, a chair, a jar of pickled artichoke hearts.

A lone figure enters.

This is **TERESA**, one of billions of women made a widow by the Plague.

But unlike so many of her friends, Teresa hasn't turned to drugs or alcohol, she hasn't contemplated suicide. She is a pillar of strength, an independent woman.

Because Teresa and her husband built a shelter in their basement after 9/11, she has enough food to last her more than a year.

Teresa will not die. She is a **survivor**.

But as she sits down to enjoy her lunch, Teresa is confronted with a problem…

146

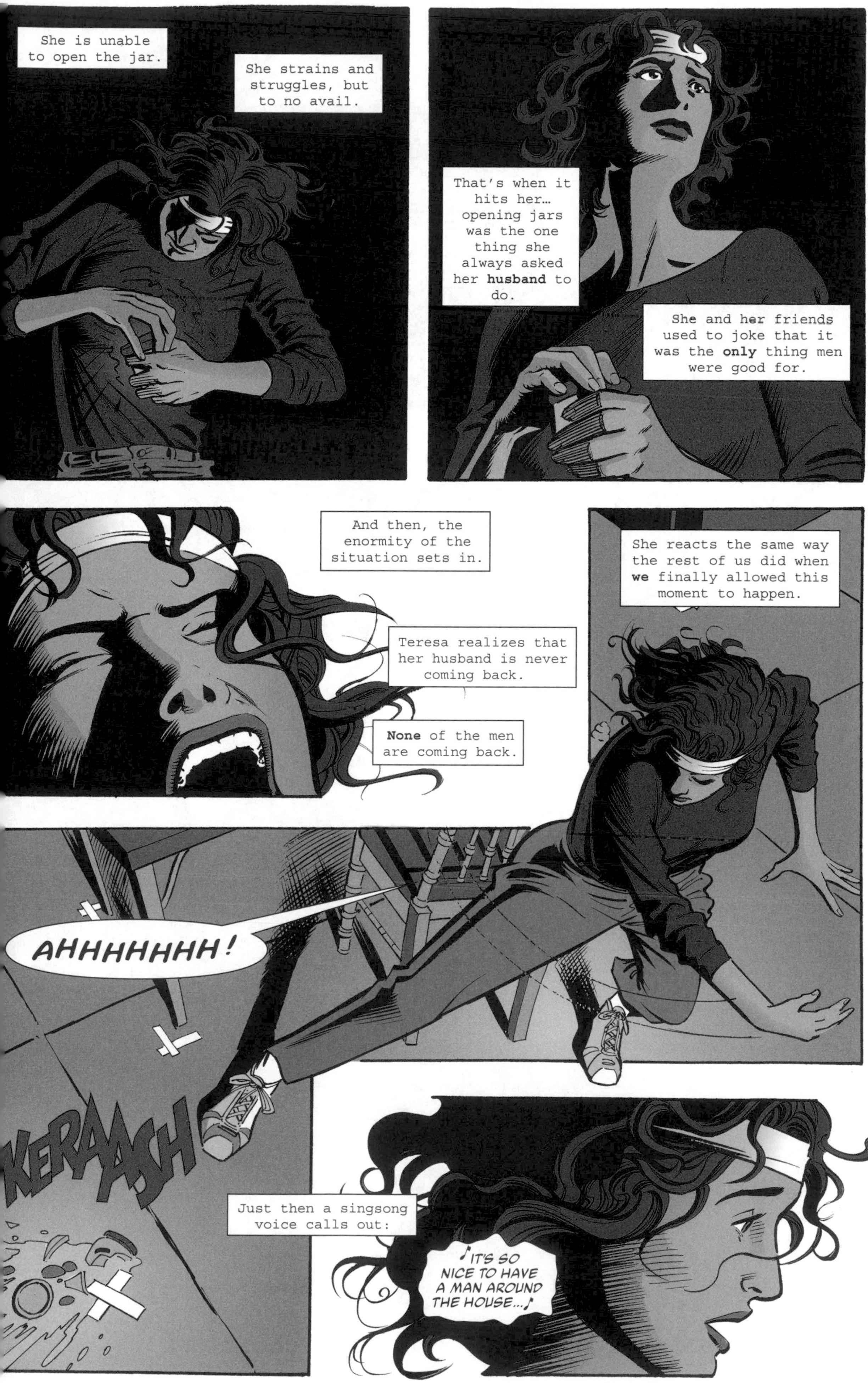

She is unable to open the jar.
She strains and struggles, but to no avail.
That's when it hits her... opening jars was the one thing she always asked her **husband** to do.
She and her friends used to joke that it was the **only** thing men were good for.
And then, the enormity of the situation sets in.
Teresa realizes that her husband is never coming back.
None of the men are coming back.
She reacts the same way the rest of us did when **we** finally allowed this moment to happen.
AHHHHHHH!
KERAASH
Just then a singsong voice calls out:
♪IT'S SO NICE TO HAVE A MAN AROUND THE HOUSE...♪

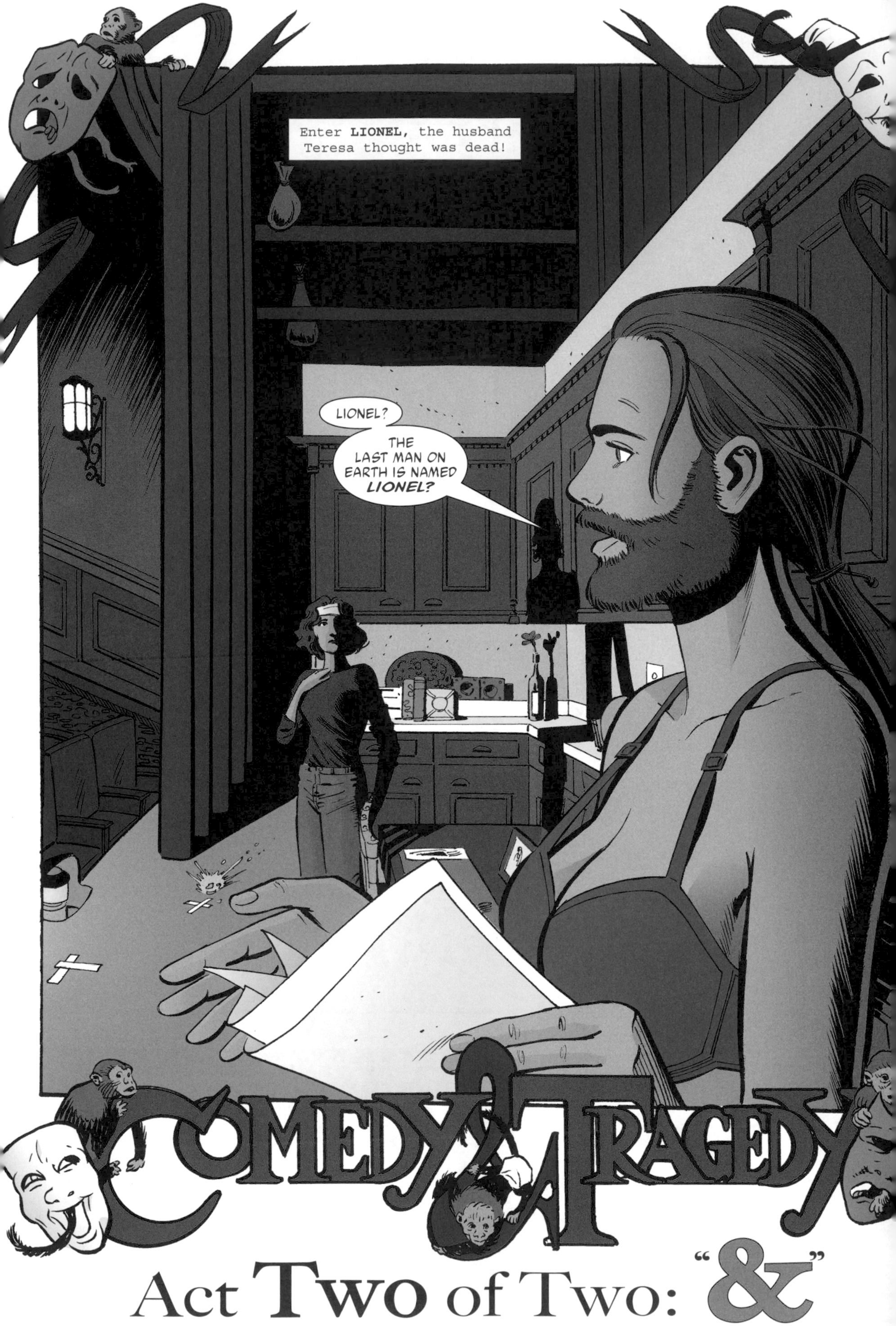

Enter LIONEL, the husband Teresa thought was dead!
LIONEL?
THE LAST MAN ON EARTH IS NAMED LIONEL?
COMEDY & TRAGEDY
Act Two of Two: "&"

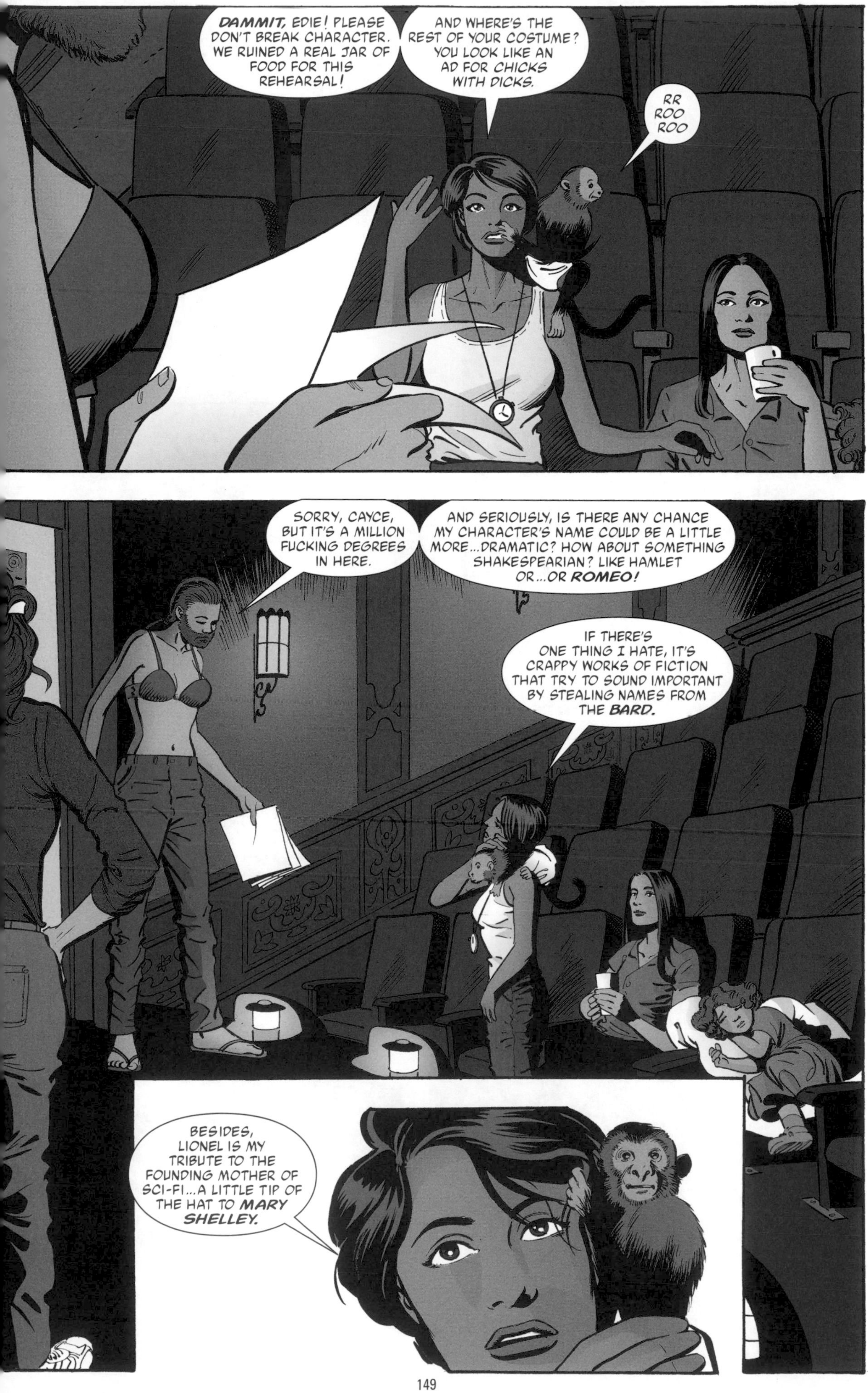
DAMMIT, EDIE! PLEASE DON'T BREAK CHARACTER. WE RUINED A REAL JAR OF FOOD FOR THIS REHEARSAL!
AND WHERE'S THE REST OF YOUR COSTUME? YOU LOOK LIKE AN AD FOR CHICKS WITH DICKS.
RR ROO ROO
SORRY, CAYCE, BUT IT'S A MILLION FUCKING DEGREES IN HERE.
AND SERIOUSLY, IS THERE ANY CHANCE MY CHARACTER'S NAME COULD BE A LITTLE MORE...DRAMATIC? HOW ABOUT SOMETHING SHAKESPEARIAN? LIKE HAMLET OR...OR ROMEO!
IF THERE'S ONE THING I HATE, IT'S CRAPPY WORKS OF FICTION THAT TRY TO SOUND IMPORTANT BY STEALING NAMES FROM THE BARD.
BESIDES, LIONEL IS MY TRIBUTE TO THE FOUNDING MOTHER OF SCI-FI...A LITTLE TIP OF THE HAT TO MARY SHELLEY.

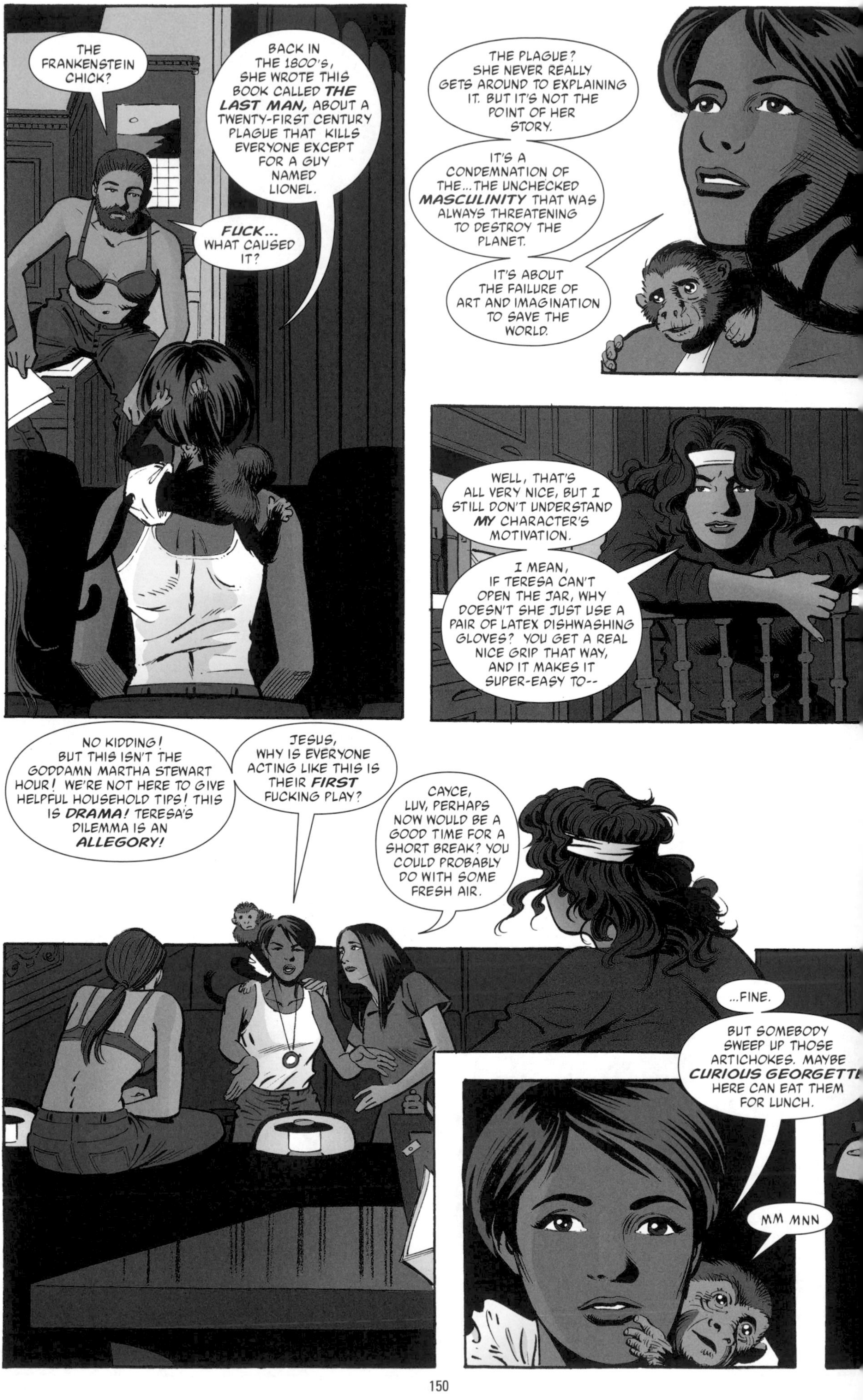
THE FRANKENSTEIN CHICK?
BACK IN THE 1800'S, SHE WROTE THIS BOOK CALLED THE LAST MAN, ABOUT A TWENTY-FIRST CENTURY PLAGUE THAT KILLS EVERYONE EXCEPT FOR A GUY NAMED LIONEL.
FUCK... WHAT CAUSED IT?
THE PLAGUE? SHE NEVER REALLY GETS AROUND TO EXPLAINING IT. BUT IT'S NOT THE POINT OF HER STORY.
IT'S A CONDEMNATION OF THE...THE UNCHECKED MASCULINITY THAT WAS ALWAYS THREATENING TO DESTROY THE PLANET.
IT'S ABOUT THE FAILURE OF ART AND IMAGINATION TO SAVE THE WORLD.
WELL, THAT'S ALL VERY NICE, BUT I STILL DON'T UNDERSTAND MY CHARACTER'S MOTIVATION.
I MEAN, IF TERESA CAN'T OPEN THE JAR, WHY DOESN'T SHE JUST USE A PAIR OF LATEX DISHWASHING GLOVES? YOU GET A REAL NICE GRIP THAT WAY, AND IT MAKES IT SUPER-EASY TO--
NO KIDDING! BUT THIS ISN'T THE GODDAMN MARTHA STEWART HOUR! WE'RE NOT HERE TO GIVE HELPFUL HOUSEHOLD TIPS! THIS IS DRAMA! TERESA'S DILEMMA IS AN ALLEGORY!
JESUS, WHY IS EVERYONE ACTING LIKE THIS IS THEIR FIRST FUCKING PLAY?
CAYCE, LUV, PERHAPS NOW WOULD BE A GOOD TIME FOR A SHORT BREAK? YOU COULD PROBABLY DO WITH SOME FRESH AIR.
...FINE.
BUT SOMEBODY SWEEP UP THOSE ARTICHOKES. MAYBE CURIOUS GEORGETT HERE CAN EAT THEM FOR LUNCH.
MM MNN

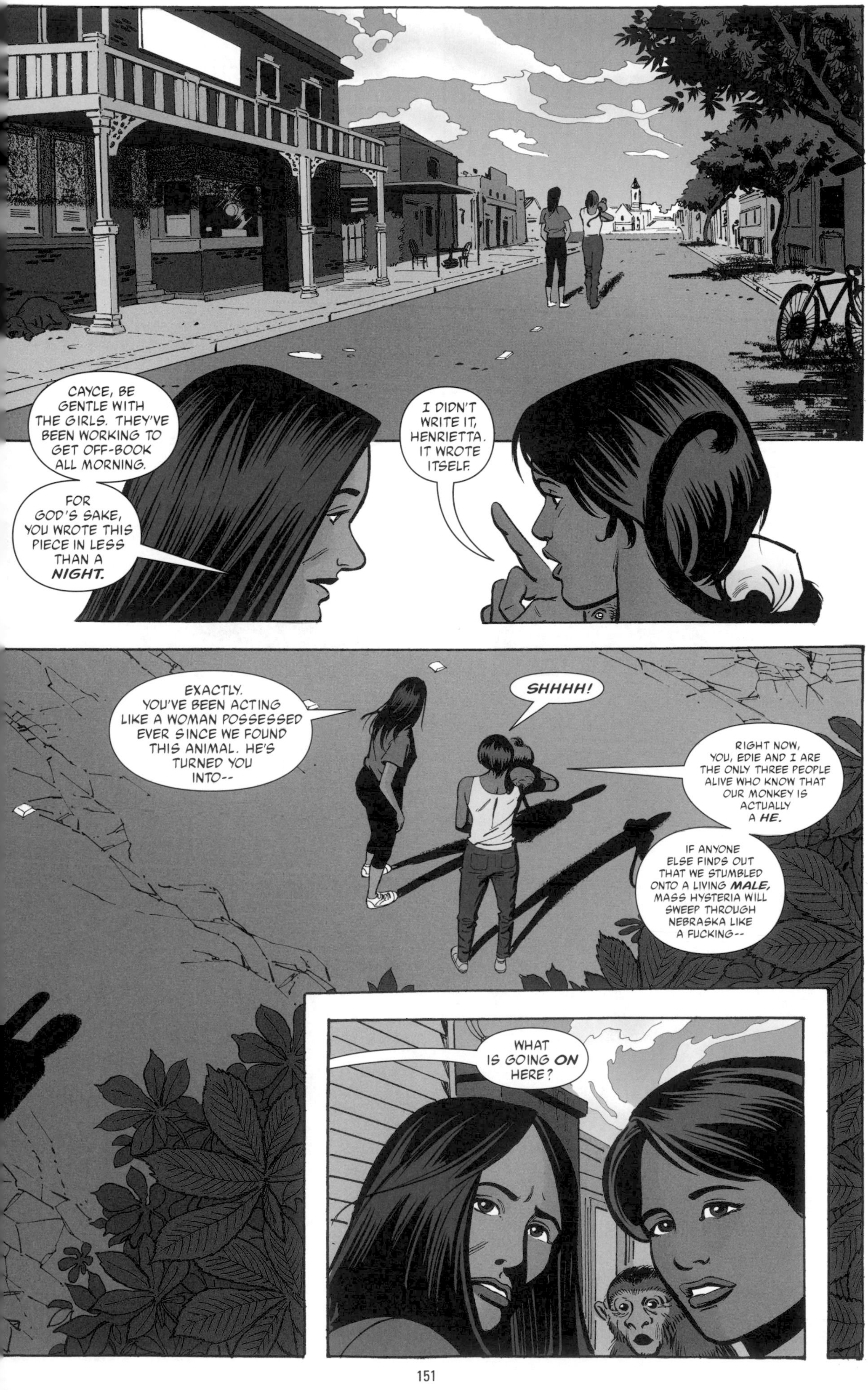
CAYCE, BE GENTLE WITH THE GIRLS. THEY'VE BEEN WORKING TO GET OFF-BOOK ALL MORNING.
FOR GOD'S SAKE, YOU WROTE THIS PIECE IN LESS THAN A **NIGHT.**
I DIDN'T WRITE IT, HENRIETTA. IT WROTE ITSELF.
EXACTLY. YOU'VE BEEN ACTING LIKE A WOMAN POSSESSED EVER SINCE WE FOUND THIS ANIMAL. HE'S TURNED YOU INTO--
SHHHH!
RIGHT NOW, YOU, EDIE AND I ARE THE ONLY THREE PEOPLE ALIVE WHO KNOW THAT OUR MONKEY IS ACTUALLY A **HE.**
IF ANYONE ELSE FINDS OUT THAT WE STUMBLED ONTO A LIVING **MALE,** MASS HYSTERIA WILL SWEEP THROUGH NEBRASKA LIKE A FUCKING--
WHAT IS GOING **ON** HERE?

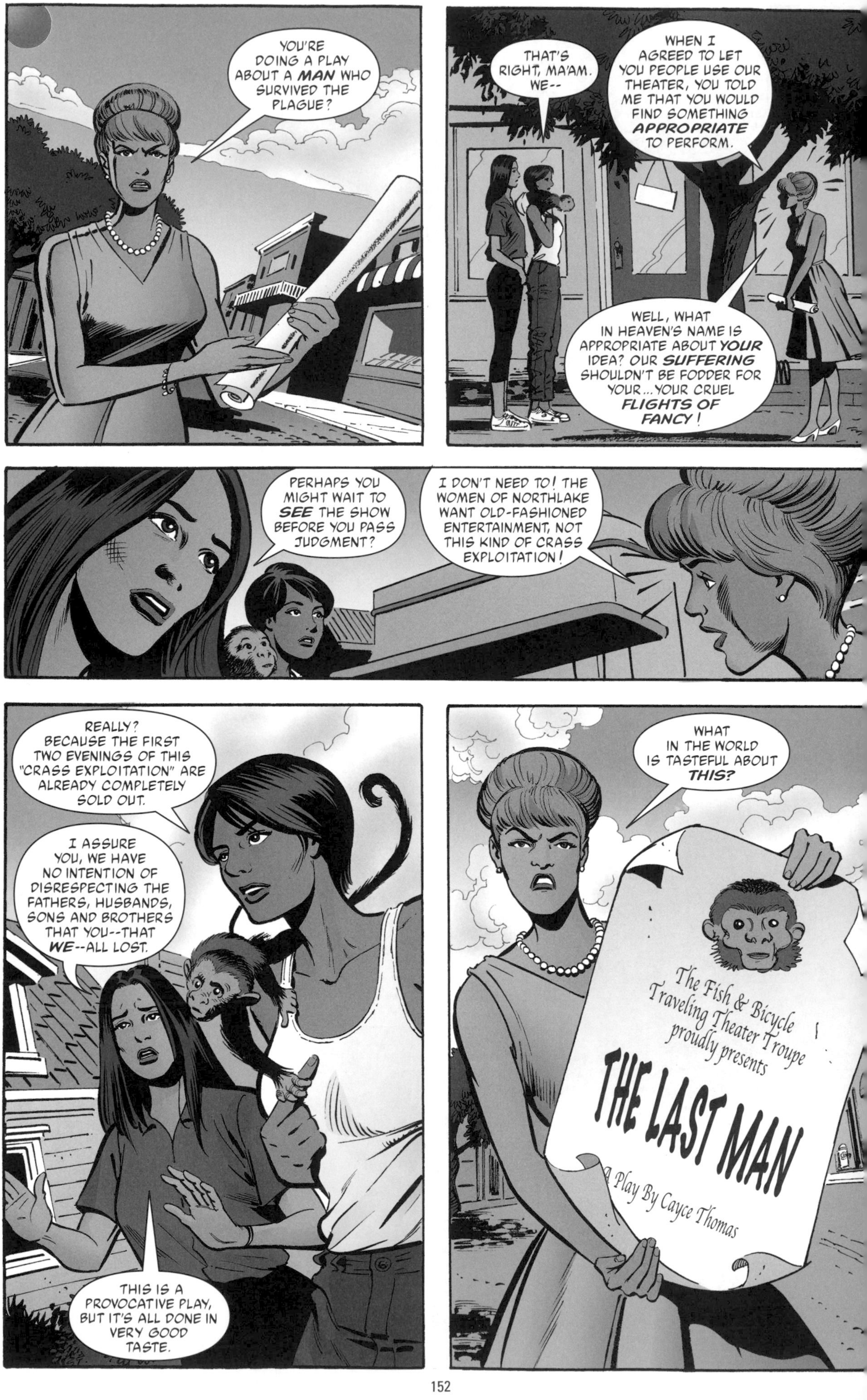
YOU'RE DOING A PLAY ABOUT A MAN WHO SURVIVED THE PLAGUE?
THAT'S RIGHT, MA'AM. WE--
WHEN I AGREED TO LET YOU PEOPLE USE OUR THEATER, YOU TOLD ME THAT YOU WOULD FIND SOMETHING APPROPRIATE TO PERFORM.
WELL, WHAT IN HEAVEN'S NAME IS APPROPRIATE ABOUT YOUR IDEA? OUR SUFFERING SHOULDN'T BE FODDER FOR YOUR... YOUR CRUEL FLIGHTS OF FANCY!
PERHAPS YOU MIGHT WAIT TO SEE THE SHOW BEFORE YOU PASS JUDGMENT?
I DON'T NEED TO! THE WOMEN OF NORTHLAKE WANT OLD-FASHIONED ENTERTAINMENT, NOT THIS KIND OF CRASS EXPLOITATION!
REALLY? BECAUSE THE FIRST TWO EVENINGS OF THIS "CRASS EXPLOITATION" ARE ALREADY COMPLETELY SOLD OUT.
I ASSURE YOU, WE HAVE NO INTENTION OF DISRESPECTING THE FATHERS, HUSBANDS, SONS AND BROTHERS THAT YOU--THAT WE--ALL LOST.
THIS IS A PROVOCATIVE PLAY, BUT IT'S ALL DONE IN VERY GOOD TASTE.
WHAT IN THE WORLD IS TASTEFUL ABOUT THIS?
The Fish & Bicycle Traveling Theater Troupe proudly presents
THE LAST MAN
A Play By Cayce Thomas

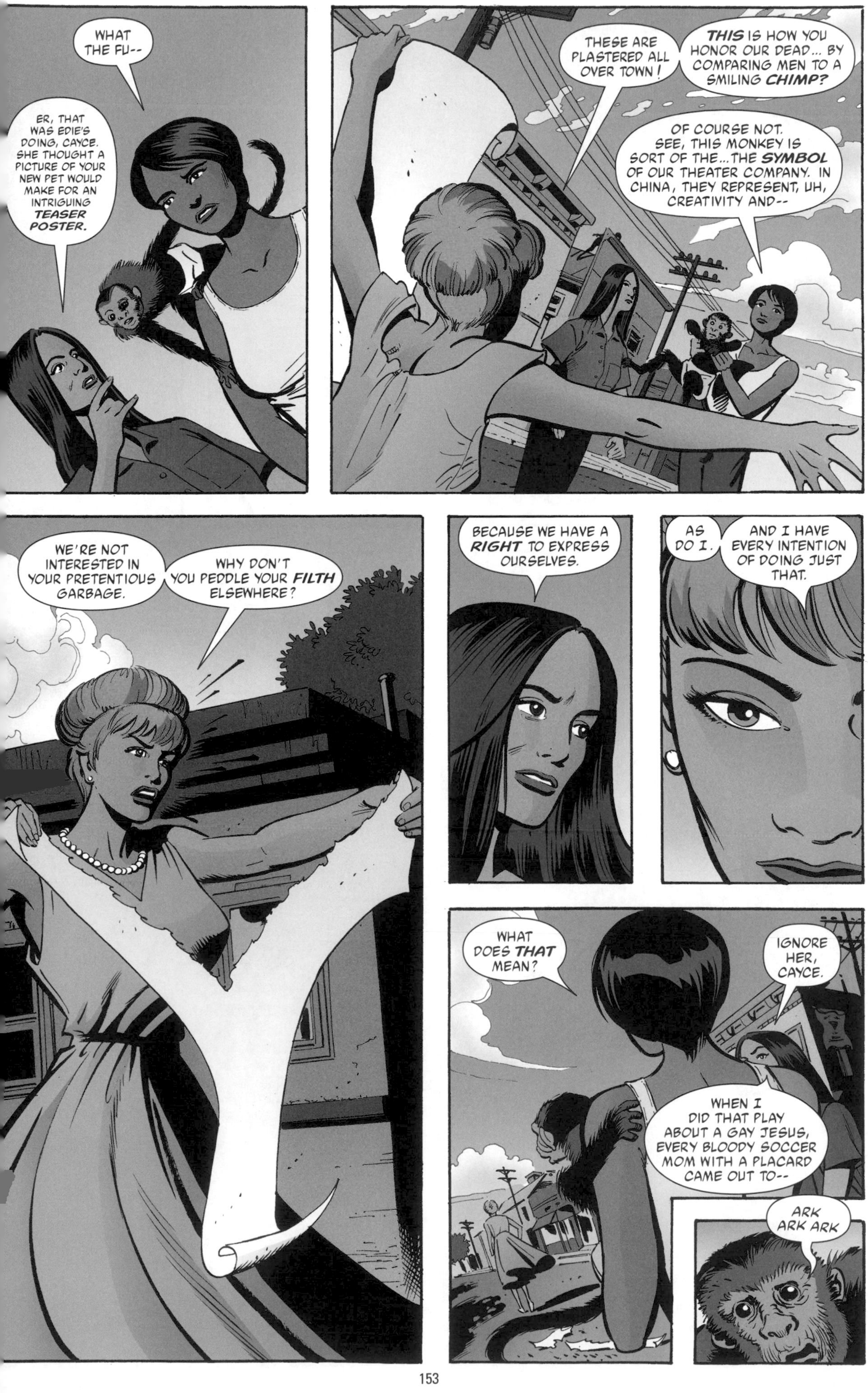

WHAT THE FU--
ER, THAT WAS EDIE'S DOING, CAYCE. SHE THOUGHT A PICTURE OF YOUR NEW PET WOULD MAKE FOR AN INTRIGUING TEASER POSTER.
THESE ARE PLASTERED ALL OVER TOWN!
THIS IS HOW YOU HONOR OUR DEAD... BY COMPARING MEN TO A SMILING CHIMP?
OF COURSE NOT. SEE, THIS MONKEY IS SORT OF THE...THE SYMBOL OF OUR THEATER COMPANY. IN CHINA, THEY REPRESENT, UH, CREATIVITY AND--
WE'RE NOT INTERESTED IN YOUR PRETENTIOUS GARBAGE.
WHY DON'T YOU PEDDLE YOUR FILTH ELSEWHERE?
BECAUSE WE HAVE A RIGHT TO EXPRESS OURSELVES.
AS DO I.
AND I HAVE EVERY INTENTION OF DOING JUST THAT.
WHAT DOES THAT MEAN?
IGNORE HER, CAYCE.
WHEN I DID THAT PLAY ABOUT A GAY JESUS, EVERY BLOODY SOCCER MOM WITH A PLACARD CAME OUT TO--
ARK ARK ARK

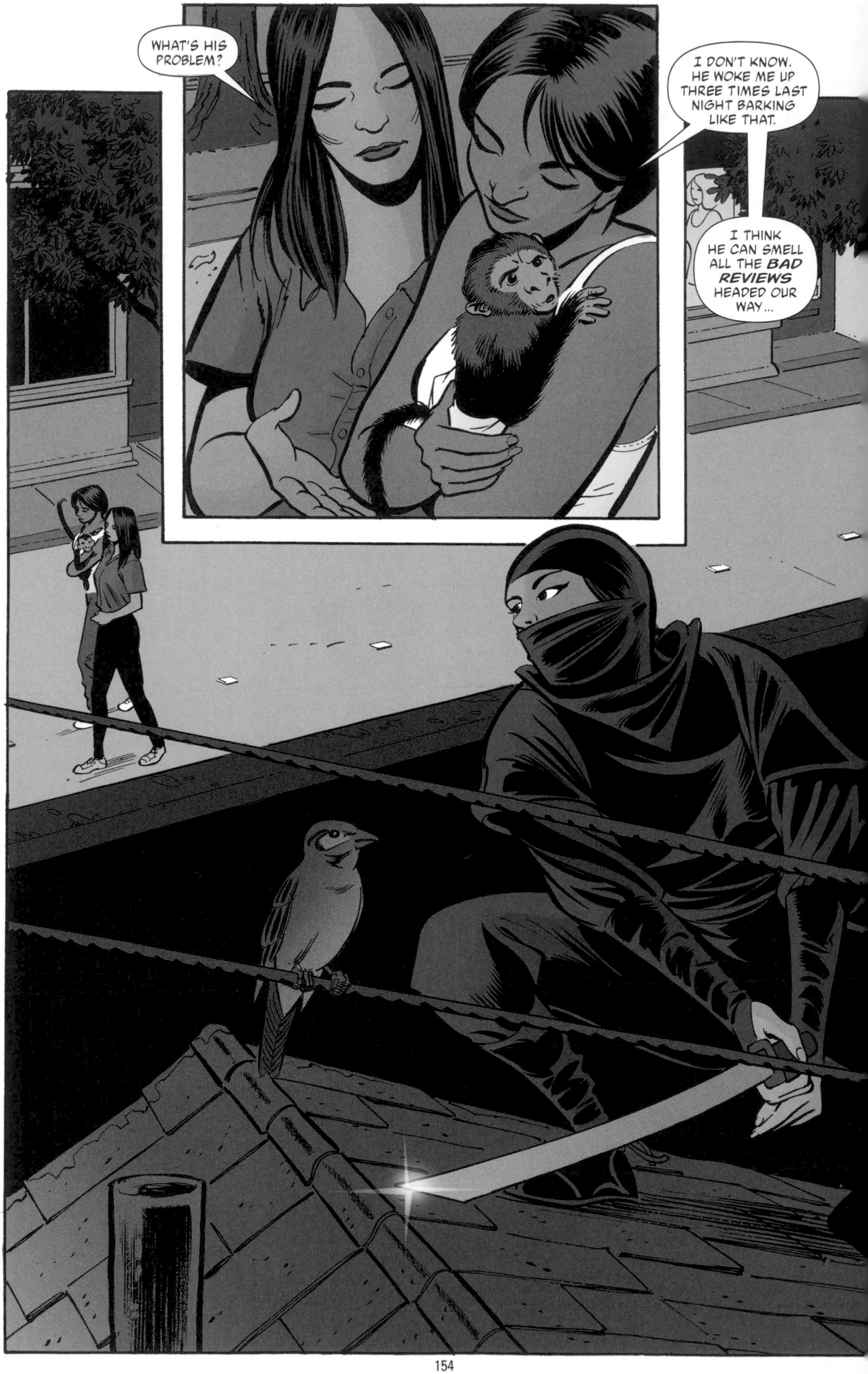

WHAT'S HIS PROBLEM?
I DON'T KNOW. HE WOKE ME UP THREE TIMES LAST NIGHT BARKING LIKE THAT.
I THINK HE CAN SMELL ALL THE *BAD REVIEWS* HEADED OUR WAY...

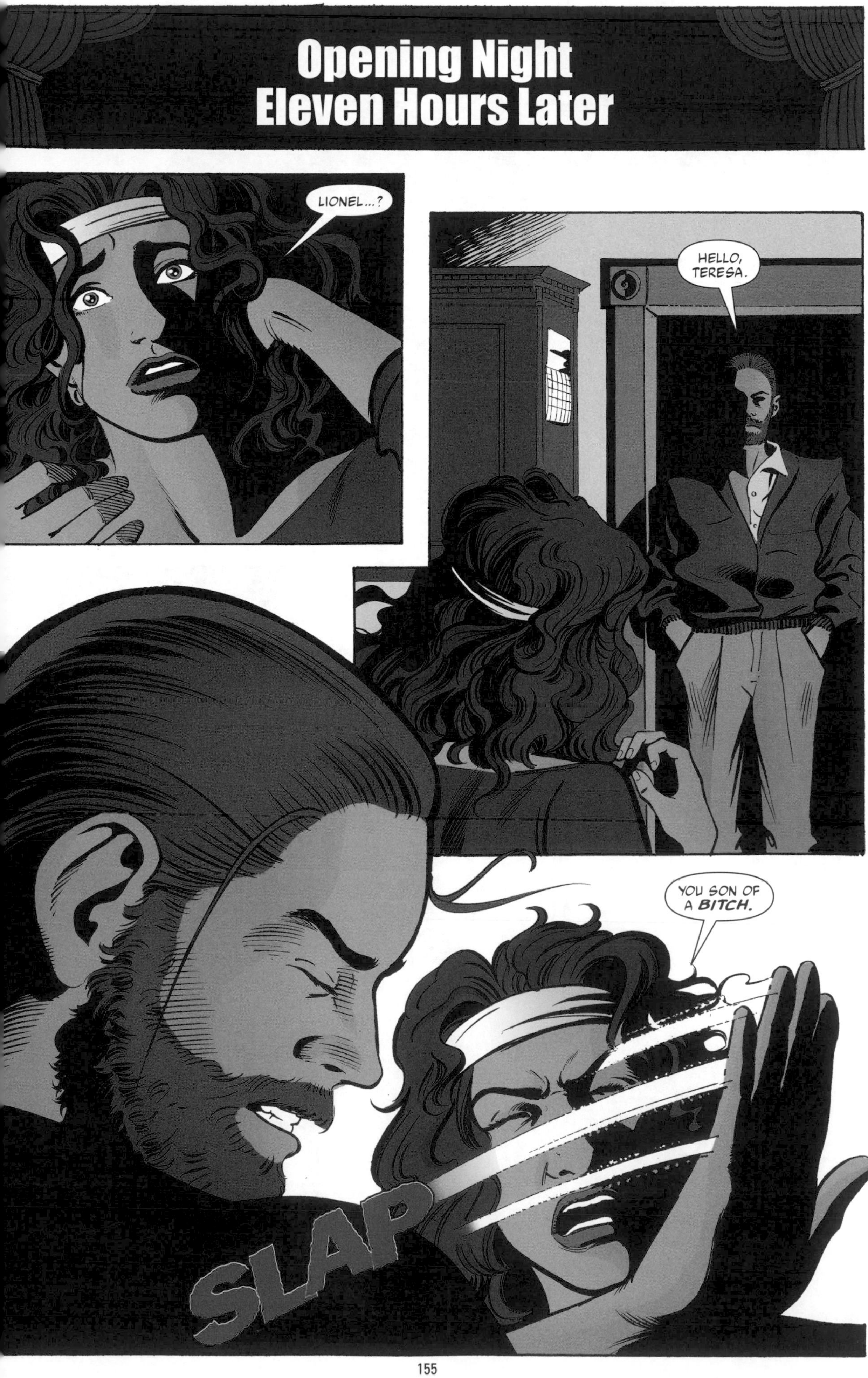
Opening Night
Eleven Hours Later
LIONEL...?
HELLO, TERESA.
YOU SON OF A BITCH.
SLAP

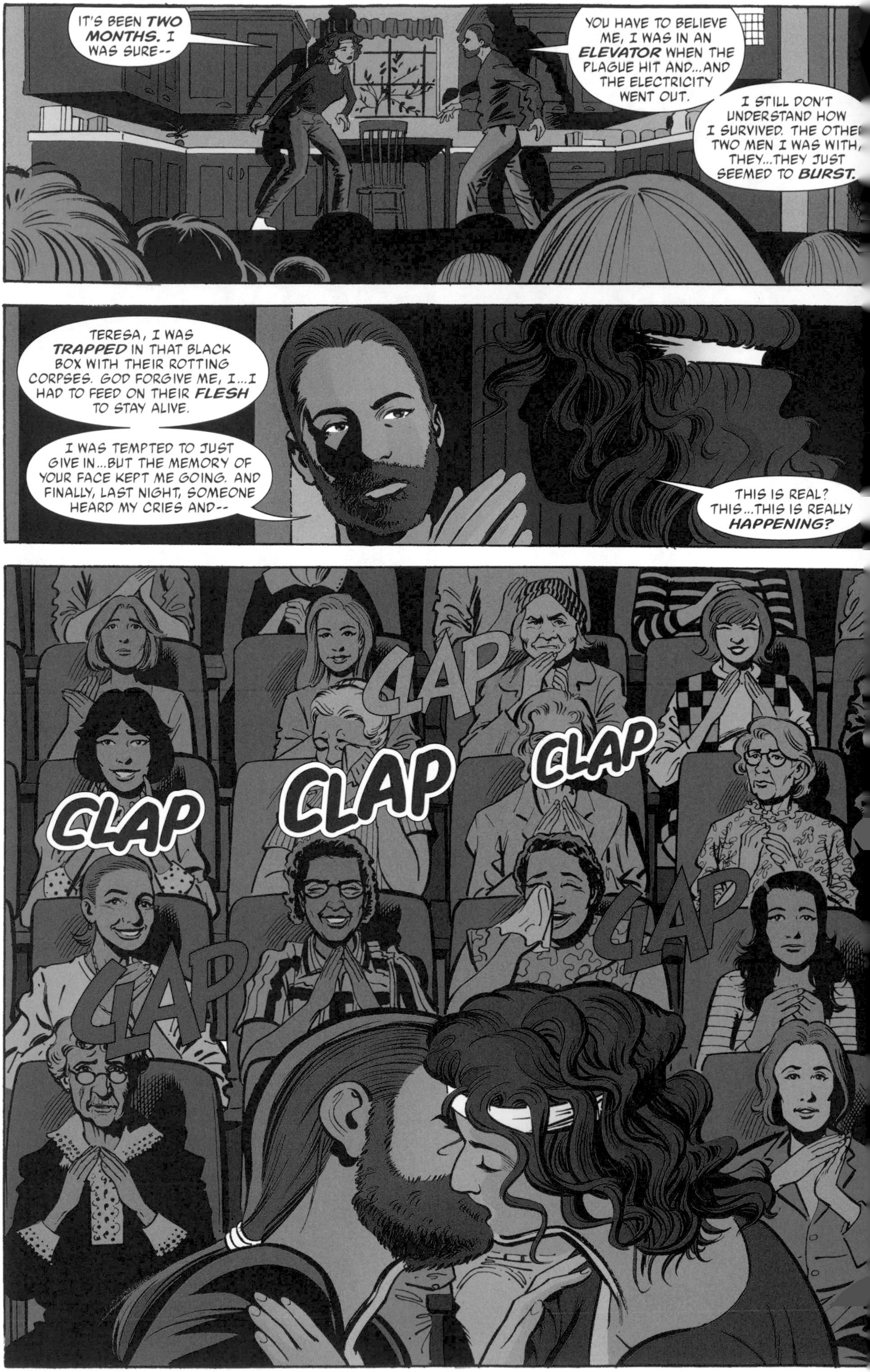
IT'S BEEN TWO MONTHS. I WAS SURE--
YOU HAVE TO BELIEVE ME, I WAS IN AN ELEVATOR WHEN THE PLAGUE HIT AND...AND THE ELECTRICITY WENT OUT.
I STILL DON'T UNDERSTAND HOW I SURVIVED. THE OTHE TWO MEN I WAS WITH, THEY...THEY JUST SEEMED TO BURST.
TERESA, I WAS TRAPPED IN THAT BLACK BOX WITH THEIR ROTTING CORPSES. GOD FORGIVE ME, I...I HAD TO FEED ON THEIR FLESH TO STAY ALIVE.
I WAS TEMPTED TO JUST GIVE IN...BUT THE MEMORY OF YOUR FACE KEPT ME GOING. AND FINALLY, LAST NIGHT, SOMEONE HEARD MY CRIES AND--
THIS IS REAL? THIS...THIS IS REALLY HAPPENING?
CLAP
CLAP
CLAP
CLAP
CLAP
CLAP

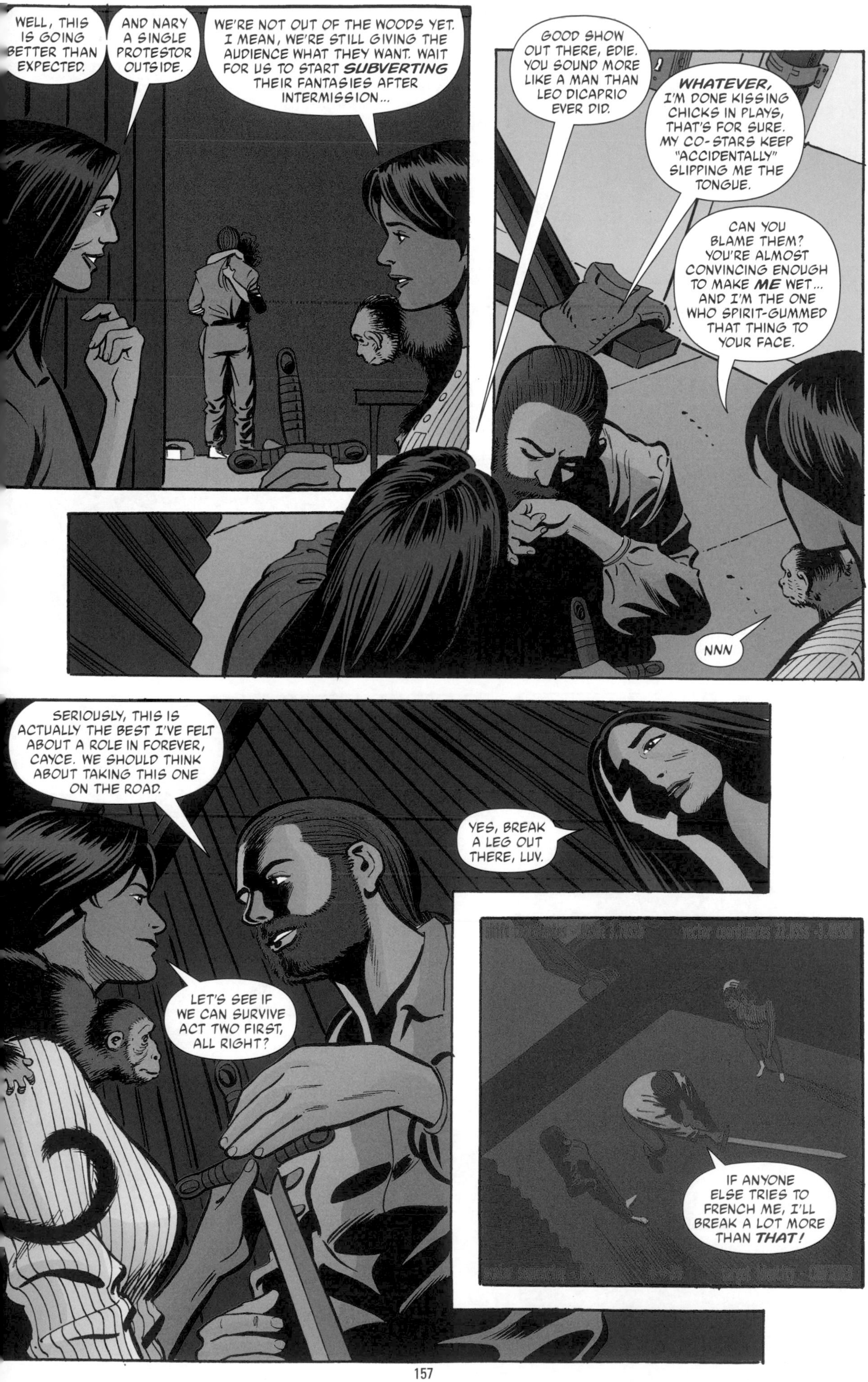
WELL, THIS IS GOING BETTER THAN EXPECTED.
AND NARY A SINGLE PROTESTOR OUTSIDE.
WE'RE NOT OUT OF THE WOODS YET. I MEAN, WE'RE STILL GIVING THE AUDIENCE WHAT THEY WANT. WAIT FOR US TO START SUBVERTING THEIR FANTASIES AFTER INTERMISSION...
GOOD SHOW OUT THERE, EDIE. YOU SOUND MORE LIKE A MAN THAN LEO DICAPRIO EVER DID.
WHATEVER, I'M DONE KISSING CHICKS IN PLAYS, THAT'S FOR SURE. MY CO-STARS KEEP "ACCIDENTALLY" SLIPPING ME THE TONGUE.
CAN YOU BLAME THEM? YOU'RE ALMOST CONVINCING ENOUGH TO MAKE ME WET... AND I'M THE ONE WHO SPIRIT-GUMMED THAT THING TO YOUR FACE.
NNN
SERIOUSLY, THIS IS ACTUALLY THE BEST I'VE FELT ABOUT A ROLE IN FOREVER, CAYCE. WE SHOULD THINK ABOUT TAKING THIS ONE ON THE ROAD.
YES, BREAK A LEG OUT THERE, LUV.
LET'S SEE IF WE CAN SURVIVE ACT TWO FIRST, ALL RIGHT?
IF ANYONE ELSE TRIES TO FRENCH ME, I'LL BREAK A LOT MORE THAN THAT!

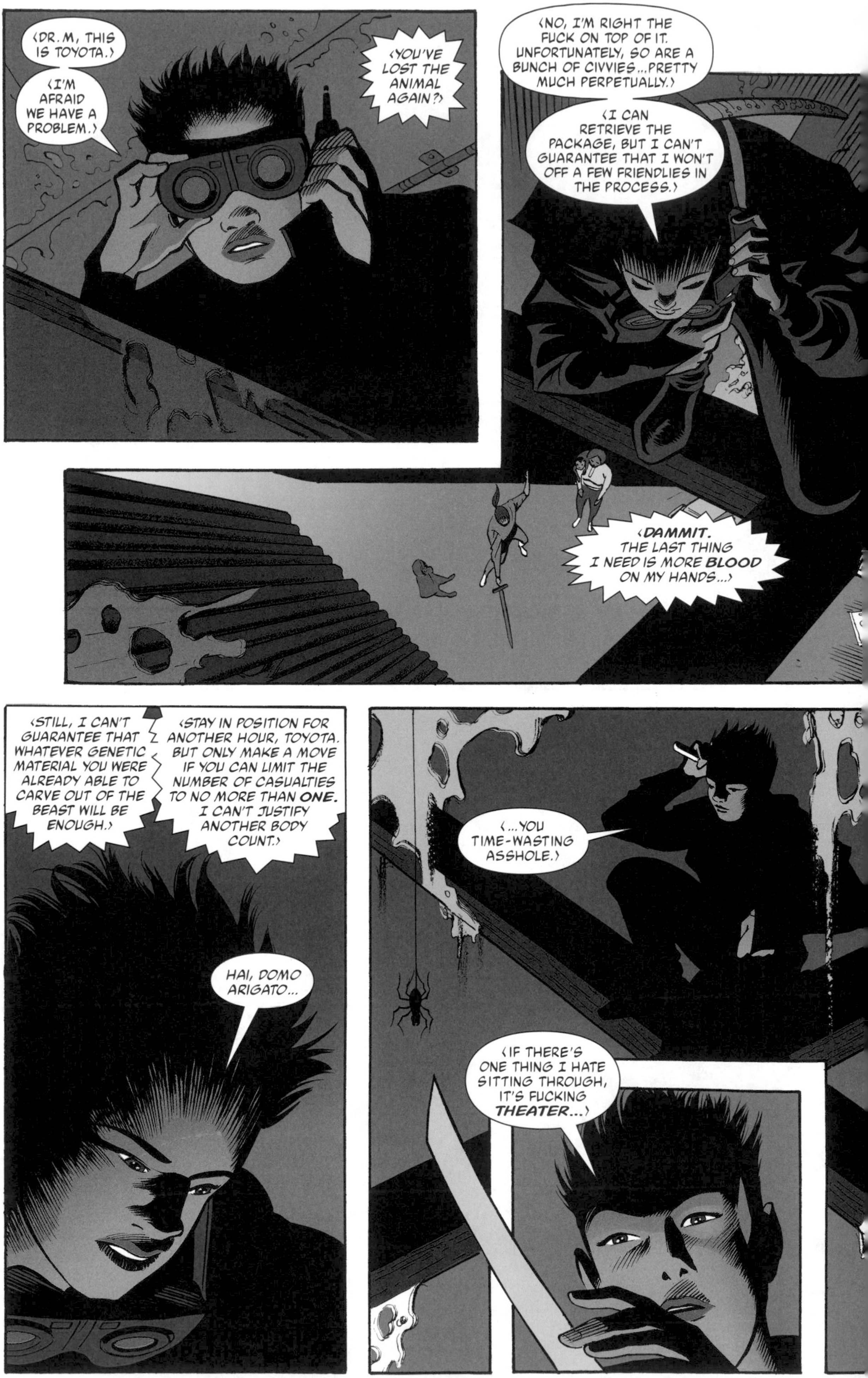
‹DR. M, THIS IS TOYOTA.›
‹I'M AFRAID WE HAVE A PROBLEM.›
‹YOU'VE LOST THE ANIMAL AGAIN?›
‹NO, I'M RIGHT THE FUCK ON TOP OF IT. UNFORTUNATELY, SO ARE A BUNCH OF CIVVIES...PRETTY MUCH PERPETUALLY.›
‹I CAN RETRIEVE THE PACKAGE, BUT I CAN'T GUARANTEE THAT I WON'T OFF A FEW FRIENDLIES IN THE PROCESS.›
‹DAMMIT. THE LAST THING I NEED IS MORE BLOOD ON MY HANDS...›
‹STILL, I CAN'T GUARANTEE THAT WHATEVER GENETIC MATERIAL YOU WERE ALREADY ABLE TO CARVE OUT OF THE BEAST WILL BE ENOUGH.›
‹STAY IN POSITION FOR ANOTHER HOUR, TOYOTA. BUT ONLY MAKE A MOVE IF YOU CAN LIMIT THE NUMBER OF CASUALTIES TO NO MORE THAN ONE. I CAN'T JUSTIFY ANOTHER BODY COUNT.›
HAI, DOMO ARIGATO...
‹...YOU TIME-WASTING ASSHOLE.›
‹IF THERE'S ONE THING I HATE SITTING THROUGH, IT'S FUCKING THEATER...›

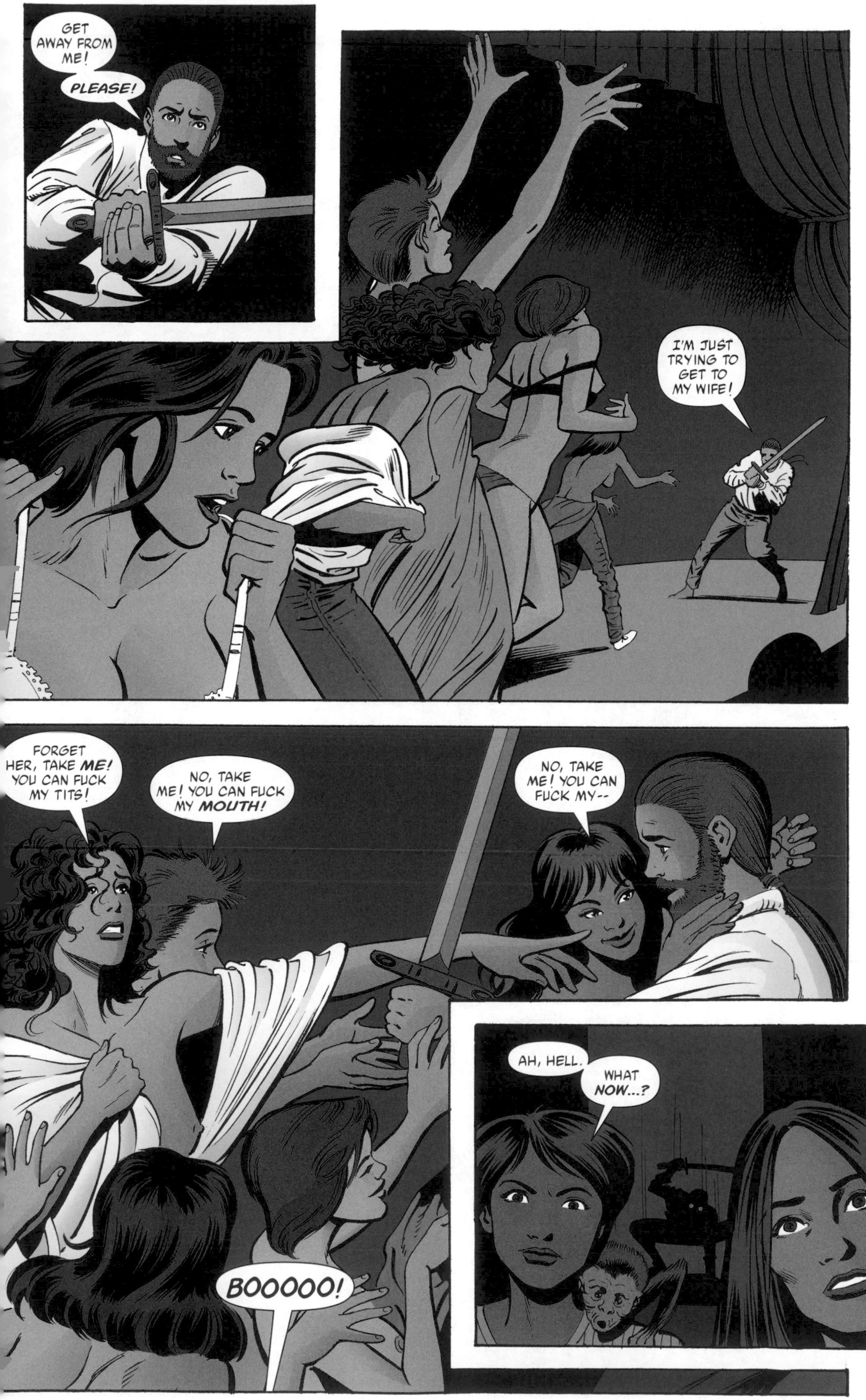

GET AWAY FROM ME!
PLEASE!
I'M JUST TRYING TO GET TO MY WIFE!
FORGET HER, TAKE ME! YOU CAN FUCK MY TITS!
NO, TAKE ME! YOU CAN FUCK MY MOUTH!
NO, TAKE ME! YOU CAN FUCK MY--
BOOOOO!
AH, HELL.
WHAT NOW...?

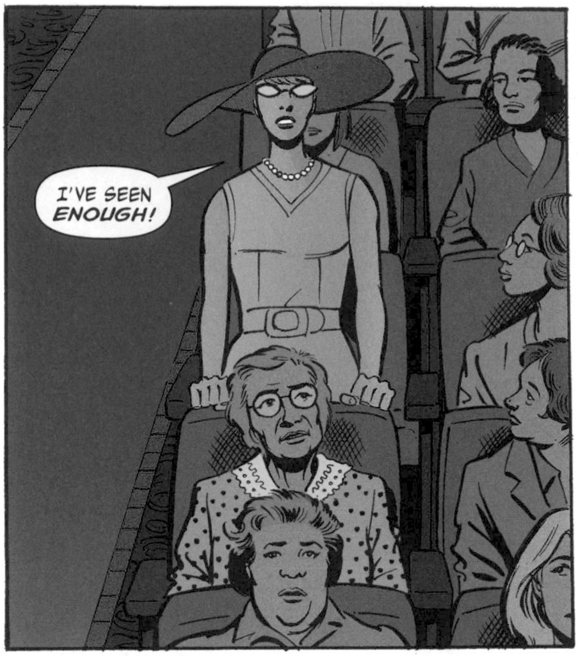
I'VE SEEN ENOUGH!

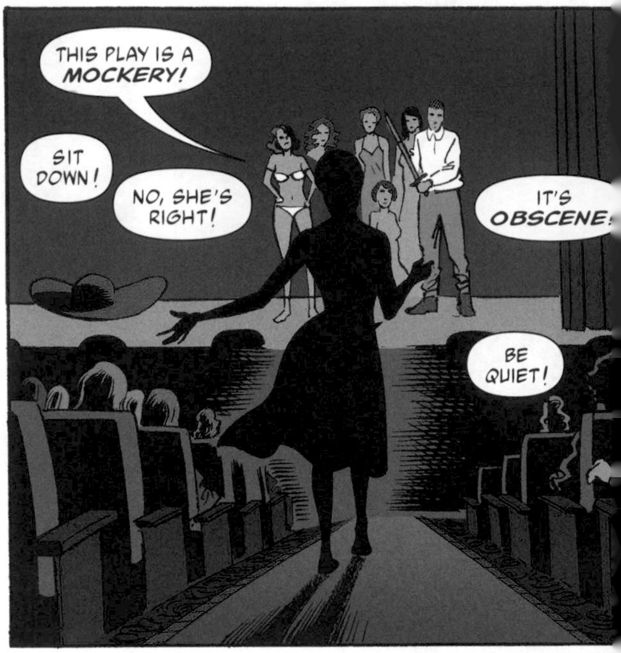
THIS PLAY IS A MOCKERY!
SIT DOWN!
NO, SHE'S RIGHT!
IT'S OBSCENE!
BE QUIET!

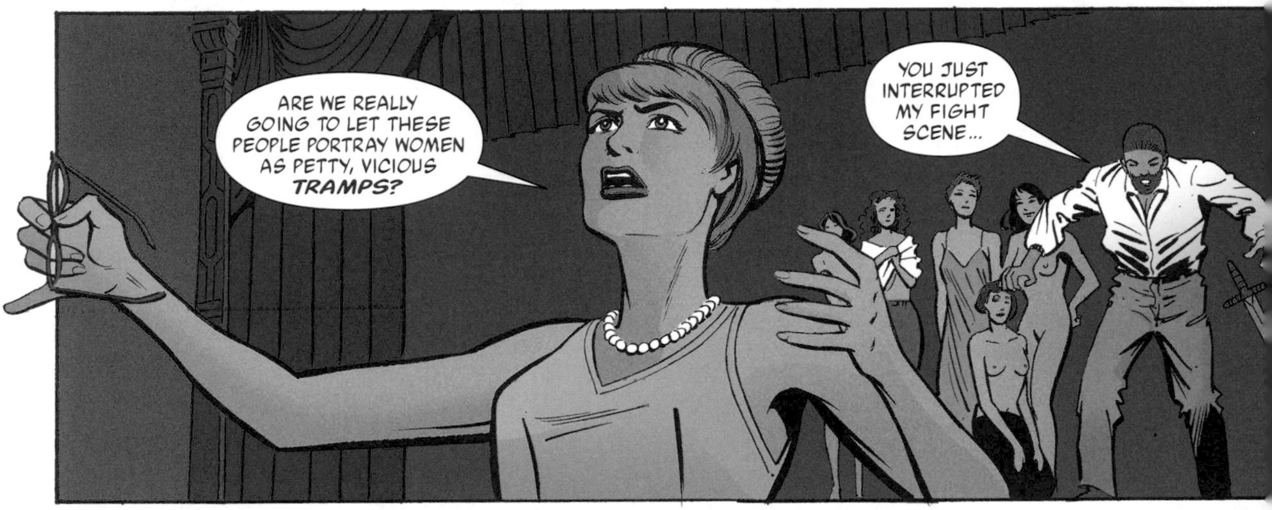
ARE WE REALLY GOING TO LET THESE PEOPLE PORTRAY WOMEN AS PETTY, VICIOUS TRAMPS?
YOU JUST INTERRUPTED MY FIGHT SCENE...

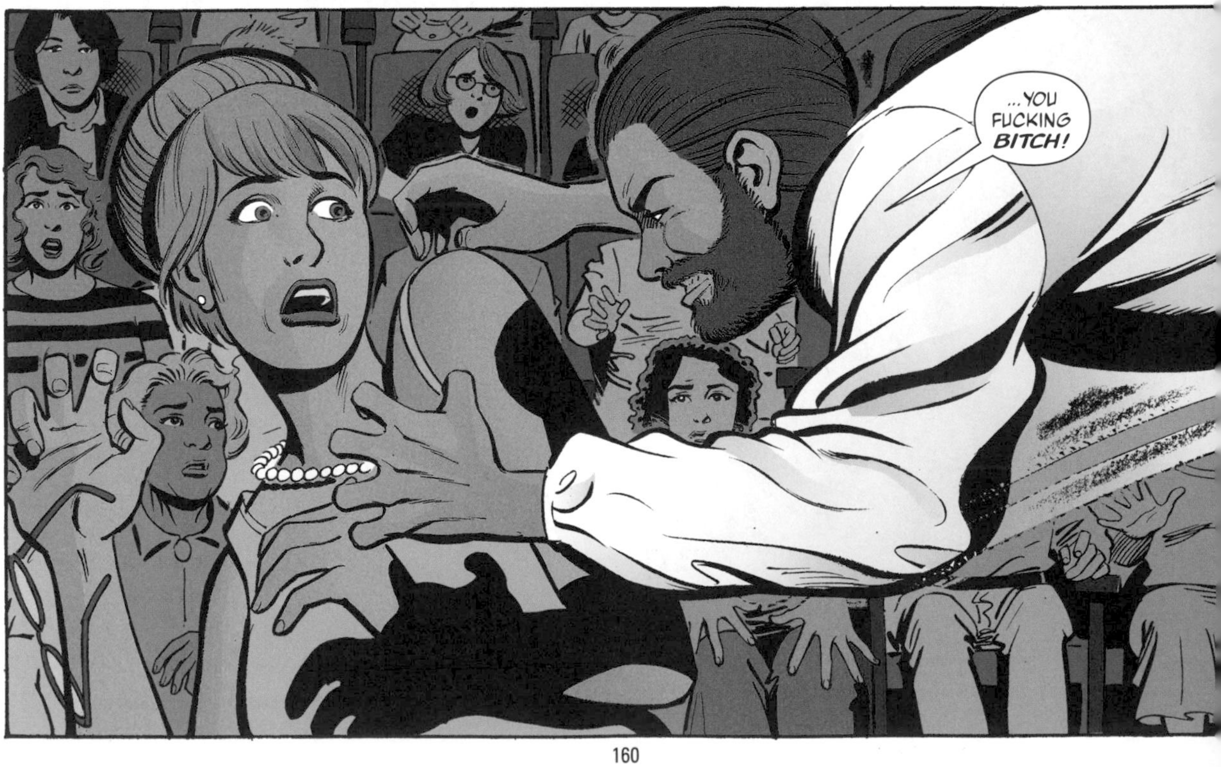
...YOU FUCKING BITCH!

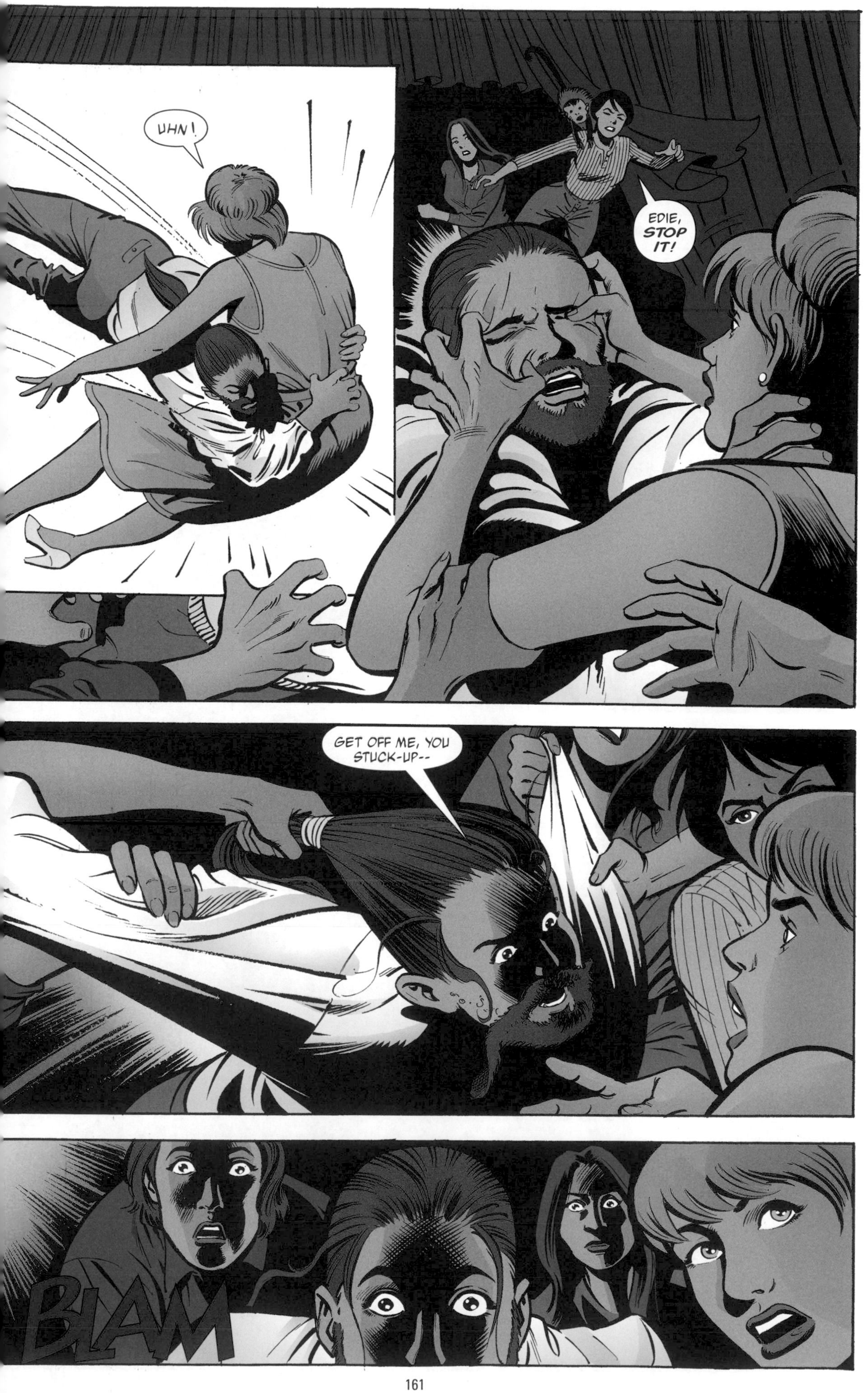
UHN!
EDIE, STOP IT!
GET OFF ME, YOU STUCK-UP--
BLAM

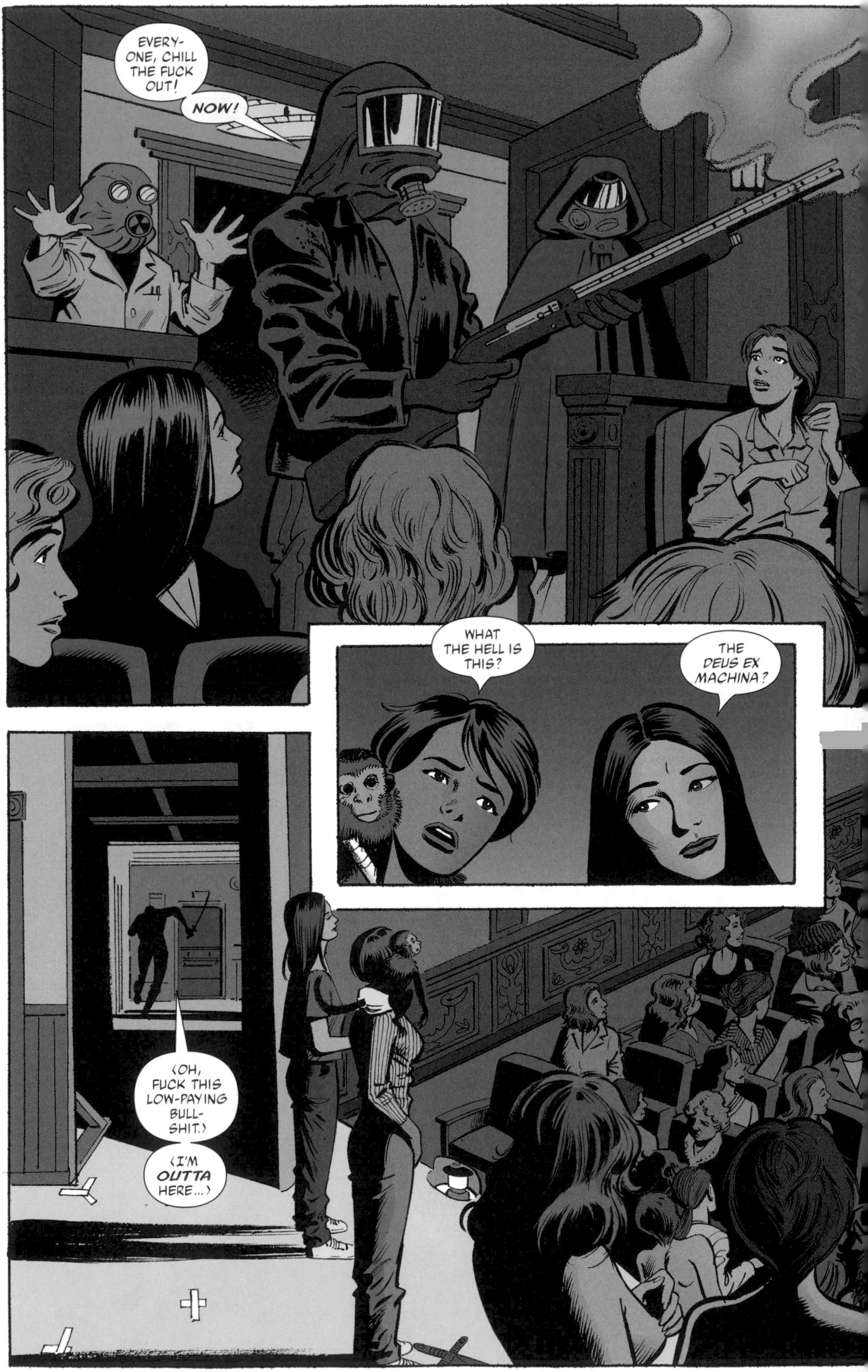
EVERY-ONE, CHILL THE FUCK OUT!
NOW!
WHAT THE HELL IS THIS?
THE DEUS EX MACHINA?
‹OH, FUCK THIS LOW-PAYING BULL-SHIT.›
‹I'M OUTTA HERE...›

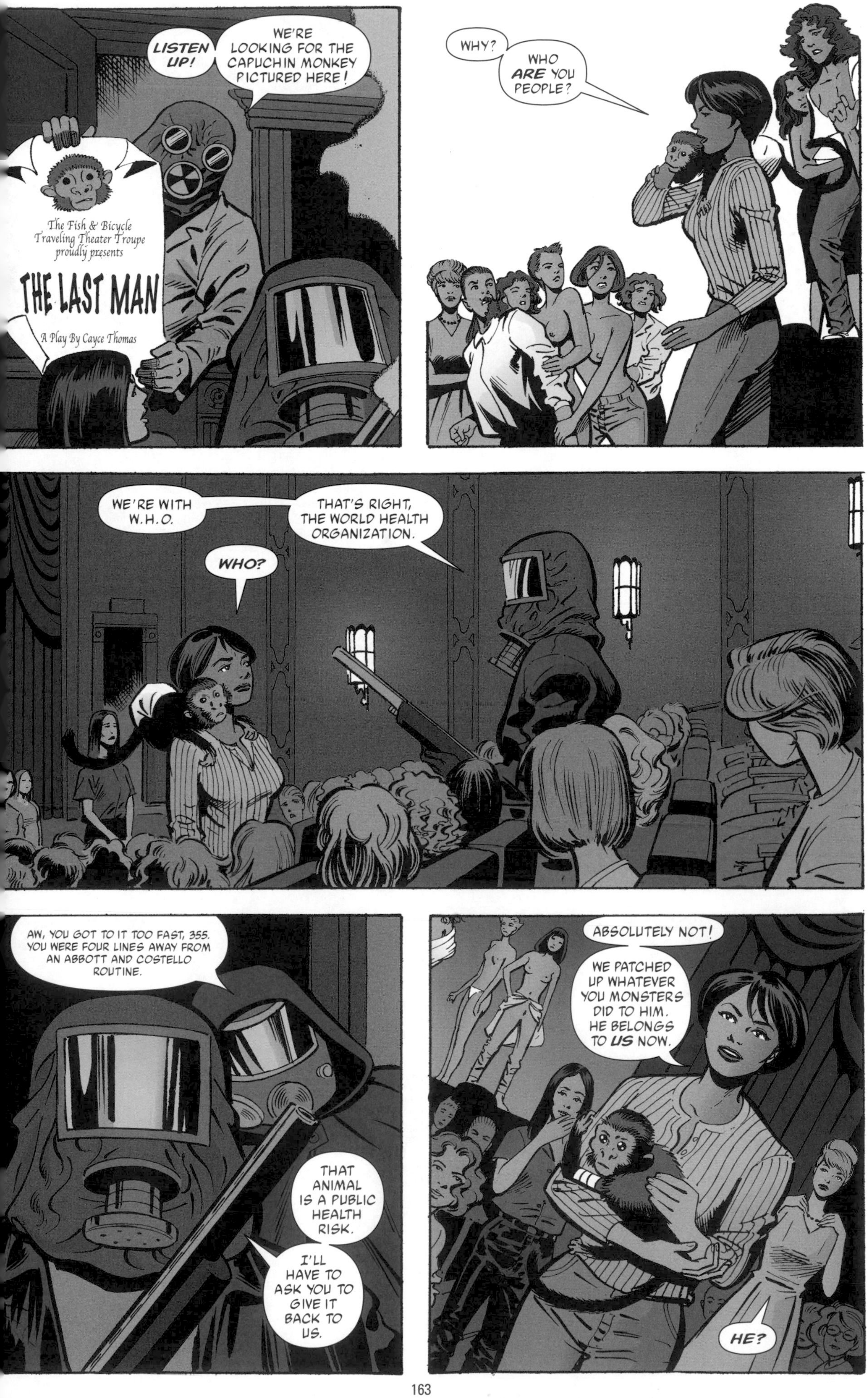
LISTEN UP!
WE'RE LOOKING FOR THE CAPUCHIN MONKEY PICTURED HERE!
The Fish & Bicycle Traveling Theater Troupe proudly presents
THE LAST MAN
A Play By Cayce Thomas
WHY?
WHO ARE YOU PEOPLE?
WE'RE WITH W.H.O.
THAT'S RIGHT, THE WORLD HEALTH ORGANIZATION.
WHO?
AW, YOU GOT TO IT TOO FAST, 355. YOU WERE FOUR LINES AWAY FROM AN ABBOTT AND COSTELLO ROUTINE.
THAT ANIMAL IS A PUBLIC HEALTH RISK.
I'LL HAVE TO ASK YOU TO GIVE IT BACK TO US.
ABSOLUTELY NOT!
WE PATCHED UP WHATEVER YOU MONSTERS DID TO HIM. HE BELONGS TO US NOW.
HE?

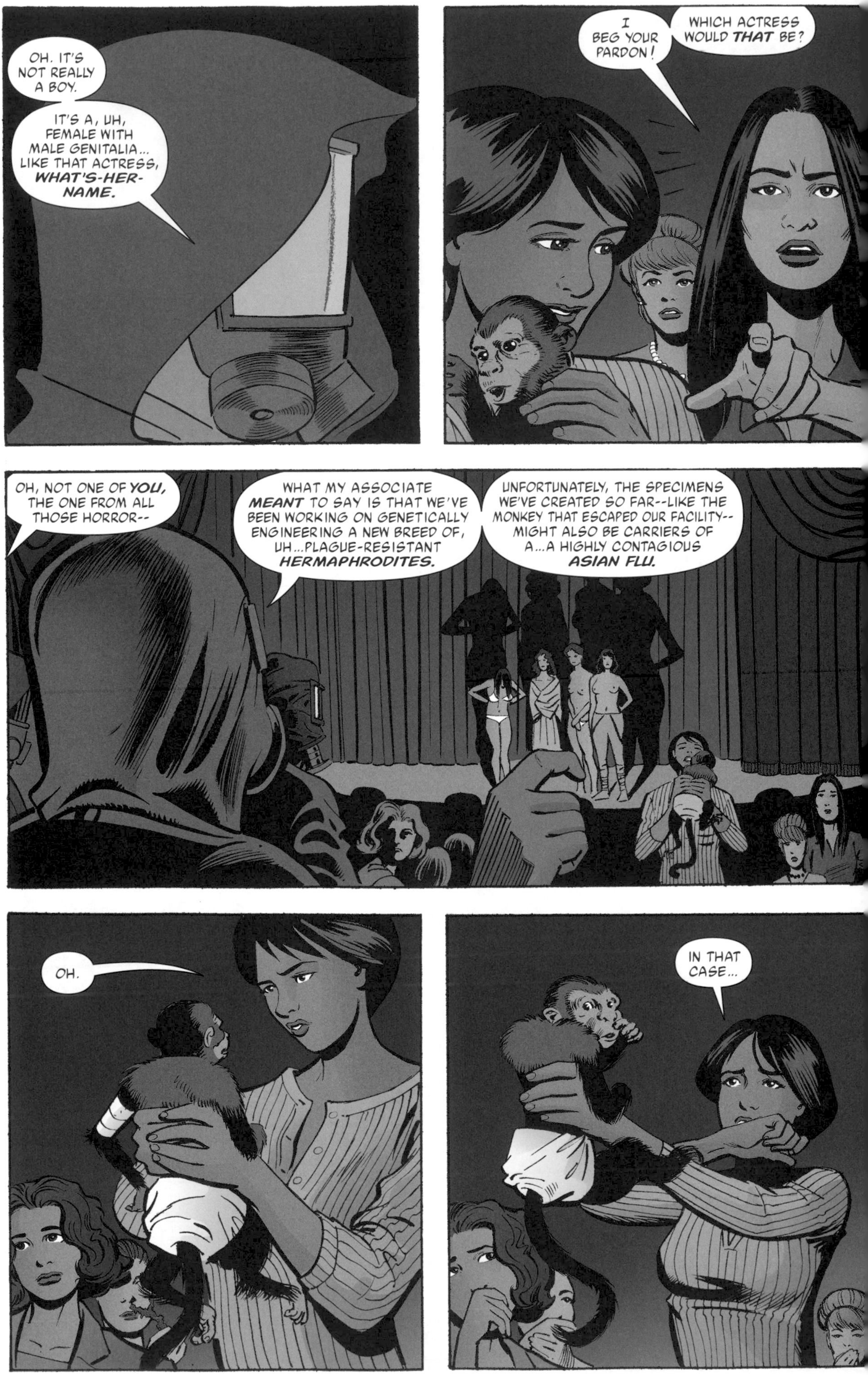
OH. IT'S NOT REALLY A BOY.
IT'S A, UH, FEMALE WITH MALE GENITALIA... LIKE THAT ACTRESS, WHAT'S-HER-NAME.
I BEG YOUR PARDON!
WHICH ACTRESS WOULD THAT BE?
OH, NOT ONE OF YOU, THE ONE FROM ALL THOSE HORROR--
WHAT MY ASSOCIATE MEANT TO SAY IS THAT WE'VE BEEN WORKING ON GENETICALLY ENGINEERING A NEW BREED OF, UH...PLAGUE-RESISTANT HERMAPHRODITES.
UNFORTUNATELY, THE SPECIMENS WE'VE CREATED SO FAR--LIKE THE MONKEY THAT ESCAPED OUR FACILITY--MIGHT ALSO BE CARRIERS OF A...A HIGHLY CONTAGIOUS ASIAN FLU.
OH.
IN THAT CASE...

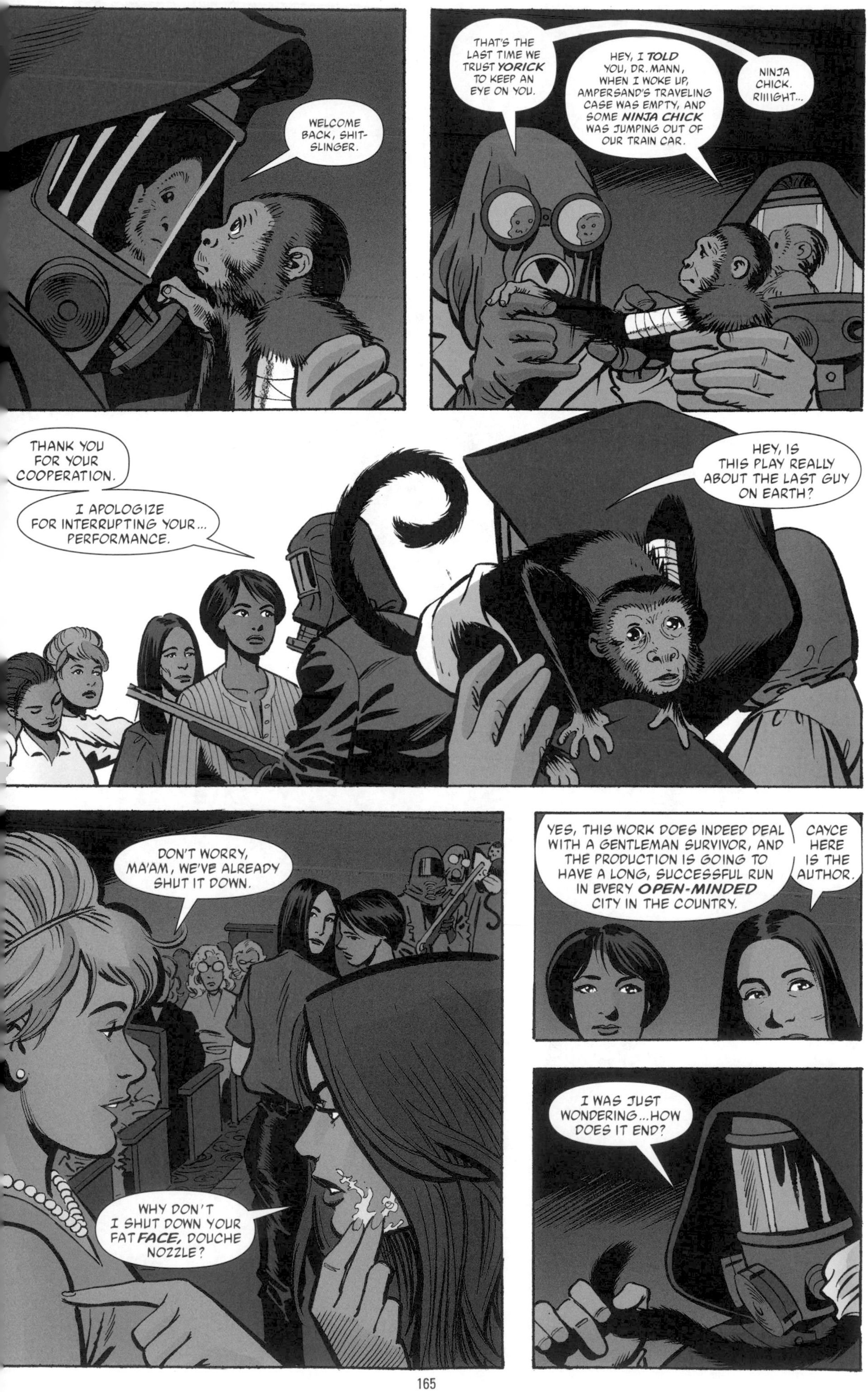
WELCOME BACK, SHIT-SLINGER.
THAT'S THE LAST TIME WE TRUST YORICK TO KEEP AN EYE ON YOU.
HEY, I TOLD YOU, DR. MANN, WHEN I WOKE UP, AMPERSAND'S TRAVELING CASE WAS EMPTY, AND SOME NINJA CHICK WAS JUMPING OUT OF OUR TRAIN CAR.
NINJA CHICK. RIIIIGHT...
THANK YOU FOR YOUR COOPERATION.
I APOLOGIZE FOR INTERRUPTING YOUR... PERFORMANCE.
HEY, IS THIS PLAY REALLY ABOUT THE LAST GUY ON EARTH?
DON'T WORRY, MA'AM, WE'VE ALREADY SHUT IT DOWN.
WHY DON'T I SHUT DOWN YOUR FAT FACE, DOUCHE NOZZLE?
YES, THIS WORK DOES INDEED DEAL WITH A GENTLEMAN SURVIVOR, AND THE PRODUCTION IS GOING TO HAVE A LONG, SUCCESSFUL RUN IN EVERY OPEN-MINDED CITY IN THE COUNTRY.
CAYCE HERE IS THE AUTHOR.
I WAS JUST WONDERING... HOW DOES IT END?

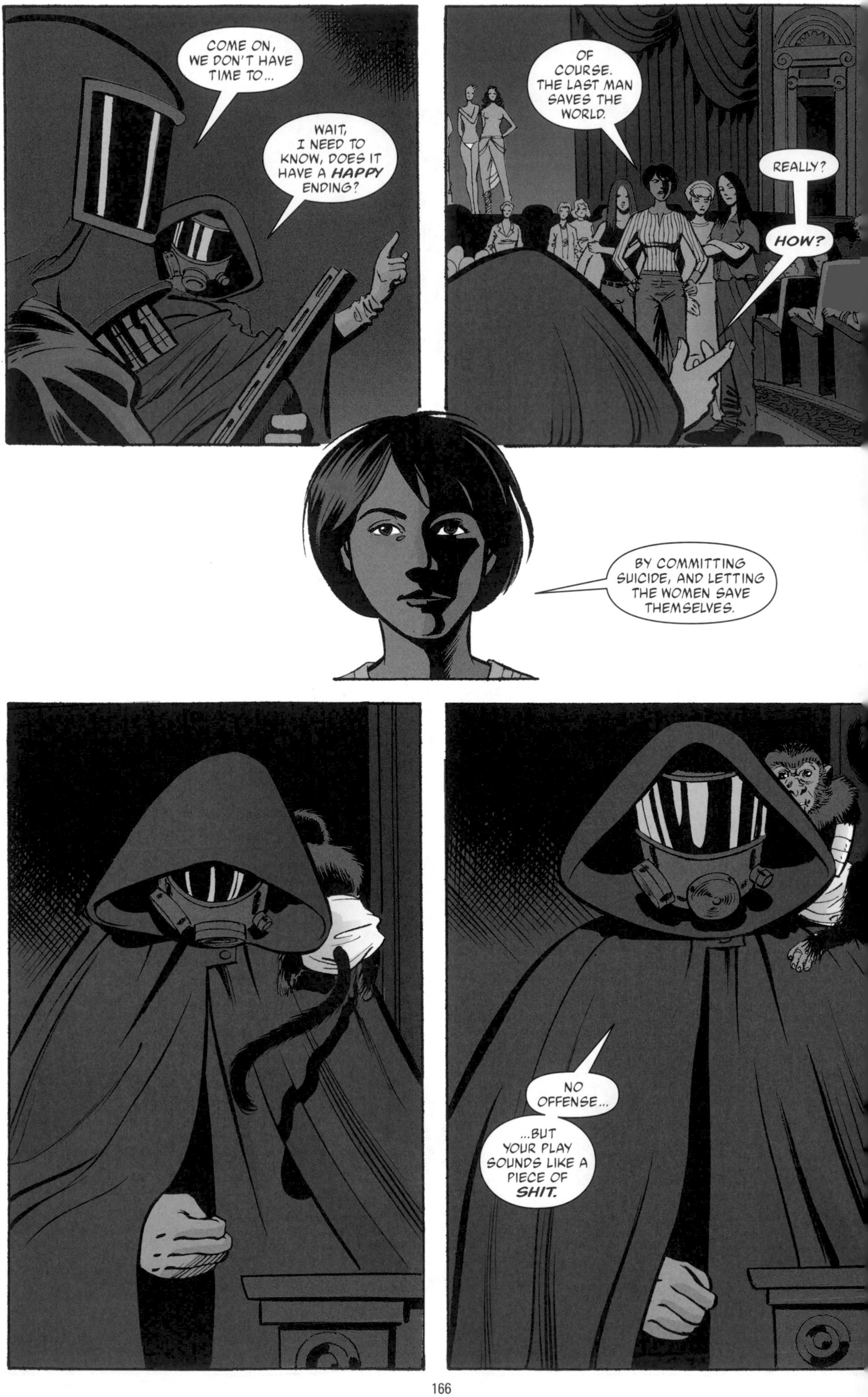
COME ON, WE DON'T HAVE TIME TO...
WAIT, I NEED TO KNOW, DOES IT HAVE A HAPPY ENDING?
OF COURSE. THE LAST MAN SAVES THE WORLD.
REALLY?
HOW?
BY COMMITTING SUICIDE, AND LETTING THE WOMEN SAVE THEMSELVES.
NO OFFENSE...
...BUT YOUR PLAY SOUNDS LIKE A PIECE OF SHIT.

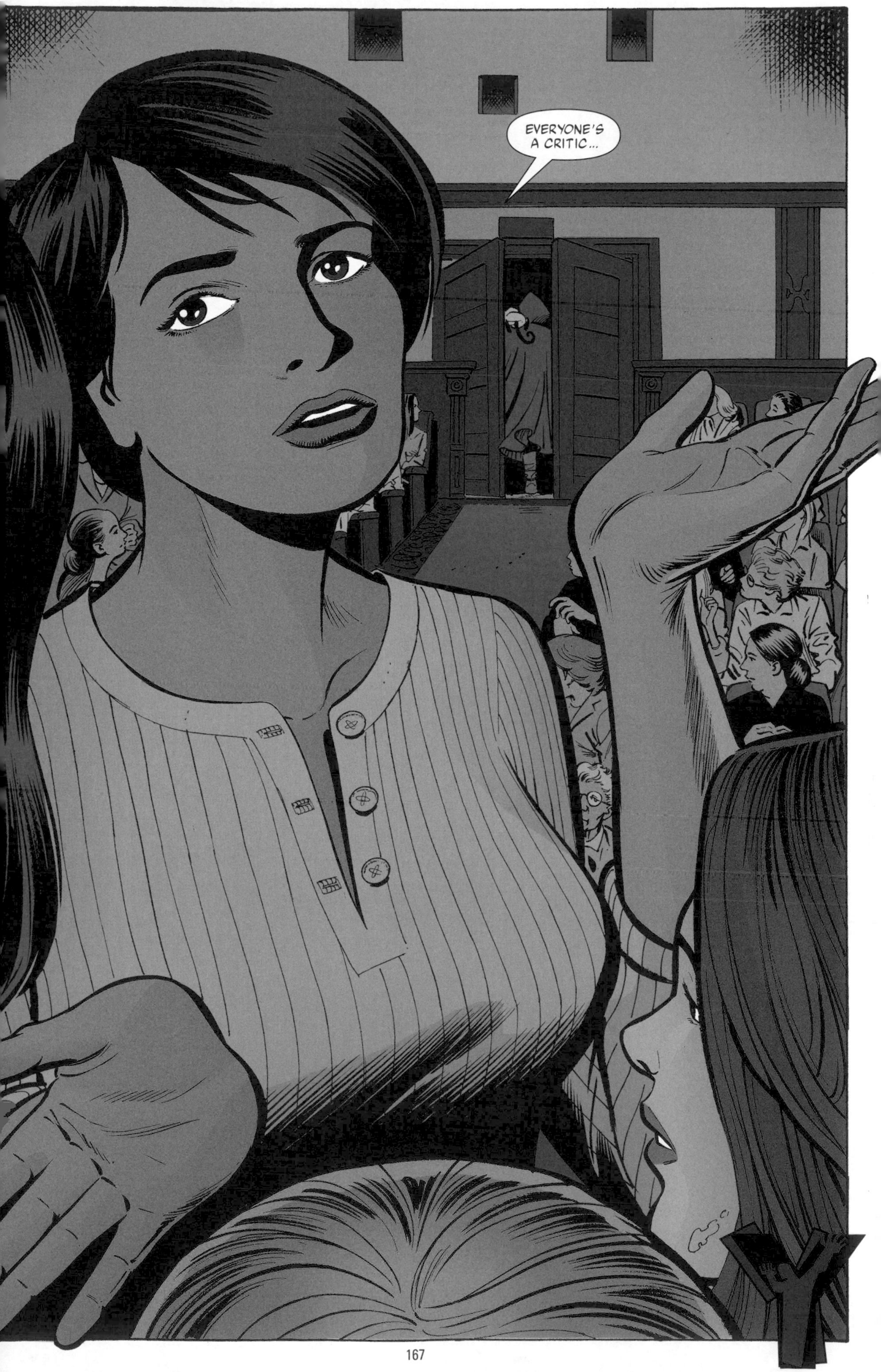
EVERYONE'S
A CRITIC...

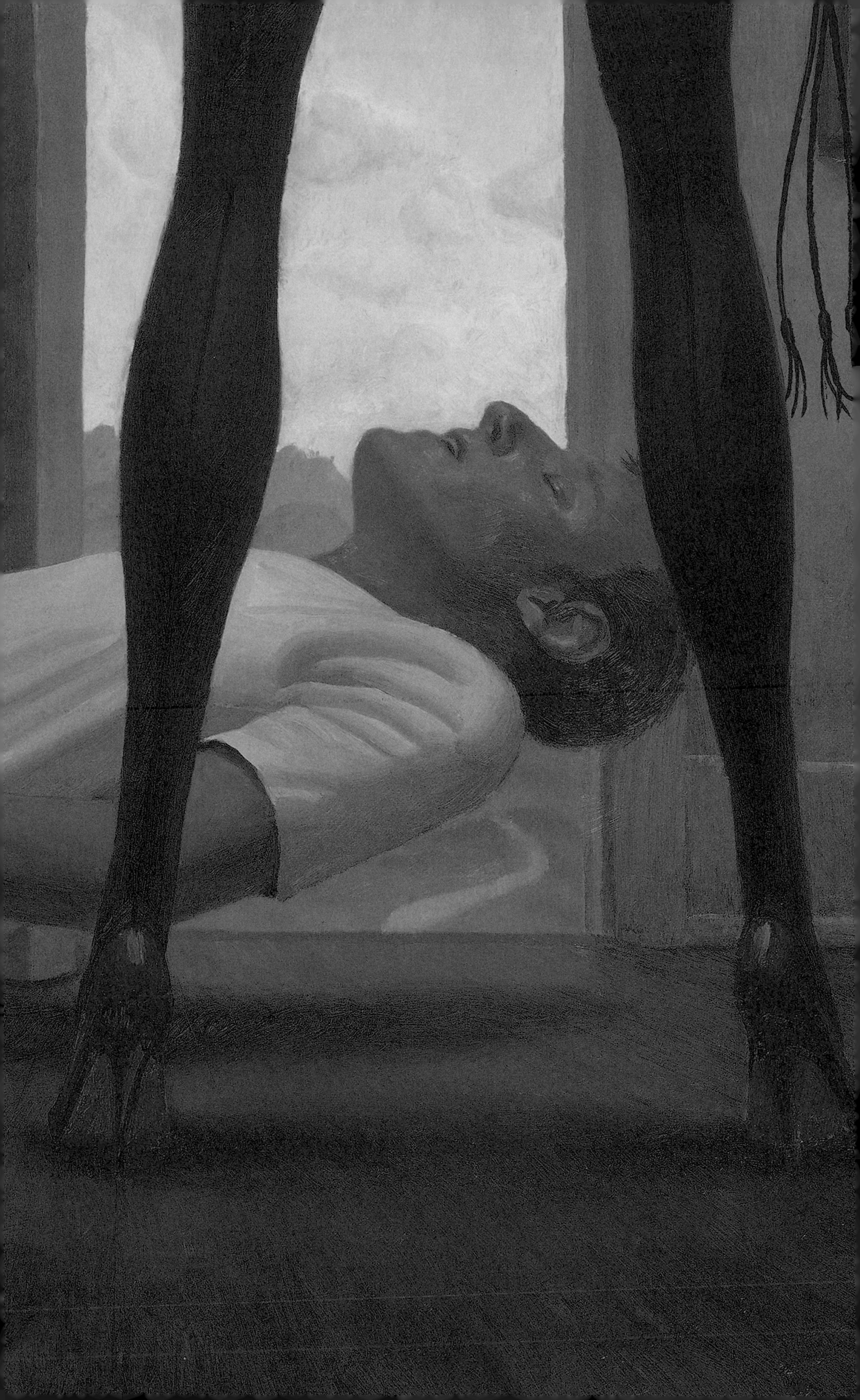

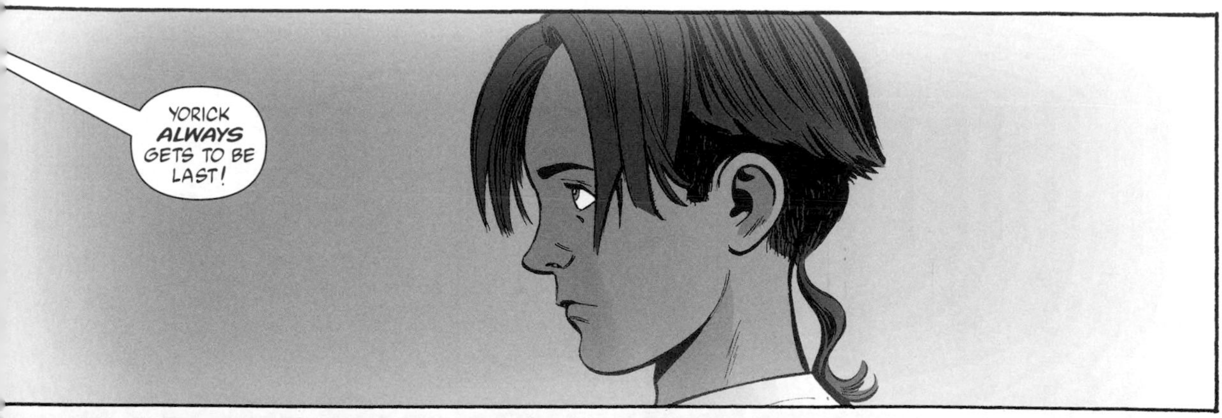
YORICK ALWAYS GETS TO BE LAST!

Cleveland, Ohio
Fifteen Years Ago

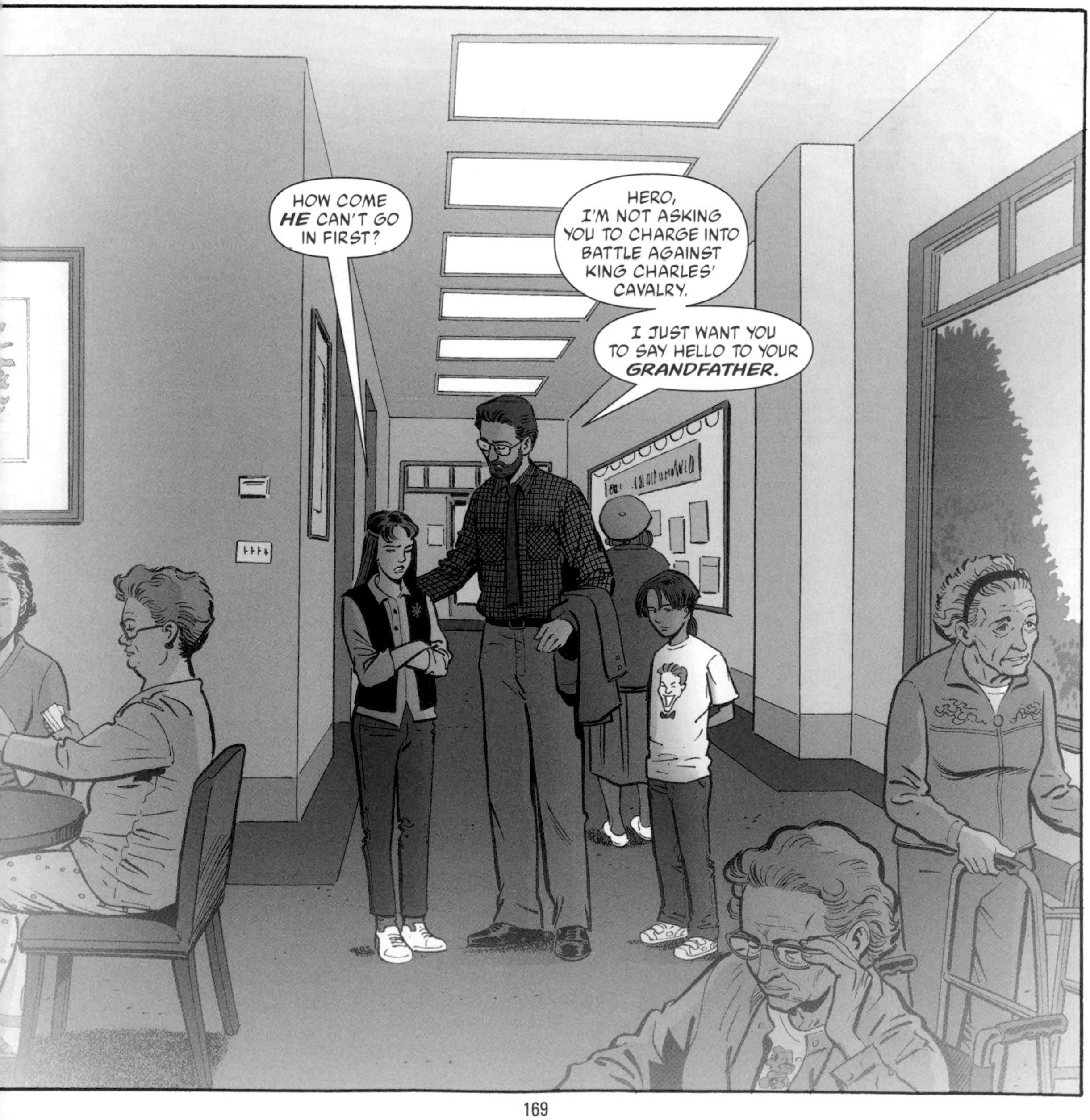
HOW COME HE CAN'T GO IN FIRST?
HERO, I'M NOT ASKING YOU TO CHARGE INTO BATTLE AGAINST KING CHARLES' CAVALRY.
I JUST WANT YOU TO SAY HELLO TO YOUR GRANDFATHER.

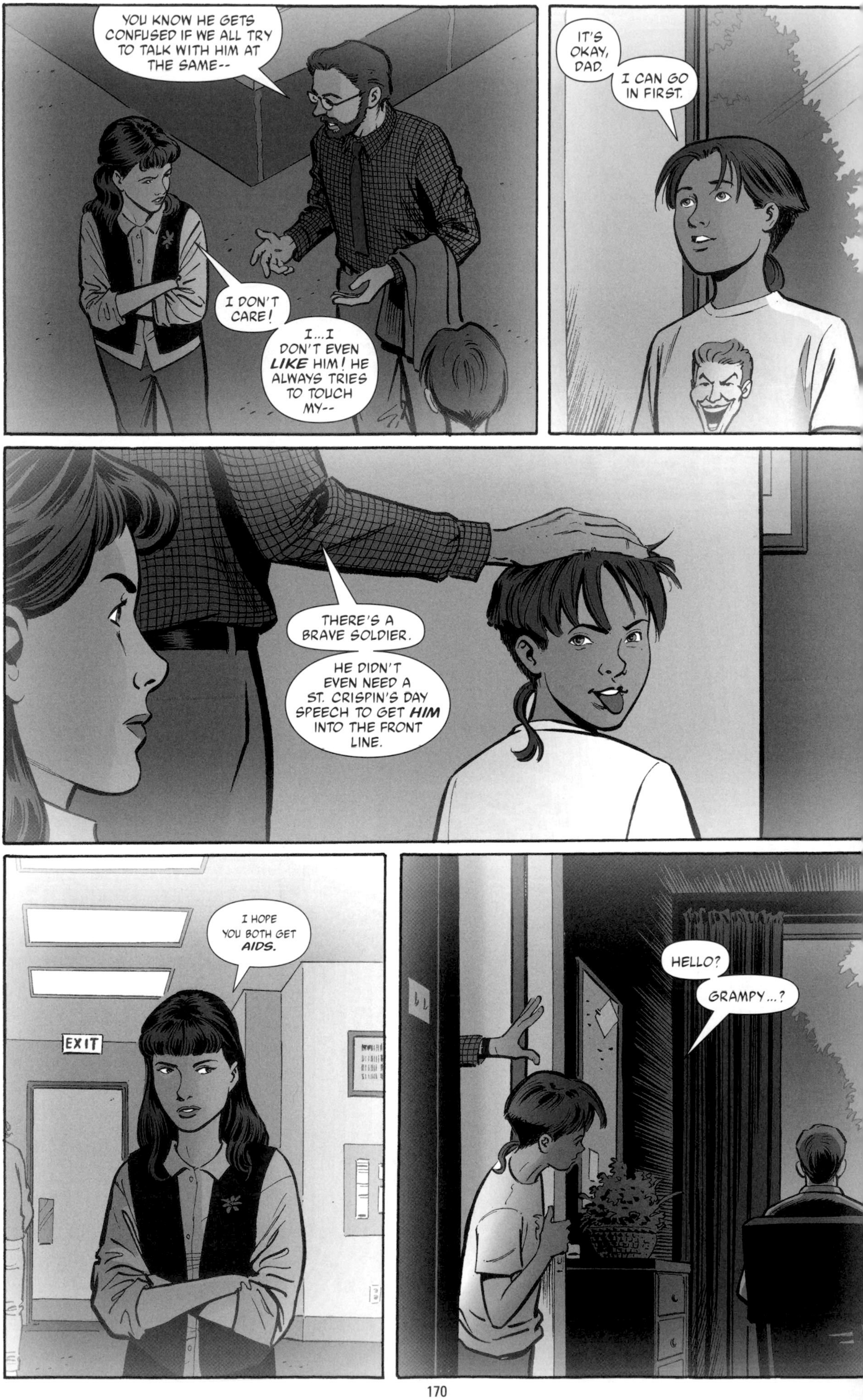
YOU KNOW HE GETS CONFUSED IF WE ALL TRY TO TALK WITH HIM AT THE SAME--
I DON'T CARE!
I...I DON'T EVEN LIKE HIM! HE ALWAYS TRIES TO TOUCH MY--
IT'S OKAY, DAD.
I CAN GO IN FIRST.
THERE'S A BRAVE SOLDIER.
HE DIDN'T EVEN NEED A ST. CRISPIN'S DAY SPEECH TO GET HIM INTO THE FRONT LINE.
I HOPE YOU BOTH GET AIDS.
EXIT
HELLO?
GRAMPY...?

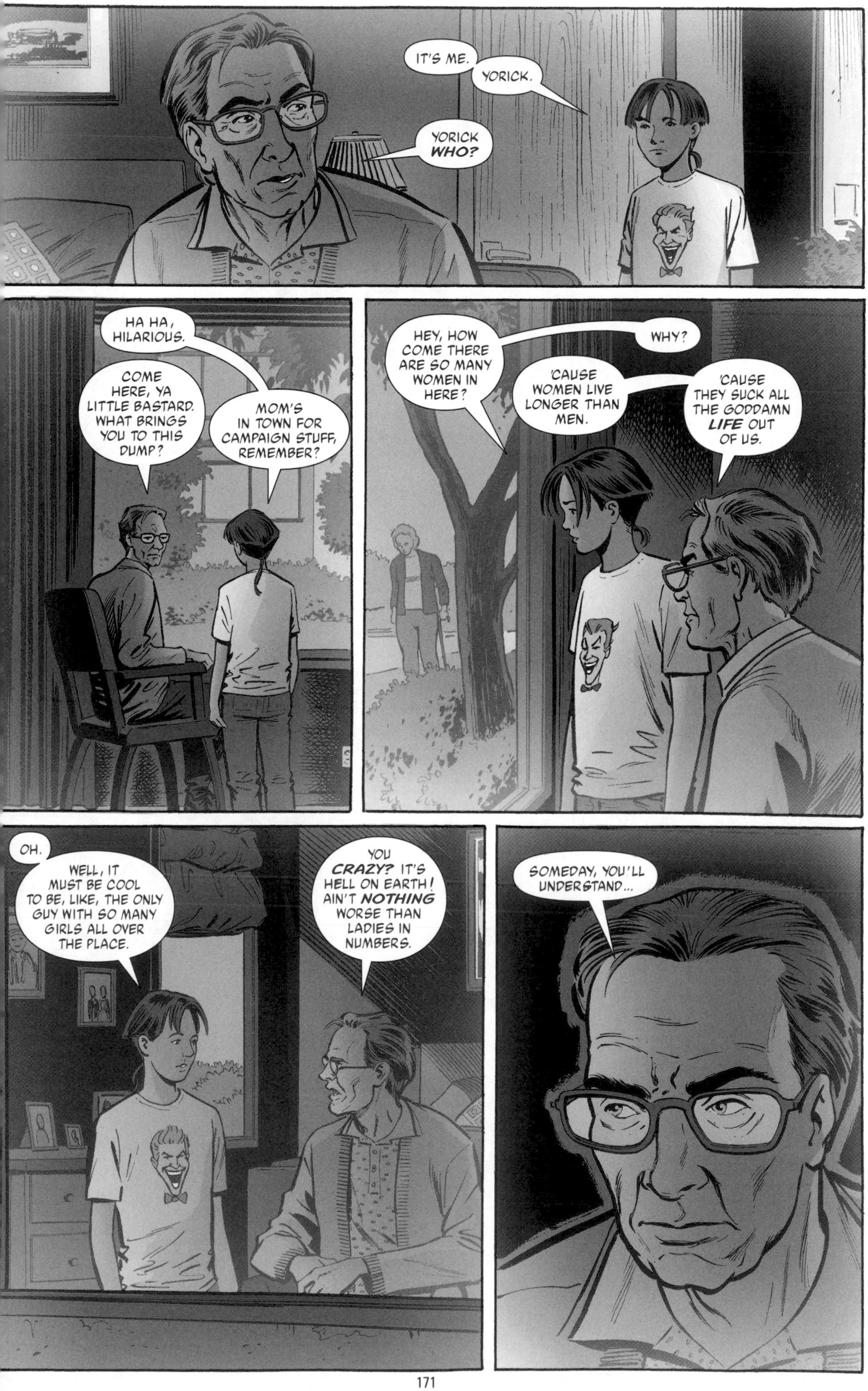
IT'S ME.
YORICK.
YORICK WHO?
HA HA, HILARIOUS.
COME HERE, YA LITTLE BASTARD. WHAT BRINGS YOU TO THIS DUMP?
MOM'S IN TOWN FOR CAMPAIGN STUFF, REMEMBER?
HEY, HOW COME THERE ARE SO MANY WOMEN IN HERE?
'CAUSE WOMEN LIVE LONGER THAN MEN.
WHY?
'CAUSE THEY SUCK ALL THE GODDAMN LIFE OUT OF US.
OH.
WELL, IT MUST BE COOL TO BE, LIKE, THE ONLY GUY WITH SO MANY GIRLS ALL OVER THE PLACE.
YOU CRAZY? IT'S HELL ON EARTH! AIN'T NOTHING WORSE THAN LADIES IN NUMBERS.
SOMEDAY, YOU'LL UNDERSTAND...

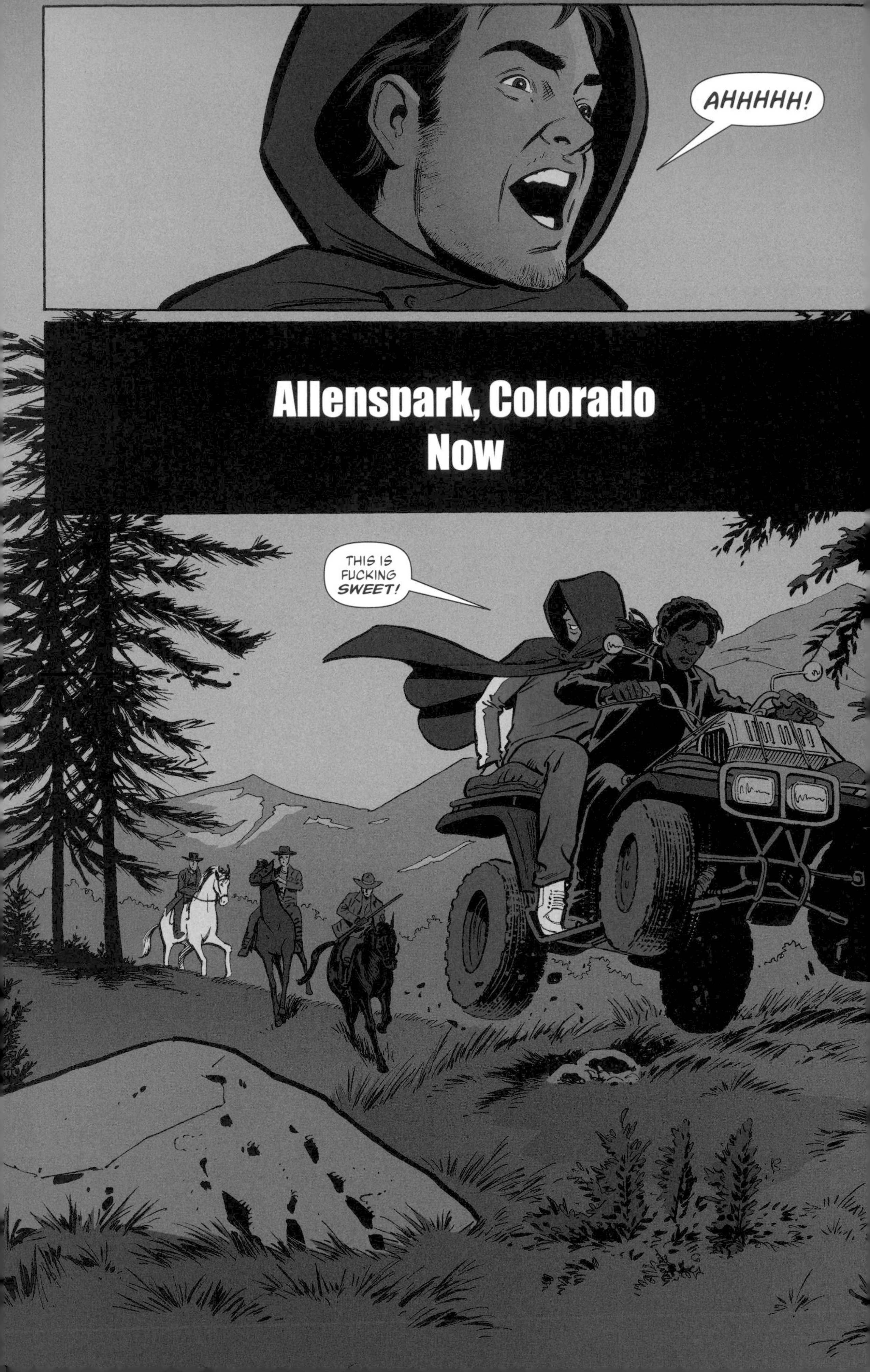
AHHHHH!
Allenspark, Colorado
Now
THIS IS FUCKING SWEET!

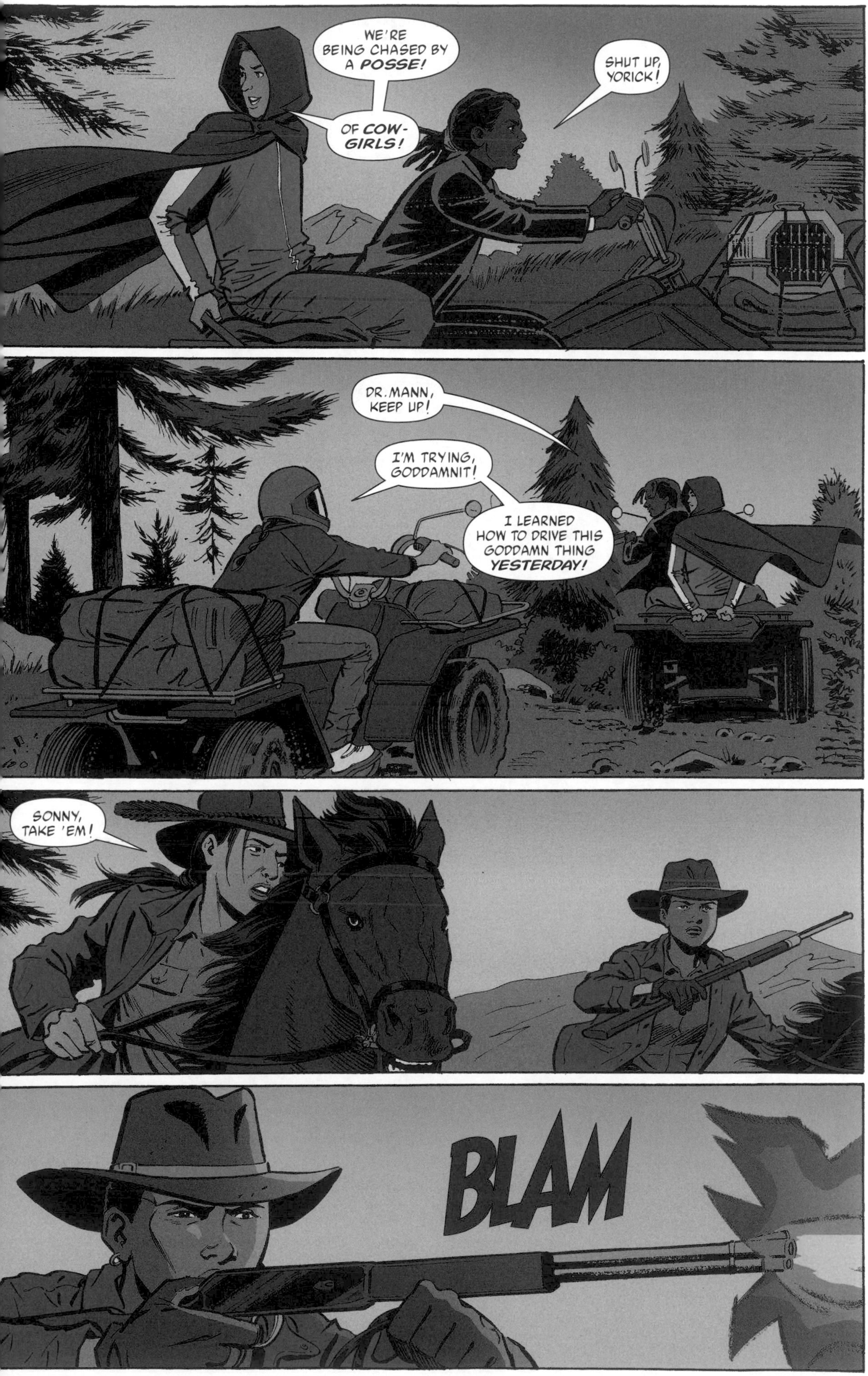
WE'RE BEING CHASED BY A POSSE!
OF COW-GIRLS!
SHUT UP, YORICK!
DR. MANN, KEEP UP!
I'M TRYING, GODDAMNIT!
I LEARNED HOW TO DRIVE THIS GODDAMN THING YESTERDAY!
SONNY, TAKE 'EM!
BLAM

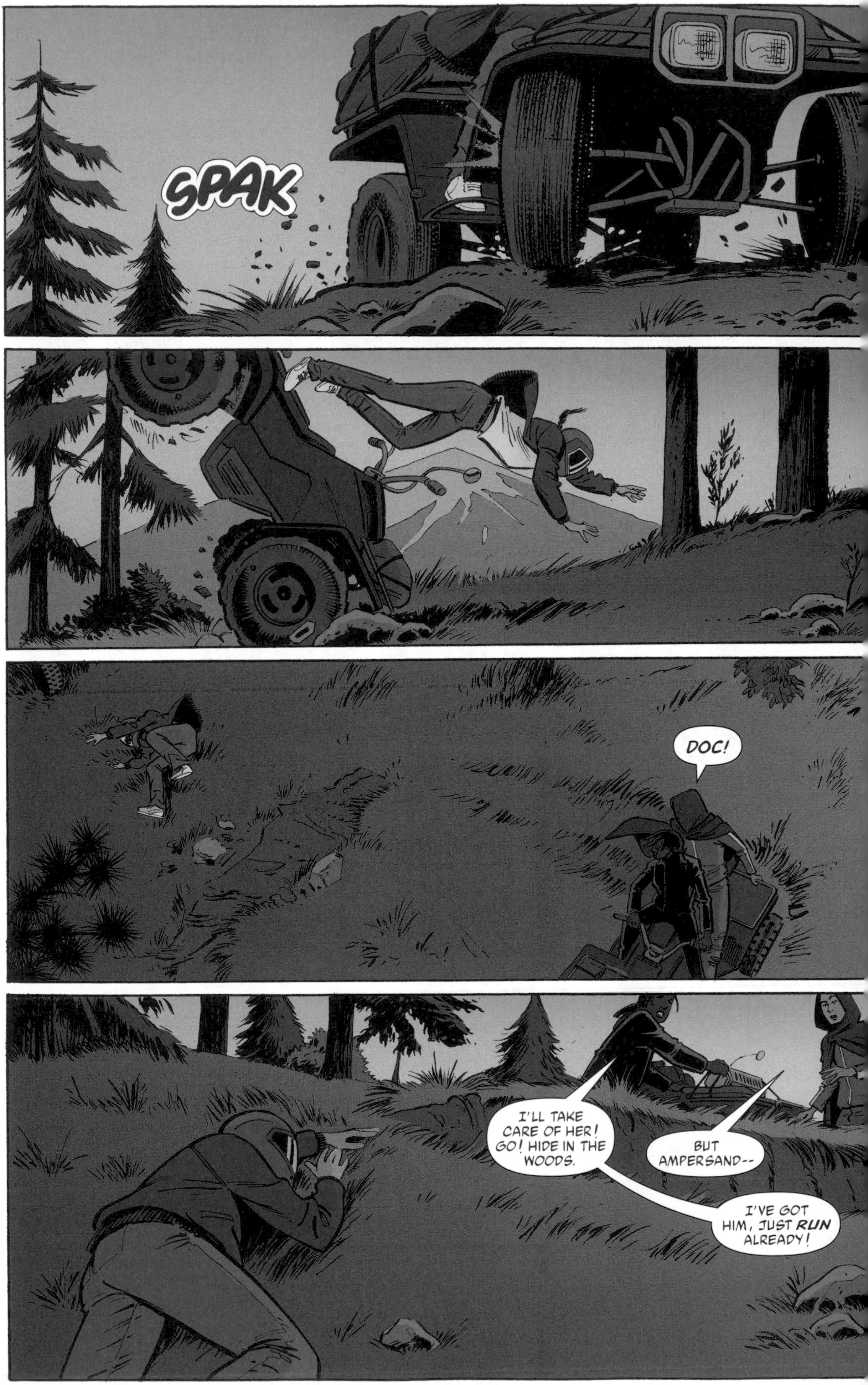
SPAK
DOC!
I'LL TAKE CARE OF HER! GO! HIDE IN THE WOODS.
BUT AMPERSAND--
I'VE GOT HIM, JUST RUN ALREADY!

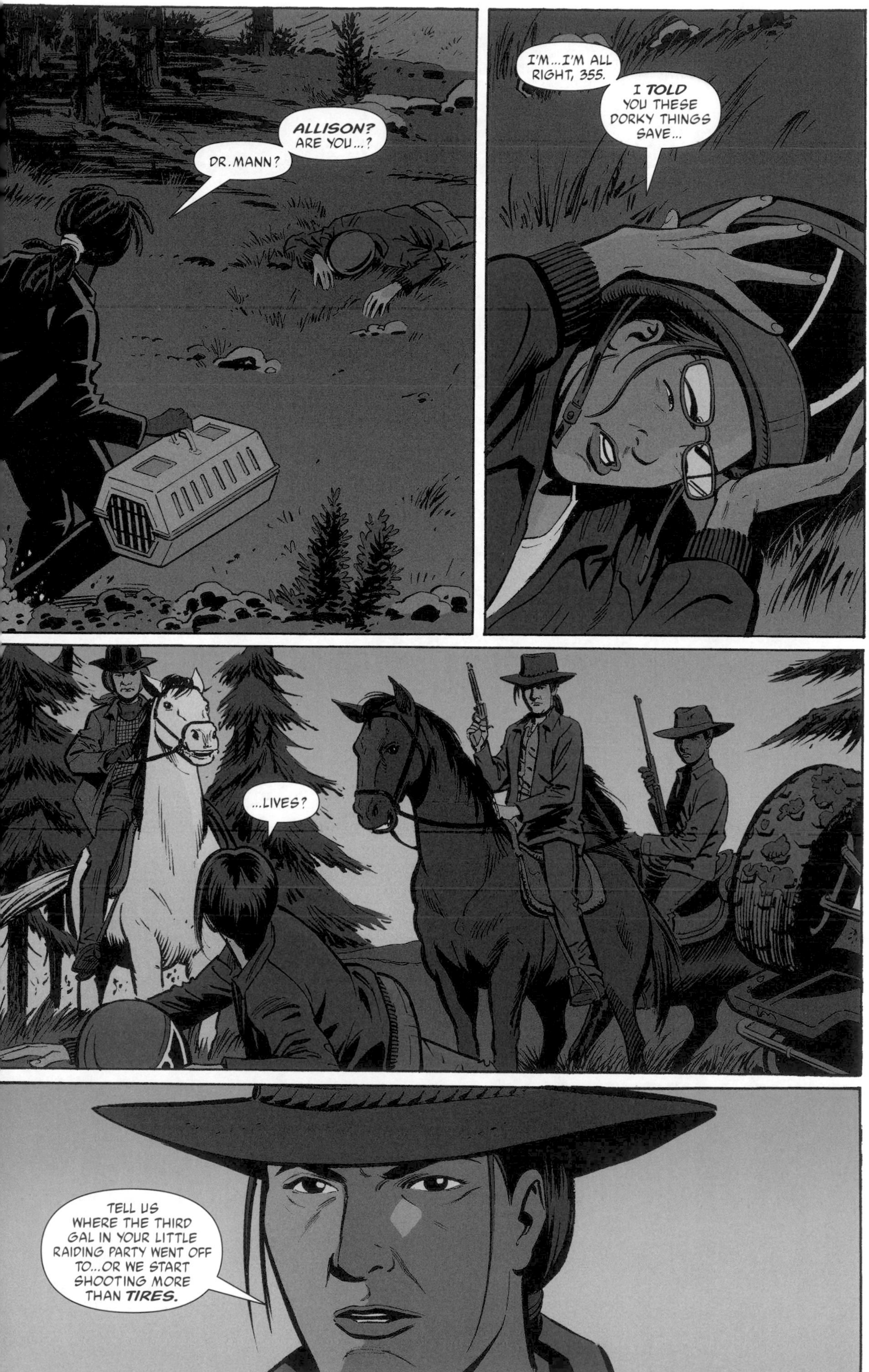
DR. MANN?
ALLISON? ARE YOU...?
I'M...I'M ALL RIGHT, 355.
I TOLD YOU THESE DORKY THINGS SAVE...
...LIVES?
TELL US WHERE THE THIRD GAL IN YOUR LITTLE RAIDING PARTY WENT OFF TO...OR WE START SHOOTING MORE THAN TIRES.

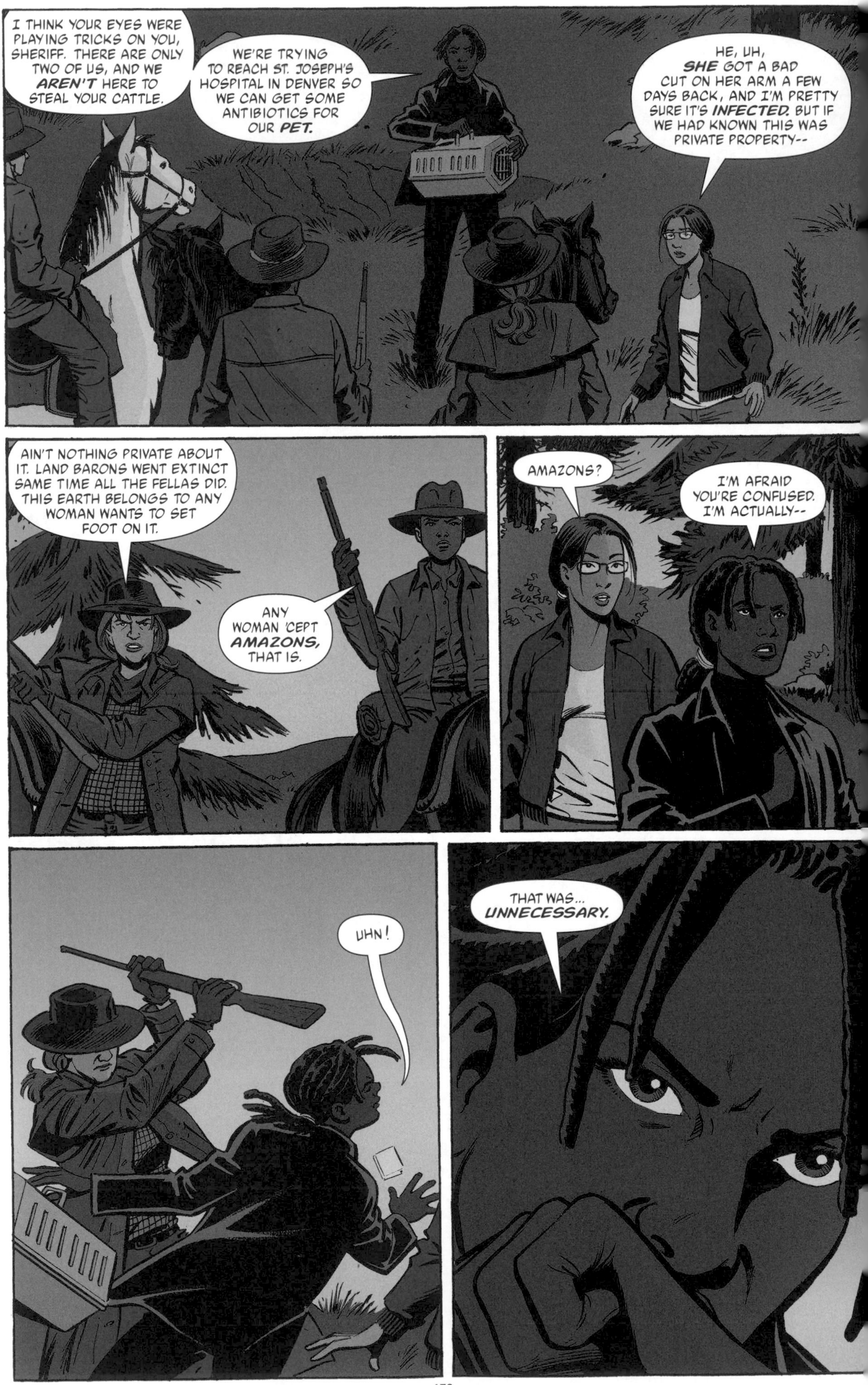
I THINK YOUR EYES WERE PLAYING TRICKS ON YOU, SHERIFF. THERE ARE ONLY TWO OF US, AND WE AREN'T HERE TO STEAL YOUR CATTLE.
WE'RE TRYING TO REACH ST. JOSEPH'S HOSPITAL IN DENVER SO WE CAN GET SOME ANTIBIOTICS FOR OUR PET.
HE, UH, SHE GOT A BAD CUT ON HER ARM A FEW DAYS BACK, AND I'M PRETTY SURE IT'S INFECTED. BUT IF WE HAD KNOWN THIS WAS PRIVATE PROPERTY--
AIN'T NOTHING PRIVATE ABOUT IT. LAND BARONS WENT EXTINCT SAME TIME ALL THE FELLAS DID. THIS EARTH BELONGS TO ANY WOMAN WANTS TO SET FOOT ON IT.
ANY WOMAN 'CEPT AMAZONS, THAT IS.
AMAZONS?
I'M AFRAID YOU'RE CONFUSED. I'M ACTUALLY--
UHN!
THAT WAS... UNNECESSARY.

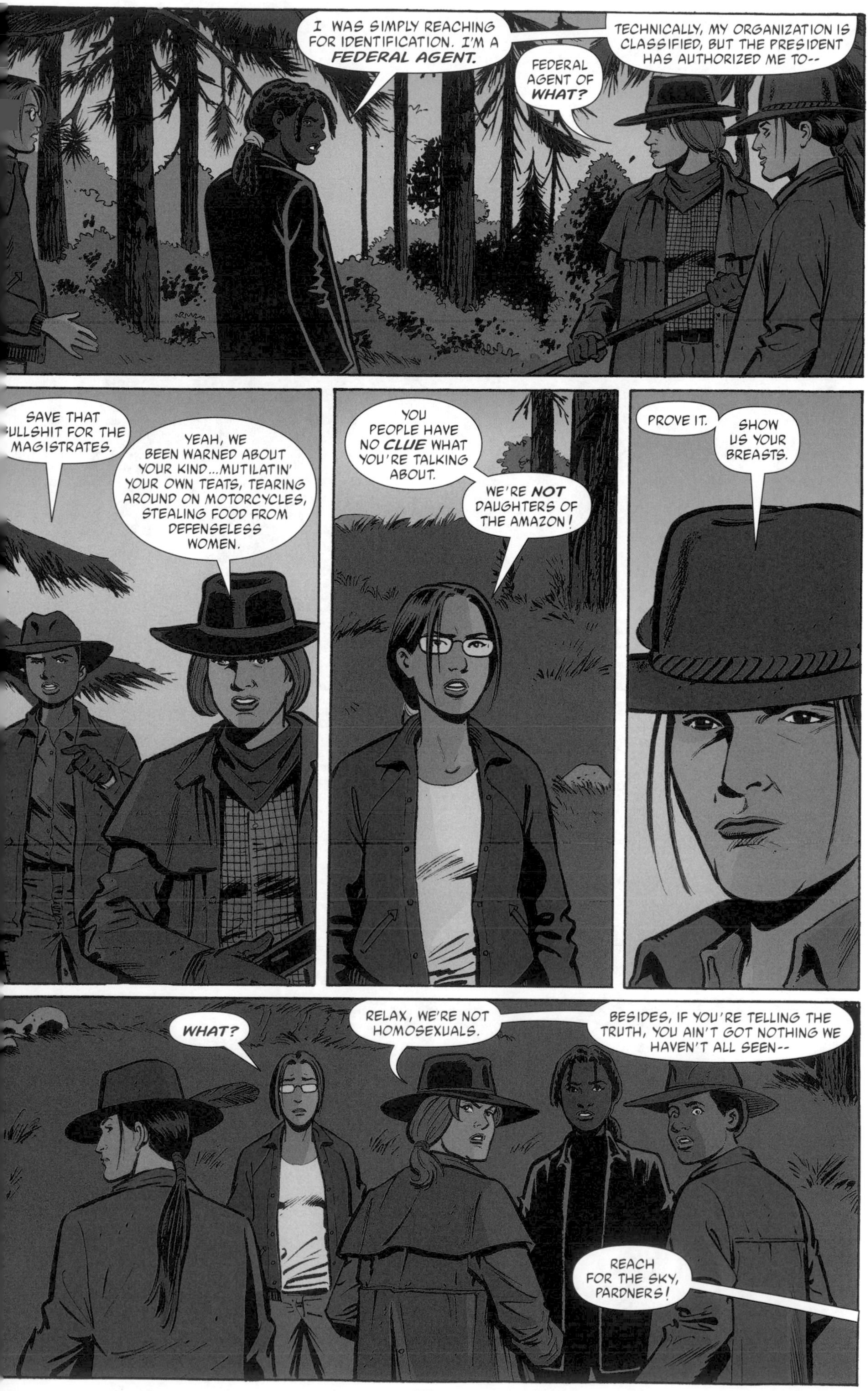
I WAS SIMPLY REACHING FOR IDENTIFICATION. I'M A FEDERAL AGENT.
FEDERAL AGENT OF WHAT?
TECHNICALLY, MY ORGANIZATION IS CLASSIFIED, BUT THE PRESIDENT HAS AUTHORIZED ME TO--
SAVE THAT ULLSHIT FOR THE MAGISTRATES.
YEAH, WE BEEN WARNED ABOUT YOUR KIND...MUTILATIN' YOUR OWN TEATS, TEARING AROUND ON MOTORCYCLES, STEALING FOOD FROM DEFENSELESS WOMEN.
YOU PEOPLE HAVE NO CLUE WHAT YOU'RE TALKING ABOUT.
WE'RE NOT DAUGHTERS OF THE AMAZON!
PROVE IT.
SHOW US YOUR BREASTS.
WHAT?
RELAX, WE'RE NOT HOMOSEXUALS.
BESIDES, IF YOU'RE TELLING THE TRUTH, YOU AIN'T GOT NOTHING WE HAVEN'T ALL SEEN--
REACH FOR THE SKY, PARDNERS!

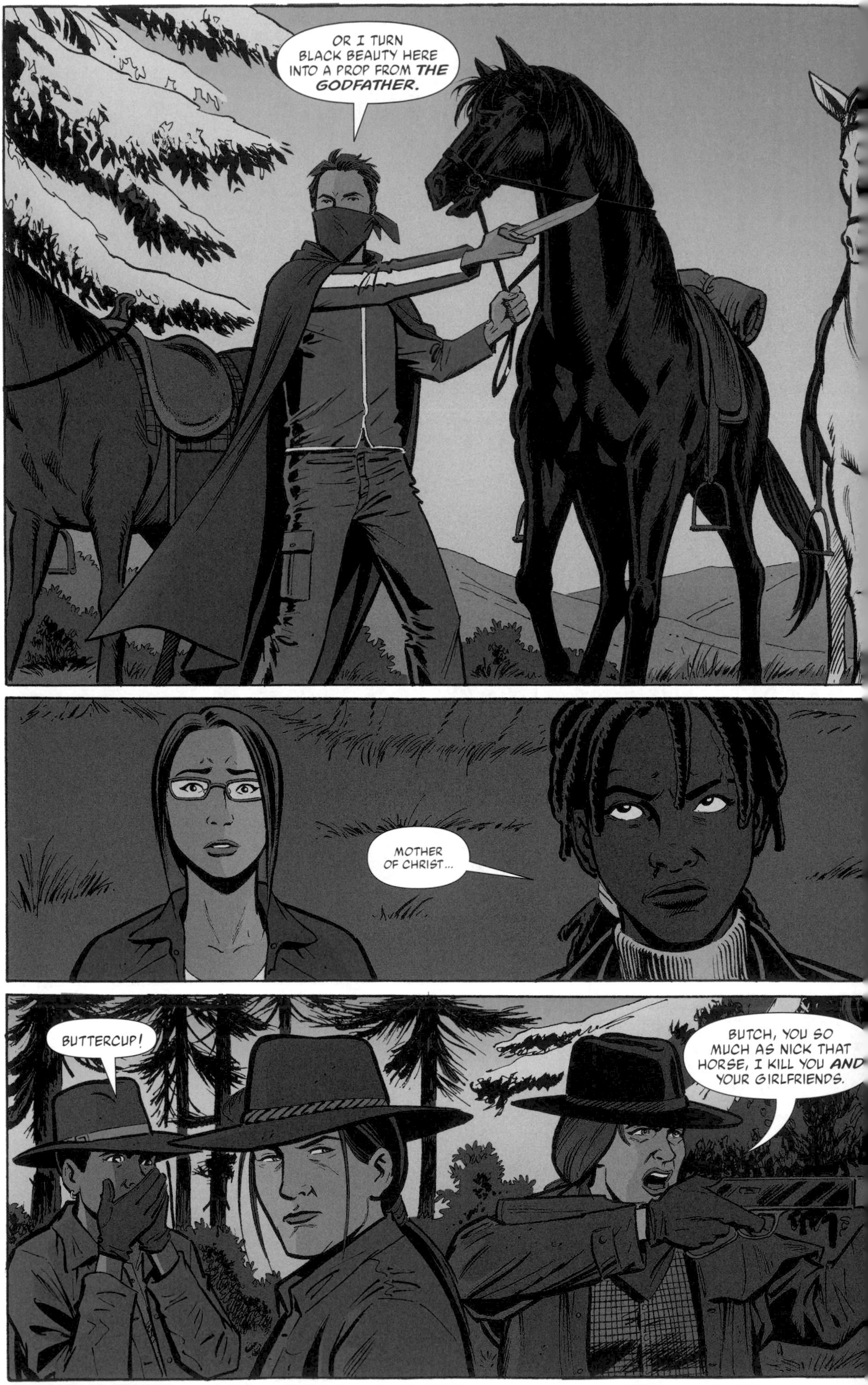
OR I TURN BLACK BEAUTY HERE INTO A PROP FROM **THE GODFATHER.**
MOTHER OF CHRIST...
BUTTERCUP!
BUTCH, YOU SO MUCH AS NICK THAT HORSE, I KILL YOU **AND** YOUR GIRLFRIENDS.

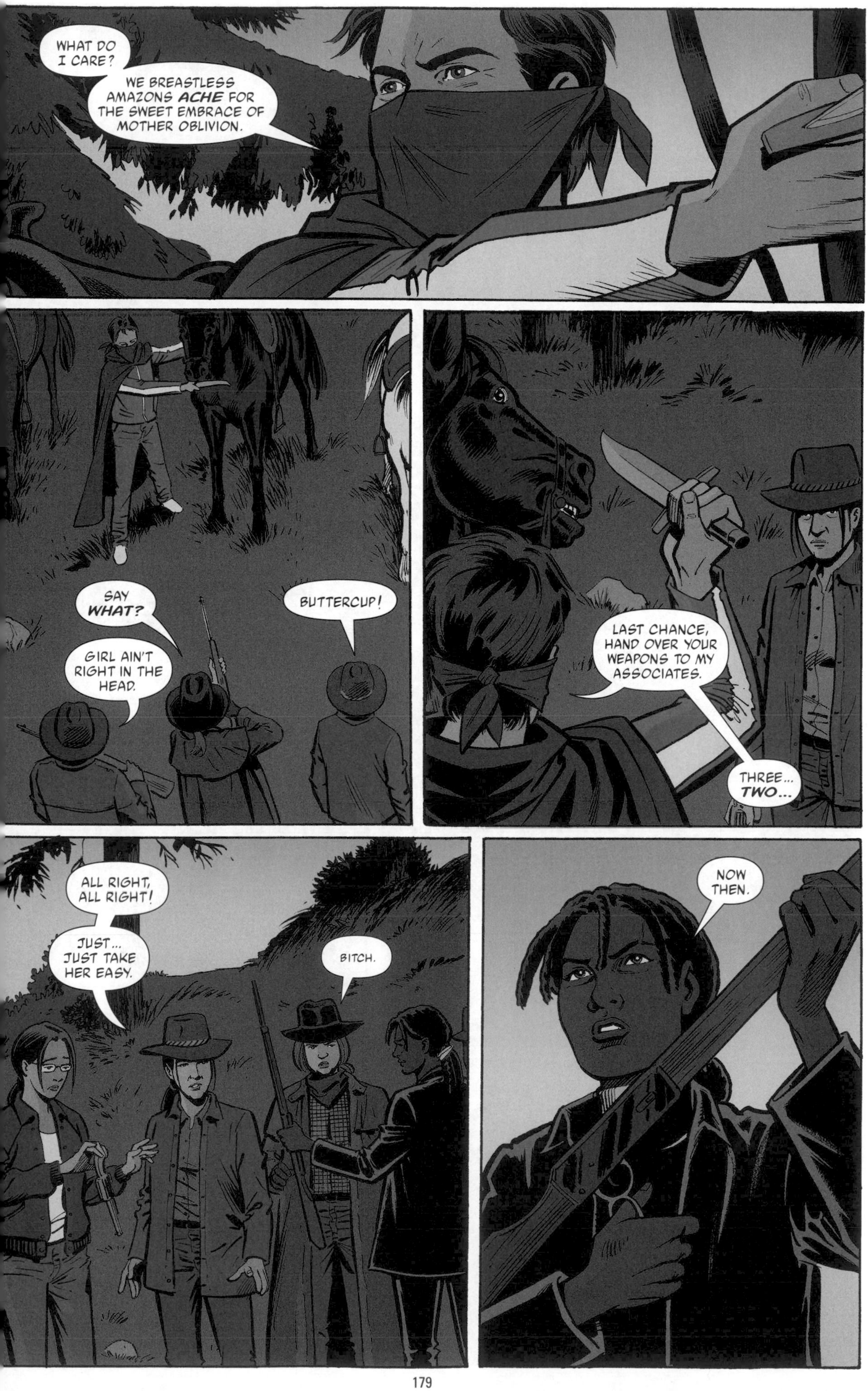
WHAT DO I CARE?
WE BREASTLESS AMAZONS ACHE FOR THE SWEET EMBRACE OF MOTHER OBLIVION.
SAY WHAT?
GIRL AIN'T RIGHT IN THE HEAD.
BUTTERCUP!
LAST CHANCE, HAND OVER YOUR WEAPONS TO MY ASSOCIATES.
THREE... TWO...
ALL RIGHT, ALL RIGHT!
JUST... JUST TAKE HER EASY.
BITCH.
NOW THEN.

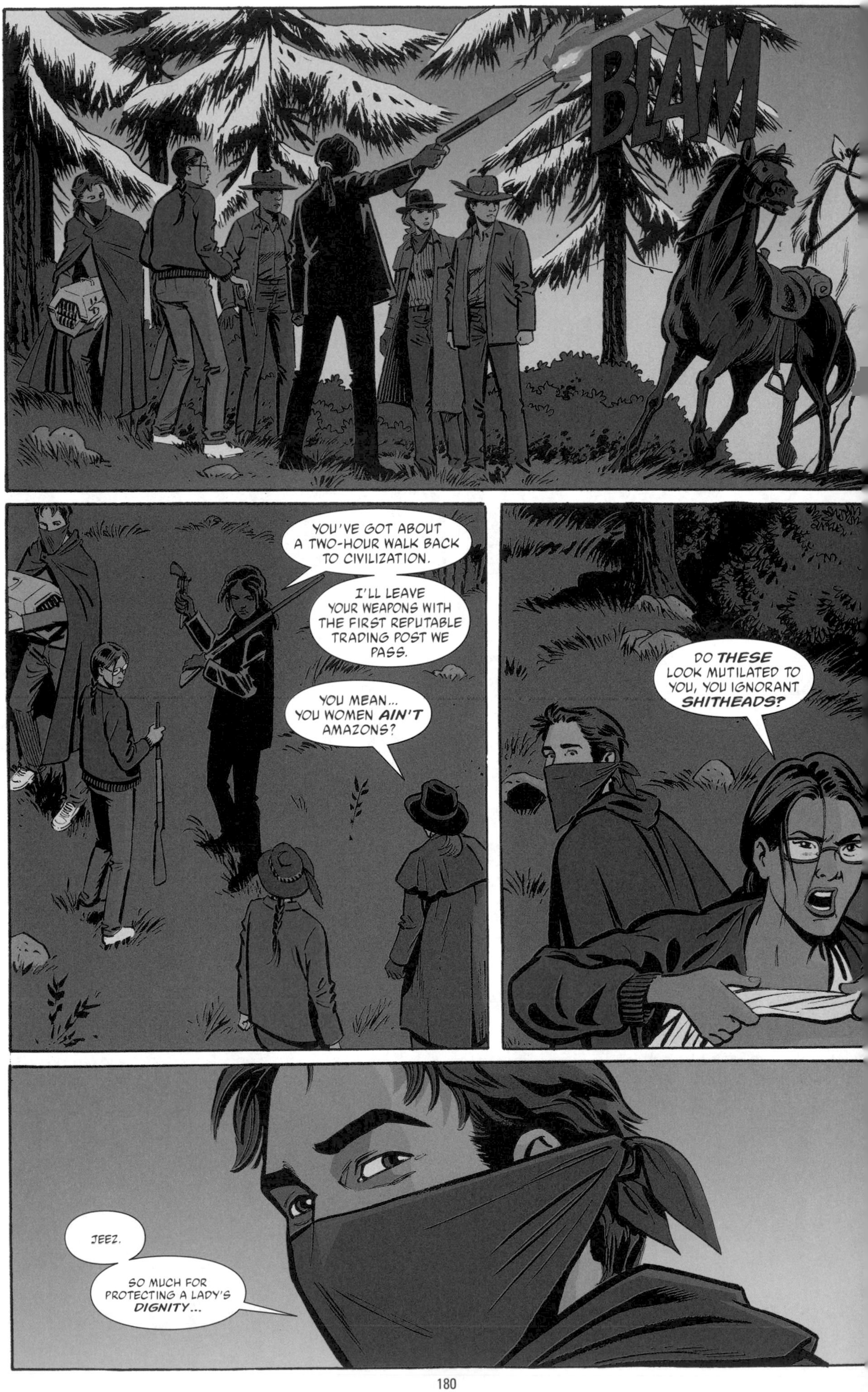
BLAM
YOU'VE GOT ABOUT A TWO-HOUR WALK BACK TO CIVILIZATION.
I'LL LEAVE YOUR WEAPONS WITH THE FIRST REPUTABLE TRADING POST WE PASS.
YOU MEAN... YOU WOMEN ***AIN'T*** AMAZONS?
DO ***THESE*** LOOK MUTILATED TO YOU, YOU IGNORANT ***SHITHEADS?***
JEEZ.
SO MUCH FOR PROTECTING A LADY'S ***DIGNITY...***

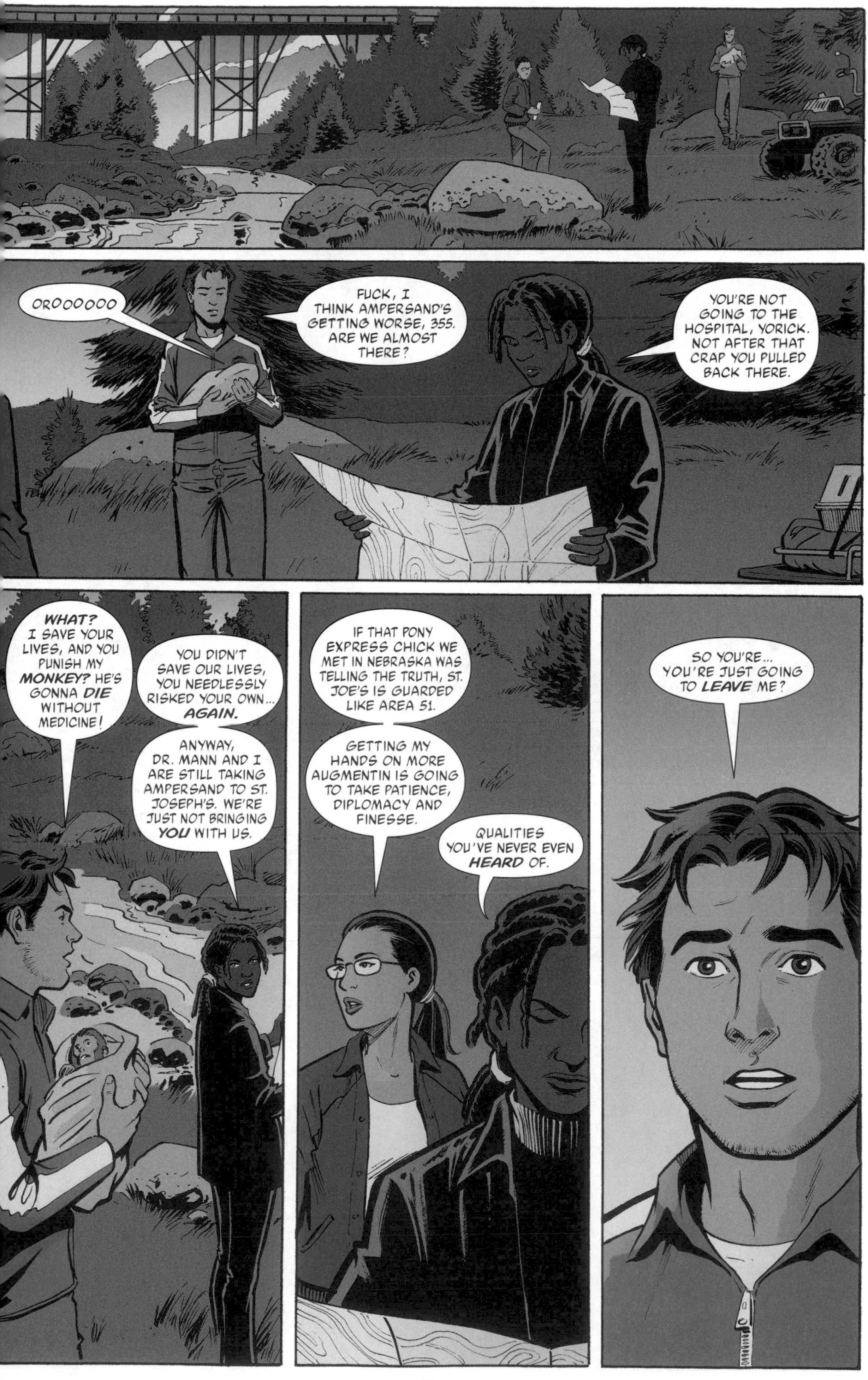
OROOOOOO
FUCK, I THINK AMPERSAND'S GETTING WORSE, 355. ARE WE ALMOST THERE?
YOU'RE NOT GOING TO THE HOSPITAL, YORICK. NOT AFTER THAT CRAP YOU PULLED BACK THERE.
WHAT? I SAVE YOUR LIVES, AND YOU PUNISH MY MONKEY? HE'S GONNA DIE WITHOUT MEDICINE!
YOU DIDN'T SAVE OUR LIVES, YOU NEEDLESSLY RISKED YOUR OWN... AGAIN.
ANYWAY, DR. MANN AND I ARE STILL TAKING AMPERSAND TO ST. JOSEPH'S. WE'RE JUST NOT BRINGING YOU WITH US.
IF THAT PONY EXPRESS CHICK WE MET IN NEBRASKA WAS TELLING THE TRUTH, ST. JOE'S IS GUARDED LIKE AREA 51.
GETTING MY HANDS ON MORE AUGMENTIN IS GOING TO TAKE PATIENCE, DIPLOMACY AND FINESSE.
QUALITIES YOU'VE NEVER EVEN HEARD OF.
SO YOU'RE... YOU'RE JUST GOING TO LEAVE ME?

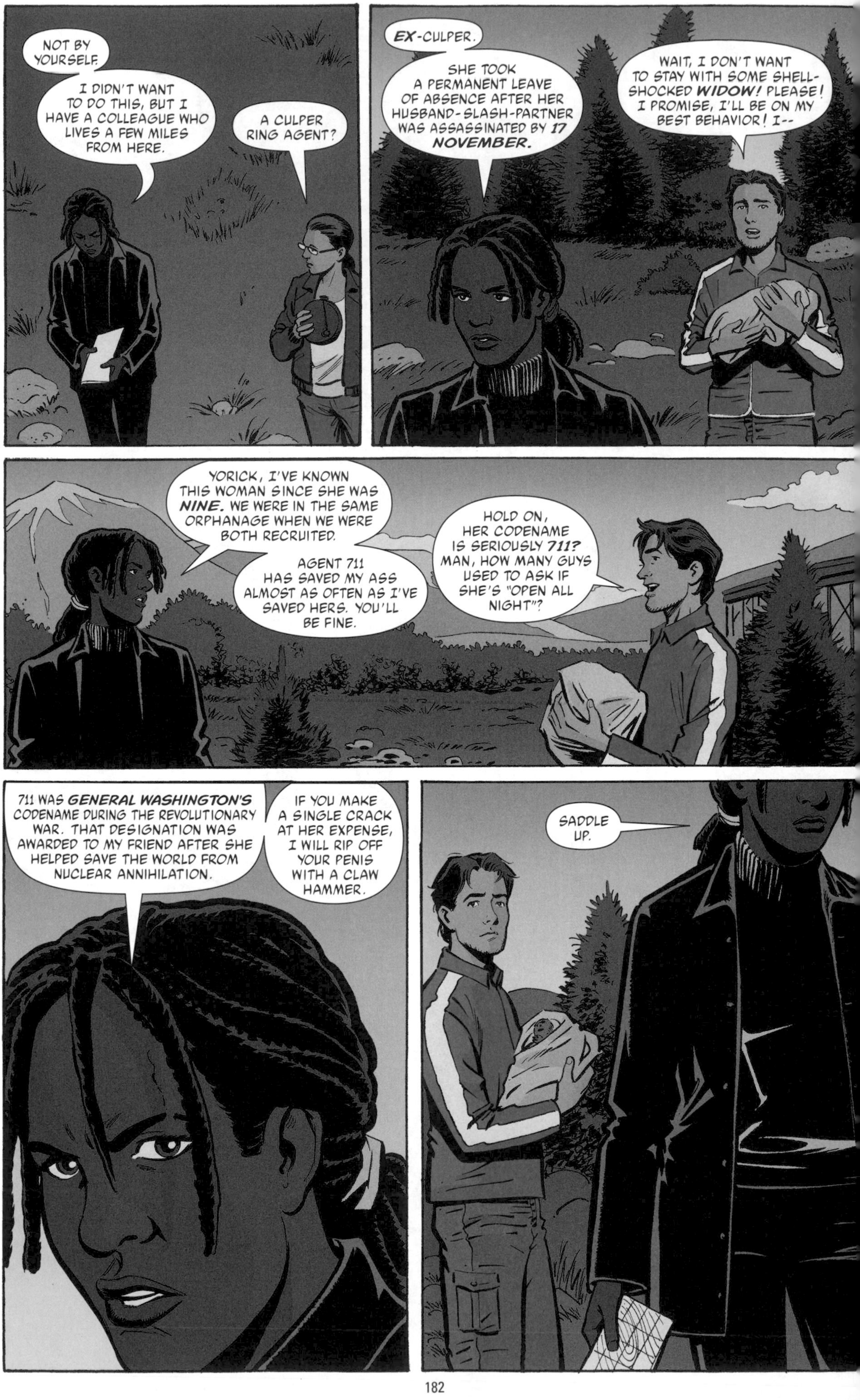
NOT BY YOURSELF.
I DIDN'T WANT TO DO THIS, BUT I HAVE A COLLEAGUE WHO LIVES A FEW MILES FROM HERE.
A CULPER RING AGENT?
EX-CULPER.
SHE TOOK A PERMANENT LEAVE OF ABSENCE AFTER HER HUSBAND-SLASH-PARTNER WAS ASSASSINATED BY 17 NOVEMBER.
WAIT, I DON'T WANT TO STAY WITH SOME SHELL-SHOCKED WIDOW! PLEASE! I PROMISE, I'LL BE ON MY BEST BEHAVIOR! I--
YORICK, I'VE KNOWN THIS WOMAN SINCE SHE WAS NINE. WE WERE IN THE SAME ORPHANAGE WHEN WE WERE BOTH RECRUITED.
AGENT 711 HAS SAVED MY ASS ALMOST AS OFTEN AS I'VE SAVED HERS. YOU'LL BE FINE.
HOLD ON, HER CODENAME IS SERIOUSLY 711? MAN, HOW MANY GUYS USED TO ASK IF SHE'S "OPEN ALL NIGHT"?
711 WAS GENERAL WASHINGTON'S CODENAME DURING THE REVOLUTIONARY WAR. THAT DESIGNATION WAS AWARDED TO MY FRIEND AFTER SHE HELPED SAVE THE WORLD FROM NUCLEAR ANNIHILATION.
IF YOU MAKE A SINGLE CRACK AT HER EXPENSE, I WILL RIP OFF YOUR PENIS WITH A CLAW HAMMER.
SADDLE UP.

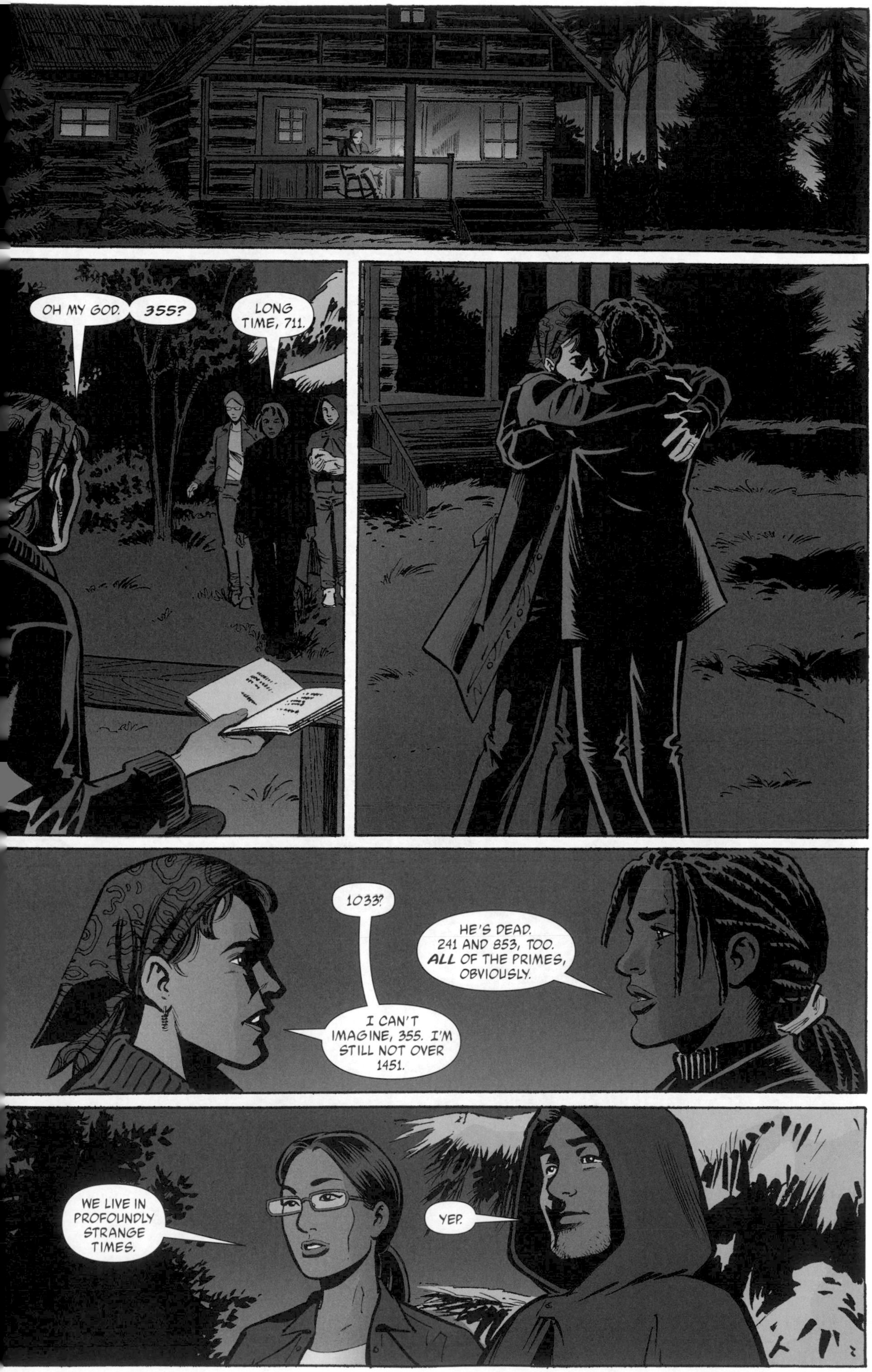
OH MY GOD. 355?
LONG TIME, 711.
1033?
HE'S DEAD. 241 AND 853, TOO. ALL OF THE PRIMES, OBVIOUSLY.
I CAN'T IMAGINE, 355. I'M STILL NOT OVER 1451.
WE LIVE IN PROFOUNDLY STRANGE TIMES.
YEP.

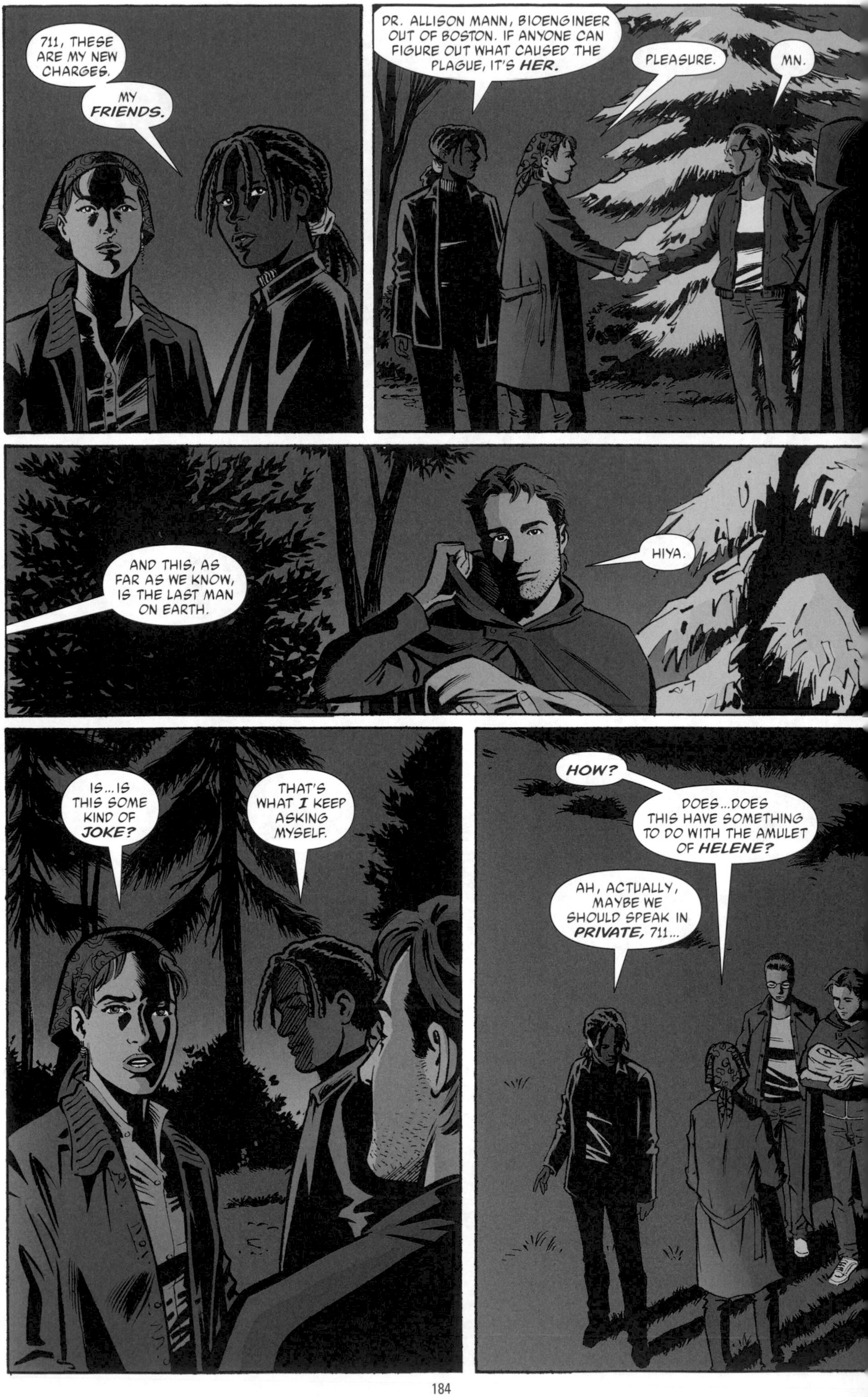
711, THESE ARE MY NEW CHARGES.
MY FRIENDS.
DR. ALLISON MANN, BIOENGINEER OUT OF BOSTON. IF ANYONE CAN FIGURE OUT WHAT CAUSED THE PLAGUE, IT'S HER.
PLEASURE.
MN.
AND THIS, AS FAR AS WE KNOW, IS THE LAST MAN ON EARTH.
HIYA.
IS... IS THIS SOME KIND OF JOKE?
THAT'S WHAT I KEEP ASKING MYSELF.
HOW?
DOES...DOES THIS HAVE SOMETHING TO DO WITH THE AMULET OF HELENE?
AH, ACTUALLY, MAYBE WE SHOULD SPEAK IN PRIVATE, 711...

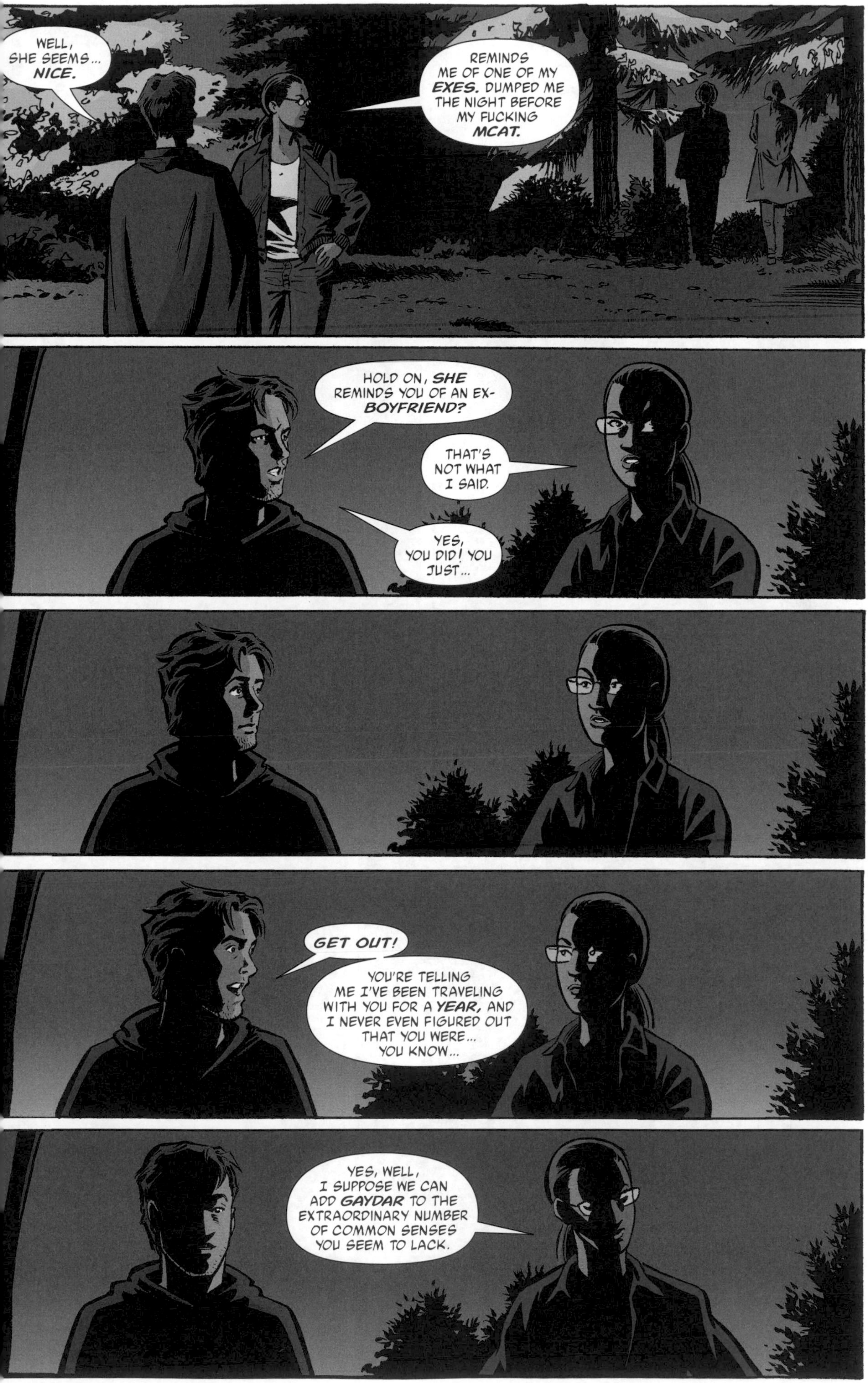

WELL, SHE SEEMS... NICE.
REMINDS ME OF ONE OF MY EXES. DUMPED ME THE NIGHT BEFORE MY FUCKING MCAT.
HOLD ON, SHE REMINDS YOU OF AN EX-BOYFRIEND?
THAT'S NOT WHAT I SAID.
YES, YOU DID! YOU JUST...
GET OUT!
YOU'RE TELLING ME I'VE BEEN TRAVELING WITH YOU FOR A YEAR, AND I NEVER EVEN FIGURED OUT THAT YOU WERE... YOU KNOW...
YES, WELL, I SUPPOSE WE CAN ADD GAYDAR TO THE EXTRAORDINARY NUMBER OF COMMON SENSES YOU SEEM TO LACK.

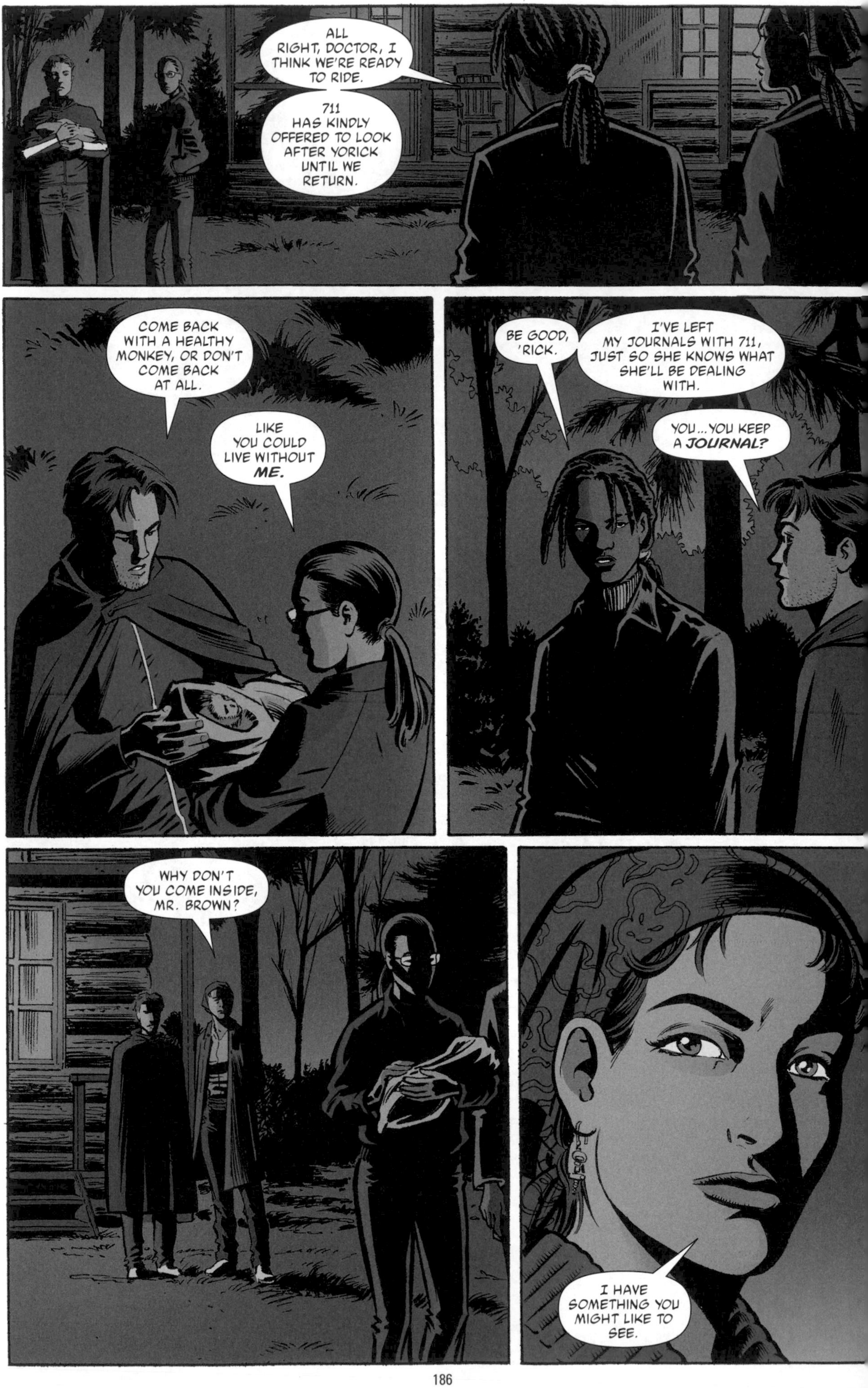
ALL RIGHT, DOCTOR, I THINK WE'RE READY TO RIDE.
711 HAS KINDLY OFFERED TO LOOK AFTER YORICK UNTIL WE RETURN.
COME BACK WITH A HEALTHY MONKEY, OR DON'T COME BACK AT ALL.
LIKE YOU COULD LIVE WITHOUT *ME.*
BE GOOD, 'RICK.
I'VE LEFT MY JOURNALS WITH 711, JUST SO SHE KNOWS WHAT SHE'LL BE DEALING WITH.
YOU...YOU KEEP A *JOURNAL?*
WHY DON'T YOU COME INSIDE, MR. BROWN?
I HAVE SOMETHING YOU MIGHT LIKE TO SEE.

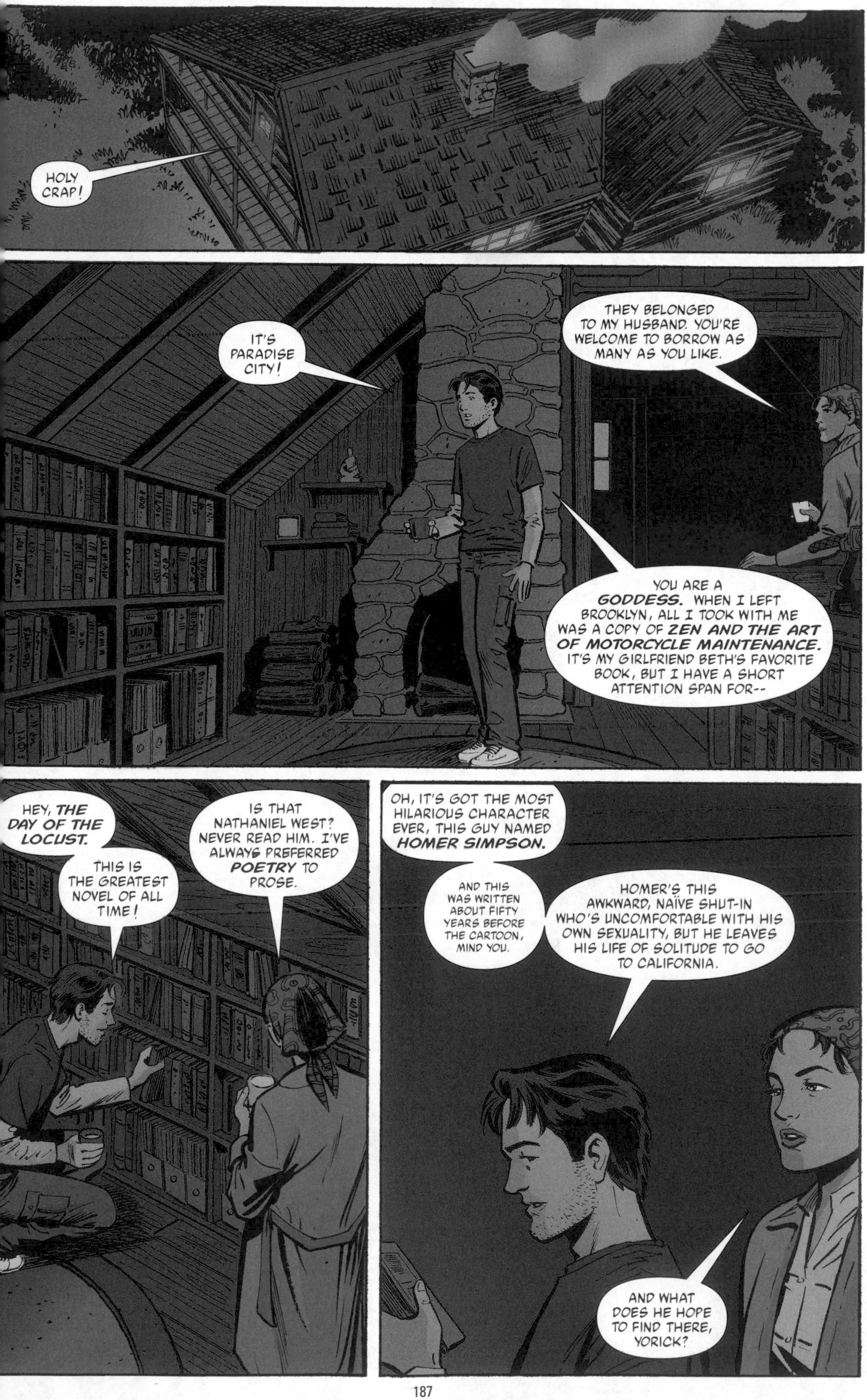
HOLY CRAP!
IT'S PARADISE CITY!
THEY BELONGED TO MY HUSBAND. YOU'RE WELCOME TO BORROW AS MANY AS YOU LIKE.
YOU ARE A **GODDESS.** WHEN I LEFT BROOKLYN, ALL I TOOK WITH ME WAS A COPY OF ***ZEN AND THE ART OF MOTORCYCLE MAINTENANCE.*** IT'S MY GIRLFRIEND BETH'S FAVORITE BOOK, BUT I HAVE A SHORT ATTENTION SPAN FOR--
HEY, ***THE DAY OF THE LOCUST.***
THIS IS THE GREATEST NOVEL OF ALL TIME!
IS THAT NATHANIEL WEST? NEVER READ HIM. I'VE ALWAYS PREFERRED ***POETRY*** TO PROSE.
OH, IT'S GOT THE MOST HILARIOUS CHARACTER EVER, THIS GUY NAMED ***HOMER SIMPSON.***
AND THIS WAS WRITTEN ABOUT FIFTY YEARS BEFORE THE CARTOON, MIND YOU.
HOMER'S THIS AWKWARD, NAÏVE SHUT-IN WHO'S UNCOMFORTABLE WITH HIS OWN SEXUALITY, BUT HE LEAVES HIS LIFE OF SOLITUDE TO GO TO CALIFORNIA.
AND WHAT DOES HE HOPE TO FIND THERE, YORICK?

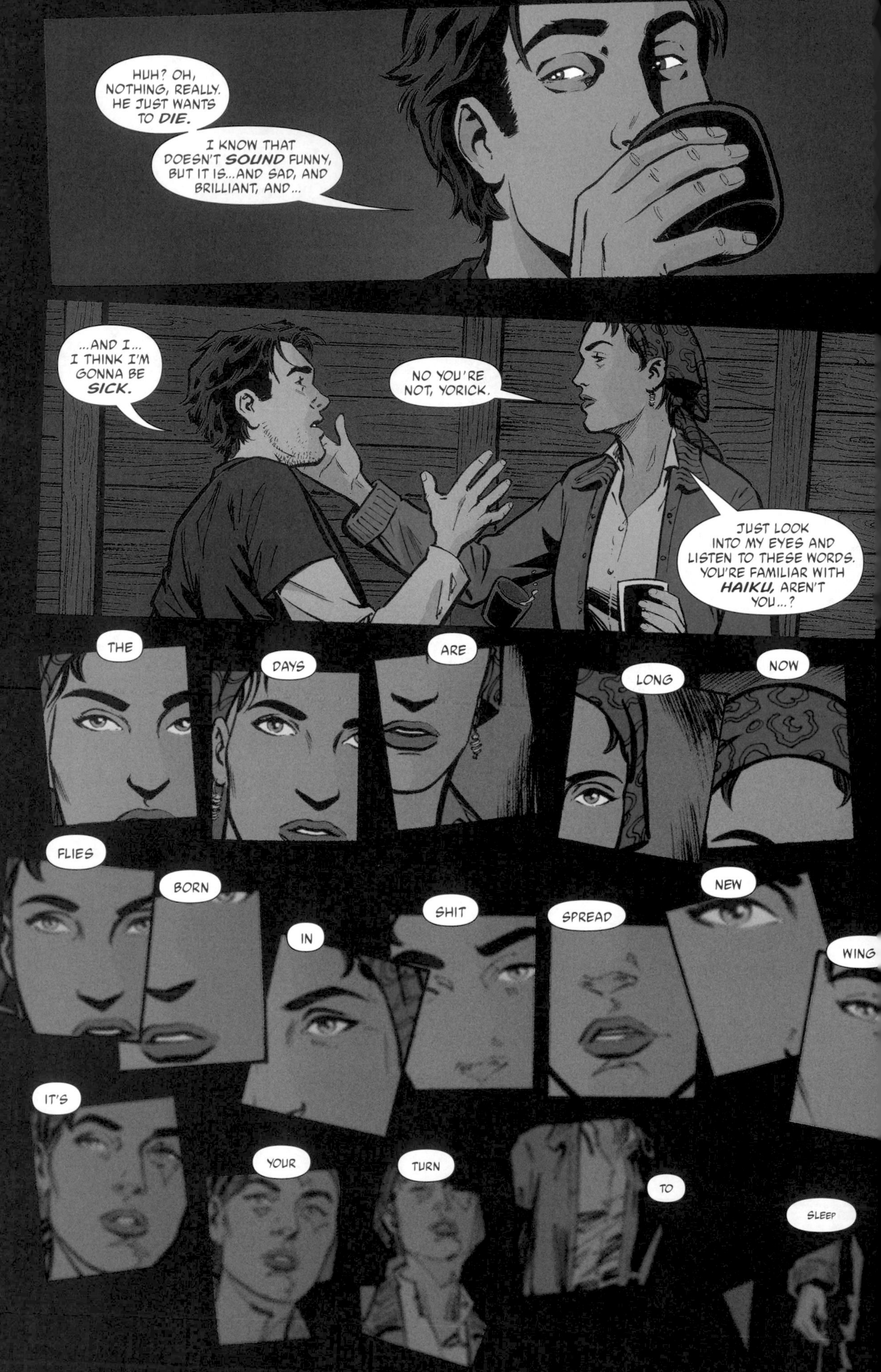
HUH? OH, NOTHING, REALLY. HE JUST WANTS TO DIE.
I KNOW THAT DOESN'T SOUND FUNNY, BUT IT IS...AND SAD, AND BRILLIANT, AND...
...AND I... I THINK I'M GONNA BE SICK.
NO YOU'RE NOT, YORICK.
JUST LOOK INTO MY EYES AND LISTEN TO THESE WORDS. YOU'RE FAMILIAR WITH HAIKU, AREN'T YOU...?
THE
DAYS
ARE
LONG
NOW
FLIES
BORN
IN
SHIT
SPREAD
NEW
WING
IT'S
YOUR
TURN
TO
SLEEP

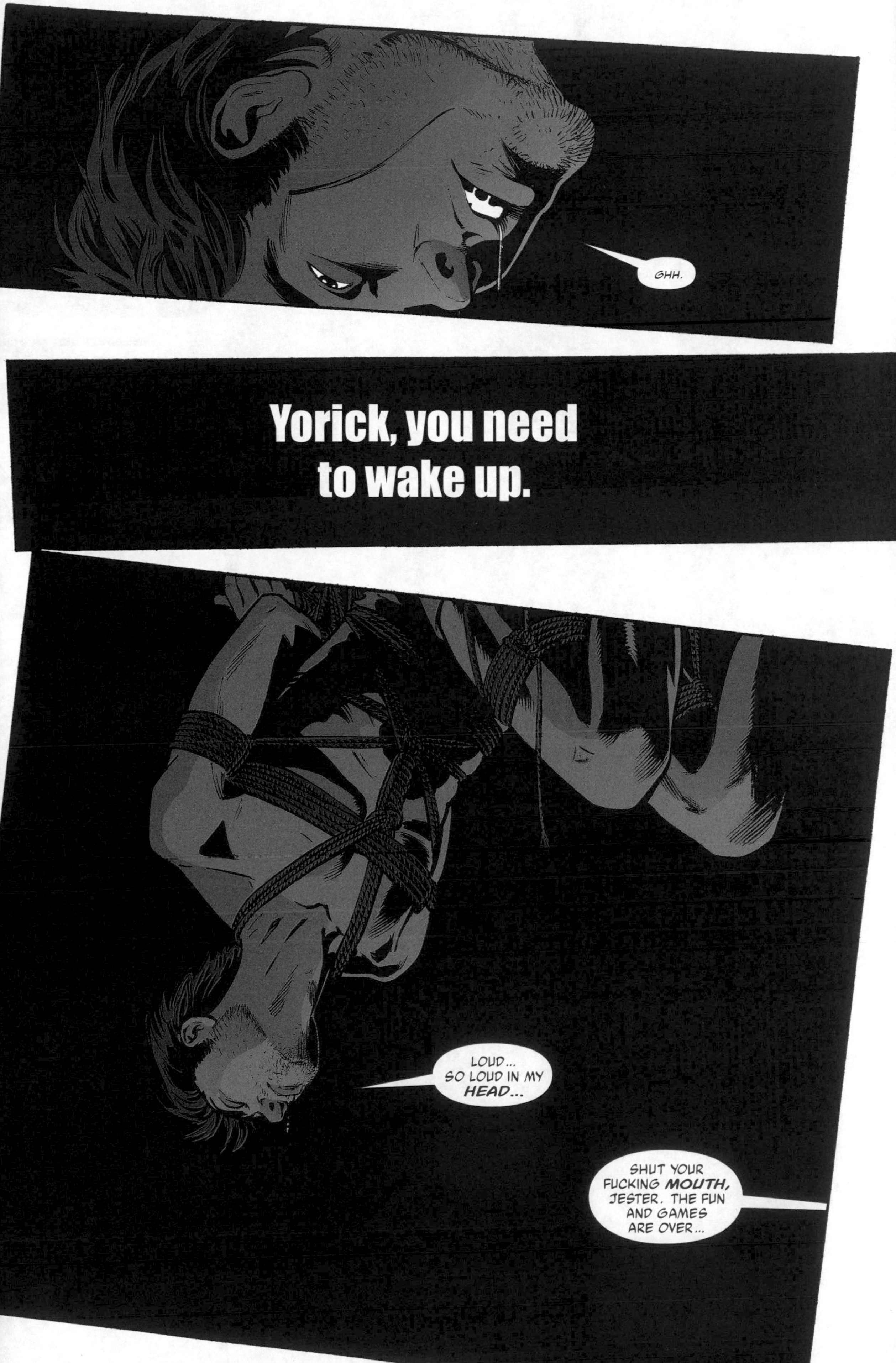
GHH.
Yorick, you need to wake up.
LOUD... SO LOUD IN MY HEAD...
SHUT YOUR FUCKING MOUTH, JESTER. THE FUN AND GAMES ARE OVER...

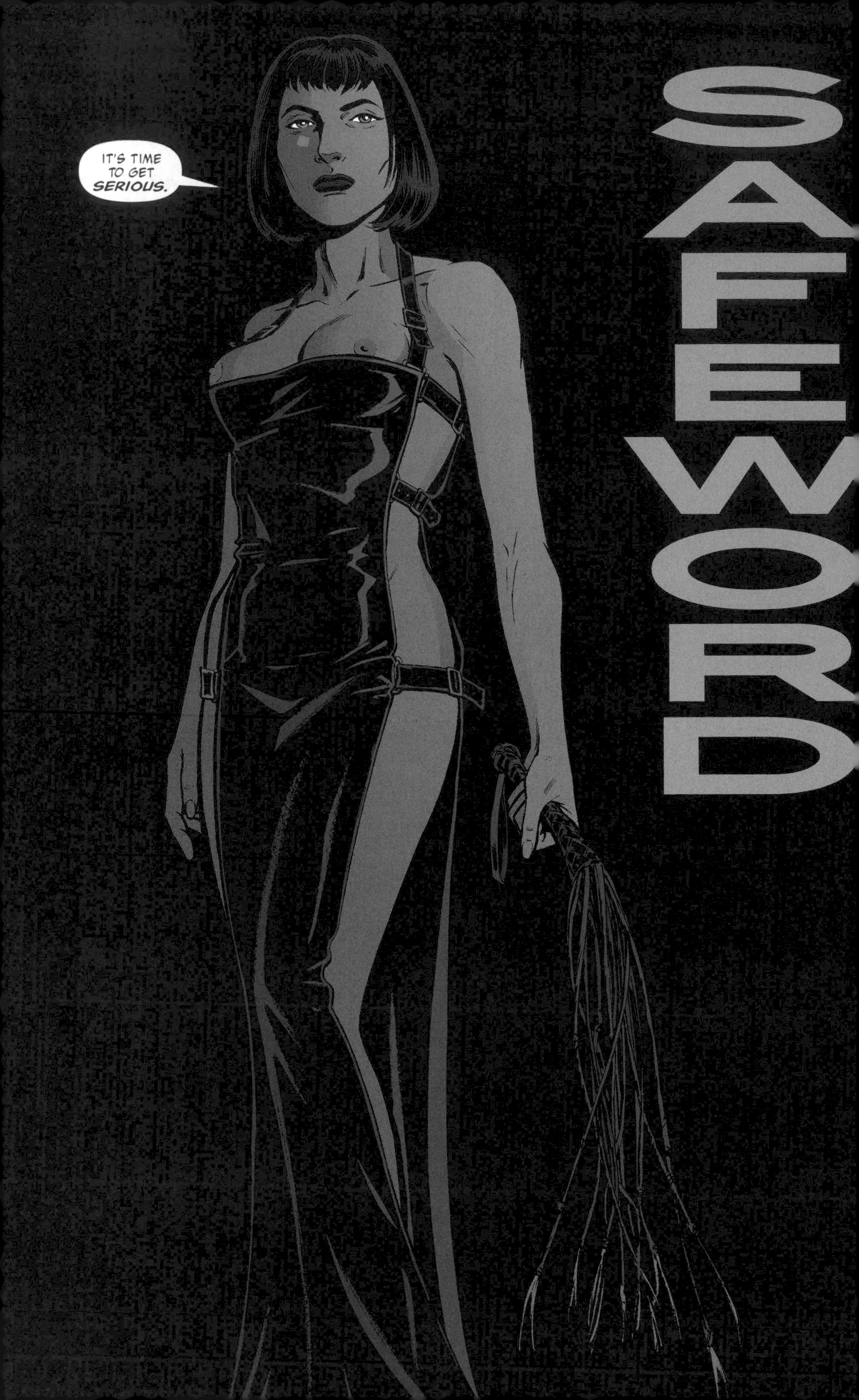
IT'S TIME TO GET SERIOUS.
SAFEWORD

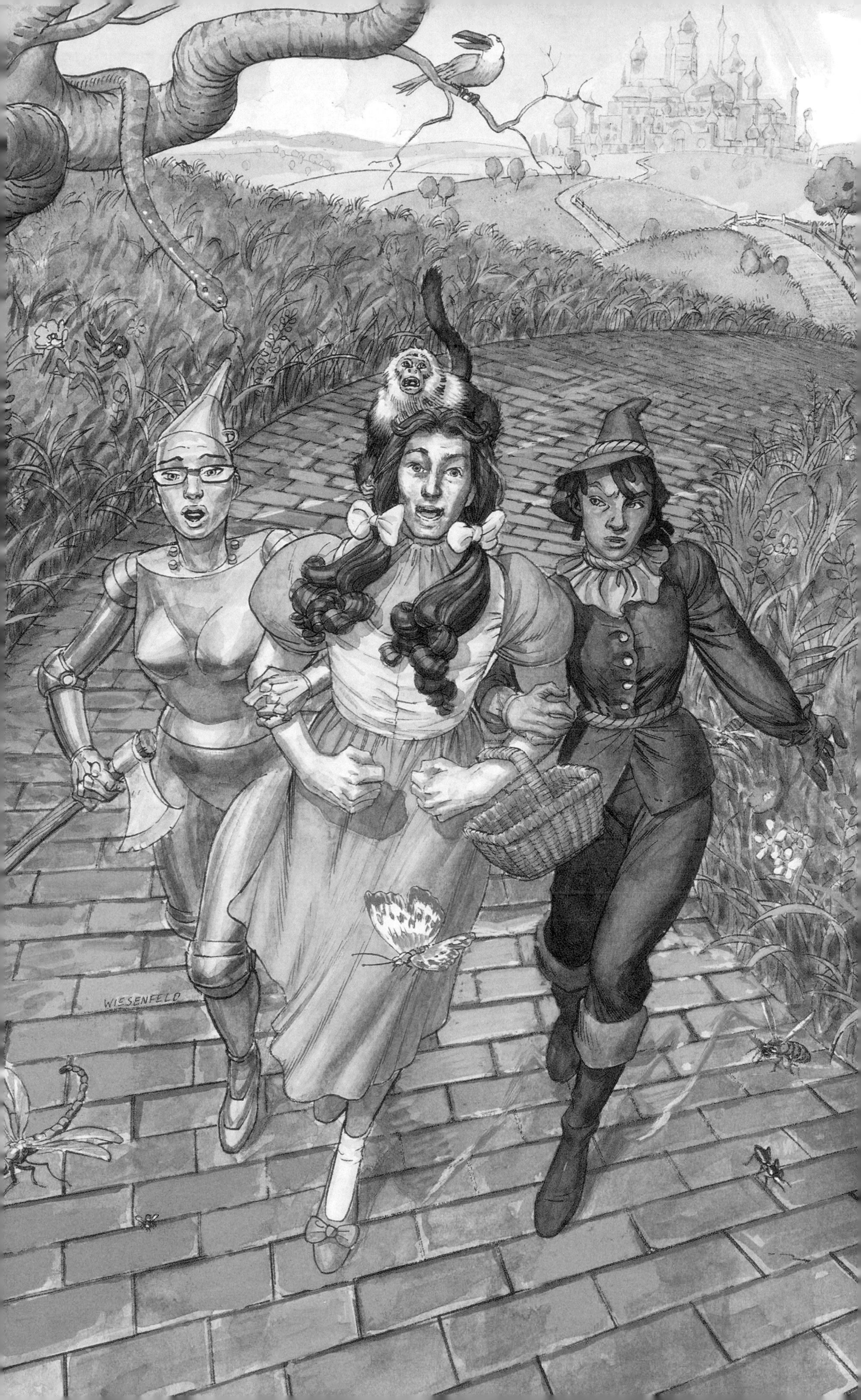
WIESENFELD

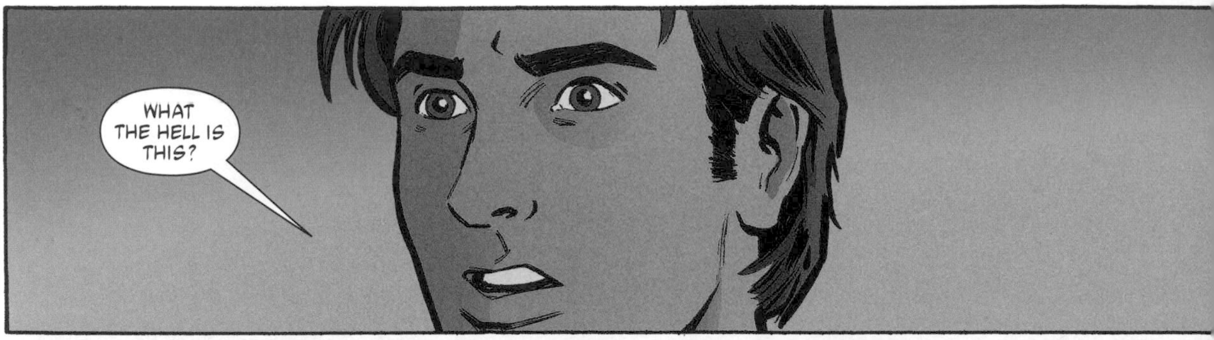
WHAT THE HELL IS THIS?

Where the Hell Am I?

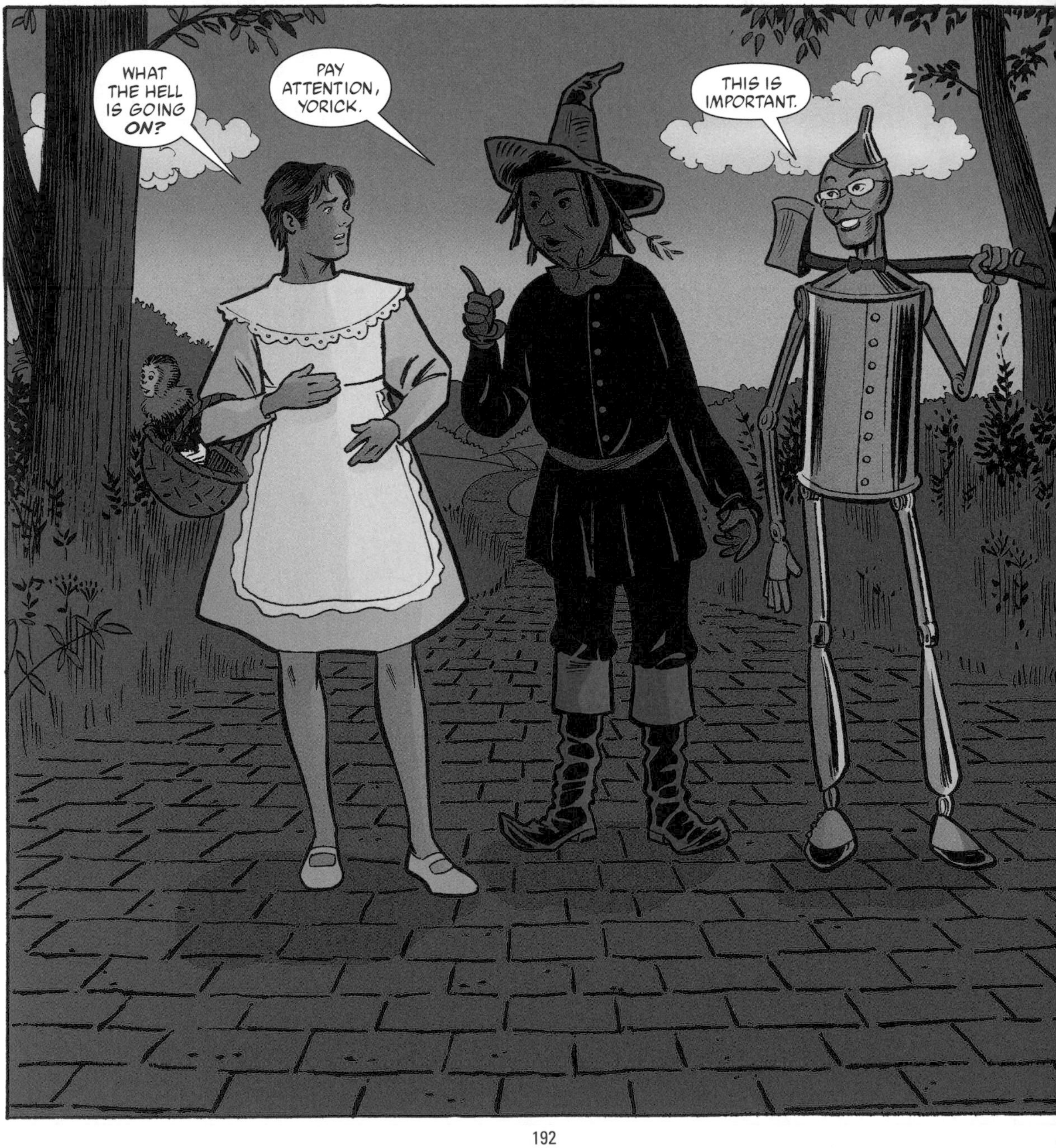
WHAT THE HELL IS GOING *ON?*
PAY ATTENTION, YORICK.
THIS IS IMPORTANT.

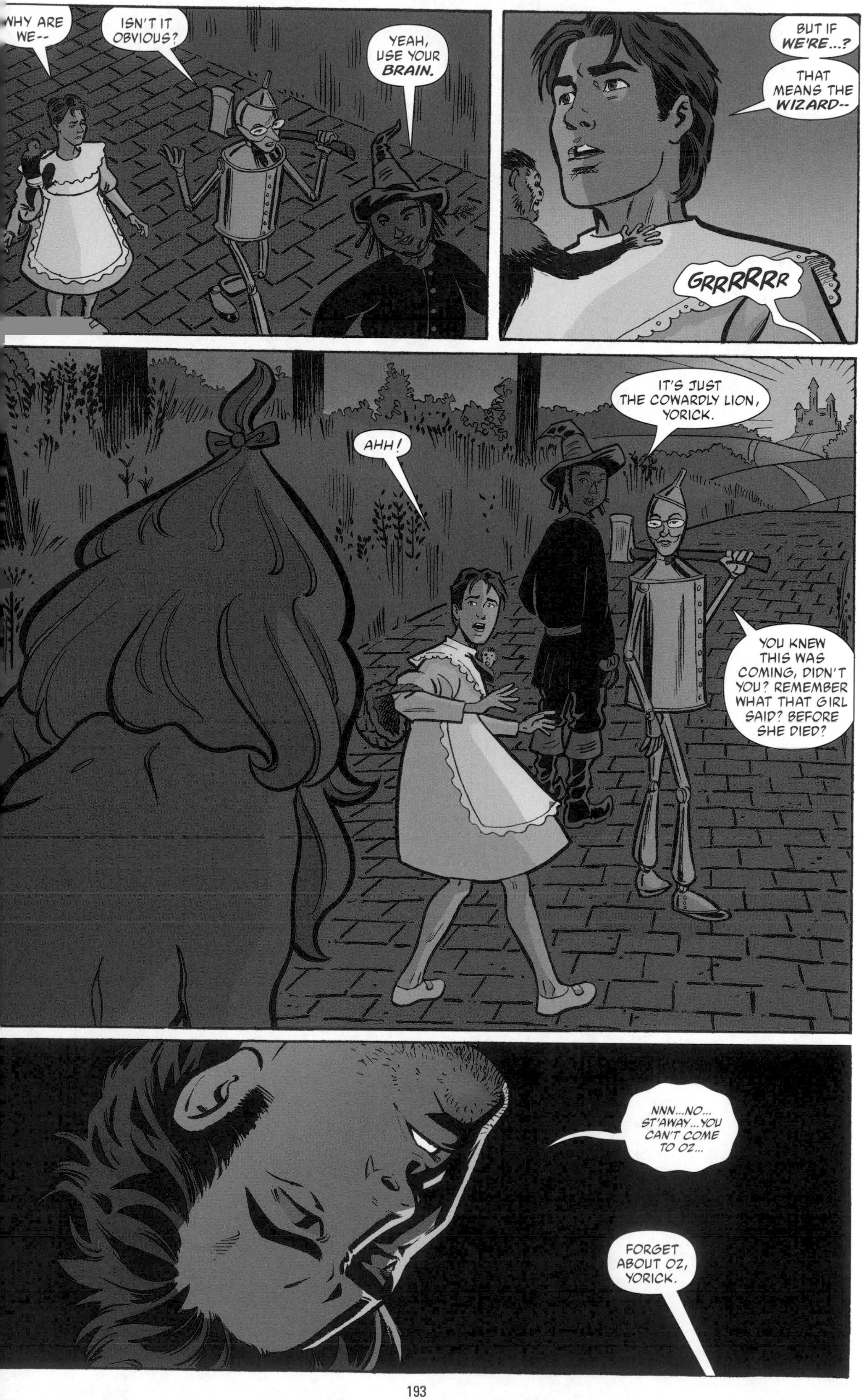
WHY ARE WE--
ISN'T IT OBVIOUS?
YEAH, USE YOUR BRAIN.
BUT IF WE'RE...?
THAT MEANS THE WIZARD--
GRRRRRR
AHH!
IT'S JUST THE COWARDLY LION, YORICK.
YOU KNEW THIS WAS COMING, DIDN'T YOU? REMEMBER WHAT THAT GIRL SAID? BEFORE SHE DIED?
NNN...NO... ST'AWAY...YOU CAN'T COME TO OZ...
FORGET ABOUT OZ, YORICK.

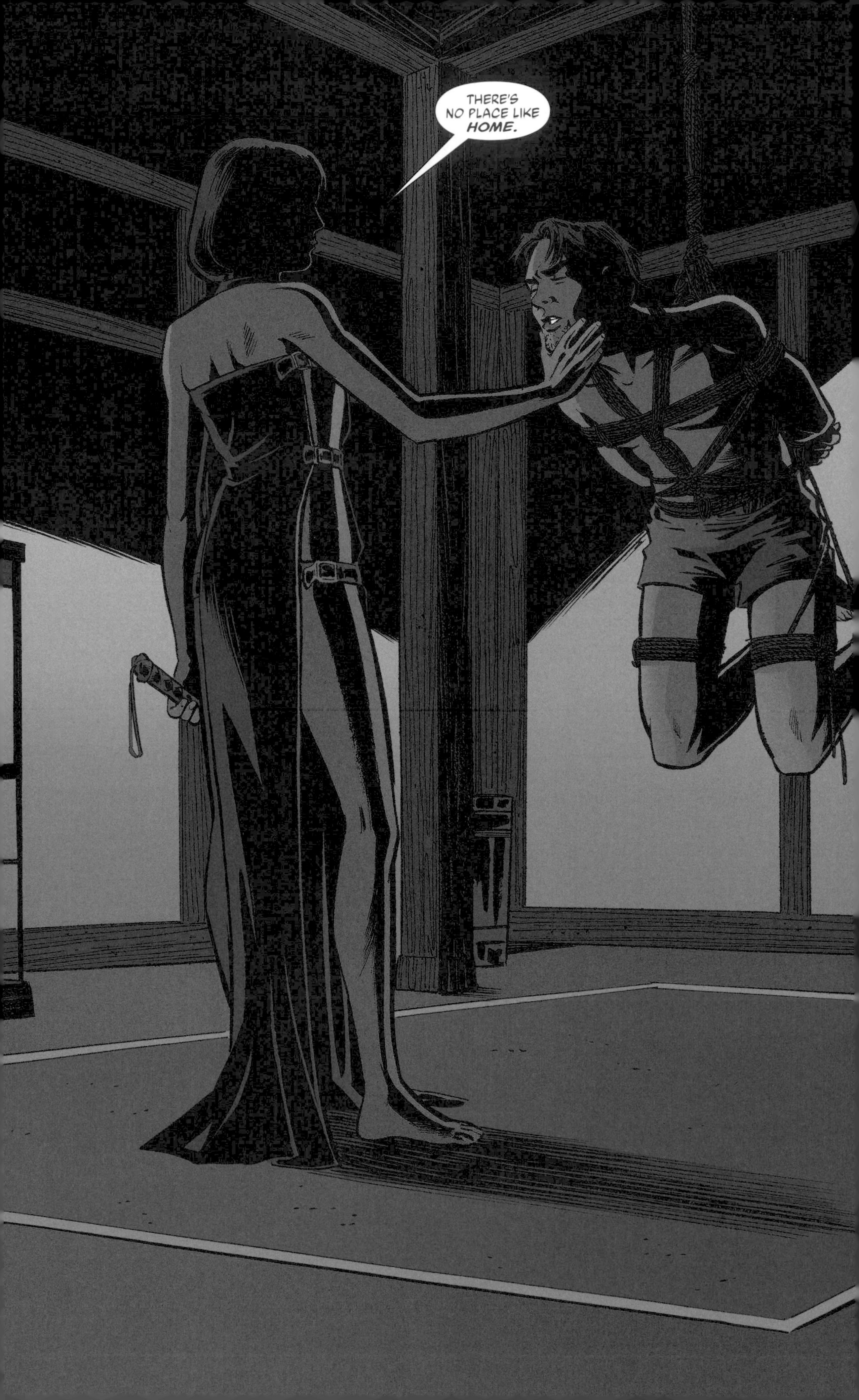
THERE'S NO PLACE LIKE HOME.

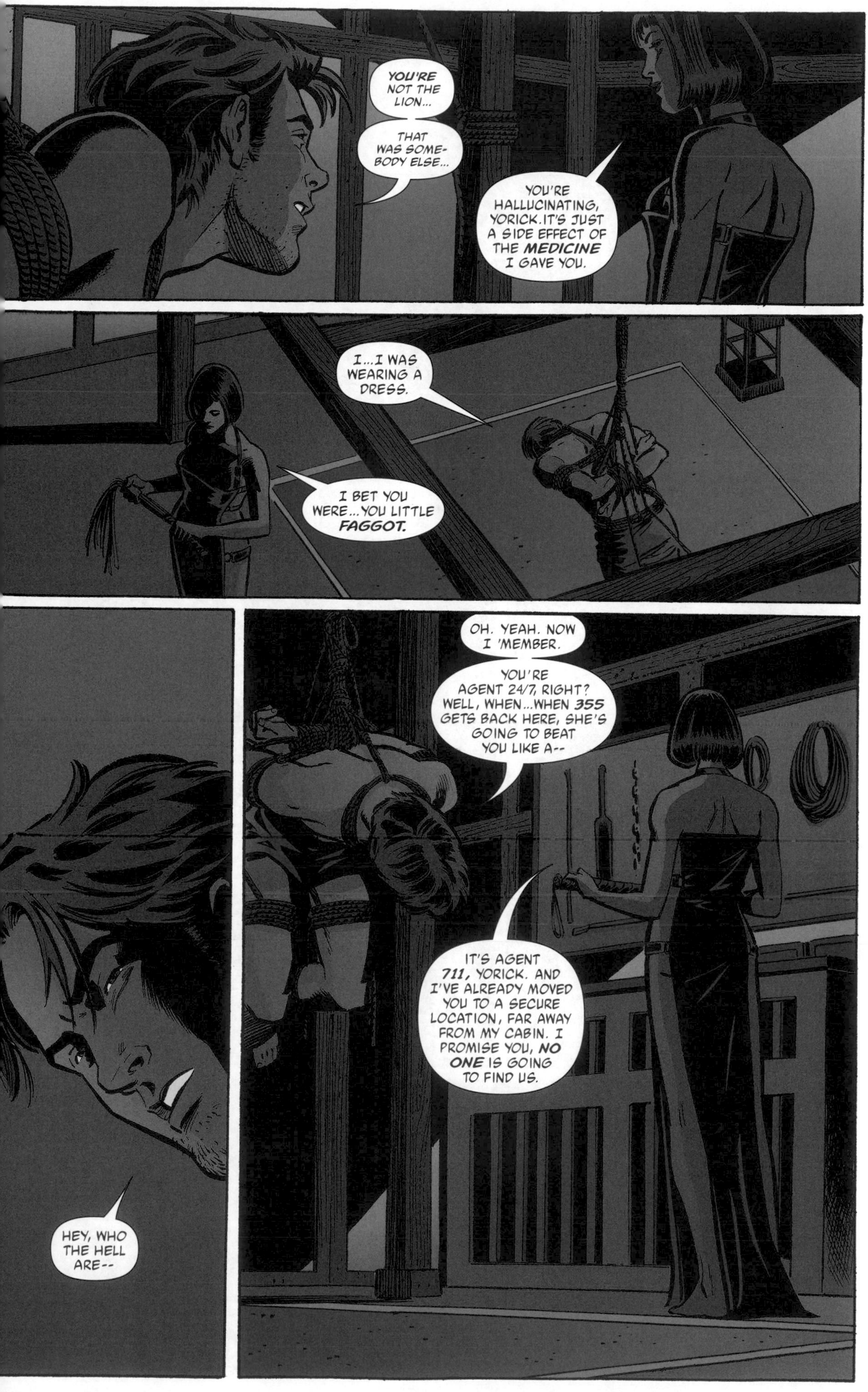
YOU'RE NOT THE LION...
THAT WAS SOMEBODY ELSE...
YOU'RE HALLUCINATING, YORICK. IT'S JUST A SIDE EFFECT OF THE MEDICINE I GAVE YOU.
I...I WAS WEARING A DRESS.
I BET YOU WERE...YOU LITTLE FAGGOT.
HEY, WHO THE HELL ARE--
OH. YEAH. NOW I 'MEMBER.
YOU'RE AGENT 24/7, RIGHT? WELL, WHEN...WHEN 355 GETS BACK HERE, SHE'S GOING TO BEAT YOU LIKE A--
IT'S AGENT 711, YORICK. AND I'VE ALREADY MOVED YOU TO A SECURE LOCATION, FAR AWAY FROM MY CABIN. I PROMISE YOU, NO ONE IS GOING TO FIND US.

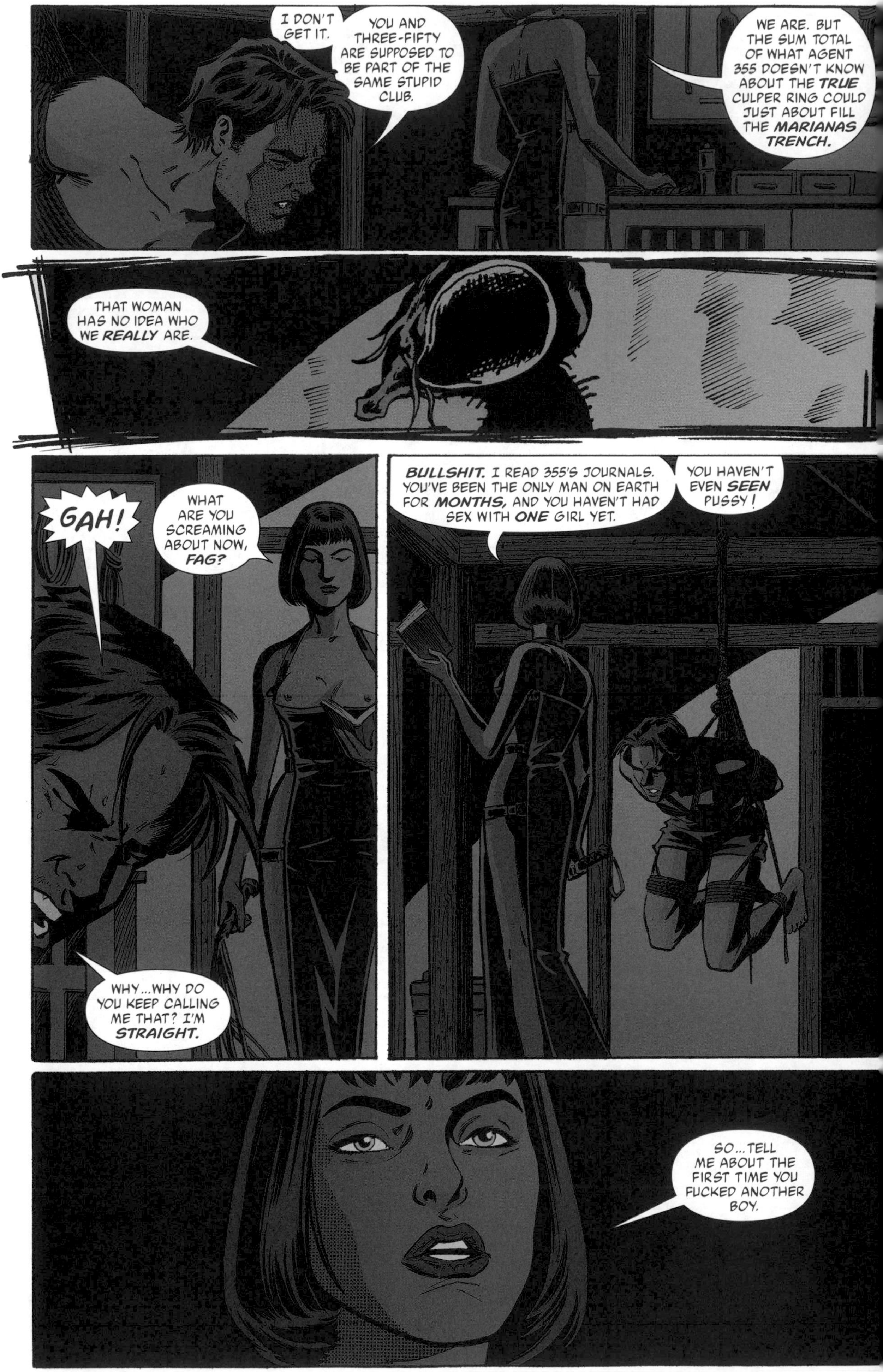
I DON'T GET IT.
YOU AND THREE-FIFTY ARE SUPPOSED TO BE PART OF THE SAME STUPID CLUB.
WE ARE. BUT THE SUM TOTAL OF WHAT AGENT 355 DOESN'T KNOW ABOUT THE **TRUE** CULPER RING COULD JUST ABOUT FILL THE **MARIANAS TRENCH.**
THAT WOMAN HAS NO IDEA WHO WE **REALLY** ARE.
GAH!
WHAT ARE YOU SCREAMING ABOUT NOW, **FAG?**
WHY...WHY DO YOU KEEP CALLING ME THAT? I'M **STRAIGHT.**
BULLSHIT. I READ 355'S JOURNALS. YOU'VE BEEN THE ONLY MAN ON EARTH FOR **MONTHS,** AND YOU HAVEN'T HAD SEX WITH **ONE** GIRL YET.
YOU HAVEN'T EVEN **SEEN** PUSSY!
SO...TELL ME ABOUT THE FIRST TIME YOU FUCKED ANOTHER BOY.

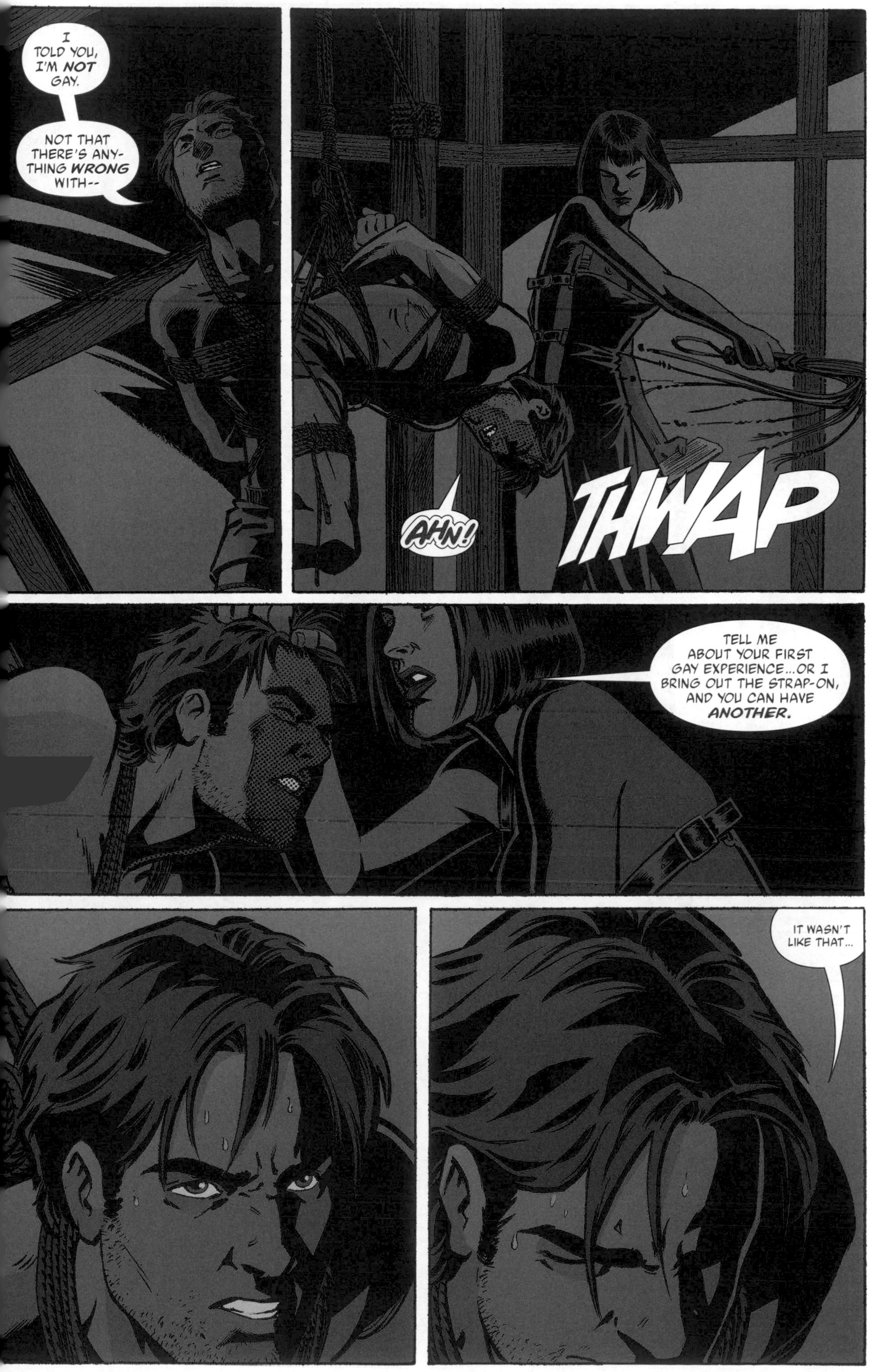
I TOLD YOU, I'M NOT GAY.
NOT THAT THERE'S ANYTHING WRONG WITH--
AHN!
THWAP
TELL ME ABOUT YOUR FIRST GAY EXPERIENCE...OR I BRING OUT THE STRAP-ON, AND YOU CAN HAVE ANOTHER.
IT WASN'T LIKE THAT...

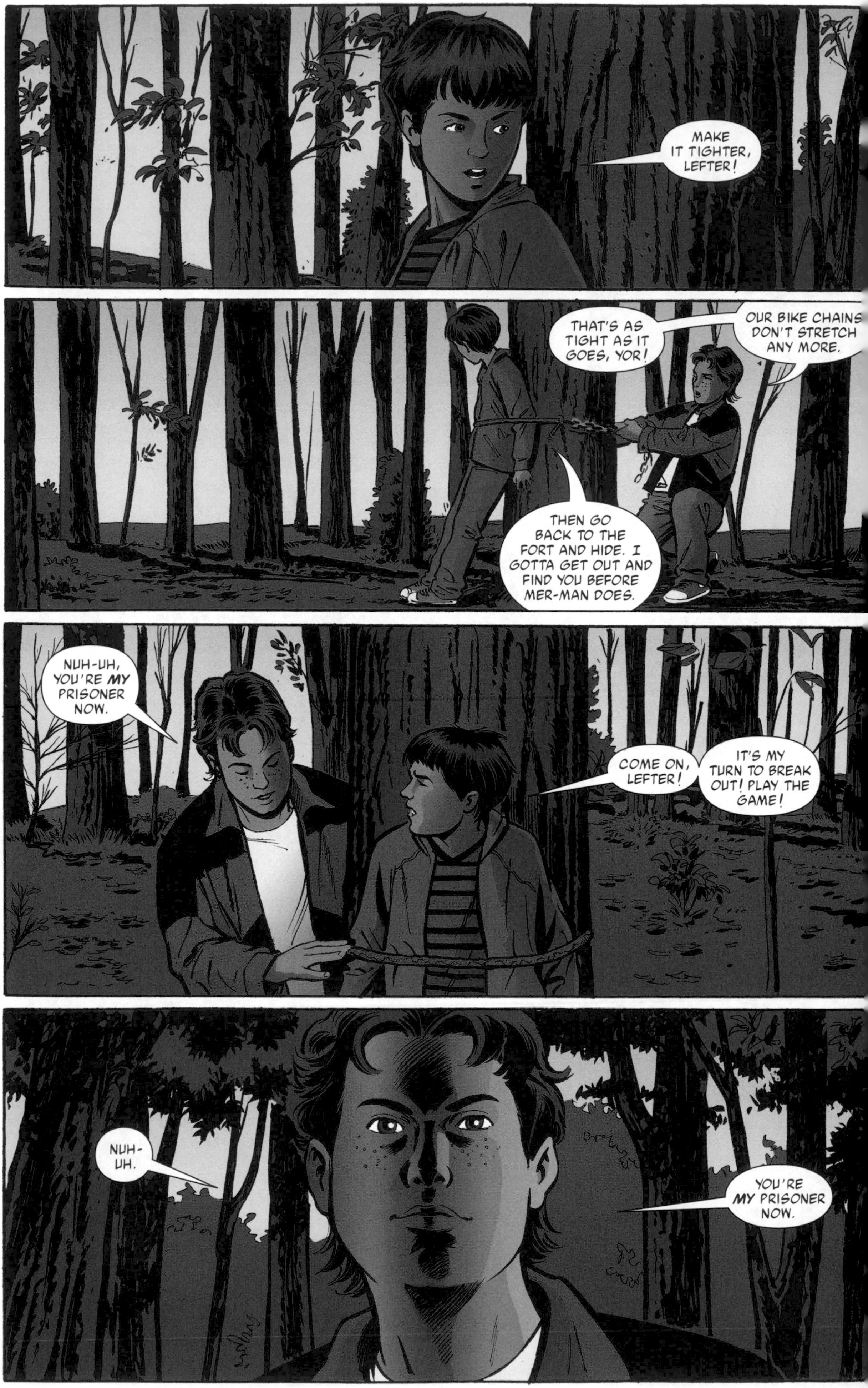
MAKE IT TIGHTER, LEFTER!
THAT'S AS TIGHT AS IT GOES, YOR!
OUR BIKE CHAINS DON'T STRETCH ANY MORE.
THEN GO BACK TO THE FORT AND HIDE. I GOTTA GET OUT AND FIND YOU BEFORE MER-MAN DOES.
NUH-UH, YOU'RE MY PRISONER NOW.
COME ON, LEFTER!
IT'S MY TURN TO BREAK OUT! PLAY THE GAME!
NUH-UH.
YOU'RE MY PRISONER NOW.

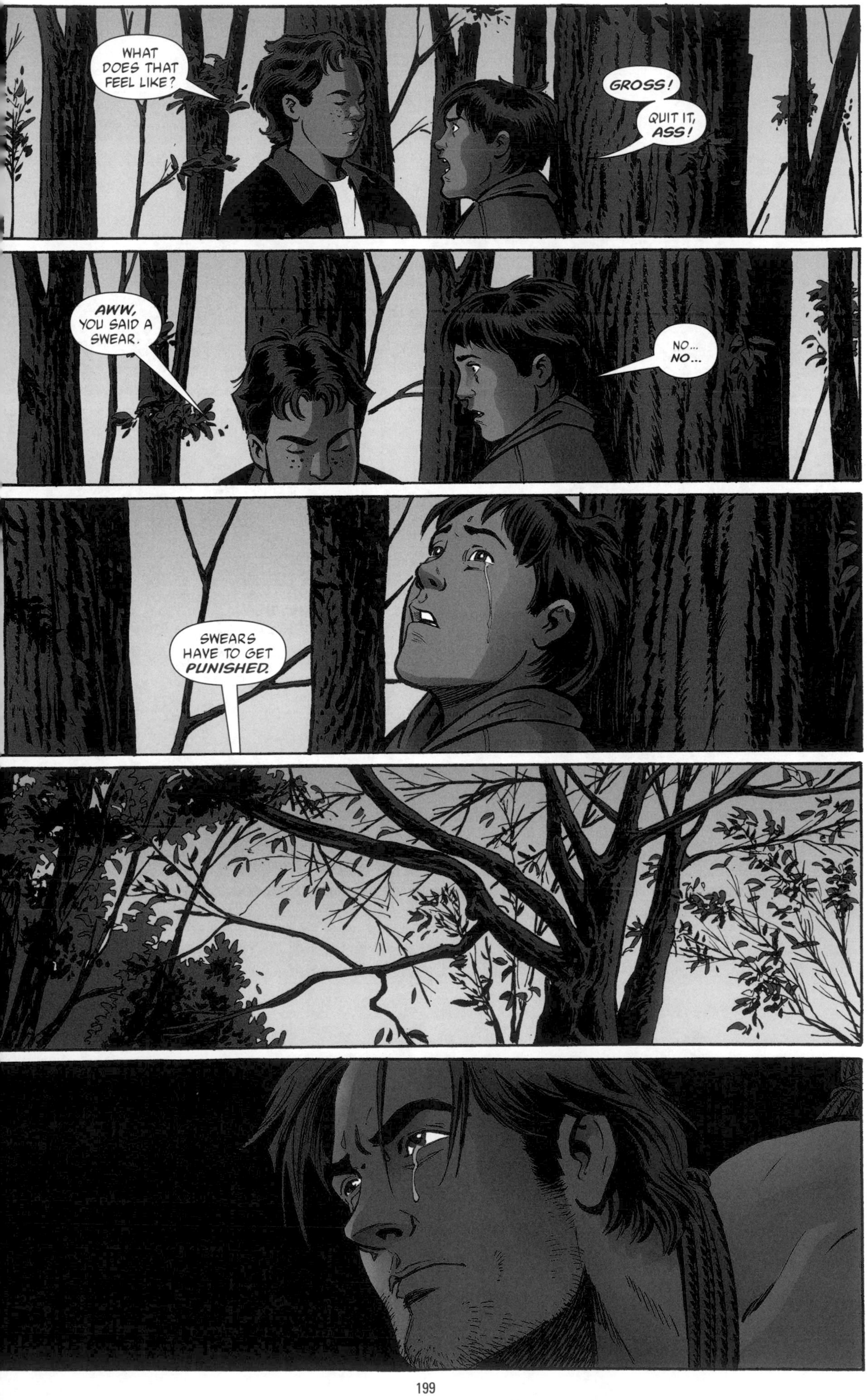
WHAT DOES THAT FEEL LIKE?
GROSS!
QUIT IT, ASS!
AWW, YOU SAID A SWEAR.
NO... NO...
SWEARS HAVE TO GET PUNISHED.

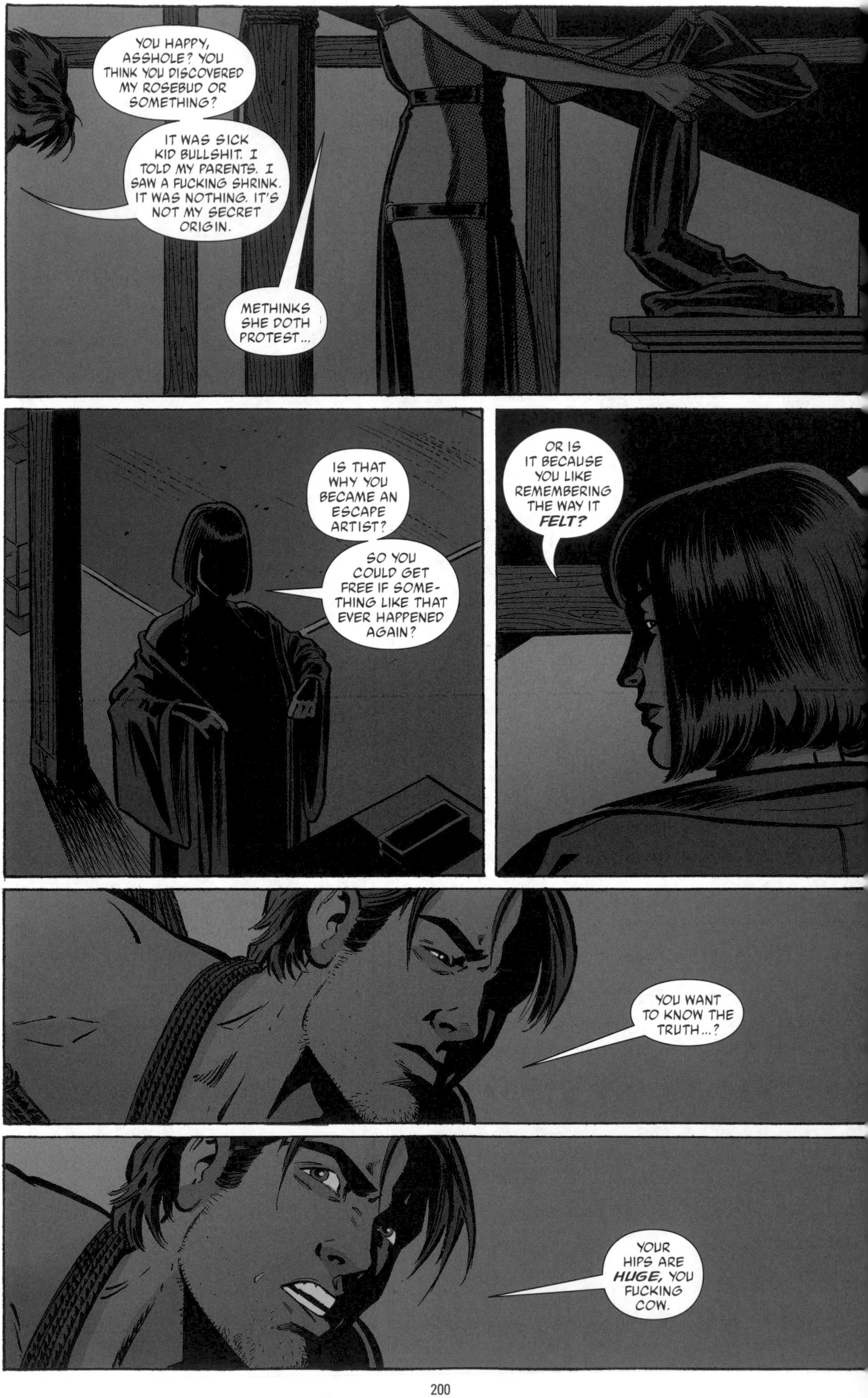
YOU HAPPY, ASSHOLE? YOU THINK YOU DISCOVERED MY ROSEBUD OR SOMETHING?
IT WAS SICK KID BULLSHIT. I TOLD MY PARENTS. I SAW A FUCKING SHRINK. IT WAS NOTHING. IT'S NOT MY SECRET ORIGIN.
METHINKS SHE DOTH PROTEST...
IS THAT WHY YOU BECAME AN ESCAPE ARTIST?
SO YOU COULD GET FREE IF SOMETHING LIKE THAT EVER HAPPENED AGAIN?
OR IS IT BECAUSE YOU LIKE REMEMBERING THE WAY IT FELT?
YOU WANT TO KNOW THE TRUTH...?
YOUR HIPS ARE HUGE, YOU FUCKING COW.

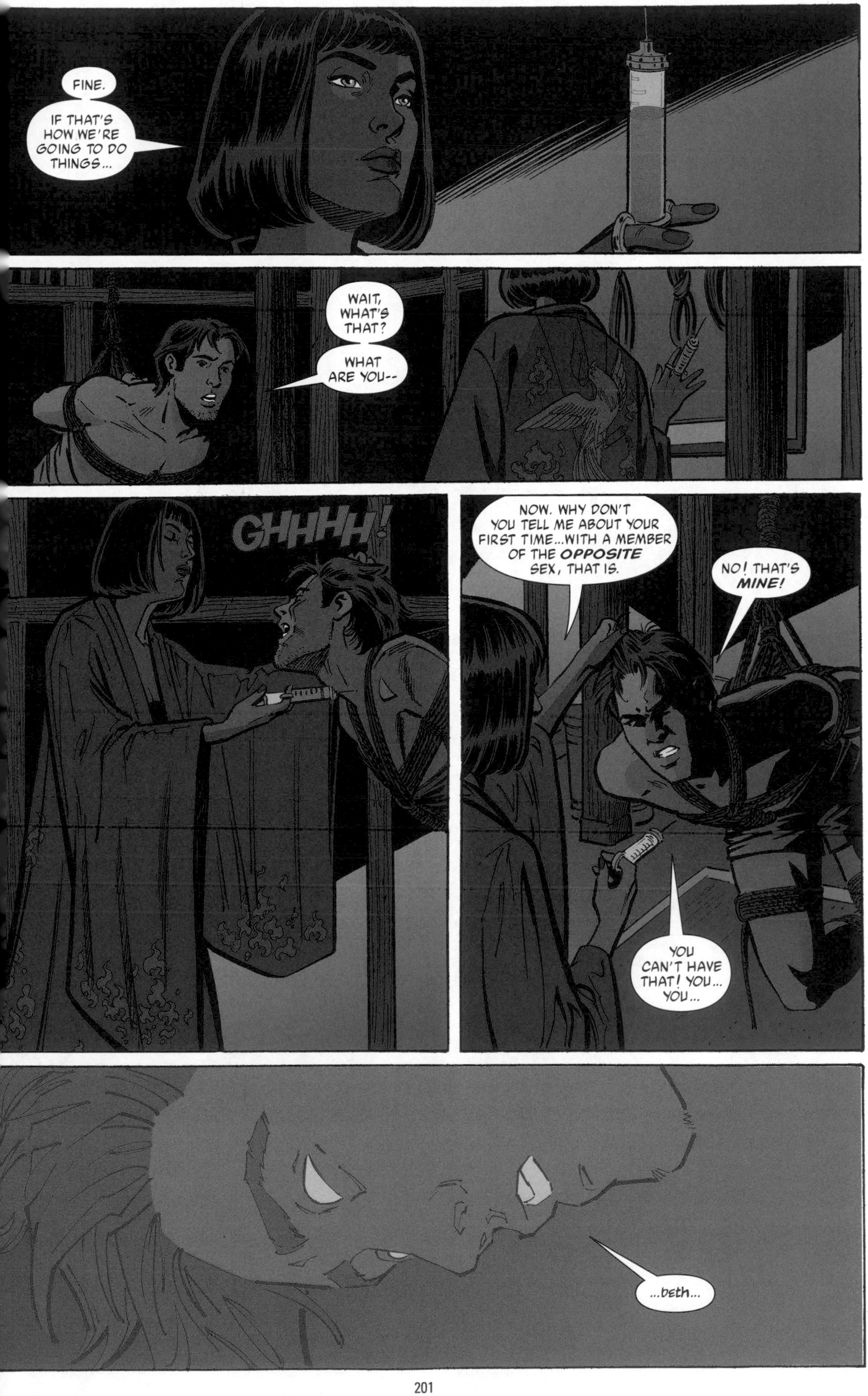
FINE.
IF THAT'S HOW WE'RE GOING TO DO THINGS...
WAIT, WHAT'S THAT?
WHAT ARE YOU--
GHHHH!
NOW. WHY DON'T YOU TELL ME ABOUT YOUR FIRST TIME...WITH A MEMBER OF THE OPPOSITE SEX, THAT IS.
NO! THAT'S MINE!
YOU CAN'T HAVE THAT! YOU... YOU...
...beth...

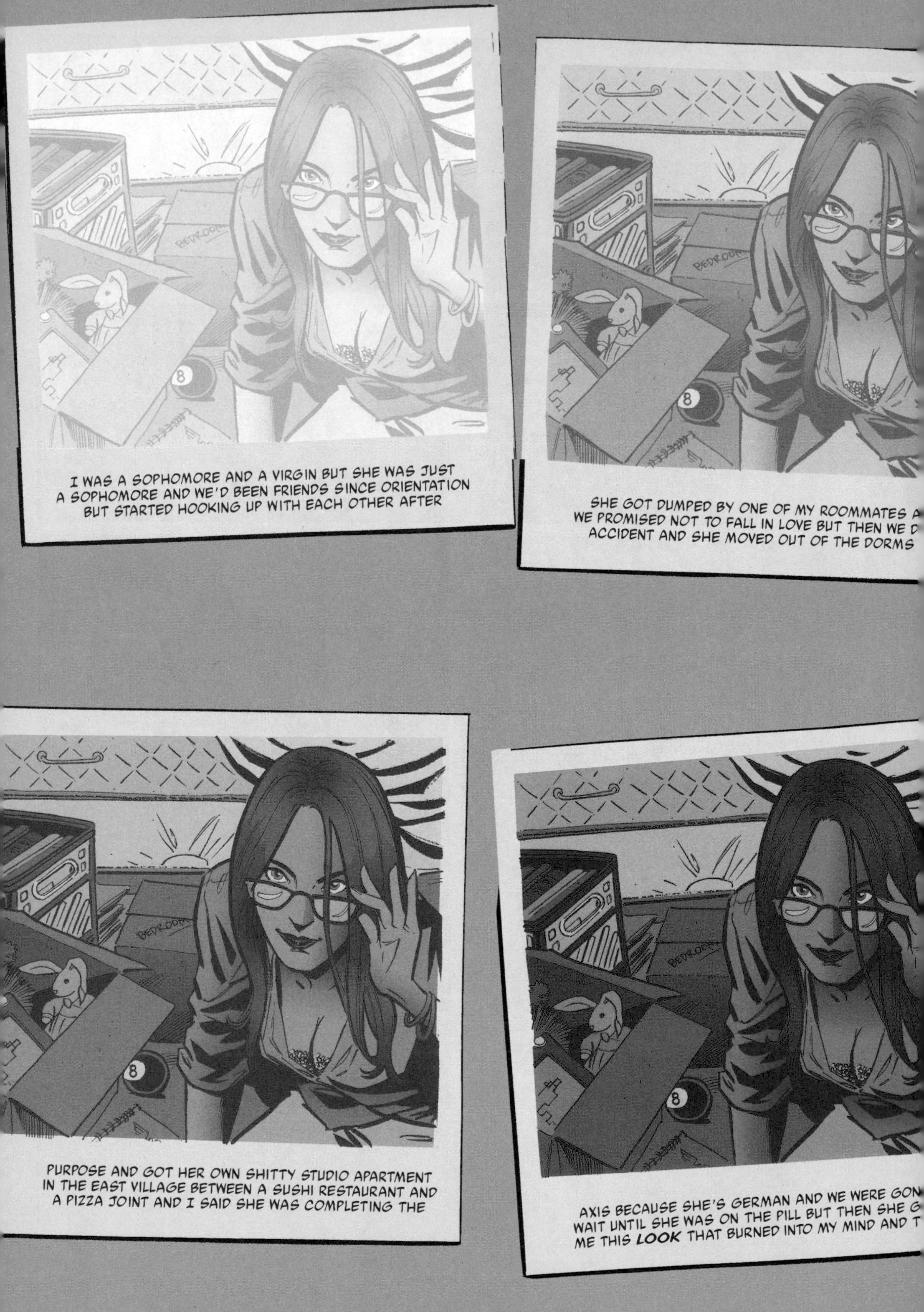

I WAS A SOPHOMORE AND A VIRGIN BUT SHE WAS JUST A SOPHOMORE AND WE'D BEEN FRIENDS SINCE ORIENTATION BUT STARTED HOOKING UP WITH EACH OTHER AFTER
SHE GOT DUMPED BY ONE OF MY ROOMMATES A
WE PROMISED NOT TO FALL IN LOVE BUT THEN WE D
ACCIDENT AND SHE MOVED OUT OF THE DORMS
PURPOSE AND GOT HER OWN SHITTY STUDIO APARTMENT IN THE EAST VILLAGE BETWEEN A SUSHI RESTAURANT AND A PIZZA JOINT AND I SAID SHE WAS COMPLETING THE
AXIS BECAUSE SHE'S GERMAN AND WE WERE GON
WAIT UNTIL SHE WAS ON THE PILL BUT THEN SHE G
ME THIS **LOOK** THAT BURNED INTO MY MIND AND T

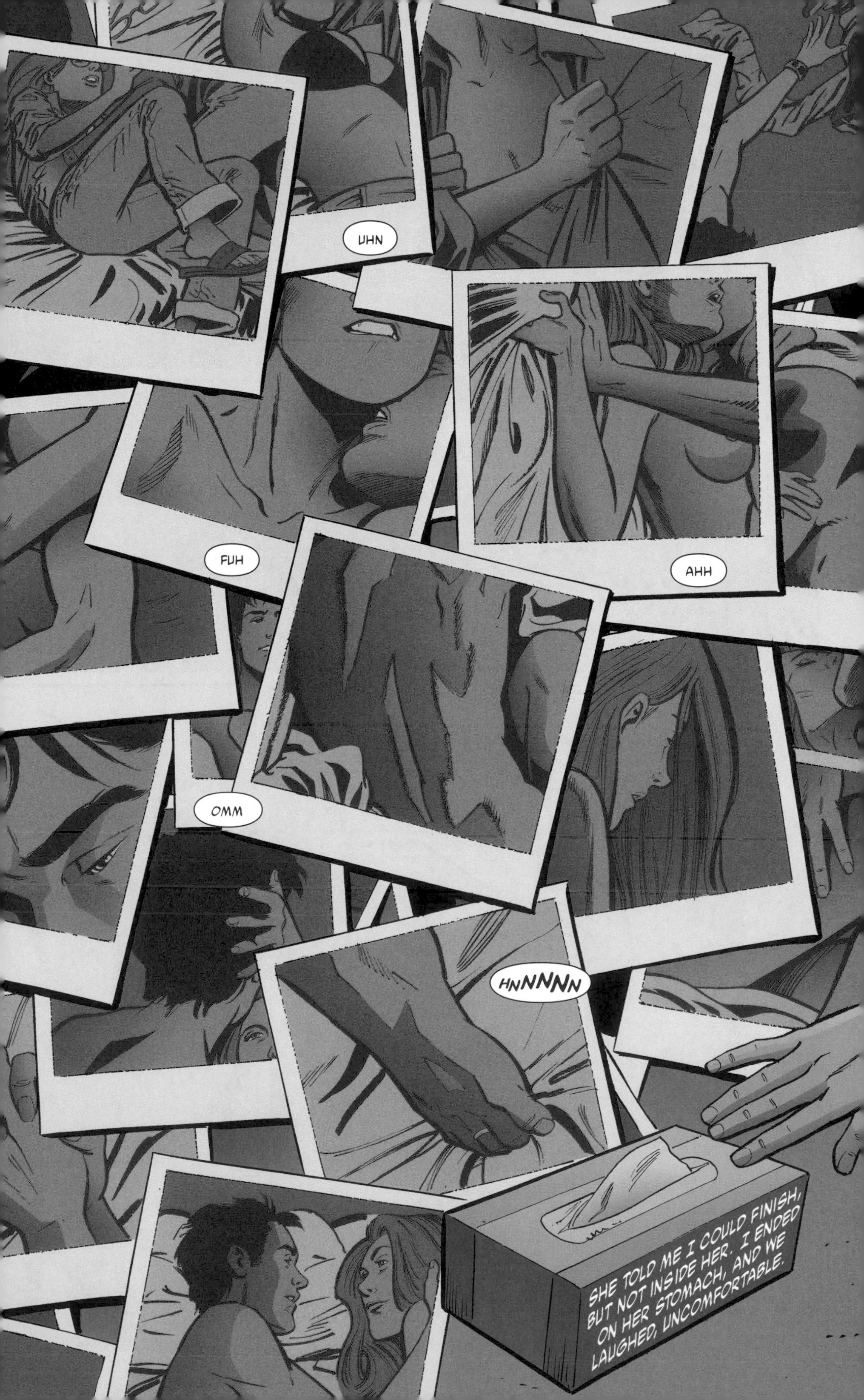
UHN
FUH
AHH
OMM
HNNNNN
SHE TOLD ME I COULD FINISH, BUT NOT INSIDE HER. I ENDED ON HER STOMACH, AND WE LAUGHED, UNCOMFORTABLE.

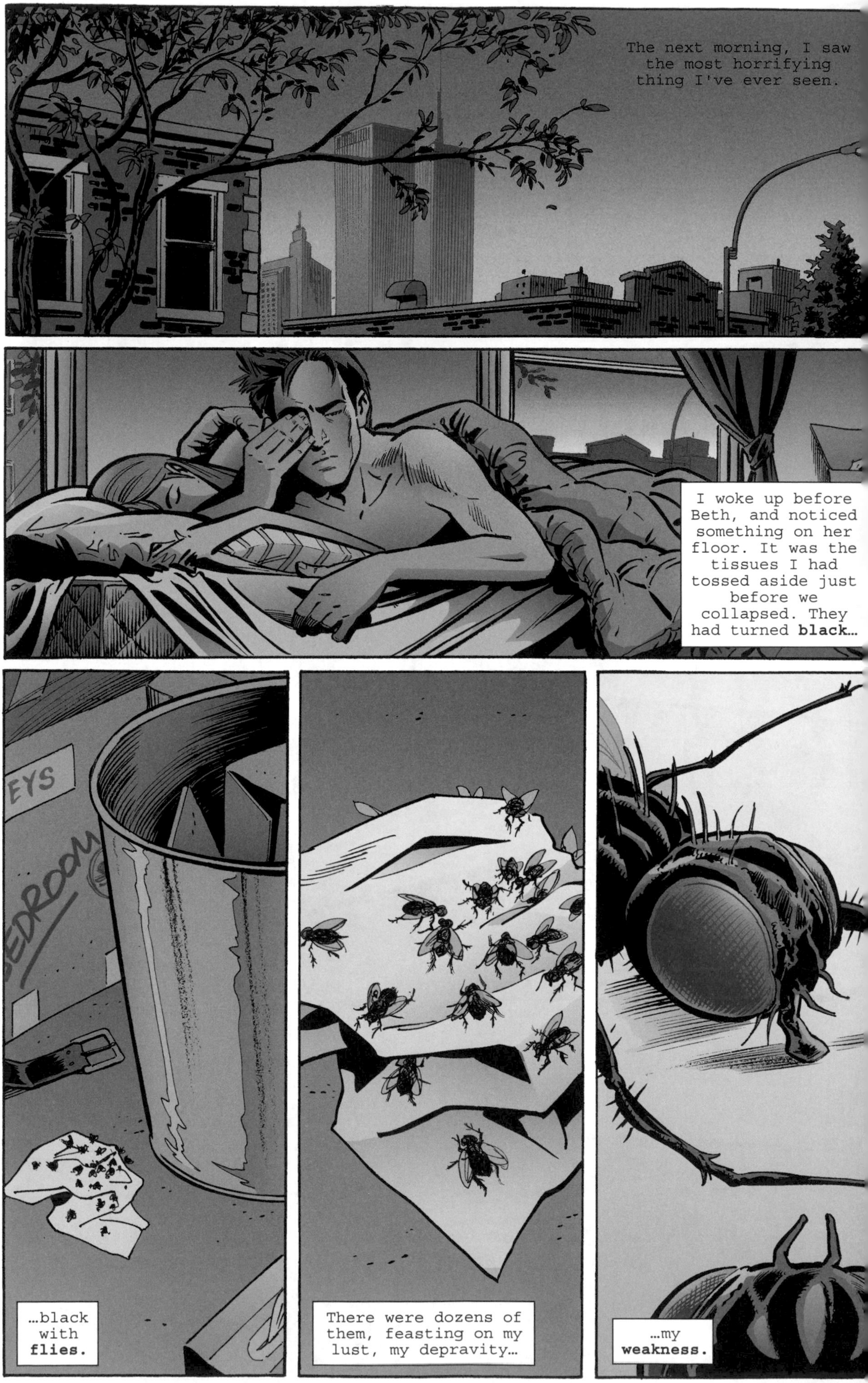
The next morning, I saw the most horrifying thing I've ever seen.
I woke up before Beth, and noticed something on her floor. It was the tissues I had tossed aside just before we collapsed. They had turned **black**…
…black with **flies.**
There were dozens of them, feasting on my lust, my depravity…
…my **weakness.**

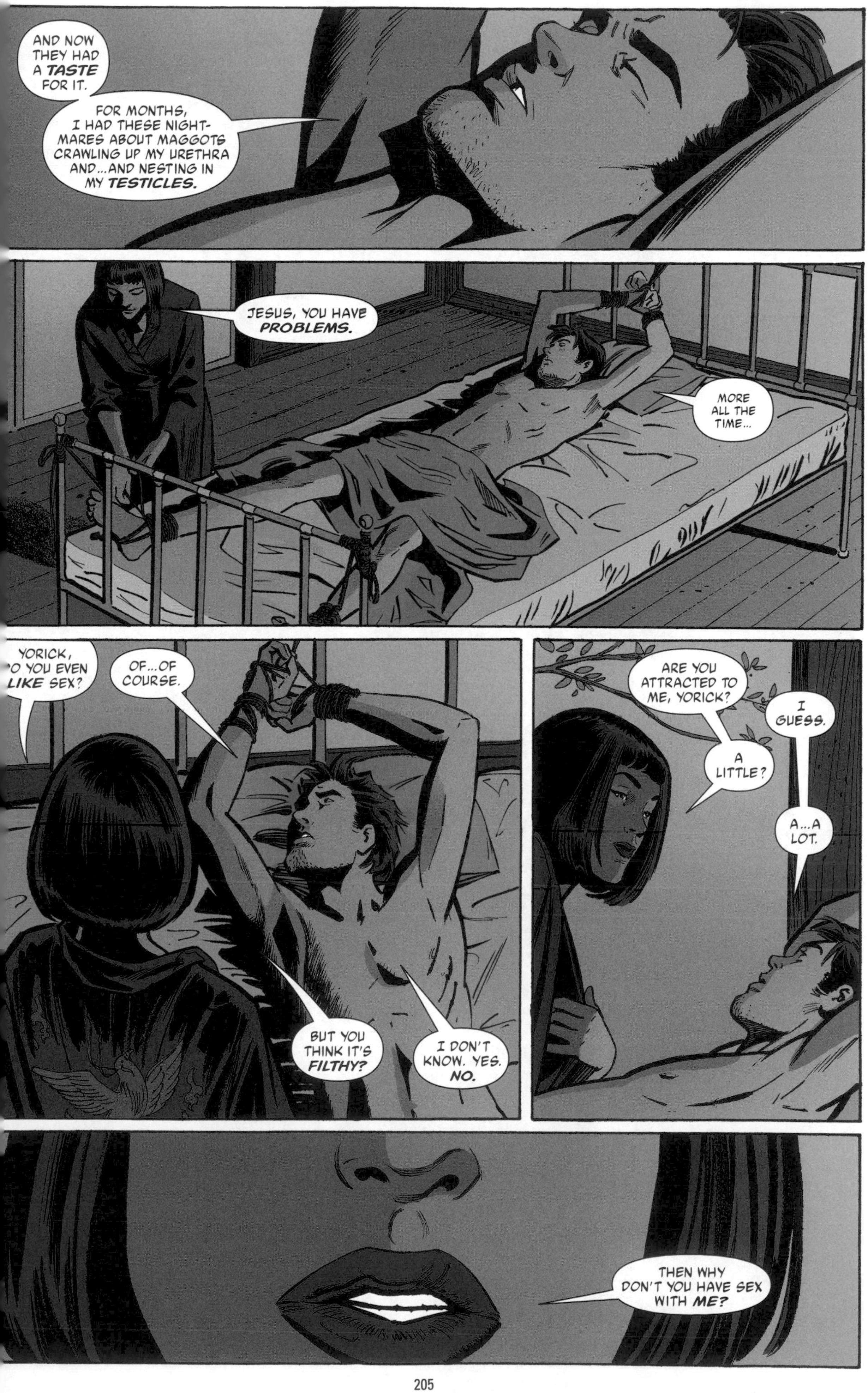
AND NOW THEY HAD A *TASTE* FOR IT.
FOR MONTHS, I HAD THESE NIGHT-MARES ABOUT MAGGOTS CRAWLING UP MY URETHRA AND...AND NESTING IN MY *TESTICLES.*
JESUS, YOU HAVE *PROBLEMS.*
MORE ALL THE TIME...
YORICK, DO YOU EVEN *LIKE* SEX?
OF...OF COURSE.
BUT YOU THINK IT'S *FILTHY?*
I DON'T KNOW. YES. *NO.*
ARE YOU ATTRACTED TO ME, YORICK?
A LITTLE?
I GUESS.
A...A LOT.
THEN WHY DON'T YOU HAVE SEX WITH *ME?*

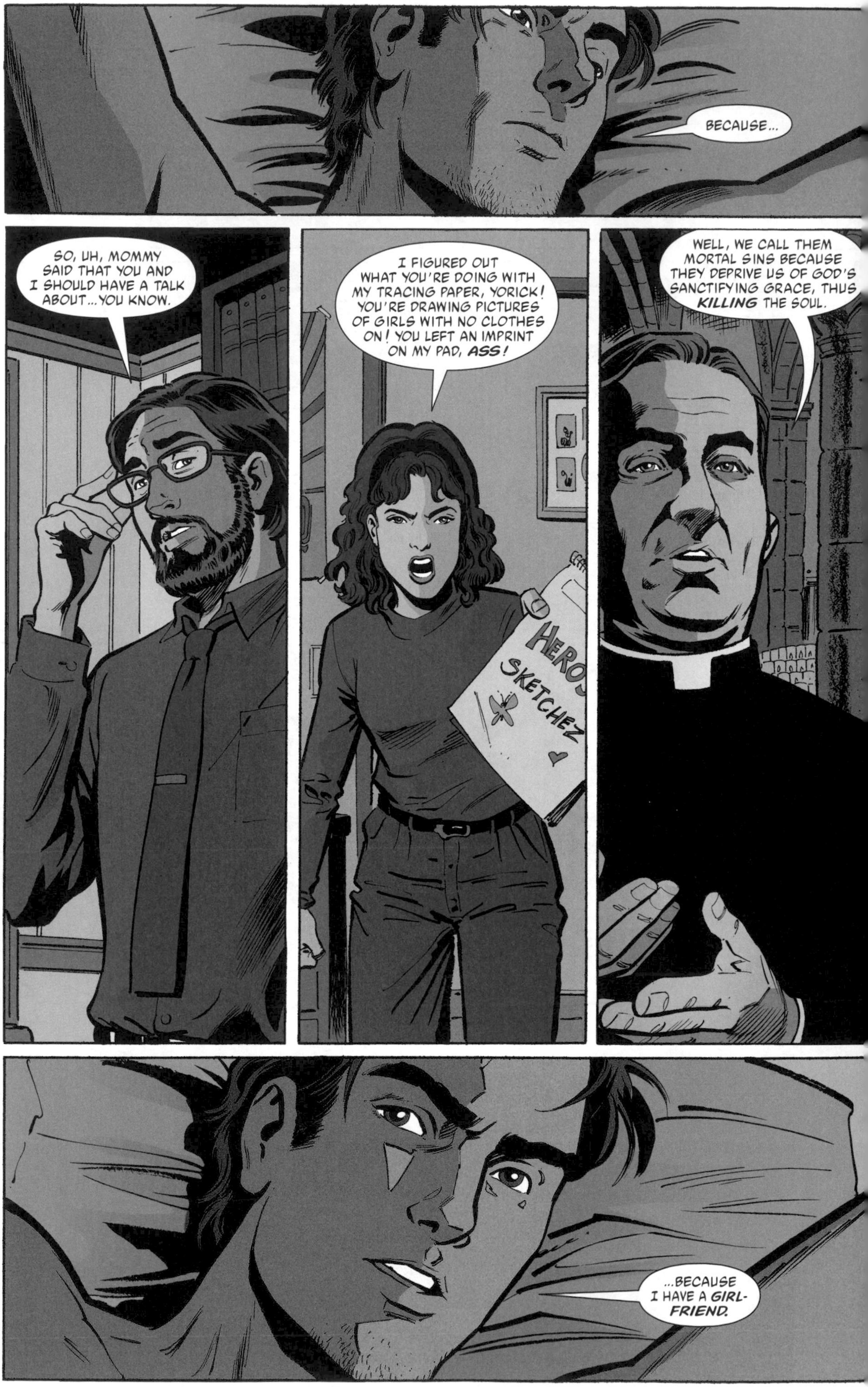
BECAUSE...
SO, UH, MOMMY SAID THAT YOU AND I SHOULD HAVE A TALK ABOUT... YOU KNOW.
I FIGURED OUT WHAT YOU'RE DOING WITH MY TRACING PAPER, YORICK! YOU'RE DRAWING PICTURES OF GIRLS WITH NO CLOTHES ON! YOU LEFT AN IMPRINT ON MY PAD, ASS!
HEROS SKETCHEZ
WELL, WE CALL THEM MORTAL SINS BECAUSE THEY DEPRIVE US OF GOD'S SANCTIFYING GRACE, THUS KILLING THE SOUL.
...BECAUSE I HAVE A GIRL-FRIEND.

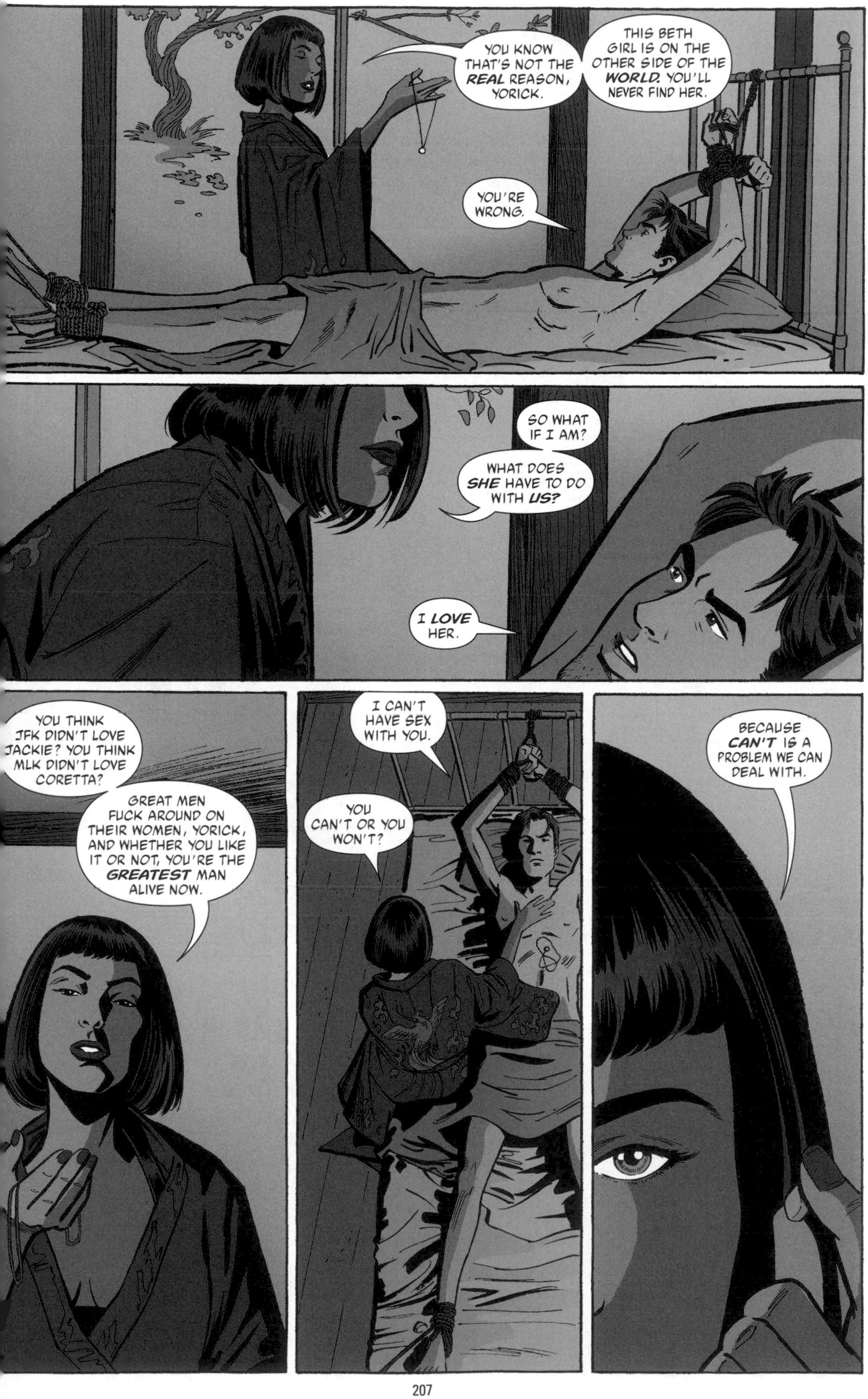
YOU KNOW THAT'S NOT THE REAL REASON, YORICK.
THIS BETH GIRL IS ON THE OTHER SIDE OF THE WORLD. YOU'LL NEVER FIND HER.
YOU'RE WRONG.
SO WHAT IF I AM?
WHAT DOES SHE HAVE TO DO WITH US?
I LOVE HER.
YOU THINK JFK DIDN'T LOVE JACKIE? YOU THINK MLK DIDN'T LOVE CORETTA?
GREAT MEN FUCK AROUND ON THEIR WOMEN, YORICK, AND WHETHER YOU LIKE IT OR NOT, YOU'RE THE GREATEST MAN ALIVE NOW.
I CAN'T HAVE SEX WITH YOU.
YOU CAN'T OR YOU WON'T?
BECAUSE CAN'T IS A PROBLEM WE CAN DEAL WITH.

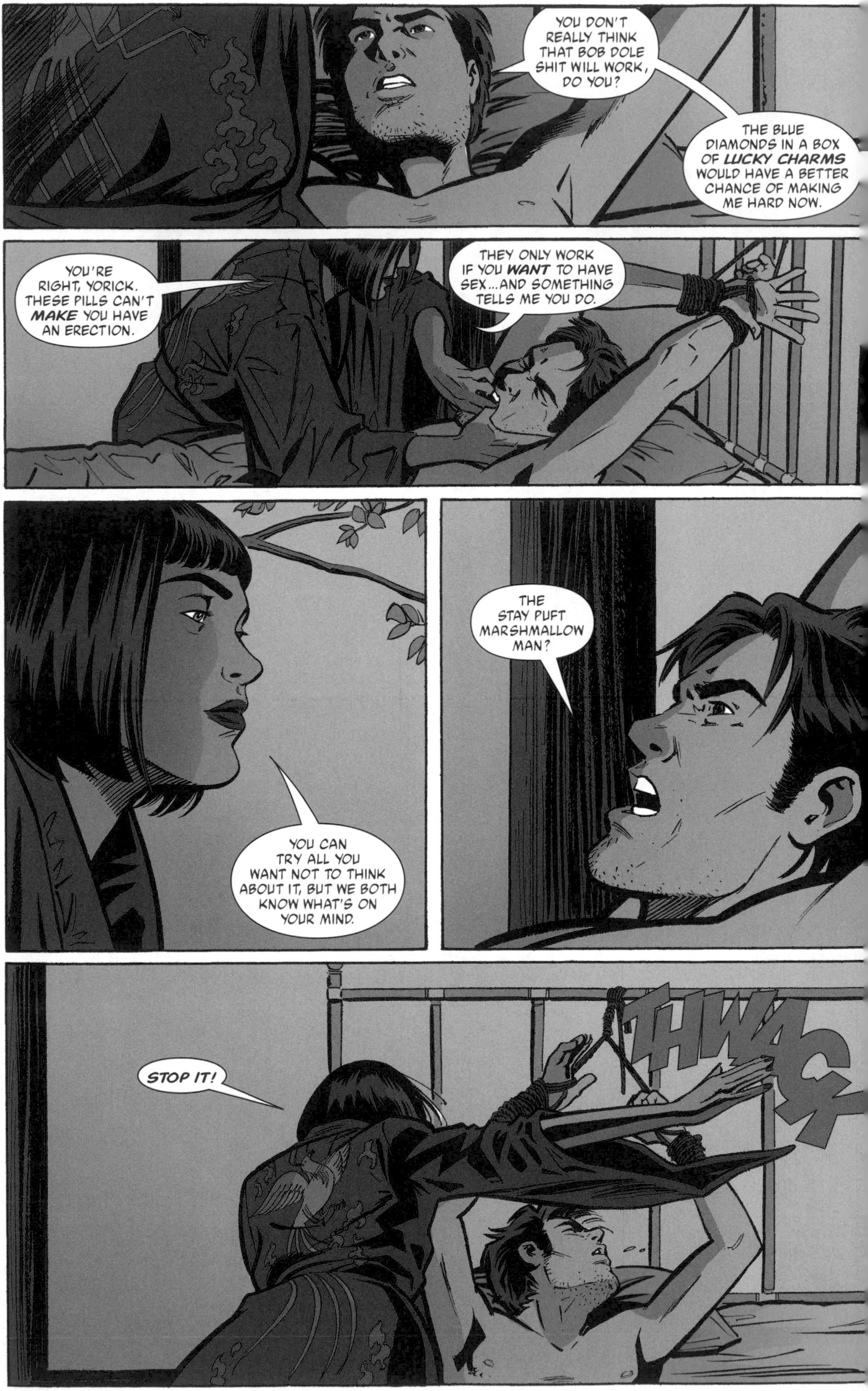
YOU DON'T REALLY THINK THAT BOB DOLE SHIT WILL WORK, DO YOU?
THE BLUE DIAMONDS IN A BOX OF LUCKY CHARMS WOULD HAVE A BETTER CHANCE OF MAKING ME HARD NOW.
YOU'RE RIGHT, YORICK. THESE PILLS CAN'T MAKE YOU HAVE AN ERECTION.
THEY ONLY WORK IF YOU WANT TO HAVE SEX...AND SOMETHING TELLS ME YOU DO.
YOU CAN TRY ALL YOU WANT NOT TO THINK ABOUT IT, BUT WE BOTH KNOW WHAT'S ON YOUR MIND.
THE STAY PUFT MARSHMALLOW MAN?
STOP IT!
THWACK

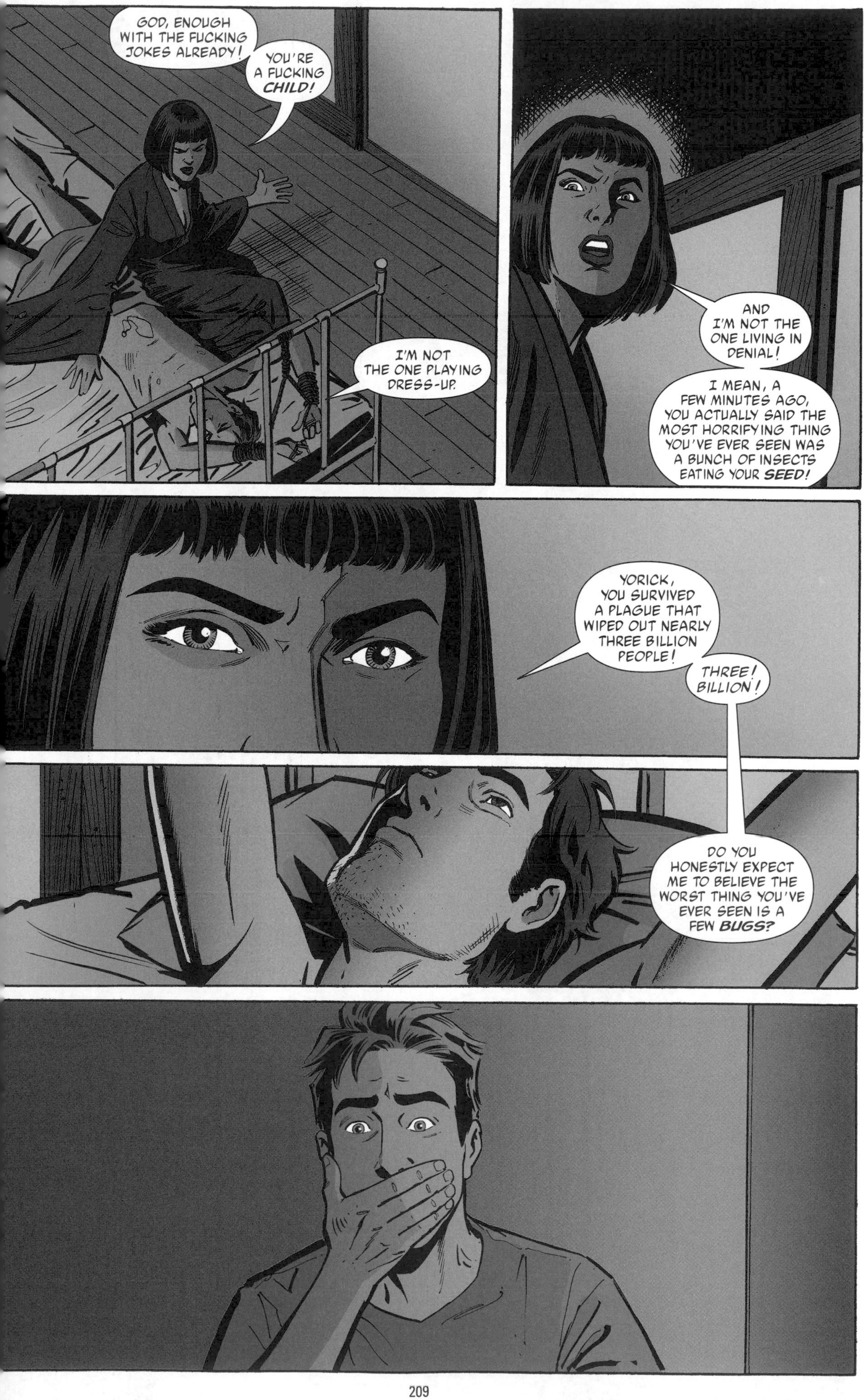
GOD, ENOUGH WITH THE FUCKING JOKES ALREADY!
YOU'RE A FUCKING CHILD!
I'M NOT THE ONE PLAYING DRESS-UP.
AND I'M NOT THE ONE LIVING IN DENIAL!
I MEAN, A FEW MINUTES AGO, YOU ACTUALLY SAID THE MOST HORRIFYING THING YOU'VE EVER SEEN WAS A BUNCH OF INSECTS EATING YOUR SEED!
YORICK, YOU SURVIVED A PLAGUE THAT WIPED OUT NEARLY THREE BILLION PEOPLE!
THREE! BILLION!
DO YOU HONESTLY EXPECT ME TO BELIEVE THE WORST THING YOU'VE EVER SEEN IS A FEW BUGS?

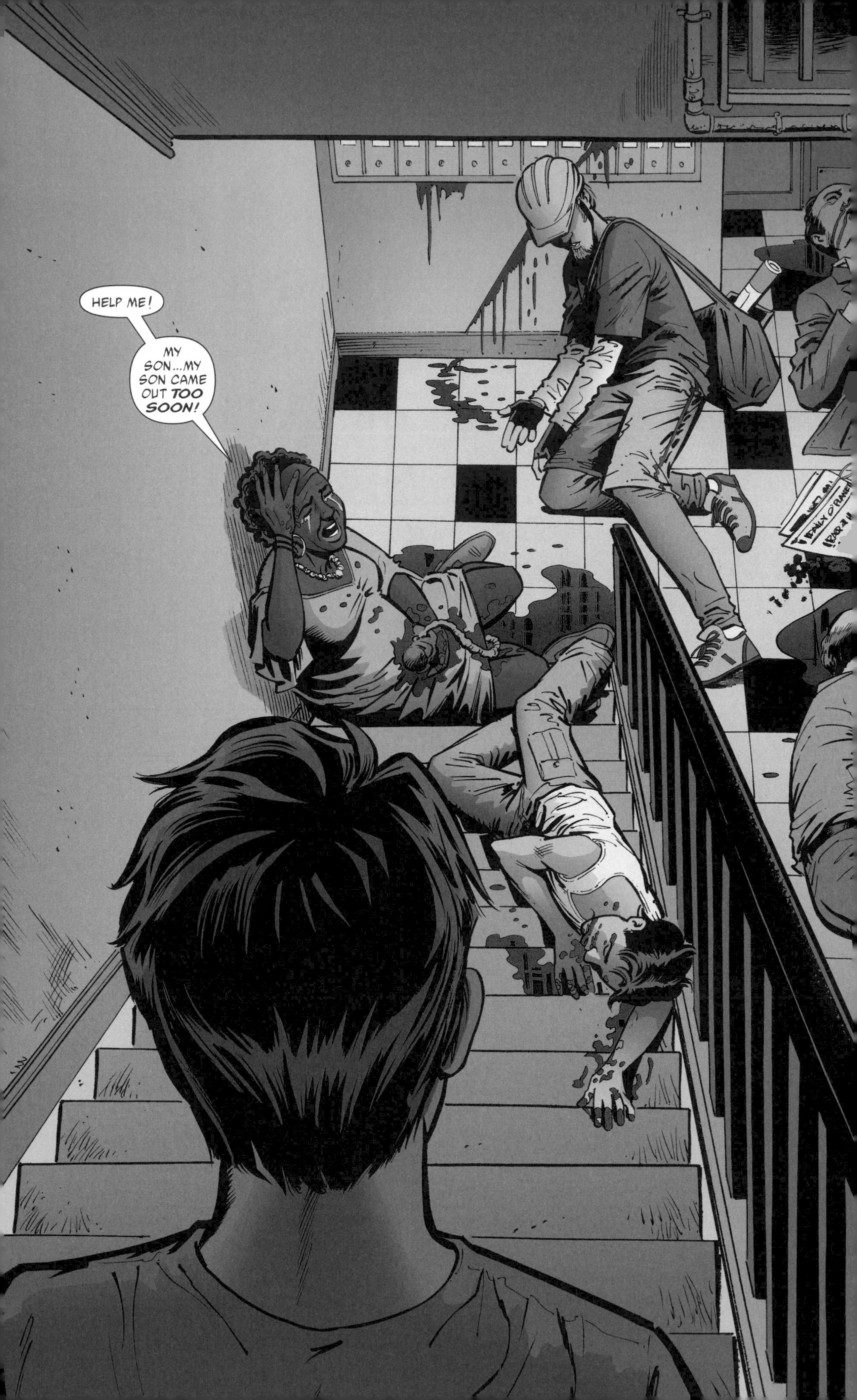
HELP ME!
MY SON...MY SON CAME OUT TOO SOON!

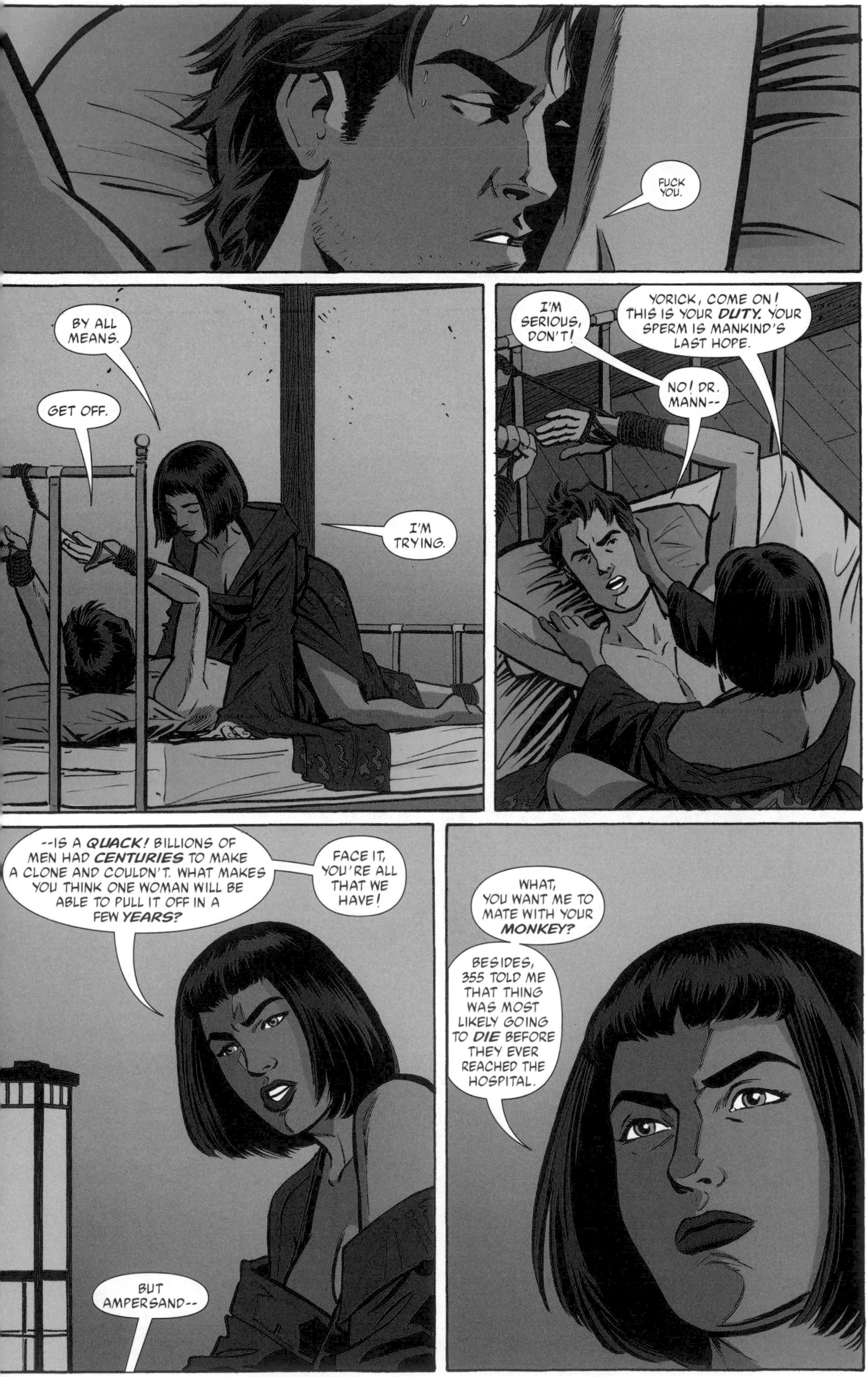
FUCK YOU.
BY ALL MEANS.
GET OFF.
I'M TRYING.
I'M SERIOUS, DON'T!
YORICK, COME ON! THIS IS YOUR DUTY. YOUR SPERM IS MANKIND'S LAST HOPE.
NO! DR. MANN--
--IS A QUACK! BILLIONS OF MEN HAD CENTURIES TO MAKE A CLONE AND COULDN'T. WHAT MAKES YOU THINK ONE WOMAN WILL BE ABLE TO PULL IT OFF IN A FEW YEARS?
FACE IT, YOU'RE ALL THAT WE HAVE!
BUT AMPERSAND--
WHAT, YOU WANT ME TO MATE WITH YOUR MONKEY?
BESIDES, 355 TOLD ME THAT THING WAS MOST LIKELY GOING TO DIE BEFORE THEY EVER REACHED THE HOSPITAL.

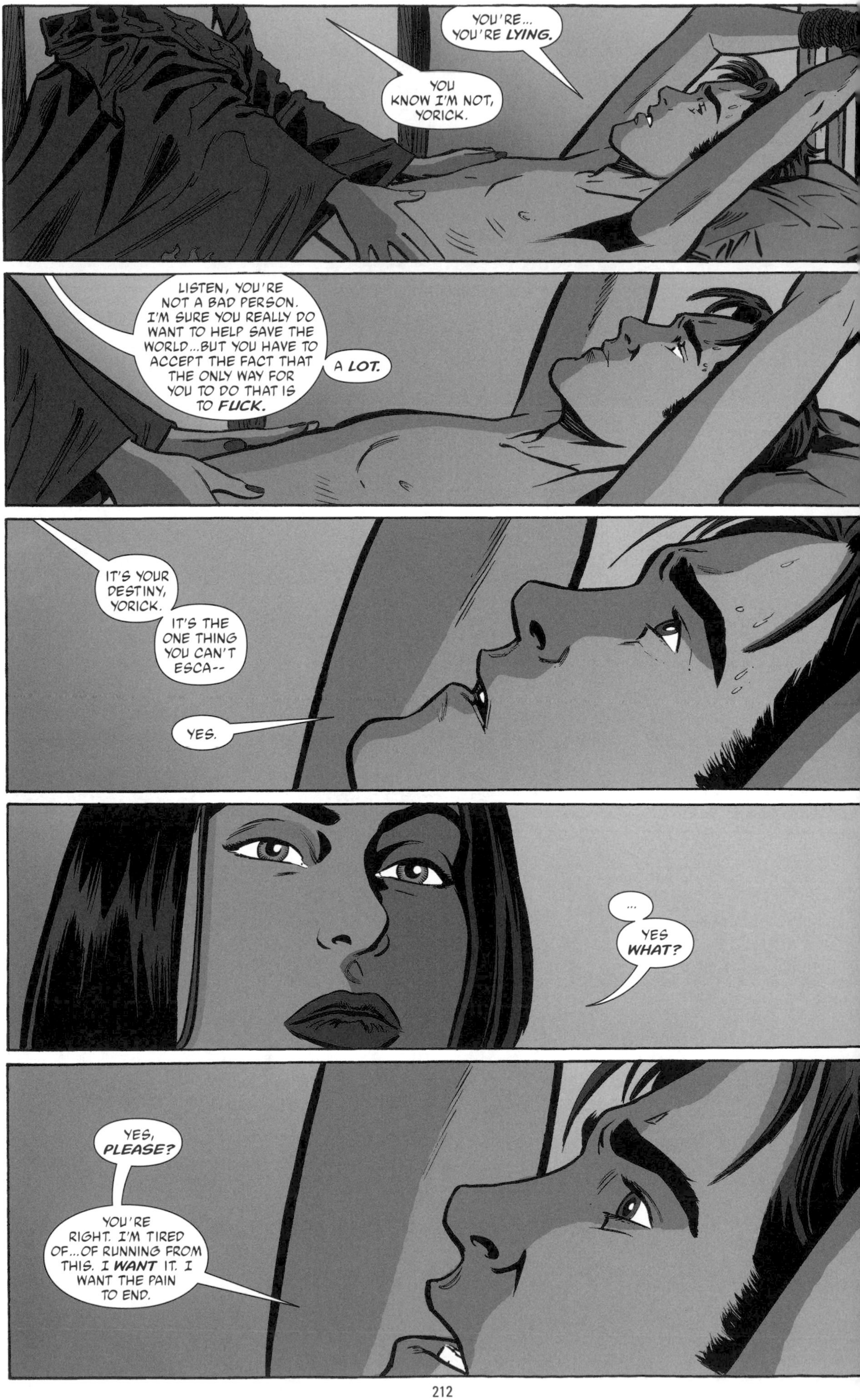
YOU'RE... YOU'RE **LYING.**
YOU KNOW I'M NOT, YORICK.
LISTEN, YOU'RE NOT A BAD PERSON. I'M SURE YOU REALLY DO WANT TO HELP SAVE THE WORLD...BUT YOU HAVE TO ACCEPT THE FACT THAT THE ONLY WAY FOR YOU TO DO THAT IS TO **FUCK.**
A **LOT.**
IT'S YOUR DESTINY, YORICK.
IT'S THE ONE THING YOU CAN'T ESCA--
YES.
...
YES **WHAT?**
YES, **PLEASE?**
YOU'RE RIGHT. I'M TIRED OF...OF RUNNING FROM THIS. I **WANT** IT. I WANT THE PAIN TO END.

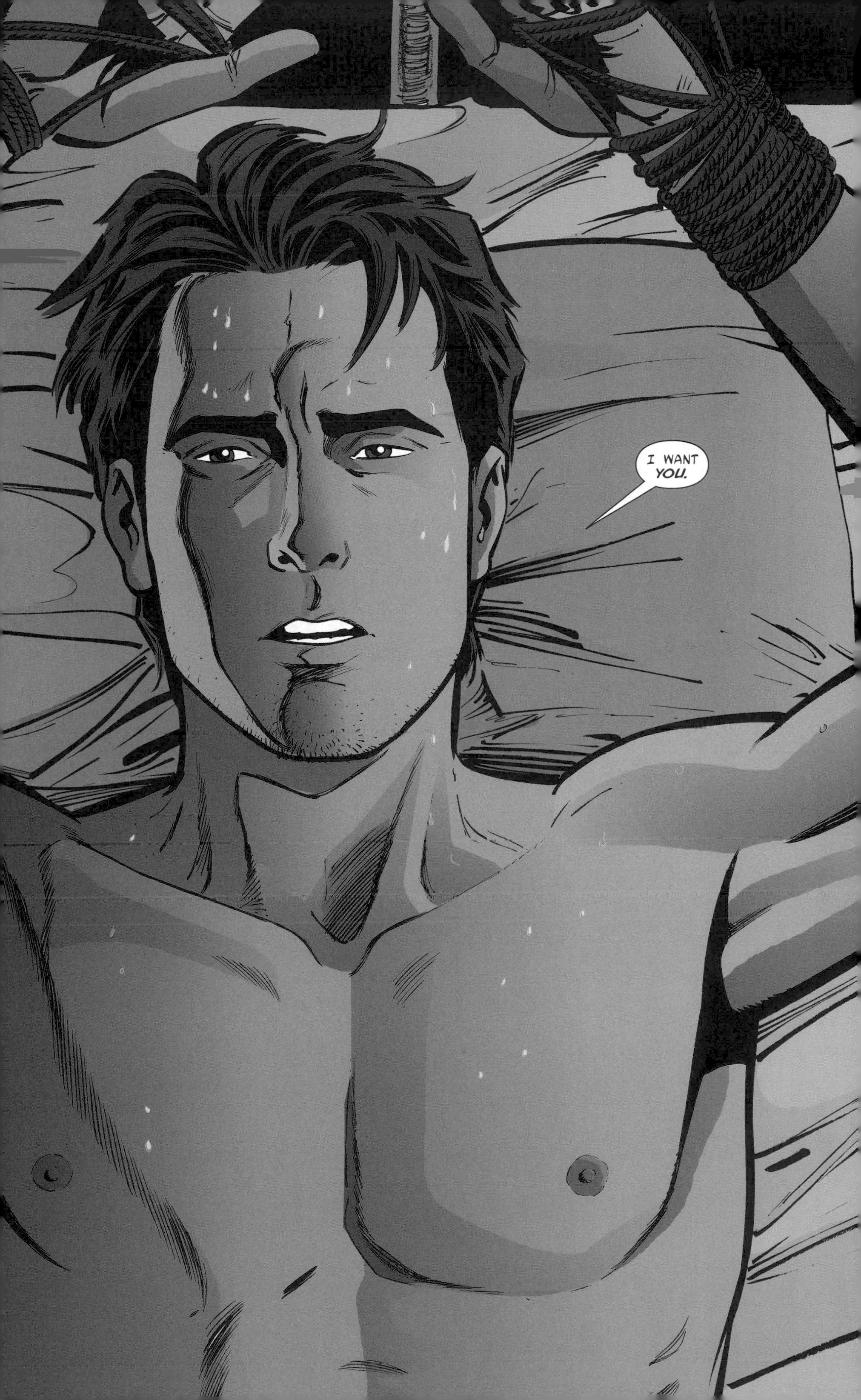
I WANT YOU.

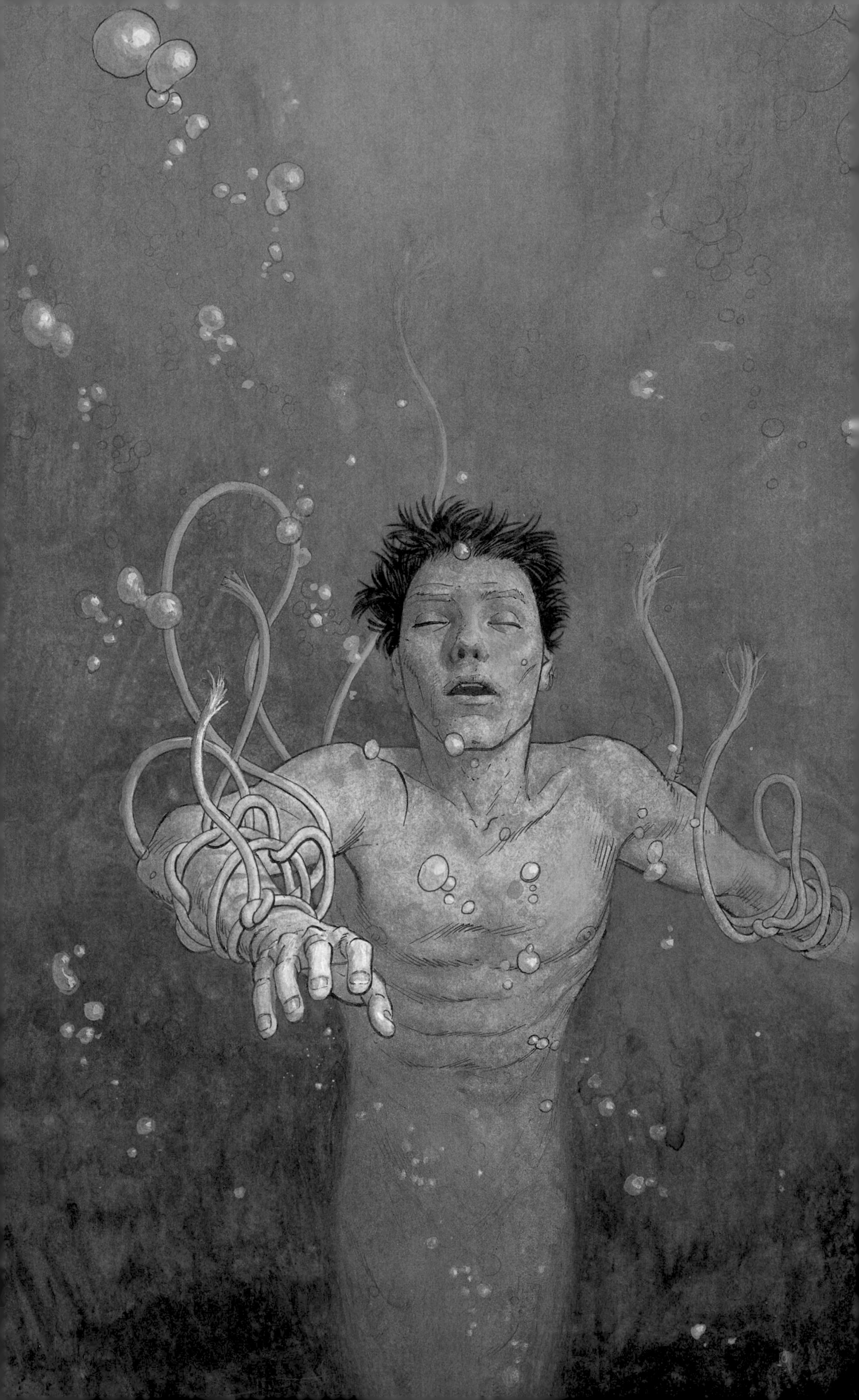

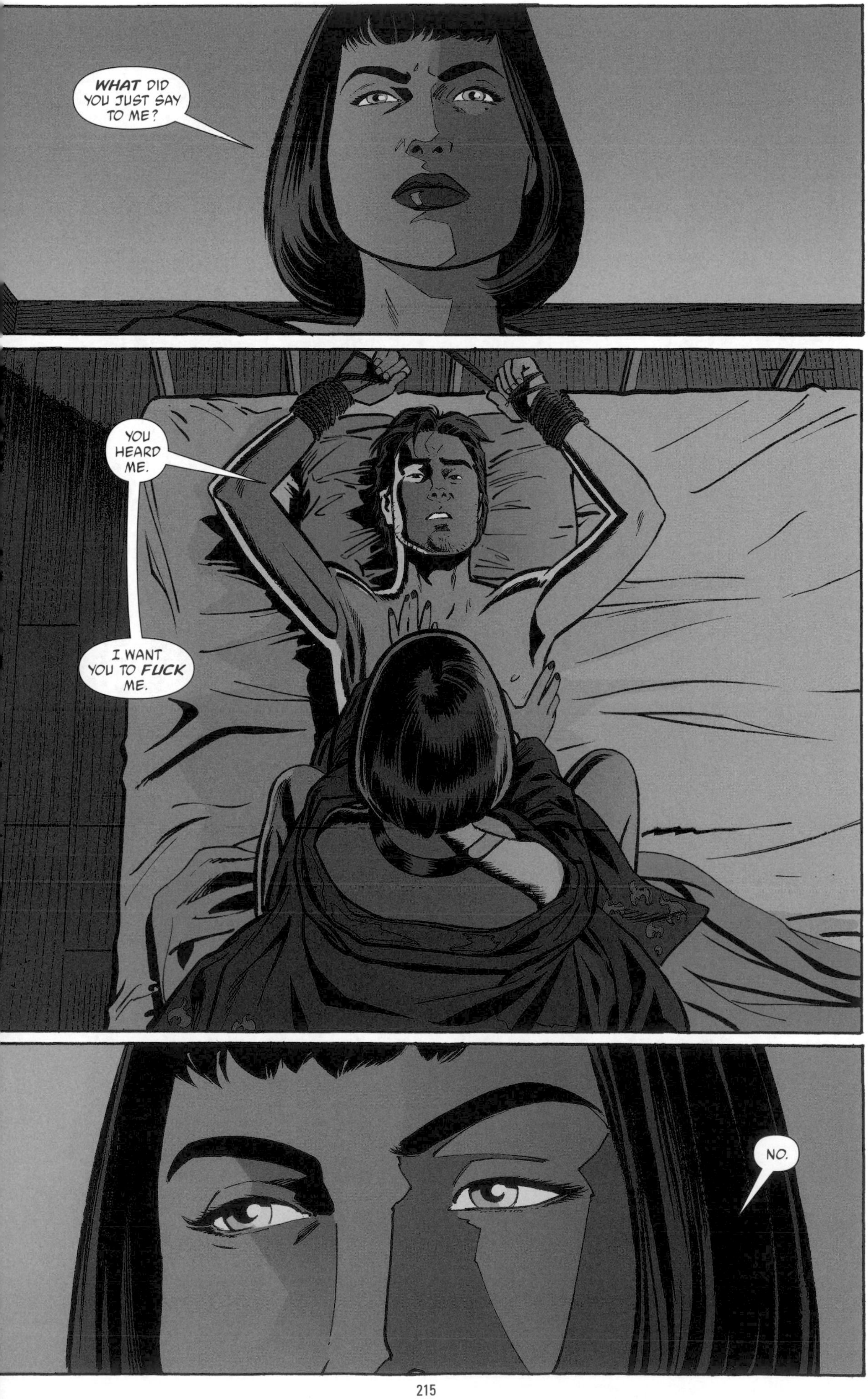
WHAT DID YOU JUST SAY TO ME?
YOU HEARD ME.
I WANT YOU TO FUCK ME.
NO.

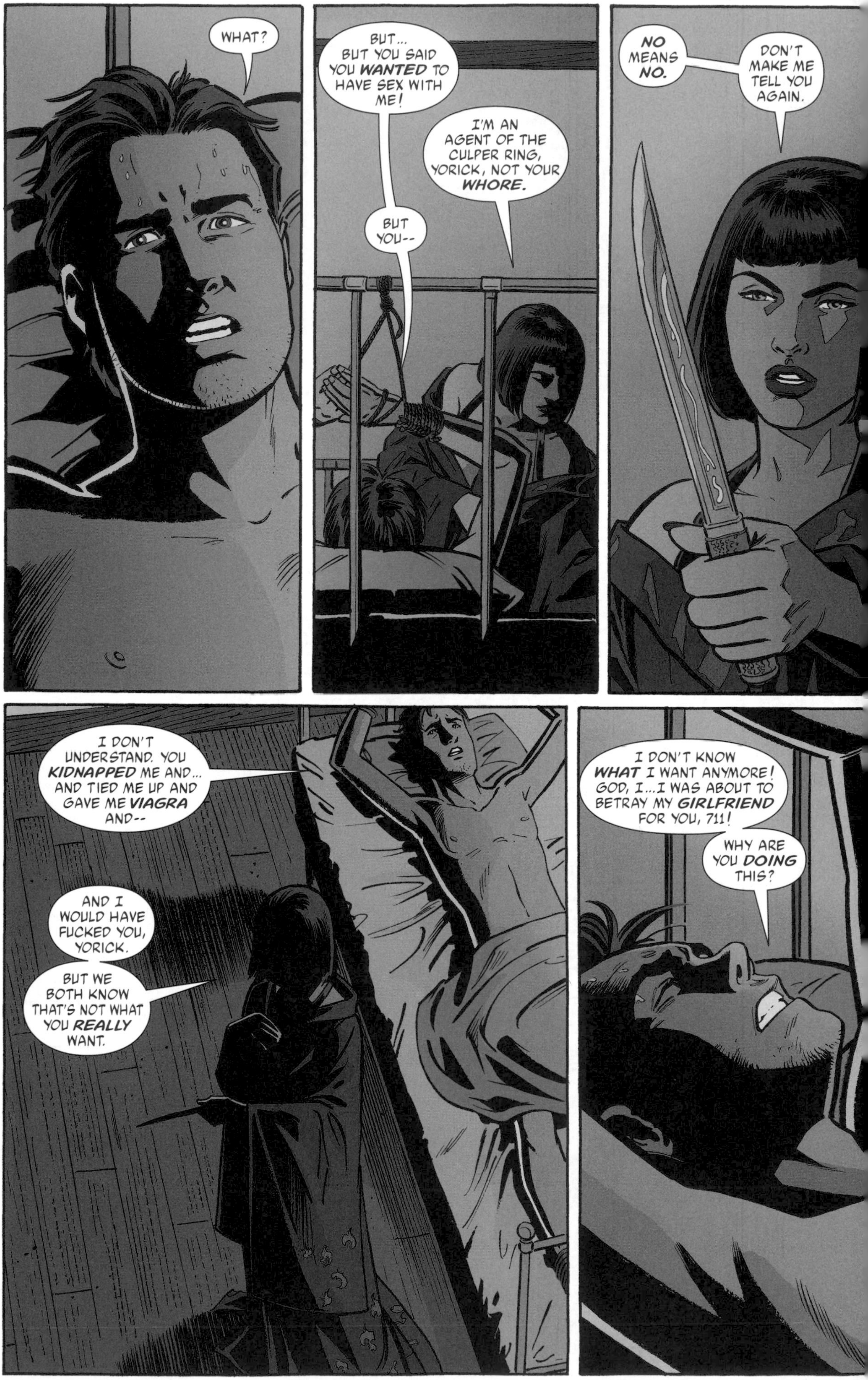
WHAT?
BUT... BUT YOU SAID YOU WANTED TO HAVE SEX WITH ME!
I'M AN AGENT OF THE CULPER RING, YORICK, NOT YOUR WHORE.
BUT YOU--
NO MEANS NO.
DON'T MAKE ME TELL YOU AGAIN.
I DON'T UNDERSTAND. YOU KIDNAPPED ME AND... AND TIED ME UP AND GAVE ME VIAGRA AND--
AND I WOULD HAVE FUCKED YOU, YORICK.
BUT WE BOTH KNOW THAT'S NOT WHAT YOU REALLY WANT.
I DON'T KNOW WHAT I WANT ANYMORE! GOD, I...I WAS ABOUT TO BETRAY MY GIRLFRIEND FOR YOU, 711!
WHY ARE YOU DOING THIS?

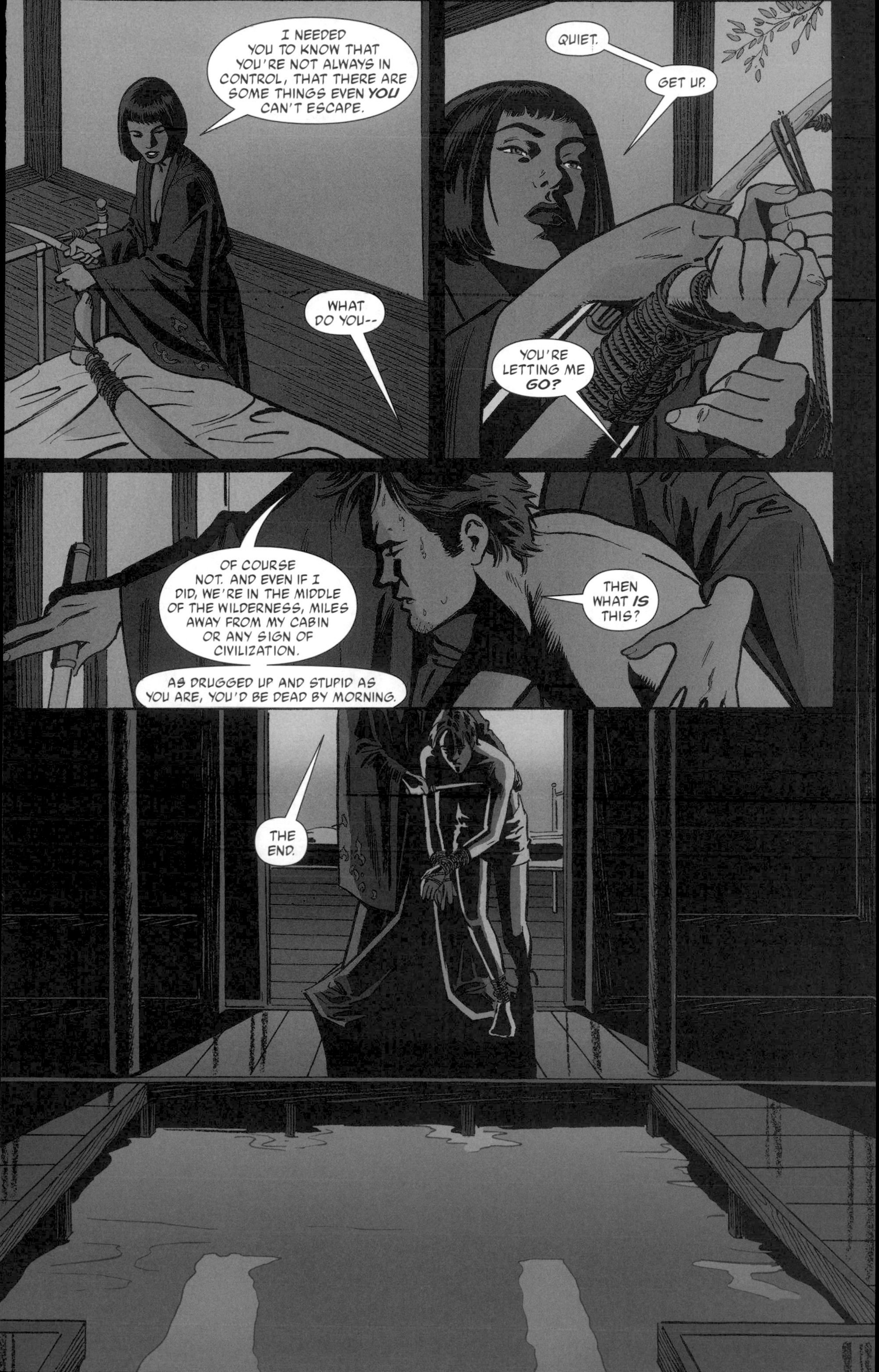
I NEEDED YOU TO KNOW THAT YOU'RE NOT ALWAYS IN CONTROL, THAT THERE ARE SOME THINGS EVEN YOU CAN'T ESCAPE.
WHAT DO YOU--
QUIET.
GET UP.
YOU'RE LETTING ME GO?
OF COURSE NOT. AND EVEN IF I DID, WE'RE IN THE MIDDLE OF THE WILDERNESS, MILES AWAY FROM MY CABIN OR ANY SIGN OF CIVILIZATION.
AS DRUGGED UP AND STUPID AS YOU ARE, YOU'D BE DEAD BY MORNING.
THEN WHAT IS THIS?
THE END.

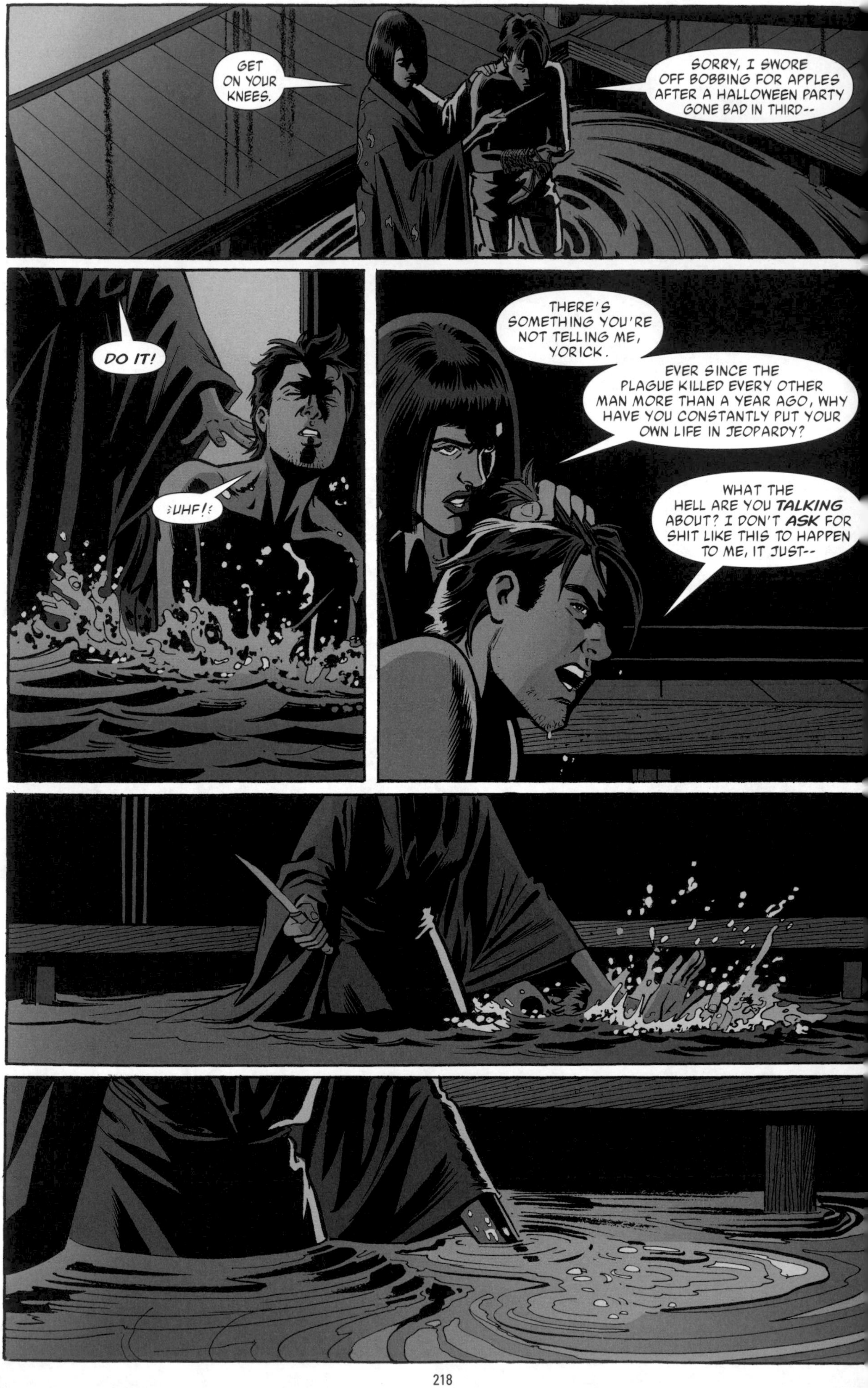
GET ON YOUR KNEES.
SORRY, I SWORE OFF BOBBING FOR APPLES AFTER A HALLOWEEN PARTY GONE BAD IN THIRD--
DO IT!
UHF!
THERE'S SOMETHING YOU'RE NOT TELLING ME, YORICK.
EVER SINCE THE PLAGUE KILLED EVERY OTHER MAN MORE THAN A YEAR AGO, WHY HAVE YOU CONSTANTLY PUT YOUR OWN LIFE IN JEOPARDY?
WHAT THE HELL ARE YOU TALKING ABOUT? I DON'T ASK FOR SHIT LIKE THIS TO HAPPEN TO ME, IT JUST--

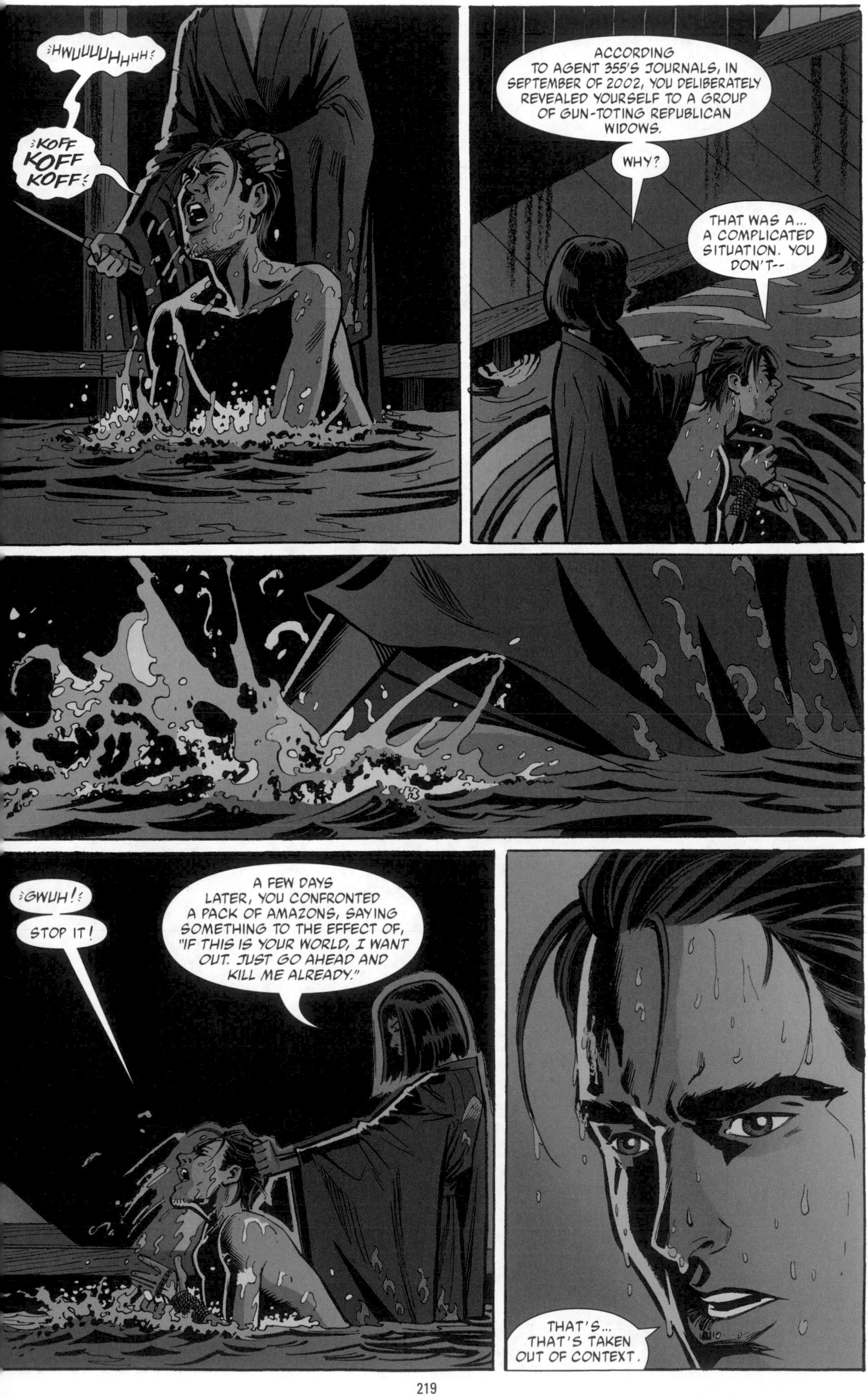
HWUUUUHHHH
KOFF KOFF KOFF
ACCORDING TO AGENT 355'S JOURNALS, IN SEPTEMBER OF 2002, YOU DELIBERATELY REVEALED YOURSELF TO A GROUP OF GUN-TOTING REPUBLICAN WIDOWS.
WHY?
THAT WAS A... A COMPLICATED SITUATION. YOU DON'T--
GWUH!
STOP IT!
A FEW DAYS LATER, YOU CONFRONTED A PACK OF AMAZONS, SAYING SOMETHING TO THE EFFECT OF, "IF THIS IS YOUR WORLD, I WANT OUT. JUST GO AHEAD AND KILL ME ALREADY."
THAT'S... THAT'S TAKEN OUT OF CONTEXT.

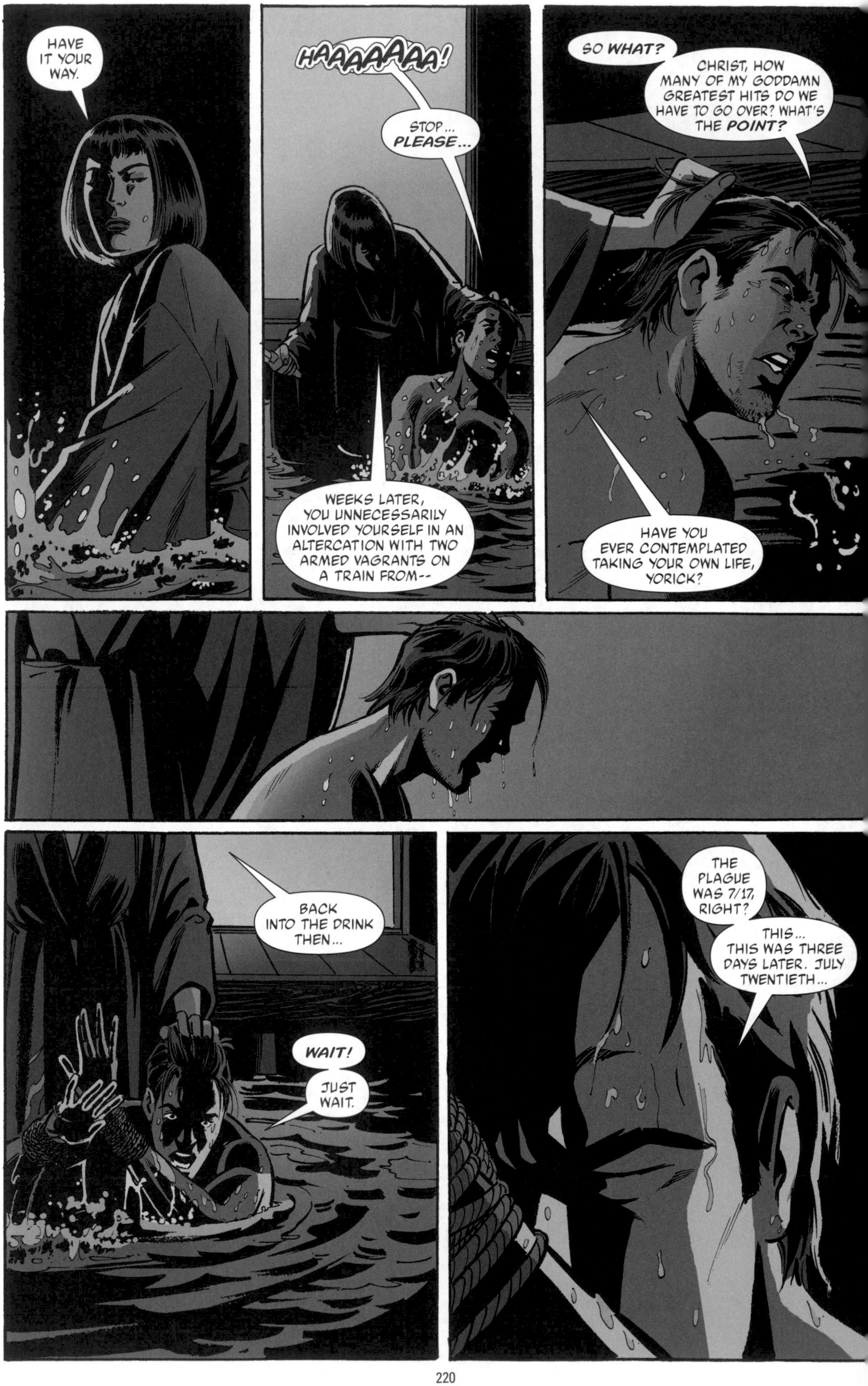
HAVE IT YOUR WAY.
HAAAAAAA!
STOP... PLEASE...
WEEKS LATER, YOU UNNECESSARILY INVOLVED YOURSELF IN AN ALTERCATION WITH TWO ARMED VAGRANTS ON A TRAIN FROM--
SO WHAT?
CHRIST, HOW MANY OF MY GODDAMN GREATEST HITS DO WE HAVE TO GO OVER? WHAT'S THE POINT?
HAVE YOU EVER CONTEMPLATED TAKING YOUR OWN LIFE, YORICK?
BACK INTO THE DRINK THEN...
WAIT!
JUST WAIT.
THE PLAGUE WAS 7/17, RIGHT?
THIS... THIS WAS THREE DAYS LATER. JULY TWENTIETH...

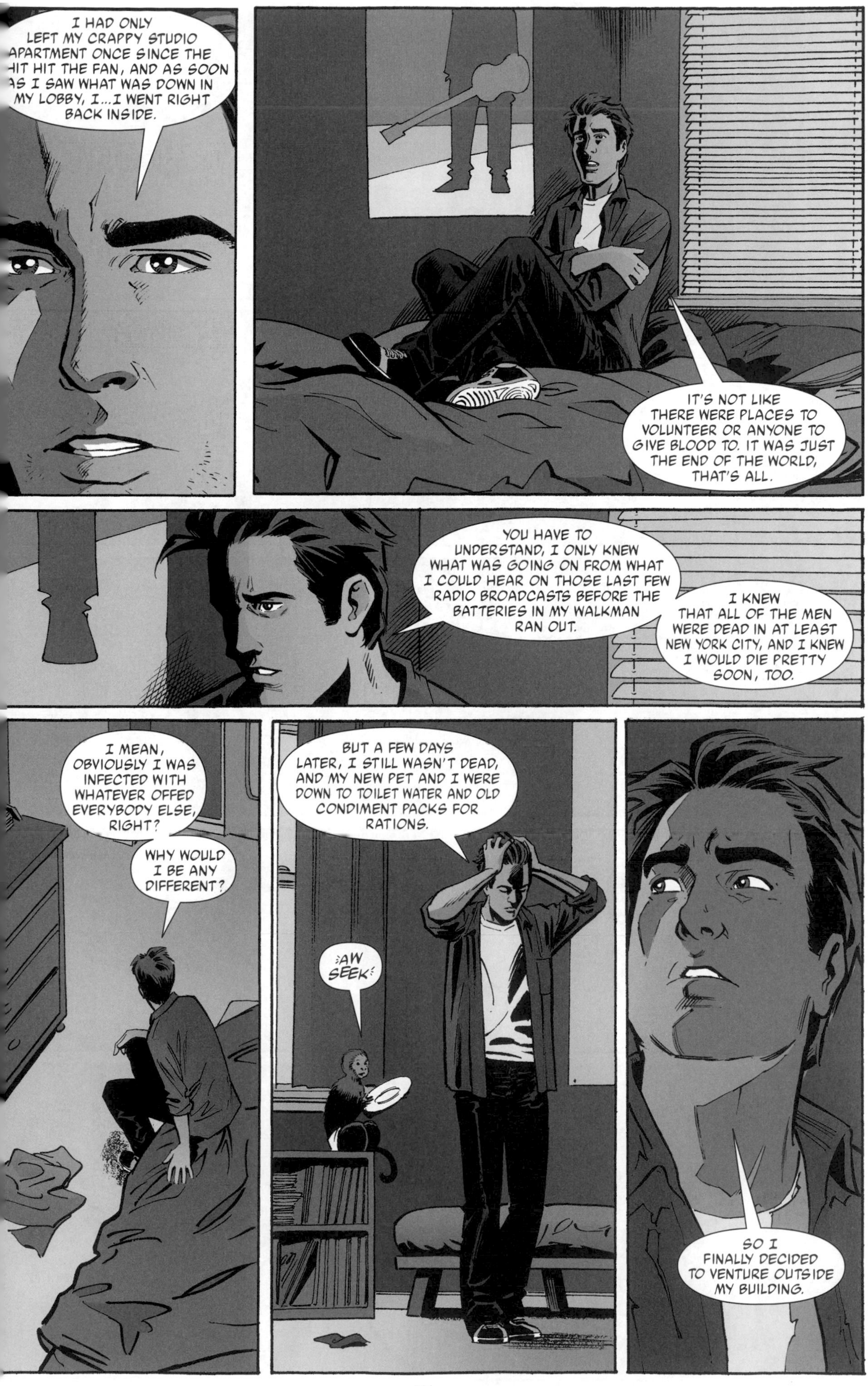
I HAD ONLY LEFT MY CRAPPY STUDIO APARTMENT ONCE SINCE THE HIT HIT THE FAN, AND AS SOON AS I SAW WHAT WAS DOWN IN MY LOBBY, I...I WENT RIGHT BACK INSIDE.
IT'S NOT LIKE THERE WERE PLACES TO VOLUNTEER OR ANYONE TO GIVE BLOOD TO. IT WAS JUST THE END OF THE WORLD, THAT'S ALL.
YOU HAVE TO UNDERSTAND, I ONLY KNEW WHAT WAS GOING ON FROM WHAT I COULD HEAR ON THOSE LAST FEW RADIO BROADCASTS BEFORE THE BATTERIES IN MY WALKMAN RAN OUT.
I KNEW THAT ALL OF THE MEN WERE DEAD IN AT LEAST NEW YORK CITY, AND I KNEW I WOULD DIE PRETTY SOON, TOO.
I MEAN, OBVIOUSLY I WAS INFECTED WITH WHATEVER OFFED EVERYBODY ELSE, RIGHT?
WHY WOULD I BE ANY DIFFERENT?
BUT A FEW DAYS LATER, I STILL WASN'T DEAD, AND MY NEW PET AND I WERE DOWN TO TOILET WATER AND OLD CONDIMENT PACKS FOR RATIONS.
AW SEEK
SO I FINALLY DECIDED TO VENTURE OUTSIDE MY BUILDING.

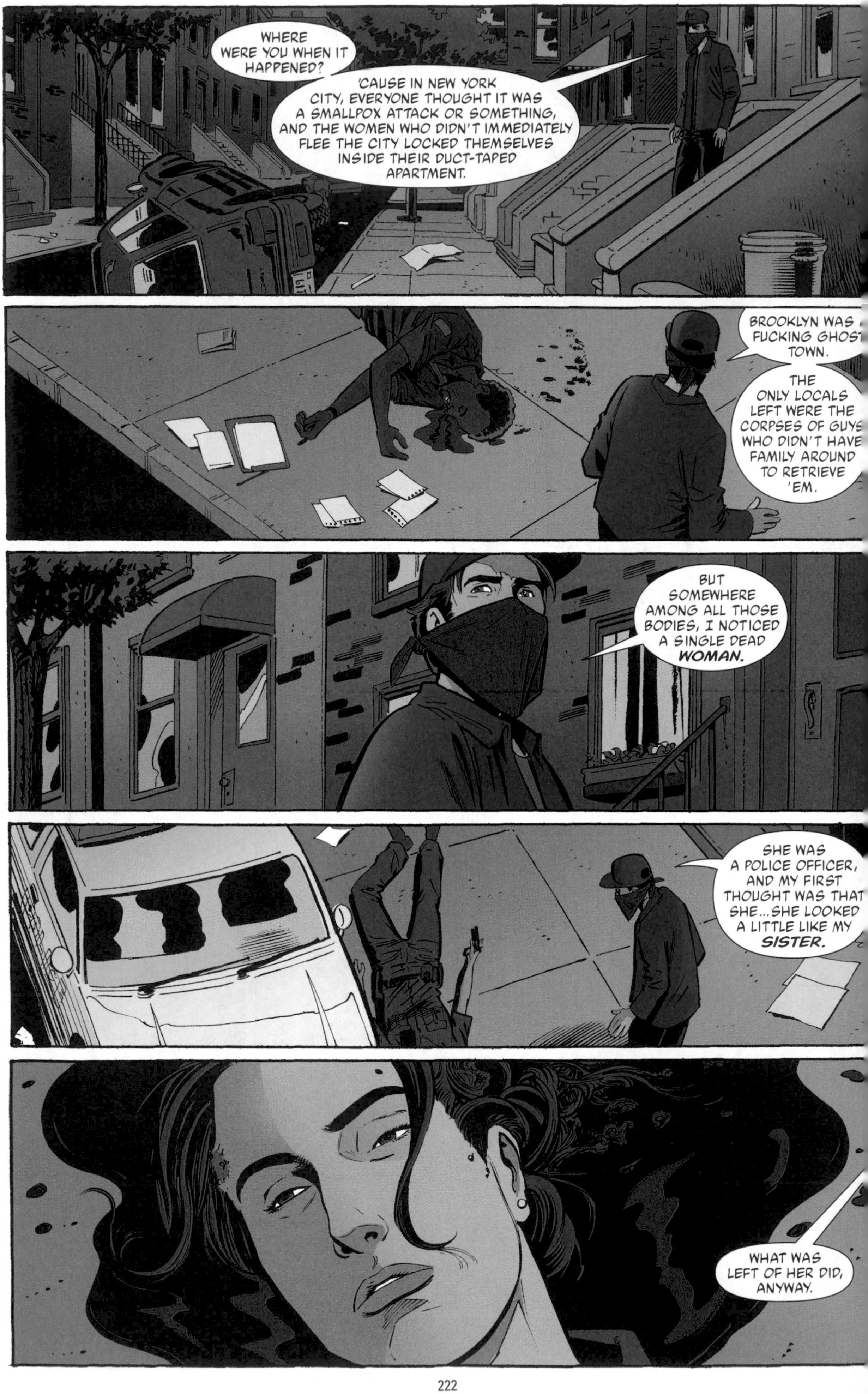
WHERE WERE YOU WHEN IT HAPPENED?
'CAUSE IN NEW YORK CITY, EVERYONE THOUGHT IT WAS A SMALLPOX ATTACK OR SOMETHING, AND THE WOMEN WHO DIDN'T IMMEDIATELY FLEE THE CITY LOCKED THEMSELVES INSIDE THEIR DUCT-TAPED APARTMENT.
BROOKLYN WAS A FUCKING GHOST TOWN.
THE ONLY LOCALS LEFT WERE THE CORPSES OF GUYS WHO DIDN'T HAVE FAMILY AROUND TO RETRIEVE 'EM.
BUT SOMEWHERE AMONG ALL THOSE BODIES, I NOTICED A SINGLE DEAD **WOMAN.**
SHE WAS A POLICE OFFICER, AND MY FIRST THOUGHT WAS THAT SHE...SHE LOOKED A LITTLE LIKE MY **SISTER.**
WHAT WAS LEFT OF HER DID, ANYWAY.

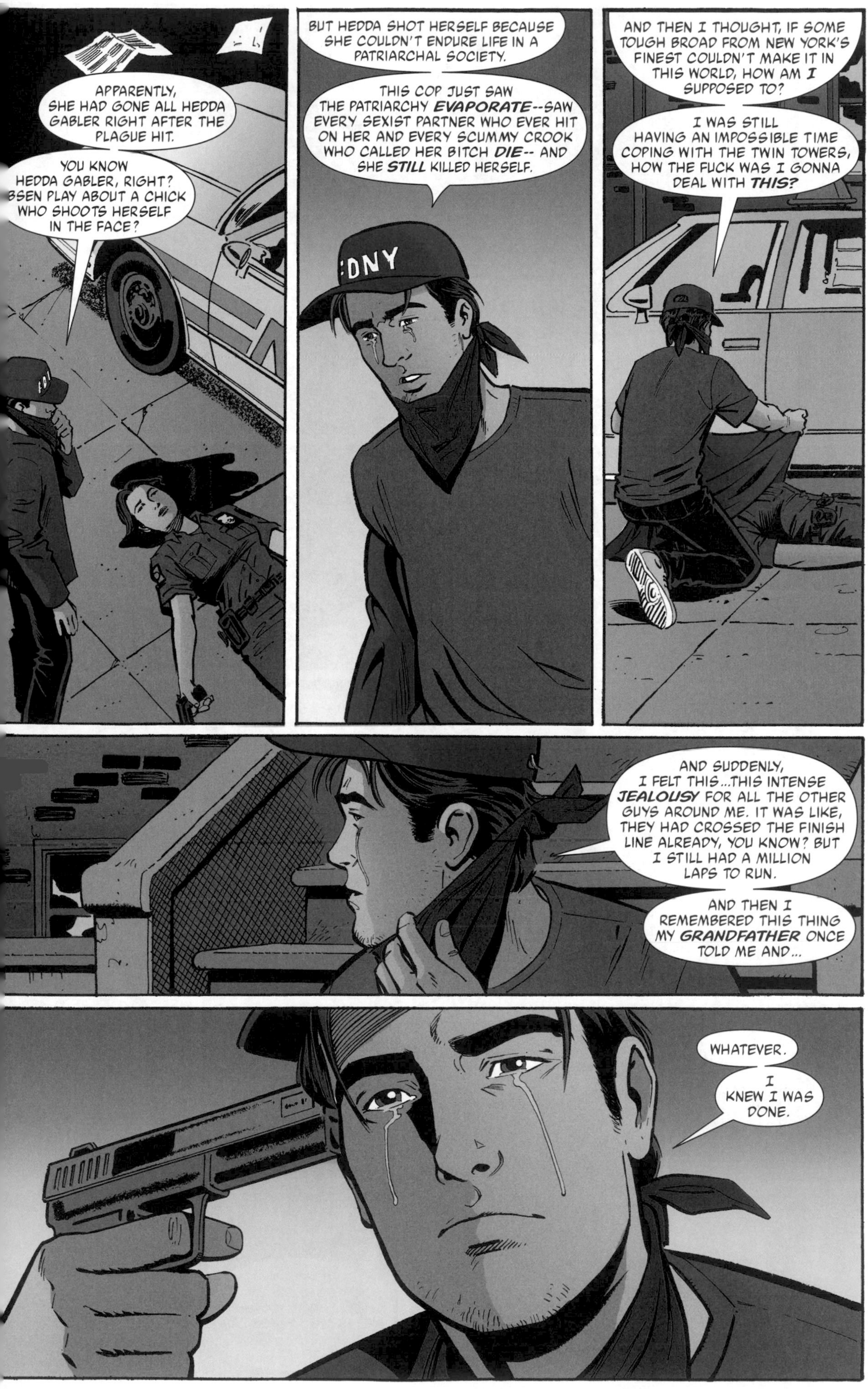
APPARENTLY, SHE HAD GONE ALL HEDDA GABLER RIGHT AFTER THE PLAGUE HIT.
YOU KNOW HEDDA GABLER, RIGHT? BSEN PLAY ABOUT A CHICK WHO SHOOTS HERSELF IN THE FACE?
BUT HEDDA SHOT HERSELF BECAUSE SHE COULDN'T ENDURE LIFE IN A PATRIARCHAL SOCIETY.
THIS COP JUST SAW THE PATRIARCHY EVAPORATE--SAW EVERY SEXIST PARTNER WHO EVER HIT ON HER AND EVERY SCUMMY CROOK WHO CALLED HER BITCH DIE-- AND SHE STILL KILLED HERSELF.
FDNY
AND THEN I THOUGHT, IF SOME TOUGH BROAD FROM NEW YORK'S FINEST COULDN'T MAKE IT IN THIS WORLD, HOW AM I SUPPOSED TO?
I WAS STILL HAVING AN IMPOSSIBLE TIME COPING WITH THE TWIN TOWERS, HOW THE FUCK WAS I GONNA DEAL WITH THIS?
AND SUDDENLY, I FELT THIS...THIS INTENSE JEALOUSY FOR ALL THE OTHER GUYS AROUND ME. IT WAS LIKE, THEY HAD CROSSED THE FINISH LINE ALREADY, YOU KNOW? BUT I STILL HAD A MILLION LAPS TO RUN.
AND THEN I REMEMBERED THIS THING MY GRANDFATHER ONCE TOLD ME AND...
WHATEVER.
I KNEW I WAS DONE.

BUT YOU WEREN'T DONE.

NOT UNLESS I'M IN HELL NOW.

YOU REALIZED THAT YOU WERE STRONGER THAN SOME PATHETIC LITTLE METER MAID.

I... I GUESS SO.

BULLSHIT!

AHN!

KRACK!

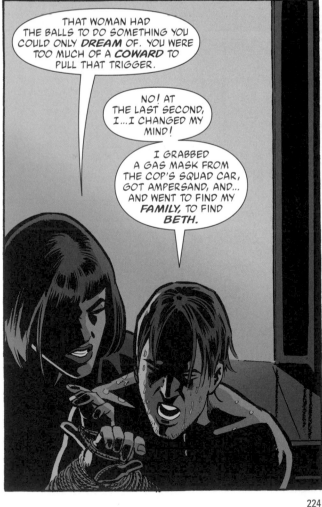

THAT WOMAN HAD THE BALLS TO DO SOMETHING YOU COULD ONLY *DREAM* OF. YOU WERE TOO MUCH OF A *COWARD* TO PULL THAT TRIGGER.

NO! AT THE LAST SECOND, I...I CHANGED MY MIND!

I GRABBED A GAS MASK FROM THE COP'S SQUAD CAR, GOT AMPERSAND, AND... AND WENT TO FIND MY *FAMILY*, TO FIND *BETH*.

IS THAT WHY YOU LEFT?

OR DEEP DOWN, DID YOU KNOW THAT IF YOU THREW YOURSELF INTO ENOUGH DANGEROUS SITUATIONS, SOONER OR LATER...

SOMEONE WOULD PUT A HOLE IN YOUR HEAD *FOR* YOU?

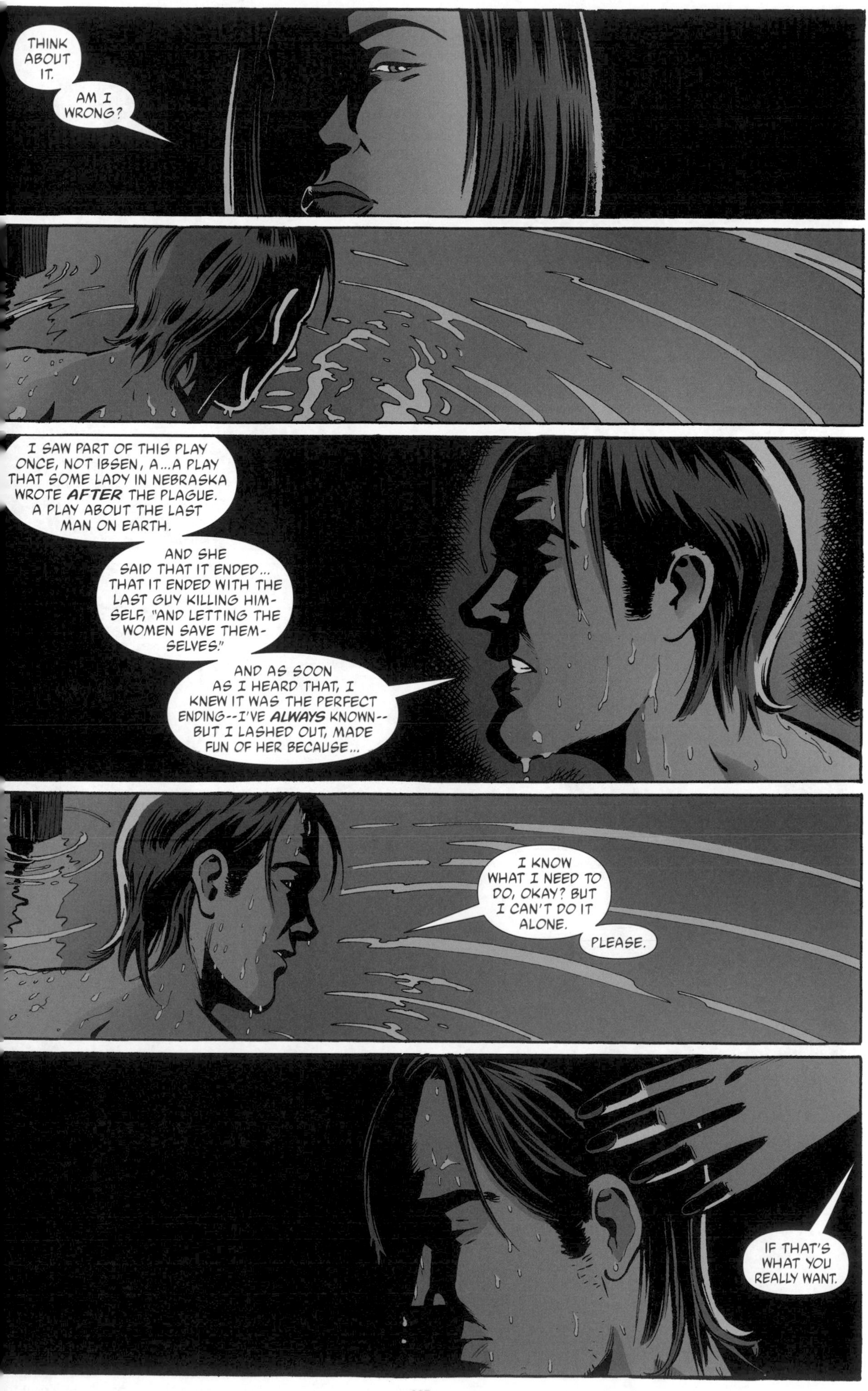
THINK ABOUT IT.
AM I WRONG?
I SAW PART OF THIS PLAY ONCE, NOT IBSEN, A...A PLAY THAT SOME LADY IN NEBRASKA WROTE AFTER THE PLAGUE. A PLAY ABOUT THE LAST MAN ON EARTH.
AND SHE SAID THAT IT ENDED... THAT IT ENDED WITH THE LAST GUY KILLING HIMSELF, "AND LETTING THE WOMEN SAVE THEMSELVES."
AND AS SOON AS I HEARD THAT, I KNEW IT WAS THE PERFECT ENDING--I'VE ALWAYS KNOWN--BUT I LASHED OUT, MADE FUN OF HER BECAUSE...
I KNOW WHAT I NEED TO DO, OKAY? BUT I CAN'T DO IT ALONE.
PLEASE.
IF THAT'S WHAT YOU REALLY WANT.

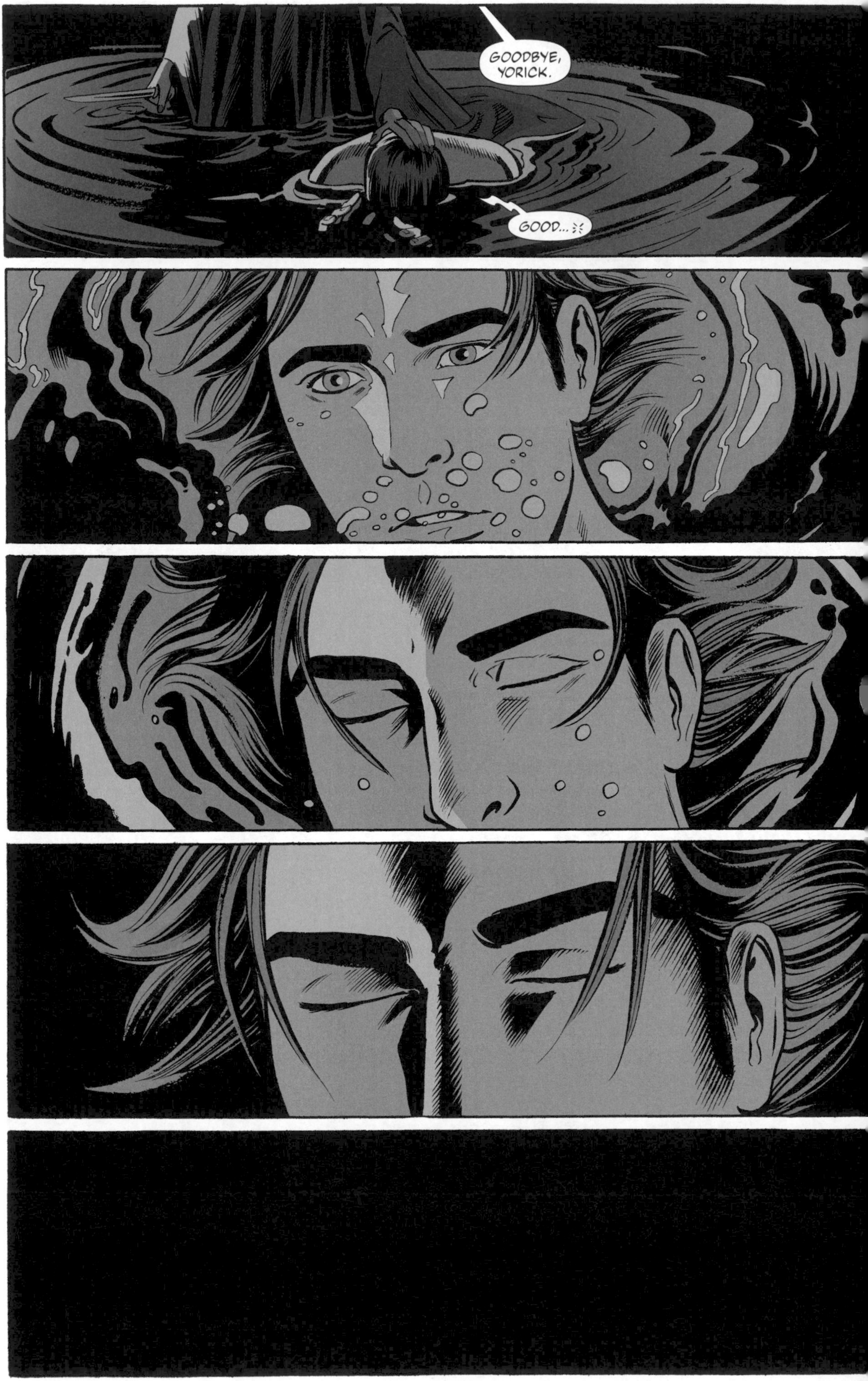
GOODBYE, YORICK.
GOOD...

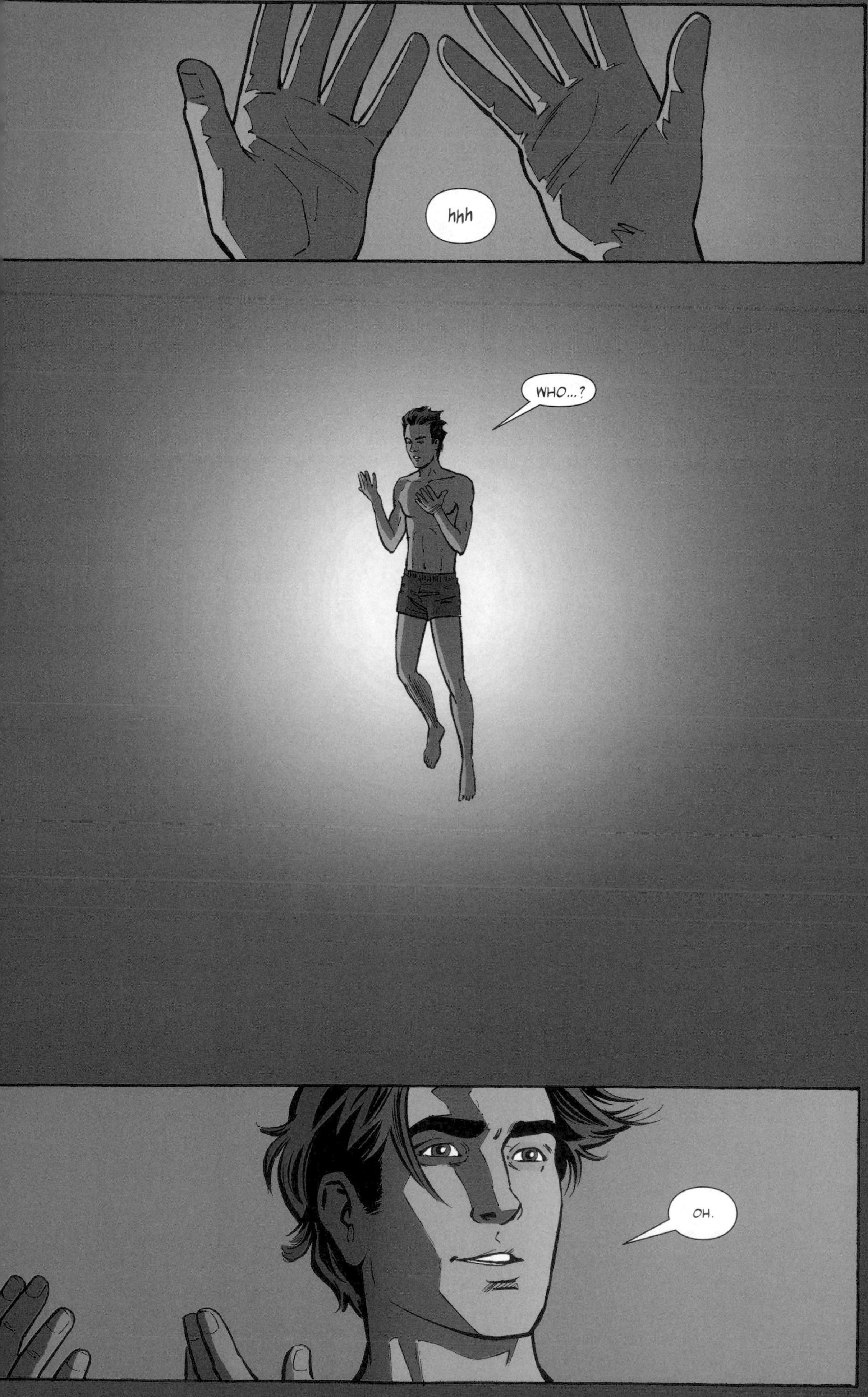
hhh
WHO...?
OH.

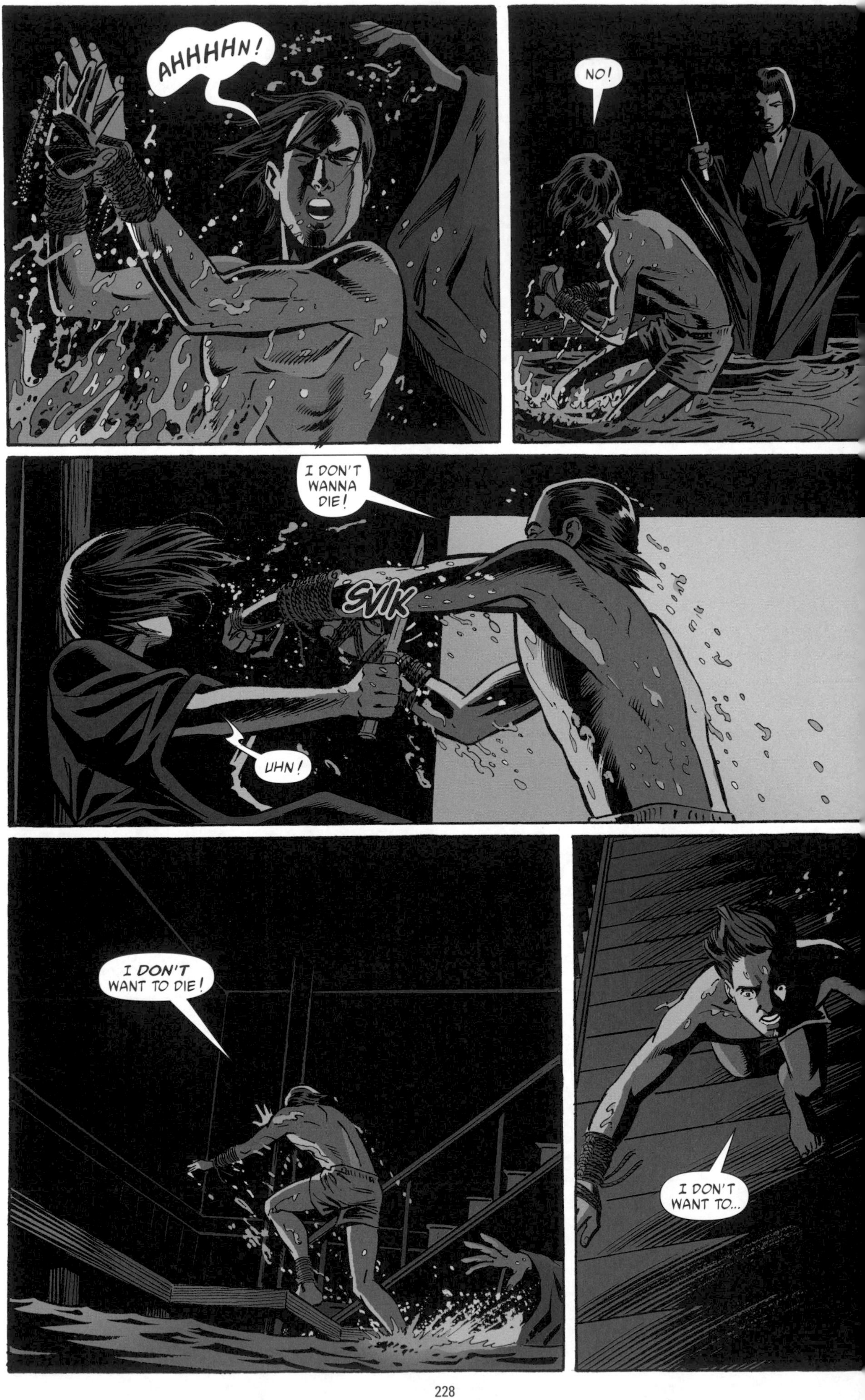

AHHHHN!
NO!
I DON'T WANNA DIE!
SVIK
UHN!
I DON'T WANT TO DIE!
I DON'T WANT TO...

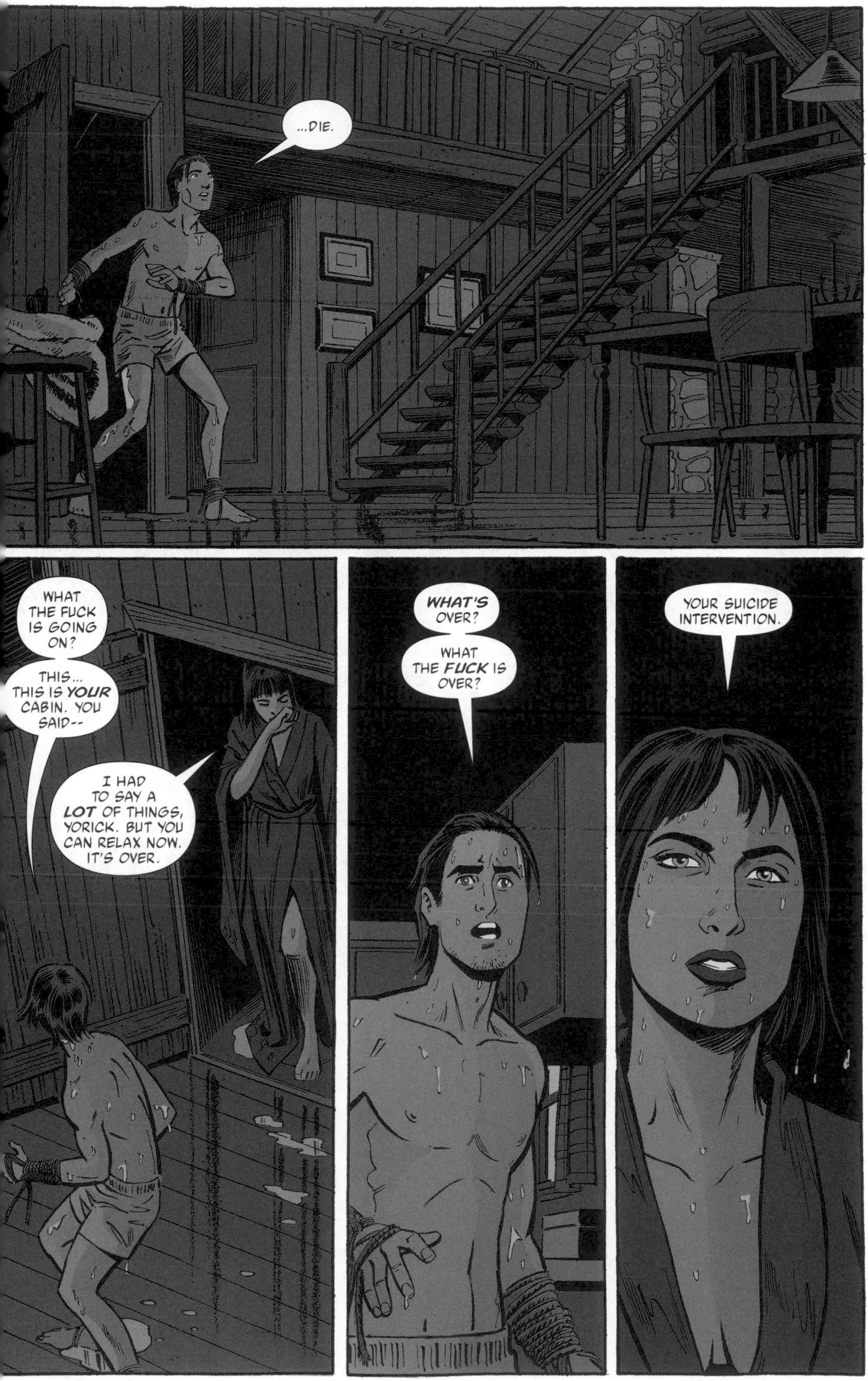
...DIE.
WHAT THE FUCK IS GOING ON?
THIS... THIS IS YOUR CABIN. YOU SAID--
I HAD TO SAY A LOT OF THINGS, YORICK. BUT YOU CAN RELAX NOW. IT'S OVER.
WHAT'S OVER?
WHAT THE FUCK IS OVER?
YOUR SUICIDE INTERVENTION.

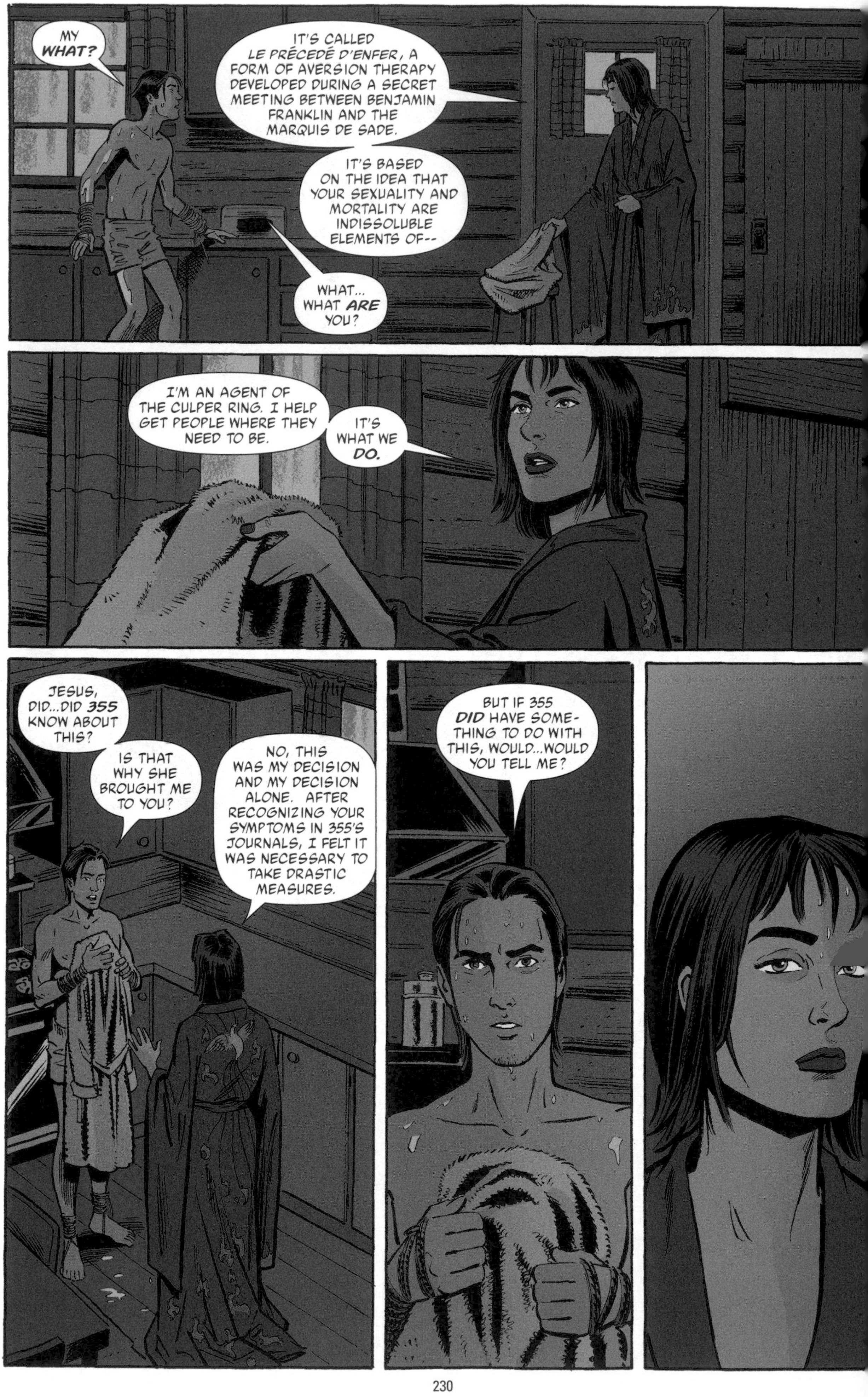
MY WHAT?
IT'S CALLED LE PRÉCEDÉ D'ENFER, A FORM OF AVERSION THERAPY DEVELOPED DURING A SECRET MEETING BETWEEN BENJAMIN FRANKLIN AND THE MARQUIS DE SADE.
IT'S BASED ON THE IDEA THAT YOUR SEXUALITY AND MORTALITY ARE INDISSOLUBLE ELEMENTS OF--
WHAT... WHAT ARE YOU?
I'M AN AGENT OF THE CULPER RING. I HELP GET PEOPLE WHERE THEY NEED TO BE.
IT'S WHAT WE DO.
JESUS, DID...DID 355 KNOW ABOUT THIS?
IS THAT WHY SHE BROUGHT ME TO YOU?
NO, THIS WAS MY DECISION AND MY DECISION ALONE. AFTER RECOGNIZING YOUR SYMPTOMS IN 355'S JOURNALS, I FELT IT WAS NECESSARY TO TAKE DRASTIC MEASURES.
BUT IF 355 DID HAVE SOME-THING TO DO WITH THIS, WOULD...WOULD YOU TELL ME?

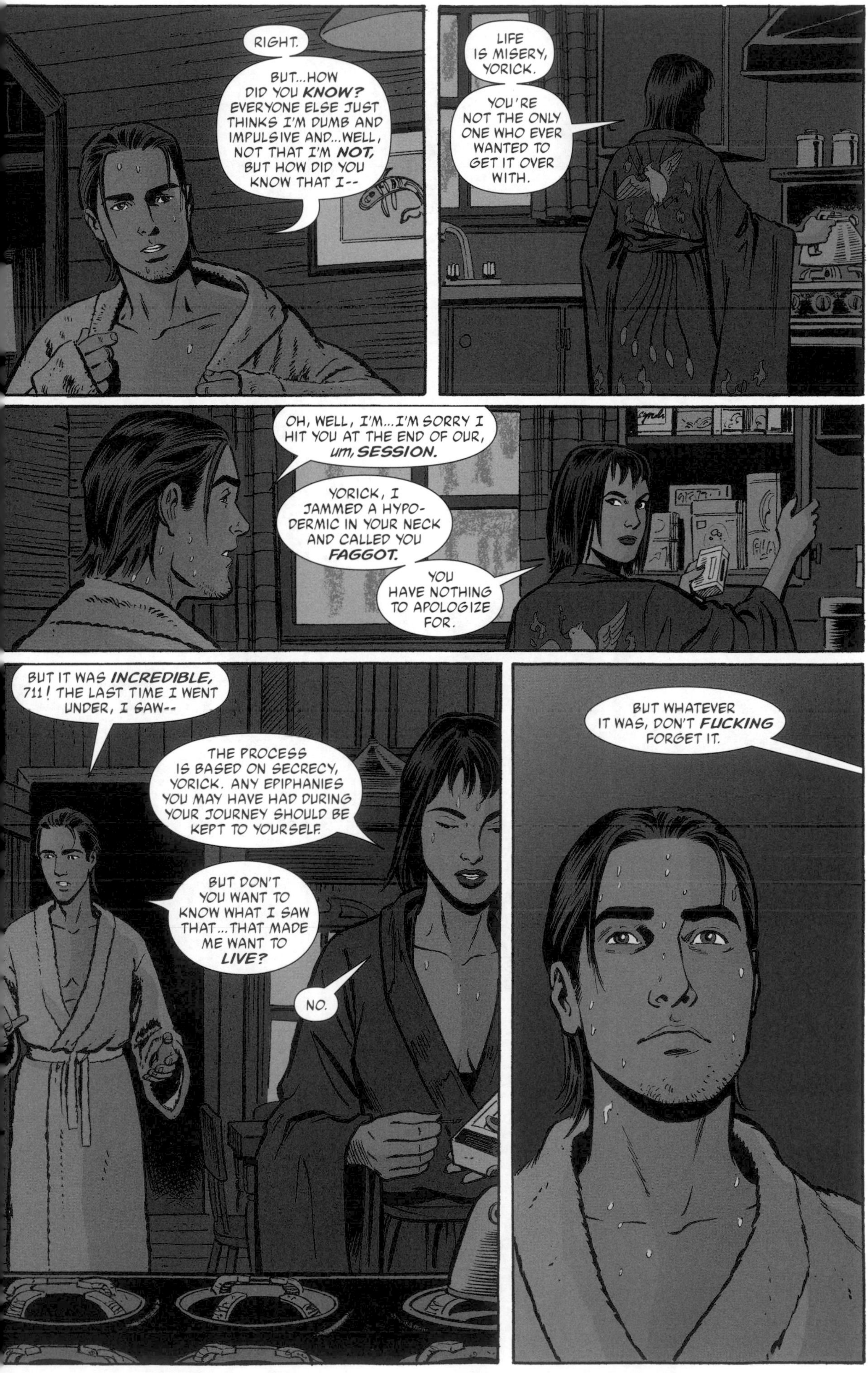
RIGHT.
BUT...HOW DID YOU KNOW? EVERYONE ELSE JUST THINKS I'M DUMB AND IMPULSIVE AND...WELL, NOT THAT I'M NOT, BUT HOW DID YOU KNOW THAT I--
LIFE IS MISERY, YORICK.
YOU'RE NOT THE ONLY ONE WHO EVER WANTED TO GET IT OVER WITH.
OH, WELL, I'M...I'M SORRY I HIT YOU AT THE END OF OUR, um, SESSION.
YORICK, I JAMMED A HYPODERMIC IN YOUR NECK AND CALLED YOU FAGGOT.
YOU HAVE NOTHING TO APOLOGIZE FOR.
BUT IT WAS INCREDIBLE, 711! THE LAST TIME I WENT UNDER, I SAW--
THE PROCESS IS BASED ON SECRECY, YORICK. ANY EPIPHANIES YOU MAY HAVE HAD DURING YOUR JOURNEY SHOULD BE KEPT TO YOURSELF.
BUT DON'T YOU WANT TO KNOW WHAT I SAW THAT...THAT MADE ME WANT TO LIVE?
NO.
BUT WHATEVER IT WAS, DON'T FUCKING FORGET IT.

355! DR. MANN!

WHERE'S AMPERSAND? IS...IS HE...?

HE'S *FINE*, YORICK.

ALTHOUGH THE ANTIBIOTICS MAKE HIS STOOL EXTREMELY SOFT, AS THE UNGRATEFUL LITTLE *FUCK* WILL BE HAPPY TO SHOW YOU.

YES!

YOU TWO FOUND A WAY INSIDE THE HOSPITAL?

EVENTUALLY, ALTHOUGH IT WAS A BIT MORE OF AN *EVENT* THAN I WOULD HAVE LIKED.

I WONDER IF ETHER-RAGGIN A SECURITY GUAR IS A VIOLATION O MY HIPPOCRATIC OATH?

HOW ABOUT YOU, YORICK?

YOU DO ANYTHING *EXCITING*?

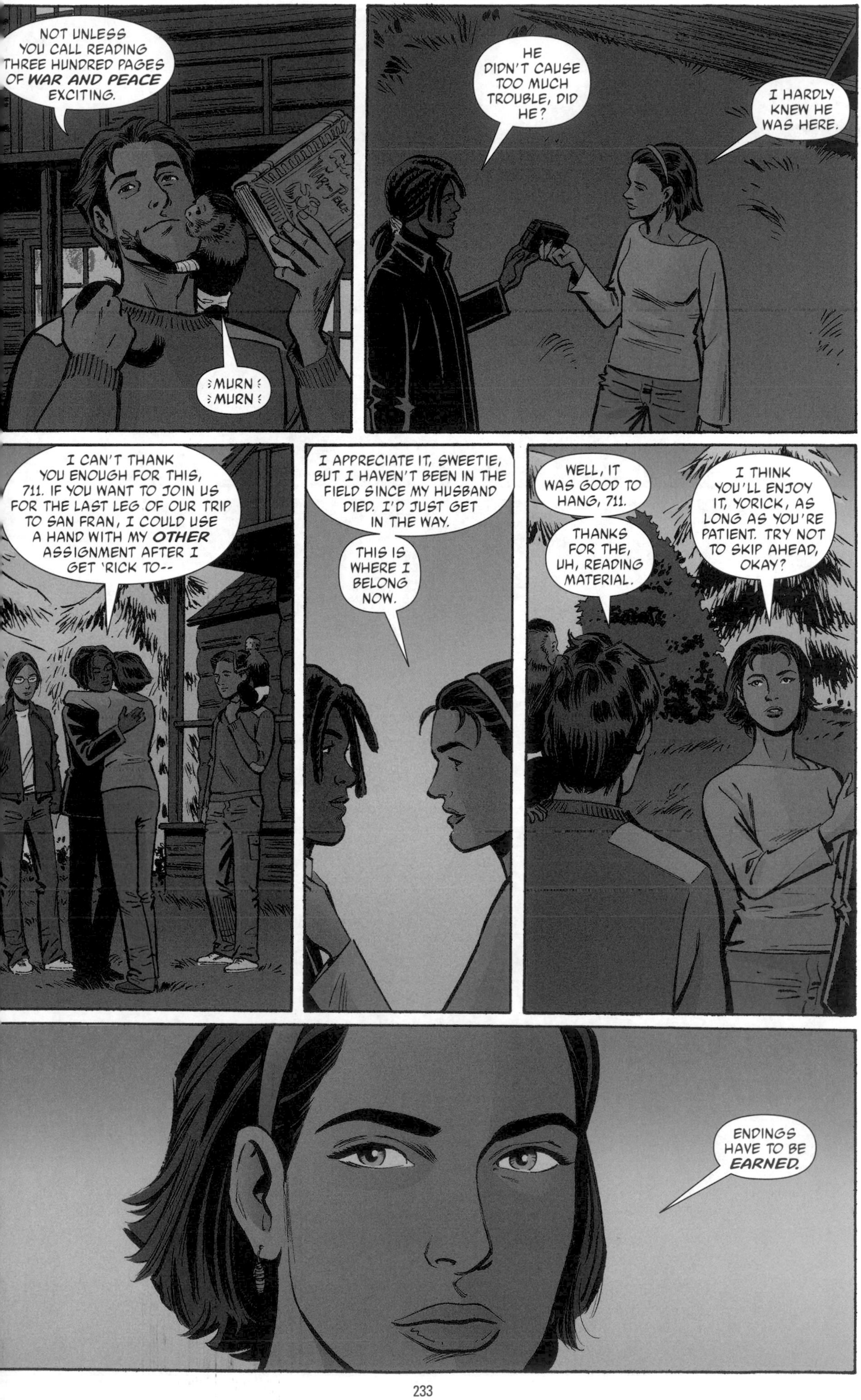
NOT UNLESS YOU CALL READING THREE HUNDRED PAGES OF WAR AND PEACE EXCITING.
WAR AND PEACE
MURN MURN
HE DIDN'T CAUSE TOO MUCH TROUBLE, DID HE?
I HARDLY KNEW HE WAS HERE.
I CAN'T THANK YOU ENOUGH FOR THIS, 711. IF YOU WANT TO JOIN US FOR THE LAST LEG OF OUR TRIP TO SAN FRAN, I COULD USE A HAND WITH MY OTHER ASSIGNMENT AFTER I GET 'RICK TO--
I APPRECIATE IT, SWEETIE, BUT I HAVEN'T BEEN IN THE FIELD SINCE MY HUSBAND DIED. I'D JUST GET IN THE WAY.
THIS IS WHERE I BELONG NOW.
WELL, IT WAS GOOD TO HANG, 711.
THANKS FOR THE, UH, READING MATERIAL.
I THINK YOU'LL ENJOY IT, YORICK, AS LONG AS YOU'RE PATIENT. TRY NOT TO SKIP AHEAD, OKAY?
ENDINGS HAVE TO BE EARNED.

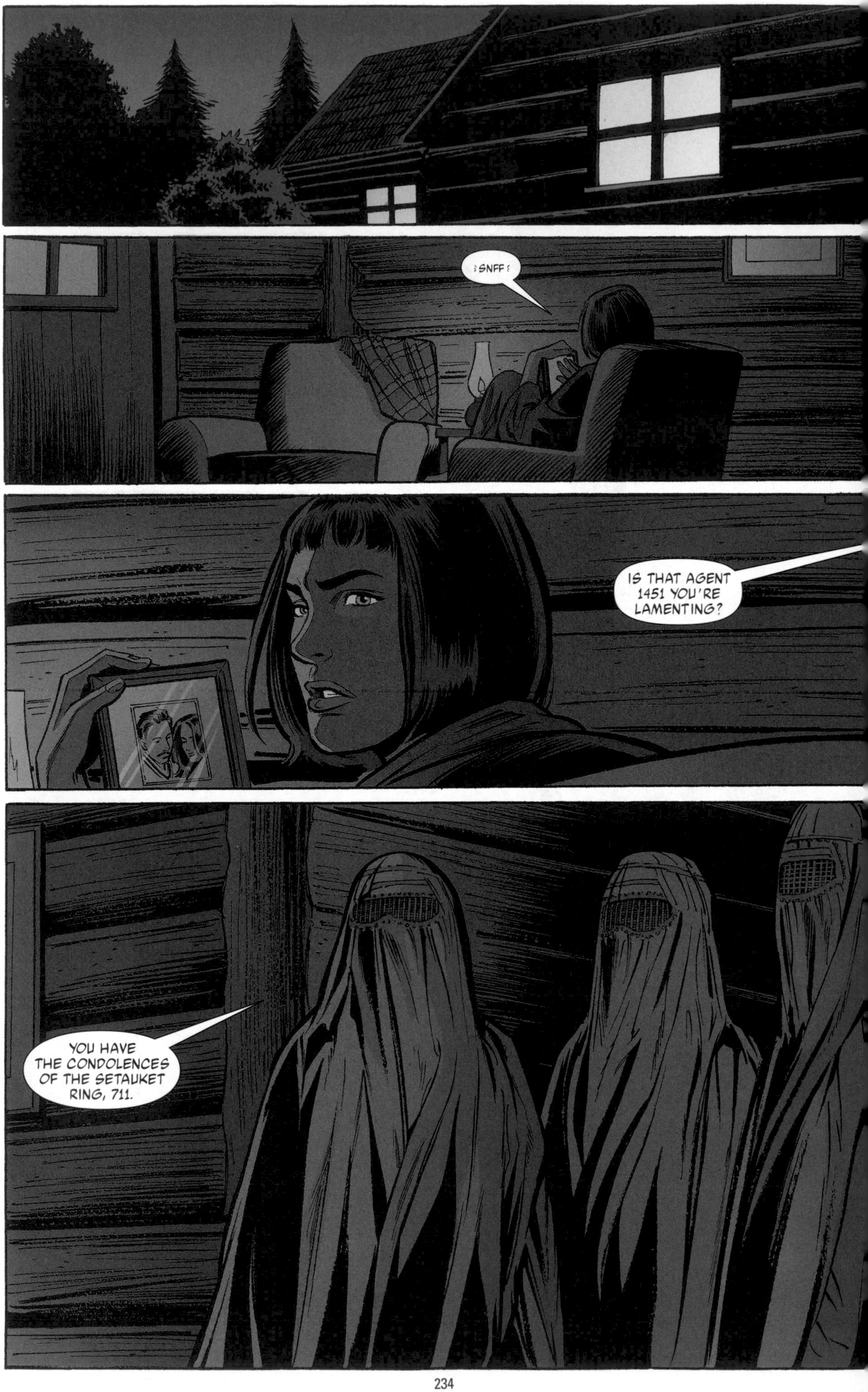
SNFF
IS THAT AGENT 1451 YOU'RE LAMENTING?
YOU HAVE THE CONDOLENCES OF THE SETAUKET RING, 711.

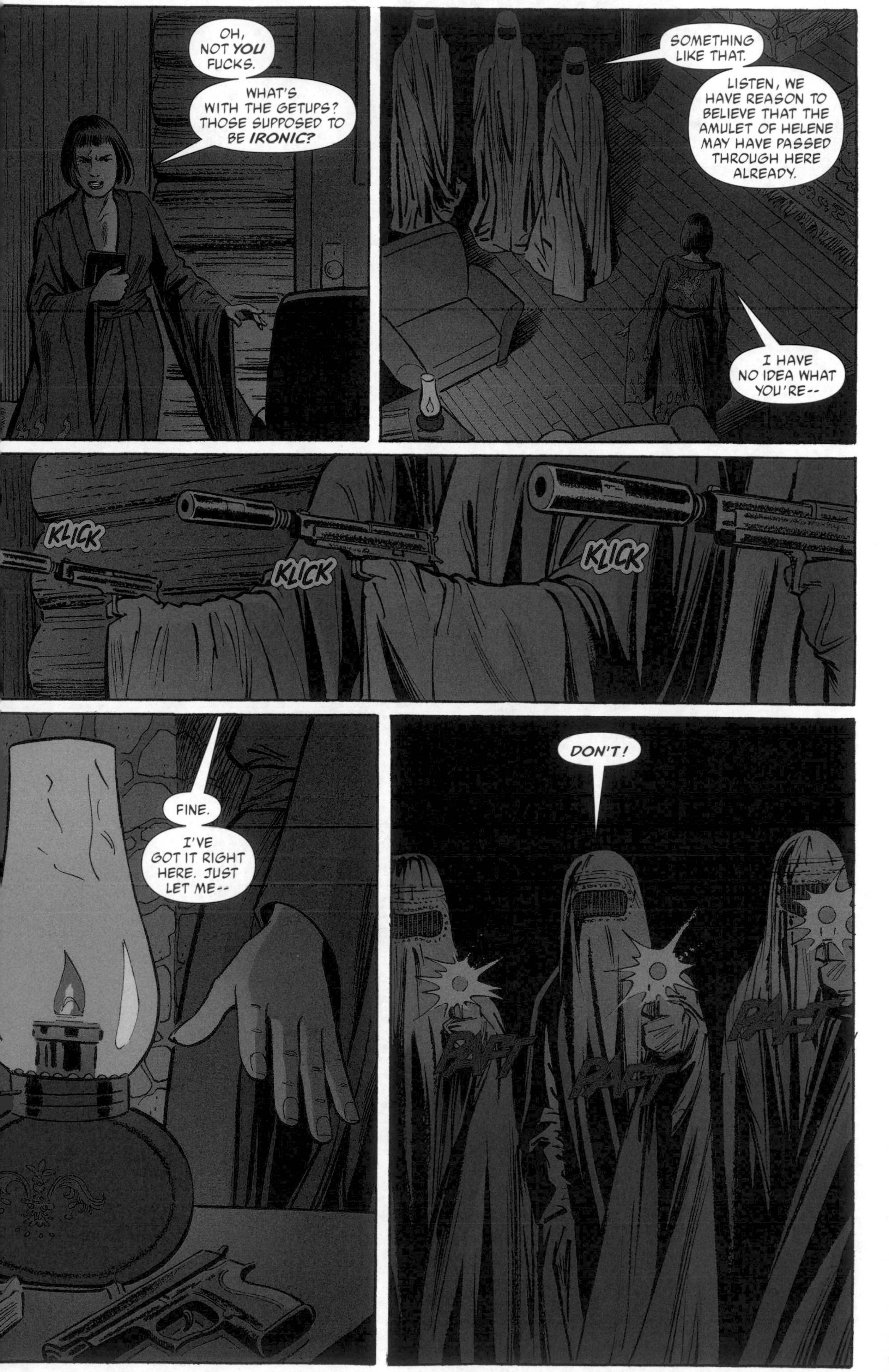
OH, NOT YOU FUCKS.
WHAT'S WITH THE GETUPS? THOSE SUPPOSED TO BE IRONIC?
SOMETHING LIKE THAT.
LISTEN, WE HAVE REASON TO BELIEVE THAT THE AMULET OF HELENE MAY HAVE PASSED THROUGH HERE ALREADY.
I HAVE NO IDEA WHAT YOU'RE--
KLICK
KLICK
KLICK
FINE.
I'VE GOT IT RIGHT HERE. JUST LET ME--
DON'T!

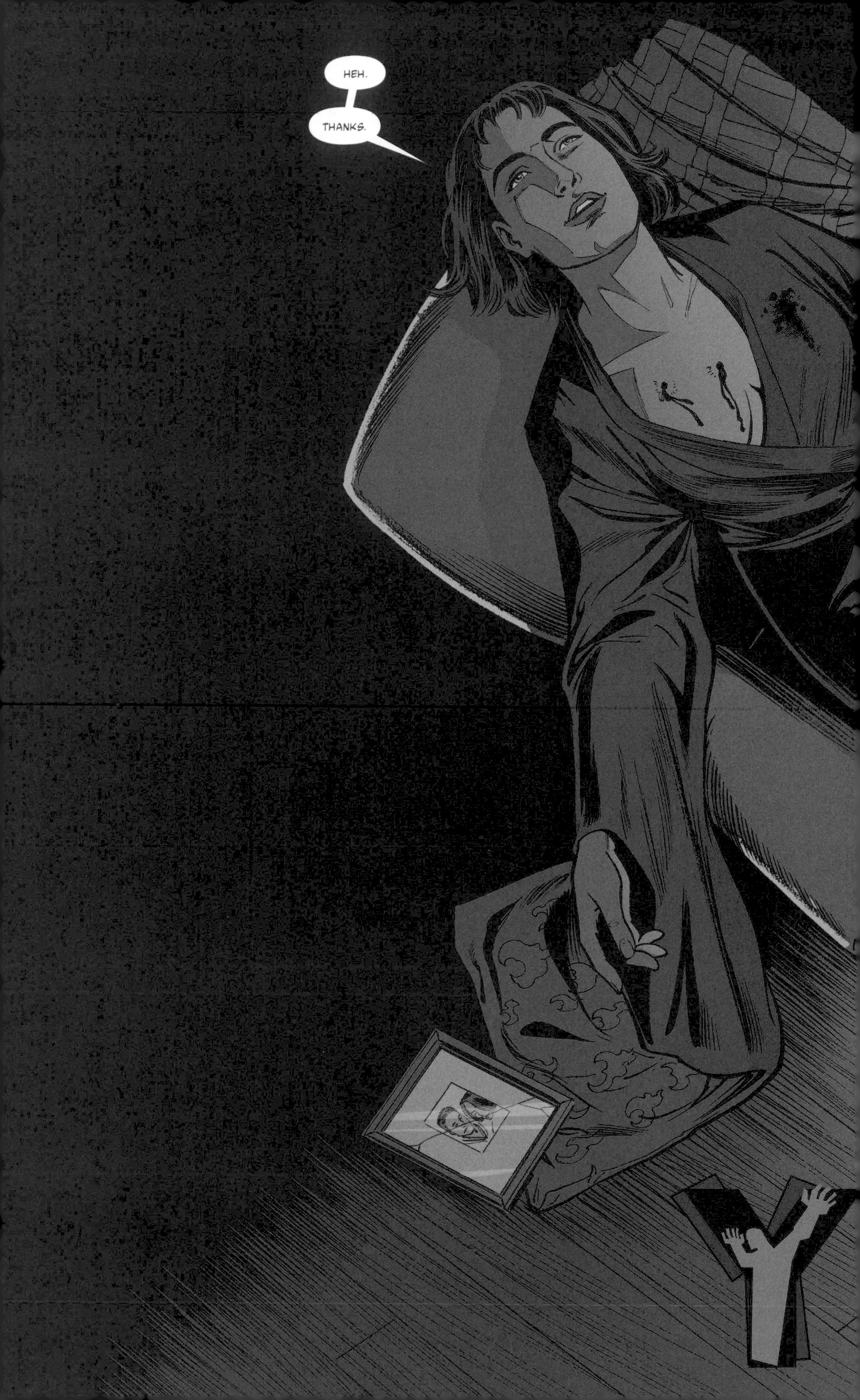
HEH.
THANKS.

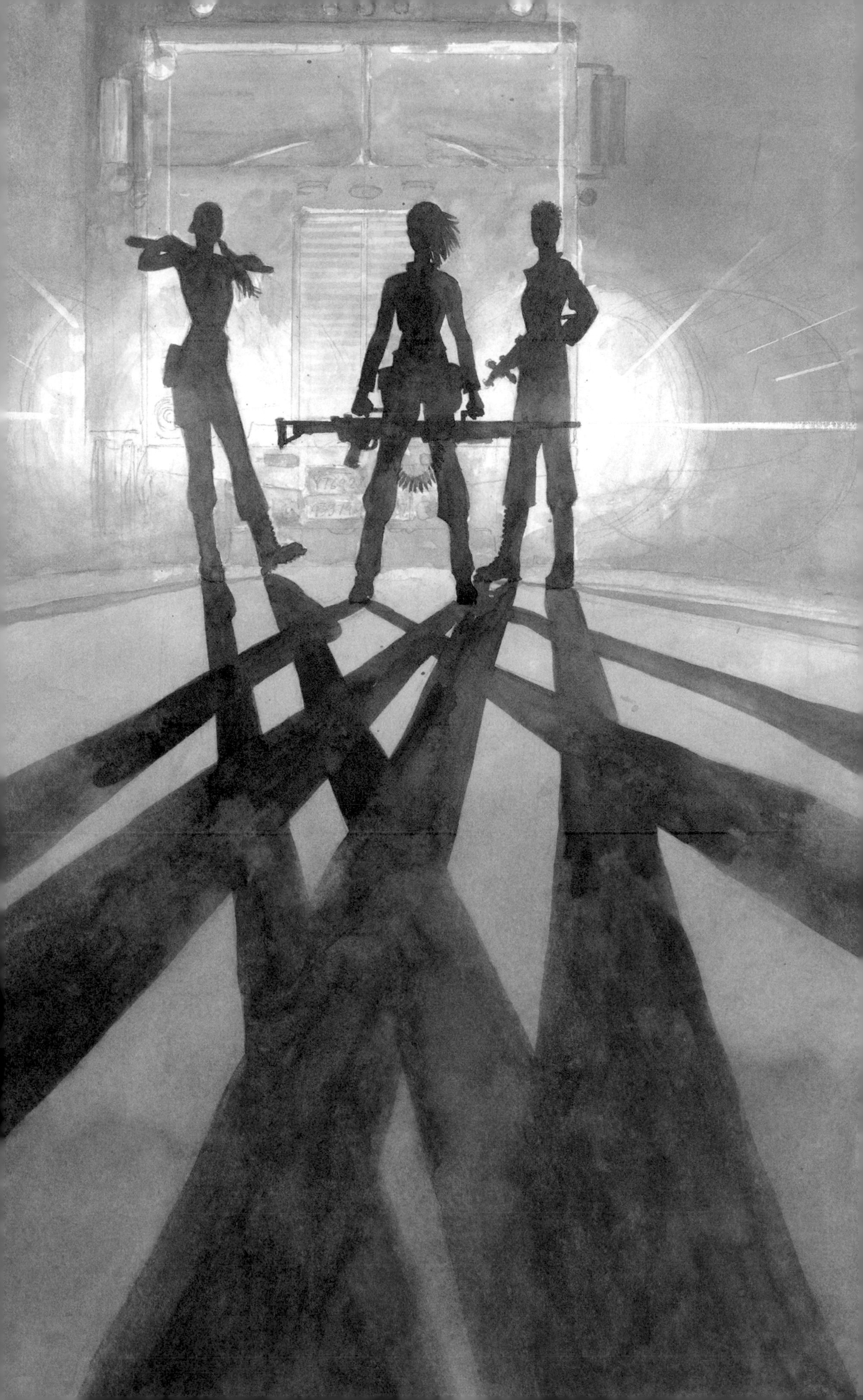

Queensbrook, Arizona
Now

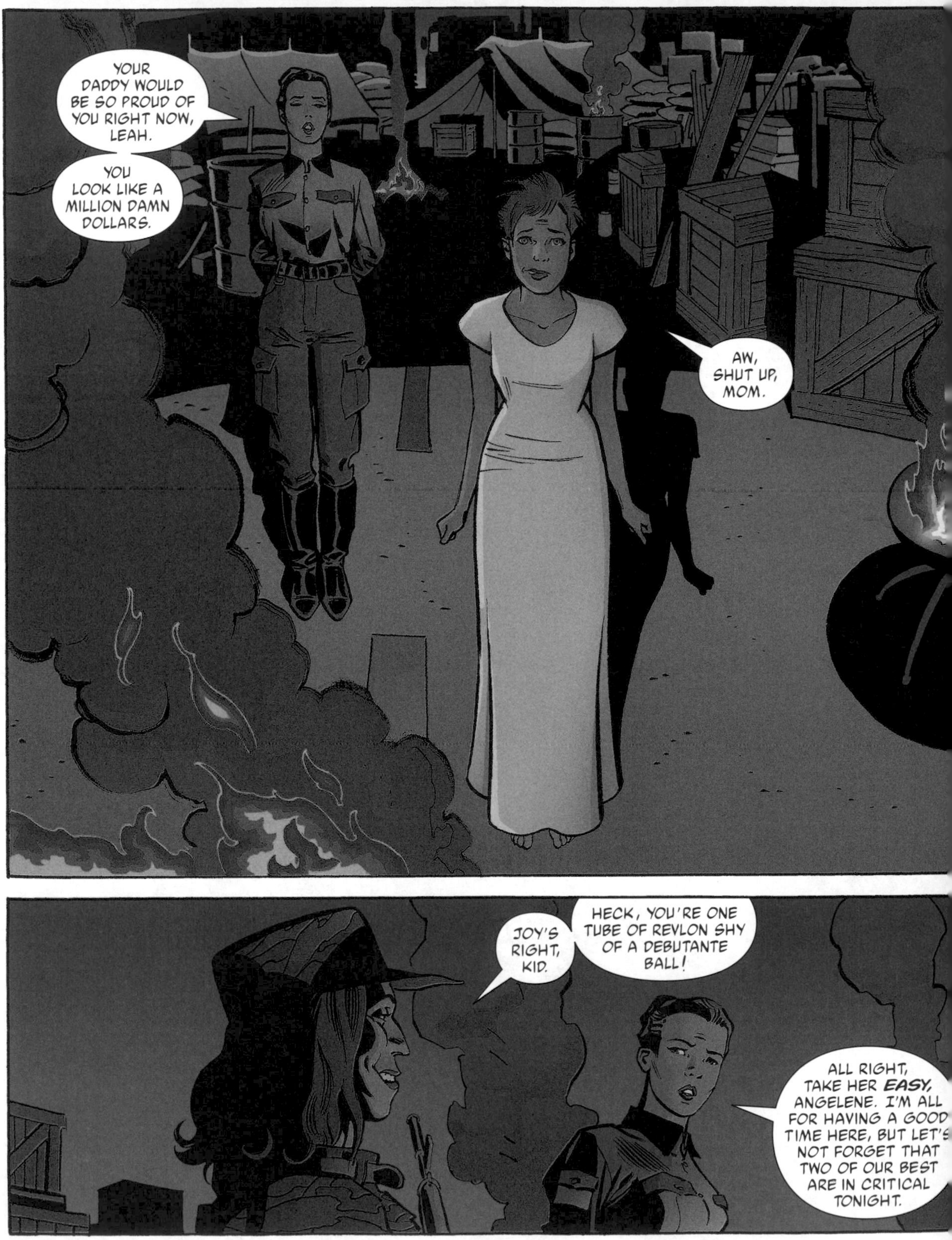
YOUR DADDY WOULD BE SO PROUD OF YOU RIGHT NOW, LEAH.
YOU LOOK LIKE A MILLION DAMN DOLLARS.
AW, SHUT UP, MOM.
JOY'S RIGHT, KID.
HECK, YOU'RE ONE TUBE OF REVLON SHY OF A DEBUTANTE BALL!
ALL RIGHT, TAKE HER *EASY,* ANGELENE. I'M ALL FOR HAVING A GOOD TIME HERE, BUT LET'S NOT FORGET THAT TWO OF OUR BEST ARE IN CRITICAL TONIGHT.

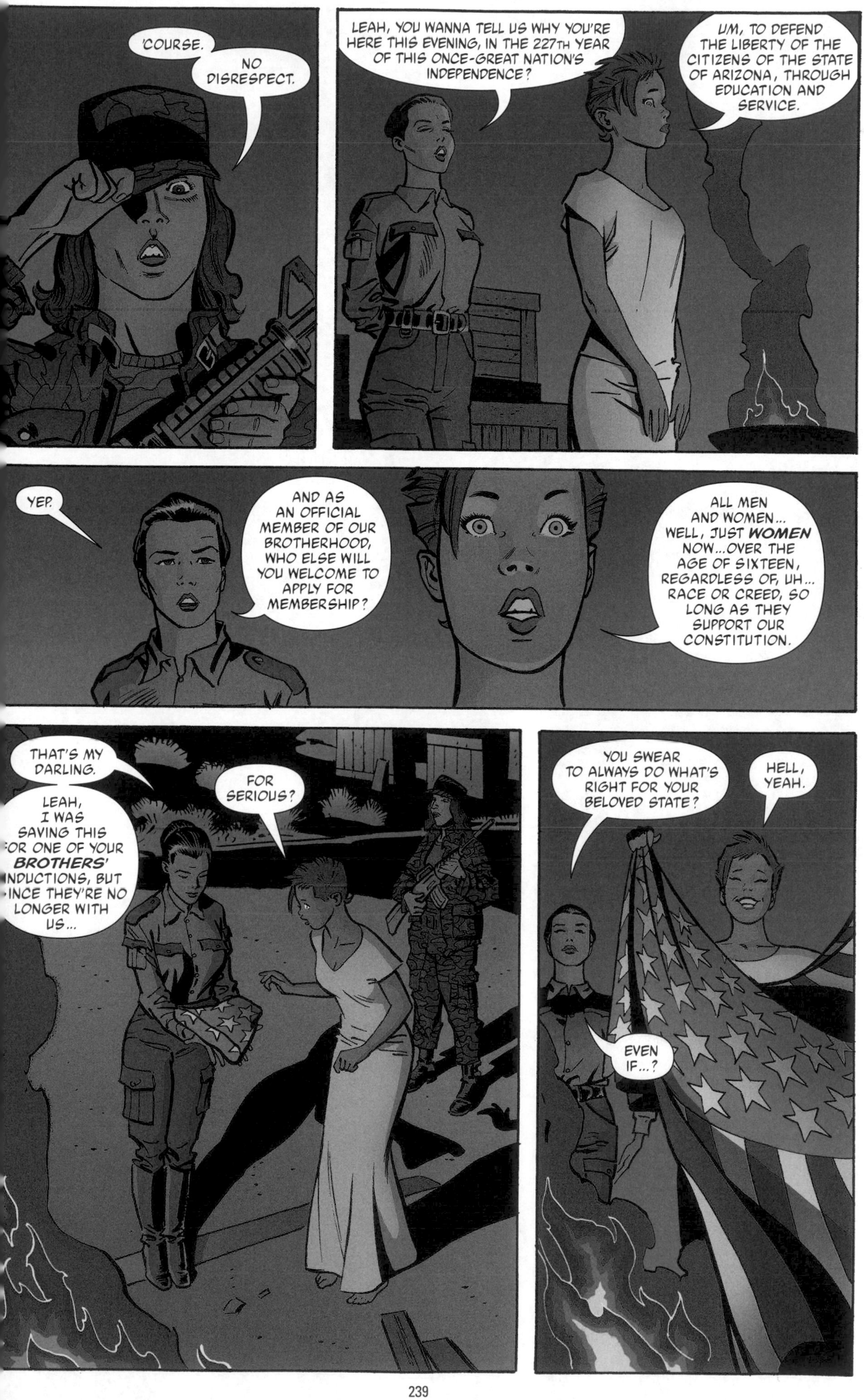
'COURSE.
NO DISRESPECT.
LEAH, YOU WANNA TELL US WHY YOU'RE HERE THIS EVENING, IN THE 227TH YEAR OF THIS ONCE-GREAT NATION'S INDEPENDENCE?
UM, TO DEFEND THE LIBERTY OF THE CITIZENS OF THE STATE OF ARIZONA, THROUGH EDUCATION AND SERVICE.
YEP.
AND AS AN OFFICIAL MEMBER OF OUR BROTHERHOOD, WHO ELSE WILL YOU WELCOME TO APPLY FOR MEMBERSHIP?
ALL MEN AND WOMEN... WELL, JUST **WOMEN** NOW...OVER THE AGE OF SIXTEEN, REGARDLESS OF, UH... RACE OR CREED, SO LONG AS THEY SUPPORT OUR CONSTITUTION.
THAT'S MY DARLING.
LEAH, I WAS SAVING THIS FOR ONE OF YOUR **BROTHERS'** INDUCTIONS, BUT SINCE THEY'RE NO LONGER WITH US...
FOR SERIOUS?
YOU SWEAR TO ALWAYS DO WHAT'S RIGHT FOR YOUR BELOVED STATE?
HELL, YEAH.
EVEN IF...?

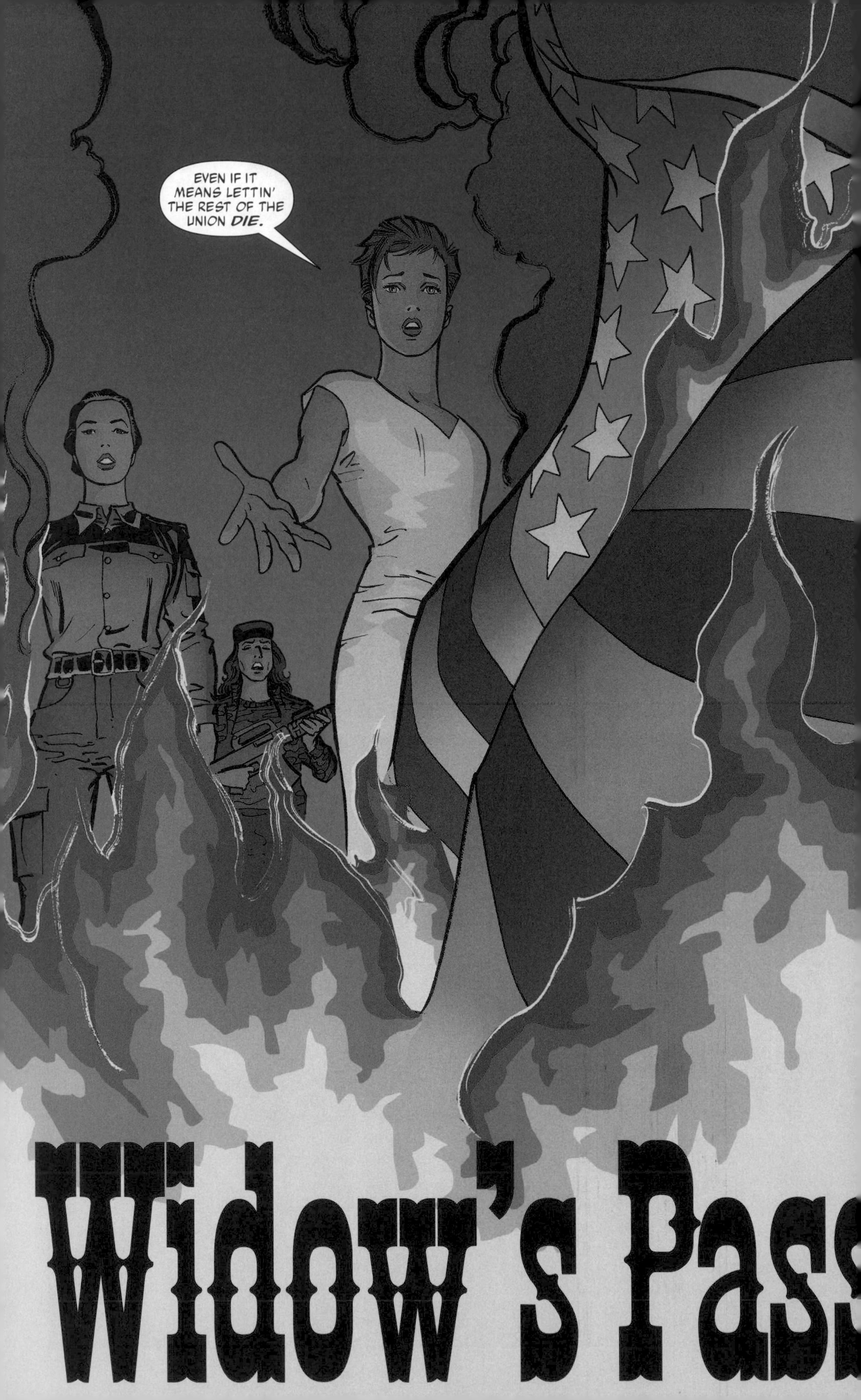
EVEN IF IT MEANS LETTIN' THE REST OF THE UNION *DIE.*
Widow's Pass

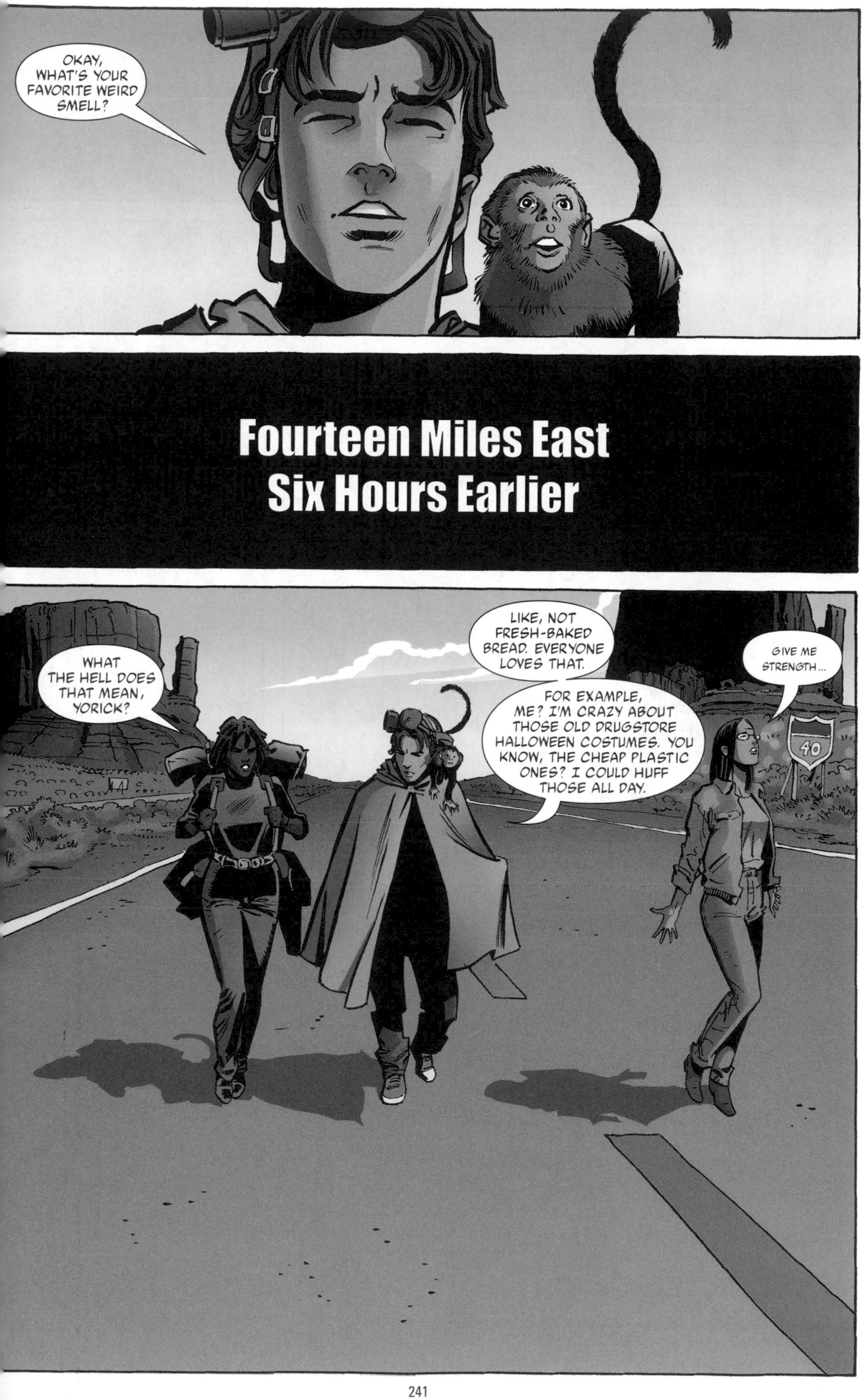
OKAY, WHAT'S YOUR FAVORITE WEIRD SMELL?
Fourteen Miles East
Six Hours Earlier
WHAT THE HELL DOES THAT MEAN, YORICK?
LIKE, NOT FRESH-BAKED BREAD. EVERYONE LOVES THAT.
FOR EXAMPLE, ME? I'M CRAZY ABOUT THOSE OLD DRUGSTORE HALLOWEEN COSTUMES. YOU KNOW, THE CHEAP PLASTIC ONES? I COULD HUFF THOSE ALL DAY.
GIVE ME STRENGTH...
40

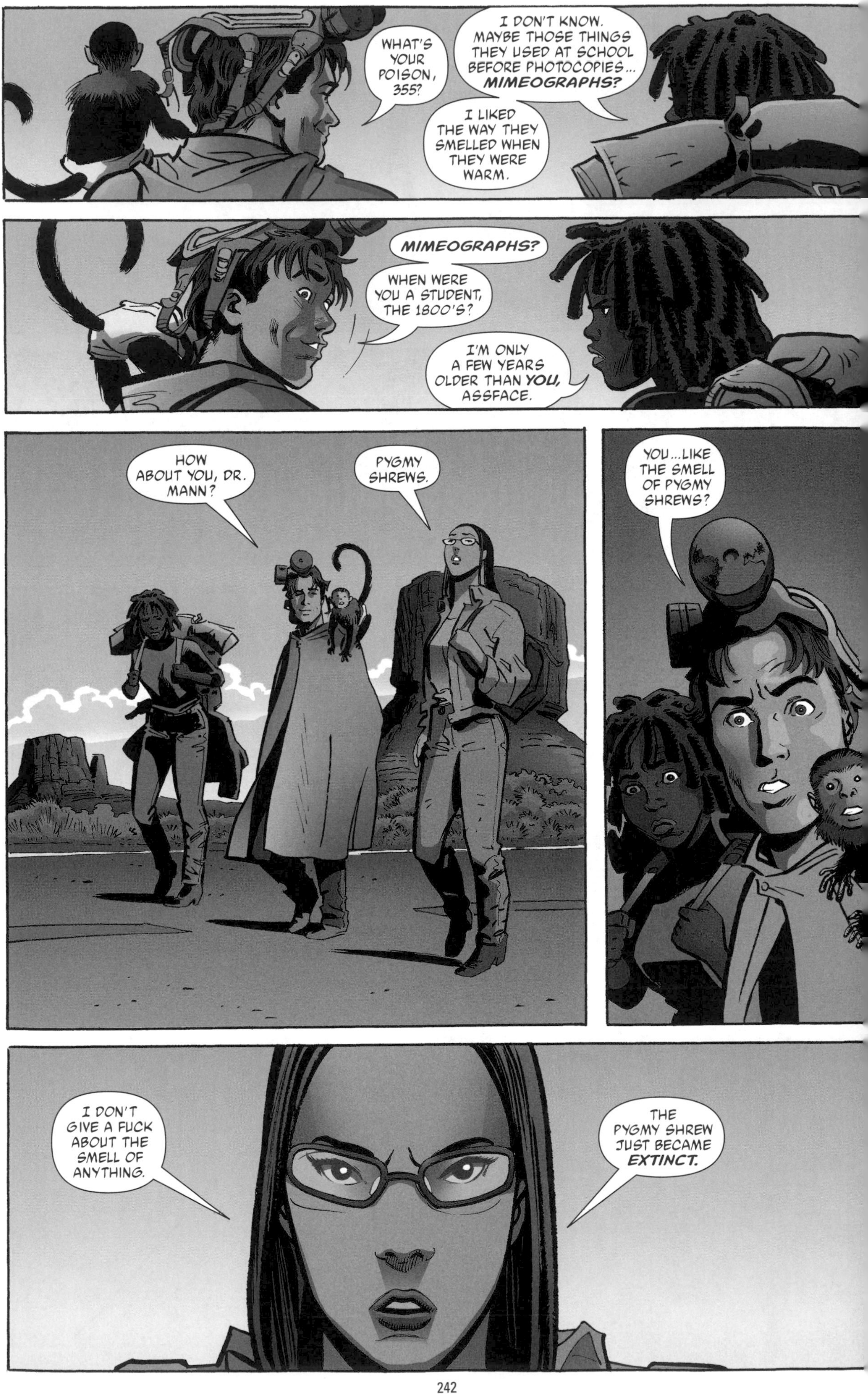

WHAT'S YOUR POISON, 355?
I DON'T KNOW. MAYBE THOSE THINGS THEY USED AT SCHOOL BEFORE PHOTOCOPIES... MIMEOGRAPHS?
I LIKED THE WAY THEY SMELLED WHEN THEY WERE WARM.
MIMEOGRAPHS?
WHEN WERE YOU A STUDENT, THE 1800'S?
I'M ONLY A FEW YEARS OLDER THAN YOU, ASSFACE.
HOW ABOUT YOU, DR. MANN?
PYGMY SHREWS.
YOU...LIKE THE SMELL OF PYGMY SHREWS?
I DON'T GIVE A FUCK ABOUT THE SMELL OF ANYTHING.
THE PYGMY SHREW JUST BECAME EXTINCT.

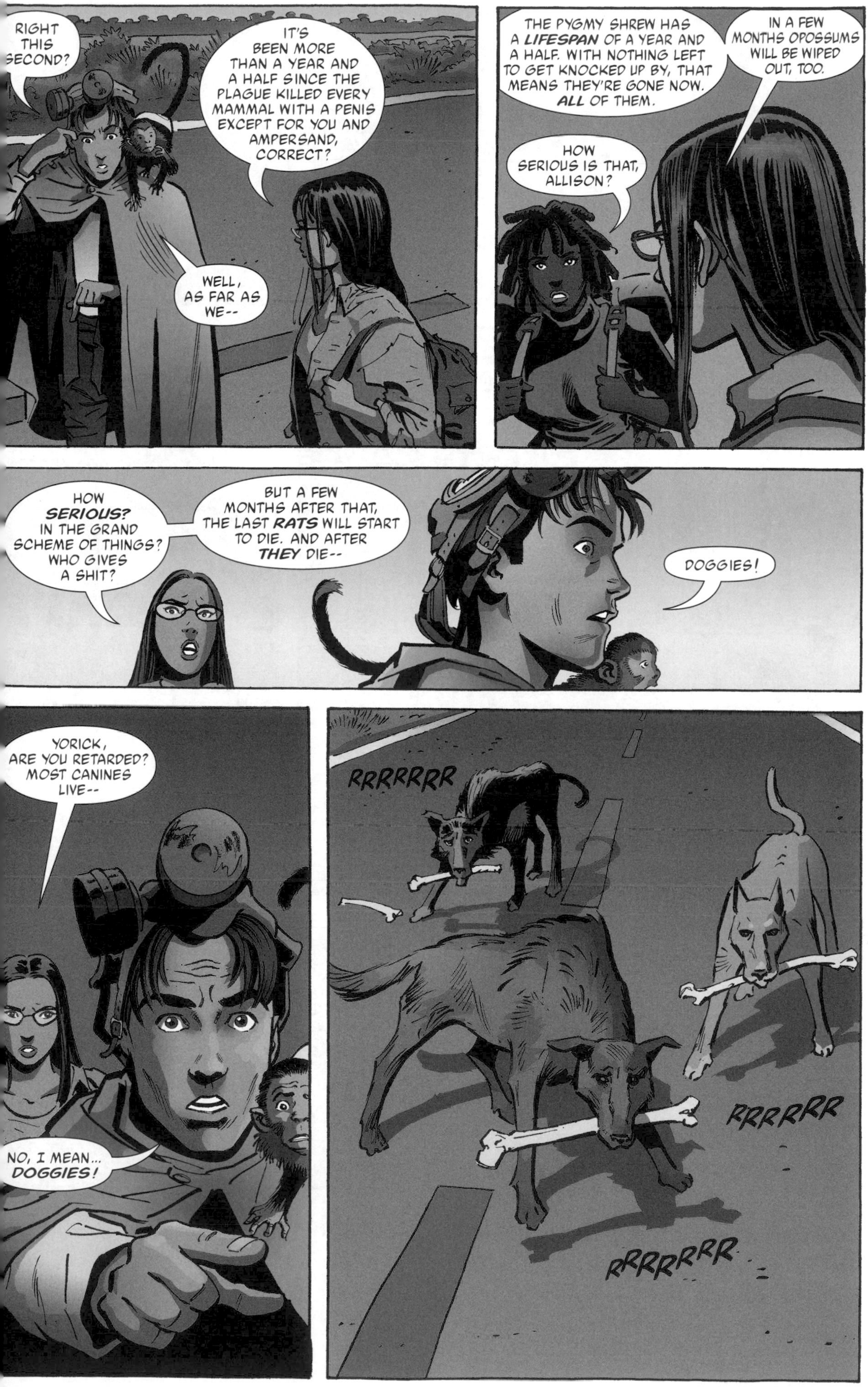
RIGHT THIS SECOND?
IT'S BEEN MORE THAN A YEAR AND A HALF SINCE THE PLAGUE KILLED EVERY MAMMAL WITH A PENIS EXCEPT FOR YOU AND AMPERSAND, CORRECT?
WELL, AS FAR AS WE--
THE PYGMY SHREW HAS A **LIFESPAN** OF A YEAR AND A HALF. WITH NOTHING LEFT TO GET KNOCKED UP BY, THAT MEANS THEY'RE GONE NOW. **ALL** OF THEM.
IN A FEW MONTHS OPOSSUMS WILL BE WIPED OUT, TOO.
HOW SERIOUS IS THAT, ALLISON?
HOW **SERIOUS?** IN THE GRAND SCHEME OF THINGS? WHO GIVES A SHIT?
BUT A FEW MONTHS AFTER THAT, THE LAST **RATS** WILL START TO DIE. AND AFTER **THEY** DIE--
DOGGIES!
YORICK, ARE YOU RETARDED? MOST CANINES LIVE--
NO, I MEAN... **DOGGIES!**
RRRRRRR
RRRRRR
RRRRRRR

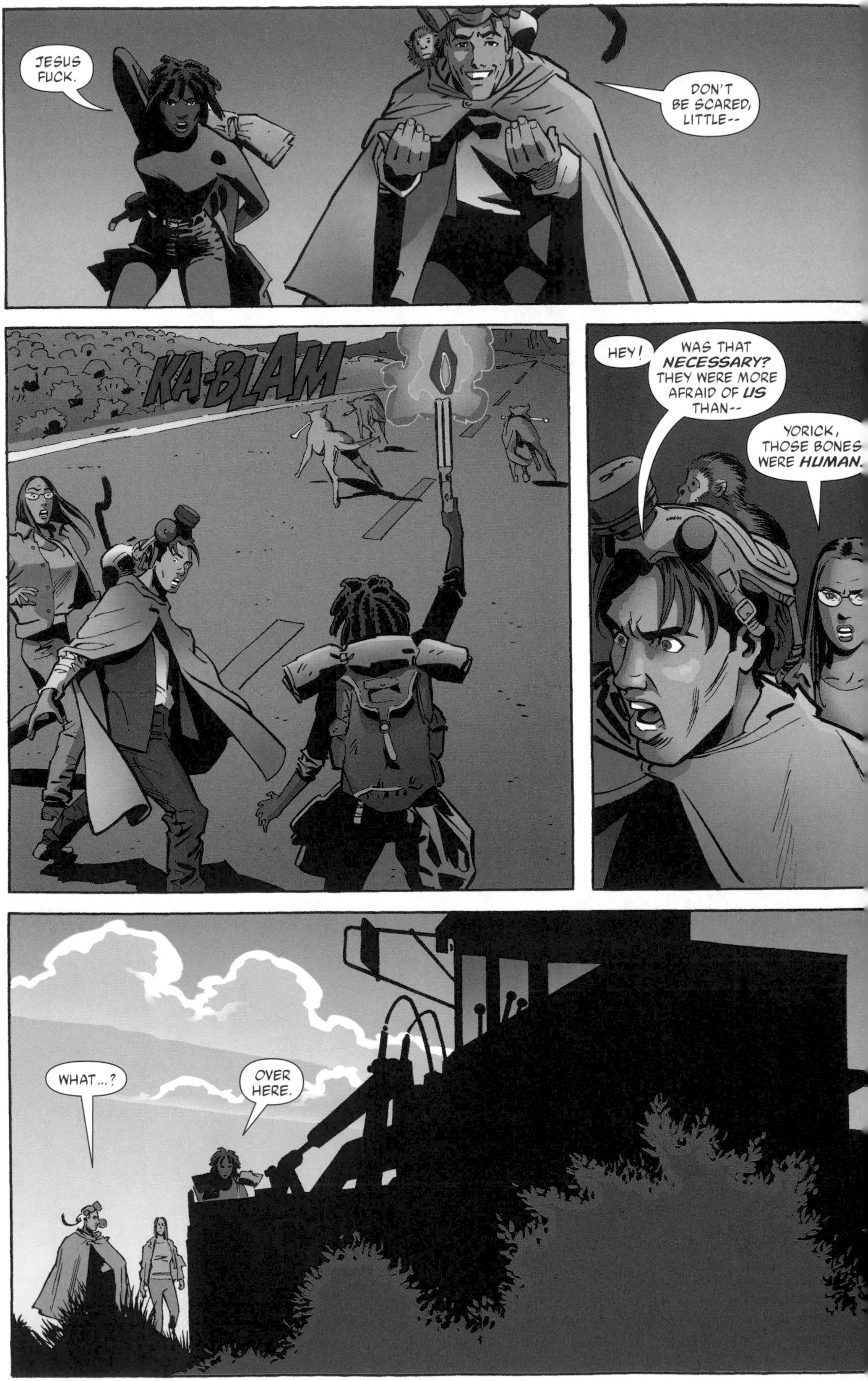
JESUS FUCK.
DON'T BE SCARED, LITTLE--
KA-BLAM
HEY!
WAS THAT NECESSARY? THEY WERE MORE AFRAID OF US THAN--
YORICK, THOSE BONES WERE HUMAN.
WHAT...?
OVER HERE.

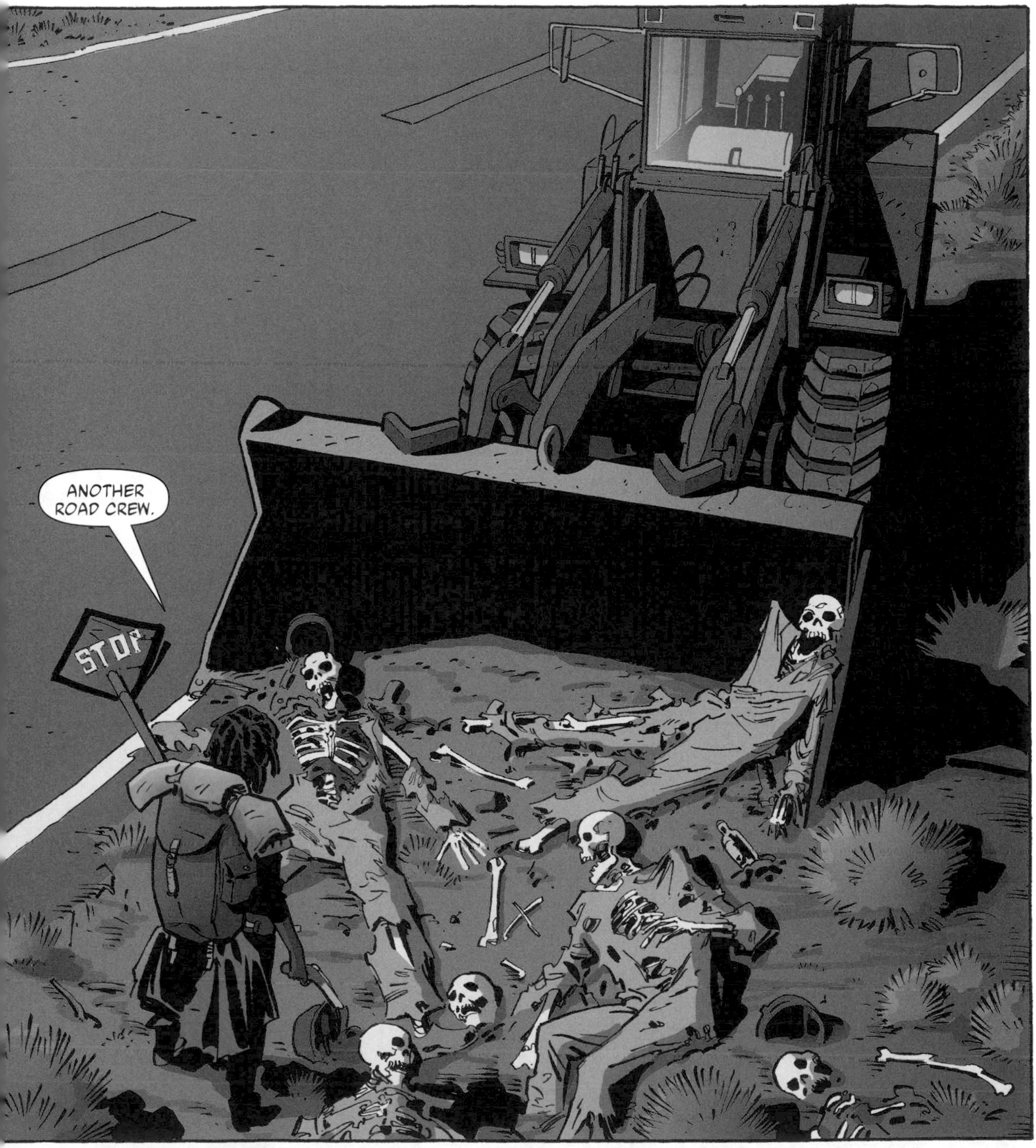
ANOTHER ROAD CREW.
STOP

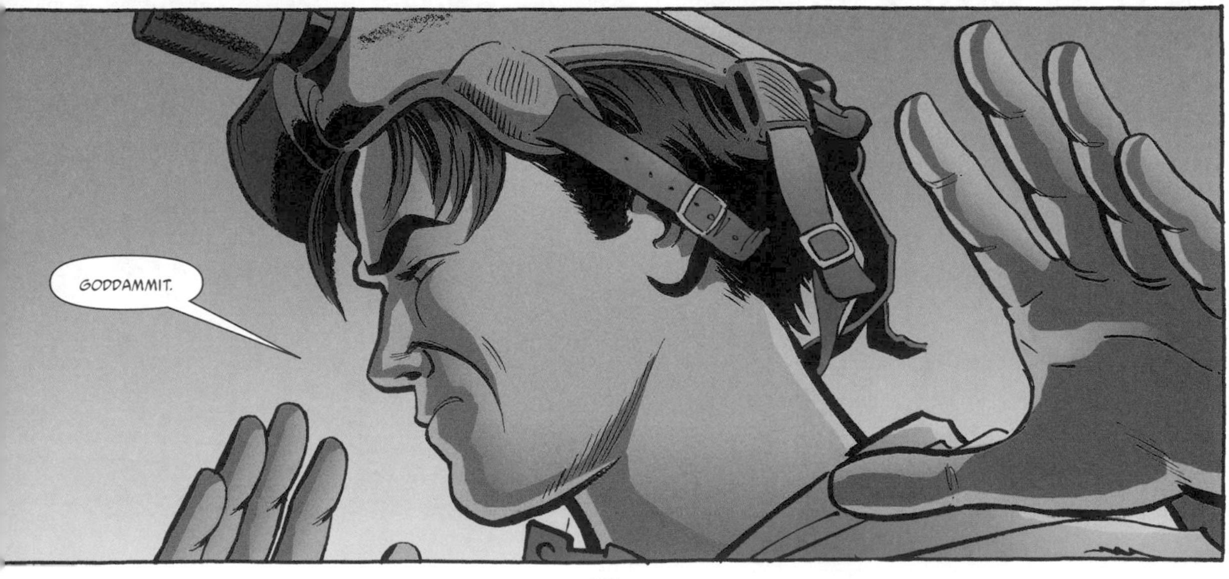
GODDAMMIT.

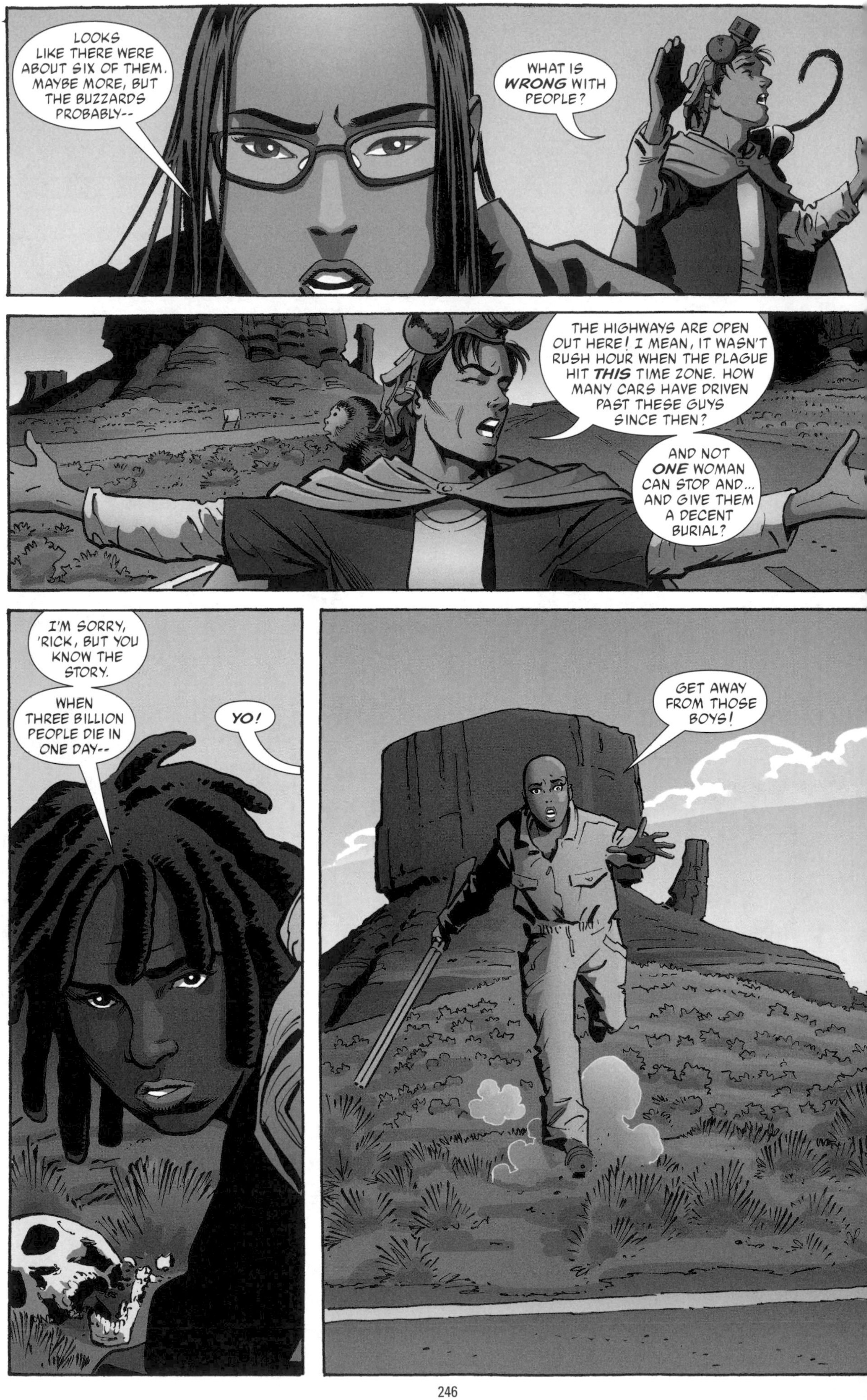
LOOKS LIKE THERE WERE ABOUT SIX OF THEM. MAYBE MORE, BUT THE BUZZARDS PROBABLY--
WHAT IS WRONG WITH PEOPLE?
THE HIGHWAYS ARE OPEN OUT HERE! I MEAN, IT WASN'T RUSH HOUR WHEN THE PLAGUE HIT THIS TIME ZONE. HOW MANY CARS HAVE DRIVEN PAST THESE GUYS SINCE THEN?
AND NOT ONE WOMAN CAN STOP AND... AND GIVE THEM A DECENT BURIAL?
I'M SORRY, 'RICK, BUT YOU KNOW THE STORY.
WHEN THREE BILLION PEOPLE DIE IN ONE DAY--
YO!
GET AWAY FROM THOSE BOYS!

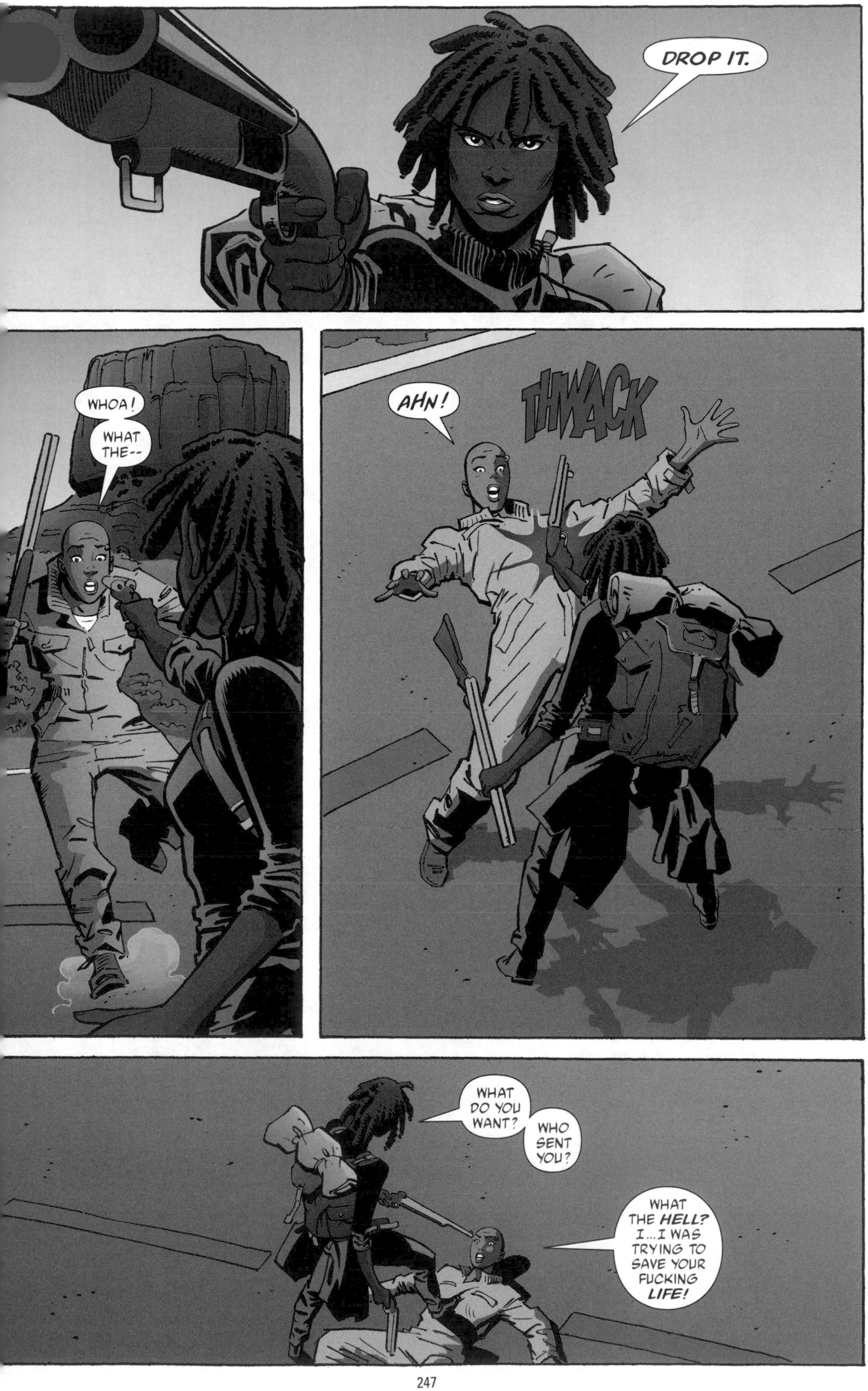
DROP IT.
WHOA!
WHAT THE--
AHN!
THWACK
WHAT DO YOU WANT?
WHO SENT YOU?
WHAT THE HELL? I...I WAS TRYING TO SAVE YOUR FUCKING LIFE!

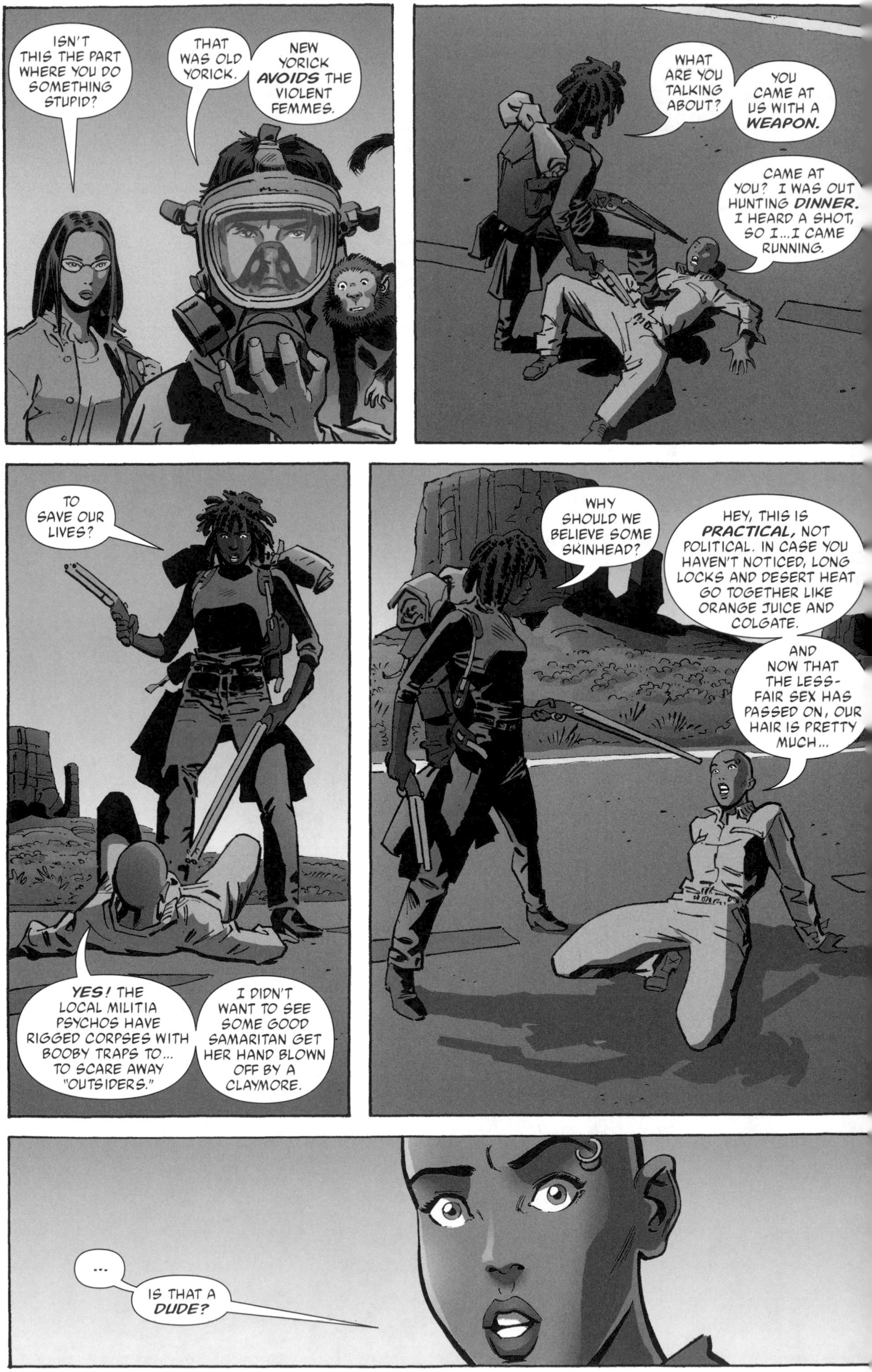

ISN'T THIS THE PART WHERE YOU DO SOMETHING STUPID?
THAT WAS OLD YORICK.
NEW YORICK AVOIDS THE VIOLENT FEMMES.
WHAT ARE YOU TALKING ABOUT?
YOU CAME AT US WITH A WEAPON.
CAME AT YOU? I WAS OUT HUNTING DINNER. I HEARD A SHOT, SO I...I CAME RUNNING.
TO SAVE OUR LIVES?
YES! THE LOCAL MILITIA PSYCHOS HAVE RIGGED CORPSES WITH BOOBY TRAPS TO... TO SCARE AWAY "OUTSIDERS."
I DIDN'T WANT TO SEE SOME GOOD SAMARITAN GET HER HAND BLOWN OFF BY A CLAYMORE.
WHY SHOULD WE BELIEVE SOME SKINHEAD?
HEY, THIS IS PRACTICAL, NOT POLITICAL. IN CASE YOU HAVEN'T NOTICED, LONG LOCKS AND DESERT HEAT GO TOGETHER LIKE ORANGE JUICE AND COLGATE.
AND NOW THAT THE LESS-FAIR SEX HAS PASSED ON, OUR HAIR IS PRETTY MUCH...
...
IS THAT A DUDE?

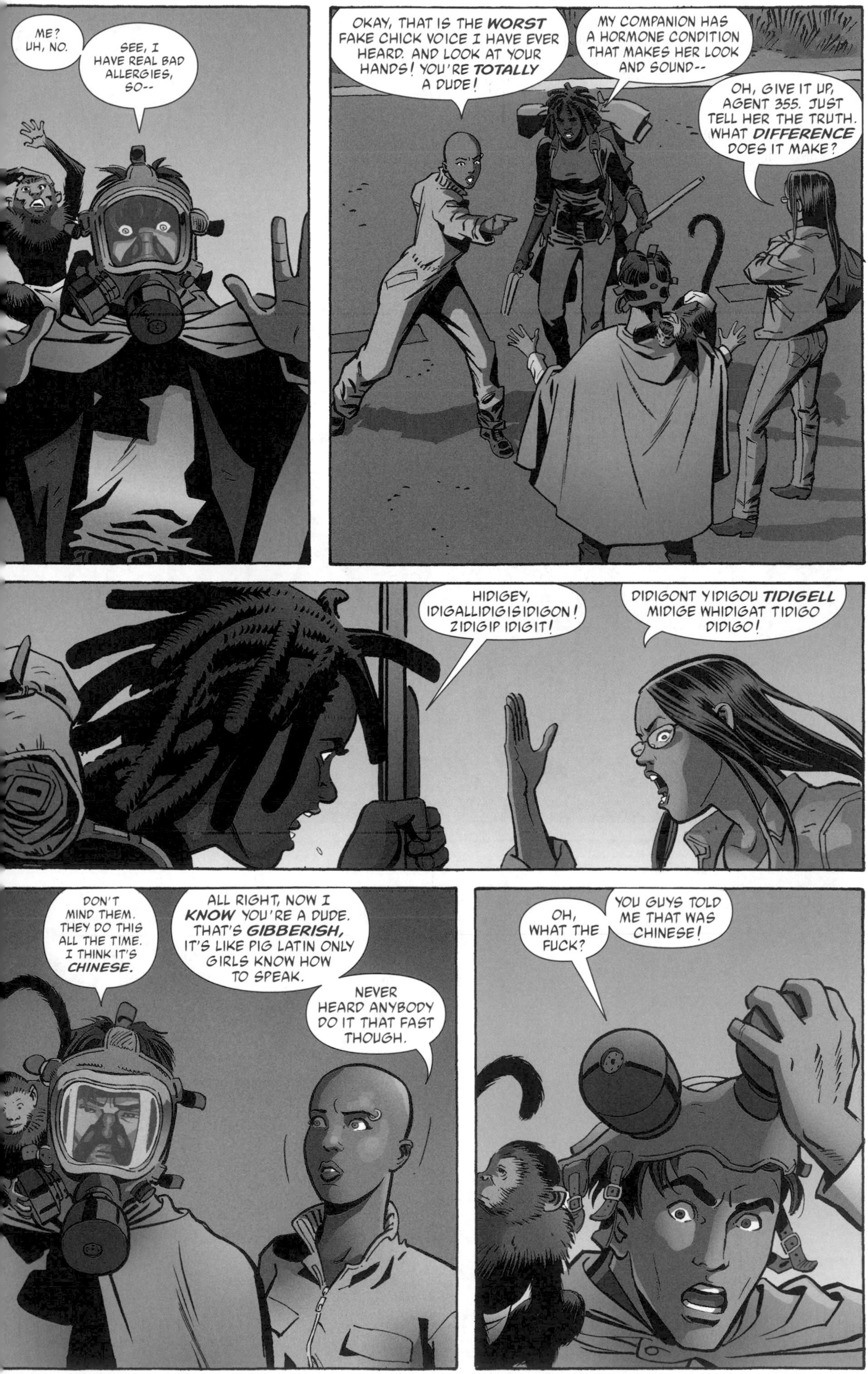
ME? UH, NO.
SEE, I HAVE REAL BAD ALLERGIES, SO--
OKAY, THAT IS THE WORST FAKE CHICK VOICE I HAVE EVER HEARD. AND LOOK AT YOUR HANDS! YOU'RE TOTALLY A DUDE!
MY COMPANION HAS A HORMONE CONDITION THAT MAKES HER LOOK AND SOUND--
OH, GIVE IT UP, AGENT 355. JUST TELL HER THE TRUTH. WHAT DIFFERENCE DOES IT MAKE?
HIDIGEY, IDIGALLIDIGISIDIGON! ZIDIGIP IDIGIT!
DIDIGONT YIDIGOU TIDIGELL MIDIGE WHIDIGAT TIDIGO DIDIGO!
DON'T MIND THEM. THEY DO THIS ALL THE TIME. I THINK IT'S CHINESE.
ALL RIGHT, NOW I KNOW YOU'RE A DUDE. THAT'S GIBBERISH, IT'S LIKE PIG LATIN ONLY GIRLS KNOW HOW TO SPEAK.
NEVER HEARD ANYBODY DO IT THAT FAST THOUGH.
OH, WHAT THE FUCK?
YOU GUYS TOLD ME THAT WAS CHINESE!

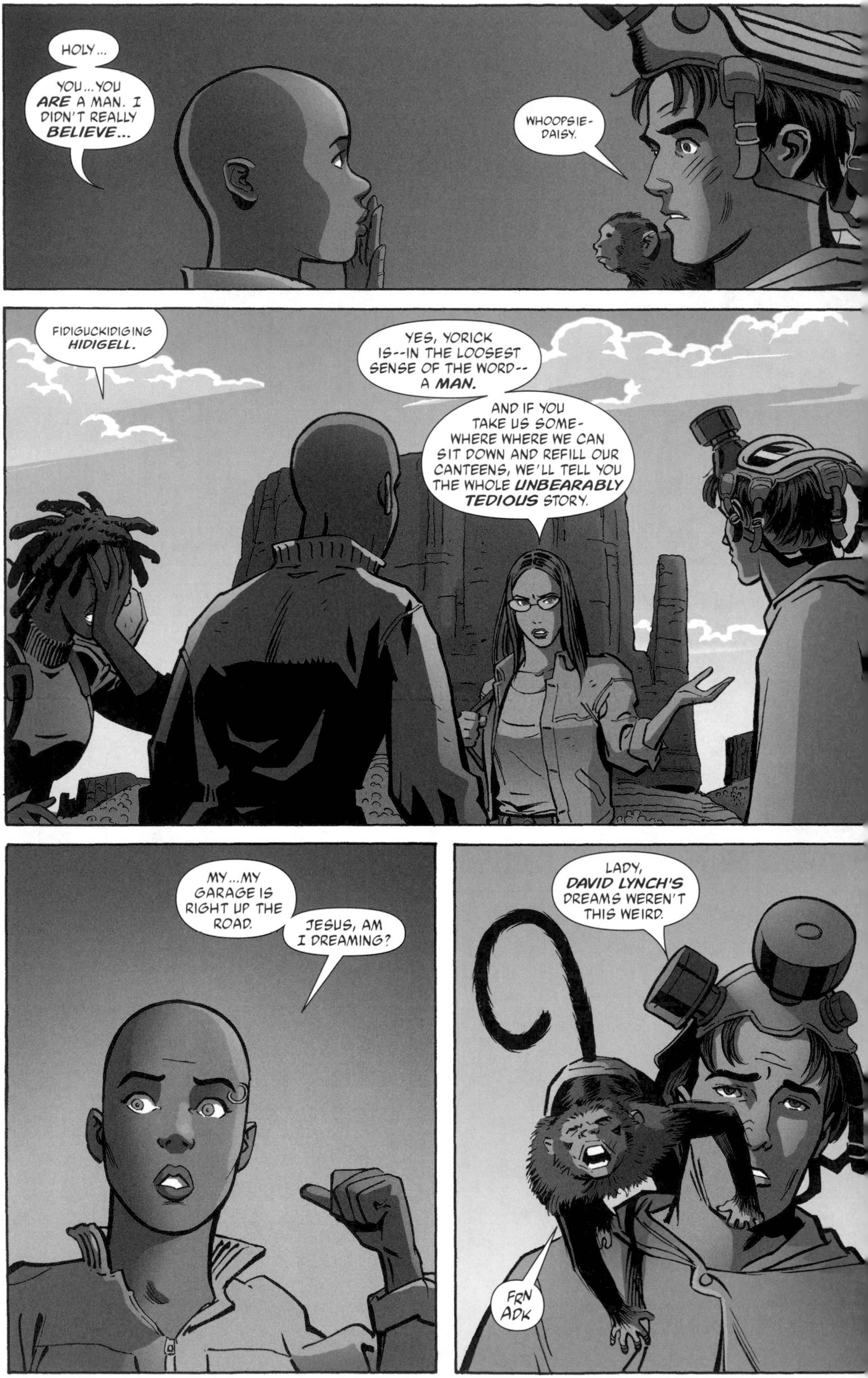
HOLY...
YOU...YOU ARE A MAN. I DIDN'T REALLY BELIEVE...
WHOOPSIE-DAISY.
FIDIGUCKIDIGING HIDIGELL.
YES, YORICK IS--IN THE LOOSEST SENSE OF THE WORD--A MAN.
AND IF YOU TAKE US SOME-WHERE WHERE WE CAN SIT DOWN AND REFILL OUR CANTEENS, WE'LL TELL YOU THE WHOLE UNBEARABLY TEDIOUS STORY.
MY...MY GARAGE IS RIGHT UP THE ROAD.
JESUS, AM I DREAMING?
LADY, DAVID LYNCH'S DREAMS WEREN'T THIS WEIRD.
FRN ADK

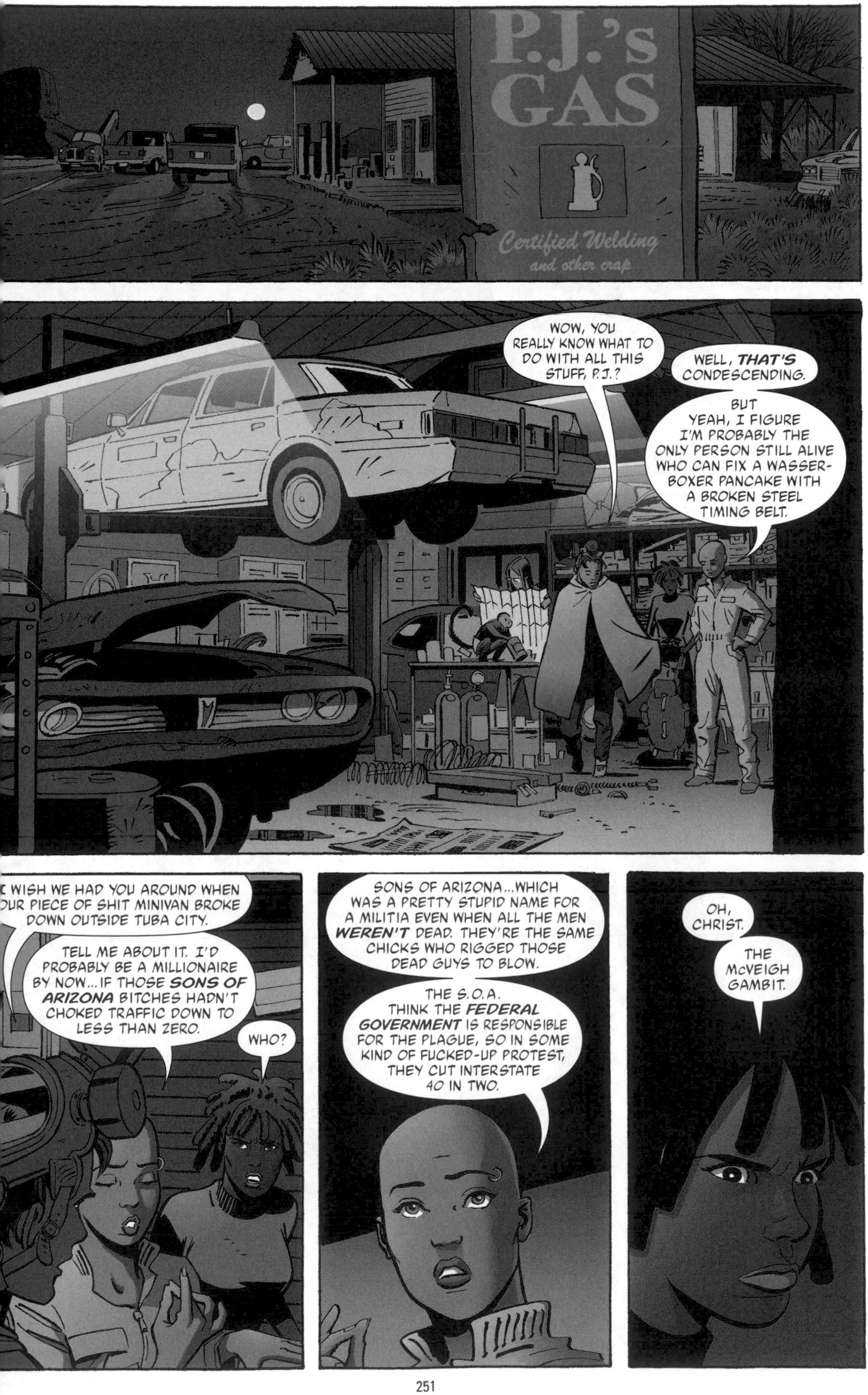
P.J.'s
GAS
Certified Welding
and other crap
WOW, YOU REALLY KNOW WHAT TO DO WITH ALL THIS STUFF, P.J.?
WELL, *THAT'S* CONDESCENDING.
BUT YEAH, I FIGURE I'M PROBABLY THE ONLY PERSON STILL ALIVE WHO CAN FIX A WASSER-BOXER PANCAKE WITH A BROKEN STEEL TIMING BELT.
I WISH WE HAD YOU AROUND WHEN OUR PIECE OF SHIT MINIVAN BROKE DOWN OUTSIDE TUBA CITY.
TELL ME ABOUT IT. I'D PROBABLY BE A MILLIONAIRE BY NOW... IF THOSE ***SONS OF ARIZONA*** BITCHES HADN'T CHOKED TRAFFIC DOWN TO LESS THAN ZERO.
WHO?
SONS OF ARIZONA... WHICH WAS A PRETTY STUPID NAME FOR A MILITIA EVEN WHEN ALL THE MEN ***WEREN'T*** DEAD. THEY'RE THE SAME CHICKS WHO RIGGED THOSE DEAD GUYS TO BLOW.
THE S.O.A. THINK THE ***FEDERAL GOVERNMENT*** IS RESPONSIBLE FOR THE PLAGUE, SO IN SOME KIND OF FUCKED-UP PROTEST, THEY CUT INTERSTATE 40 IN TWO.
OH, CHRIST.
THE McVEIGH GAMBIT.

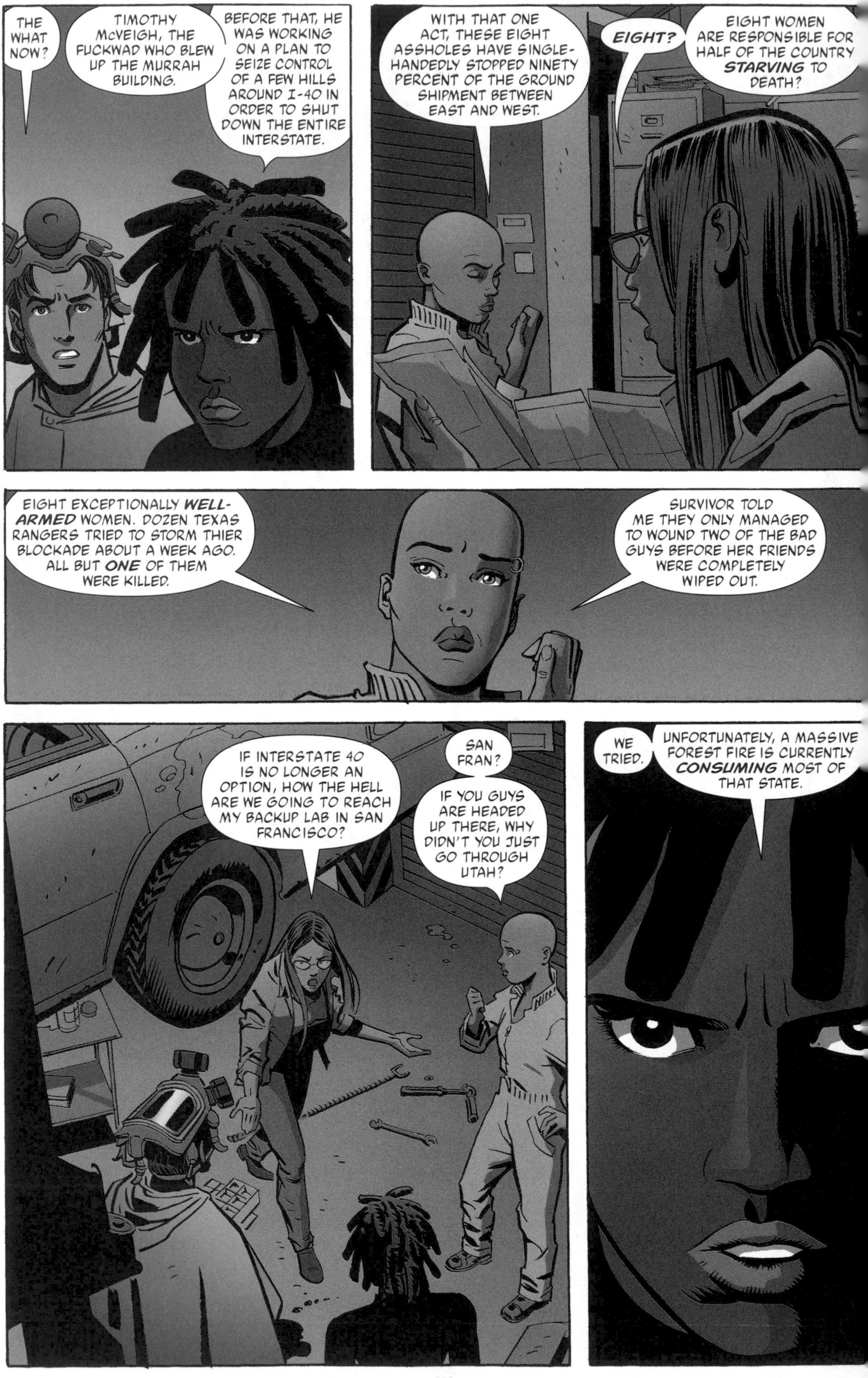
THE WHAT NOW?
TIMOTHY McVEIGH, THE FUCKWAD WHO BLEW UP THE MURRAH BUILDING.
BEFORE THAT, HE WAS WORKING ON A PLAN TO SEIZE CONTROL OF A FEW HILLS AROUND I-40 IN ORDER TO SHUT DOWN THE ENTIRE INTERSTATE.
WITH THAT ONE ACT, THESE EIGHT ASSHOLES HAVE SINGLE-HANDEDLY STOPPED NINETY PERCENT OF THE GROUND SHIPMENT BETWEEN EAST AND WEST.
EIGHT?
EIGHT WOMEN ARE RESPONSIBLE FOR HALF OF THE COUNTRY STARVING TO DEATH?
EIGHT EXCEPTIONALLY WELL-ARMED WOMEN. DOZEN TEXAS RANGERS TRIED TO STORM THIER BLOCKADE ABOUT A WEEK AGO. ALL BUT ONE OF THEM WERE KILLED.
SURVIVOR TOLD ME THEY ONLY MANAGED TO WOUND TWO OF THE BAD GUYS BEFORE HER FRIENDS WERE COMPLETELY WIPED OUT.
IF INTERSTATE 40 IS NO LONGER AN OPTION, HOW THE HELL ARE WE GOING TO REACH MY BACKUP LAB IN SAN FRANCISCO?
SAN FRAN?
IF YOU GUYS ARE HEADED UP THERE, WHY DIDN'T YOU JUST GO THROUGH UTAH?
WE TRIED.
UNFORTUNATELY, A MASSIVE FOREST FIRE IS CURRENTLY CONSUMING MOST OF THAT STATE.

WITH SO FEW FEMALE FIGHTERS AROUND, 355 THOUGHT IT WOULD BE SAFER TO DETOUR THROUGH ARIZONA THAN TO RISK A TRIP THROUGH MORMON HELLFIRE.

OUT OF THE FRYING PAN, HUH?

WELL, YOU CAN ALWAYS HAVE A TRUCK FROM MY FLEET, TAKE YOUR CHANCES WITH AN ALTERNATE ROUTE.

HOW MANY CHOICES DO WE HAVE LEFT? I-10? I-8?

WHAT IF RUBY RIDGE LUNATICS HAVE TAKEN *THOSE* ROADS HOSTAGE?

THEN WE'LL GO DOWN TO MEXICO AND COME UP THROUGH SAN DIEGO.

BULLSHIT! WE CAN'T AFFORD TO WASTE ANY MORE TIME, 355!

WHAT DO YOU WANT ME TO DO, ALLISON? DRAG YOU AND YORICK THROUGH A WARZONE?

ISN'T THAT WHAT YOU'VE BEEN DOING FOR THE LAST EIGHTEEN MONTHS? BESIDES, I THOUGHT YOUR LITTLE CLUB WAS *CREATED* TO DEAL WITH CRAP LIKE THIS!

THE REST OF THE CULPER RING AND I WILL WORK ON OPENING INTERSTATE 40...*AFTER* I GET YOU AND YORICK TO OUR FINAL DESTINATION.

WHEN WILL THAT BE, A *YEAR* FROM NOW?

BY THEN, SOME AMAZON WILL HAVE PROBABLY TORCHED *EVERYTHING* I USED TO MAKE MY DAUGHTER!

DAUGHTER?

DOC, YOU TOLD US THAT CLONE YOU GAVE BIRTH TO WAS A *BOY.*

AND THIS ISN'T THE FIRST TIME YOU'VE SUGGESTED OTHERWISE...

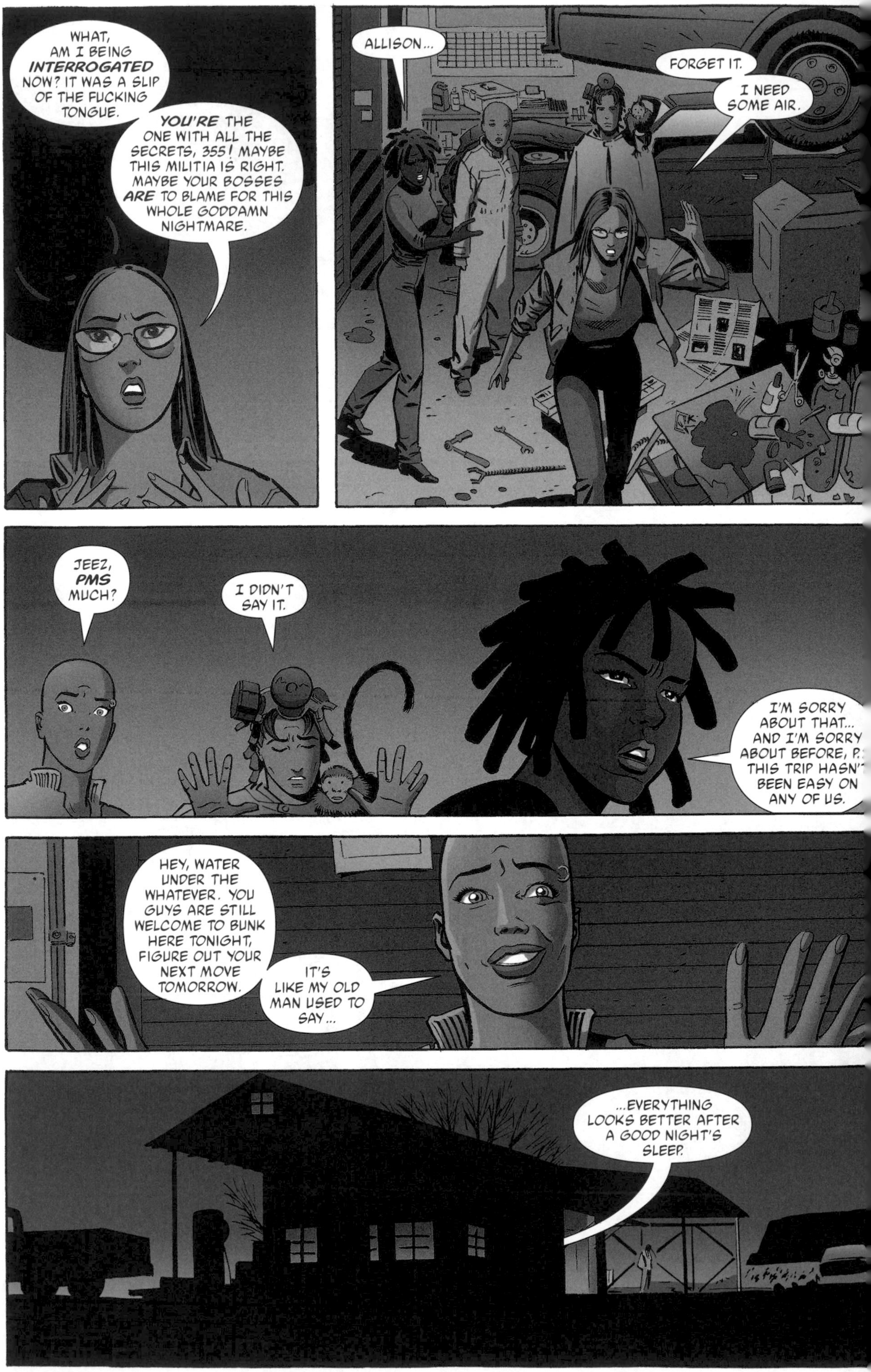
WHAT, AM I BEING INTERROGATED NOW? IT WAS A SLIP OF THE FUCKING TONGUE.
YOU'RE THE ONE WITH ALL THE SECRETS, 355! MAYBE THIS MILITIA IS RIGHT. MAYBE YOUR BOSSES ARE TO BLAME FOR THIS WHOLE GODDAMN NIGHTMARE.
ALLISON...
FORGET IT.
I NEED SOME AIR.
JEEZ, PMS MUCH?
I DIDN'T SAY IT.
I'M SORRY ABOUT THAT... AND I'M SORRY ABOUT BEFORE, P. THIS TRIP HASN'T BEEN EASY ON ANY OF US.
HEY, WATER UNDER THE WHATEVER. YOU GUYS ARE STILL WELCOME TO BUNK HERE TONIGHT, FIGURE OUT YOUR NEXT MOVE TOMORROW.
IT'S LIKE MY OLD MAN USED TO SAY...
...EVERYTHING LOOKS BETTER AFTER A GOOD NIGHT'S SLEEP.

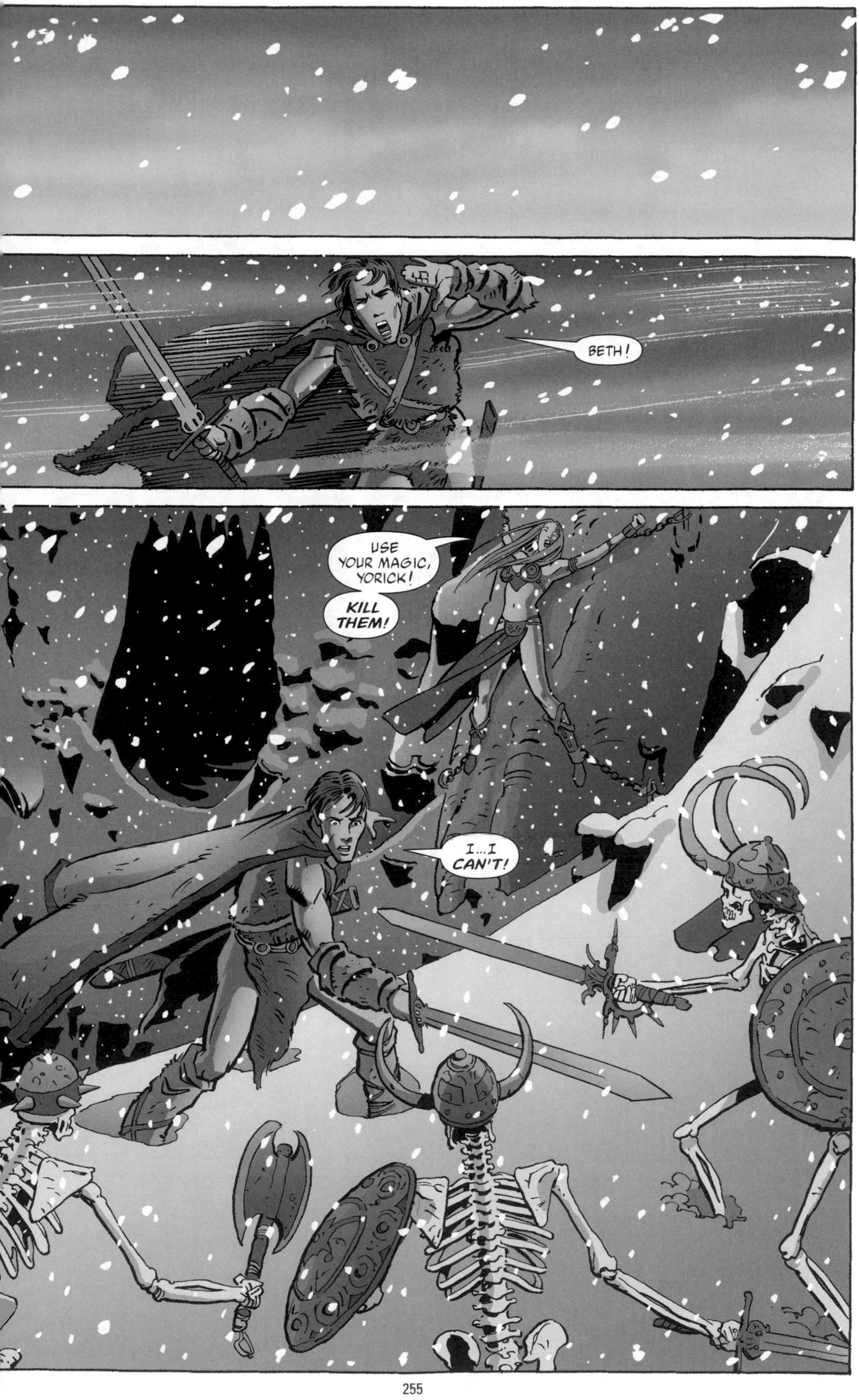
BETH!
USE YOUR MAGIC, YORICK!
KILL THEM!
I...I CAN'T!

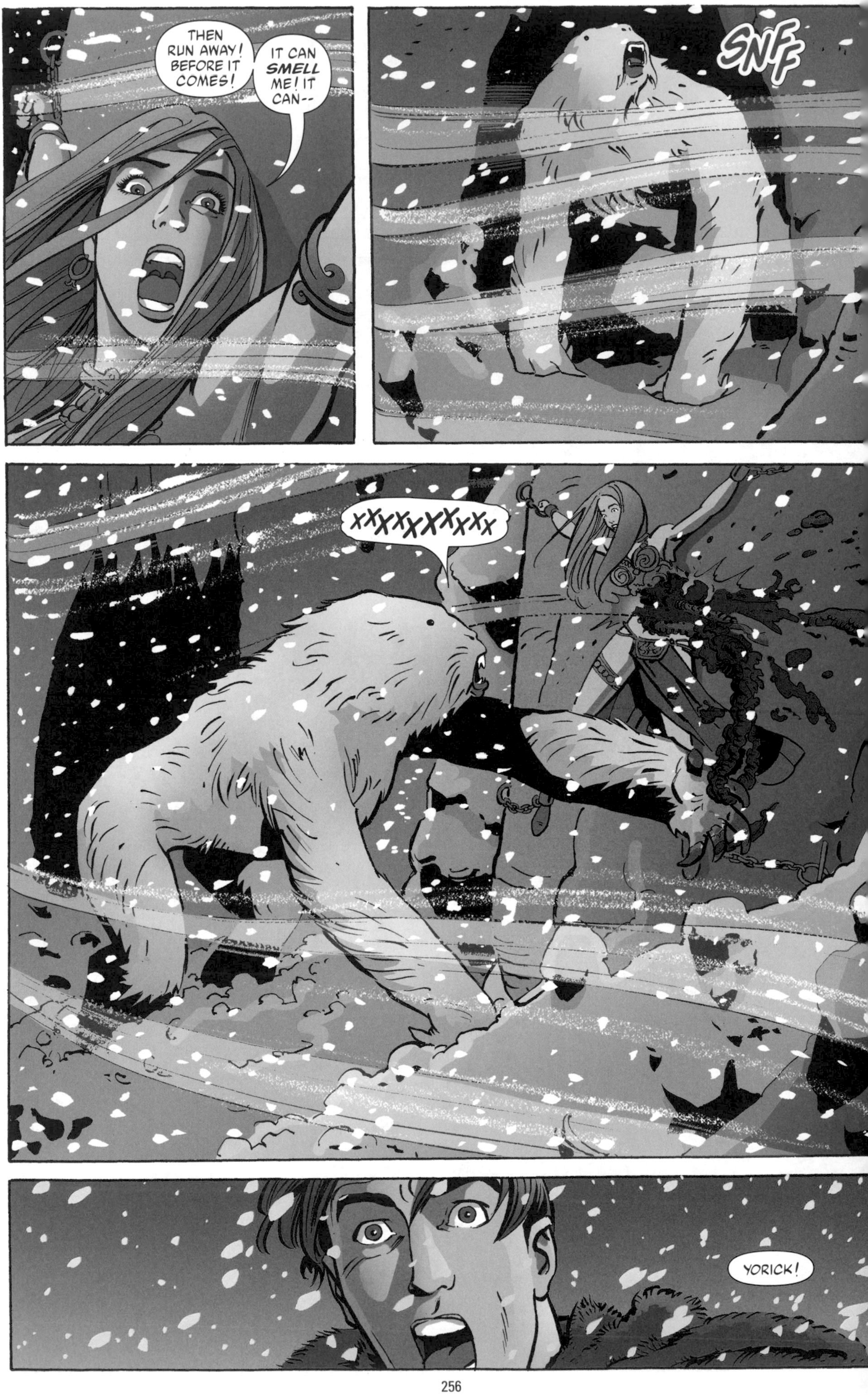
THEN RUN AWAY! BEFORE IT COMES!
IT CAN SMELL ME! IT CAN--
SNFF
XXXXXXXXXX
YORICK!

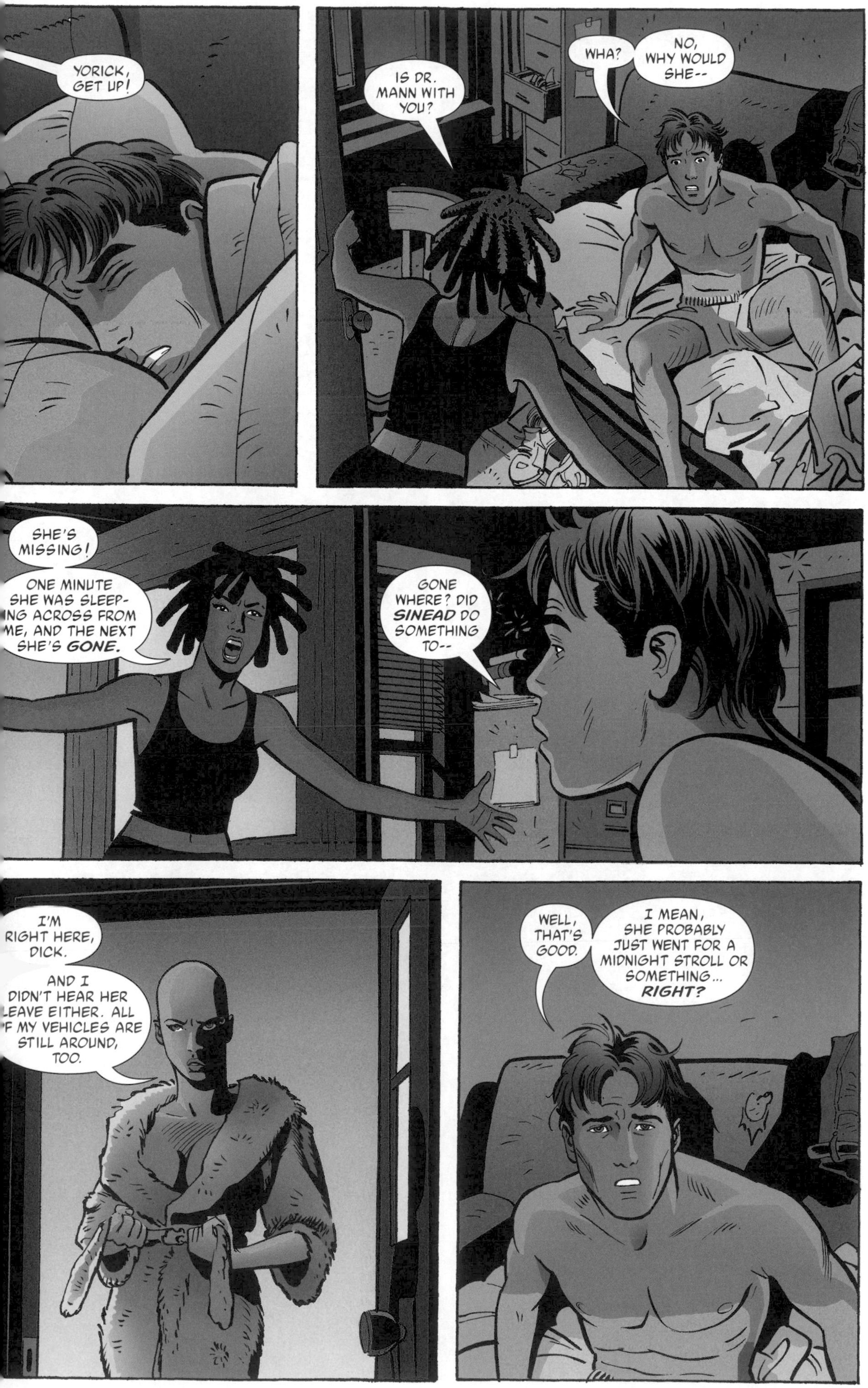

YORICK, GET UP!
IS DR. MANN WITH YOU?
WHA?
NO, WHY WOULD SHE--
SHE'S MISSING!
ONE MINUTE SHE WAS SLEEP-ING ACROSS FROM ME, AND THE NEXT SHE'S GONE.
GONE WHERE? DID SINEAD DO SOMETHING TO--
I'M RIGHT HERE, DICK.
AND I DIDN'T HEAR HER LEAVE EITHER. ALL OF MY VEHICLES ARE STILL AROUND, TOO.
WELL, THAT'S GOOD.
I MEAN, SHE PROBABLY JUST WENT FOR A MIDNIGHT STROLL OR SOMETHING... RIGHT?

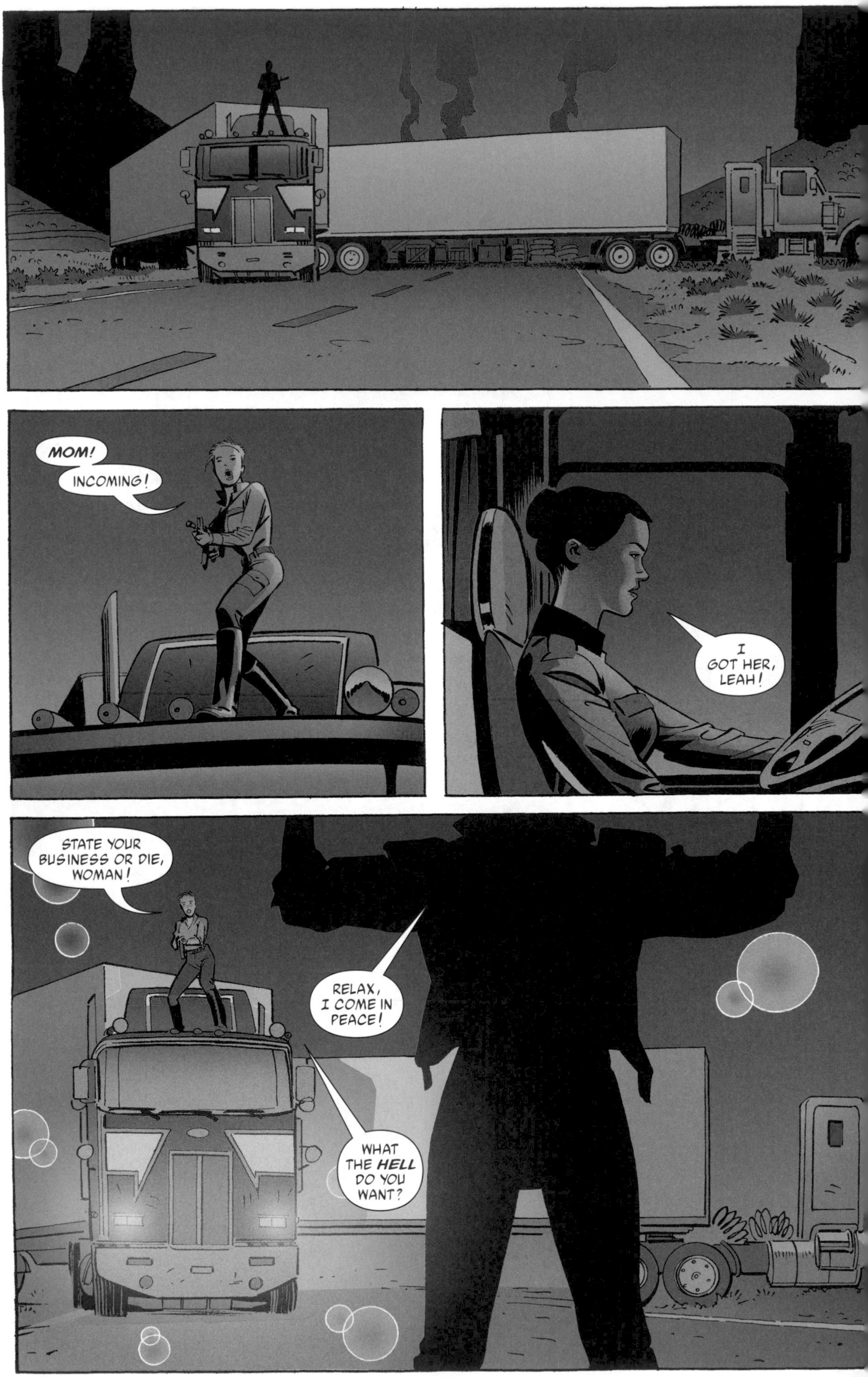
MOM!
INCOMING!
I GOT HER, LEAH!
STATE YOUR BUSINESS OR DIE, WOMAN!
RELAX, I COME IN PEACE!
WHAT THE HELL DO YOU WANT?

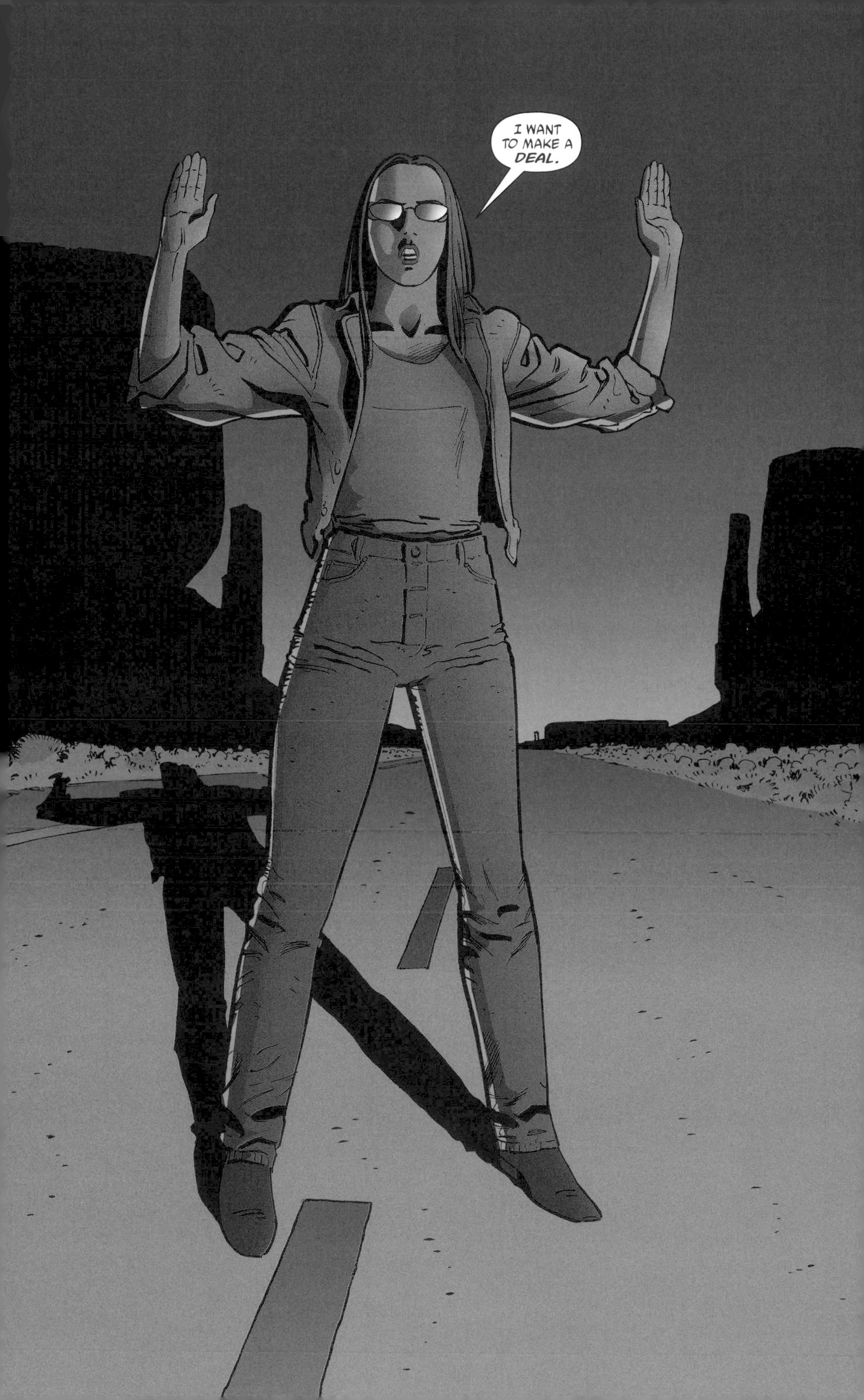
I WANT TO MAKE A DEAL.

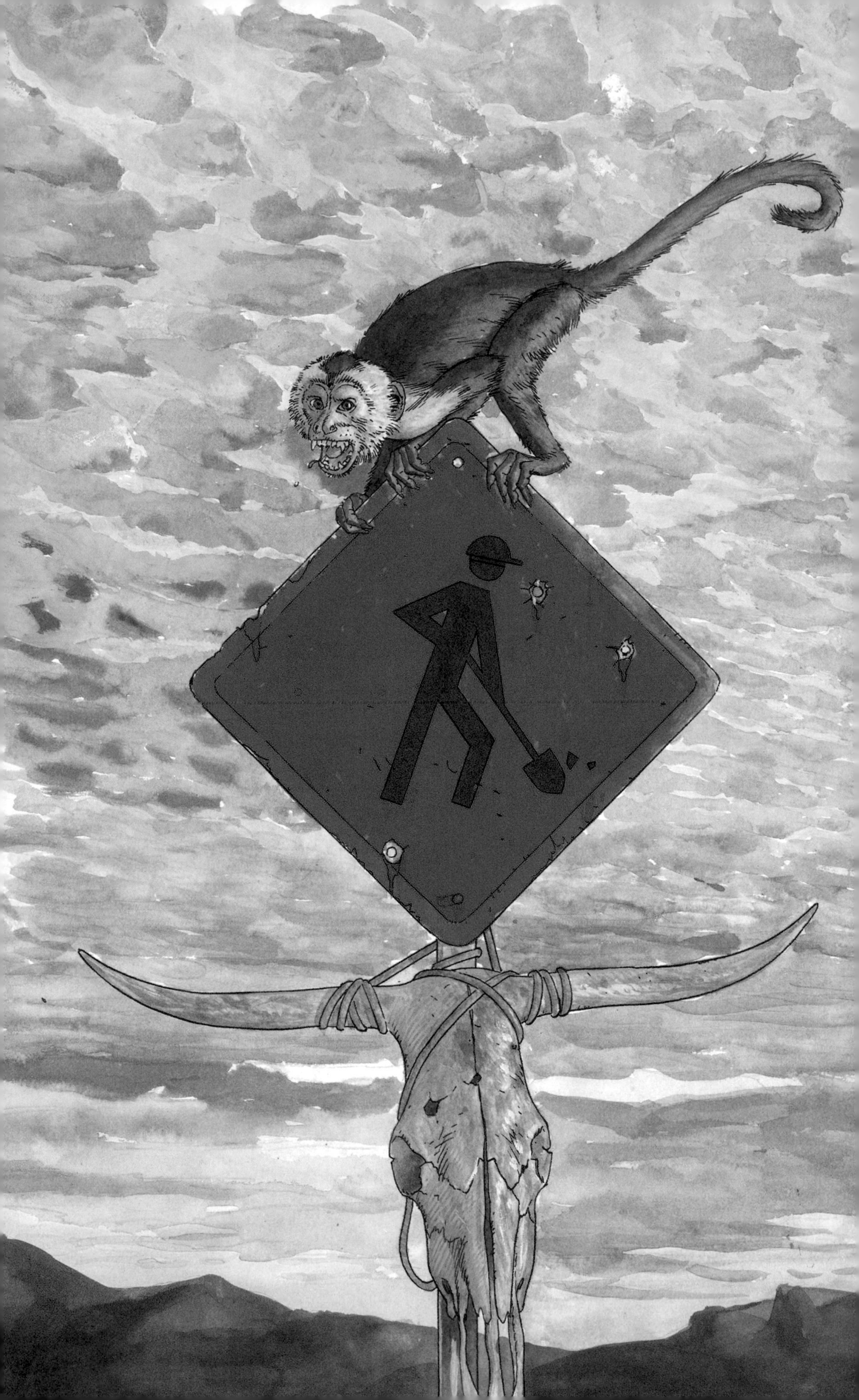

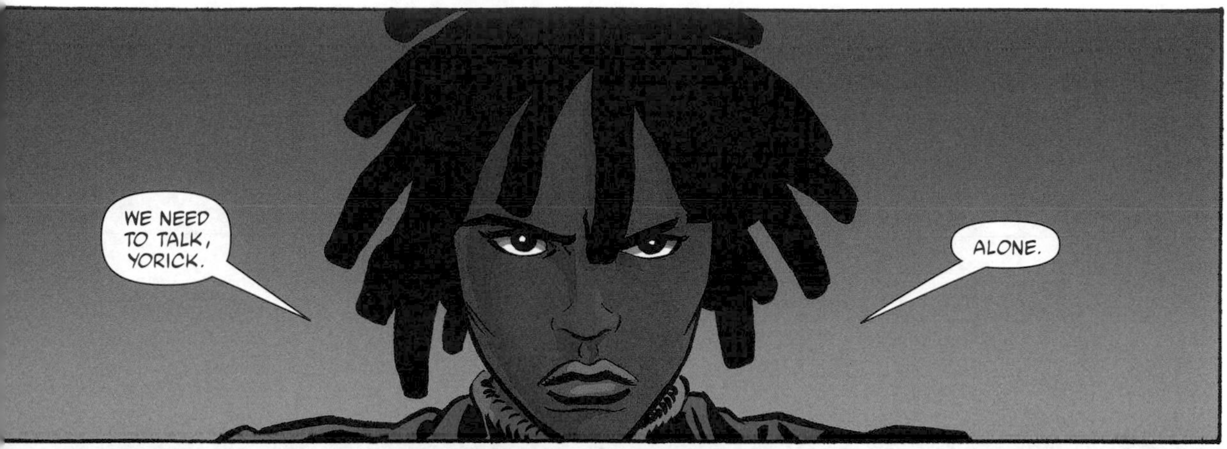
WE NEED TO TALK, YORICK.
ALONE.

Queensbrook, Arizona
Now

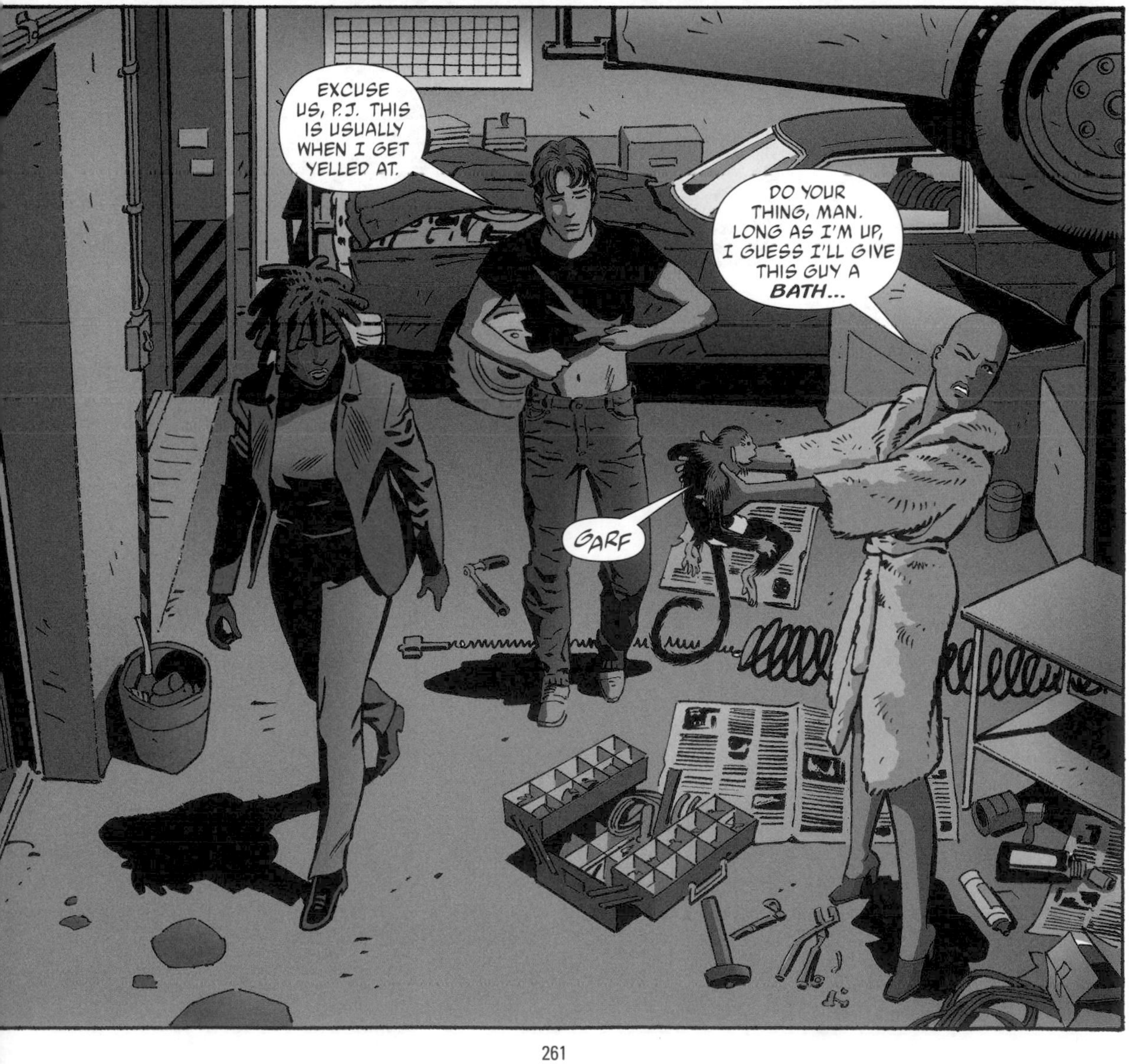
EXCUSE US, P.J. THIS IS USUALLY WHEN I GET YELLED AT.
DO YOUR THING, MAN. LONG AS I'M UP, I GUESS I'LL GIVE THIS GUY A BATH...
GARF

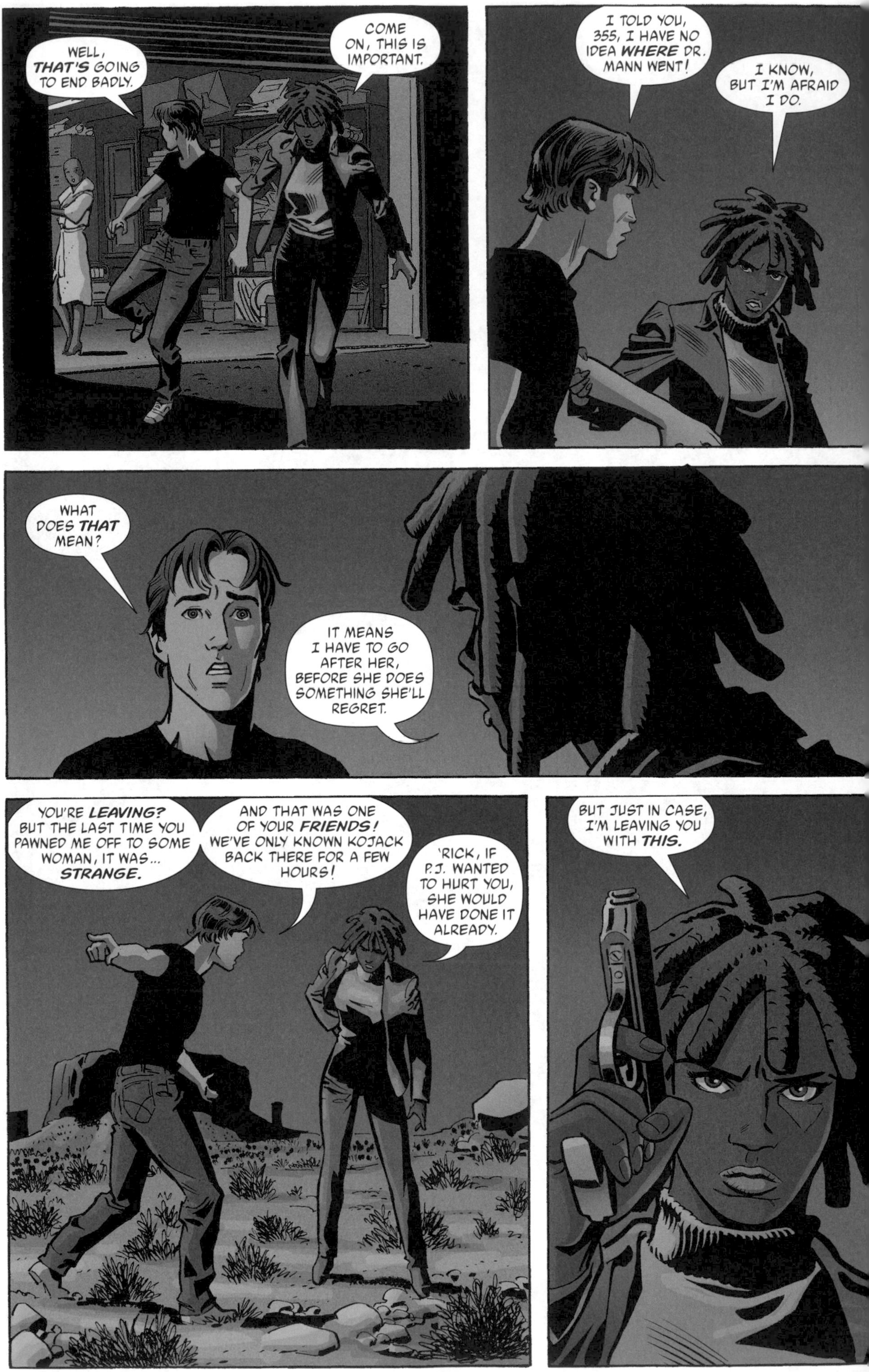
WELL, THAT'S GOING TO END BADLY.
COME ON, THIS IS IMPORTANT.
I TOLD YOU, 355, I HAVE NO IDEA WHERE DR. MANN WENT!
I KNOW, BUT I'M AFRAID I DO.
WHAT DOES THAT MEAN?
IT MEANS I HAVE TO GO AFTER HER, BEFORE SHE DOES SOMETHING SHE'LL REGRET.
YOU'RE LEAVING? BUT THE LAST TIME YOU PAWNED ME OFF TO SOME WOMAN, IT WAS... STRANGE.
AND THAT WAS ONE OF YOUR FRIENDS! WE'VE ONLY KNOWN KOJACK BACK THERE FOR A FEW HOURS!
'RICK, IF P.J. WANTED TO HURT YOU, SHE WOULD HAVE DONE IT ALREADY.
BUT JUST IN CASE, I'M LEAVING YOU WITH THIS.

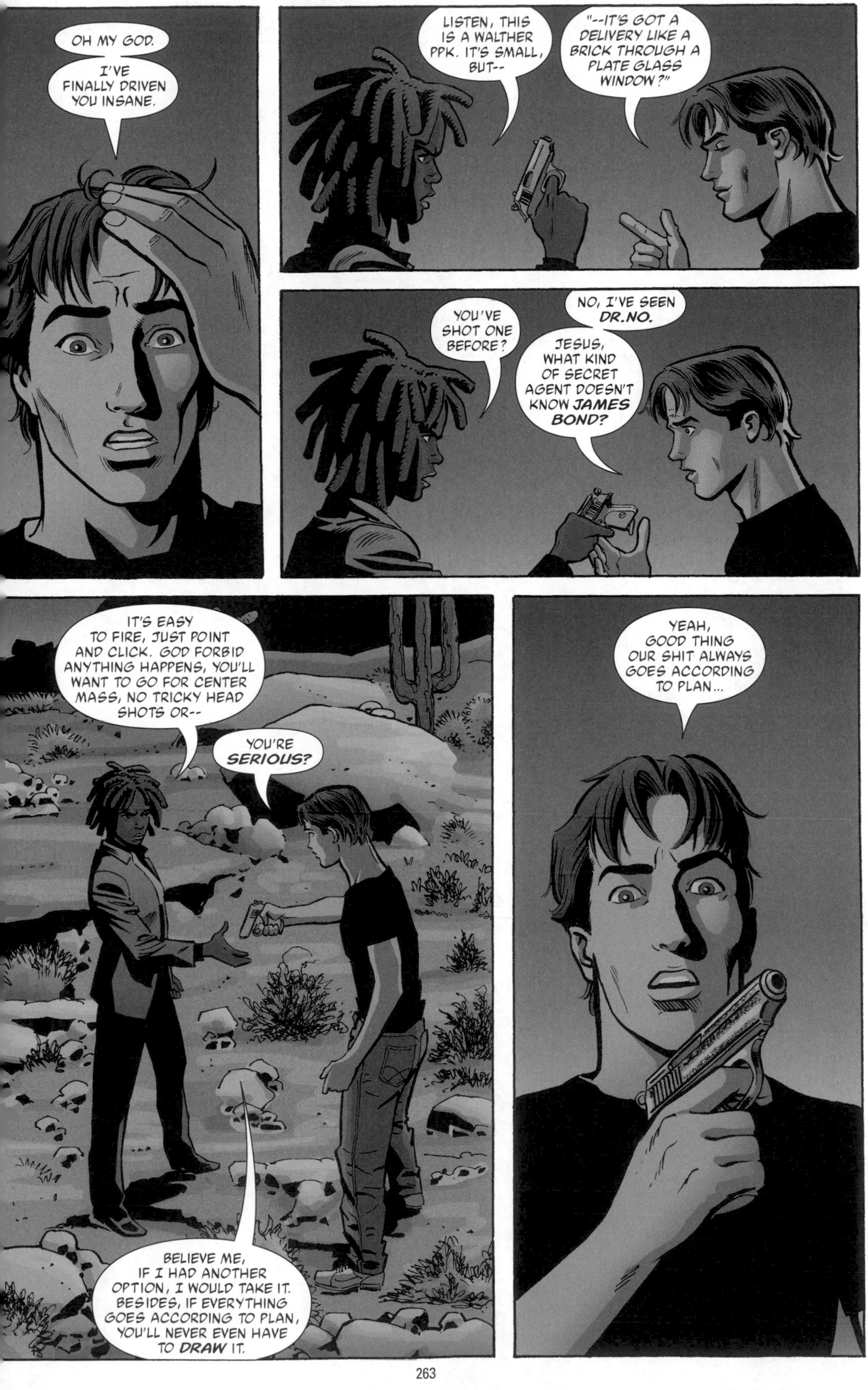
OH MY GOD.
I'VE FINALLY DRIVEN YOU INSANE.
LISTEN, THIS IS A WALTHER PPK. IT'S SMALL, BUT--
"--IT'S GOT A DELIVERY LIKE A BRICK THROUGH A PLATE GLASS WINDOW?"
YOU'VE SHOT ONE BEFORE?
NO, I'VE SEEN DR.NO.
JESUS, WHAT KIND OF SECRET AGENT DOESN'T KNOW JAMES BOND?
IT'S EASY TO FIRE, JUST POINT AND CLICK. GOD FORBID ANYTHING HAPPENS, YOU'LL WANT TO GO FOR CENTER MASS, NO TRICKY HEAD SHOTS OR--
YOU'RE SERIOUS?
BELIEVE ME, IF I HAD ANOTHER OPTION, I WOULD TAKE IT. BESIDES, IF EVERYTHING GOES ACCORDING TO PLAN, YOU'LL NEVER EVEN HAVE TO DRAW IT.
YEAH, GOOD THING OUR SHIT ALWAYS GOES ACCORDING TO PLAN...

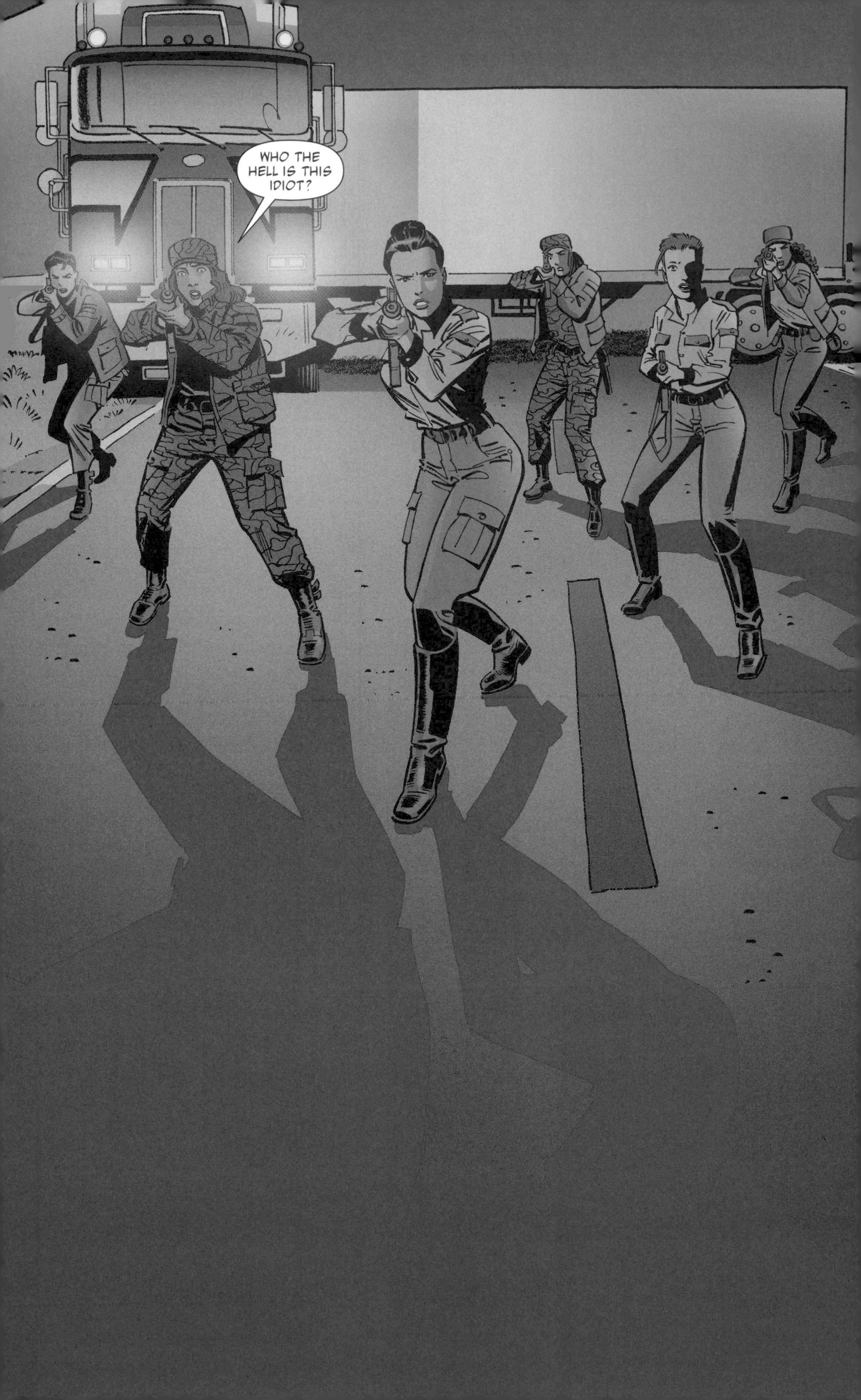
WHO THE HELL IS THIS IDIOT?

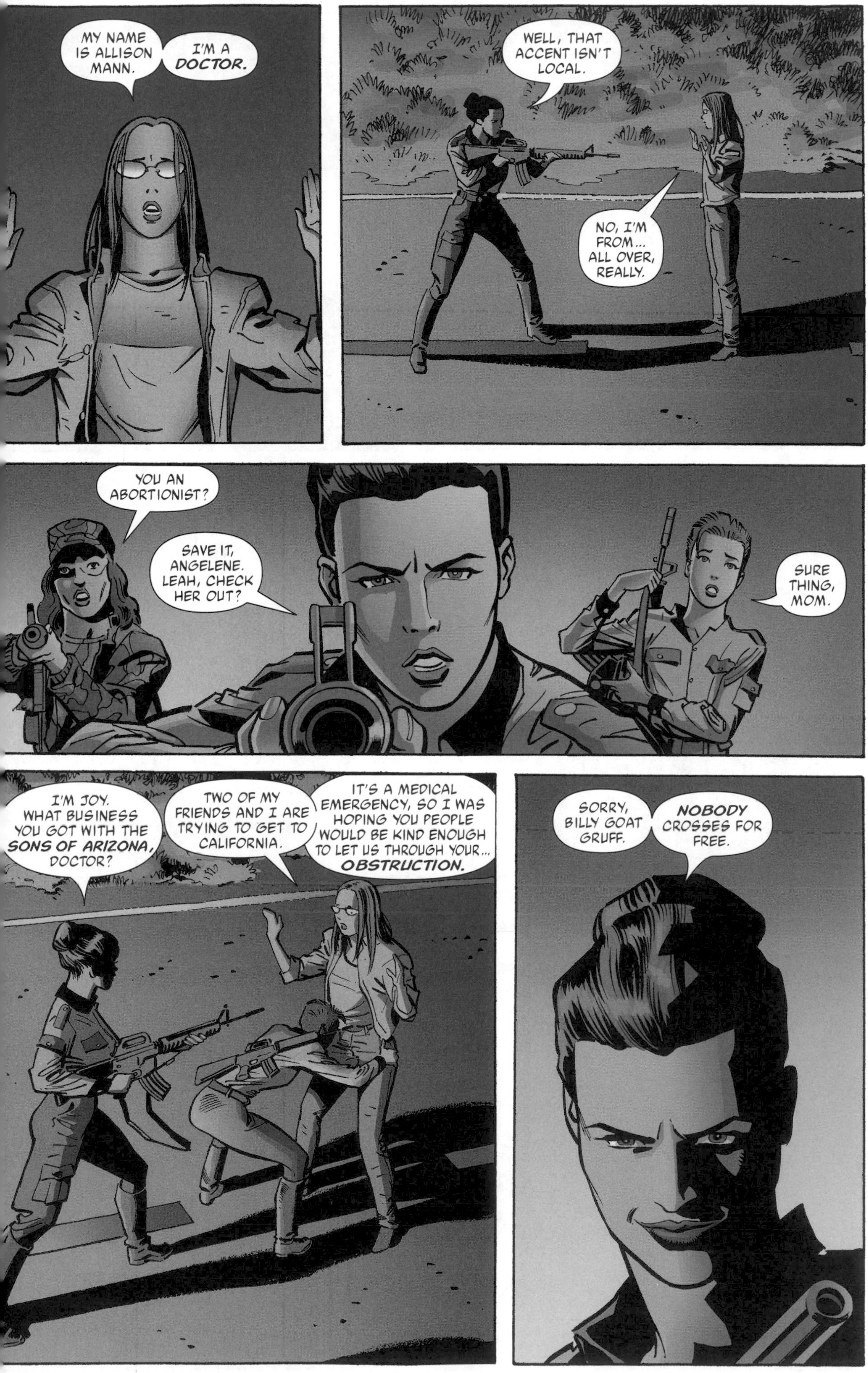
MY NAME IS ALLISON MANN.
I'M A DOCTOR.
WELL, THAT ACCENT ISN'T LOCAL.
NO, I'M FROM... ALL OVER, REALLY.
YOU AN ABORTIONIST?
SAVE IT, ANGELENE. LEAH, CHECK HER OUT?
SURE THING, MOM.
I'M JOY. WHAT BUSINESS YOU GOT WITH THE SONS OF ARIZONA, DOCTOR?
TWO OF MY FRIENDS AND I ARE TRYING TO GET TO CALIFORNIA.
IT'S A MEDICAL EMERGENCY, SO I WAS HOPING YOU PEOPLE WOULD BE KIND ENOUGH TO LET US THROUGH YOUR... OBSTRUCTION.
SORRY, BILLY GOAT GRUFF.
NOBODY CROSSES FOR FREE.

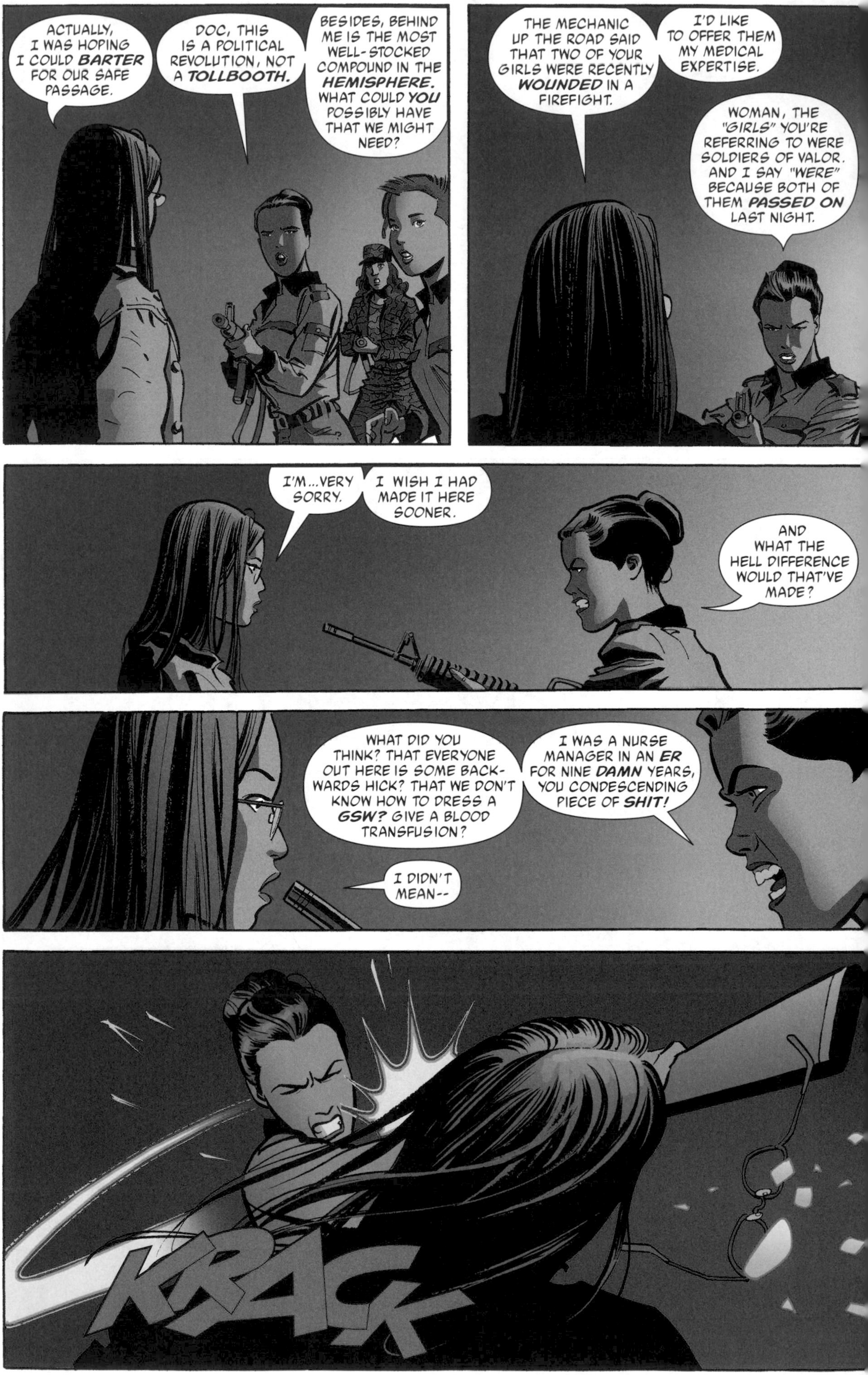
ACTUALLY, I WAS HOPING I COULD BARTER FOR OUR SAFE PASSAGE.
DOC, THIS IS A POLITICAL REVOLUTION, NOT A TOLLBOOTH.
BESIDES, BEHIND ME IS THE MOST WELL-STOCKED COMPOUND IN THE HEMISPHERE. WHAT COULD YOU POSSIBLY HAVE THAT WE MIGHT NEED?
THE MECHANIC UP THE ROAD SAID THAT TWO OF YOUR GIRLS WERE RECENTLY WOUNDED IN A FIREFIGHT.
I'D LIKE TO OFFER THEM MY MEDICAL EXPERTISE.
WOMAN, THE "GIRLS" YOU'RE REFERRING TO WERE SOLDIERS OF VALOR. AND I SAY "WERE" BECAUSE BOTH OF THEM PASSED ON LAST NIGHT.
I'M...VERY SORRY.
I WISH I HAD MADE IT HERE SOONER.
AND WHAT THE HELL DIFFERENCE WOULD THAT'VE MADE?
WHAT DID YOU THINK? THAT EVERYONE OUT HERE IS SOME BACK-WARDS HICK? THAT WE DON'T KNOW HOW TO DRESS A GSW? GIVE A BLOOD TRANSFUSION?
I DIDN'T MEAN--
I WAS A NURSE MANAGER IN AN ER FOR NINE DAMN YEARS, YOU CONDESCENDING PIECE OF SHIT!
KRACK

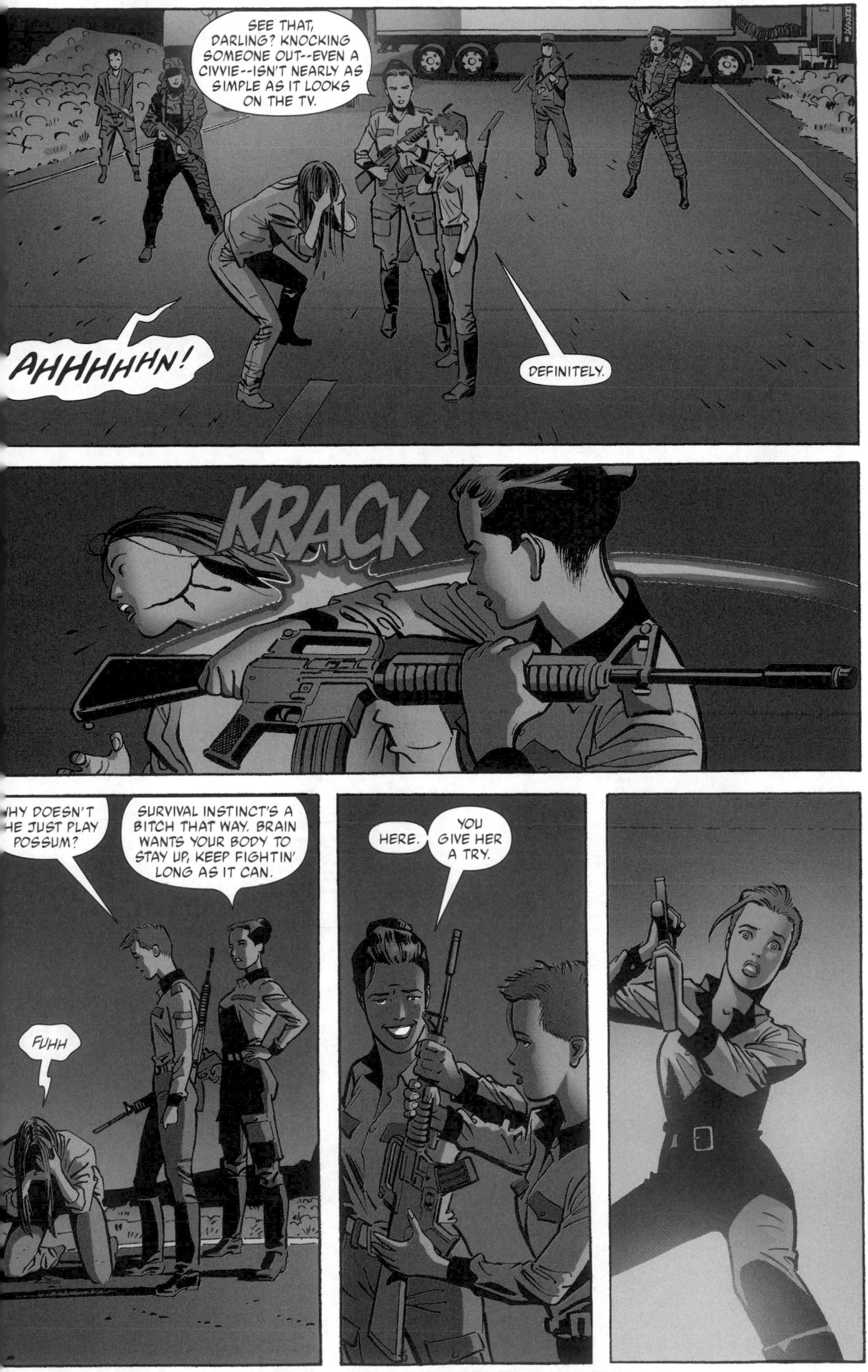
SEE THAT, DARLING? KNOCKING SOMEONE OUT--EVEN A CIVVIE--ISN'T NEARLY AS SIMPLE AS IT LOOKS ON THE TV.
AHHHHHN!
DEFINITELY.
KRACK
WHY DOESN'T HE JUST PLAY POSSUM?
SURVIVAL INSTINCT'S A BITCH THAT WAY. BRAIN WANTS YOUR BODY TO STAY UP, KEEP FIGHTIN' LONG AS IT CAN.
FUHH
HERE.
YOU GIVE HER A TRY.

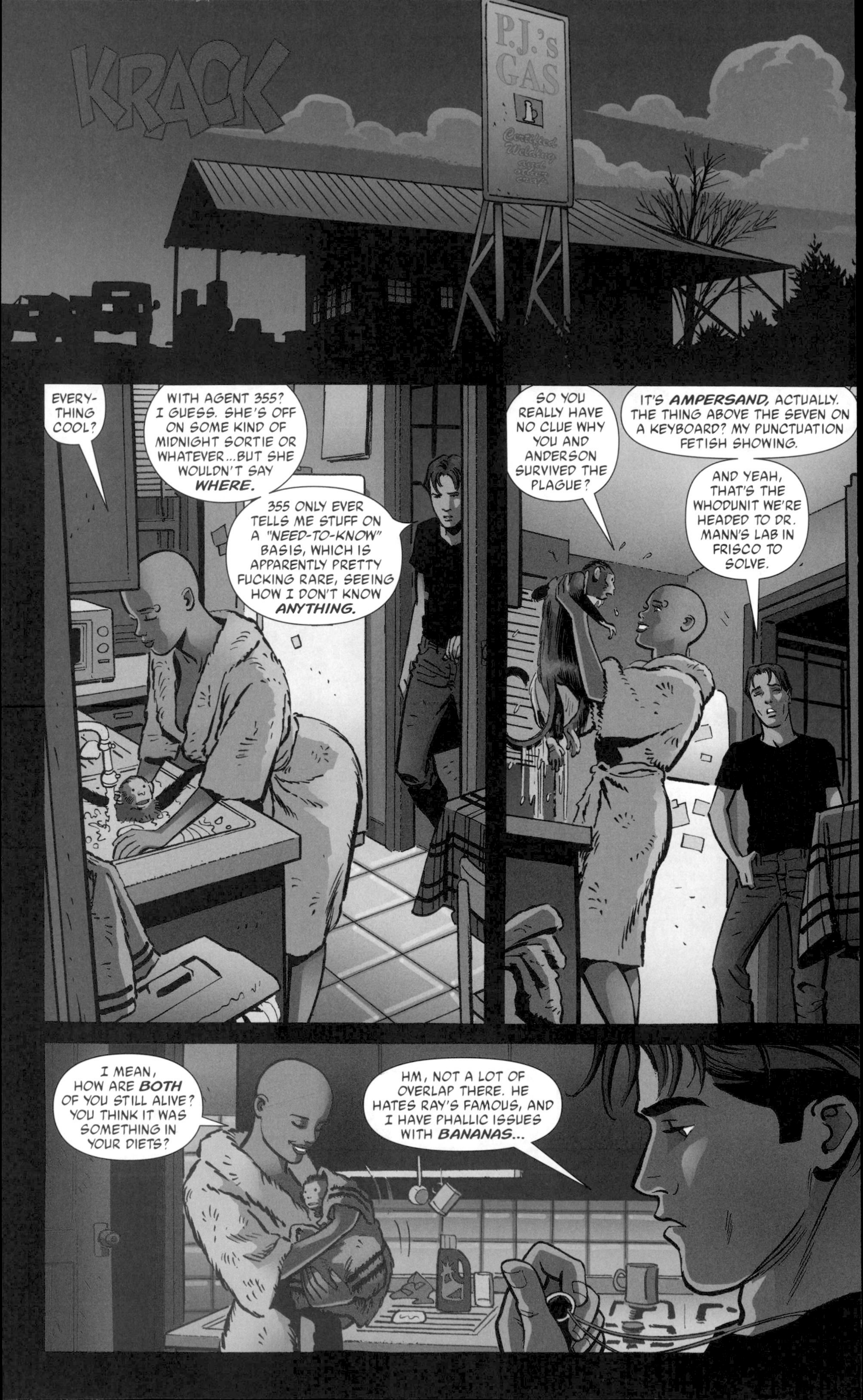

KRACK
P.J.'s GAS
Certified Welding
EVERY-THING COOL?
WITH AGENT 355? I GUESS. SHE'S OFF ON SOME KIND OF MIDNIGHT SORTIE OR WHATEVER...BUT SHE WOULDN'T SAY WHERE.
355 ONLY EVER TELLS ME STUFF ON A "NEED-TO-KNOW" BASIS, WHICH IS APPARENTLY PRETTY FUCKING RARE, SEEING HOW I DON'T KNOW ANYTHING.
SO YOU REALLY HAVE NO CLUE WHY YOU AND ANDERSON SURVIVED THE PLAGUE?
IT'S AMPERSAND, ACTUALLY. THE THING ABOVE THE SEVEN ON A KEYBOARD? MY PUNCTUATION FETISH SHOWING.
AND YEAH, THAT'S THE WHODUNIT WE'RE HEADED TO DR. MANN'S LAB IN FRISCO TO SOLVE.
I MEAN, HOW ARE BOTH OF YOU STILL ALIVE? YOU THINK IT WAS SOMETHING IN YOUR DIETS?
HM, NOT A LOT OF OVERLAP THERE. HE HATES RAY'S FAMOUS, AND I HAVE PHALLIC ISSUES WITH BANANAS...

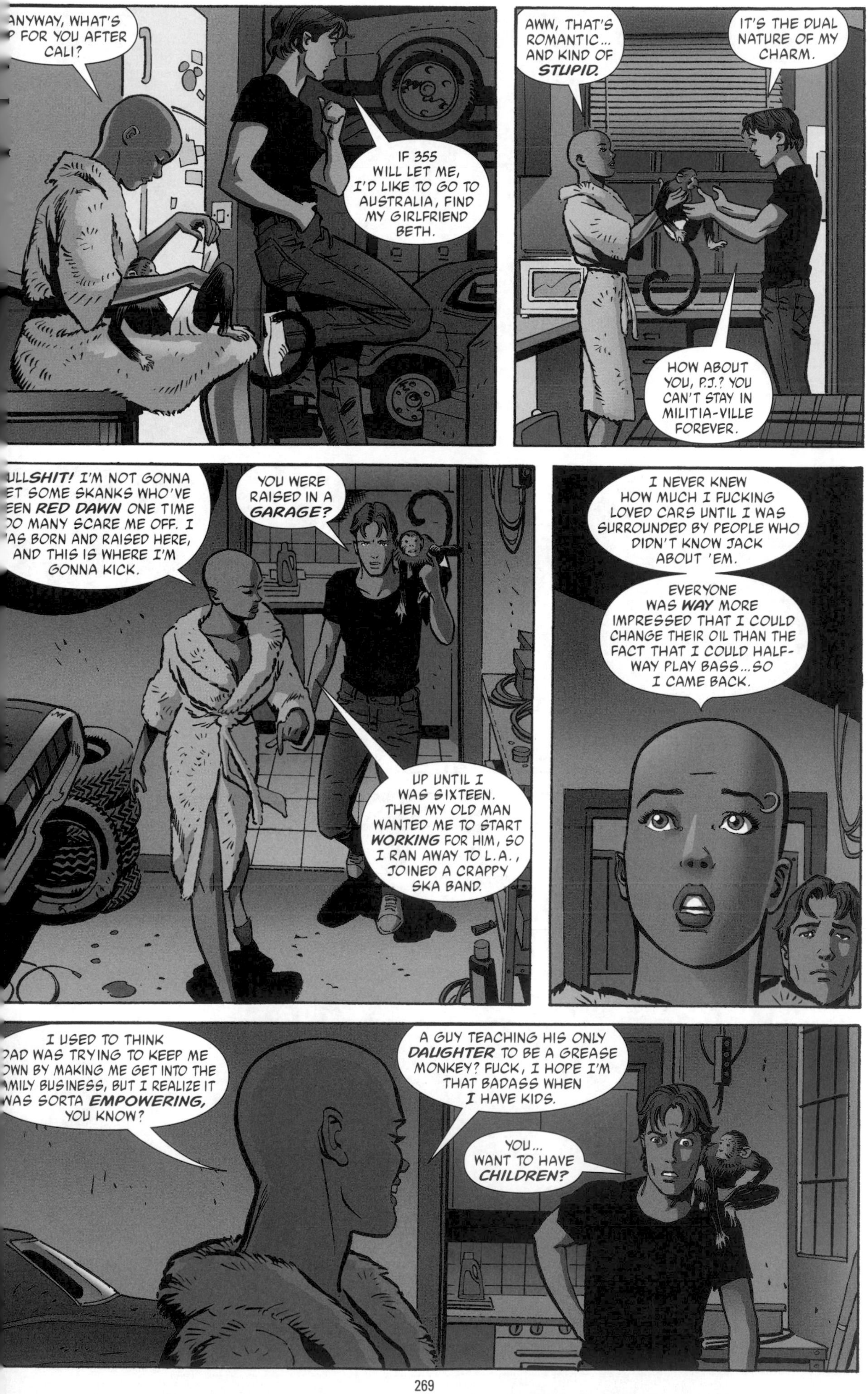

ANYWAY, WHAT'S P FOR YOU AFTER CALI?
IF 355 WILL LET ME, I'D LIKE TO GO TO AUSTRALIA, FIND MY GIRLFRIEND BETH.
AWW, THAT'S ROMANTIC... AND KIND OF STUPID.
IT'S THE DUAL NATURE OF MY CHARM.
HOW ABOUT YOU, P.J.? YOU CAN'T STAY IN MILITIA-VILLE FOREVER.
ULLSHIT! I'M NOT GONNA ET SOME SKANKS WHO'VE EEN RED DAWN ONE TIME OO MANY SCARE ME OFF. I 'AS BORN AND RAISED HERE, AND THIS IS WHERE I'M GONNA KICK.
YOU WERE RAISED IN A GARAGE?
UP UNTIL I WAS SIXTEEN. THEN MY OLD MAN WANTED ME TO START WORKING FOR HIM, SO I RAN AWAY TO L.A., JOINED A CRAPPY SKA BAND.
I NEVER KNEW HOW MUCH I FUCKING LOVED CARS UNTIL I WAS SURROUNDED BY PEOPLE WHO DIDN'T KNOW JACK ABOUT 'EM.
EVERYONE WAS WAY MORE IMPRESSED THAT I COULD CHANGE THEIR OIL THAN THE FACT THAT I COULD HALF-WAY PLAY BASS... SO I CAME BACK.
I USED TO THINK AD WAS TRYING TO KEEP ME OWN BY MAKING ME GET INTO THE AMILY BUSINESS, BUT I REALIZE IT WAS SORTA EMPOWERING, YOU KNOW?
A GUY TEACHING HIS ONLY DAUGHTER TO BE A GREASE MONKEY? FUCK, I HOPE I'M THAT BADASS WHEN I HAVE KIDS.
YOU... WANT TO HAVE CHILDREN?

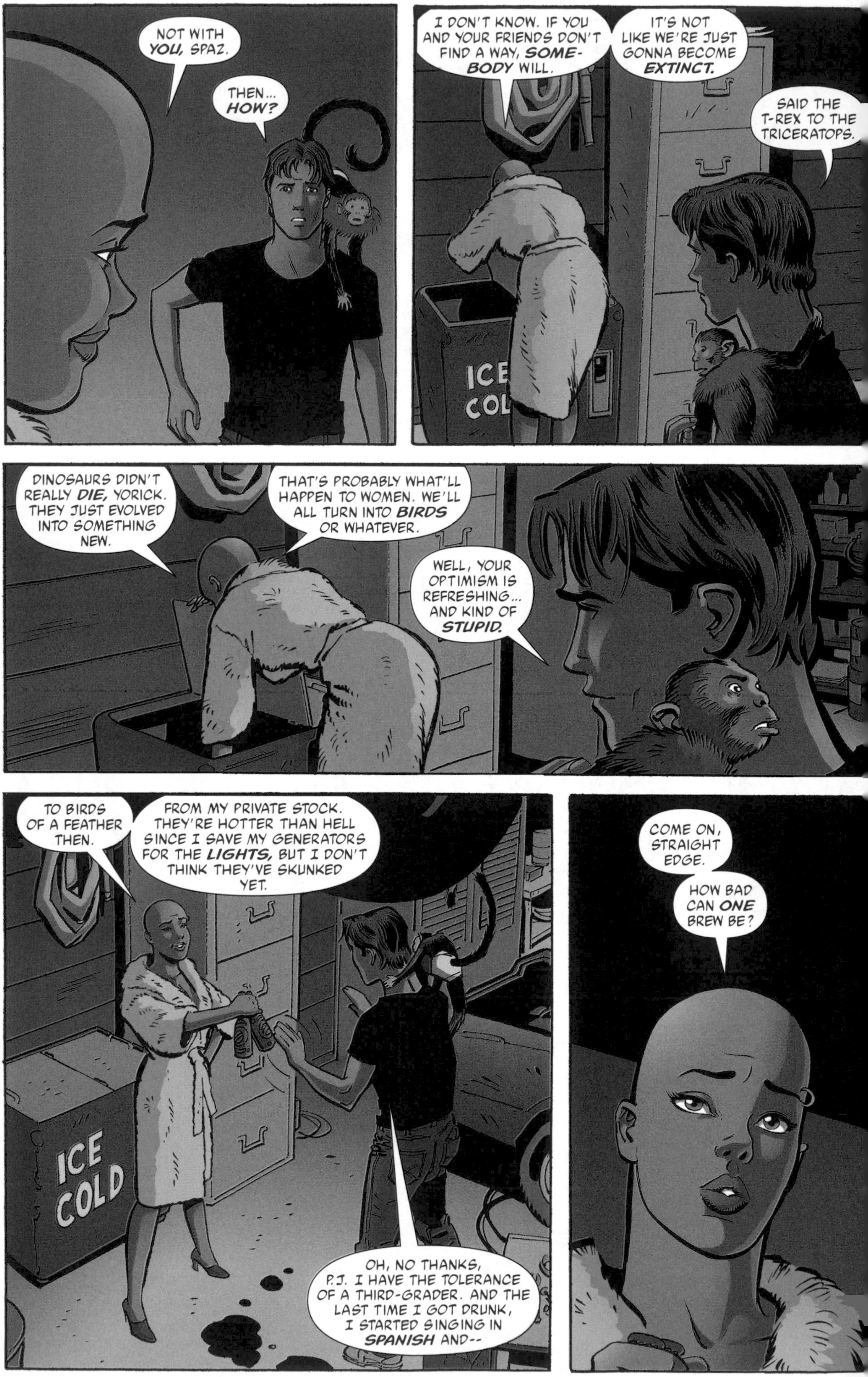
NOT WITH YOU, SPAZ.
THEN... HOW?
I DON'T KNOW. IF YOU AND YOUR FRIENDS DON'T FIND A WAY, SOMEBODY WILL.
IT'S NOT LIKE WE'RE JUST GONNA BECOME EXTINCT.
SAID THE T-REX TO THE TRICERATOPS.
ICE COL
DINOSAURS DIDN'T REALLY DIE, YORICK. THEY JUST EVOLVED INTO SOMETHING NEW.
THAT'S PROBABLY WHAT'LL HAPPEN TO WOMEN. WE'LL ALL TURN INTO BIRDS OR WHATEVER.
WELL, YOUR OPTIMISM IS REFRESHING... AND KIND OF STUPID.
TO BIRDS OF A FEATHER THEN.
FROM MY PRIVATE STOCK. THEY'RE HOTTER THAN HELL SINCE I SAVE MY GENERATORS FOR THE LIGHTS, BUT I DON'T THINK THEY'VE SKUNKED YET.
ICE COLD
OH, NO THANKS, P.J. I HAVE THE TOLERANCE OF A THIRD-GRADER. AND THE LAST TIME I GOT DRUNK, I STARTED SINGING IN SPANISH AND--
COME ON, STRAIGHT EDGE.
HOW BAD CAN ONE BREW BE?

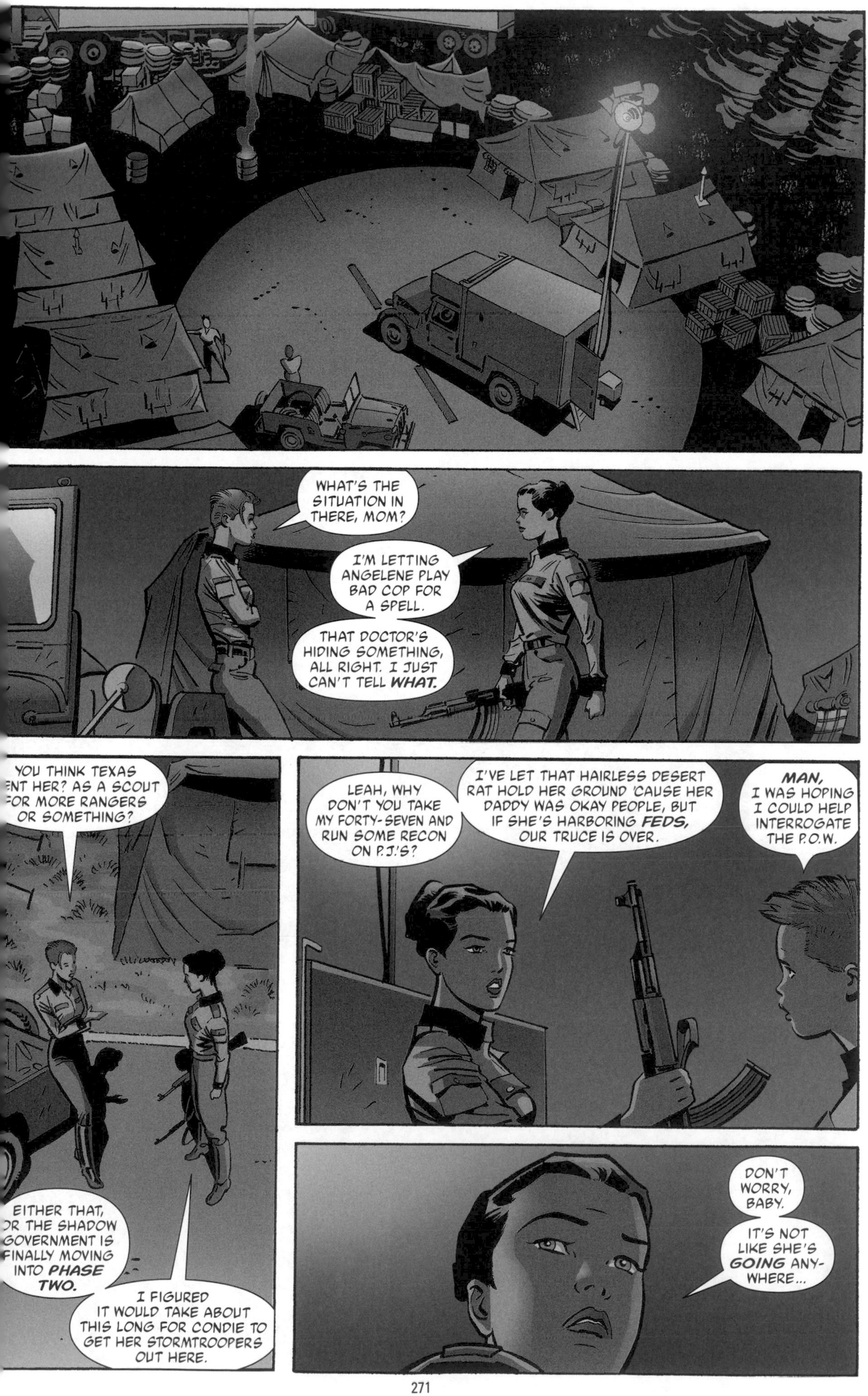
WHAT'S THE SITUATION IN THERE, MOM?
I'M LETTING ANGELENE PLAY BAD COP FOR A SPELL.
THAT DOCTOR'S HIDING SOMETHING, ALL RIGHT. I JUST CAN'T TELL **WHAT.**
YOU THINK TEXAS ENT HER? AS A SCOUT FOR MORE RANGERS OR SOMETHING?
EITHER THAT, OR THE SHADOW GOVERNMENT IS FINALLY MOVING INTO **PHASE TWO.**
I FIGURED IT WOULD TAKE ABOUT THIS LONG FOR CONDIE TO GET HER STORMTROOPERS OUT HERE.
LEAH, WHY DON'T YOU TAKE MY FORTY-SEVEN AND RUN SOME RECON ON P.J.'S?
I'VE LET THAT HAIRLESS DESERT RAT HOLD HER GROUND 'CAUSE HER DADDY WAS OKAY PEOPLE, BUT IF SHE'S HARBORING **FEDS,** OUR TRUCE IS OVER.
MAN, I WAS HOPING I COULD HELP INTERROGATE THE P.O.W.
DON'T WORRY, BABY.
IT'S NOT LIKE SHE'S **GOING** ANYWHERE...

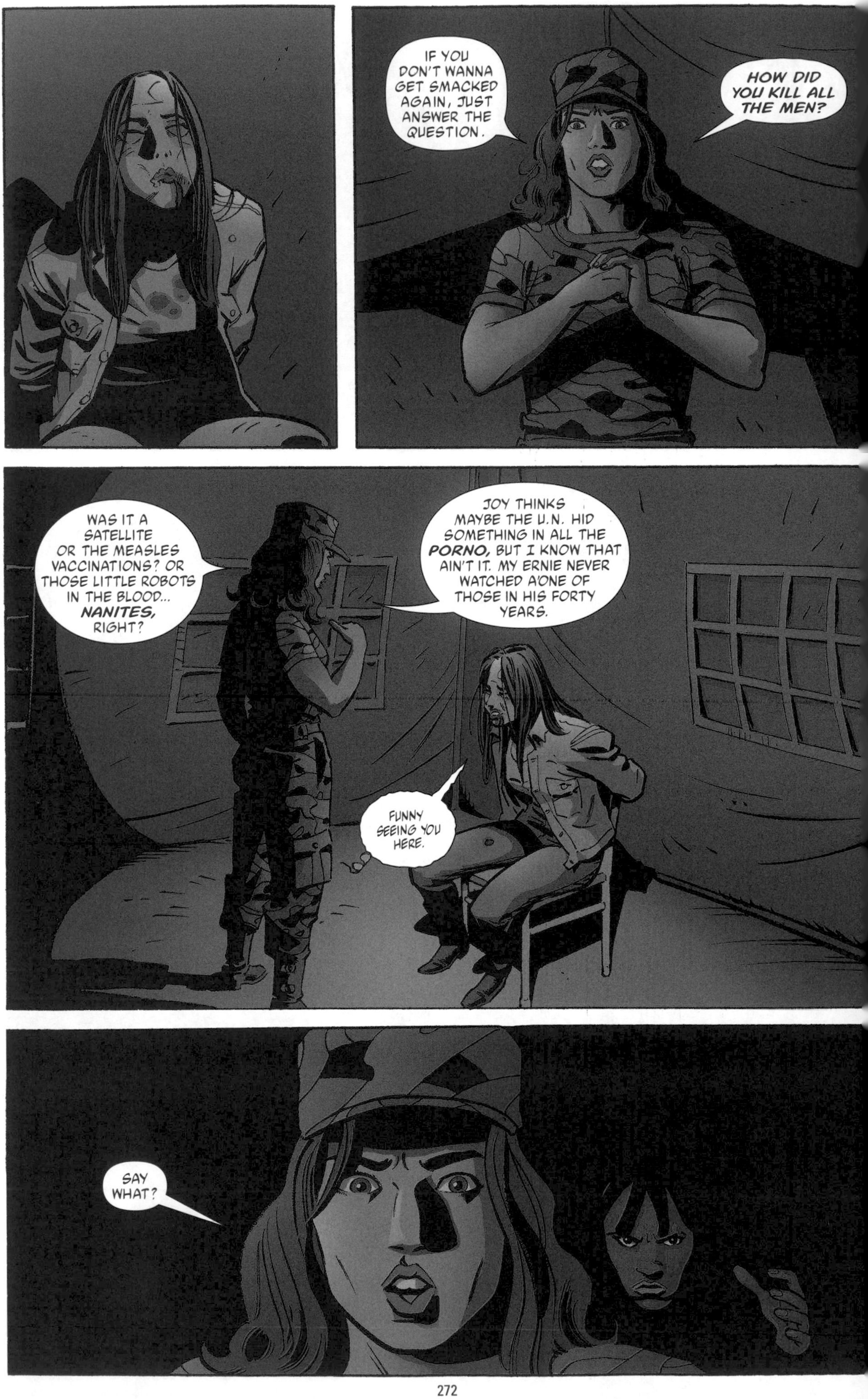

IF YOU DON'T WANNA GET SMACKED AGAIN, JUST ANSWER THE QUESTION.
HOW DID YOU KILL ALL THE MEN?
WAS IT A SATELLITE OR THE MEASLES VACCINATIONS? OR THOSE LITTLE ROBOTS IN THE BLOOD... NANITES, RIGHT?
JOY THINKS MAYBE THE U.N. HID SOMETHING IN ALL THE PORNO, BUT I KNOW THAT AIN'T IT. MY ERNIE NEVER WATCHED A'ONE OF THOSE IN HIS FORTY YEARS.
FUNNY SEEING YOU HERE.
SAY WHAT?

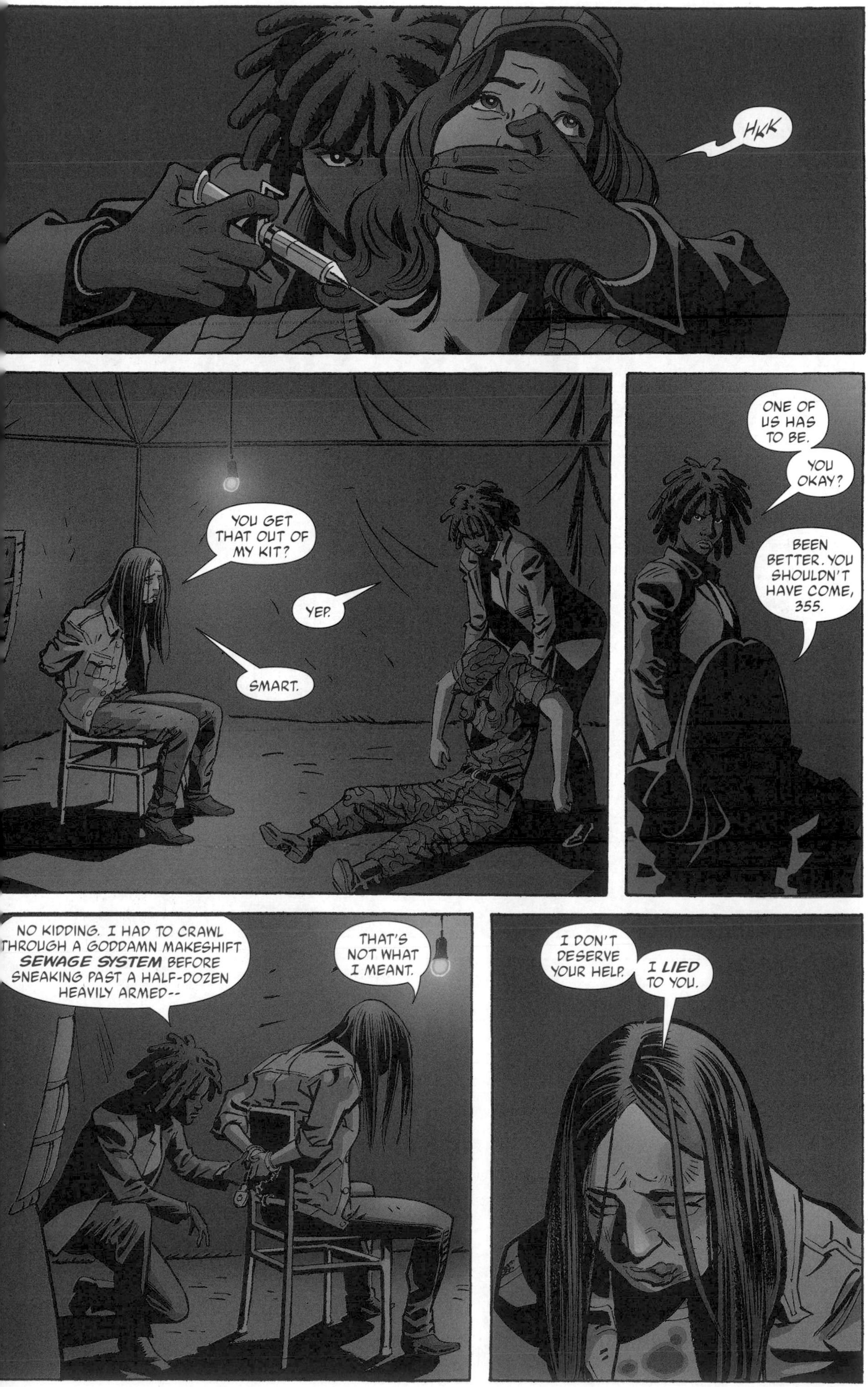
HKK
YOU GET THAT OUT OF MY KIT?
YEP.
SMART.
ONE OF US HAS TO BE.
YOU OKAY?
BEEN BETTER. YOU SHOULDN'T HAVE COME, 355.
NO KIDDING. I HAD TO CRAWL THROUGH A GODDAMN MAKESHIFT SEWAGE SYSTEM BEFORE SNEAKING PAST A HALF-DOZEN HEAVILY ARMED--
THAT'S NOT WHAT I MEANT.
I DON'T DESERVE YOUR HELP.
I LIED TO YOU.

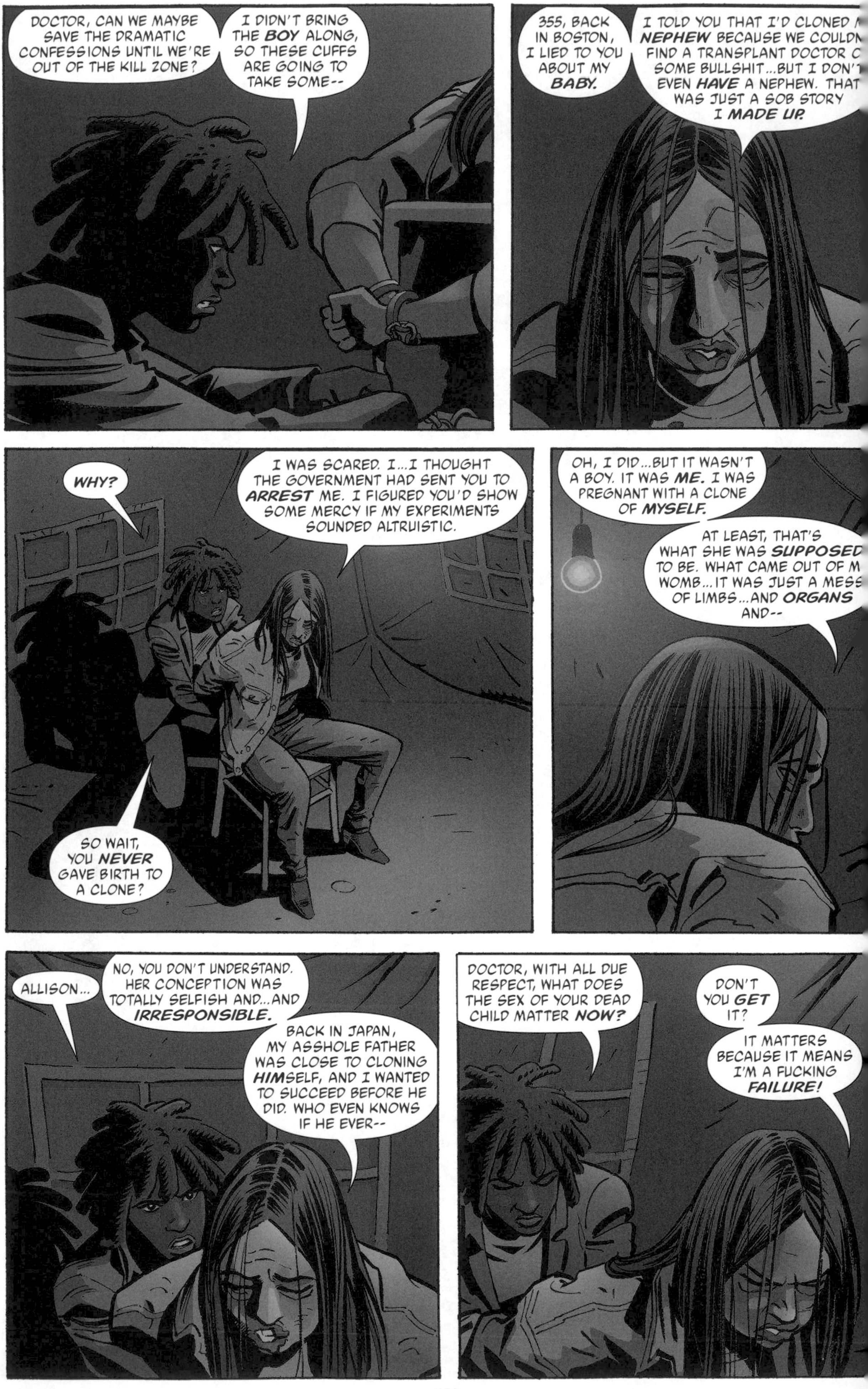

DOCTOR, CAN WE MAYBE SAVE THE DRAMATIC CONFESSIONS UNTIL WE'RE OUT OF THE KILL ZONE?
I DIDN'T BRING THE BOY ALONG, SO THESE CUFFS ARE GOING TO TAKE SOME--
355, BACK IN BOSTON, I LIED TO YOU ABOUT MY BABY.
I TOLD YOU THAT I'D CLONED M NEPHEW BECAUSE WE COULDN FIND A TRANSPLANT DOCTOR C SOME BULLSHIT...BUT I DON'T EVEN HAVE A NEPHEW. THAT WAS JUST A SOB STORY I MADE UP.
WHY?
I WAS SCARED. I...I THOUGHT THE GOVERNMENT HAD SENT YOU TO ARREST ME. I FIGURED YOU'D SHOW SOME MERCY IF MY EXPERIMENTS SOUNDED ALTRUISTIC.
SO WAIT, YOU NEVER GAVE BIRTH TO A CLONE?
OH, I DID...BUT IT WASN'T A BOY. IT WAS ME. I WAS PREGNANT WITH A CLONE OF MYSELF.
AT LEAST, THAT'S WHAT SHE WAS SUPPOSED TO BE. WHAT CAME OUT OF M WOMB...IT WAS JUST A MESS OF LIMBS...AND ORGANS AND--
ALLISON...
NO, YOU DON'T UNDERSTAND. HER CONCEPTION WAS TOTALLY SELFISH AND...AND IRRESPONSIBLE.
BACK IN JAPAN, MY ASSHOLE FATHER WAS CLOSE TO CLONING HIMSELF, AND I WANTED TO SUCCEED BEFORE HE DID. WHO EVEN KNOWS IF HE EVER--
DOCTOR, WITH ALL DUE RESPECT, WHAT DOES THE SEX OF YOUR DEAD CHILD MATTER NOW?
DON'T YOU GET IT?
IT MATTERS BECAUSE IT MEANS I'M A FUCKING FAILURE!

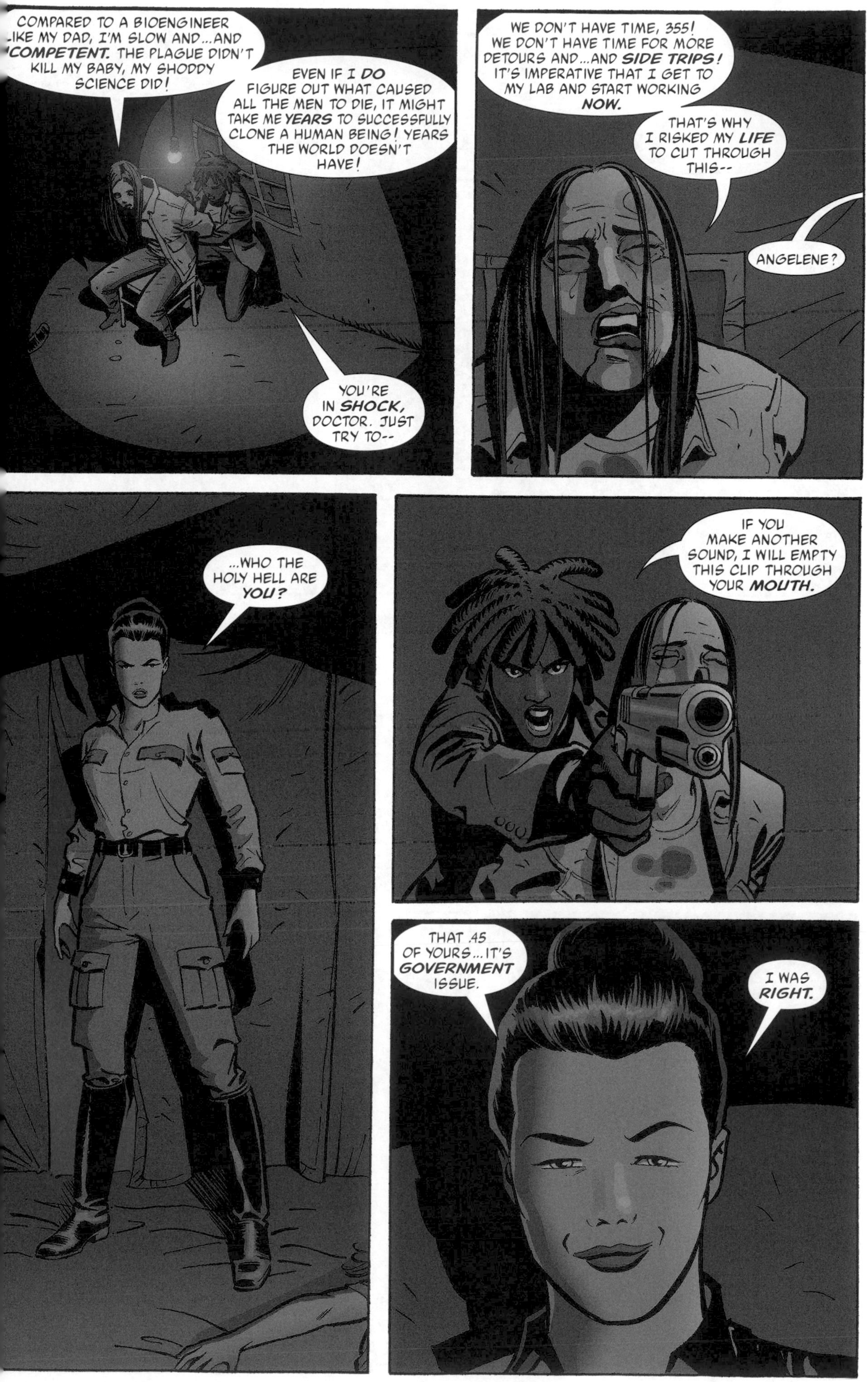
COMPARED TO A BIOENGINEER
IKE MY DAD, I'M SLOW AND...AND
COMPETENT. THE PLAGUE DIDN'T KILL MY BABY, MY SHODDY SCIENCE DID!
EVEN IF I DO FIGURE OUT WHAT CAUSED ALL THE MEN TO DIE, IT MIGHT TAKE ME YEARS TO SUCCESSFULLY CLONE A HUMAN BEING! YEARS THE WORLD DOESN'T HAVE!
YOU'RE IN SHOCK, DOCTOR. JUST TRY TO--
WE DON'T HAVE TIME, 355! WE DON'T HAVE TIME FOR MORE DETOURS AND...AND SIDE TRIPS! IT'S IMPERATIVE THAT I GET TO MY LAB AND START WORKING NOW.
THAT'S WHY I RISKED MY LIFE TO CUT THROUGH THIS--
ANGELENE?
...WHO THE HOLY HELL ARE YOU?
IF YOU MAKE ANOTHER SOUND, I WILL EMPTY THIS CLIP THROUGH YOUR MOUTH.
THAT .45 OF YOURS...IT'S GOVERNMENT ISSUE.
I WAS RIGHT.

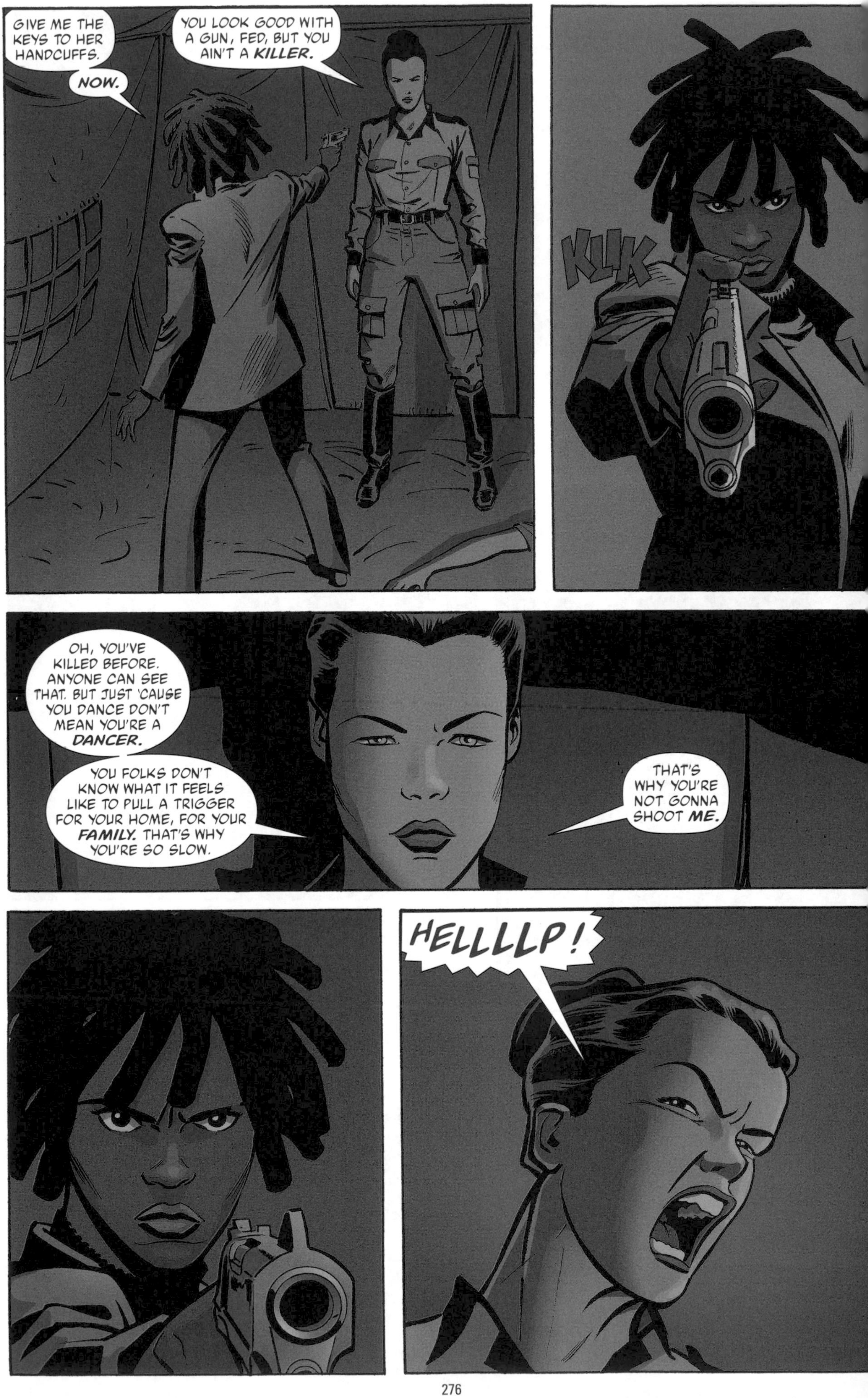
GIVE ME THE KEYS TO HER HANDCUFFS.
NOW.
YOU LOOK GOOD WITH A GUN, FED, BUT YOU AIN'T A KILLER.
KLIK
OH, YOU'VE KILLED BEFORE. ANYONE CAN SEE THAT. BUT JUST 'CAUSE YOU DANCE DON'T MEAN YOU'RE A DANCER.
YOU FOLKS DON'T KNOW WHAT IT FEELS LIKE TO PULL A TRIGGER FOR YOUR HOME, FOR YOUR FAMILY. THAT'S WHY YOU'RE SO SLOW.
THAT'S WHY YOU'RE NOT GONNA SHOOT ME.
HELLLLP!

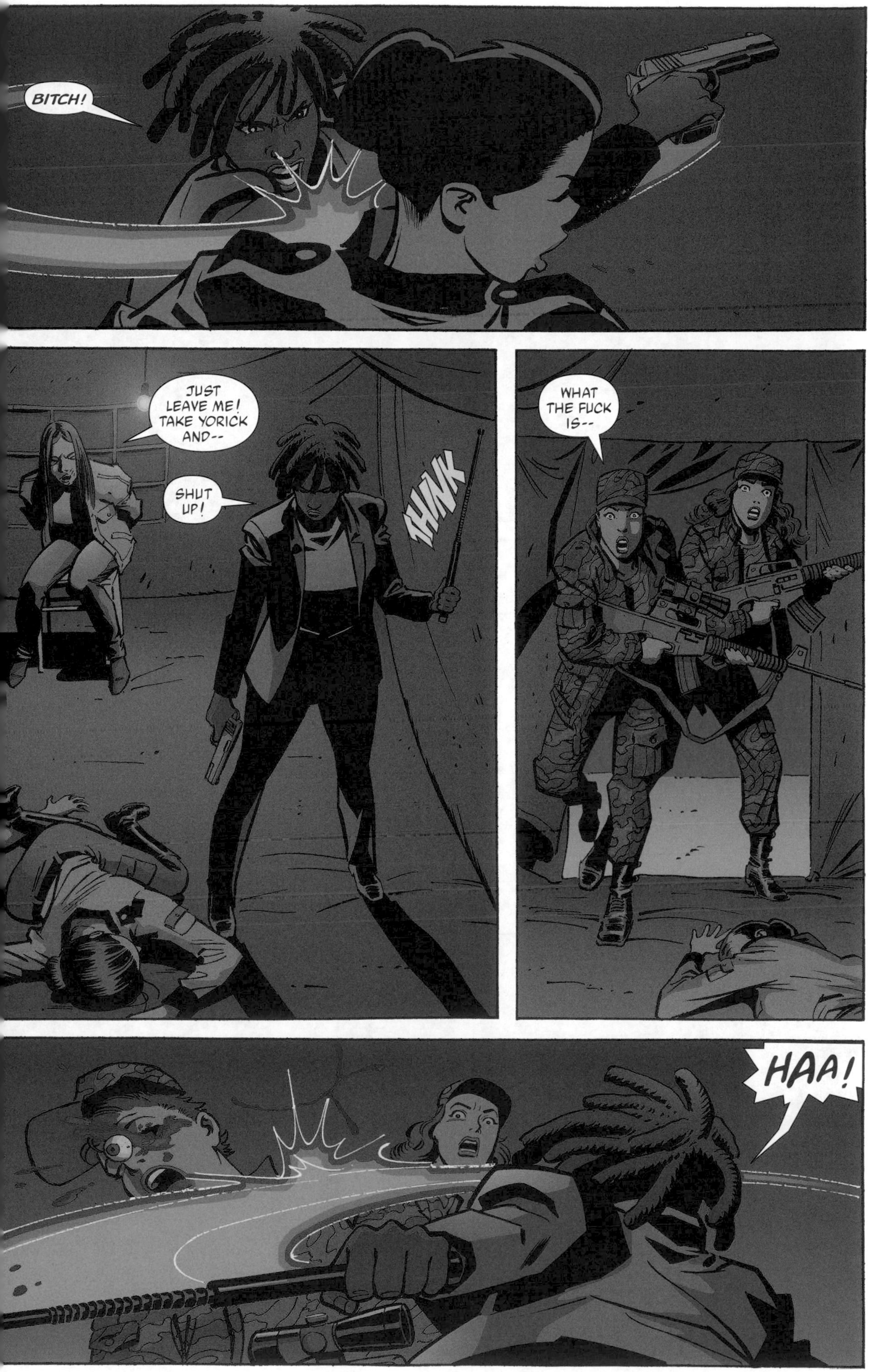
BITCH!
JUST LEAVE ME! TAKE YORICK AND--
SHUT UP!
THINK
WHAT THE FUCK IS--
HAA!

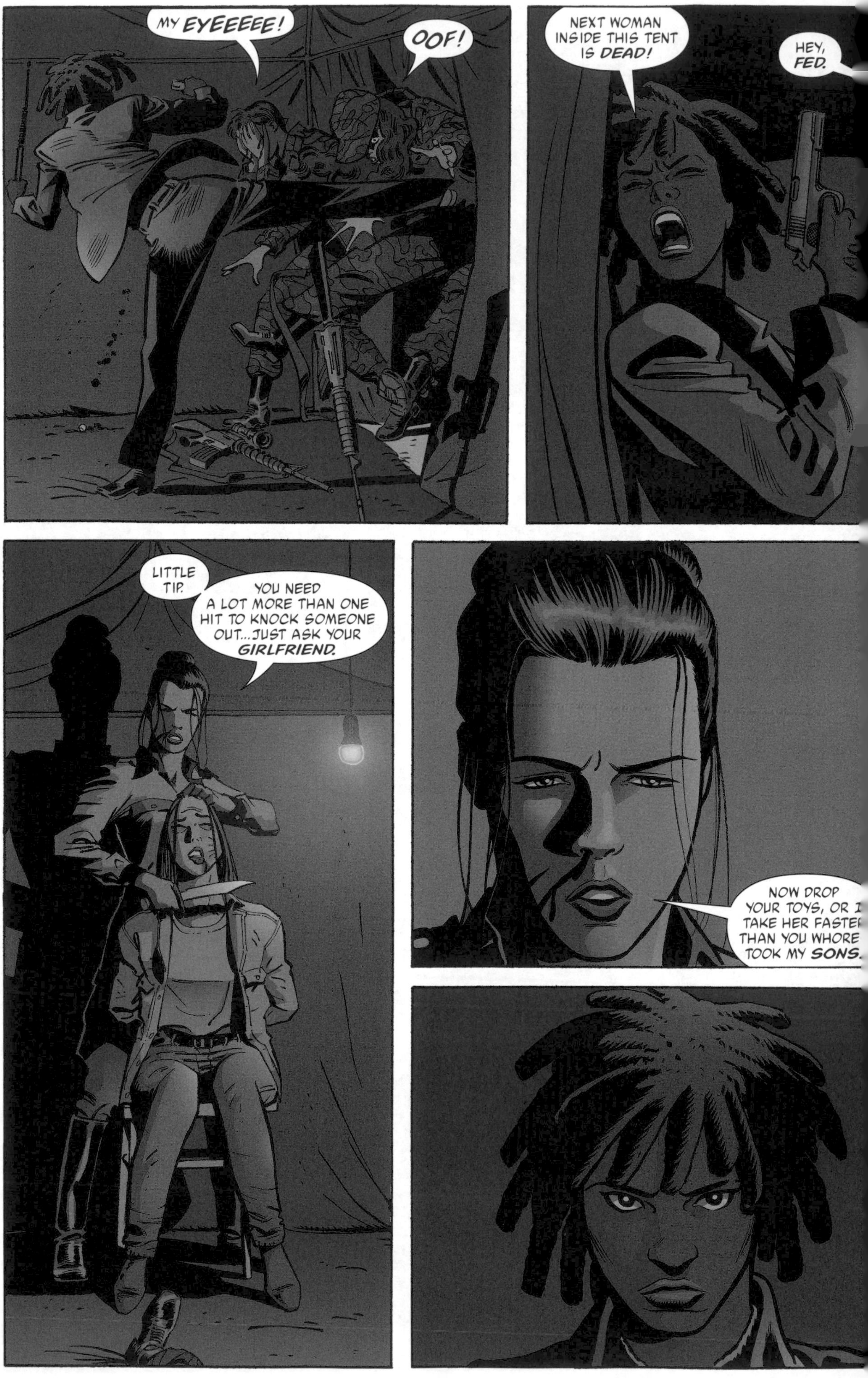
MY EYEEEEE!
OOF!
NEXT WOMAN INSIDE THIS TENT IS DEAD!
HEY, FED.
LITTLE TIP.
YOU NEED A LOT MORE THAN ONE HIT TO KNOCK SOMEONE OUT...JUST ASK YOUR GIRLFRIEND.
NOW DROP YOUR TOYS, OR I TAKE HER FASTER THAN YOU WHORE TOOK MY SONS.

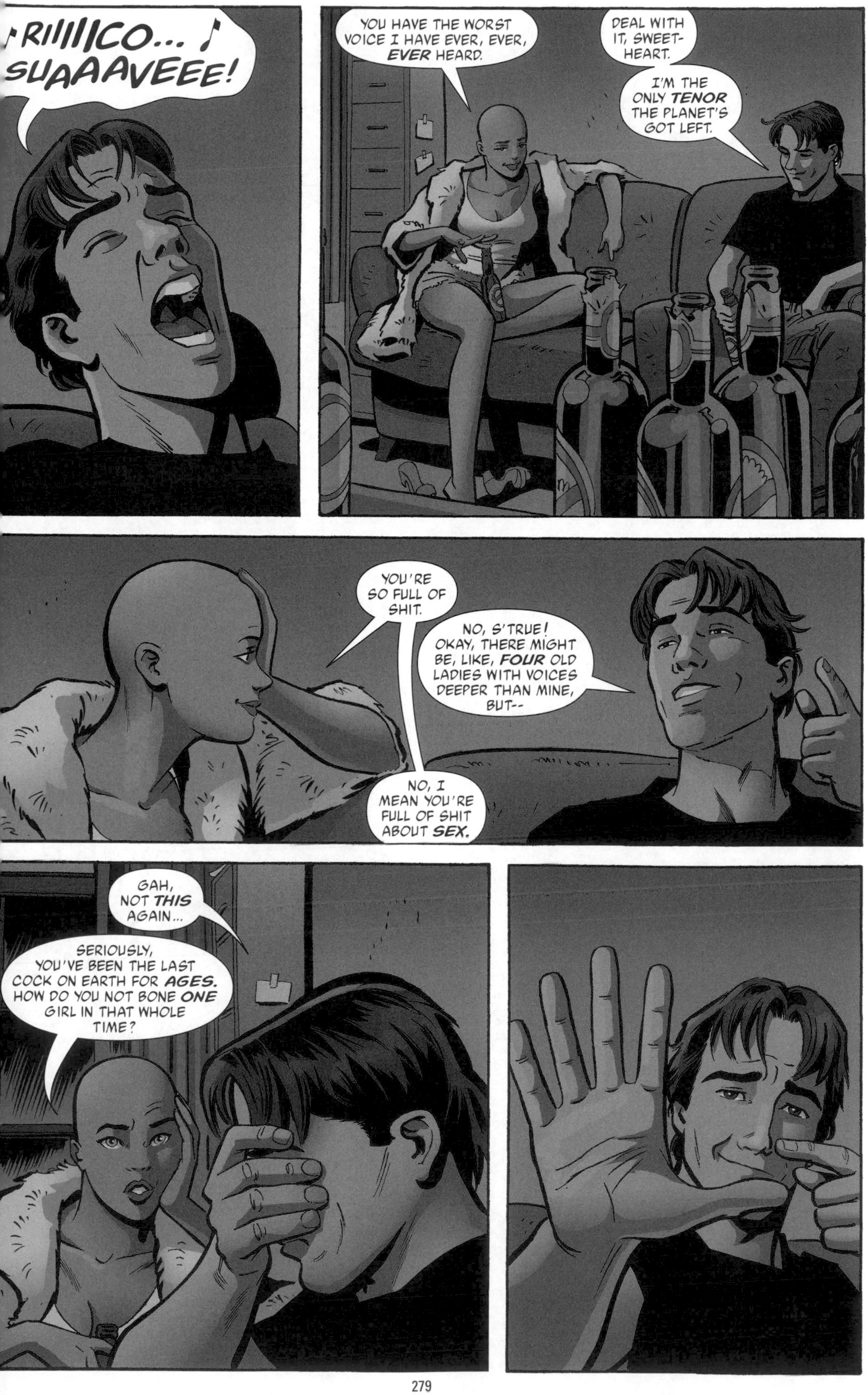
♪ RIIIIICO... ♪ SUAAAVEEE!
YOU HAVE THE WORST VOICE I HAVE EVER, EVER, EVER HEARD.
DEAL WITH IT, SWEET-HEART.
I'M THE ONLY TENOR THE PLANET'S GOT LEFT.
YOU'RE SO FULL OF SHIT.
NO, S'TRUE! OKAY, THERE MIGHT BE, LIKE, FOUR OLD LADIES WITH VOICES DEEPER THAN MINE, BUT--
NO, I MEAN YOU'RE FULL OF SHIT ABOUT SEX.
GAH, NOT THIS AGAIN...
SERIOUSLY, YOU'VE BEEN THE LAST COCK ON EARTH FOR AGES. HOW DO YOU NOT BONE ONE GIRL IN THAT WHOLE TIME?

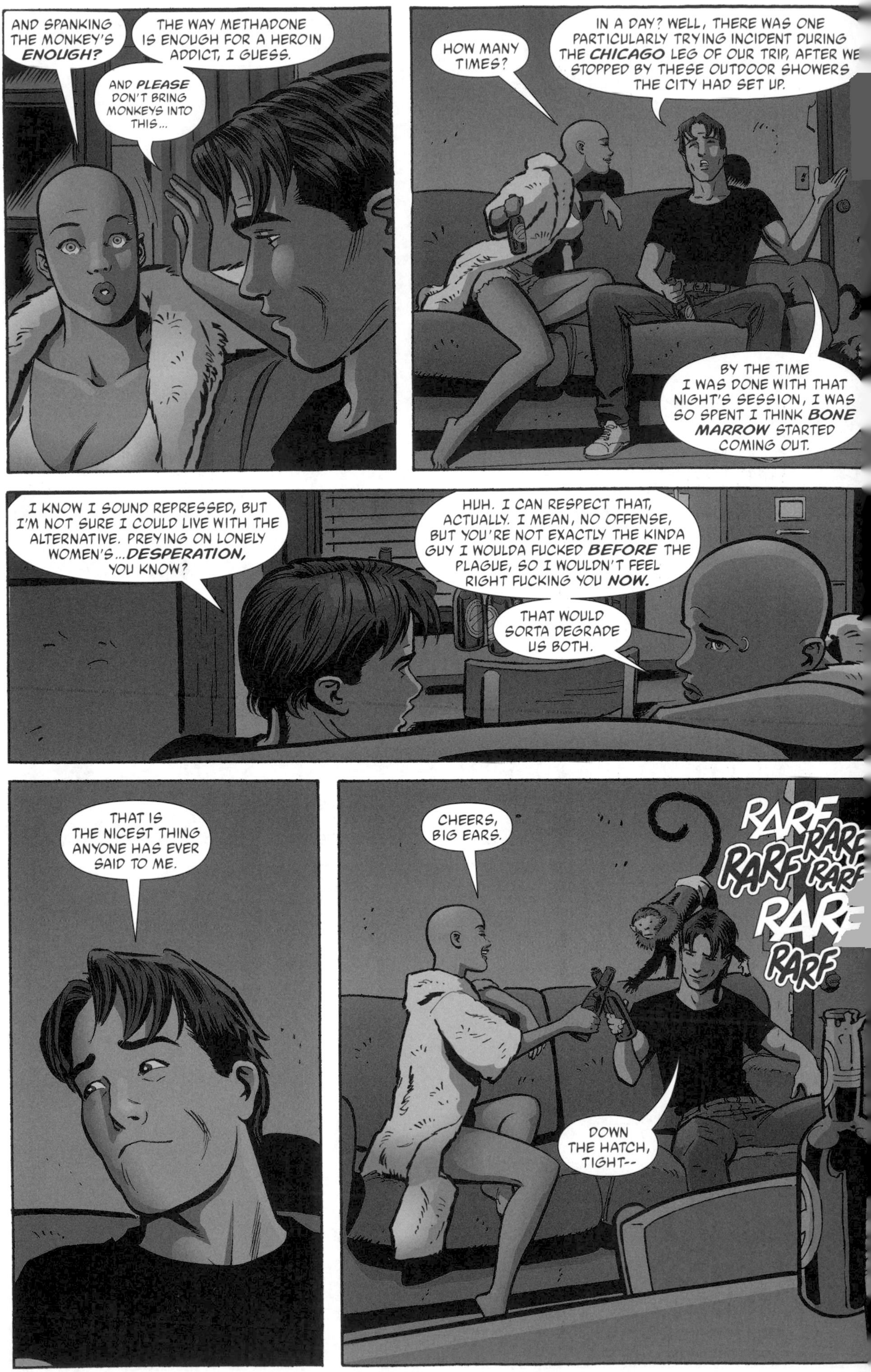
AND SPANKING THE MONKEY'S ENOUGH?
THE WAY METHADONE IS ENOUGH FOR A HEROIN ADDICT, I GUESS.
AND PLEASE DON'T BRING MONKEYS INTO THIS...
HOW MANY TIMES?
IN A DAY? WELL, THERE WAS ONE PARTICULARLY TRYING INCIDENT DURING THE CHICAGO LEG OF OUR TRIP, AFTER WE STOPPED BY THESE OUTDOOR SHOWERS THE CITY HAD SET UP.
BY THE TIME I WAS DONE WITH THAT NIGHT'S SESSION, I WAS SO SPENT I THINK BONE MARROW STARTED COMING OUT.
I KNOW I SOUND REPRESSED, BUT I'M NOT SURE I COULD LIVE WITH THE ALTERNATIVE. PREYING ON LONELY WOMEN'S...DESPERATION, YOU KNOW?
HUH. I CAN RESPECT THAT, ACTUALLY. I MEAN, NO OFFENSE, BUT YOU'RE NOT EXACTLY THE KINDA GUY I WOULDA FUCKED BEFORE THE PLAGUE, SO I WOULDN'T FEEL RIGHT FUCKING YOU NOW.
THAT WOULD SORTA DEGRADE US BOTH.
THAT IS THE NICEST THING ANYONE HAS EVER SAID TO ME.
CHEERS, BIG EARS.
RARF RARF RARF RARF RARF RARF
DOWN THE HATCH, TIGHT--

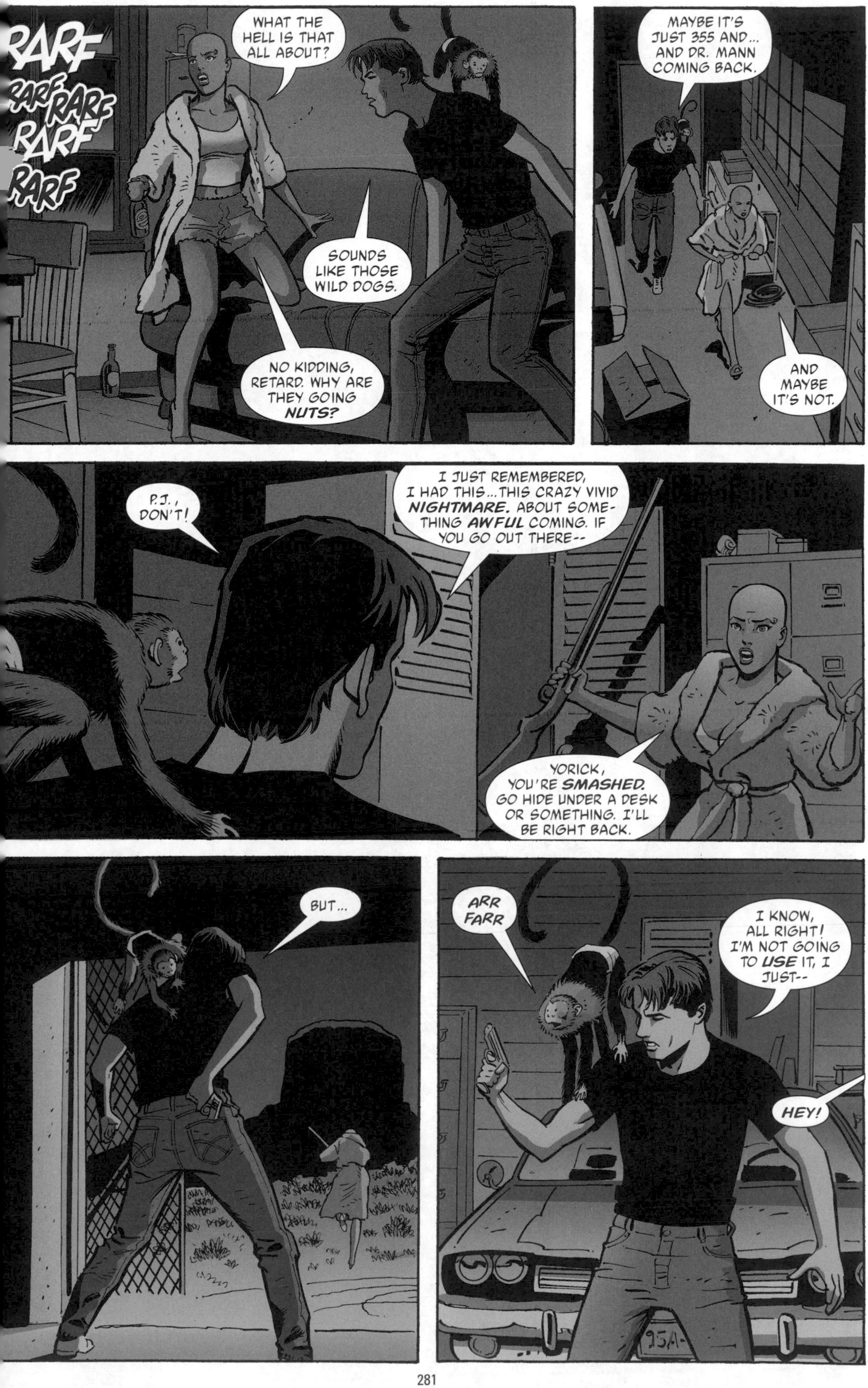
RARF RARF RARF RARF RARF
WHAT THE HELL IS THAT ALL ABOUT?
SOUNDS LIKE THOSE WILD DOGS.
NO KIDDING, RETARD. WHY ARE THEY GOING NUTS?
MAYBE IT'S JUST 355 AND... AND DR. MANN COMING BACK.
AND MAYBE IT'S NOT.
P.J., DON'T!
I JUST REMEMBERED, I HAD THIS...THIS CRAZY VIVID NIGHTMARE. ABOUT SOMETHING AWFUL COMING. IF YOU GO OUT THERE--
YORICK, YOU'RE SMASHED. GO HIDE UNDER A DESK OR SOMETHING. I'LL BE RIGHT BACK.
BUT...
ARR FARR
I KNOW, ALL RIGHT! I'M NOT GOING TO USE IT, I JUST--
HEY!

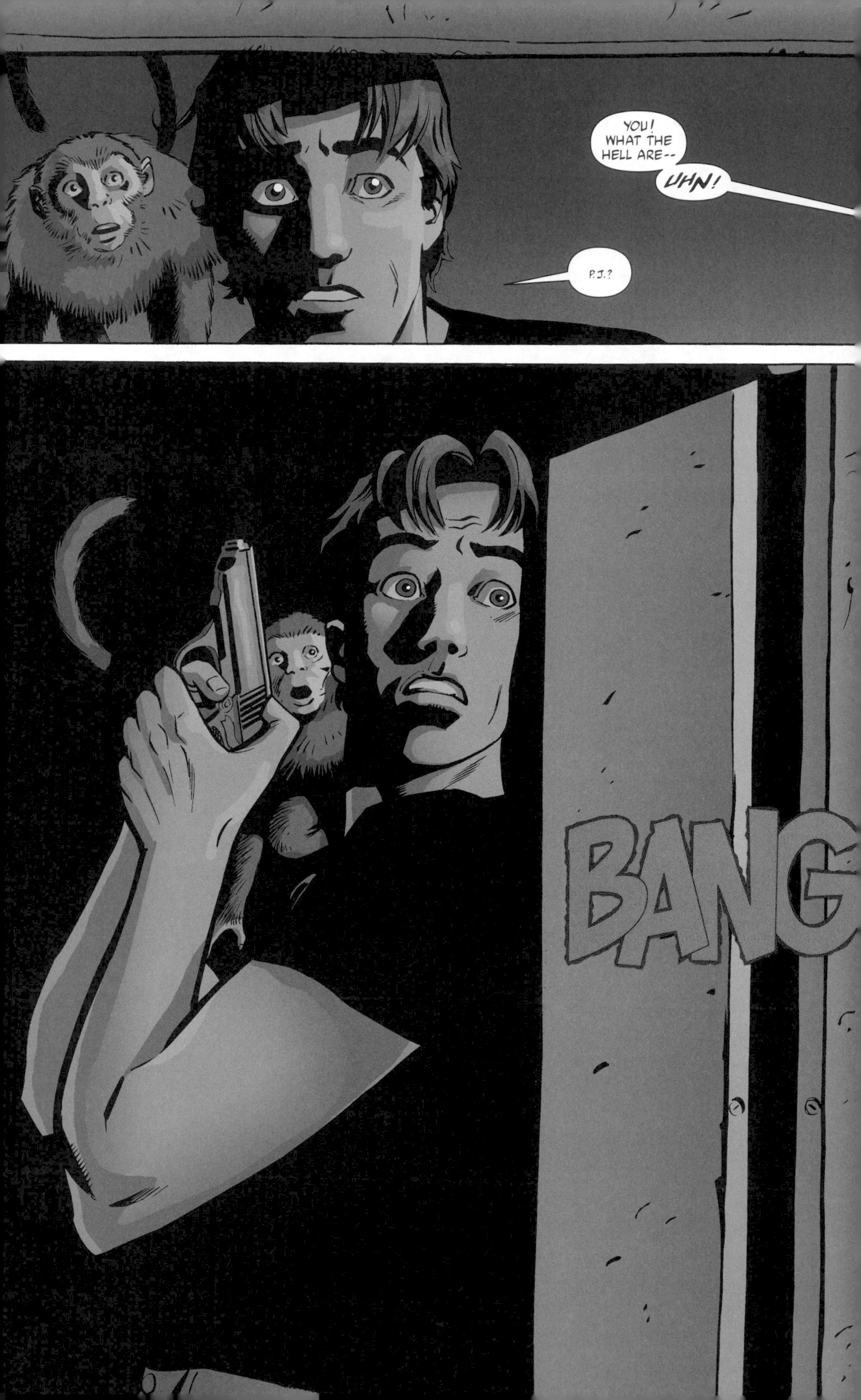
YOU! WHAT THE HELL ARE--
UHN!
P.J.?
BANG

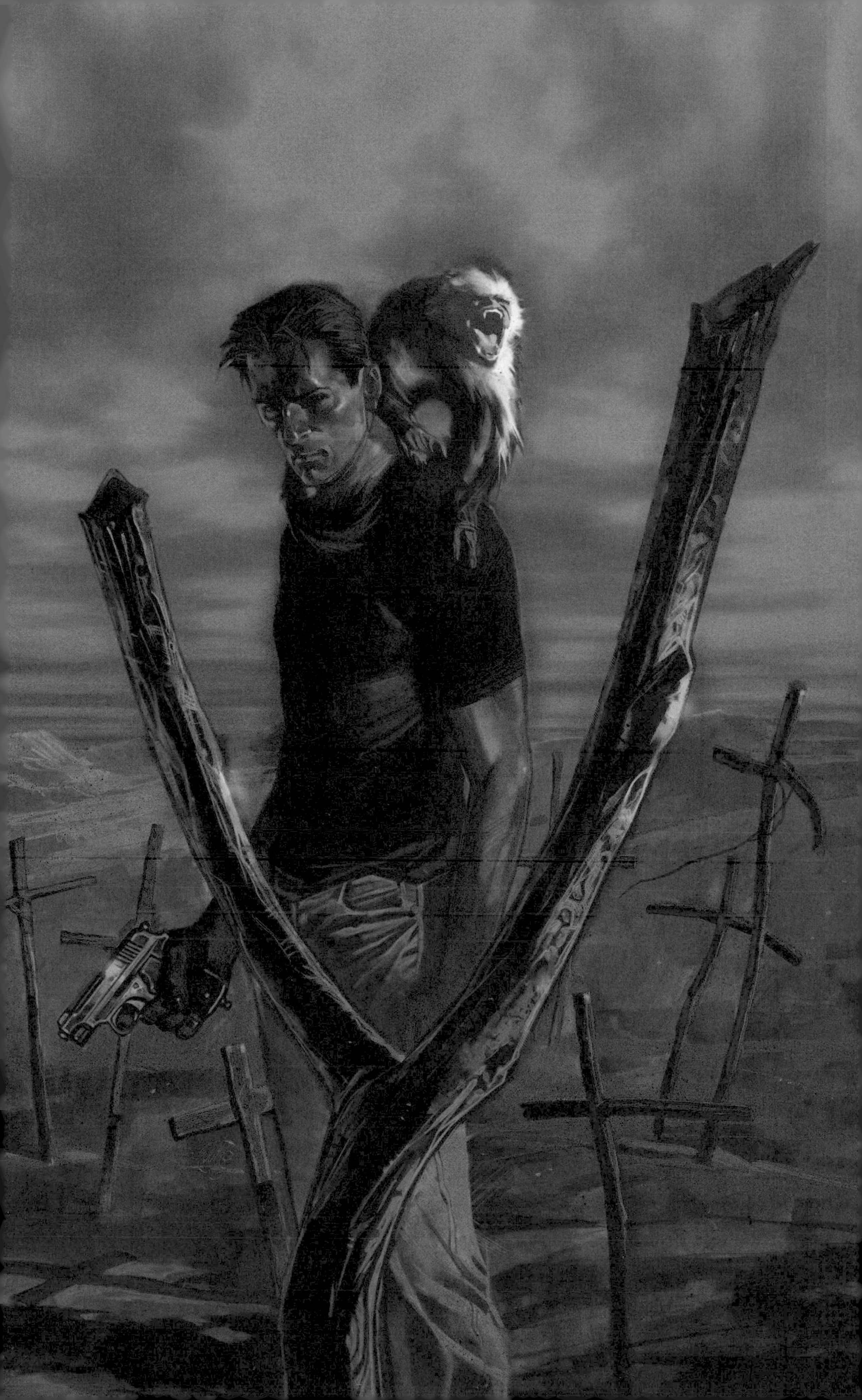

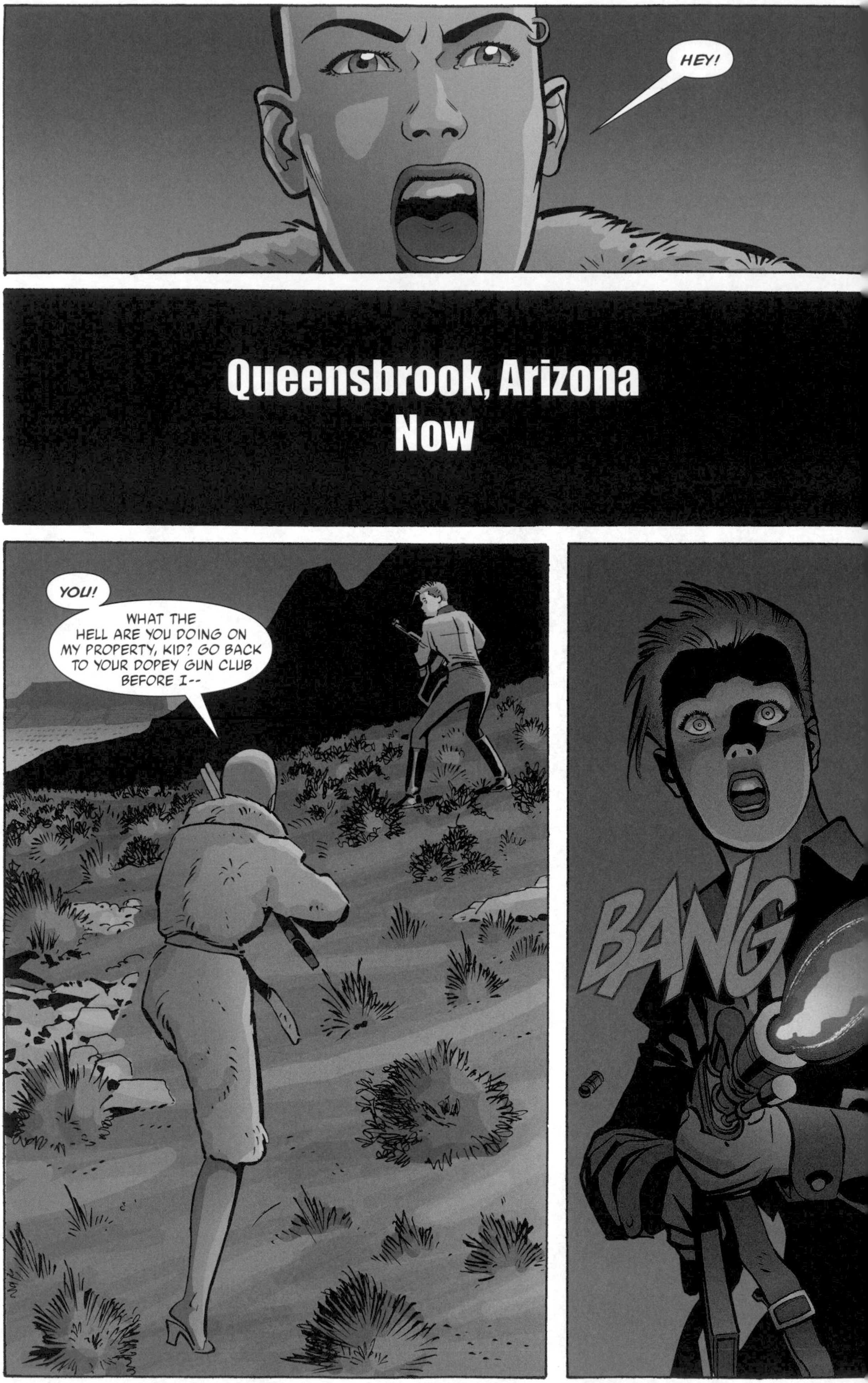
HEY!
Queensbrook, Arizona
Now
YOU!
WHAT THE HELL ARE YOU DOING ON MY PROPERTY, KID? GO BACK TO YOUR DOPEY GUN CLUB BEFORE I--
BANG

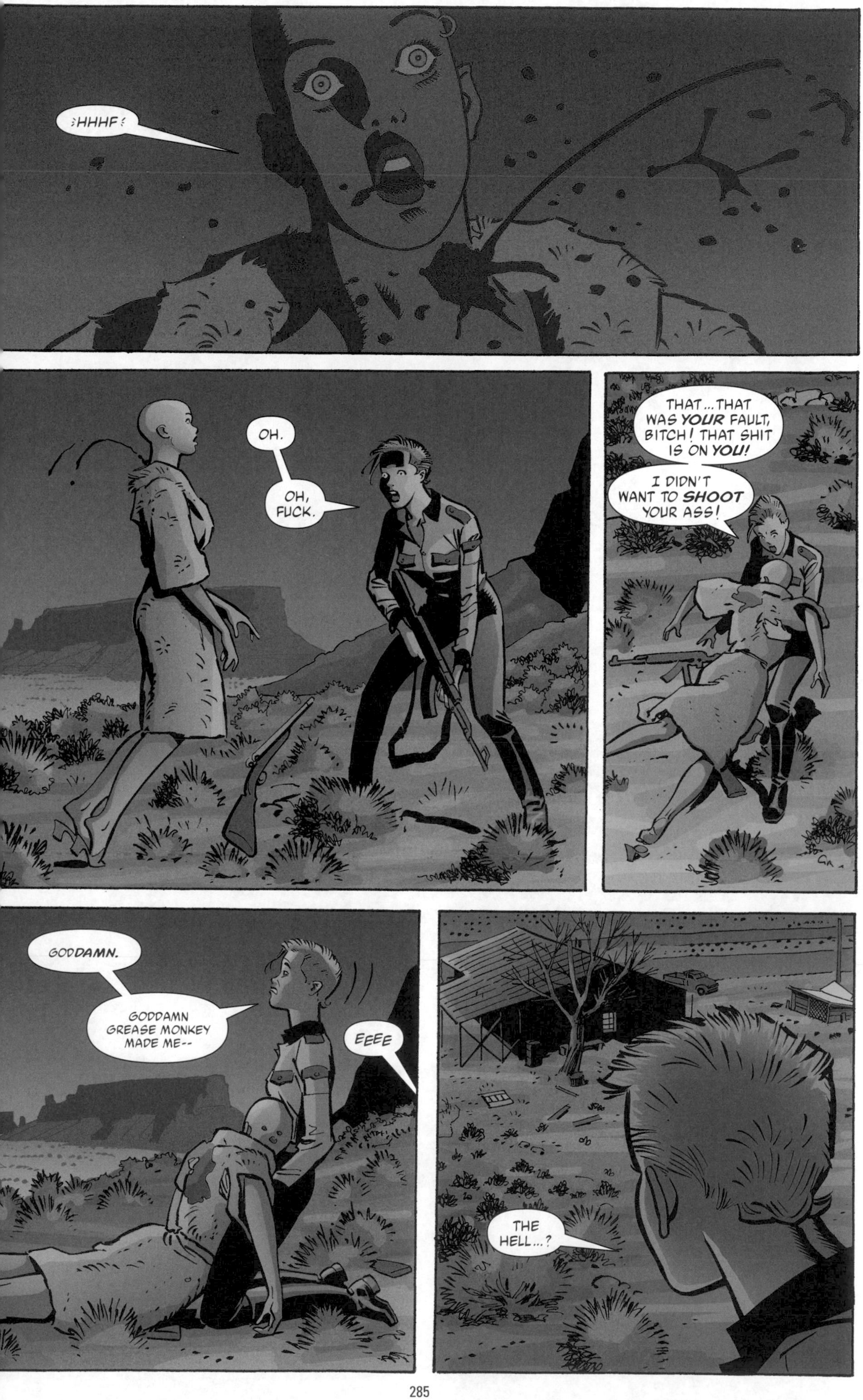
HHHF
OH.
OH, FUCK.
THAT...THAT WAS YOUR FAULT, BITCH! THAT SHIT IS ON YOU!
I DIDN'T WANT TO SHOOT YOUR ASS!
GODDAMN.
GODDAMN GREASE MONKEY MADE ME--
EEEE
THE HELL...?

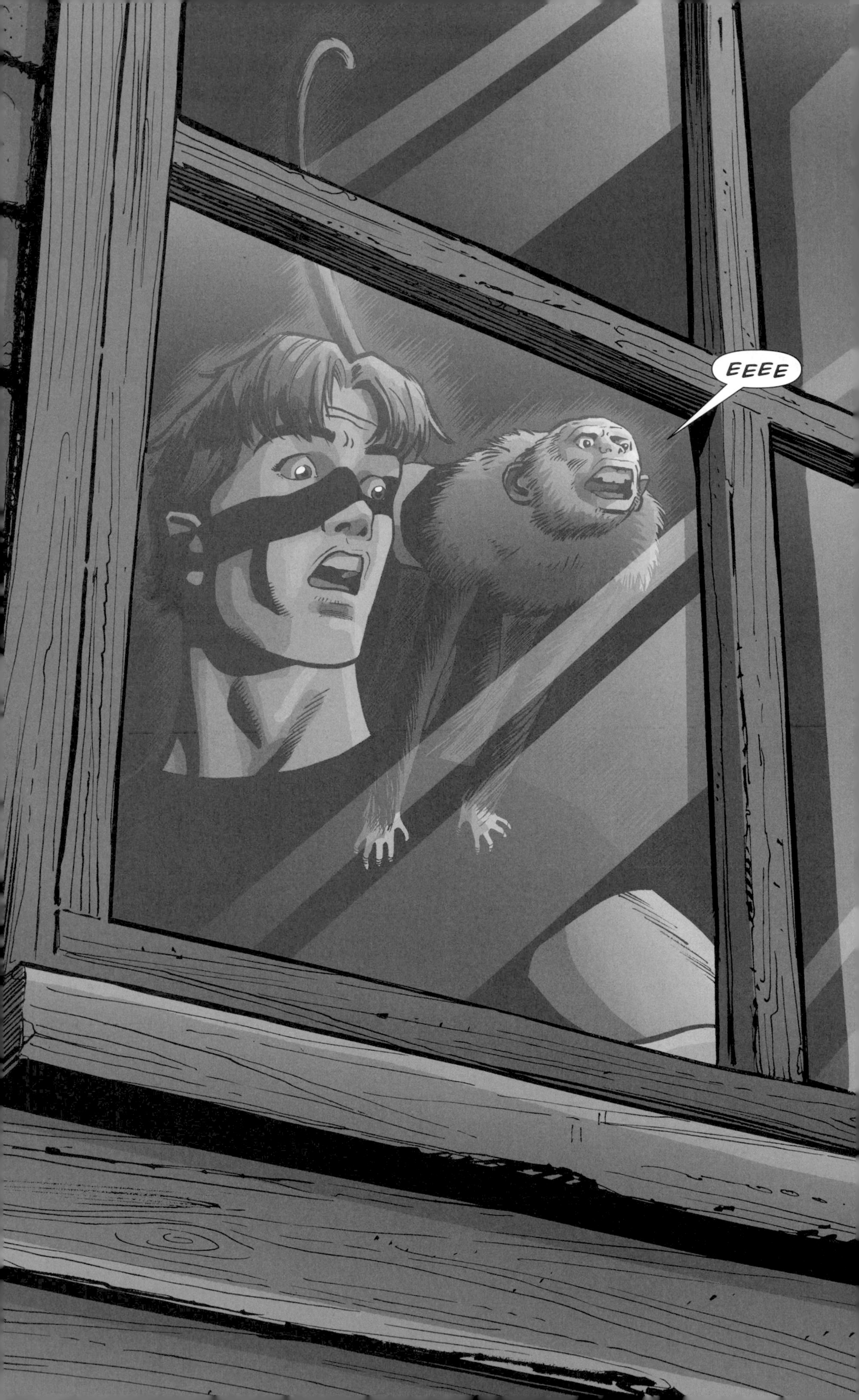
EEEE

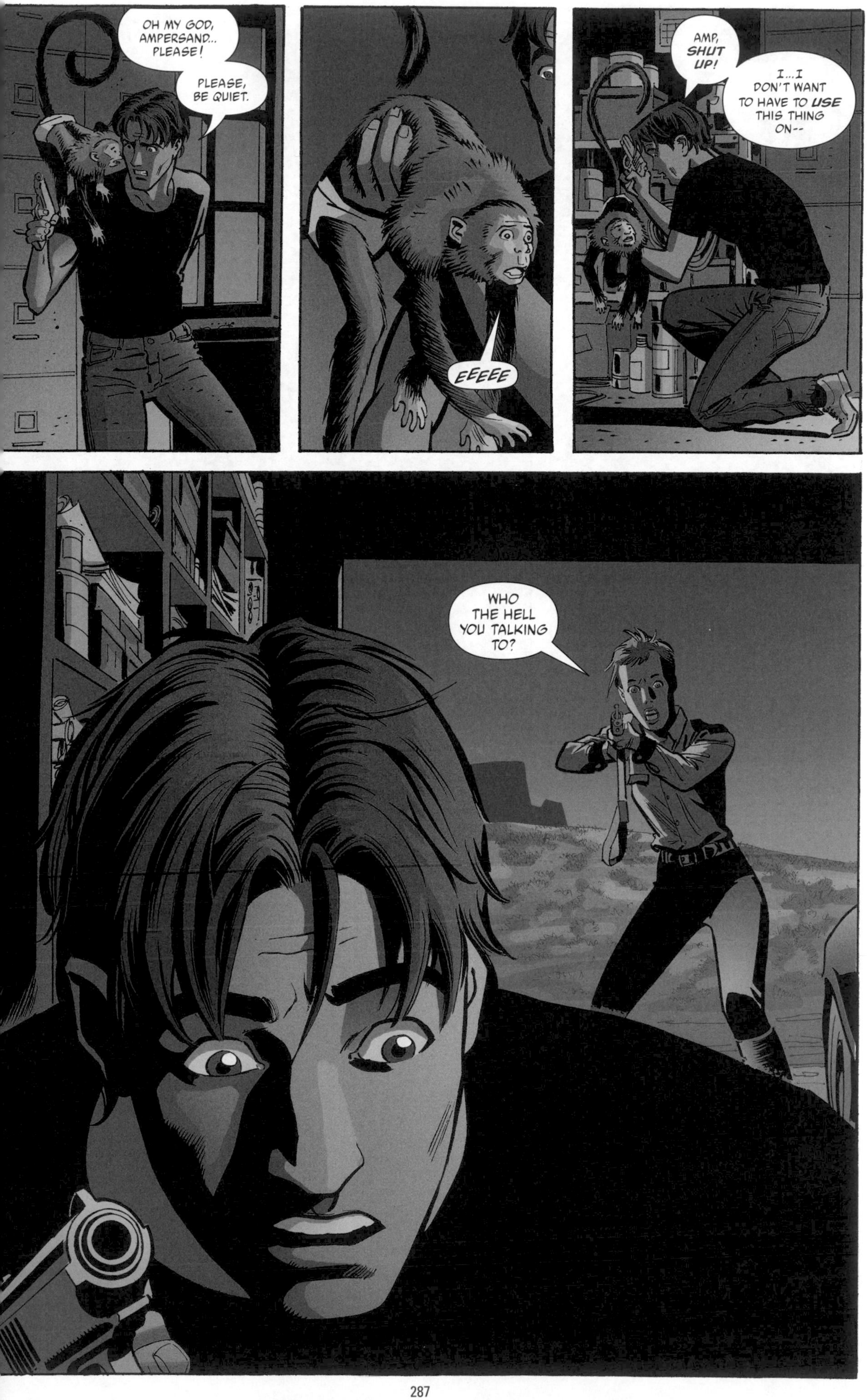
OH MY GOD, AMPERSAND... PLEASE!
PLEASE, BE QUIET.
EEEEE
AMP, SHUT UP!
I...I DON'T WANT TO HAVE TO USE THIS THING ON--
WHO THE HELL YOU TALKING TO?

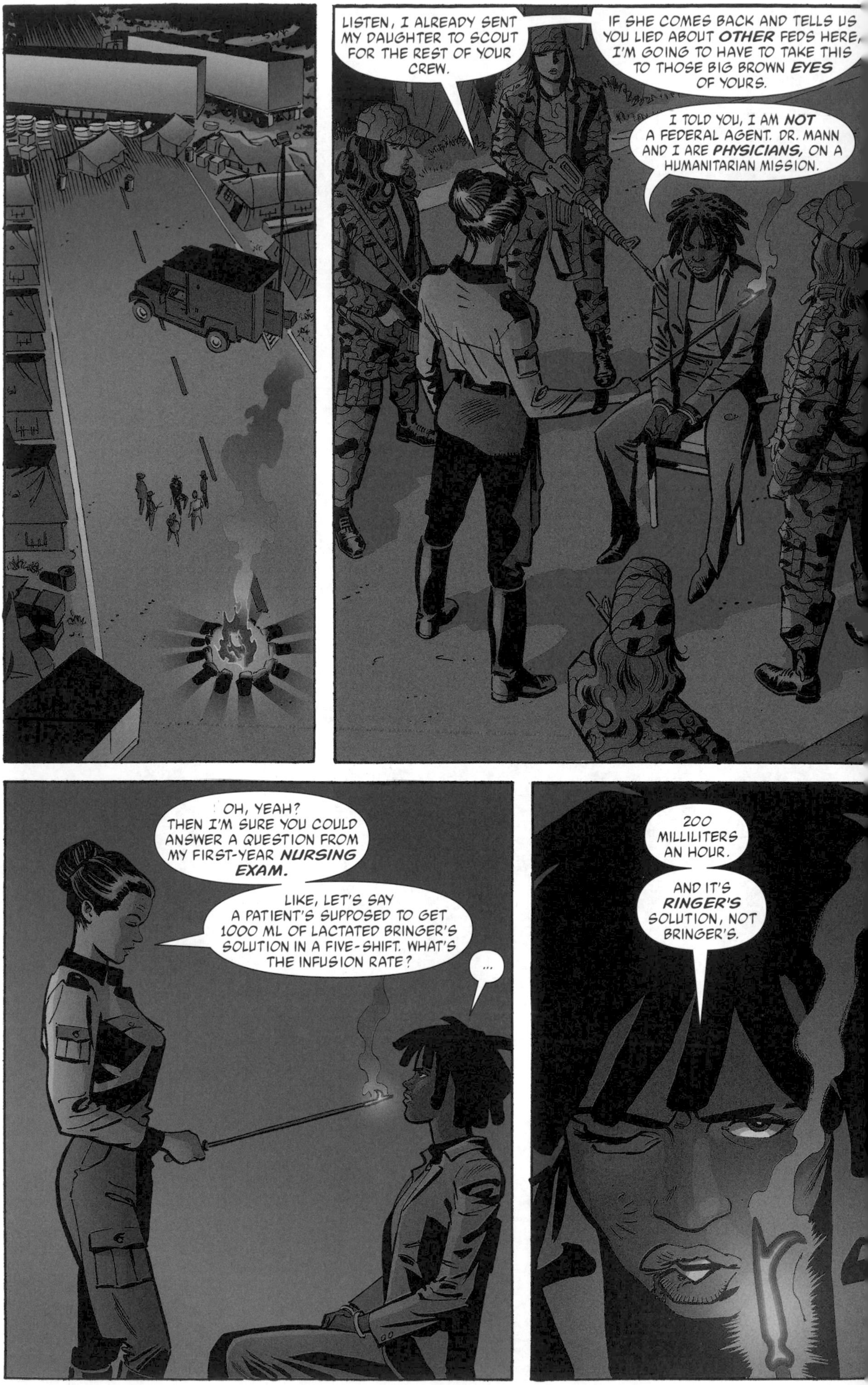
LISTEN, I ALREADY SENT MY DAUGHTER TO SCOUT FOR THE REST OF YOUR CREW.
IF SHE COMES BACK AND TELLS US YOU LIED ABOUT OTHER FEDS HERE, I'M GOING TO HAVE TO TAKE THIS TO THOSE BIG BROWN EYES OF YOURS.
I TOLD YOU, I AM NOT A FEDERAL AGENT. DR. MANN AND I ARE PHYSICIANS, ON A HUMANITARIAN MISSION.
OH, YEAH? THEN I'M SURE YOU COULD ANSWER A QUESTION FROM MY FIRST-YEAR NURSING EXAM.
LIKE, LET'S SAY A PATIENT'S SUPPOSED TO GET 1000 ML OF LACTATED BRINGER'S SOLUTION IN A FIVE-SHIFT. WHAT'S THE INFUSION RATE?
...
200 MILLILITERS AN HOUR.
AND IT'S RINGER'S SOLUTION, NOT BRINGER'S.

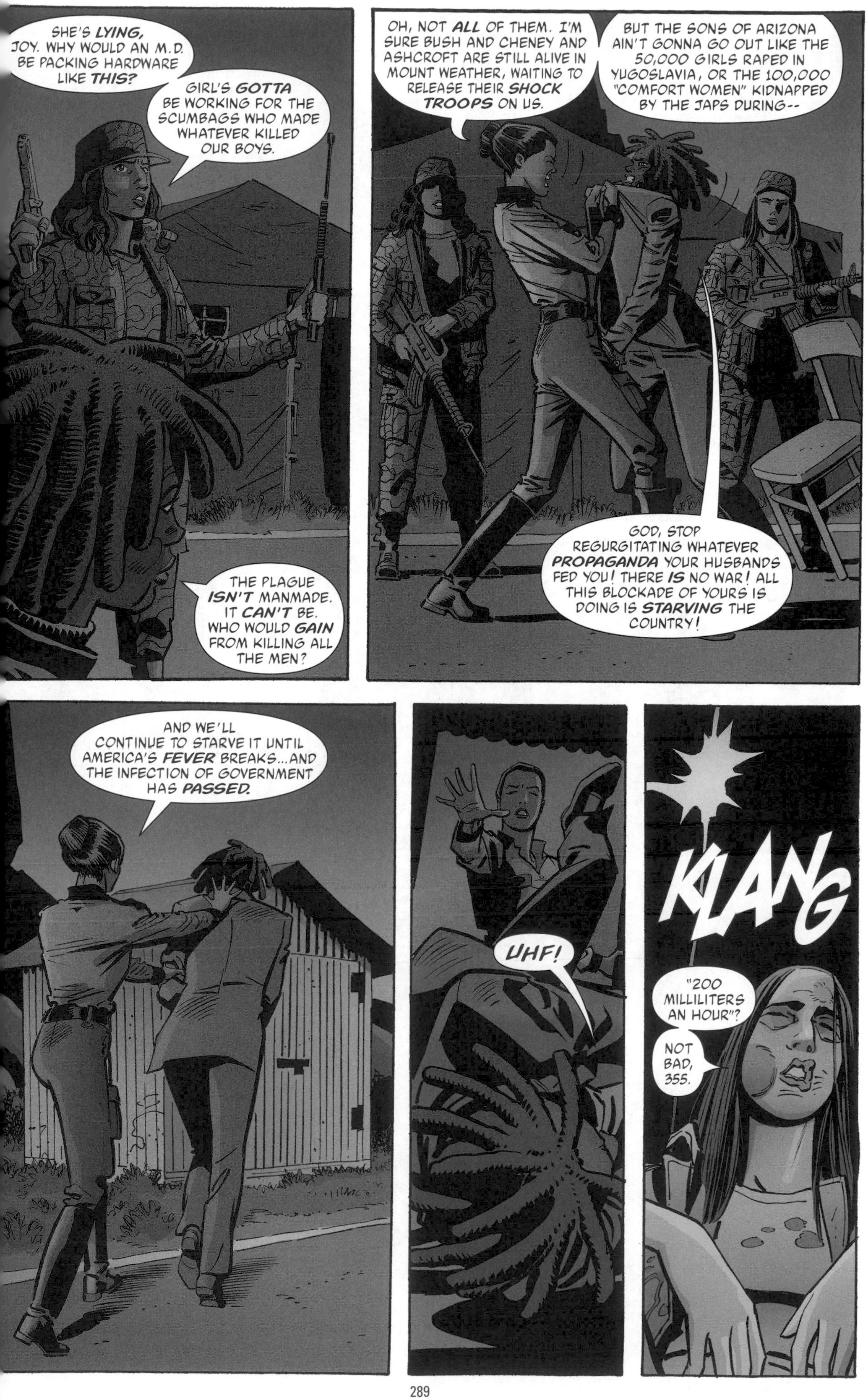
SHE'S LYING, JOY. WHY WOULD AN M.D. BE PACKING HARDWARE LIKE THIS?
GIRL'S GOTTA BE WORKING FOR THE SCUMBAGS WHO MADE WHATEVER KILLED OUR BOYS.
THE PLAGUE ISN'T MANMADE. IT CAN'T BE. WHO WOULD GAIN FROM KILLING ALL THE MEN?
OH, NOT ALL OF THEM. I'M SURE BUSH AND CHENEY AND ASHCROFT ARE STILL ALIVE IN MOUNT WEATHER, WAITING TO RELEASE THEIR SHOCK TROOPS ON US.
BUT THE SONS OF ARIZONA AIN'T GONNA GO OUT LIKE THE 50,000 GIRLS RAPED IN YUGOSLAVIA, OR THE 100,000 "COMFORT WOMEN" KIDNAPPED BY THE JAPS DURING--
GOD, STOP REGURGITATING WHATEVER PROPAGANDA YOUR HUSBANDS FED YOU! THERE IS NO WAR! ALL THIS BLOCKADE OF YOURS IS DOING IS STARVING THE COUNTRY!
AND WE'LL CONTINUE TO STARVE IT UNTIL AMERICA'S FEVER BREAKS...AND THE INFECTION OF GOVERNMENT HAS PASSED.
UHF!
KLANG
"200 MILLILITERS AN HOUR"?
NOT BAD, 355.

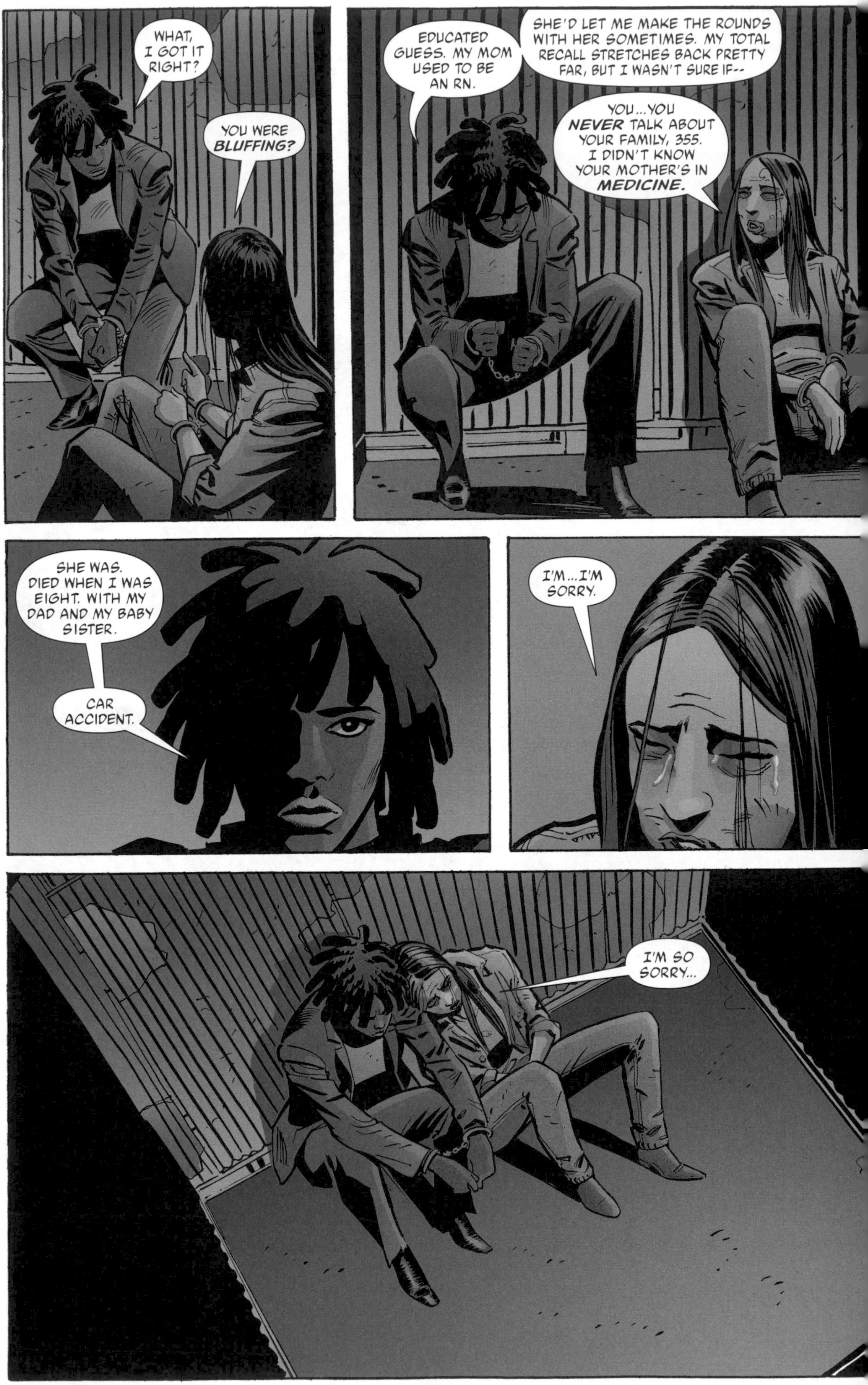
WHAT, I GOT IT RIGHT?
YOU WERE *BLUFFING?*
EDUCATED GUESS. MY MOM USED TO BE AN RN.
SHE'D LET ME MAKE THE ROUNDS WITH HER SOMETIMES. MY TOTAL RECALL STRETCHES BACK PRETTY FAR, BUT I WASN'T SURE IF--
YOU...YOU *NEVER* TALK ABOUT YOUR FAMILY, 355. I DIDN'T KNOW YOUR MOTHER'S IN *MEDICINE.*
SHE WAS. DIED WHEN I WAS EIGHT. WITH MY DAD AND MY BABY SISTER.
CAR ACCIDENT.
I'M...I'M SORRY.
I'M SO SORRY...

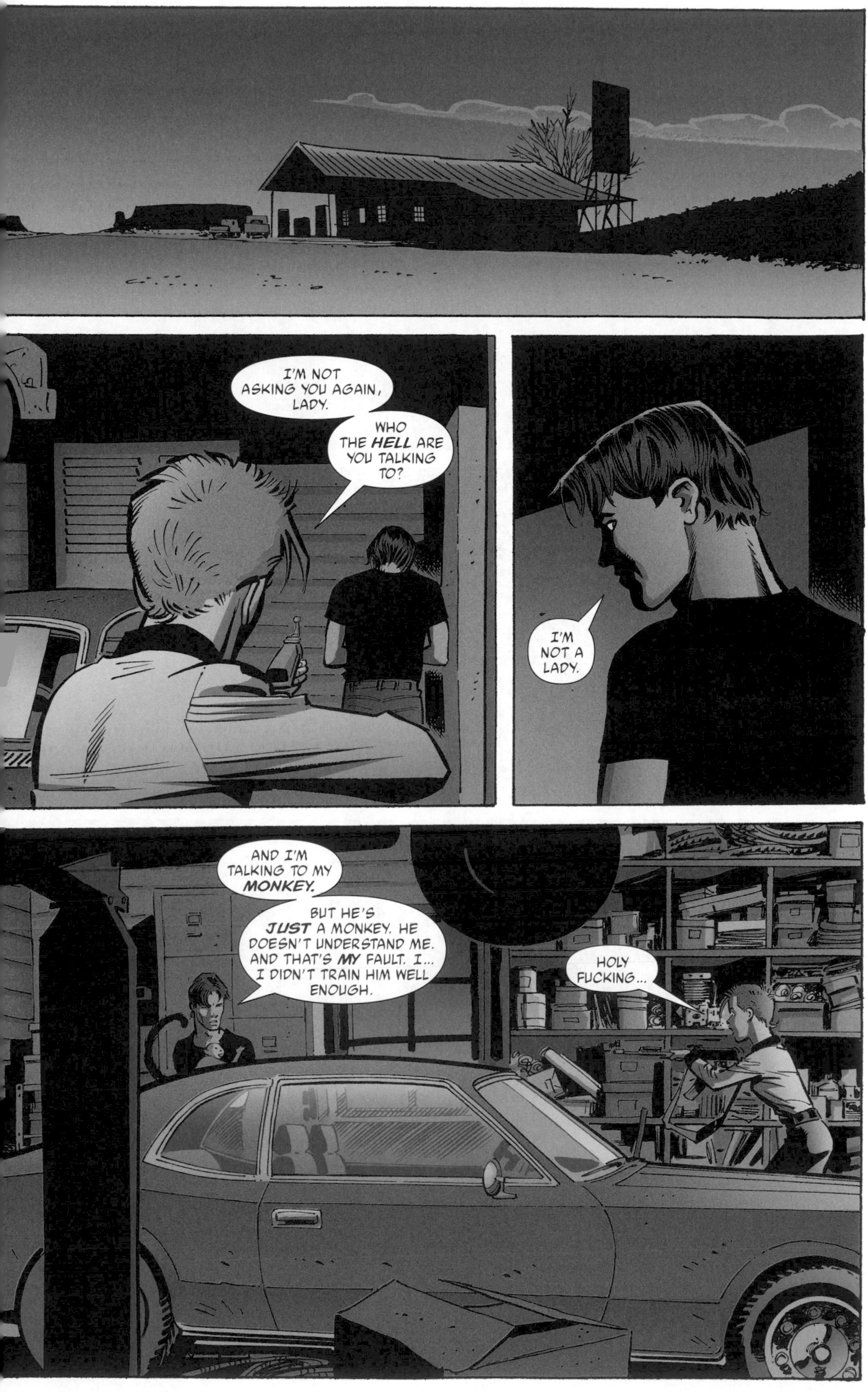
I'M NOT ASKING YOU AGAIN, LADY.
WHO THE **HELL** ARE YOU TALKING TO?
I'M NOT A LADY.
AND I'M TALKING TO MY **MONKEY.**
BUT HE'S **JUST** A MONKEY. HE DOESN'T UNDERSTAND ME. AND THAT'S **MY** FAULT. I... I DIDN'T TRAIN HIM WELL ENOUGH.
HOLY FUCKING...

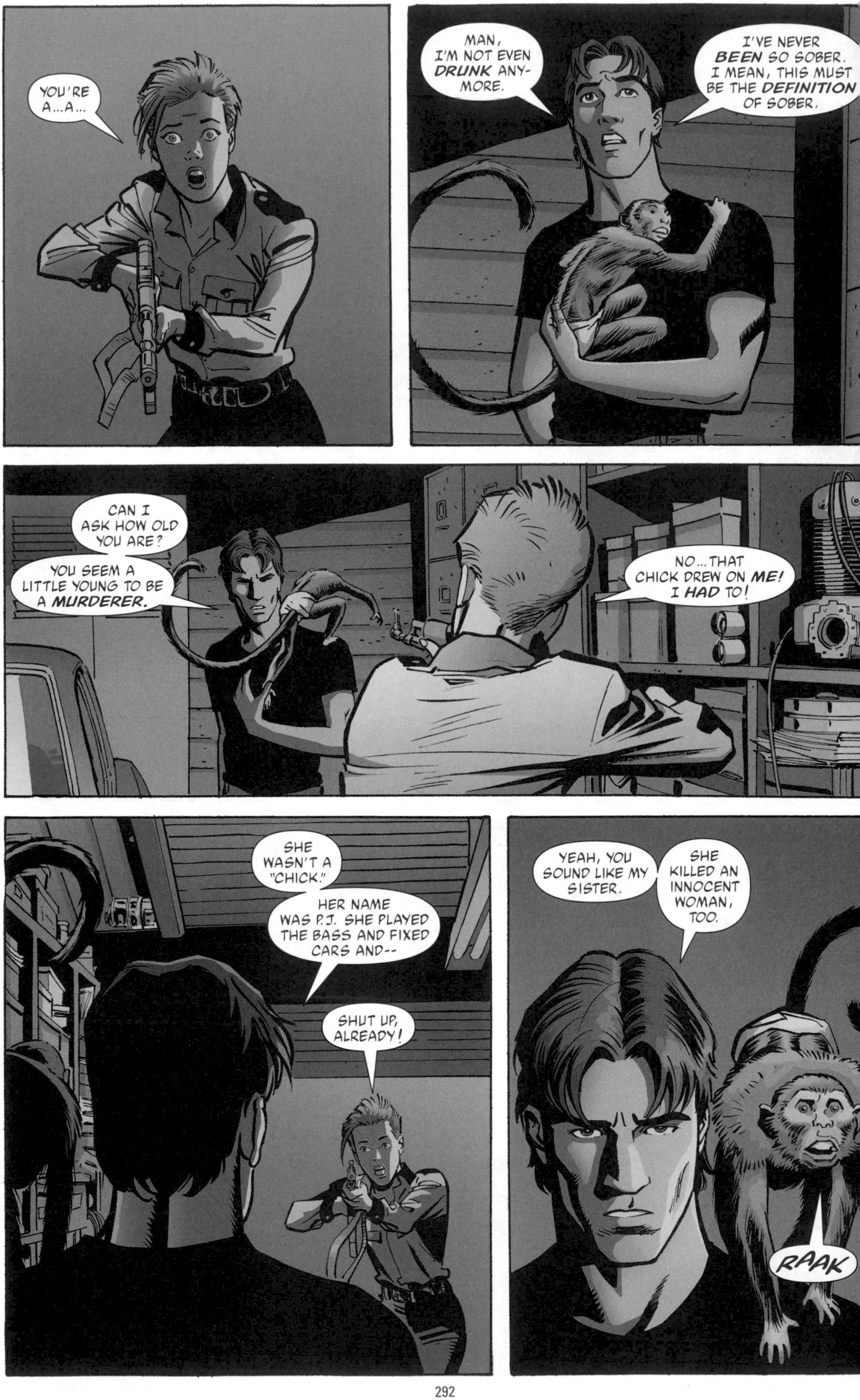
YOU'RE A...A...
MAN, I'M NOT EVEN DRUNK ANYMORE.
I'VE NEVER BEEN SO SOBER. I MEAN, THIS MUST BE THE DEFINITION OF SOBER.
CAN I ASK HOW OLD YOU ARE?
YOU SEEM A LITTLE YOUNG TO BE A MURDERER.
NO...THAT CHICK DREW ON ME! I HAD TO!
SHE WASN'T A "CHICK."
HER NAME WAS P.J. SHE PLAYED THE BASS AND FIXED CARS AND--
SHUT UP, ALREADY!
YEAH, YOU SOUND LIKE MY SISTER.
SHE KILLED AN INNOCENT WOMAN, TOO.
RAAK

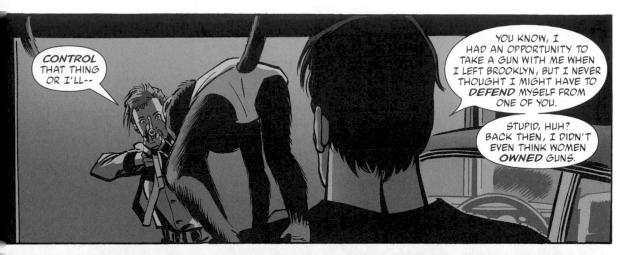

CONTROL THAT THING OR I'LL--

YOU KNOW, I HAD AN OPPORTUNITY TO TAKE A GUN WITH ME WHEN I LEFT BROOKLYN, BUT I NEVER THOUGHT I MIGHT HAVE TO *DEFEND* MYSELF FROM ONE OF YOU.

STUPID, HUH? BACK THEN, I DIDN'T EVEN THINK WOMEN *OWNED* GUNS.

BUT THESE PAST FEW MONTHS HAVE BEEN A REAL EDUCATION.

DROP IT!

I WILL. RIGHT AFTER YOU DROP YOURS.

PLEASE, I DON'T WANT TO--

BANG   BANG

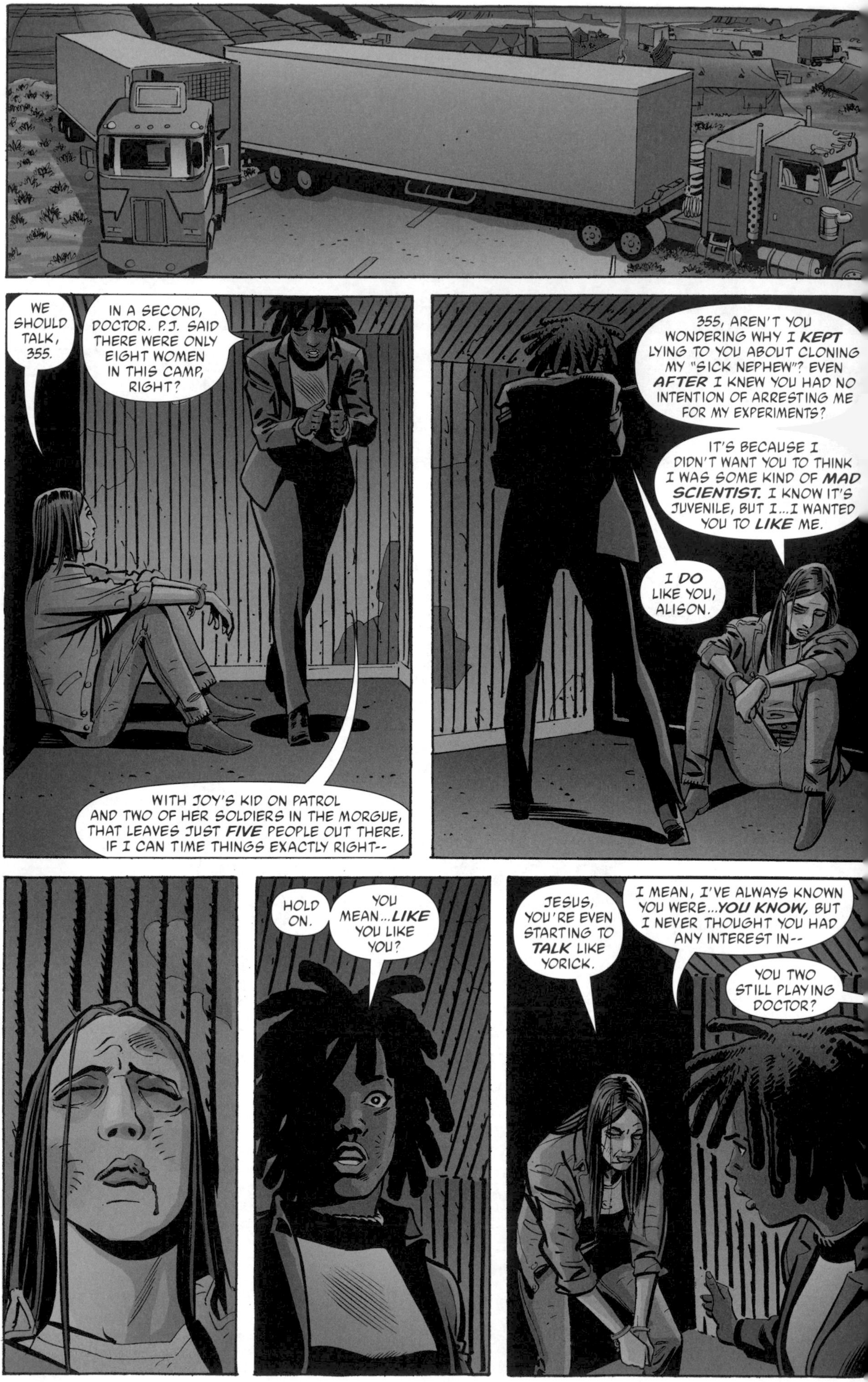

WE SHOULD TALK, 355.
IN A SECOND, DOCTOR. P.J. SAID THERE WERE ONLY EIGHT WOMEN IN THIS CAMP, RIGHT?
WITH JOY'S KID ON PATROL AND TWO OF HER SOLDIERS IN THE MORGUE, THAT LEAVES JUST FIVE PEOPLE OUT THERE. IF I CAN TIME THINGS EXACTLY RIGHT--
355, AREN'T YOU WONDERING WHY I KEPT LYING TO YOU ABOUT CLONING MY "SICK NEPHEW"? EVEN AFTER I KNEW YOU HAD NO INTENTION OF ARRESTING ME FOR MY EXPERIMENTS?
IT'S BECAUSE I DIDN'T WANT YOU TO THINK I WAS SOME KIND OF MAD SCIENTIST. I KNOW IT'S JUVENILE, BUT I...I WANTED YOU TO LIKE ME.
I DO LIKE YOU, ALISON.
HOLD ON.
YOU MEAN...LIKE YOU LIKE YOU?
JESUS, YOU'RE EVEN STARTING TO TALK LIKE YORICK.
I MEAN, I'VE ALWAYS KNOWN YOU WERE...YOU KNOW, BUT I NEVER THOUGHT YOU HAD ANY INTEREST IN--
YOU TWO STILL PLAYING DOCTOR?

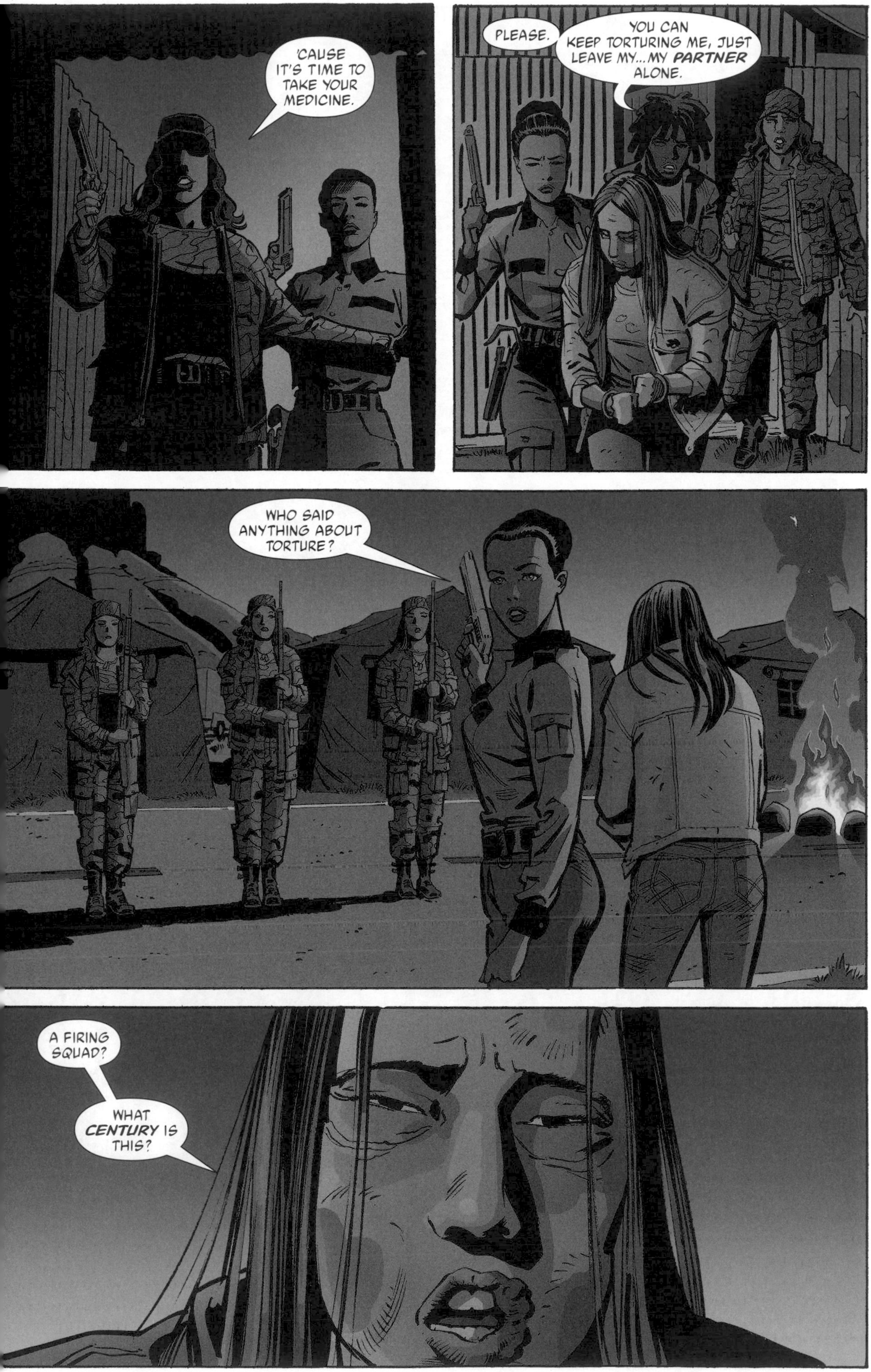
'CAUSE IT'S TIME TO TAKE YOUR MEDICINE.
PLEASE.
YOU CAN KEEP TORTURING ME, JUST LEAVE MY...MY PARTNER ALONE.
WHO SAID ANYTHING ABOUT TORTURE?
A FIRING SQUAD?
WHAT CENTURY IS THIS?

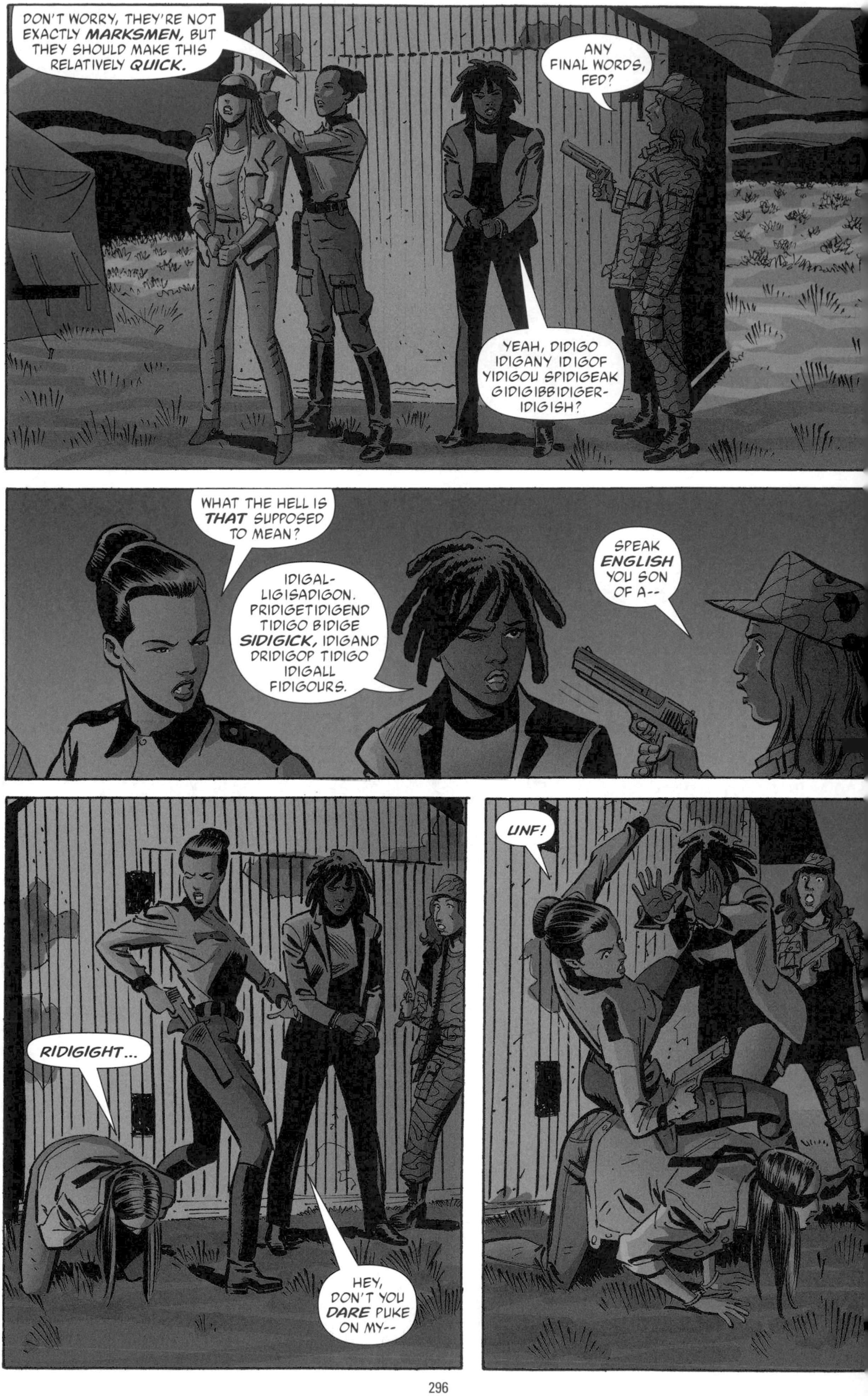
DON'T WORRY, THEY'RE NOT EXACTLY MARKSMEN, BUT THEY SHOULD MAKE THIS RELATIVELY QUICK.
ANY FINAL WORDS, FED?
YEAH, DIDIGO IDIGANY IDIGOF YIDIGOU SPIDIGEAK GIDIGIBBIDIGER-IDIGISH?
WHAT THE HELL IS THAT SUPPOSED TO MEAN?
IDIGAL-LIGISADIGON. PRIDIGETIDIGEND TIDIGO BIDIGE SIDIGICK, IDIGAND DRIDIGOP TIDIGO IDIGALL FIDIGOURS.
SPEAK ENGLISH YOU SON OF A--
RIDIGIGHT...
HEY, DON'T YOU DARE PUKE ON MY--
UNF!

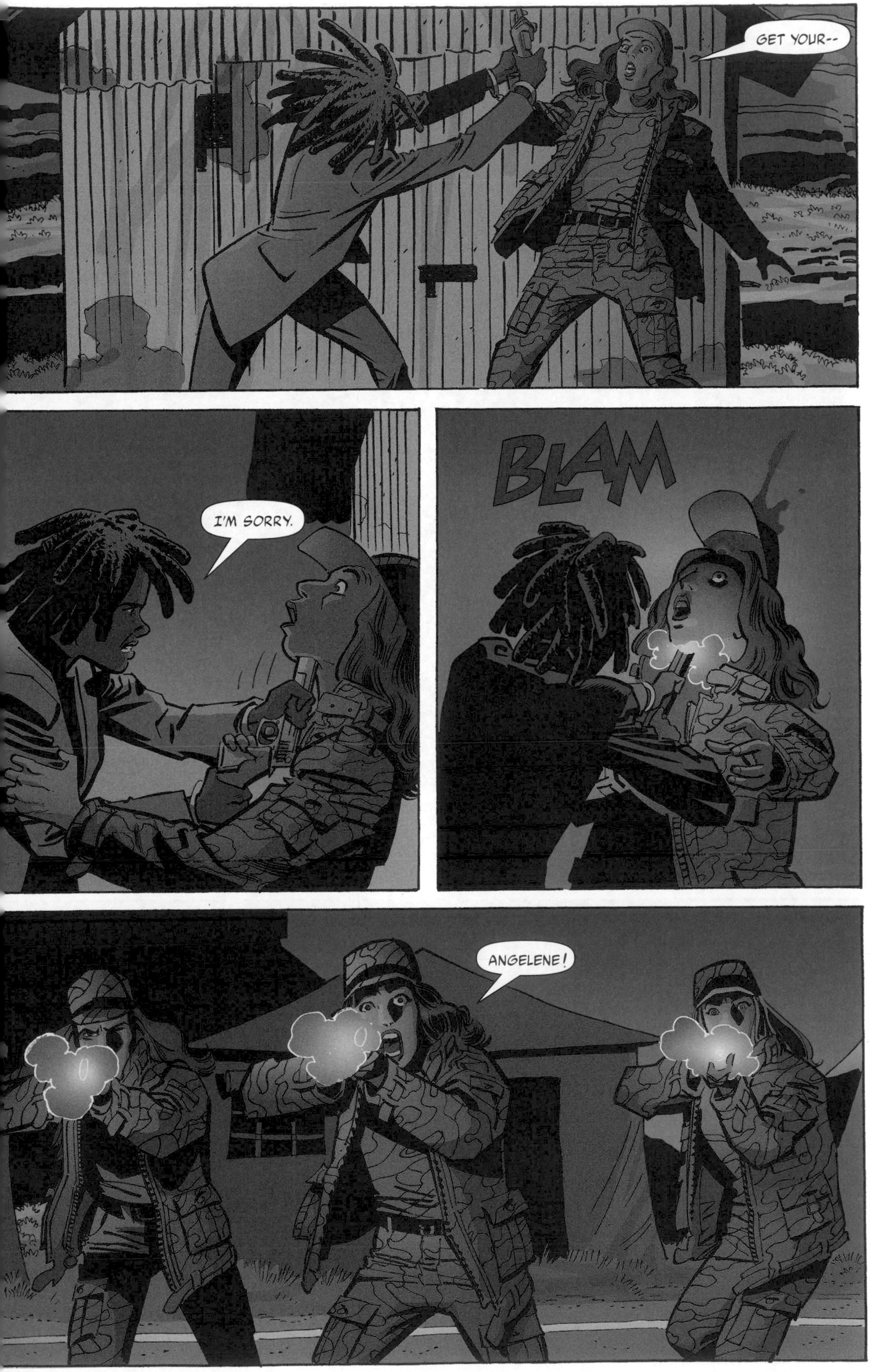
GET YOUR--
I'M SORRY.
BLAM
ANGELENE!

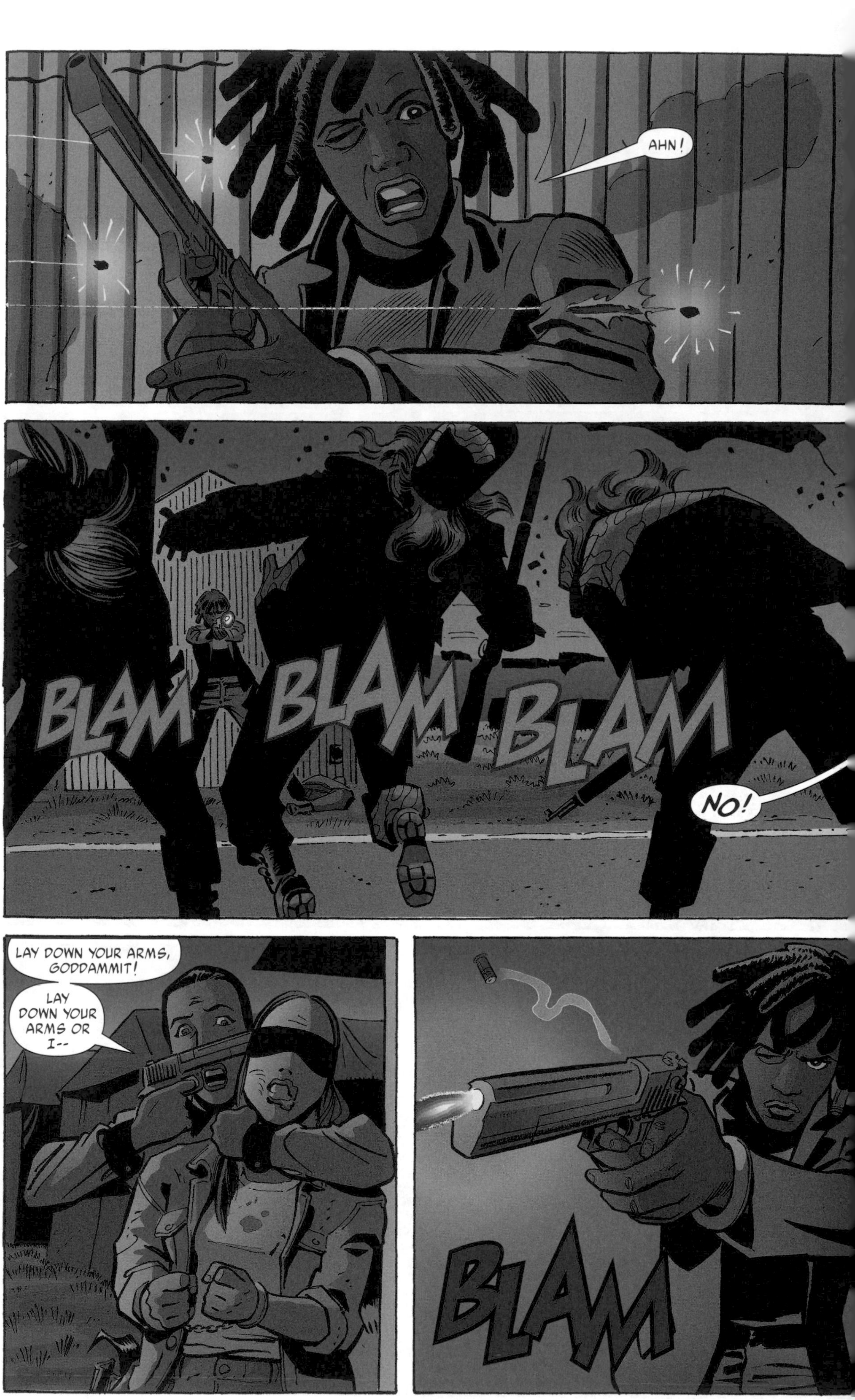
AHN!
BLAM
BLAM
BLAM
NO!
LAY DOWN YOUR ARMS, GODDAMMIT!
LAY DOWN YOUR ARMS OR I--
BLAM

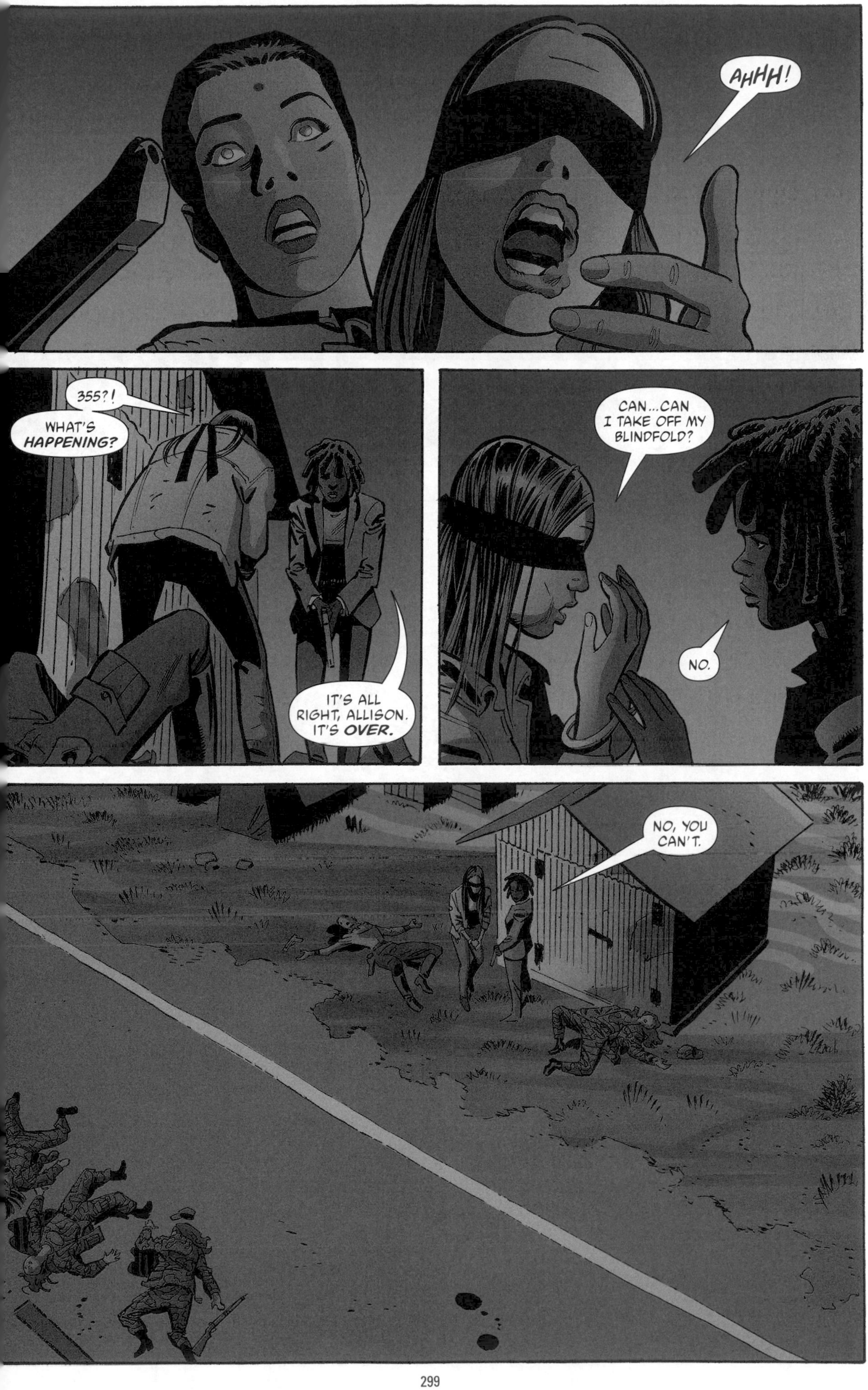
AHHH!
355?!
WHAT'S HAPPENING?
IT'S ALL RIGHT, ALLISON. IT'S OVER.
CAN...CAN I TAKE OFF MY BLINDFOLD?
NO.
NO, YOU CAN'T.

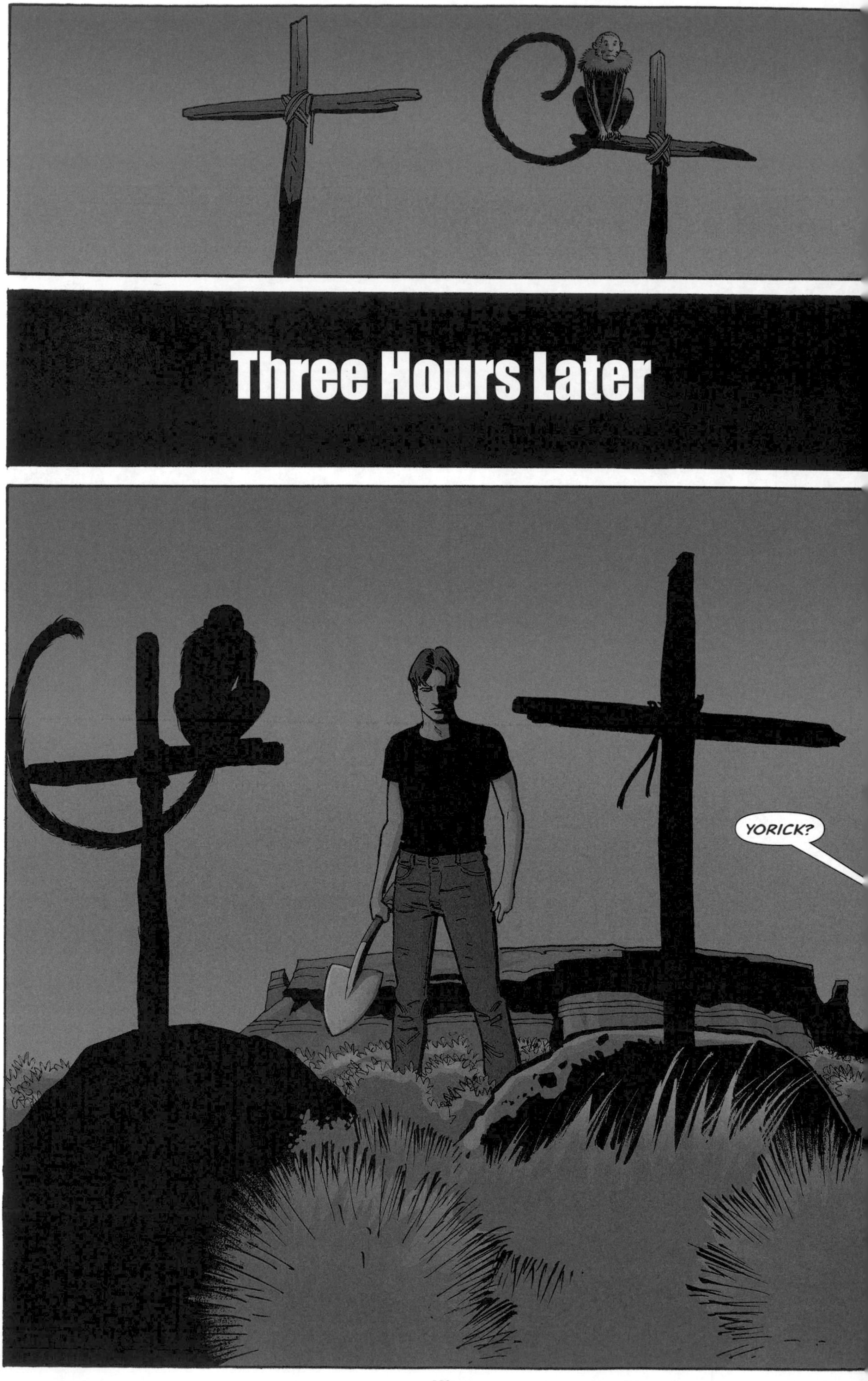
Three Hours Later
YORICK?

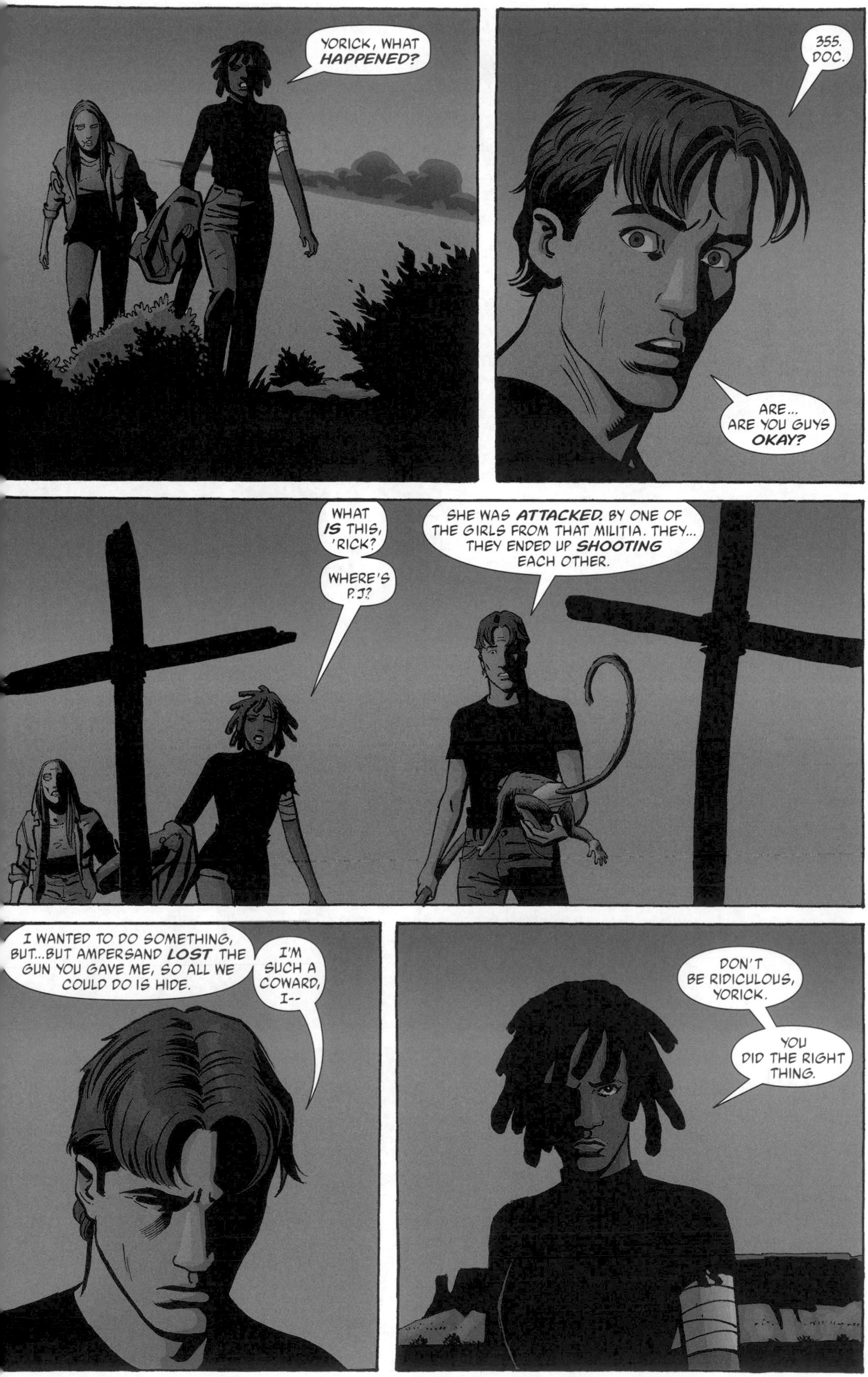
YORICK, WHAT HAPPENED?
355. DOC.
ARE... ARE YOU GUYS OKAY?
WHAT IS THIS, 'RICK?
WHERE'S P.J.?
SHE WAS ATTACKED. BY ONE OF THE GIRLS FROM THAT MILITIA. THEY... THEY ENDED UP SHOOTING EACH OTHER.
I WANTED TO DO SOMETHING, BUT...BUT AMPERSAND LOST THE GUN YOU GAVE ME, SO ALL WE COULD DO IS HIDE.
I'M SUCH A COWARD, I--
DON'T BE RIDICULOUS, YORICK.
YOU DID THE RIGHT THING.

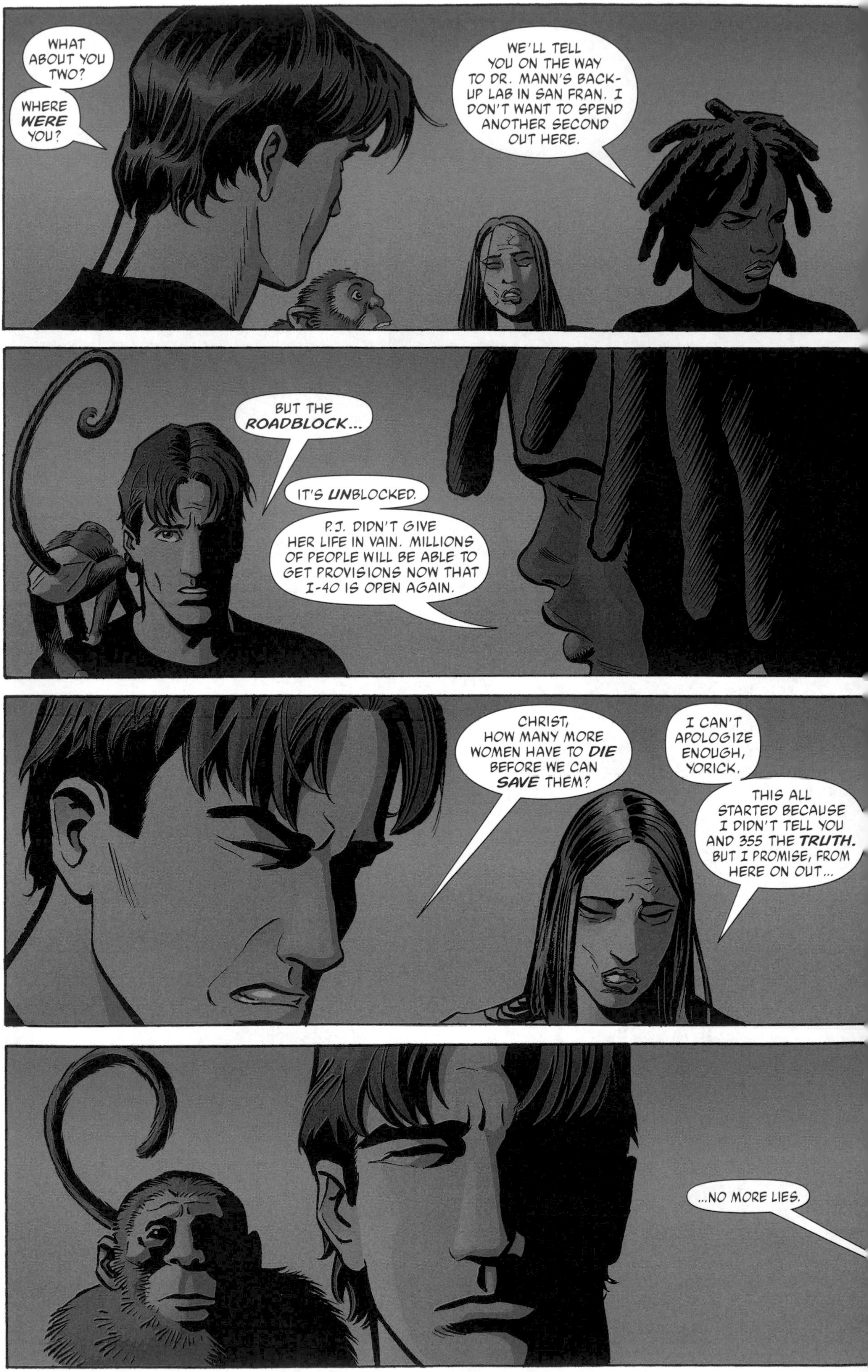
WHAT ABOUT YOU TWO?
WHERE WERE YOU?
WE'LL TELL YOU ON THE WAY TO DR. MANN'S BACK-UP LAB IN SAN FRAN. I DON'T WANT TO SPEND ANOTHER SECOND OUT HERE.
BUT THE ROADBLOCK...
IT'S UNBLOCKED.
P.J. DIDN'T GIVE HER LIFE IN VAIN. MILLIONS OF PEOPLE WILL BE ABLE TO GET PROVISIONS NOW THAT I-40 IS OPEN AGAIN.
CHRIST, HOW MANY MORE WOMEN HAVE TO DIE BEFORE WE CAN SAVE THEM?
I CAN'T APOLOGIZE ENOUGH, YORICK.
THIS ALL STARTED BECAUSE I DIDN'T TELL YOU AND 355 THE TRUTH. BUT I PROMISE, FROM HERE ON OUT...
...NO MORE LIES.

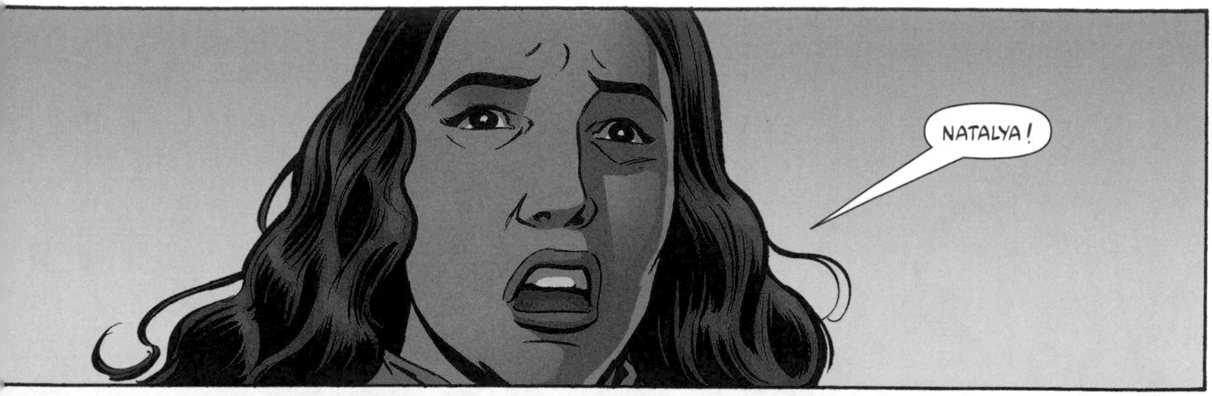
NATALYA!

**Oldenbrook, Kansas
Now**

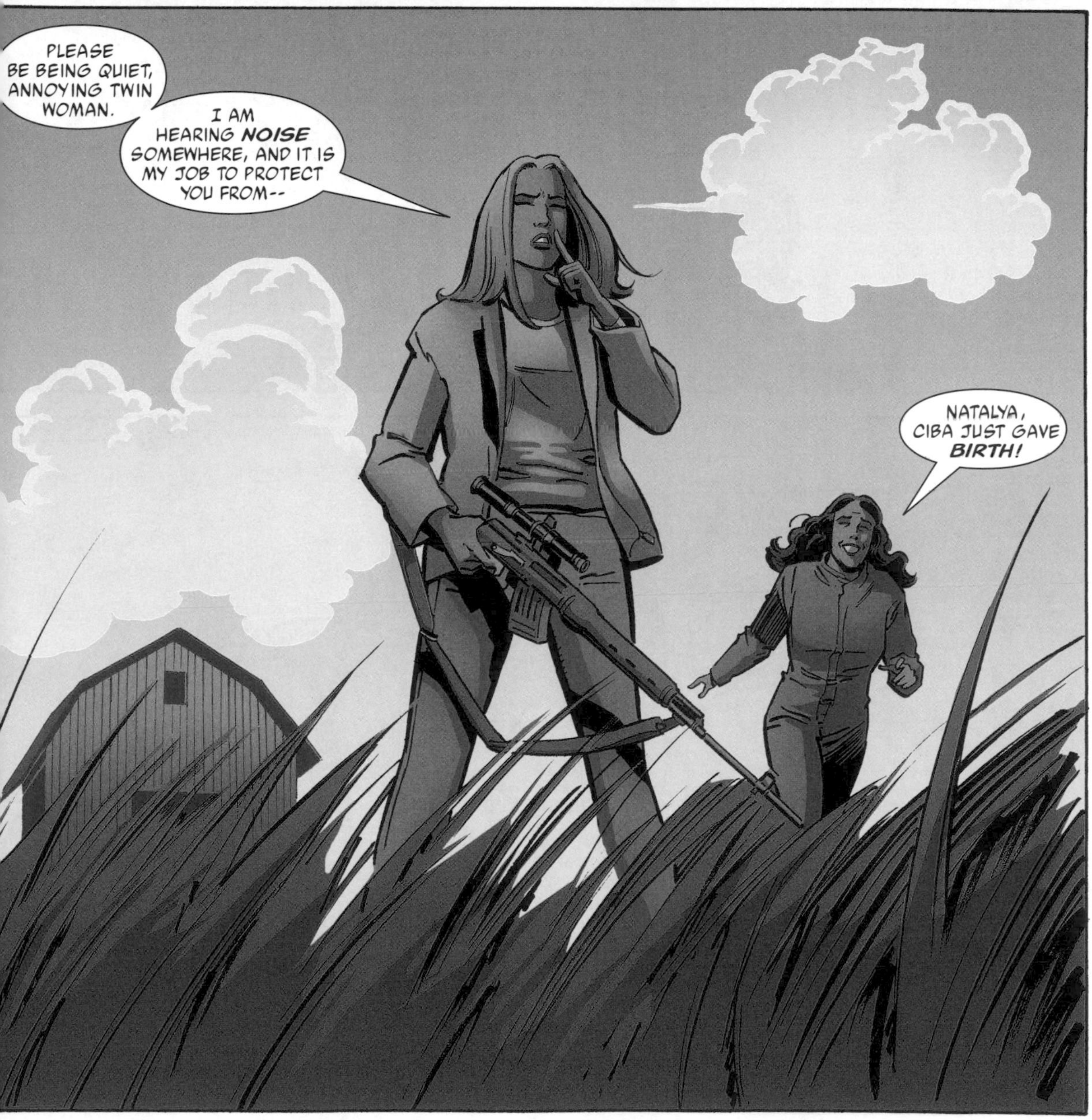
PLEASE BE BEING QUIET, ANNOYING TWIN WOMAN.
I AM HEARING NOISE SOMEWHERE, AND IT IS MY JOB TO PROTECT YOU FROM--
NATALYA, CIBA JUST GAVE BIRTH!

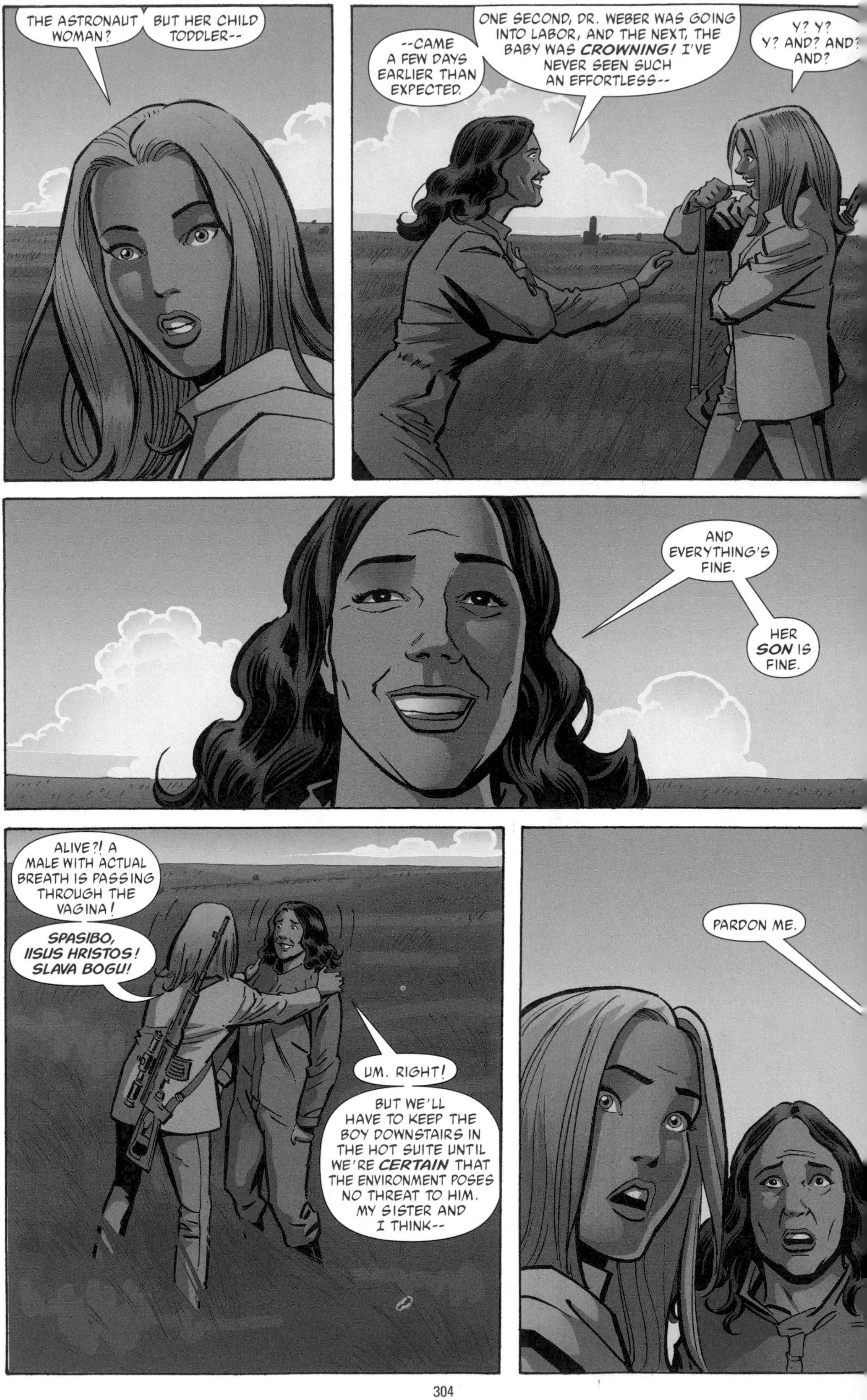
THE ASTRONAUT WOMAN?
BUT HER CHILD TODDLER--
--CAME A FEW DAYS EARLIER THAN EXPECTED.
ONE SECOND, DR. WEBER WAS GOING INTO LABOR, AND THE NEXT, THE BABY WAS CROWNING! I'VE NEVER SEEN SUCH AN EFFORTLESS--
Y? Y? Y? AND? AND? AND?
AND EVERYTHING'S FINE.
HER SON IS FINE.
ALIVE?! A MALE WITH ACTUAL BREATH IS PASSING THROUGH THE VAGINA!
SPASIBO, IISUS HRISTOS! SLAVA BOGU!
UM. RIGHT!
BUT WE'LL HAVE TO KEEP THE BOY DOWNSTAIRS IN THE HOT SUITE UNTIL WE'RE CERTAIN THAT THE ENVIRONMENT POSES NO THREAT TO HIM. MY SISTER AND I THINK--
PARDON ME.

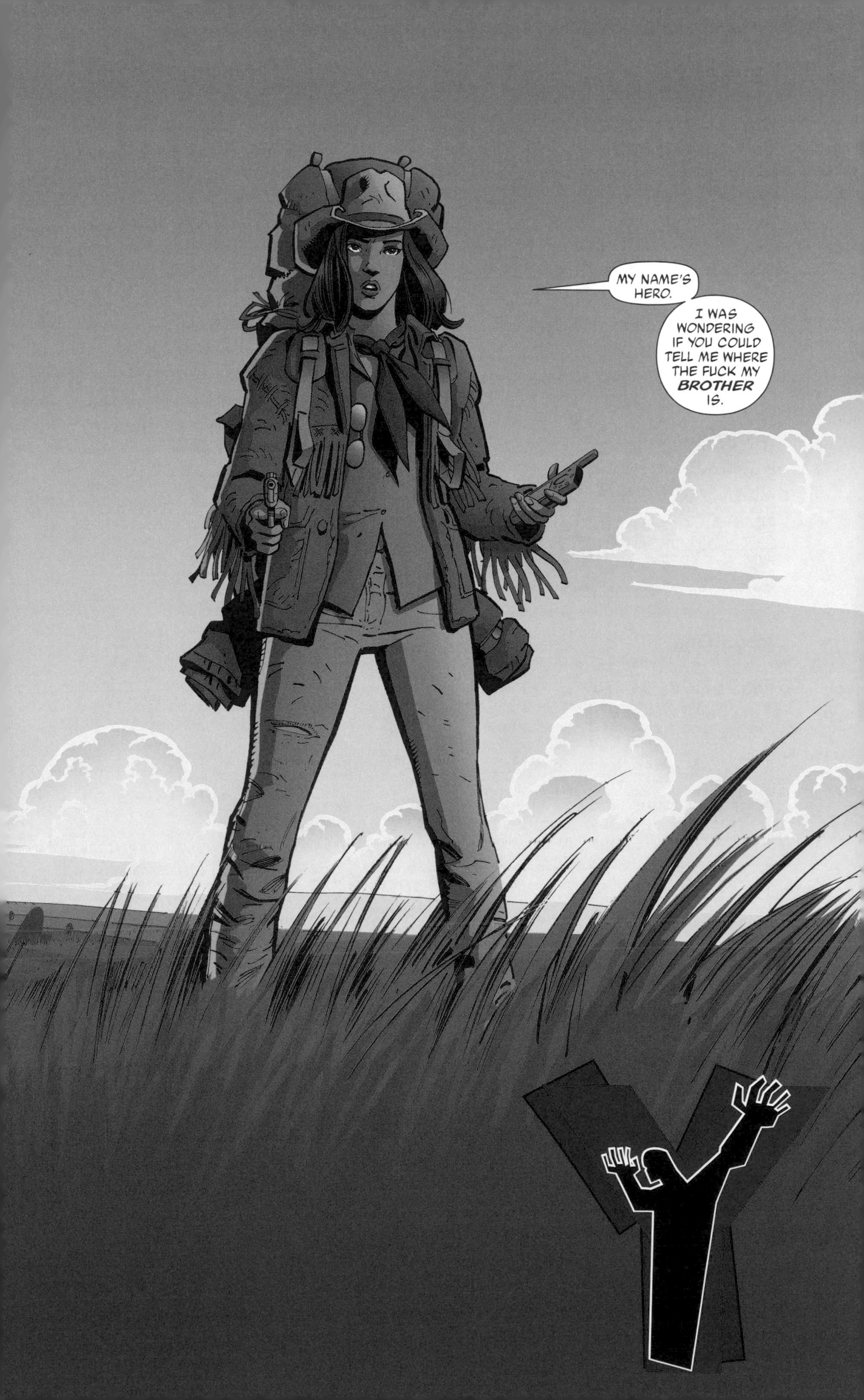
MY NAME'S HERO.
I WAS WONDERING IF YOU COULD TELL ME WHERE THE FUCK MY BROTHER IS.

VERTIGO
NEW STORYLINE
Y
THE LAST MAN
ISSUE 18
VAUGHAN GUERRA MARZAN JR.
SUGGESTED FOR MATURE READERS

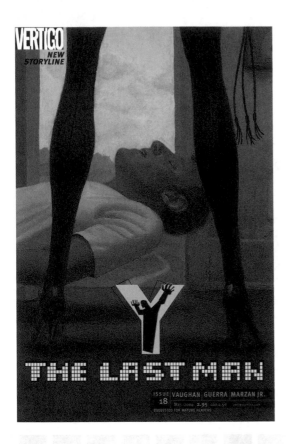

"Safeword, Chapter One"

The Full Script for Y #18

Prepared for Vertigo Comics,

June 30, 2003

Brian K. Vaughan

Page One

Page One, Panel One

We open with this close-up of YORICK BROWN, age *eight* (or so). It's 1989. He has braces and a stupid haircut, but he's still our Yorick.

1) Someone's Voice (from off): Yorick *always* gets to be last!

Page One, Panel Two

White text, black background, etc.

2) White text on black background:

Cleveland, Ohio
Fifteen Years Ago

Page One, Panel Three

Pull out for this largest panel of the page, at least a half-SPLASH. We can now see that we're inside of a "retirement home." ELDERLY WOMEN are shuffling along, playing bridge in the background, etc., but there should be no elderly *males* in this shot. Standing outside of a doorway to one of the nursing facility rooms are Yorick, HERO, and their father, PROFESSOR BROWN (the bearded guy we saw in a photo back in Issue #11, I think). Hero is twelve or eleven here, and she's throwing a little fit. Prof. Brown is trying to calm her down. Watching this confrontation with interest is Yorick, who we can now see is wearing an oversized purple T-shirt with a picture of Jack Nicholson as the Joker on the front of it. *(Will, please give us a heads-up now if that will be a problem with legal or anything. This is actually an important bit of costuming, since this story is about "Yorick the Jester" in a lot of ways.)*

3) Hero: How come *he* can't go in first?

4) Prof. Brown: Hero, I'm not asking you to charge into battle against King Charles' cavalry.

5) Prof. Brown: I just want you to say hello to your *grandfather.*

Page Two

Page Two, Panel One
Push in closer on the Professor and his daughter, who almost looks frightened here.

1) <u>Prof. Brown</u>: You know he gets confused if we all try to talk with him at the same—

2) <u>Hero</u>: I don't care!
3) <u>Hero</u>: I... I don't even *like* him! He always tries to touch my—

Page Two, Panel Two
Cut over to Yorick, nobly volunteering.

4) <u>Yorick</u>: It's okay, Dad.
5) <u>Yorick</u>: I can go in first.

Page Two, Panel Three
This largest panel of the page can be from Hero's point-of-view. The Professor affectionately musses Yorick's hair as he addresses his off-panel daughter. Now that his father isn't looking, Yorick crosses his eyes and sticks out his tongue at the off-panel Hero.

6) <u>Prof. Brown</u>: There's a brave soldier.
7) <u>Prof. Brown</u>: He didn't even need a St. Crispin's Day speech to get *him* onto the front line.

Page Two, Panel Four
This is just a shot of the pissed-off young Hero, crossing her arms and muttering under her breath.

8) <u>Hero (small, under her breath)</u>: I hope you both get *AIDS*.

Page Two, Panel Five
We're behind Yorick here, cheated so we can see some of his expression, as he knocks on the frame of the open door. Inside this room, we can see an elderly man in the background. He's seated with his back to us, and we can't see his face. He's apparently staring out the window. This shot should be creepy and ominous, Pia.

9) <u>Yorick</u>: Hello?
10) <u>Yorick</u>: Grampy... ?

Page Three

Page Three, Panel One
Change angles for this largest panel of the page. We're now in the foreground with Yorick's gruff, eighty-year-old GRANDFATHER (a man that Yorick will look almost identical to when we see *him* at this age... oops, did I give something away?). In the background, Yorick cautiously steps into the dimly lit room.

1) <u>Yorick</u>: It's me.
2) <u>Yorick</u>: Yorick.

3) <u>Grandpa</u>: Yorick *who*?

Page Three, Panel Two
Push in closer on the two, as "Grampy" smiles and turns to greet his smirking grandchild.

4) <u>Yorick</u>: Ha ha, hilarious.

5) <u>Grandpa</u>: Come here, ya little bastard. What brings you to this dump?

6) <u>Yorick</u>: Mom's in town for campaign stuff, remember?

Page Three, Panel Three
   Change angles, as a curious Yorick interrogates his surly elder. Please leave some room between them for this exchange:

   7) <u>Yorick</u>: Hey, how come there are so many women in here?

   8) <u>Grandpa</u>: 'Cause women live longer than men.

   9) <u>Yorick</u>: Why?

   10) <u>Grandpa</u>: 'Cause they suck all the goddamn life out of us.

Page Three, Panel Four
   Similar framing, but now Yorick's frail grandfather becomes fairly irate.

   11) <u>Yorick</u>: Oh.
   12) <u>Yorick</u>: Well, it must be cool to be, like, the only guy with so many girls all over the place.

   13) <u>Grandpa</u>: You *crazy*? It's hell on earth! Ain't nothing worse than ladies in numbers.

Page Three, Panel Five
   And we end with this portentous close-up of Yorick's grandfather, as he warns:

   14) <u>Grandpa</u>: Someday, you'll understand...

Page Four

Page Four, Panel One
   Cut to the present day for this close-up of a clean-shaven ADULT YORICK. He has the hood of his dark blue poncho up, but no gas mask on. He's screaming at the top of his lungs.

   1) <u>Yorick</u>: AHHHHH!

Page Four, Panel Two
   What's black and white and a recurring panel gimmick that this writer seemingly never tires of?

   2) <u>White text on black background</u>:
Allenspark, Colorado
Now

Page Four, Panel Three
   Pull out to the largest panel of the page, at least a half-SPLASH. We're in the fore-ground with the still-screaming Yorick, who we can now see is sitting behind AGENT 355 on a large two-passenger ATV. Tied to the front of this speeding all-terrain vehicle is a pet carrier, which we will eventually learn houses a sickly Ampersand.
   More importantly, we can see that 355 and Yorick are currently being pursued by THREE COWGIRLS ON HORSEBACK, all carrying rifles and wearing sheriff stars. The lead cowgirl is a Native American woman named TAD. Next to her is an angry white girl named JANE. And riding a beautiful black stallion is an African-American cowgirl named SONNY.
   It's early afternoon now, and we're in the middle of a gorgeous open field. There are woods to either side of our riders, and we can see the Rocky Mountains in the background. Oh, and we should now be able to tell that Yorick is screaming with *excitement*, not fear.
   Have fun with this, pardner!

   3) <u>Yorick</u>: This is fucking *sweet*!

Page Five

Page Five, Panel One

Change angles for this profile shot of 355 and the hooded Yorick, on top of their speeding ATV.

　　1) Yorick: We're being chased by a *posse*!
　　2) Yorick: Of *cowgirls*!

　　3) Agent 355: Shut up, Yorick!

Page Five, Panel Two

Pull out to the largest panel of the page as we reveal that 355 is riding next to DR. MANN, who is awkwardly driving her own (smaller) ATV. She's wearing a helmet that covers much of her face.

　　4) Agent 355: Dr. Mann, keep up!

　　5) Dr. Mann: I'm trying, goddammit!
　　6) Dr. Mann: I learned how to drive this goddamn thing *yesterday*!

Page Five, Panel Three

Cut back to the pursuing cowgirls, as Tad orders the African-American Sonny to raise her rifle.

　　7) Tad: Sonny, take 'em!

Page Five, Panel Four

This is just a shot of Sonny, as she FIRES at the off-panel women she's pursuing.

　　8) SFX: *BLAM*

Page Six

Page Six, Panel One

Cut to the helmeted Dr. Mann, as one of the front tires of her ATV suddenly EXPLODES.

　　1) SFX: *SPAK*

Page Six, Panel Two

Change angles, as the ATV pitches forward and LAUNCHES Dr. Mann over its handlebars.

　　No Copy

Page Six, Panel Three

Change angles for this largest panel of the page. We're with the fallen and seemingly lifeless Dr. Mann in the extreme foreground of this shot. In the background, 355 breaks hard and brings the ATV screeching to a sideways halt. Yorick screams in horror.

　　2) Yorick: DOC!

Page Six, Panel Four

Push in on Yorick and 355, as they both hop off of the vehicle. We can see some dense woods in the immediate background. Yorick looks concerned, but 355 screams for him to get moving, while she starts to take the pet carrier off of the front of the ATV.

　　3) Agent 355: I'll take care of her! Go! Hide in the woods!

　　4) Yorick: But Ampersand—

　　5) Agent 355: I've got him, just *run* already!

Page Seven

Page Seven, Panel One
We're behind Agent 355 now, cheated so we can see some of her concerned expression. She's holding the pet carrier now, and she's approaching the unmoving Dr. Mann.

1) <u>Agent 355</u>: Dr. Mann?
2) <u>Agent 355</u>: *Allison*? Are you... ?

Page Seven, Panel Two
This is just a shot of the winded Dr. Mann, as she sits up and starts to remove her helmet.

3) <u>Dr. Mann</u>: I'm... I'm all right, 355.
4) <u>Dr. Mann</u>: I *told* you these dorky things save...

Page Seven, Panel Three
Pull out for this largest panel of the page. We're behind Dr. Mann here, as she finishes taking off her helmet (maybe she's still on one knee). Behind her, 355 has turned around to see what both women are now staring at: the super-posse. The three cowgirls have just stopped their horses in front of Mann and 355, and they have their rifles aimed at both women.

5) <u>Dr. Mann</u>: ... lives?

Page Seven, Panel Four
This is just a badass close-up of Tad, the Native American leader of these marshals.

6) <u>Tad</u>: Tell us where the third gal in your little raiding party went off to... or we start shooting more than *tires*.

Page Eight

Page Eight, Panel One
Change angles for this shot of 355 and the now-standing Dr. Mann. 355 holds up the sealed animal carrier as evidence, and Dr. Mann nervously tries to back up her friend's story.

1) <u>Agent 355</u>: I think your eyes were playing tricks on you, sheriff. There are only two of us, and we *aren't* here to steal your cattle.
2) <u>Agent 355</u>: We're trying to reach St. Joseph's Hospital in Denver so we can get some antibiotics for our *pet*.

3) <u>Dr. Mann</u>: He, uh, *she* got a bad cut on her arm a few days back, and I'm pretty sure it's *infected*. But if we had known this was private property—

Page Eight, Panel Two
Change anglers for this shot of the three cowgirls, as they deftly DISMOUNT their horses.

4) <u>Jane</u>: Ain't nothing private about it. Land barons went extinct same time all the fellas did. This earth belongs to any woman wants to set foot on it.

5) <u>Sonny</u>: Any woman 'cept *Amazons*, that is.

Page Eight, Panel Three
Cut back to Dr. Mann and 355. Mann is visibly stunned by this accusation, while 355 uses her free hand to calmly reach inside of her jacket for something.

6) <u>Dr. Mann</u>: *Amazons*?

7) <u>Agent 355</u>: I'm afraid you're confused. I'm actually—

Page Eight, Panel Four

Change angles for this largest panel of the page, as Jane uses the butt of her rifle to SMASH 355 in the mouth.

8) <u>Agent 355</u>: Uhn!

Page Eight, Panel Five

This is just a menacing extreme close-up of 355, her gritted teeth now stained red with blood. She's trying her best not to hulk out.

9) <u>Agent 355</u>: That was... *unnecessary.*

Page Nine

Page Nine, Panel One

Pull out for this shot of 355 and the dubious Tad.

1) <u>Agent 355</u>: I was simply reaching for identification. I'm a *federal agent.*

2) <u>Tad</u>: Federal agent of *what?*

3) <u>Agent 355</u>: Technically, my organization is classified, but the President has authorized me to—

Page Nine, Panel Two

Cut over to Sonny and Jane, who both look impatient.

4) <u>Sonny</u>: Save that bullshit for the magistrates.

5) <u>Jane</u>: Yeah, we been warned about your kind... mutilatin' your own teats, tearing around on motorcycles, stealing food from defenseless women.

Page Nine, Panel Three

This is just a shot of Dr. Mann, screaming in protest.

6) <u>Dr. Mann</u>: You people have no *clue* what you're talking about!
7) <u>Dr. Mann</u>: We're *not* Daughters of the Amazon!

Page Nine, Panel Four

And this is just a close-up of Tad, as she matter-of-factly says:

8) <u>Tad</u>: Prove it.
9) <u>Tad</u>: Show us your breasts.

Page Nine, Panel Five

Pull out to this largest panel of the page for a group shot of Mann, 355 and the three cowgirls (who have all walked away from their off-panel horses).

10) <u>Dr. Mann</u>: *What?*

11) <u>Tad</u>: Relax, we're not homosexuals. Besides, if you're telling the truth, you ain't got nothing we haven't all seen—

12) <u>Someone's Voice (from off)</u>: Reach for the sky, pardners!

Page Ten

Page Ten, Panel One

Change angles for this largest panel of the page, at least a half-SPLASH. We're looking at the horses here, and we can now see that Yorick is standing next to the black stallion. He has a decent-sized BOWIE KNIFE pressed to the neck of the frightened animal. No longer wearing his hood, Yorick is now covering his mouth with a red bandana, bandit-style. He's holding the black horse hostage by its reins.

    1) <u>Yorick</u>: Or I turn Black Beauty here into a prop from *The Godfather*.

Page Ten, Panel Two
    Cut over to 355 and Mann. Mann looks baffled by this development, but 355 rolls her eyes knowingly.

    2) <u>Agent 355 (small, annoyed)</u>: Mother of Christ...

Page Ten, Panel Three
    Cut over to the three cowgirls. Tad is calmly formulating a plan, while Sonny screams in fear at the thought of something happening to her precious horse. Jane raises her rifle and aims it at the off-panel Yorick.

    3) <u>Sonny</u>: Buttercup!

    4) <u>Jane</u>: Butch, you so much as knick that horse, I kill you *and* your girlfriends.

Page Eleven

Page Eleven, Panel One
    This is just a shot of the bandana-clad Yorick.

    1) <u>Yorick</u>: What do I care?
    2) <u>Yorick</u>: We breastless Amazons *ache* for the sweet embrace of Mother Oblivion.

Page Eleven, Panel Two
    Cut back to the cowgirls. Jane and Tad look confused, but Sonny is still screaming in fear.

    3) <u>Jane</u>: Say *what*?

    4) <u>Tad</u>: Girl ain't right in the head.

    5) <u>Sonny</u>: Buttercup!

Page Eleven, Panel Three
    Cut back to Yorick, as he threatens to PLUNGE his knife into the throat of the captive steed.

    6) <u>Yorick</u>: Last chance, hand over your weapons to my associates.
    7) <u>Yorick</u>: Three... *two*...

Page Eleven, Panel Four
    Pull out to the largest panel of the page for a group shot of the whole crowd, as the three cowgirls reluctantly hand over their firearms to 355 and Dr. Mann (who looks extremely uncomfortable holding the two rifles she's just been handed). Tad keeps her eyes on Yorick as she relinquishes her weapon, while Jane curses under her breath.

    8) <u>Tad</u>: All right, all right!
    9) <u>Tad</u>: Just... just take her easy.

    10) <u>Jane (small, under her breath)</u>: Bitch.

Page Eleven, Panel Five
    This is just a kick-ass shot of 355, COCKING one of the old-fashioned rifles (by pulling down that lever-thing *underneath* the trigger). She looks hungry for revenge.

    11) <u>Agent 355</u>: Now then.

Page Twelve

Page Twelve, Panel One
Pull out to the largest panel of the page for this group shot. The cowgirls flinch as 355 FIRES the rifle... into the *air*. This causes the three horses to GALLOP AWAY at top speed.

1) SFX: *BLAM*

Page Twelve, Panel Two
Change angles, as 355 starts to load Ampersand's carrying case and the rifles onto the ATV. Behind her, Jane looks confused.

2) Agent 355: You've got about a two-hour walk back to civilization.
3) Agent 355: I'll leave your weapons with the first reputable trading post we pass.

4) Jane: You mean... you women *ain't* Amazons?

Page Twelve, Panel Three
We're behind Dr. Mann in the foreground of this shot, cheated so we can see some of her annoyed expression. We can clearly tell that she's opening her shirt to bare her breasts to the stunned cowgirls in the background, though we shouldn't actually *see* her Dr. Mammaries. (Sorry...)

5) Dr. Mann: Do these look mutilated to you, you ignorant shitheads?

Page Twelve, Panel Four
This is just a small shot of Yorick (still wearing his bandana).

6) Yorick (small, under his breath): Jeez.
7) Yorick (small, under his breath): So much for protecting a lady's *dignity*...

Page Thirteen

Page Thirteen, Panel One
Cut to a few hours later for this page-wide, wide-angle establishing shot (the sun is starting to set in the distance). We can see our crew's ATV parked overlooking a cliff. 355, Mann and Yorick (standing around the vehicle) can just be tiny figures in this shot.

No Copy

Page Thirteen, Panel Two
Push in on the trio for this largest panel of the page. On our left, Yorick is cradling an ailing Ampersand, who is howling in pain. Next to him, 355 is consulting a large foldout map of Colorado. Dr. Mann can be sitting on the parked ATV behind them.

1) Ampersand: *oroooooo*

2) Yorick: Jesus, I think Ampersand's getting worse, 355. Are we almost there?

3) Agent 355: You're not going to the hospital, Yorick. Not after that crap you pulled back there.

Page Thirteen, Panel Three
Change angles for this shot of an indignant Yorick and 355, who calmly looks up from her map.

4) Yorick: *What?* I save your lives, and you punish my *monkey*? He's gonna *die* without medicine!

5) Agent 355: You didn't save our lives, you needlessly risked your own... *again*.

6) <u>Agent 355</u>: Anyway, Dr Mann and I are still taking Ampersand to St. Joseph's. We're just not bringing *you* with us.

Page Thirteen, Panel Four
Change angles for this shot of Mann and 355, who are both looking at the off-panel Yorick.

7) <u>Dr. Mann</u>: If that Pony Express chick we met in Nebraska was telling the truth, St. Joe's is guarded like Area 51.
8) <u>Dr. Mann</u>: Getting my hands on more Augmentin is going to take patience, diplomacy and finesse.

9) <u>Agent 355</u>: Qualities you've never even *heard* of.

Page Thirteen, Panel Five
This is just a small shot of Yorick, looking genuinely worried.

10) <u>Yorick</u>: So you're... you're just going to *leave* me?

Page Fourteen

Page Fourteen, Panel One
Change angles for this shot of 355 and Mann, as 355 returns to her map.

1) <u>Agent 355</u>: Not by yourself.
2) <u>Agent 355</u>: I didn't want to do this, but I have a colleague who lives a few miles from here.

3) <u>Dr. Mann</u>: A Culper Ring agent?

Page Fourteen, Panel Two
Change angles for this shot of 355, and the now-pleading Yorick, still cradling his sickly pet.

4) <u>Agent 355</u>: *Ex*-Culper.
5) <u>Agent 355</u>: She took a permanent leave of absence after her husband-slash-partner was assassinated by *17 November*.

6) <u>Yorick</u>: Wait, I don't want to stay with some shell-shocked *widow*! Please! I promise, I'll be on my best behavior! I—

Page Fourteen, Panel Three
Similar framing, but now Yorick looks more skeptical than alarmed.

7) <u>Agent 355</u>: Yorick, I've known this woman since she was *nine*. We were in the same orphanage when we were both recruited.
8) <u>Agent 355</u>: Agent 711 has saved my ass almost as often as I've saved hers. You'll be fine.

9) <u>Yorick</u>: Hold on, her codename is seriously *711*? Man, how many guys used to ask if she's "open all night"?

Page Fourteen, Panel Four
This is just a close-up of Agent 355, looking deadly serious.

10) <u>Agent 355</u>: 711 was *General Washington's* codename during the Revolutionary War. That designation was awarded to my friend after she helped save the world from nuclear annihilation.
11) <u>Agent 355</u>: If you make a single crack at her expense, I will rip off your penis with a claw hammer.

Page Fourteen, Panel Five

Pull out for this largest panel of the page, as 355 walks towards us in the foreground. Behind her in the background, Yorick looks understandably nervous.

12) <u>Agent 355</u>: Saddle up.

Page Fifteen

Page Fifteen, Panel One

Cut to later that night (the sun has set now) for this page-wide establishing shot of a small cabin nestled in the woods of Colorado. We can see a woman sitting in a rocking chair on the porch, reading by the light of a Coleman gas lamp. We'll eventually learn that this is AGENT 711, a former Culper Ring operative in her late twenties (somewhat conservatively dressed). Maybe she can look like your original design for 355, Pia, back when she was a raven-haired white girl?

No Copy

Page Fifteen, Panel Two

Change angles for this largest panel of the page. We're with a stunned Agent 711 in the foreground of this shot, as she rises to greet the approaching Agent 355 and her two companions (Yorick is still holding Ampersand, and he has his hood up again).

1) <u>Agent 711</u>: Oh my god.
2) <u>Agent 711</u>: *355?*

3) <u>Agent 355</u>: Long time, 711.

Page Fifteen, Panel Three

Change angles, as 355 and 711 rush towards each other and EMBRACE.

No Copy

Page Fifteen, Panel Four

Similar framing, but now the two women pull apart and look at each other. Please leave some room between them for this rapid-fire exchange:

4) <u>Agent 711</u>: 1033?

5) <u>Agent 355</u>: He's dead. 241 and 853, too. *All* of the primes, obviously.

6) <u>Agent 711</u>: I can't imagine, 355. I'm still not over 1451.

Page Fifteen, Panel Five

Cut over to Dr. Mann and Yorick, who are eavesdropping on this bizarre dialogue.

7) <u>Dr. Mann</u>: We live in profoundly strange times.

8) <u>Yorick</u>: Yep.

Page Sixteen

Page Sixteen, Panel One

This is just a shot of 355, as she gestures at her off-panel friends.

1) <u>Agent 355</u>: 711, these are my new charges.
2) <u>Agent 355</u>: My *friends*.

Page Sixteen, Panel Two

Change angles, as 355 introduces 711 to Mann. 711 warmly shakes the doctor's hand, but Mann just stares at her icily.

     3) <u>Agent 355</u>: Dr. Allison Mann, bioengineer out of Boston. If anyone can figure out what caused the Plague, it's *her*.

     4) <u>Agent 711</u>: Pleasure.

     5) <u>Dr. Mann</u>: Mn.

Page Sixteen, Panel Three
     Change angles again, as 355 introduces Yorick, who nonchalantly waves with his free hand (the one not cradling Ampersand).

     6) <u>Agent 355</u>: And this, as far as we know, is the last man on earth.

     7) <u>Yorick</u>: Hiya.

Page Sixteen, Panel Four
     Pull out to the largest panel of the page, as a floored 711 inspects the suddenly uncomfortable Yorick. 355 watches in the background.

     8) <u>Agent 711</u>: Is... is this some kind of *joke*?

     9) <u>Agent 355</u>: That's what *I* keep asking myself.

Page Sixteen, Panel Five
     Change angles for this shot of the two Culper agents, as 711 turns to talk with 355. Her question clearly makes 355 uneasy.

     10) <u>Agent 711</u>: *How?*
     11) <u>Agent 711</u>: Does... does this have something to do with the Amulet of *Helene*?

     12) <u>Agent 355</u>: Ah, actually, maybe we should speak in *private*, 711...

Page Seventeen

Page Seventeen, Panel One
     Pull out for this largest panel of the page. We're with Yorick and Mann in the foreground of this shot, as they watch 711 and 355 walk into the shadows in the background in order to speak in private.

     1) <u>Yorick</u>: Well, she seems... *nice*.

     2) <u>Dr. Mann</u>: I guess.
     3) <u>Dr. Mann</u>: Reminds me of one of my *exes*. Dumped me the night before my fucking MCAT.

Page Seventeen, Panel Two
     Change angles for this shot of an emotionless Dr. Mann and the puzzled Yorick. (I'm picturing these next four panels all being equal-sized page-wide letterbox shots, but as always, stick with what you think works best).

     4) <u>Yorick</u>: Hold on, *she* reminds you of an ex-*boyfriend*?

     5) <u>Dr. Mann</u>: That's not what I said.

     6) <u>Yorick</u>: Yes, you did! You just...

Page Seventeen, Panel Three
     Exact same framing, but now Yorick falls silent.

No Copy

Page Seventeen, Panel Four
Exact same framing, but now Yorick's jaw drops as a light bulb goes off over his head. He shouldn't look disgusted, just surprised.

7) <u>Yorick</u>: Get out!
8) <u>Yorick</u>: You're telling me I've been traveling with you for a *year*, and I never even figured out that you were... you know...

Page Seventeen, Panel Five
Exact same framing one last time, as Mann and Yorick exchange two tiny (nearly imperceptible!) smiles.

9) <u>Dr. Mann</u>: Yes, well, I suppose we can add *gaydar* to the extraordinary number of common senses you seem to lack.

Page Eighteen

Page Eighteen, Panel One
Pull out to the largest panel of the page. We're with Mann and Yorick in the foreground of this shot, as they turn to see 355 and 711 walking out of the shadows in the background. 711 is now holding a small black journal.

1) <u>Agent 355</u>: All right, Doctor, I think we're ready to ride.
2) <u>Agent 355</u>: 711 has kindly offered to look after Yorick until we return.

Page Eighteen, Panel Two
Change angles for this shot of Yorick and Mann, as Yorick reluctantly hands the weary Ampersand over to the doctor.

3) <u>Yorick</u>: Come back with a healthy monkey, or don't come back at all.

4) <u>Dr. Mann</u>: Like you could live without me.

Page Eighteen, Panel Three
Change angles for this shot of 355 and Yorick, as she says goodbye to the suddenly troubled young man.

5) <u>Agent 355</u>: Be good, 'Rick.
6) <u>Agent 355</u>: I've left my journals with 711, just so she knows what she'll be dealing with.

7) <u>Yorick</u>: You... you keep a *journal*?

Page Eighteen, Panel Four
Change angles again, as Yorick and 711 watch their off-panel companions depart.

8) <u>Agent 711</u>: Why don't you come inside, Mr. Brown?

Page Eighteen, Panel Five
This is just an alluring close-up of 711, as she looks at us and arches an eyebrow.

9) <u>Agent 711</u>: I have something you might like to see.

Page Nineteen

Page Nineteen, Panel One
Cut to later that night for a different page-wide establishing shot of 711's cabin. There's smoke coming out of its small chimney here.

1) <u>From Cabin</u>: Holy crap!

Page Nineteen, Panel Two
　　　　Cut inside for this largest panel of the page. We're now inside of an expansive study that is lined from floor to ceiling with a billion and a half books. Yorick is awestruck by this sight, which makes his hostess smile. Yorick and 711 are both holding tea cups here.

　　　　2) <u>Yorick</u>: It's Paradise City!

　　　　3) <u>Agent 711</u>: They belonged to my husband. You're welcome to borrow as many as you like.

　　　　4) <u>Yorick</u>: You are a *goddess*. When I left Brooklyn, all I took with me was a copy of *Zen and the Art of Motorcycle Maintenance*. It's my girlfriend Beth's favorite book, but I have a short attention span for—

Page Nineteen, Panel Three
　　　　Change angles on the two, as Yorick suddenly notices a hardcover book on one of the shelves. He's pulling it out with a free hand here.

　　　　5) <u>Yorick</u>: Hey, *The Day of the Locust*!
　　　　6) <u>Yorick</u>: This is the greatest novel of all time!

　　　　7) <u>Agent 711</u>: Is that Nathaniel West? Never read him. I've always preferred *poetry* to prose.

Page Nineteen, Panel Four
　　　　Push in closer on the two, as Yorick looks down at the book. 711 is looking at him the way a therapist looks at a patient.

　　　　8) <u>Yorick</u>: Oh, it's got the most hilarious character ever, this guy named *Homer Simpson*.
　　　　9) <u>Yorick (small, an aside)</u>: And this was written about fifty years before the cartoon, mind you.
　　　　10) <u>Yorick</u>: Homer's this awkward, naïve shut-in who's uncomfortable with his own sexuality. The book's about how he leaves his life of solitude to go to California.

　　　　11) <u>Agent 711</u>: And what does he hope to find there, Yorlck?

Page Twenty

Page Twenty, Panel One
　　　　This is just a shot of Yorick, nervously talking as he sips from his teacup. Gulp, gulp, gulp...

1) <u>Yorick</u>: Huh? Oh, nothing, really. He just wants to *die*.
2) <u>Yorick</u>: I know that doesn't *sound* funny, but it is... and sad, and brilliant, and...

Page Twenty, Panel Two
　　　　Pull out to the largest panel of the page, as Yorick groggily lowers the teacup from his mouth. All of the color has drained from his face. 711 stares into the boy's half-mast eyes.

　　　　3) <u>Yorick</u>: ... and I... I think I'm gonna be *sick*.

　　　　4) <u>Agent 711</u>: No you're not, Yorick.
　　　　5) <u>Agent 711</u>: Just look into my eyes and listen to these words. You're familiar with *haiku*, aren't you... ?

Page Twenty, Panels Three through Seven
　　　　Okay, Pia, please don't get freaked out by the number of panels we have on this page! The next <u>seventeen</u> panels should all be literally the size of postage stamps in the final comic, so keep 'em small. We're essentially turning the lower 50% of this page into a graphic haiku. In this first tier, there are five panels, all with the same shot of 711's head from Yorick's

P.O.V. 711 will say one word in each panel:

> 6) <u>Agent 711</u>: The

> 7) <u>Agent 711</u>: days

> 8) <u>Agent 711</u>: are

> 9) <u>Agent 711</u>: long

> 10) <u>Agent 711</u>: now

Page Twenty, Panels Eight through Fourteen

Second tier will have seven panels (again with one word in each), as 711's face becomes progressively more distorted.

> 11) <u>Agent 711</u>: Flies

> 12) <u>Agent 711</u>: born

> 13) <u>Agent 711</u>: in

> 14) <u>Agent 711</u>: shit

> 15) <u>Agent 711</u>: spread

> 16) <u>Agent 711</u>: new

> 17) <u>Agent 711</u>: wings

Page Twenty, Panels Fifteen through Nineteen

And this last tier will have five panels. 711's distorted face will get progressively darker, until we reach the final panel, which will be entirely **black**, and should ideally blend into this page's solid black background.

> 18) <u>Agent 711</u>: It's

> 19) <u>Agent 711</u>: your

> 20) <u>Agent 711</u>: turn

> 21) <u>Agent 711</u>: to

> 22) <u>Agent 711</u> (**tailless**): sleep

Page Twenty-one

Page Twenty-one, Panel One

Cut to an hour later for this close-up of an exhausted Yorick, as he struggles to open one eye. A little drool is coming out of his mouth. We're not playing this for laughs, so Yorick should look genuinely *awful*.

> 1) <u>Yorick (small, groggy)</u>: Ghh.

Page Twenty-one, Panel Two

Okay, Clem, lettered into the center of this black panel is white text, but instead of a location caption, it's this line of dialogue (which should be in the same font/size as our standard location captions):

> 2) <u>White text on black background</u>:
> ## Yorick, you need to wake up.

Page Twenty-one, Panel Three

Pull out to this largest panel of the page, at least a half-SPLASH. We're in some kind of dark, dank cellar now, where Yorick is trussed in the most elaborate Japanese rope bondage set-up in the history of the art. All of the reference you found is amazing, Pia, but I particularly liked the ones where the subject is completely suspended over the floor (though

Yorick's head should be pulled back so that it's looking at "us" here). Either way, he should be completely naked, with his genitals covered by shadows or ropes (as I don't think we can get away with full-frontal male nudity). Again, this needs to be shocking and unpleasant.

    3) <u>Yorick (small, groggy)</u>: Loud... so loud in my *head*...

    4) <u>Someone's Voice (from off)</u>: Shut your fucking *mouth*, jester. The fun and games are over...

Page Twenty-two

Page Twenty-two, SPLASH

    Cut over to the entrance of this cellar for this three-quarter SPLASH (please leave some negative space at the bottom of our page for the credits and title). Standing here is Agent 711, who's now wearing an extraordinary DOMINATRIX OUTFIT (this should be a nice full-figure shot, thigh-high boots and all). Go with whatever leather/latex/etc. floats your boat, Pia, but I really think we should put her in one of those underwire push-up bustiers that leaves the breasts exposed, since we've held off showing any female nudity until now, and this is certainly the moment to make it count. Either way, 711 should also be holding a whip (or some instrument of torture), and she looks like she could dish out more punishment than any one man could survive. Keeping with our darker shift in tone, 711 should *not* be smiling here. Instead, her expression is stern and determined.

    1) <u>Agent 711</u>: It's time to get serious.

    2) <u>Title</u>:

Safeword
chapter one

    3) <u>Credits</u>:

Brian K. Vaughan Pia Guerra
Writer/Co-creators/Penciller

Jose Marzan, Jr.
Inker

Clem Robins
Letterer

Pamela Rambo
Colorist

Digital Chameleon
Separations(?)

J.G. Jones
Cover Artist

Zachary Rau
Assistant Editor

Will Dennis
Editor

Y: The Last Man Created by Brian K. Vaughan and Pia Guerra